MANAGING ENERGY PRICE RISK

Second Edition

MANAGING ENERGY PRICE RISK

Second Edition

Published by Risk Books, a division of Risk Publications.

Haymarket House
28–29 Haymarket
London SW1Y 4RX
Tel: +44 (0)171 484 9700
Fax: + 44 (0)171 930 2238

©Financial Engineering Ltd 1999
First published 1995
Second Edition 1999

ISBN 1 899332 545

British Library Cataloguing in Publication Data
A catalogue record for this book is available from the British Library

Risk Books Commissioning Editor: Rob Jameson
Project Editor: Avril Eglinton
Desk Editor: Lindsey Hofmeister
Copy Editor: Romilly Hambling
Typesetter: Miles Smith-Morris

Printed and bound in Great Britain by Bookcraft (Bath) Ltd, Somerset.

PREFACE

In recent years, finding effective ways of managing energy price risk has emerged as one of the great challenges facing both practitioners and academics in the field. Management of exposures to price level and volatility is a complicated task in any business, but it is especially difficult in a commodity market characterised by rapid structural change and a growing degree of integration, both geographically and across different market segments. This book brings together papers by a cross-section of industry leaders and academic thinkers. The contributions reflect the current state of the discipline of price risk management in the energy industry; they also identify some key unanswered questions and point to the direction of future research.

The book consists of four sections. The first section reviews the range of risk management tools available to practitioners; from swaps and standard options, across more complicated option structures to the use of derivatives pricing technology for the valuation of real assets.

The second section reviews the fast-changing landscape of the energy industry. Three consecutive chapters cover developments in the oil markets, US and UK natural gas markets and worldwide developments in electricity markets. The final chapter in this section describes regulatory developments in the US, especially from the point of view of the legality and enforceability of derivative contracts.

The third section addresses the issues of how to measure, manage and record risk exposures. It includes a chapter that reviews the value-at-risk methodology for the measurement of market and credit risks. Subsequent chapters provide a perspective on credit risk analysis and credit risk management; and a review of developments in energy derivatives accounting.

The fourth section provides an extensive review of risk analysis tools that researchers have either created specifically for the energy industry, or which can be applied to address problems facing industry practitioners. The first chapter deals with how to construct forward price curves for power markets. The next chapter offers a unified framework for the valuation of energy derivatives. This is followed by a review of new and powerful techniques for modelling and forecasting volatility. The final chapter analyses the important concepts of correlation and cointegration, which are critical in any statistical analysis of price co-movement in any market and are particularly important in the establishment of hedge ratios.

Vincent Kaminski, Vice President of Research, Enron Corp

CONTENTS

RISK MEASUREMENT AND REPORTING

TOOLS FOR RISK ANALYSIS

CONTRIBUTORS

Carol Alexander is based in London, working as an independent consultant and writing "Financial Markets Data Analysis: A Practitioner's Guide" for John Wileys. Previously Carol was director and head of market risk modelling at Nikko Securities in London, and before that the academic director for Algorithmics Inc. She lectured in mathematics and economics at the University of Sussex from 1986 to 1998 and has published over 30 papers in international journals. Her editorial experience includes 12 books on mathematics and finance, most recently the two volumes on risk management and analysis published by Wileys in 1998. Carol was also the founding editor-in-chief of *NetExposure*, the electronic journal of financial risk, sponsored by Algorithmics. Since 1990 Carol has been consulting, training and developing models of risk management and investment analysis and has a visiting research fellowship at Oxford University.

Etienne Amic is responsible for structured transactions at Elf Trading, the international supply, trading and shipping division of Elf Aquitaine. Before this position, he was a project cost controller in China for Elf Atochem, the chemicals branch of Elf Aquitaine. He is a graduate from Ecole Normale Supérieure des Mines de Paris. He holds a MSc in quantum physics from the University of Paris Jussieu and a MSc in international financial markets from Dauphine Univesity.

Kaushik Amin is currently a managing director and head of USD swaps and options at Lehman Brothers. Previously, he was an associate professor of finance at the School of Business Administration of the University of Michigan. He has published various articles on option pricing in leading journals.

William Falloon is corporate editor for *Risk* magazine. He has reported on financial and energy risk management and the derivatives market since graduating from the University of Chicago in 1983. He is author of three books; "Strategic Risk Management: How Global Corporations Manage Financial Risk for Competitive Advantage"; "Charlie D: The Story of the Legendary Bond Trader"; and "Market Maker: A Sesquicentennial Look at the Chicago Board of Trade".

Stinson Gibner has worked in the research group at Enron for seven years and is currently a vice-president. His areas of responsibility include valuation of derivatives and real options in the energy markets. Stinson received a BA in physics from Rice University and a PhD in physics from Caltech.

Stephen Gray is associate professor of finance at the University of Queensland and Duke University. His research interests include asset pricing, time series analysis, and derivative valuation. Stephen has consulted widely in Australia on

matters relating to derivative valuation, risk management, and the cost of capital. He has degrees in commerce and law from the University of Queensland and a PhD from Stanford University.

Alison Gregory is the deputy general counsel of Long-Term Capital Management, L.P. She serves on various industry committees, including the Futures Industry Association's Law and Compliance Executive Committee and the American Bar Association's Committee on Regulation of Futures and Derivative Instruments. Alison annually teaches the securities regulation course at Yale Law School. In addition, she speaks at various conferences and is the annual co-chair of the PLI "Swaps and Other Derivatives Conference" with Kenneth Raisler. After graduating from the University of Virginia, Alison traded derivatives for Morgan Stanley, before graduating from Stanford Law School.

Michael Hampton joined HDS Shipping in 1997 where he develops commodity and derivative related transactions. He also acts as a trading advisor to Excalibur Global Investments Ltd. Michael worked for Chase Manhattan Bank in the global shipping department as a lending officer before becoming vice president. At Chase Investment Bank he played a seminal role in the pioneering of commodity derivatives and was promoted to Managing Director. In

1991 Michael moved to SBC/O'Connor where he was co-head of Swiss Bank's commodity derivatives operation. After this he worked for Cedef Finance where he developed commodity related business opportunities. He has written several articles and books on related subjects including a monograph "Long and Short Shipping Cycles". Michael is a graduate from Harvard College.

Philip Hoang is a PhD student at the University of Queensland. His research interests include asset pricing, time series analysis, and their applications to emerging world electricity markets. He has a BSc and a MSc in commerce from the University of Queensland.

Richard Hunter is a senior director in Fitch IBCA's London office. Richard is primarily responsible for the agency's coverage of the European energy sector, including entities in the oil and gas and power industries. Prior to joining Fitch IBCA in 1996 Richard worked for DG Bank, the wholesale German co-operative bank, in Frankfurt and London. Richard earned an MA in modern languages from Lincoln College, Oxford and studied at the European School of Management in Paris.

Vincent Kaminski is a vice-president and head of research in the risk management group of Enron. Previously, he was a vice-president in the research department of Salomon Brothers in New York (bond portfolio analysis group) and a manager in AT&T Communications (Long Lines) in Bedminster, New Jersey. In his current position, Vince is responsible for the development of analytical tools for pricing of commodity options and other commodity transactions, hedging strategies, optimisation of financial and physical transactions, as well as the

development of value-at-risk systems. He is a recipient of the 1999 James H. McGraw Award for Energy Risk Management (Energy Risk Manager of the Year). Vince holds an MSc in international economics and a PhD in mathematical economics from the Main School of Planning and Statistics in Warsaw, Poland, and an MBA from Fordham University in New York.

Jack Kellett joined Credit Lyonnais Rouse Derivatives in 1997 in order to develop the marketing and trading of energy derivatives to end users, refiners, and producers in the oil markets. He began his career in the sector as a broker of physical crude and products in Ireland, moving to derivatives in 1996. Jack has been actively developing new applications for derivative markets with a special focus upon the deregulation of the European utility sector.

Louise Kitchen is Vice President of Enron Corp, and is currently responsible for Enron's trading of natural gas in the UK and Europe. Louise has been involved in the natural gas trading market in the UK since 1993 and has been a key player in its development, sitting on several industry panels for the IPE Gas Steering Committee and Network Code. Prior to joining Enron in spring 1994, she was employed by PowerGen, where she worked in electricity trading before taking responsibility for PowerGen's gas trading activities. Louise is an economics graduate and has honours degrees from universities in England and France.

Fred Lagrasta is vice-president of Enron North America where he manages the energy risk management marketing group. The group markets price risk management structures to both producers and end users of natural gas, crude oil, refined products, and natural gas

liquids. He has marketed both physical and financial energy structures with Enron for the last 10 years. Prior to that he was vice-president of gas supply for Houston Pipe Line Company and Enron Gas Marketing.

Ellen Lapson is a senior director of Fitch IBCA Inc, an international credit rating agency. Ellen is one of the senior members of the Global Power Group and is responsible for policy matters affecting credit ratings of companies in the electricity and gas industries. She is also a member of the Credit Advisory Board, which reviews credit criteria throughout the firm. Ellen is actively involved in rating utilities, generation companies, and energy marketers in North and South America. Prior to joining Fitch IBCA in 1994, Ellen worked for Chemical Bank and Chemical Securities Inc, where she structured financings and provided advisory services for energy, telecommunications, and utility clients. She holds an MBA from New York University's Stern School of Business and is a Chartered Financial Analyst.

Philippe Lautard is currently deputy general manager of products trading and risk management and is involved with the marketing and development of new energy markets. He started working for Elf Trading in 1988 as a derivatives trader within the oil markets. Philippe then became manager of the OTC derivatives, then Head of Marketing at the start of the European natural gas trading activity in 1995. He graduated as a civil engineer of the French Ecole Nationale Supérieure des Points et Chaussées and oil economist of the French Institute Petroleum.

Tom Lewthwaite is a partner in the financial services industry practice of Arthur Andersen with responsibility for both investment banking and financial investigations in London. Tom has extensive experience of operational risk issues through his involvement in the investigations of major financial failures including: Barings Bank; Daiwa Bank and Morgan Grenfell. He has also undertaken numerous operational consulting assignments and advised major financial institutions in the process of mega mergers. Tom's investment banking experience has been applied to numerous energy and commodity clients in relation to their management and control of risks related to their hedging and trading activities.

Hassaan Majid is a senior manager in Arthur Andersen's energy trading and marketing practice, focusing on the deregulating UK, European and US gas and electricity sectors. Hassaan has led and participated in numerous projects in the energy trading and marketing sector. These include reviews of risk management policies and strategies; reviews and "health checks" of trading and associated support processes compared to industry best practices; design and implementation of front, middle and back office functions and processes; the selection and implementation of risk management software and supporting internal and external audits of energy trading operations.

Grant Masson is a vice president with the risk analytics and control unit of Enron. He oversees quantitative support for market analysis, forward curve development and asset and derivative structure valuations for both domestic and international electricity trading operations. Prior to joining Enron, Grant spent five years at the University of Basel as a research scientist specialising in experimental nuclear physics. He received a BA cum laude from Rice University

in Houston and MSc and PhD degrees in physics from the University of Wisconsin–Madison.

Shankar Nagarajan is the lead quantitative risk management specialist in the capital markets group of Deloitte & Touche L.L.P, dedicated to serving power, energy, commodity and telecom market participants. He was previously a senior member of the risk advisory group at Bankers Trust, which won the *Euromoney* award for the best risk advisor of the year, three years in a row. In that capacity, Shankar has advised major international and US corporate, energy and power companies on various tactical and strategic risk management issues. Previously, he was a tenured professor of finance at McGill University, Montreal. He has also taught at Northwestern University, Columbia University and New York University, and has been a consultant to the Federal Reserve and the People's Bank of China. Shankar has published extensively in leading academic and trade journals and has been an invited speaker at various conferences all over the world. He holds a MSc and PhD from Northwestern University and a BTech from the Indian Institute of Technology.

Victor Ng is currently a vice-president at Goldman Sachs and Company in New York. He is also an associate editor of the *Journal of Business and Economic Statistics*. Previously, he was an assistant professor of finance at the School of Business Administration of the University of Michigan and has also been an economist in the capital market and financial studies division of the International Monetary Fund. Victor has published numerous articles in leading journals on volatility modelling, option pricing, commodity futures and econometric techniques.

Krishnarao Pinnamaneni is a director in the research group at Enron Corp. He joined Enron in November 1993 and is currently responsible for the overall research support for Enron Energy Services – the retail division of Enron. His research interests are in the areas of commodity finance, valuation of assets and contracts as real options, and the application of optimisation methods for risk management and trading. He received an engineering degree from the Indian Institute of Technology at Madras, an MBA in Finance from Rice Unversity in Houston, and a PhD in operation research from Stanford University.

Craig Pirrong is an associate professor of business economics at Washington University in St Louis. He is the author of "Grain Futures Markets: An Economic Appraisal"; "Corners and Squeezes: The Economics, Law and Public Policy of Derivative Market Manipulation"; and several articles on pricing and regulatory issues in futures markets. He has also consulted extensively in the derivatives area.

Ross Prevatt is an Associate with Enron Corp, currently working in a Research Group in Houston, Texas. There he is a member of the Market Fundamentals team, which supports Enron's trading desks. Prior to joining Enron he worked for Ernst & Young, L.L.P., in its Financial Services group. He holds a BSc and MSc in finance.

Kenneth M. Raisler is a partner in Sullivan & Cromwell's New York office and head of the firm's Commodities, Futures and Derivatives Group. He joined the Commodity Futures Trading Commission as deputy general counsel in 1982 and was the general counsel of the commission from 1985 to 1987. From 1988 to

1991 he was chairman of the Association of the Bar of the City of New York. In 1992 to 1993 he was a member of the working group of The Group of Thirty Derivatives Project and is currently a member of the board of directors of the Futures Industry Association. Mr Raisler is a graduate of Yale University and New York University School of Law.

Brian Senior is responsible for creating and operating an integrated global energy risk management unit within National Power. His unit includes risk management for UK, Australian and Nord Pool trading operations, together with a strong interface with National Power's JV energy trading operations in the US. Brian has held a number of commercial posts in the last few years, including managing the analysis, modelling and settlement team within the UK's energy management centre, and the market studies group supporting international business development. His first commercial appointment was as head of the trading and planning group within the research and engineering function in 1993. Prior to this, Brian headed projects to develop risk analysis methods for generation operations, including forced outages and reliability studies. He graduated from Liverpool University with a BSc in metallurgy

and materials science, and took a PhD in a related subject in 1985.

Lloyd Spencer joined Bankers Trust (now Deutsche Bank) in 1998. As a member of the Risk Advisory Group, Lloyd advises energy companies on a broad range of risk related issues. His primary focus is in the utilities sector helping firms assess the impact of deregulation on their strategy, particularly as it relates to the risks in power trading and marketing and asset acquisition /disposition. Prior to working at Bankers Trust, Lloyd has worked in project risk management within Enron's Treasury group, and in a risk management group at Edison International, the parent company of Southern California Edison. He holds a BSc in Applied mathematics and a B. Comm. in Finance from Auckland University and a MSc in Operations Research from Stanford University.

Nicholas Swingler is a manager in Arthur Andersen's financial markets division and has responsibility for reviewing and auditing the trading operations of a major international energy group. Recent projects have included reviewing and improving front, middle and back office controls at a major investment bank and being involved in piloting continuous improvement in process and con-

trols for a major investment bank.

Ravi Thuraisingham is a member of Enron's research group that is responsible for developing trading, risk management and quantitative business models for the corporation across all lines of business. He supports selected new product development initiatives from concept to quantitative modelling. Ravi also serves as a corporate specialist on SFAS 133 related quantitative issues pertaining to new product and risk management models development. Before joining Enron, Ravi worked as a capital markets consultant in New York and as an energy industry consultant. Ravi holds a MSc in nuclear engineering, BSc engineering science and a Chartered Financial Analyst (CFA) Charter.

David Turner is editor of *Euro* magazine, a Risk Publications monthly, which covers European capital markets. Previously he was editor for *Energy & Power Risk Management* magazine, reporting on all aspects of energy risk across the world, including oil, gas, electricity, weather and emission trading. David has also edited the 1998 Risk Publications weather risk special report. He has an MA from St John's College, Cambridge.

INTRODUCTION

The Evolution of a Market

William Falloon[1] and David Turner
Risk Publications

Energy risk management is no longer the gauche younger brother of the risk management family. Energy derivatives may be newer than foreign exchange derivatives, interest rate derivatives or other similar instruments, but over the last five years the market has attracted some of the keenest minds in risk management. They have been attracted in part by the novelty of the market, but also by the severity of the challenge.

Plotting the electricity forward curve, for example, is proving one of the most taxing intellectual conundrums in finance, while weather risk management presents formidable problems in terms of data assessment. High time, then, that a revised edition of *Managing Energy Price Risk*, with a revised introduction, should grapple anew with some of the problems the field presents.

While the volumes traded in most energy risk management markets have risen dramatically, the most startling development since the first edition of this book was published in 1995 is the birth of wholly new market sectors. In the first edition we included a chapter on risk management in the UK electricity market, together with some tentative but well-aimed comments by John Woodley of Morgan Stanley on the possible development of a US power risk management market. Since then power risk management in the United States and other liberalising markets has taken off to the extent that (at last count) 11 sets of futures contracts have been launched.

True, the volume of electricity hedging, whether exchange-traded or OTC, is still pretty paltry compared to the huge underlying physical market. But the range of contracts listed is impressive – no fewer than eight sets of contracts in the US (from three exchanges, Nymex, the Chicago Board of Trade and the Minneapolis Grain Exchange), electricity futures for the Nordic market on Nord Pool in Oslo, contracts for New South Wales and Victoria on the Sydney Futures Exchange, a South Island contract on the New Zealand Futures & Options Exchange. Talk of a set of futures contracts for the UK market seems progressively less idle, with two rivals, the International Petroleum Exchange and OMLX, both considering their positions. In April 1999 Deutsche Borse and Nymex announced they would be working together to set up a German energy exchange.

Inevitably, some of these contracts will falter. Yet anyone doubting the importance of these new arrivals would do well to read our account below of the early history of oil futures contracts.

Whether trading in electricity futures will indeed take off is perhaps *the* question in energy risk management, even more than the prospects for weather derivatives (of which more later). The irony is that the very price spikes that define the purpose of derivatives have, as of spring 1999, stunted their growth. The extreme price spikes which occurred in the US, and most strikingly in the midwest, in the summer of 1998 pushed many traders out of the electricity forward market. From the journalists' point of view, the story was spectacular: prices as high as $7,500 a megawatt hour (MWh), sudden corporate collapses and allegations of market manipulation all served to turn the financial repercussions of that summer's heatwave into high drama. But while derivatives thrive during periods of price volatility, they don't in periods of price madness, when prices don't seem to show any relation to the underlying supply/demand fundamentals.

Though bruised and battered, electricity risk management will pick itself up off the floor before the 10-second countdown is over. Since we published the first edition of this book energy risk management in general has survived some fair old disasters – aside from the collapse of top 15 US power marketer Power Company of America in summer 1998 we have seen losses amounting to 560 million Finnish markka ($100 million) at Finnish state-owned oil company

Neste, for example. But the market soldiers on, just as it did after what remains the biggest loss in energy risk management: the $1–1.3 billion deficit of MG Corp, the US oil marketing subsidiary of German metals and mining company Metallgesellschaft, in oil derivatives in the early 1990s.

New markets are still appearing. One example is coal, whose first derivatives instruments were agreed in the late 1990s as the world market moved closer to deregulation. Probably the most interesting new instruments are weather derivatives. Weather risk management is, of course, as old as agriculture, which is supposed, according to the old saw, to be the world's oldest profession. Farmers have always taken precautions to protect their crops against the risk of inclement weather, and the commodity futures markets that developed in the 19th century to protect agricultural positions and revenues eventually also spawned the first oil contract. This said, weather derivatives had something of a false start in the mid-1990s, achieving some degree of success in 1997, and only then in the US market. As of March 1999 the first handful of European deals have begun to appear, and the US market is steadily growing, though the market is still dominated by, if not exclusively restricted to, the so-called degree-day options and swaps. These instruments essentially allow parties to hedge against warmer or cooler temperatures.

Weather derivatives represent an interesting departure for energy risk management (most of the deals currently involve energy companies, and this is hardly surprising, when one considers how weather-dependent their revenues are). Indeed, the difference between weather derivatives and all previous derivative instruments is as great as that between those very first oil swaps and their progenitors in the interest-rate and foreign exchange markets. Weather derivatives are unlike previous instruments for several reasons: the underlying can't be traded, the hedge is against changes in volume (caused by changes in heating or cooling demand) rather than price, and the markets' outlook does not change from minute to minute with new information as it does in the markets for natural gas, oil, power or indeed interest rates. Weather derivatives also give a new twist to the old problem of data scarcity and validity. Few locations in the world have long time series of data on temperature, or precipitation, and in any case recent global warming puts in doubt the validity of historical information.

But weather derivatives also create new opportunities. The concept intrigues a broad range of the public – after all, everyone has their own opinion on the weather. Moreover, companies from a wide range of industries are affected by the weather, from energy companies to fruit growers to ski resorts to beach resorts to thermal underwear manufacturers. Energy derivative providers such as Koch Industries say they find weather risk portfolio benefits from their involvement in both the agricultural and energy risk management markets. Maybe energy companies will at last be able to solve, to some degree, the perennial problem of energy risk management – a lack of end-user counterparties and a consequent one-sided market.

Weather risk management is also helping to bring new blood into energy risk management: the insurance companies. Players such as Swiss Re, the reinsurer, are making their presence felt in the weather-related sector. Indeed, insurers are appearing in other areas of energy risk management. US insurance company AIG, for example, is offering to US power companies cover against price spikes, as part of the same policy which also protects them against property damage. This is healthy for energy risk management, which needs new entrants to replace the gang of investment banks that have quit the market.

The inelegant retreat of the investment bankers is the other striking story in energy risk management in recent years. When the first edition of this book appeared the investment banks seemed about to take the energy risk management market by storm – they, after all, were past masters in the art of structuring and trading derivatives. At the end of the millennium, the market they helped to create remains, but the banking players have dwindled: among the battle-scarred survivors are Goldman Sachs, Morgan Stanley and (having swallowed the old NationsBank energy team) Bank of America.

Others, such as Lehmans, Merrill Lynch, JP Morgan and UBS, have substantially left the market over the past few years. Official statements from the banks about wishing to concentrate on "core areas" may obscure a more fundamental explanation. Energy companies involved in derivatives trading argue that banks have a permanent disadvantage arising from their lack of knowledge of inventories and other aspects of the physical market. Even so, those banks still in the market seem to be thriving.

Insurers say that they have a big advantage in the energy markets over banks owing to the huge capital reserves that they are required by law to set aside. Only massive amounts of capital can insulate a company in the energy markets against "tail end" market risk (the risk of unlikely but devastating market price moves) and counterparty risk. Counterparty risk is clearly something which the energy sector needs to pay more attention to: the extreme summer 1998 price spikes in the US power market were caused at root by power marketer defaults, which in turn exacerbated power shortages. Understandably, the first focus of energy traders is price risk. But they also need to watch the credit profile of those they rely on to perform.

Back to the beginning

The energy risk management market all started with oil, of course – not exactly way back in the past, but all of 13 years ago. With Cathay Pacific Airways Ltd in Hong Kong, and Koch Industries in Wichita, Kansas as counterparties, Chase Manhattan Bank entered into the world's first oil-indexed price swaps in October 1986. These back-to-back swaps, with Chase in the middle, represented the first time that hedging concepts developed for the interest rate and currency swap market had been successfully transferred to the energy markets.

The first historic transaction, in the form of a cash-settled, four-month swap on 25,000 barrels of crude oil per month, took place just after the price of oil had collapsed to around $14 per barrel. Koch agreed to pay the average spot price of oil over the period, while Cathay Pacific hoped that by agreeing to pay a fixed price of $14–15 per barrel of oil, it would gain an effective hedge against any rise in the price of jet fuel in the coming months.[2] The success of the deal prompted Koch to make swap transactions with a notional value of more than 1 million barrels over the next 24 months, including deals in which oil prices were swapped for as much as five years into the future.

The original stimulus for these back-to-back swaps came from Chase, which quickly attracted Cathay Pacific's interest by explaining to the airline how it might manage energy price volatility and its overall impact on fuel consumption costs through a swap.[3] Unfortunately, Chase had not been able to find an oil company willing to take the "other side" of this new-fangled instrument. After a couple of months searching, Chase's enthusiasm sparked interest at privately-held Koch Industries. Assisting Koch Industries to assess the worth of these pioneering transactions

were Corky Nelson, treasurer at that time, and Lawrence Kitchen, a well-known energy derivative expert. Charles Koch, the chief executive officer of Koch Industries, gave them the green light to go ahead with this initial deal. His degrees in mechanical (nuclear) and chemical engineering from MIT were invaluable in helping him to understand the implications of this new hedging instrument – and perhaps also made him more receptive to using it than other oil producers and refiners.

Prior to Koch's deal, the concept of "commodity swaps" had been brainstormed in a series of seminars attended by senior managers at Chase.[4] Leading the way in turning these ideas into commercial deals were Chase's Gaylen Byker and Ron Liesching.[5] Byker remembers having long talks with Liesching about the concept; in turn, Liesching frequently discussed which energy indices might be appropriate benchmarks for swaps with Colin Carter, an oil analyst at Chase who has since died. Although Liesching had been toying with the idea since 1984, he became seriously interested in applying the concept after a meeting with Amerada Hess Corporation, which was considering funding some of its activities in British pounds and Norwegian kroner. The sensitivity of those currencies to oil prices jogged a wild thought in Liesching's mind: given the close links these currencies have to oil prices, why not fund yourselves in another currency – oil?

The gregarious Byker, in contrast, seemed willing to take Liesching's conceptual notions and hammer them into a project on which he could focus his entrepreneurial energies. "I was rotating through the interest rate and currency swap area at the time, after doing my doctorate in foreign exchange risk management", recalls Byker. "I had practiced law and taught finance, but I didn't really have any practical experience. Frankly, I don't think Chase knew quite what to do with me. I had some long talks with Ron. If this was such a good idea, I told him, then why don't we do it?"

Byker found a loyal internal sponsor in the form of Chase's chief operating officer at the time, Richard Urfer.[6] Over the months following the first Koch–Cathay Pacific deal, Chase executed two sizeable oil price swaps with Canadian and US railways, so that within a short period of time deals had been booked in the bank's New York, Toronto and London offices.

In the same period, some of Chase's competitors such as Bankers Trust, Citibank and Phibro

Energy (owned by Salomon Brothers) were tinkering with their own ideas. Through a subsidiary that was allowed to trade in the physical market, Citibank International Trading Co (Citco), Citibank had begun to offer six-month hedging protection against energy cargoes coming from the Middle East and the Far East. The bank's initial short-term programmes met with minimal success, but they predated Chase's first transactions and seem to represent the first attempt by a bank to get involved with risk transfer in the energy markets. Citibank's efforts lasted only a few months, as the bank found it very difficult to manage basis risk – the uncertain relationship between Citco's forward contract price on these cargoes and the price of the futures contracts at the New York Mercantile Exchange (Nymex) that the bank then used as a way of hedging this obligation. The problem was that the bank was trying to hedge the price of energy cargoes arriving outside the United States with exchange-traded instruments whose prices reflected directly only what was happening in the New York Harbor market.

The pioneering efforts to market energy swaps prompted one of the first media references to the nascent energy derivatives industry in the April 9, 1987 edition of the *Wall Street Journal*. This identified Chase and Phibro Energy as two intermediaries getting involved in newfangled hedging instruments linked to commodity prices. Journalist Ann Monroe wrote: "A handful of banks and investment banks are betting that if corporations liked interest rate swaps, they'll love oil price swaps". The article explained that the idea was to give producers, refiners, marketers and consumers of oil products a longer-term and more customised hedge than they could achieve in the futures market. Rather than using an interest rate benchmark to determine the exchange of cashflows, payments on an oil price swap would be determined by the average spot market price of oil.

Bankers Trust began playing with ideas about energy derivatives in late 1986, and from that date received occasional queries from interested customers. By late 1987, Allen Levinson, then a Bankers Trust managing director, had proposed a formal business plan to former Bankers Trust president Eugene Shanks. The thrust of this proposal was to make energy and other commodity derivatives an official line of products at the bank. Over the next decade, Bankers Trust would become one of the most important providers of energy-based derivative instruments.

However, unlike Chase, Bankers Trust would emphasise OTC option-based hedging instruments and would later become the first bank to successfully apply average rate option pricing methodologies.[7] According to Mark Standish, formerly Bankers Trust's vice-president in interest rate derivatives, Bankers Trust started to see interest from end-users in options at about the same time that Chase began to market swaps. "During the latter half of 1987, I started spending my time looking at the potential for commodity derivatives", explains Standish. "We had a couple of enormous trades come in. One European customer was interested in buying put options on Brent [crude oil] to the tune of 250 million barrels over a period of five years. It was an enormous trade, just totally outrageous. And who had a clue at that time what the price of five-year Brent was?"

As a result of this query, Standish flew to Tokyo in search of an eligible counterparty. In his mind, "as massive consumers of oil, the Japanese were the only ones who would sell put options of that type". While the transaction proved too large for anyone to handle at the time, it was during his trip to Tokyo that Standish came upon David Spaughton (formerly with Bankers Trust International and now a managing director of product development with Credit Suisse Financial Products in London). Together, the men were to create the first commercially used option-pricing methodology to be based on the average price of crude oil over time.

Spaughton had already started using this exotic option technology in some long-term currency warrant issues that Bankers Trust had devised for Svensk Exportkredit (SEK); in these warrants the stipulated settlement price was an average exchange rate, not one discrete price, at maturity. However, as Standish points out, "There was really no compelling reason to have an average price option model until commodity derivatives came along. Whereas in financial markets you have explicit risk on a particular day or at the end of the year, a standard physical contract in crude is typically based on an average price over the month". As for the name, "We were in Tokyo at the time we developed this pricing methodology, so we called it the 'Asian option'. It's as simple as that".

This option-pricing innovation made it possible for dealers to cope with the historical volatility of the crude oil market. As the comparative volatility illustrated in Figure 1 shows, while

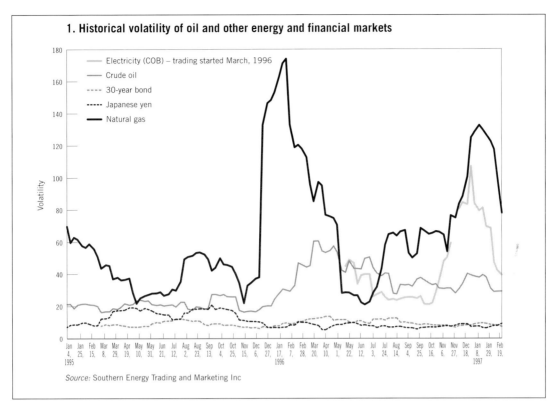

1. Historical volatility of oil and other energy and financial markets

- Electricity (COB) – trading started March, 1996
- Crude oil
- 30-year bond
- Japanese yen
- Natural gas

Source: Southern Energy Trading and Marketing Inc

crude oil is relatively tame compared to the volatility in energy risk management markets that have developed in natural gas and electricity over the last decade, it is still markedly higher than the volatility in traditional financial markets, for example, 30-year bond volatility. Without the breakthrough, the price of offering option-based hedges to end-users, and managing the associated risks, might have slowed down the development of OTC commodity options.

Bankers Trust first applied the idea in March 1989 to 18-month WTI oil-linked average price warrants and to gold-indexed notes with embedded four-year gold options.[8] The warrants were launched in two series: the first issue cost $2.58 and gave the holder the right to buy oil at $17 a barrel, 18 months ahead. This issue was aimed largely at corporate treasurers who wanted to manage oil price exposures, and at bond portfolio managers interested in an inflation hedge. The second issue was an "up and in" warrant: if the closing price of the WTI contract reached $21.50 at least once over the next two months, the warrants automatically became fungible with the first issue. This second issue was aimed at speculators and investors looking to gain more leveraged exposure to the energy markets.

These deals were early predecessors of the rash of commodity-linked warrants and structured notes that appeared in 1994, as the commodity markets again seemed to offer a good inflationary hedge, and many dealers followed in

Goldman Sachs' footsteps to launch proprietary commodity-based indices.

The regulatory rollercoaster

When Chase began to develop energy swaps, the bank was keenly aware that it was wading into uncharted legal and regulatory waters. As a first step, Byker made use of his legal training to begin to convert an interest rate swap document into a user-friendly oil swap document. With the help of Schuyler Henderson, formerly with Sidley & Austin and now a partner with Baker & MacKenzie in London, Chase polished a final draft of a legal document that would be used by its original four-man commodity index and swap financing team for its initial ground-breaking deals.

The concept of commodity derivatives received a major boost on July 20, 1987, when Chase's attorney, Margery Waxman at Sidley & Austin, received a "no-action" letter from the Office of the Comptroller of the Currency – the regulator of US commercial banks (Figure 2 overleaf). The letter stated that Chase's commodity price index swaps represented both a traditional banking function and "a modern concept of banking as funds intermediation". Henderson notes that since Chase was operating as a credit intermediary and not involving itself in commodity markets directly, banking regulators saw only one major difference between commodity swaps and interest rate swaps: a commodity price

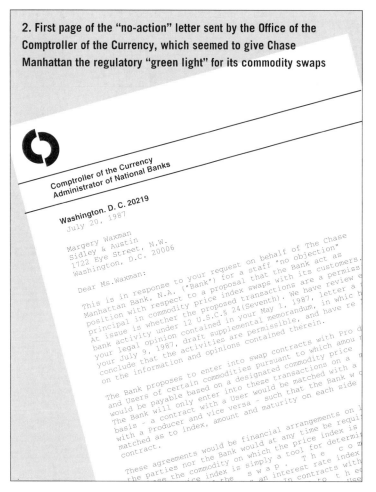

2. First page of the "no-action" letter sent by the Office of the Comptroller of the Currency, which seemed to give Chase Manhattan the regulatory "green light" for its commodity swaps

Comptroller of the Currency
Administrator of National Banks

Washington. D. C. 20219
July 20, 1987

Margery Waxman
Sidley & Austin
1722 Eye Street, N.W.
Washington, D.C. 20006

Dear Ms.Waxman:

This is in response to your request on behalf of The Chase Manhattan Bank, N.A. ("Bank") for a staff "no objection" position with respect to a proposal that the Bank act as principal in commodity price index swaps with its customers. At issue is whether the proposed transactions are a permissible bank activity under 12 U.S.C.§ 24(Seventh). We have review your legal opinion contained in your May 1, 1987, letter a your July 9, 1987, draft supplemental memorandum, in whic conclude that the activities are permissible, and have re on the information and opinions contained therein.

The Bank proposes to enter into swap contracts with Pro d and Users of certain commodities pursuant to which amou would be payable based on a designated commodity price The Bank will only enter into these transactions on a basis - a contract with a User would be matched with a with a Producer and vice versa - such that the Bank w matched as to index, amount and maturity on each side contract.

These agreements would be financial arrangements on the parties nor the Bank would at any time be requi the commodity on which the price index is simply a tool for determi the index is simply a tool for determi the s w a p . T h e c o m index an interest rate index ice index the an interest rate ro t h e use

index was being used as a pricing reference.

"That was truly an amazing letter", admits Byker. "Up until that point there had never been one shred of paper in which a federal government entity had explicitly approved the legality of any kind of swaps. So even our interest rate and currency swap people were ecstatic when we got it. We had already made some pretty good money and were basically all alone in this market. After that letter, we were about as high as you could get from being at the threshold of a new industry".

That emotional high did not last long. On August 1, 1987, not long after printing up a glossy blue brochure to promote its expertise in energy derivative instruments, Chase received a subpoena from the Commodity Futures Trading Commission (CFTC) and was threatened with enforcement actions – including possible criminal charges. Ironically, the glossy brochure became the basis for the CFTC's queries. "If you look at their original questions to us", says Byker, "it's as if the CFTC staff went through the brochure line by line to form its questions". Implicit in this regulatory action was the accusation that Chase was marketing and trading off-exchange futures contracts – an activity out-

lawed by the Commodity Exchange Act of 1974. According to the CFTC, this act of law specifically required that all futures contracts be traded on a designated exchange by a member of that contract market, and that all commodity-linked forward contracts be settled with physical delivery.

The critical debate was about to begin. In the view of the CFTC, oil price swaps posed a jurisdictional challenge to the CFTC because they possessed characteristics of both futures contracts and forward contracts. Prodding the CFTC to take this view were the US futures exchanges – notably the two Chicago exchanges. The exchanges had watched the interest rate swap market grow to $313 billion in notional principal contracts outstanding by the end of 1986, and were unconvinced at that time by the argument that a major OTC energy market would complement, rather than compete with, their own activities. They therefore dropped a few sharp tacks on the commodity swap market's road to Washington – it was even suggested to the CFTC that the familiar Chase corporate logo resembled a futures trading pit.

Chase was not alone in running into this regulatory quicksand. The legality of a gold-linked certificate of deposit (CD) offered by Wells Fargo Bank in July had been challenged by the CFTC on November 17, 1987, in the Central District Court of California. Wells Fargo subsequently closed down its offering and returned money to investors to appease the CFTC (which, in its legal suit, likened the offering to commodity options), but the legally conservative Chase seemed willing to take up the fight. "Chase did not go into this market blind", explains Henderson. "They were very aware of the legal issues involved and comfortable that their activities in this market were defensible".

While the CFTC proceeded in its attempt to pigeonhole commodity swaps as "off-exchange futures", Chase took its commodity swap business offshore and continued its legal battle to conduct such activities in the United States. On December 11, 1987, the CFTC issued an advance notice of proposed rulemaking as prepared by the CFTC's Off-Exchange Task Force. The notice, entitled "Regulation of Hybrid and Related Instruments", established the Commission's hardline position on the regulation of hybrid instruments, including oil-index price swaps.

Lauren S. Klett summarised the CFTC's position in the *Dickinson Law Review* in Winter 1989, in an essay she wrote about oil price swaps[9]:

Specifically, the Commission takes the position that, in all likelihood, the swaps are illegal. The CFTC, however proposes a blanket no-action position with respect to transactions solely involving commercial participants, such that oil producers and consumers are permitted to participate in the transactions. The CFTC's proposal, however, prohibits intermediaries, such as Chase Manhattan Bank, from participating in the swaps. In proposing to prohibit swap transactions involving intermediaries, the CFTC states that these types of transactions "substantially depart from the context in which the forward contract exclusion has historically operated".

The battle was hardly over, however. That advance notice for public comment resulted in 61 responses to the CFTC's rulemaking proposal, with the overwhelming majority opposing them.[10] The only support for the proposed rule came from exchanges such as the Chicago Board of Trade, Chicago Mercantile Exchange, Coffee, Sugar & Cocoa Exchange, Commodity Exchange and the New York Mercantile Exchange. Quite legitimately, many of the exchanges also questioned the CFTC's authority even to make a legal ruling on this complex issue.

On July 17, 1989, under the helm of CFTC chairwoman Wendy Gramm, the CFTC released Safe Harbor provisions for commodity swaps and hybrid instruments. "Wendy Gramm and her staff finally made the rational decision", explains Byker. "An overly literal interpretation of the Commodity Exchange Act would have brought down not only our business but the whole interest rate swap market, which by that time had hundreds of billions of dollars in notional contracts outstanding".

Ironically, soon after it exempted swaps and hybrid instruments, the CFTC's legal authority to interpret and enforce the Commodity Exchange Act in this way was itself questioned. Those concerns were heightened when, in 1990, another OTC market – Brent Oil forward contracts – suffered a major disruption as a result of a federal district court holding that those contracts were unenforceable futures.[11] The CFTC promptly issued yet another regulatory interpretation seeking to give legal sanction to such contracts. However, many US participants in the Brent Oil market complained that foreign firms remained reluctant to deal with them.

Only in 1992 was the legality of the CFTC's decisions made official, when Congress passed the Futures Trading Practices Act. "It's fascinating to look back on those early days", says Byker, "There's a lot more 'boilerplate' in the [contracts] we use now, but the substance is exactly what we came up with at Chase in 1986".

There continues to be some uncertainty about the role of the CFTC in regulating OTC commodity derivatives. On May 12, 1998, the CFTC published a Concept Release on Over-the-Counter Derivatives. It was issued despite objections, including the dissent of one CFTC Commissioner. During 1999 and 2000, Congress will address the reauthorisation of the CFTC due to expire on September 30, 2000. Chapter 8 of this book follows the story of the regulation and documentation of the industry up to the summer of 1999.

Meeting of the markets

Since those early days, energy swap dealers and futures exchanges have come to regard their respective markets as mutually beneficial. The first evidence of this came when Chase and others began pushing their commodity swap business offshore when oil was fluctuating consistently at around $20 per barrel in 1987–88. At this price, the bank was not always able to match up producers with consumers "back-to-back" because of the different views in the market about the ideal price levels at which to transact. Unfortunately, there were not as many consumers of oil looking to manage price risk as there were producers and refiners.

By that time, however, some derivative participants had started to use the futures markets and physical markets to intermediate energy risk in ways that banks, legally, could not. Phibro Energy, for example, had started to use the energy futures market to offset the risk of one leg of a swap while waiting for a price level in which an opposing counterparty would be willing to take the other side. In this way, swaps could be "warehoused" for short periods. Phibro would do so by going "short" a strip of energy futures to offset the risk of an unmatched swap position, and closing out the "short" position once a natural counterparty had taken the other side. Being allowed to take physical delivery of oil – and to do this flexibly at different delivery points through the exchange of futures for physicals (EFPs) – gave the major oil and natural gas companies an early competitive advantage. (The Federal Reserve only started to allow selected US commercial banks, such as Bankers Trust and JP Morgan, this facility from around 1992.)

Indeed, between 1987 and 1991, a "second wave" of cutting-edge energy derivative teams entered the market in Europe as the CFTC controversy drove business outside the United States. It included the likes of Elf Aquitaine, British Petroleum, Phibro Energy and later J Aron, Morgan Stanley and Shell International Trading Company (Sitco). Unlike counterparties such as Chase, these oil companies and so-called "Wall Street refiners" represented a class of counterparties that was willing to run unmatched positions on their books, or assume calculated levels of basis risk, on behalf of their derivative customers. Elf and Phibro, in particular, aggressively marketed to sectors such as shipping companies and airlines. "Very few firms were willing to take on oil yield curve risk", explains Scott Marinchek, a one-time member of Phibro Energy's team in London. "The market liquidity was limited because the banks' propensity for risk was limited. The banks were some of our biggest customers".

Marinchek, for example, remembers selling Chase six-month $50 call options on WTI crude oil when the market price shot up to $43 per barrel during the Gulf War. "The bid/offer spreads at that time could sometimes be exorbitant", he says. "I recall volatilities at that time of 210–215%. Only a few days later, volatilities dropped 100% and the oil price was down $10–15. But we were happy to assume risks when it fitted our outlook on market fundamentals".

Another key development in the market during this critical period was the arrival of inter-bank brokers. These companies were able to facilitate two-way prices among the wholesale participants in the energy derivative markets and their customers. In particular, Intercapital Brokers and Tradition Financial Services built a handsome business while creating greater price transparency and liquidity for all involved. "A two-way market really only started to develop in 1990", says Paul Newman, at that time managing director of commodity swaps for Intercapital in London. "The first deals were brokered in August 1990, and what was a field for a privileged few suddenly became more of a public forum".

The importance of energy futures exchanges to the OTC market cannot be overestimated – in the early days or at present. Futures contracts such as No 2 Heating Oil, to cite just one exam-

ple, can be used as a "proxy" hedge against swap contracts that dealers offer in refined product markets such as jet fuel. But the differential between the price of the product that has to be risk managed, and its proxy on the exchanges, is never absolutely predictable – indeed, one of the main reasons the OTC market exists is the desire on the part of end-users to isolate themselves from this basis risk.

Sometimes even the banks and oil majors themselves get bitten by basis risk. For a three-month period from December 1988, and during the Gulf Crisis, a sharp spike in the price for jet fuel was not matched in the No 2 heating oil market. This meant that energy risk managers who had relied on close-fitting "proxy" hedges in the futures markets, or who ran mismatched books that relied on their trading skills in the physical markets, lost millions.

In general, however, highly liquid contracts of this sort on the exchanges have allowed swap dealers to warehouse positions, manage portfolio imbalances, and to assume and manage basis risk. Partly because of the demand from the OTC sector, Nymex has been able to push the expiration dates for the contracts that it offers as far as 36 months into the future in the cases of crude and natural gas, and out as far as 18 months in the case of refined product futures contracts. The International Petroleum Exchange (IPE) has become the other big hub of managing energy price risk for dealers and end-users, with no fewer than seven other exchanges listing their own energy and power derivatives contracts.

A key difference between the energy risk management markets and the pure financial risk management markets (such as the interest rate derivatives) is the challenge of managing the relationship between the physical product and the paper markets. Barry Schaps, who was business manager of risk management at Shell Oil Co in Houston at the time, explains why an EFP (the exchange of a futures position for a physical position in the underlying cash market, or vice versa) is so important to participants in OTC energy derivatives:[12]

> Suppose a bank is writing a swap for an
> independent crude oil producer. The pro-
> ducer promises to deliver to a bank a
> physical volume of oil, so many barrels
> per month for so many months. In
> exchange, he may get an immediate
> inflow of cash. In essence, the indepen-
> dent is selling his product forward at a

fixed price and is getting paid for it today.

What does the bank do with the stream of crude? More than likely, the bank will turn around and try to entirely lay off the risk in the futures market. It may wish to place the physical oil with a refiner in exchange for a futures contract. Essentially, it will do an EFP on the opposite side of the swap. It will offer to a refiner a one-year physical supply of 100,000, 200,000 or 300,000 barrels per month in exchange for an equal volume of futures contracts at a price to be determined today. The banker just unwinds an entire year's strip of EFPs at that one time. The refiner, who needs the wet barrels, has the flexibility of locking in his supply without committing a price. It's a flexible tool for a refiner, and helps the bank unwind the swap position it has entered into with the producer.

Although a futures markets in energy is taken for granted today, launching exchange-traded contracts was not easy. Nymex first introduced heating oil and residual oil futures with a Rotterdam delivery point in the early 1970s. But trading in those contracts was patchy at best, and died away soon after the contracts were launched.

However, after two potato delivery failures at Nymex in the mid-1970s, the CFTC refused to approve any new contract submissions from the exchange. Nymex was forced to develop products from a list of contract markets that had already been approved by the CFTC, including apples, silver coins, nickel, currencies and oil (from the Rotterdam days). Joel Faber, president of Faber's Futures Inc, has remarked of Nymex's entrance into the energy markets: "The revival of the Nymex energy contracts wasn't obvious, and it wasn't some brilliant brainstorm, it was a matter of circumstance. Because of the potato problems, the exchange was in danger of losing its franchise. The days of potato trading were numbered, platinum was essentially the only viable commodity traded".[13]

Despite these haphazard beginnings, the alchemy of launching a new heating oil contract on November 14, 1978 proved fortuitous. It would later give Nymex its identity as a leader in energy-related futures and options, and pave the way for other successful contract launches in leaded gasoline (1981), unleaded gasoline (1984), West Texas Intermediate crude oil

(1983), propane (1987), natural gas (1990) and electricity (1996 for two sets of contracts, and then 1998 for two more).

To create the successful heating oil futures contracts for the energy industry (and ultimately a successful complex of energy futures and options), Nymex broke ranks with futures industry convention and the preferences of its local members. The contract was launched with a $4.20 minimum tick per contract at a time when virtually no-one in the futures industry used a minimum tick move of less than $5. This mechanism, which equated one tick to 1/100th of a cent per gallon, would later turn out to be a key factor when overcoming challenges from competing contracts launched by the Chicago Board of Trade (CBOT) and Chicago Mercantile Exchange (CME).

Steven Errera, one of the creators of the heating oil contract at Nymex and a veteran in energy futures, explains:[14]

In 1978, I rewrote the contract and changed it to a 42,000-gallon contract from 30,000 gallons because 42,000 gallons was equal to 1,000 barrels, and I wanted the ability to talk about "barrels" in heavy oils and "gallons" in gasoline and heating oil, which is how they are sold in the physical market.

When I sat down to work out the minimum price fluctuation, I bumped into a particular problem. A minimum fluctuation of $0.0001, which reflected the way the oil industry calculated its pricing for refined products, meant the minimum tick would be $4.20 per contract.... Many of the locals [on the exchange] wanted a $5 minimum tick [which would] cover their commissions. They didn't like $4.20, because they might have had to trade through two ticks.

We didn't listen to the locals. Today, we have a 1,000-barrel (42,000-gallon) contract in crude oil and we have a 42,000-gallon (1,000-barrel) contract in heating oil, gasoline and propane. It worked out to connect the markets better and obviously assisted in the development of crack spreads.

Errera notes that, a few years later, the Chicago Board of Trade wrote a crude oil contract with a tick of $0.00025, giving a minimum fluctuation of $10.50 per contract; the contract failed because the oil industry did not trade in halves (five decimals) and thus could not relate to it.

Nymex would ultimately be rewarded handsomely for carefully thinking through the logic of its contract specifications. Heating oil futures volume began to pick up in October 1979. By that time, prices were strong and frequently moved "limit up" – the maximum that contract prices are allowed to move over one day of trading, as specified by the CFTC – after a period in the United States in which energy consumption had actually declined for a number of years after the 1973 oil embargo. As a result, many companies started to buy as many barrels as possible on both the spot and futures market to assure themselves of adequate supply, while traders sold futures as part of their arbitrage strategy.

By November 14, 1980, the second anniversary of the contract, open interest was more than 10,000, while average daily volume often exceeded 3,000 contracts. During the Iran-Iraq war, which broke out in September 1980, the heating oil contract became a refuge of risk transfer for oil price risk managers and speculators. From that point, trading volume and liquidity rapidly grew, reaching a trading volume of 8,625,061 contracts and 185,425 open interest by the end of 1993. As we reach the end of the millennium, the trading volume reported by Nymex for 1999 up to the end of April is 168,233 with 171,204 open interest.

By the time Nymex launched the light sweet crude oil futures contract on March 30, 1983, the exchange was becoming a hub of trading and risk transfer for the oil industry. "The industry's successful transfer of risk from the cash crude oil market onto the floor of the exchange through heating oil futures made it easier for the oil industry to accept crude futures", in the words of former Nymex chairman Lou Guttman.

By the mid-1980s, market conditions were ripe for both OTC and exchange-traded markets to grow synergistically. One reason for this was the dramatic price collapse of crude oil from $31.75 per barrel in November 1985 to $9.75 on April 1, 1986, which spurred on trading in all of the exchange energy contracts. Heating oil volume for that year finished 48.3% ahead of the previous year, with a total volume of 3,275,044 contracts, an average of 13,100 per day. Crude oil futures, in contrast, traded 8,313,529 contracts that year, 2472.6% more than they did in their first year of trading in 1983.

At the same time, the banks involved in OTC energy derivatives were encroaching on the turf of major oil companies and refiners. Products such as energy price swaps meant that purchasing decisions made by airlines, mass transit authorities, chemical companies, shipping and trucking companies, refiners and marketers, and other industrial companies could be decoupled from risk-management decisions.

This put pressure on major oil companies – first in Europe, and later in the United States and Canada – to offer many of the same risk management services that were being offered by major commercial and investment banks. "That definitely was important", says Standish. "BP started getting more aggressive. Shell did. The French started coming in. It was a matter of necessity. And then brokers in London such as Intercapital started making pricing in short-dated product derivatives such as jet fuel very plain vanilla. That was a milestone in the European market – when you could start to see one-, two-, three-month swaps in products like jet quoted on the screen".

Energy swap dealers account for a significant proportion of the open interest in energy futures and options contracts traded at Nymex and the IPE. Likewise, oil and natural gas producers such as British Petroleum, Chevron, Enron, Mobil, Texaco and Shell Oil have come to play an essential role in the OTC energy derivative markets – as a result, many of the world's major oil producers are presently listed as Nymex members.

Enron, in fact, provides an excellent example of how intertwined the exchange-traded and OTC energy derivative markets have become with the underlying physical business activities of many energy firms. As the largest US integrated natural gas company, Enron embarked on a strategy of creating a "gas bank" in March 1989, shortly before the Nymex natural gas contract began to be traded on April 3, 1990. Enron's idea had been to intermediate between buyers and sellers of gas, earning a spread in the same way that a traditional bank earns a spread when intermediating. In this instance, however, the spread earned by standing in the middle of producers and consumers would be a function of natural gas prices, not interest rates.

The benefits of decoupling physical gas delivery from pricing issues through a swap structure – even though it was not called this at the time – became obvious in 1989 when Enron was attempting to negotiate a fixed-price gas deal with a Louisiana-based aluminium producer. The producer was not interested in a long-term fixed-price deal because the cost of physically transporting gas made the deal economically inefficient. To solve the problem, Enron entered into a "financial" contract in which the aluminium producer agreed to pay Enron fixed sums whilst Enron paid the producer's floating prices. With hindsight, this deal can be seen as one of the market's first natural gas swaps.

As a result of these sorts of derivative activities, Enron eventually complemented its "gas bank" with a large risk management services group designed to manage the credit and price risk exposures created by the array of financial settlement contracts that Enron was building up with natural gas producers and consumers.

The key to running a natural gas book, which potentially represents large credit and market risk exposures, is to match it off. To do this for fixed-price contracts with local distribution companies, which are shorter in term, Enron makes use of the exchange-traded futures and options markets out to 18 months. For fixed-price contracts of three to five years, which are of interest to industrial users and cogeneration plants, Enron is obliged to find offsetting transactions in the OTC market.

Meanwhile, certain business deals such as the volumetric production payments (VPPs) discussed below create long-term exposures for Enron that also have to be managed. The counterparties to these longer-term commitments are usually other major oil and gas companies, or the energy derivative groups at major financial institutions.

It is this interconnection between the markets when managing a broad spectrum of risks that causes many dealers to suggest that the success of the exchange market is reliant upon the success of the OTC market – and vice versa.

Back to the future

In terms of volume, the energy risk management market is likely to remain dominated by standard products of one- to two-years' duration, as the core business is driven by corporate budgeting and opportunistic investment. However, the range of products that the market feels familiar with is continually expanding.

Although "plain vanilla" instruments will continue to dominate in terms of volume, new instruments have proved successful in the energy risk management markets when they have been carefully tailored to the needs of end-users. Chapter 1 demonstrates how, even within the swaps market, a relatively wide range of instruments is now

in common use, while Chapters 2 and 3 chart the huge advances in modern option technology. As the authors of these chapters point out, however, end-users have proved resistant to buying the full range of exotic options available in financial risk management markets. They are also rightly wary of "black boxes" – today's derivative end-user wants to know the risks that more complex instruments entail and how to value them accurately and independently.

Another interesting sector, and one, which has made increasing use of innovative structures, is project financing. The most important instrument type here is perhaps the prepaid swap, whereby the fixed payments of a classic swap are brought forward and paid upfront. In effect, this sort of swap creates a synthetic financing which is amortised as the proceeds from energy production are realised.

Many variations of this prepaid swap theme have been applied in the market already. As described in Chapter 6, in the natural gas risk management market this type of structure is often called a volumetric production payment (VPP). In a VPP deal, actual physical gas or oil production is committed as payment to a counterparty. On the other side of the deal, a counterparty such as Enron calculates the net present value of the future commodity flows to be realised from the reserves financed under the VPP contract. The buyer of the gas secures the contract by securing its rights to the physical gas, or by obtaining a financial guarantee such as a letter of credit, to avoid potential complications resulting from a counterparty that goes into default. In the event of bankruptcy, a VPP entitles a counterparty to receive a predetermined volume of produced gas over a certain time period, and provides it with a direct legal claim on the reserves.

This book focuses on energy risk management, but many uses are now being found for energy derivative technology that do not involve altering risk profiles. Prepaid commodity swaps, for example, are used to manage liability and tax positions – a development driven by the fact that such a swap may not be eligible for withholding tax and may not be recorded on the balance sheet as debt.

One difficulty in looking to the future of the energy risk management market is that there are few reliable indicators even of the present size of the market, still less statistical evidence of sector growth. However, in 1998 one US energy company estimated the total value of all OTC energy derivative contracts outstanding as $1 trillion. This compares to previous estimates by analysts of around $50 billion to $75 billion of contracts at the end of 1993. Certainly growth in the market has been huge, though cynics would say that both the historical and the current estimates represent little more than educated guesswork.

Growth – and the lack of it

While the energy risk management market is certainly only a fraction of the size of the OTC interest rate and currency derivative market, dealers are keen to point out that many potential hedgers remain on the sidelines. The single most striking example is the US oil major Exxon, which in 1999 created the largest company in the world in terms of revenue by merging with fellow US oil major Mobil. Exxon is known to regard itself as large enough and integrated enough to be self-hedged. It is certainly large – with revenues of $182 billion in the 1997 financial year – though those who market derivatives instruments have their own arguments against the theory that an oil major involved in both production and refining does not need to protect itself from price risk with derivatives instruments.

But more significant than Exxon's absence is the official lack of interest among member states of the Organisation of the Petroleum Exporting Countries (Opec) in using derivatives for risk management. At a public level, the governments and nationalised oil companies of most of the 11 member states are indifferent at best and hostile at worst to derivatives, on the grounds that they contribute to instability in oil prices. Whether this is true is an entirely different matter from the subject in hand, which is that even in 1999, with oil prices dipping for a short period to $10 a barrel (the exact price depending on which benchmark one uses), Opec member states do not generally admit to having used oil derivatives. Venezuela, Opec's only Latin American member and a member state whose high level of overproduction has given it a bit of a reputation

as a maverick, was as of early 1999 the only one to have admitted derivatives use, though the hedging about which its state oil company, Petróleos de Venezuela (PDVSA), had come clean was fairly small-time in volume. Even PDVSA's tentative move was attacked by other Opec member states. Although Iran is rumoured to have used derivatives, and the Singapore International Monetary Exchange indicated back in 1996 that it had held training sessions in how to use futures contracts in the Middle East, Opec's member states still remain a large untapped area for energy derivatives marketers.

Conclusion

This introduction has talked about market growth in terms of new areas of risk management, technical innovation, regulatory evolution and the increasing sophistication of market participants. But no introduction to the history of energy price risk management should conclude without underlining the role of "event risk". In the short history of the industry, energy-related calamities and the price volatility they bring have arguably proven as important in market growth and change as any of the factors discussed above.

The Gulf War, for example, played a key role in increasing oil and refining product derivative volumes, while the havoc wreaked by Hurricane Andrew along the US Gulf Coast helped fuel the dramatic growth of the natural gas derivative market in 1993. To this list we can now add the credit and market price risk explosion in the power markets in the summer of 1998. In a risk management industry, the importance of these events largely speaks for itself. A senior derivatives practitioner pointed out in the first edition of this book, "There's only one predictable aspect of such event-induced chaos. The more disruptive it is, the more fertile its effect on the energy risk management market overall". As for its effect on individual players, well, that is another story...

1 *The historical section of this introduction could not have been written without the advice and views of numerous experienced risk management practitioners. In particular we would like to thank Gaylen Byker, Nachamah Jacobovits, Ron Liesching, Jennifer Modesett, Paul Newman, Kate Smith, Jon Wheeler and Mildred Ford for directing us to many sources of information that we could not have found without their help. We would also like to thank the larger cast of energy derivative participants – both those named in the introduction and those who are not – who*

freely gave their time in contributing to this whirlwind history.

2 *Later in the market's development it became clear that hedging exposure to jet fuel prices by fixing the price of crude oil left hedgers badly exposed if the price of jet fuel rose much faster and further than crude prices.*

3 *The negotiations with Cathay Pacific were conducted by Van Lessig of Chase Hong Kong, who began talking to*

Cathay Pacific after attending one of the Advanced Financial Risk seminars described in Note 4.

4 *Chase's head start in oil swaps grew out of a series of Advanced Financial Risk seminars held at the bank from 1984. These AFR seminars were designed to bring together a critical mass of ideas and people to stimulate new product development. Ironically, they were also designed as a "mindstretcher" for corporate clients: if an oil producer considered the possibility of swapping oil cash flows for Libor flows, then more conventional interest rate caps and currency swaps might start to seem almost old-fashioned. The seminars were organised by Sykes Wilford . Other key figures included Bruce Smith, a some-time lecturer at the seminars, who took the first swap proposal to Chase's senior management, and Michael Hampton, author of Chapter 2 of this book, who helped to build the energy swaps concept and to start up Chase's commodity swaps business in Europe.*

5 *Gaylen Byker is now president of Calvin College and Ron Liesching is now with Pareto Partners in London.*

6 *Also backing up his efforts at that time were Peter Foggin and Michael Hampton (who pushed the commodity swap concept to airlines, shipping companies and utilities), Mark Harrison (head of Chase commodities), Michael Hudson (head of Chase's project finance group), Yoram Kimberg (a new products specialist who served on Chase's risk management committee) and Bob Lichten (head of North American capital markets at Chase).*

7 *Market sources say that Howard Sosin and Drexel Burnham Lambert were also hot on the trail of average price options at this time. In an academic setting, the concept of an average price option, or Asian option, was first developed by David Emanuel, professor of finance at the University of Texas at Dallas, and Phelim P. Boyle, the J. Page R. Wadsworth chair in finance in the School of Accountancy at the University of Waterloo in Waterloo, Ontario. Boyle says they first had a conversation on this topic in the foyer of the Faculty Club at the University of British Columbia in Vancouver (where both of them were professors in the faculty of commerce) in the autumn of 1979. In working papers, they subsequently generalised the average price option concept to include different types of averages as well as the arithmetic average: notably the geometric average and the harmonic average. They demonstrated how to value these options using the Monte Carlo method, and in later research, showed how to use the geometric mean as a control variate to increase the accuracy of the answer.*

In an interview in the mid-1990s Prof Boyle shared this interesting anecdote about the perceived value of their dis-covery early on: "When we submitted our paper, the Journal of Finance rejected it, mostly on the grounds that the proposed new options did not then exist and would have limited practical interest. We put the paper in a drawer and went on to work on other topics. Our general approach was rediscovered several times in the 1980s by Ton Vorst and Angelien Kemna, as well as Peter Ritchken and many others. I had always wanted to develop a closed-form solution for the European Asian option with continuous averaging and spent several hours on this problem. I posed this problem while visiting UC Berkeley in 1989. Eric Reiner's roommate was in my class and he gave it to Eric. At the time, Eric was completing his doctorate in Chemical Engineering. I recall first meeting Eric in a coffee shop on Telegraph Avenue and discussing the problem with him. Eric was the first person to solve this problem with a closed-form solution; unfortunately, he did not publish it. The problem has also been solved by Marc Yor, the eminent French probabilist".

8 *This is not to claim that Bankers Trust devised the first examples of oil-linked financial engineering. This accolade belongs to Standard Oil of Ohio (Sohio), a semi-independent subsidiary of British Petroleum, which in 1985 became the first company to develop and market oil-indexed securities. Sohio issued $300 million in oil-linked notes to raise money in the debt markets at sub-Libor rates. These notes included two tranches of embedded oil call warrants.*

9 *"Oil-Price Swaps: Should These Innovative Financial Instruments Be Subject to Regulation by the Commodity Futures Trading Commission or the Securities and Exchange Commission?", by Lauren S. Klett.* Dickinson Law Review, *Winter 1989, p. 398.*

10 *Including responses from the American Bankers Association, Federal Reserve System Board of Governors, the Comptroller of the Currency, the Securities and Exchange Commission, Chase, Citicorp, JP Morgan, Morgan Stanley, and oil companies such as BP America, Chevron, Exxon, Koch Industries and Mobil.*

11 *Transnor (Bermuda) Limited v. BP North America Petroleum, 783 F. Supp. 1472 (S.D.N.Y. 1990). This case is discussed in more detail in Chapter 8 of this book.*

12 *"10th Anniversary of Crude Oil Futures",* Energy in the News, *New York Mercantile Exchange, Spring 1991, p. 21.*

13 *"15th Anniversary Edition",* Energy in the News, *New York Mercantile Exchange, Fall/Winter 1993, p. 5.*

14 *"15th Anniversary Edition",* Energy in the News, *New York Mercantile Exchange, Fall/Winter 1993, p.7.*

ENERGY INSTRUMENTS

Section Introduction

Vincent Kaminski

Enron Corp

From the late 1980s through into the late 1990s, derivatives and derivative-based valuation techniques have proliferated across the energy industry. This financial revolution came about as a result of structural developments in both the financial services sector and the energy industry.

During the 1990s, financial institutions faced shrinking profit margins and increasing over-brokering of their traditional lines of business, such as interest rate swaps and currency trading. They reacted to these trends by trying to "push the envelope" of their portfolio of financial products in three dimensions: product complexity; the range of instruments underlying the derivative contracts; and customer base (in terms of client diversity and geographical location).

In many cases, these attempts were futile. Product complexity tends to backfire, as customers are reluctant to enter into derivatives transactions they do not fully comprehend and cannot independently price and evaluate in terms of the inherent risks. The expansion of the scope of the underlying instruments into areas such as emerging markets securities has run into difficulties because these markets are (as yet) relatively illiquid; also, the heterogeneous nature of the underlying instruments makes trading and hedging quite difficult. Finally, expanding the customer base of derivatives users to new industries and new geographic locations is a time-consuming process that demands a substantial initial investment in staffing and client education – and considerable patience.

The difficulty of creating and expanding new lines of business explains the growing interest in trading energy commodities and financial and physical options related to energy. The sheer size of the energy markets suggests that they can support the infrastructure necessary for derivative transactions of considerable volume; the size of the markets also creates enough room for a large number of market makers.

At the same time, and more importantly, there is significant interest in risk management tools from end-users of derivatives. This is largely because of the rapid deregulation of production, and to some extent transportation and distribution, in many sectors of the energy industry.

In the past, risk management for many companies in the energy industry simply meant maintaining good relationships with their regulator. For example, electric utilities in regulated markets used to purchase fuel at the current market price and transfer all the costs incurred to their customers using so-called "fuel-adjustment clauses". Meanwhile, regulatory action often actively discouraged hedging. If a utility hedged its feedstock risk, for example, and the market price for the fuel fell below the fixed price of the long-term fuel purchase contract, the regulators would often deny the inclusion of such "imprudent" costs in the rate base. "Hedging gains", on the other hand, would have to be shared with the customers.

Deregulation in the US has given the energy industry freedom to conduct its business in a more rational way, but at the same time exposes the industry to the risk of price variability. For the first time in their history, energy corporations are now obliged to control price risk through the use of modern hedging techniques. Especially important for power generators and refiners is the management of the so-called "spread risk" between the prices of inputs and their end products: electricity and petrochemical products. Utilities are also interested in selling options on generation capacity. Writing covered calls on excess capacity is regarded by the utilities as a convenient way of enhancing their short-term returns.

End-users of energy expect to gain significant benefits from the deregulation of the industry, but they also will face increased exposure to highly volatile prices. In the past, the industrial customers of electric utilities, for example, had little room to manoeuvre in any contract negotiations. In order to extract rate concessions the only threat they could make was that of moving their manufacturing plants to another location, or of resorting to self generation. After deregulation, industrials will easily be able to solicit competitive bids from multiple sources of supplies.

One important factor in the popularity of energy derivatives is the heterogeneous nature of energy commodities. It is true that electrons or natural gas molecules are perfectly homogeneous in terms of their physical characteristics. What is often missed is that physical fungibility does not necessarily translate into fungibility in an economic sense. Power or natural gas supplies made available at a different time of the day, or at different geographical locations, represent significantly different commodities.

In the case of the power markets, this lack of economic homogeneity is exacerbated by the perishable nature of electricity and of transportation/transmission. Power can be stored only indirectly, as a spinning reserve or as a supply of water behind a dam or in a pump storage facility. These factors contribute jointly to what is known in the financial industry as basis risk: the danger that the prices of two or more commodities will decouple. Such exposures can be managed efficiently through options offered by institutions that are well equipped to handle such risks.

The interest of financial institutions, the quest of producers and end-users of energy for risk management tools, and the size of the underlying market, all created the conditions for explosive growth in energy-related derivatives. One can already distinguish several stages in the early history of the derivatives market. The first stage, from the late 1980s to the early 1990s can be characterised as the bronze age of the industry: a period of rapid adaptation of option structures developed in the financial markets to the needs of the energy industry. This period was characterized by the relatively strong presence of financial institutions such as investment banks – compared to physical/financial players such as energy majors – and by a tendency to copy indiscriminately option and swap structures from the equity and fixed-income markets to the energy markets. In fact the pricing paradigms, models

and software used by energy businesses were almost indistinguishable from similar tools applied elsewhere.

Somewhat to the credit of the energy industry, many of these transplants from other markets were eventually rejected. They simply did not answer the needs of the market. One special feature of the problems faced by the energy industry is the need to control – at the same time and often within the same derivative structures - risks related to both market price fluctuations and volume uncertainty. In the first section of this book, we review some of the special challenges in the structuring and valuation of energy-related contracts. The first two chapters describe how various financial tools are applied in the energy industry and review the contract structures that have survived the test of time. The first chapter, contributed by Jack Kellett, examines the family of swap contracts while the second, by Michael Hampton, offers a sophisticated introduction to energy options.

The next stage, the silver age of the industry, dating from the mid 1990s up to the present, might be characterised as a period of "confrontation with reality". During this period, professional quantitative analysts ("quants", in derivatives industry jargon) working in the energy business recognised that energy markets have many special features that distinguish them from financial markets. One obvious challenge, highlighted by the recent development of competitive power markets, is the nature of the price processes followed by the energy prices. Traditional approaches from the financial markets, based on diffusion models, simply do not work that well in energy markets – mainly because energy markets tend to "gap" and "jump" for reasons related to economic fundamentals and political events.

In a related development, analysts began to recognise the full importance of the physical characteristics of energy markets – and how these affect any financial market in an energy commodity. Perhaps this recognition lies behind another recent trend: players straddling both physical and financial markets seem to be prospering and increasing their market share. The third chapter in this section, by Vincent Kaminski, Stinson Gibner and Krishnarao Pinnamaneni, offers a partial review of developments on the theoretical side of option valuation and risk management and relates these to the fundamentally different nature of the energy business as compared to the financial markets.

There are reasons to hope that we are entering today the golden age: a period of extensive use of derivatives in the energy industry across all markets. Option pricing technology is being pushed upstream and is increasingly used to value fixed assets such as generation plant, gas pipelines and gas storage facilities. Chapter 4 in this section, by Lloyd Spencer, offers some examples of how option-related tools can be used to evaluate such investment projects.

Other developments explored in this section of chapters include the creation of a market for weather instruments, which should help power companies control volume risk, and the integration of the various sectors of the energy markets. This integration is leading to a creation of a liquid Btu market for "energy", with the physical form, delivery point and timing of delivery of that energy left to the discretion of one of the counterparties of a contract. This is a radical concept for energy markets in the new millennium, and Chapter 3 offers a review of certain option structures that can be used to model such multi-commodity transactions.

1

Energy Swaps

Jack Kellett[1]
Credit Lyonnais Rouse Derivatives

The development of the swaps derivatives markets in the oil industry has been fraught with many difficult events. Metallgesellschaft foundered, and various other experienced oil markets participants have owned up to problems in swap risk management. These issues have not prevented the explosive rise of the swap contract as an effective management tool for the energy industry. The opening of electricity and natural gas markets has increased the scope of this market many fold. In fact it seems clear that the energy market will emerge into the next century as one of the greatest commodity markets the world has seen.

The driving force behind this growth has been the increasing involvement of financial intermediaries. Banks and trading companies that understand market-making and risk management have acted as middlemen. They have bridged the gap between market participants who wanted protection from falling prices and those that wanted protection from rising prices. Without the intermediaries, it is unlikely that consumers of oil would be able to match themselves with producers to offset risks of similar size and duration.

Another principal reason why we have experienced this growth is the increase in technical knowledge about the market and the instruments available. As end-users develop a deeper understanding of the mechanics of risk control, their inclination to enter into complex swaps, that are tailored to specific risks, increases.

One of the aims of this chapter is to extend that understanding through analysis of the range of energy swap structures now available. We will also review the various market sectors, and examine the role played by intermediaries. As well as surveying some of the problems of using the energy swaps market from the point of view of the end-user, we will explore some of the strategic considerations in pricing and hedging swaps faced by the intermediary. We will conclude by highlighting how we think that the energy swaps market will evolve in the near future.

The structure of energy swaps

The basic or "plain vanilla" energy swap differs little from swaps in other derivative markets, and is really a very simple financial instrument. However, several interrelated factors have combined to cause an increase in the diversity of the instruments used in the oil swap market. In particular, a more liquid and competitive market for swaps has attracted oil industry participants that are very aware of the specific price risks that they face – particularly in the low profit margin environment since 1993–94 – and are demanding more customised structures. Therefore, after briefly describing the basic building-block, we will outline the most important tailored instruments; the practical application of these structures is demonstrated throughout this chapter in a series of separate panels.

"PLAIN VANILLA" SWAP

A simple oil swap is an agreement whereby a floating price is exchanged for a fixed price over a specified period. It is an off-balance-sheet financial arrangement which involves no transfer of physical oil; both parties settle their contractual obligations by means of a transfer of cash. The agreement defines the volume, duration, fixed price and floating price. Differences are settled in cash for specific periods – usually monthly, but sometimes quarterly, six-monthly or annually.

Swaps are also known as "contracts for differences" and as "fixed-for-floating" contracts – terms which summarise the essence of these arrangements.

Producers sell swaps to lock in their sales price. The producer and the intermediary agree a fixed price, for example, $18 per barrel for an agreed oil specification index, and a floating price, often a reference price derived from Platt's or one of the futures markets.

For the period agreed, the producer receives

PLAIN VANILLA SWAP

In 1998, Rhumba Reefers A/S, a refrigerated vessel operator consuming about 400,000 tonnes of fuel per annum, decided to hedge some of the company's exposure to heavy fuel oil price risk, as the current price was low relative to the company's budget levels. It was new to the market and unfamiliar with the jargon, settlement processes, etc. It therefore chose a "plain vanilla" or straightforward swap as the simplest vehicle for its first hedge. Such a swap is a simple exchange of fixed prices for floating prices, whereby the consumer fixes his price today for a period some time into the future. The cash settlements under the swap mirror the ups and downs of the physical market, so Rhumba Reefers knew that the final price it would pay would be the fixed price agreed under the swap.

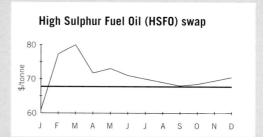

High Sulphur Fuel Oil (HSFO) swap

On October 27, 1998, Rhumba Reefers locked into a swap at $68.00/t for calendar year 1999. By December, prices had fallen even further, but the company remained comfortable with the fixed price that it had locked in, which was some $7/t lower than its budgeted figure; it was happy to take advantage of lower prices on its remaining, unhedged consumption. In the New Year, prices rallied strongly as a result of lower stocks, cold weather and, more significantly, tight supply due to the lack of the sour crudes usually exported from Russia. On balance, the hedging strategy looked wise, and the company decided to add additional volume at a similar level if the market dipped.

Fixed price buyer:	Rhumba Reefers A/S
Fixed price seller:	CLRD
Fixed price:	$68.00
Reference prices:	HSFO 3.5% Barges FOB Rotterdam
Duration:	Calendar year 1999
Volume:	5,000 tonnes per month. Total of 60,000t
Settlement:	Monthly cash settlement

from the intermediary the difference between fixed and floating if the latter is lower. If the floating price is higher, the difference is paid by the producer to the intermediary.

The simplest formula for calculating the difference is:

Contracted monthly volume × (fixed price minus floating price)

An example of a Brent swap for January 1994 might be:

50,000 bbl × ($18.00–$17.20) = $40,000

In this case, a seller of Brent crude which took on an $18 swap for 50,000 bbl per month would have received $40,000 for January. Had the average of the floating price been higher, the producer would have paid the difference to the intermediary.

The consumer of energy uses a swap in order to stabilise the buying price (see Panel 1). An airline buying jet fuel, for example, would contract to buy a jet swap with a fixed-price element of,

for example, $140 per tonne. If the floating average was $150 per tonne, then the airline would receive a monthly settlement of $10 per tonne multiplied by the volume hedged. If the floating price averaged $135 per tonne, then the airline pays out $5 per tonne.

DIFFERENTIAL SWAP

Whereas a standard swap is based on the differential between fixed and floating prices, a "diff" swap is based on the difference between a fixed differential for two products, and the actual or floating differential over time.

Some examples of energy products which might attract diff swaps include jet versus gasoil, physical (Platt's) gasoil versus futures, 3.5% fuel versus 1% fuel, and Brent versus WTI Crude oil.

Diff swaps are typically used by refiners to hedge changing margins between refined products. Refiners usually receive the fixed-price side of the swap, ensuring a known, forward relationship for the price of their various products. If they sell the diff and the diff narrows, then the refiner receives the difference; if it expands, the refiner pays out.

DIFFERENTIAL SWAP

Foxtrot Flyers, a European scheduled carrier, uses a mixture of jet fuel and IPE gasoil swaps to hedge its jet fuel exposure for the immediate budget year. It tends to use gasoil swaps when it perceives the forward jet fuel premium to be too high.

Due to a sustained period of weakness in the physical jet fuel market, the forward jet-gasoil premiums have recently narrowed quite significantly. Foxtrot Flyers decides to take this opportunity to eliminate the basis risk inherent in its gasoil hedges – that is, the risk that the gasoil price would move out of tandem with the price of jet fuel – by effectively converting these hedges to jet fuel by means of a jet-gasoil differential swap.

Differential:	Jet Cargoes CIF NWE minus IPE Gasoil
Differential buyer:	Foxtrot Flyers
Differential seller:	CLRD
Differential price:	$21.00 per tonne
Reference prices:	Platt's mean quotes for Jet Cargoes CIF NWE
	IPE frontline settlements for gasoil

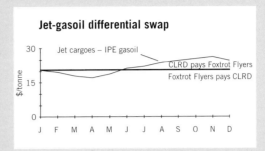

Jet-gasoil differential swap

Duration:	April to March inclusive
Volume:	10,000 tonnes per month. Total of 120,000 tonnes
Settlement:	Monthly cash settlement

If the average differential between the price of gasoil and jet fuel for each month is above $21 per tonne, then Foxtrot Flyers will receive the difference multiplied by the monthly volume. It will pay the difference if the monthly average is less than $21. Consequently, the company has eliminated the risk that jet fuel prices will increase more than gasoil prices.

Diff swaps may also be used by companies as a way of managing the basis risk assumed during their normal hedging activity. For example, an airline which prefers to hedge its jet exposure with gasoil swaps, because of the perceived value of these deals, may enter into a jet/gasoil diff swap to hedge this potential basis risk (see Panel 2).

MARGIN OR CRACK SWAP

Refiners who prefer to fix a known refining margin can construct elaborate forward (physical) and futures (exchange) deals for their products. However, such constructions can be costly and rarely provide complete cover.

Alternatively, they can enter into a refining margin swap, whereby the product output of the refinery and the crude (or feedstock) input are simultaneously hedged, ie the products are sold and the crude is bought for forward periods. At settlement, the refiner either pays or receives the difference between the margins; the calculation is based on the prices in the spot markets and those locked in (see Panel 3 overleaf). In this way, the profitability of a refinery can be guaranteed for a few years forward. This kind of hedging is often integrated into development projects

and upgrading schemes when the financiers are keen to ensure the viability of the project and to underwrite a minimum revenue stream.

PARTICIPATION SWAP

A participation swap is similar to a regular swap in that the fixed price payer is 100% protected when prices rise above the agreed price but, unlike an ordinary swap, the client "participates" in the downside (see Panel 4 overleaf). If, for example, a participation swap is agreed at a level of $80 per tonne for high sulphur fuel oil, with a 50% participation, the buyer would be fully protected against prices above $80 per tonne, but would also retain 50% of the savings generated when prices fell below $80 per tonne. If prices fall to $70 per tonne, the client would only pay out $5 per tonne rather than the $10 per tonne due under a regular swap. The level agreed determines the percentage of the participation, or vice versa.

DOUBLE-UP SWAP

By using this instrument, swap users can achieve a swap price which is better than the prevailing market price, but the swap provider will retain the option to double the swap volume before

MARGIN SWAP

Rock 'N Roll Refiners Ltd, a refiner based in Rotterdam, wishes to protect a proportion of its exposure to oil prices. Because it is both a consumer of crude oil and a producer of refined products, its exposure is to adverse movements in the value of crude oil relative to products. This is referred to as "crack spread" risk. Refiners such as Rock 'N Roll are therefore attracted to "margin swaps". This means that the company can fix feedstock cost and sell the refined products forward in a proportion that matches the refinery's output profile in order to lock in the margin. Refiners tend to have a good appetite for such structures. Margins can often be negative for sustained periods of time, especially in simple or hydro-skimming refineries where upgrading capacity is limited, .

Reference prices:	IPE Brent crude oil 1st nearby contract
Duration:	Calendar year 1999
Volume:	100,000 bbls per month.
	Total of 1,200,000 bbls
Settlement:	Monthly cash settlement

Refined products leg

Fixed price buyer:	CLRD
Fixed price seller:	R 'N R Refiners Ltd
Reference prices:	Platt's European Marketscan
	mean prices

Product	Fixed Price	%
Unl. Gasoline Cargoes CIF NWE	$190.00	20
Jet Fuel CIF Cargoes NWE	$181.50	10
Gasoil 0.2 CIF Cargoes	$159.50	30
LSFO 1% Cargoes CIF NWE	$101.00	37
Losses		3

By using the above structure, the refiner is able to lock into a margin of $1.98 per barrel for the whole of calendar year 1999.

Crude oil leg

Fixed price buyer:	R 'N R Refiners Ltd
Fixed price seller:	CLRD
Fixed price:	$17.00/bbl (landed equivalent)

the pricing period starts. The mechanism by which this is achieved involves consumers (who are buying a fixed price) selling a put swaption, or producers (who are selling a fixed price) selling a call swaption; in either case, the premium earned from the sale is used to subsidise the swap price.

For example, an airline might be able to negotiate a swap price of $150 per tonne for the winter period. This swap price could be reduced to $145 by selling the put option on the same swap to the counterparty. On the swaption exercise date, the swap provider will decide whether or not to double the swap volume (depending upon market prices at the time).

EXTENDABLE SWAP
The extendable swap is constructed on the same principle as the double-up swap, except that the provider has the right to extend the swap, at the end of the agreed period, for a further predetermined period (see Panel 5).

PRE-PAID SWAP
By means of a pre-paid swap, the fixed payment cash-flow line can be discounted back to its net present value and paid to the user. Pre-paid

swaps are often used as a source of pre-export financing, and they are discussed in detail in the section devoted to that topic below.

OFF-MARKET SWAP
In this type of swap the "fixed price" does not reflect the prevailing market. A premium is built into the swap price to fund the purchase of options or to allow for the restructuring of a hedge portfolio. Off-market swaps are generally used to restructure or cancel old swap/hedge deals: essentially, they simulate a refinancing package.

For example, imagine that a shipping company has entered into a three-year swap at $90 per tonne for heavy fuel oil. For the first two years, the swap proves advantageous, and provides the company with a significant positive cashflow (as market prices remain high). However a very mild winter then causes fuel oil prices to fall rapidly at the start of the third year of the contract.

The company believes that this price slump will not last long and, due to a lull in business, it decides it would rather not have this additional strain on its cashflow. Consequently, it decides to extend the swap for a further year, at the

PANEL 4

PARTICIPATION SWAP

Tango Trucking Company, a small distribution company, has only a relatively small volume of gasoil (diesel) exposure. However, it sees a dip in market prices as an ideal opportunity to protect its budget for the next financial year. In the past, the company had preferred to use straightforward swaps as a hedging instrument due to their simplicity. But, in this instance, it has a strong view that prices may go lower and so it wants an instrument that allows it to benefit from any downside move without having to pay any up-front premium. To achieve these objectives, Tango Trucking opts for a 50% participation swap.

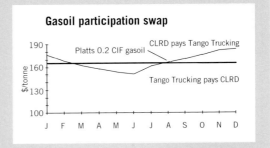

Gasoil participation swap

Fixed price buyer:	Tango Trucking
Fixed price seller:	CLRD
Fixed price:	$165/tonne
Buyers participation:	50%
Reference prices:	Platt's Gasoil 0.2 CIF Cargoes
Duration:	January to December inclusive
Volume:	5,000 tonnes per month. Total of 60,000 tonnes

Settlement: Monthly cash settlement

Tango Trucking was correct in its view that the gasoil price would drop lower for a time. With the 50% participation swap, it had only to pay out half of the normal settlement amount when the average price for the month was below $165 (that is, the price difference times 2,500 tonnes). When the average gasoil price for the month then rose above $165, Tango Truckers received the price difference times 5,000 tonnes.

---

price of $93. As the price of fuel oil is now lower, the price of this extension is actually $10 above the normal swap price. The discounted value of the extension is then deducted from the price of the current-year swap.

CURVE-LOCK AND BACKWARDATION SWAPS
These structures are variations on the same theme, and are basically plays on the shape of the oil price curve. By oil price curve, we mean here the series of prices for a given commodity contract reflecting settlement at successive dates into the future, which can be represented as a "curve" on a graph. By locking into a spread between different points on this curve, a market participant can lock into either backwardation or contango in the market.

For example, by buying October 1999 WTI contracts and selling March 2000 WTI contracts, a trader could lock into a spread of six cents; that is, the trader sells the forward contract at six cents below the prompter contract. If at the end of the pricing period, the average daily spread between these two contracts was 16 cents, then the trader will collect 10 cents profit. If, on the other hand, March averaged four cents above October, the trader will pay out 10 cents.

The rationale behind such a trade is that the

trader believes that the backwardation in the market will become steeper (which typically reflects a bullish view of the market). A strategy such as this, therefore, is essentially speculative.

However, the strategy can be viewed as an indirect hedge in that, if the market goes into contango while a market participant is locked into this kind of structure, it is because prompt prices have become very weak. And if prices are weak then obviously any consumer of fuel will benefit from cheaper physical supplies. The problem with using curve-lock swaps as a base hedge is that the user often remains vulnerable to basis risk.

Applying energy swaps: end-user benefits and concerns

The various swap arrangements described in the previous section allow companies to manage their exposure to energy price risk with considerable flexibility:

❏ producers and processors can offer fixed-price products to their consumers;

❏ refiners can fix their margins;

❏ production margins can be guaranteed in development projects;

❏ banks can offer more attractive financing when price exposure is controlled;

EXTENDABLE SWAP

Pogo Producers, an independent Brent crude oil producer, has decided that the timing is right to enter the market to fix the revenue for a portion of its production for the next 12 months. At the current market swap price, it will comfortably beat its budget forecasts. However, the company believes that prices are unlikely to continue at the relatively high levels. To take advantage of this view, and its naturally long oil position, it decides to enter into an extendable swap. In this case, Pogo Producers will be selling the swap provider the right to extend a one-year swap into two years. The swap provider will have the right to extend the swap at the end of the first year. The price for the second year will be the same as the first year. The actual swap price which the company achieves will be an improvement on the normal market price, equating to the market price plus the premium value of the swaption (option on a swap) that they are selling.

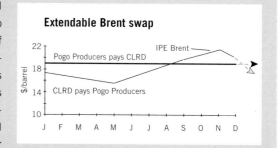

Extendable Brent swap

Fixed price buyer:	CLRD
Fixed price seller:	Pogo Producers
Fixed price:	$19/bbl
Extendable price:	$19/bbl
Reference prices:	IPE Brent frontline settlement prices

Duration: January to December inclusive

Volume: 100,000 bbls per month. Total of 1,200,000 bbls

(same for extendable swap)

Settlement: Quarterly cash settlement

For the duration of the swap for the first year, Pogo Producers will be benefiting from the fact that it has a higher swap price. It will be receiving cash settlements when the average quarterly Brent price is below $19, and paying out when the market price is above $19. At the end of this first year, the swap will be extended for another 12 months if the forward swap value for the period is higher than $19. This price also complements the company's longer-term budget forecast.

❏ pre-export financing can be secured on net present values of swap cash-flows;

❏ exposure to one oil product can be switched to another, for example, an airline fixing futures prices in gasoil can eliminate the inherent basis risk by using a jet-gasoil differential swap;

❏ competitive advantage can be secured by locking into high/low prices;

❏ certain limitations of the exchanges (notably liquidity, duration, the need for margin adjustments and the limited range of product specifications) can be overcome.

Despite these benefits, few companies hedge all of their price exposure, particularly in the longer term. Instead, the convention among end-users is to hedge the current financial year plus one, while the percentage of this exposure that companies seek to cover is usually somewhere between 40–60%. A growing number of companies are also using swaps to part-protect their three- to five-year budgets.

One reason why companies only hedge a fraction of their exposure is because they do not

want to risk foregoing gains if the market moves favourably. Companies may also be concerned that they will be left at a relative price disadvantage compared to their competitors. But it would still appear that most companies are under-utilising the risk management potential of energy swaps.

One of the main limiting factors is a lack of knowledge about derivatives. Another problem is that, in the past, the energy swaps market has been inefficient with regard to competition and liquidity. There is gradual improvement on these counts – particularly for longer-dated products. Swap spreads (the difference between the cost of a swap to a buyer and a seller), have narrowed, although in some of the less mainline products, and in less active geographical areas, illiquidity still leads to inconsistencies and inefficiencies.

A further specific improvement in efficiency is that the market can generate swap prices in non-dollar currencies. Users may want only the fixed-price part of a swap in the local currency,

PRIVATE PLACEMENT INDEXED TO JET FUEL

Waltzing Wings, a relatively small but profitable regional carrier, has decided that, in the current circumstances, the best way to raise significant financing is in the private placement market. The best offer that its bankers achieve is from a US insurance company which is willing to invest $100 million for a return of Libor plus 50bp over 10 years. The bank has offered to swap this floating rate into a fixed rate of 8.00% for the airline. Waltzing Wings is happy with this price; however, as its business is so marginal it is concerned that the maintenance on this financing may prove excessive during periods when other costs are high.

In the past, its most significant and volatile cost has been jet fuel, which generally accounts for about 15% of operating costs. From experience, it knows that its cash flows, particularly, suffer during periods of high oil prices. Thus, it wants to ensure that, with such burdensome financing costs, this fuel exposure is appropriately managed. After weighing up the options, the com-

pany decides to enter into a structure which simply indexes the financing cost to the price of jet fuel.

This fuel-indexed financing is arranged so that, over the 10-year term, when the price of jet fuel (cargoes CIF NWE) is above $195 per tonne there is an offsetting reduction in the loan interest. Conversely, when the jet fuel price is below this level, the interest cost will rise. The net payments are bi-annual. This relationship can be expressed using the simple formula:

$$8.00\% \times (1 + (195 - FPF)/195)$$

where FPF = Future Price of Fuel, calculated as the daily average of the mean price of Jet Fuel Cargoes CIF NWE as published by Platt's for each six-month period. Note that this is the opposite of one much-discussed structure recently offered to energy companies and airlines. In this case, put premiums were used to secure sub-Libor financing up-front. However, this led to large unhedged losses as the market declined through 1998.

if they buy oil in dollars. However, if they buy oil in the local currency then it is possible to arrange both the fixed and floating side in that currency. Clearly the currency risk element in a swap out of dollars into any other currency will need a certain amount of management. In the latter case, the risk rests with the swap issuer, whereas in the usual dollar-denominated case the risk will be borne by the consumer. (In most cases non-dollar swaps are sought by smaller companies with limited foreign exchange lines, such as local charter airlines. In other cases, they may simply reflect the fact that most of the company's transactions are in the local currency, and that dollar-denominated oil is an awkward but significant element in the equation.)

The true cost of any kind of swap can be difficult to resolve, and this is of legitimate concern to end-users. Given that almost all oil swaps are executed through intermediaries, it is clear that there must be a cost. A transaction in which a consumer swap is directly offset by a producer swap is the ideal transaction from the intermediary's point of view: the lack of risk(excepting credit exposure to each counterpart) means that the price difference between the two can be minimised, and no additional hedging is required by

the intermediary. However, precise fits are rare, and thus the swap price will reflect the intermediary's perception of the degree of risk that it will be obliged to assume (temporarily, at least).

Even in the case of "vanilla" swaps, users tend to be unfamiliar with the process of costing. Novelty breeds suspicion, and this in turn inhibits trading. But this disadvantage is being eroded: a survey of airlines reveals that a range of quotes for a given swap now produces fairly even prices. This procedure is of no use in the case of tailored swaps, of course, and most users are unlikely to possess the techniques necessary to price complex long-term swaps themselves.[2]

The structure of the swap market: a providers' perspective

COMPARISON WITH OTHER SWAP MARKETS
The mechanics of exchanging fixed-for-floating prices did not originate in the commodity markets, but in foreign currency and interest rate markets. Although commodity swaps are virtually identical to other swaps in terms of rationale and structure, providing and using them presents some quite specific problems.

Conventionally, the credit risk of commodity

counterparties is regarded as greater than that of participants in the foreign exchange and interest rate market. The strains on credit-backed arrangements, such as swaps, are also stretched by the greater price volatility on commodity markets – particularly oil.

This volatility also generates different problems. The global and highly liquid markets in foreign exchange and interest rates provide an efficient medium for swaps providers to lay off their risk. There is no structural difference between the cash and the forward markets; there are virtually no geographical concerns; and the relationships between different instruments, such as government and commercial paper, are generally well-established.

None of this is true for energy derivatives. Markets move in and out of contango and backwardation according to shifts in the balance of demand and supply. Local shortages and surpluses cannot be overcome quickly, simply because of the cost and time of moving product into and out of these areas. And, in the short term, even the established relationships between crude and downstream product can vary considerably. It is not uncommon, for example, for Brent crude FOB Sullom Voe to be in backwardation at the same time that Mediterranean MoGas or jet is in contango.

These variations in the "normal" price relationship between crude and downstream products, additional local variations and shifts in the spot/forward price relationship mean that dealing in energy swaps is relatively complex.

Perhaps the biggest challenge for energy swap providers is the volatility in oil price curves, particularly for downstream product, which require them to adopt a more flexible approach to hedging than their money-market counterparts. Such problems are exacerbated during times of uncertainty, when the psychological comfort of holding physical oil pushes up short-term buying, causing the spot premium or backwardation to rise sharply.

In the longer term, oil prices are determined by market expectations. But these expectations are themselves influenced by the amount of business being executed. Practitioners are well aware that a single large swap for three or four years out, for example, can influence the perception of the market.

Oil markets are also highly exposed international barometers of key political and military activity. Brent prices increased by 18% the day after Iraq invaded Kuwait. Traded option volatili-ty soared to over 100%, and settled at 70–80% for some weeks after. The pressure on jet prices, based on expectations of a large increase in military flying activity, was even greater. Swaps providers trying to hedge in such markets faced considerable difficulty, and the provider should be cautious about being short in the short term. Supply problems can lead to a spike in near-end prices while having little effect on longer-term prices.

Finally, because of the industrial culture of the oil sector, the responsibility for hedging often falls on the purchasing or operations manager of the end-user corporations. In contrast, currency and interest rate hedging is normally undertaken by the treasury manager. While we would not want to imply that purchasing managers are less capable, it is certainly true that they are often less familiar with measuring and offsetting risk. A swap provider in the energy markets therefore needs to be able to explain the conceptual basis for hedging, as well as proving the operational advantages of particular deals.

MARKET SECTORS: A BRIEF REVIEW

Oil companies Most major oil companies maintain specific derivatives trading or risk management teams. In addition to dealing in forwards, futures and options, these teams also use swaps to manage some physical exposure, more commonly to hedge particular deals with their own clients and, increasingly, to trade for profit. Derivatives are also used in project finance to risk manage major energy projects, as described below and in more detail in Chapter 4.

The main application of swaps, however, is the managed hedge, which enables an oil company to offer a fixed-price deal to its client. The offer of fixed-price product often generates a competitive advantage over other suppliers, and the oil producer hedges the assumed fixed/floating risk by means of a swap.

Airlines The jet fuel sector is the most mature and developed oil product sector. Airlines were the first serious users of commodity swaps, largely because jet fuel accounts for up to 20% of airline operating costs, and is the cost that is most exposed to short- and medium-term price fluctuation.

The Iraq-Kuwait crisis reinforced the need to manage this risk, as jet prices rose even further than the 80–100% price rise in crude oil.

Most major airlines now manage their jet exposure to some extent. Tight competition in the US airline sector has discouraged airlines from adopting new exposure management practices until recently. This is now beginning to change.

Since the growth of this business in the mid-1980s, airlines have become adept at combining swaps with various option structures. Typically, an airline will concentrate on hedging the next budget year (that is, 12–18 months out). Given present, historically low, price levels, there is also a growing tendency to hedge part of the medium-term exposure (three to five years forward). The latter strategies are usually implemented using a basis of swaps, with option structures added on.

Shipping companies The variable costs of a shipping company are dominated by bunker-fuel prices. In particular, fuel is often the only variable when ships are chartered for fixed terms. As with airlines, there is an increasing tendency to hedge forward with swaps, beyond annual budget periods. The shipping business is a long-term business: freight contracts of around 10 years' duration are common, and ship owners are therefore used to dealing with long-term risk. Long-term derivatives are a natural means of managing the oil price risk in such contracts, and although shipping companies tend not to hedge as large a percentage of their total consumption as airlines, they tend to hedge for longer periods.

Whereas airlines have no traditional alternative risk management tools, the shipping industry has used "bunker adjustment clauses" for many years to hedge oil price risk. It is only because such clauses are much less efficient and flexible that shipowners are switching to OTC derivative transactions.

Transport companies Like other sectors of the transportation sector, road haulage firms are exposed to diesel fuel prices. The biggest barrier to their participation in the OTC markets is the fragmentation of this risk. The majority of consumers are very small firms or independent truck owners working on a contract basis, and the price risk is thus spread relatively thinly.

Power companies Power generators that use gasoil or fuel oil (or indeed natural gas that is predominantly linked to a fueloil/gasoil index) are exposed to fluctuations that comprise a very large proportion of their variable cost base. The ability of generators to vary their power prices is very limited, particularly when selling to the household sector. Some companies have started hedging their fuel exposure, but without an adequate reference price mechanism (for example, Platt's) it is difficult to define a settlement price.

The developing market in electricity swaps (known as contracts for differences and EFAs) is analysed in Chapter 7.

Industrial groups Firms with a high energy consumption (for example, metal smelting and refining companies, cement manufacturers, glass makers) are increasing their use of swaps to manage fuel oil exposures. Some of these firms, such as metal producers, are experienced in managing other commodity price risks.

Chemical companies Petrochemical producers are typically exposed to naphtha price fluctuations but, apart from a few companies, this sector has yet to use swaps to any significant degree.

Financing organisations Banks and institutions which provide development finance for oil projects often carry a risk that is related to oil price. This may be because repayment is linked directly to the oil output of the completed project or, less directly, because credit risks associated with new projects are dependent on the forward price of energy.

Companies may also link oil swaps directly to bonds, warrants or other securities. There is also a specialist fund management market which uses certain commodity market instruments such as oil swaps.

Below, we provide a brief summary of the financing structures associated with energy derivatives.

ENERGY SWAPS IN FINANCING STRUCTURES
There are certain forms of finance which require long-term oil price risk management. In each case, the basic principle is the same: to use a swap to fix a known forward oil price (that is, income stream or cost factor). The following sections survey the range of financing problems that can be solved using swap-based structures.

Project finance Finance for a new field, large well or refinery is often provided by banks on a limited recourse basis. The bank's recourse to the development firm, for example, may be limited by the failure of the developer to achieve set income levels according to plan. There may be a number of reasons for this (technical, political, etc.), but one risk which can be removed by a swap structure is the market risk.

If selling prices are too low, then the income generated by a new project may be insufficient to repay the loan according to agreed terms. Engaging in a fixed-for-floating swap protects the prospective oil producer from any subsequent decline in oil prices (at the same time, of course, it gives up the right to participate in higher prices should they develop).

A particular risk in the context of project finance is the danger that the project will not even have come on line by the date that the swap comes into force. However, given the generally long lead times for such projects, it is usually possible to renegotiate these arrangements.

The role of swaps in financing such developments is particularly appropriate where the project is a high-cost producer, and the projected production costs are close to market prices. In this instance, the sensitivity of producers to adverse market fluctuations will increase the risks to the lenders, and thus increase the cost of financing. In a low price environment this becomes particularly pertinent.

Pre-export financing Swap-based financing does not only apply to commercial operations, such as mining and refining companies. Most oil-producing countries raise a production/export levy on oil output, particularly where oil exports are the major foreign exchange earner.

This makes such countries susceptible to changes in oil prices. Governments with a two- or three-year spending programme, or fixed loan repayments, are at risk from market-driven changes in the level of royalties. Many producer countries are heavily loaded with long-term debt arising from the upgrading of oil production, or the development of downstream capacity. As oil prices fall, their ability to finance this debt diminishes in tandem with their ability to raise new loans.

By means of pre-export financing, oil-exporting countries can pledge future production as collateral against immediate cash. Banks are usually more comfortable about advancing finance on the basis of receiving future oil flows, although clearly there can be considerable "country" or political risk to be taken account of.

Pre-export financing has been around for over a decade, since the famous deal in 1982 between the United States and Mexico. In this deal, the United States offered $1 billion cash in exchange for the transfer of Mexican oil into the US Strategic Petroleum Reserve. Although this kept the oil off the market, thereby helping to maintain stable prices, the effective interest rate on this debt, payable in the form of additional oil, amounted to 30%. Repayment schedules have become considerably less burdensome since.

In the Middle East, this type of pre-export financing has been popular due to the Islamic prohibition on interest rate financing. Iran, for example, has raised $2.5 billion in pre-export credits, primarily from three French banks: Crédit Lyonnais, BNP and Paribas. Repayment was in the form of physical oil, assigned to the banks at the time of loading. Simultaneously, oil trading companies made payments directly to the banks and were, in turn, assigned the cargoes. (British Aerospace and Saudi Arabia have a similar deal in place for payment of military air equipment.)

Since the repayment schedules have traditionally been written in the form of "oil to the value of", the market risk of this kind of deal to the intermediaries is negligible – especially as they are able to lay the risk off immediately on receipt. However, it seems only logical, now that the swaps market is large and liquid enough to handle country volumes, that the market risk element of pre-export finance will in the future be covered by a swap.

Asset finance Companies with a need to invest in new capital equipment or assets can link the cost of financing that asset to their fuel exposure. For example, aircraft or ship finance can be indexed to jet or bunker prices. Alternatively, refinery equipment costs can be linked to refinery margins.

Bond issues, equity issues and placements Bond and equity financing is a variation on direct financing (in the sense that it creates tradeable paper for the issuer or lender). The capital value of the debt and the income/coupon/dividend stream can be indexed to oil in much the same way as asset or pre-export finance deals.

The role of the intermediary

In theory, there is no reason why producers should not issue fixed-price swaps for purchase directly by consumers. In practice, the wide range of variables affecting oil markets – specification, geography, timing etc – would make this a choppy business. Thus intermediaries such as Crédit Lyonnais play a vital role in matching these various needs.

In addition to smoothing out the flows, intermediaries have added a considerable amount of professional skill. They have, as a group, effectively assumed some of the characteristics of a clearing system. They channel trades between buyers and sellers, they absorb and flatten out some of the imbalances which occur in the market and they provide a greater degree of price transparency.

An intermediary requires significant price making and risk management skills, a high degree of sophisticated structuring skills, and a detailed knowledge of the cash markets for energy. Perhaps the most important, however, given the bilateral financial risks which swap participants incur, is that the intermediary should be well-capitalised and financially strong. Some firms in this sector, and not simply the intermediaries, have established high credit rating, big balance sheet subsidiaries, specifically in order to trade swaps.

Banks and commodity trading companies comprise the largest group of swaps intermediaries, although there is a newer breed of "pure" swaps companies developing too. Originally, banks were involved in swaps as an extension of their lending activities, while trading companies incorporated swaps into their trading activities. Some of these trading companies are subsidiaries of banks, however, which blurs these lines somewhat.

PRICING AND HEDGING

Swap prices are initially derived from an extrapolation of futures and OTC contract prices. Included in this extrapolation will be forward interest rates and elements of the cost of financing physical production and storage. A margin is added to allow for any basis risk, forward curve shift or hedge execution risk (the risk of not achieving the assumed hedge price for the desired volume).

Swaps for a product with no exchange-traded equivalent are priced from a curve of a related product. Heavy or sour crudes, for example, can be measured against light sweet crudes with a reasonable accuracy. By contrast, Mediterranean MoGas has no easy equivalent; although a ratio hedge with WTI is acceptable during stable periods, this leaves open a potentially high basis risk if the price relationship veers away from the historical norm.

The OTC market has begun to evolve mechanisms which signal long-term levels for non-standard products. There is a market for long-term WTI spreads, for example, whereby the relationship of crude prices from one year to another enables product swappers to infer forward product price curves at one remove from the crude market.

Perhaps the clearest way to explain how traders price swaps is to look at a specific example. Imagine that a trader wants to sell a jet fuel CIF NWE swap to an airline. If the term of the swap is about a year forward, then quotes are generally available from other traders or brokers; that is, the market is quite liquid and pricing is unproblematic. However, pricing is more complicated if the swap has to be priced further forward than 3 years. Although a specific quote could still be obtained from another trader, or from brokers, it is dangerous to let the market know your intentions prior to dealing in an illiquid market (such as longer-term jet fuel). This is because other traders may try to bid the forward prices in front of you, knowing that you will still be forced to pay up to cover your position. Even so, many banks and trading companies adopt these tactics because their mandate obliges them to cover much of each position "back-to-back".

The alternative is to devise a price by calculating the different elements of the equation: the underlying crude oil swap; the Brent/IPE Gasoil differential; and the IPE Gasoil/jet fuel differential.

With regard to the crude oil swap, a relatively liquid market exists in WTI and Brent swaps for up to five years forward. Beyond this, as we have said, there is a market in WTI year spreads (that is, brokers will offer prices on the time spread between, say, June 199X and June 200Y). The swap price can be extrapolated from these spreads. For jet fuel CIF NWE it would be easiest to use the underlying crude price in Brent (the more common benchmark for European products). The Brent price can then be calculated from the WTI swap by subtracting the arbitrage spread; this spread can be readily obtained from brokers.

The next part of the equation is the Brent/IPE Gasoil differential (or crack). Again, it is fairly easy to get a market price for this from brokers for up to two years forward. Beyond this, traders rely on historical analysis, experience and common sense when calculating the mark-up. The Brent/IPE Gasoil crack is quoted in $ per barrel; for ease of calculation, the sum of the Brent and the gasoil crack is therefore converted to tonnes at 7.45 barrels per tonne.

PRICING A SWAP: JET FUEL CARGOES CIF NWE SWAP

In this example, we assume that the client, an airline, has asked the trader to price a swap of jet CIF NWE for three years forward, starting in January 1999.

	1999	2000	2001
Brent	15.30	14.96	15.17
Brent/gasoil crack	2.76	3.59	3.51
Jet/gasoil differential	27.50	25.50	26.50

Note: Prices above are offer prices

STEP ONE

The Brent price for 1999 is obtained from a market-maker as $15.30.

STEP TWO

The gasoil prices are calculated by adding the gasoil cracks to the Brent swap prices. The cracks for the last two years have been deduced:

1999: $15.30 + 2.76 \times 7.45 = 134.55$/tonne
2000: $14.96 + 3.59 \times 7.45 = 138.19$
2001: $15.17 + 3.51 \times 7.45 = 139.16$

STEP THREE

The jet fuel prices are calculated by adding the jet differential to the gasoil swap prices. The differentials for the two years furthest out have been deduced.

1999: $134.55 + 27.50 = 162.05$
2000: $138.19 + 25.50 = 163.69$
2001: $139.16 + 26.50 = 165.66$

STEP FOUR

The average offer price for this swap equates to $163.80. The trader will probably round this number up or down depending on the risk/reward assumptions built into the above prices.

This is because the final element in the equation, the IPE Gasoil/jet differential, is quoted in $ per tonne. Prices for this differential can be obtained through a broker for 18 months to two years forward. Beyond this, the trader must make an individual calculation.

By means of the calculations demonstrated in Panel 7, the trader can arrive at an offer price without implying that he is likely to be a buyer of fixed-price jet fuel in the near future. Furthermore, even if the trader finds that it is impossible to hedge the impending position with a back-to-back jet fuel swap, the deal can be hedged step by step. That is, the trader can buy a crude oil swap, and then add a crude/gasoil crack and jet/gasoil differential to this at a later date. The crude should be quick and easy to purchase, as the market is quite liquid; the crack and the differential are much less volatile, and thus the trader will have more time to cover them.

Of course, it is possible that the trader will not be able to find reasonable quotes for the crack and the differential. The trader must, therefore, feel secure that the deal with the airline is sufficient to preserve a margin of profitability even if these positions have to be bought back some weeks or months into the future. The trader always has the option of running the position

until it matures – but the natural desire to realise profits militates against this!

The methodology described above and in Panel 7 can be applied to many other oil products, given the appropriate product differentials. These differentials, and the resulting price, will be marked up or down to reflect liquidity, volatility and basis risk.

Where structures are especially complex or difficult to hedge, swap issuers will build this risk factor into the swap price using correlation coefficients. (The technical process of measuring how closely correlated different contracts are, and of calculating hedge ratios is explained in Chapter 15 of this book.) However, it may be very difficult for them to realise any profit – that is, to trade out of the positions.

Competitive pricing is also sometimes a feature of deals between intermediaries and new clients. A swap issuer may price the first swap to a new client more aggressively than other indicators would suggest.

Apart from assuming risk, swaps issuers also make money from market-making. In an ideal world, an intermediary would generate profits from "bid/offer" activity, where a fixed-price buyer (a consumer) receives the offered side of the swap price while producers, as fixed-price sellers, receive the bid price. As long as the swap price to the buyer is higher than the bid price to the seller then the swap issuer, the intermediary, makes a profit. The variation in bid-offer spreads is largely determined by:

❏ term (that is, it tends to be narrower for short dates);

❏ liquidity of the market (that is, the number of active traders); and

❏ the volatility of the commodity.

However, while intermediaries would like to "back-to-back" all their various deals, so that the risk in their portfolios balanced out, this is rarely possible. Differences in size, timing, product specification and geography are such that intermediaries end up with composite positions.

The ideal hedge for a long swap position is a short swap position at the same price levels and for similar duration. Failing that, the net exposure will need to be hedged, unless the issuer deliberately leaves a position exposed as a form of surrogate trading. Futures exchanges, with their increasing range of product and liquidity, are important risk-offset markets. However, swaps traders are often forced to warehouse certain market risks, such as product or time-spread risks. A trader's willingness to take on a position that may lead to warehousing will depend partly on its "appetite for risk", and partly on how confident it is that the position will eventually be profitable, even if kept to maturity.

Of course, each institution will try to draw a line between warehousing risk and what is, in effect, speculative trading. Most traders, like most market-makers, regard the level of risk implied in speculative trading as unacceptable – their ambition is to minimise their exposure to price movements.

THE LIQUIDITY PROBLEM

Equally important is the question of liquidity, which is one of the key practical issues in swaps markets. Liquidity here does not only refer to the liquidity of the swaps market itself – which has a bearing on bid-offer spreads – but to the liquidity of the wider market in oil for the purpose of risk management.

Infrequently traded or illiquid product markets will be more liable to basis risk, as hedging the exposure may be slow and difficult. Before embarking on a deal, a swap provider needs to know that further-out liquidity is sufficient to establish some prospect of a reasonable hedge. Although basis shifts are considered to be disruptive, as far as the issuer is concerned, forward curve risks can be more damaging; this is because they can affect the whole range of swaps rather than individual products. Therefore, the trader will try to limit the number of situations where it is likely to be forced to "stack" its hedge in short-dated positions against a longer-dated swap.

This focus on further-out risk suggests that the problems are concentrated in this area. But, in practice, short-term risks also need to be managed. The need to hedge a large exposure in any given month itself generates a hedge risk, because any major trade in the futures market is liable to move the price.

Where the degree of exposure is clear some time ahead, all these problems can be overcome. But a busy swaps issuer operates in a dynamic market. New deals change the balance of exposure, sometimes reducing overall exposure, sometimes increasing it. In practice, each new deal is weighed up for its effect on the existing net position. A swap issuer already short on fixed-price jet in a market with a steepening curve, and where the jet premium over refining margins is also growing, will not want to exacerbate this exposure by entering into additional keenly priced swaps. (Unless of course the issuer believes that these pressures are going to subside, in which case an element of market judgement may enter the equation.)

Future developments

OVERVIEW

There has been massive growth in the recent history of the energy swaps markets. Although intermediaries have helped drive this growth through aggressive marketing, trading, and innovation into new products the true explosion has come from the demand side.

Refiners, consumers, and the producers of energy have actively recruited from the banking and trading world in order to build their knowledge of these markets. Their investment in systems and understanding has allowed them to step into otherwise illiquid markets and hedge with confidence and intelligence. They have seized upon the opportunities presented by more sophisticated products that have narrowed basis risks and reduced the costs of hedging. This pattern will continue at an ever-increasing pace.

The impact of de-regulation in the energy markets is probably the next most important factor for future trade in swaps and all forms of derivative structure. The utilities in Europe are

SUCCESS IN THE SWAPS MARKET: SOME CRITICAL COMMENTS

As far as the end-user is concerned, the criteria for success in the energy swap markets are often dangerously simple. The successful use of a swap seems all too evident to a crude oil producer that sold fixed for floating in a falling market. A jet-fuel hedger that bought fixed for floating in a rising market will be the first to recommend a similar strategy to his colleagues. Unfortunately, this criterion for success is essentially speculative. It necessarily leads to risk management operations taking the blame for hedges which supposedly go "wrong" – that is, when the hedge subsequently proved unnecessary or led to "opportunity loss".

As far as providers are concerned, success in the market is often confused with success in technical innovation. Pricing and administration technologies are constantly evolving, but it is important that providers use these developments to generate products which buyers want, and that they are able themselves to cope with the additional risks that the new range of products entails.

In a mature market, the ability to provide swaps with properly constructed and priced embedded options is bound to attract attention and business. But too many "whistles and bells" may be counter-productive. It is insufficient to be able to offer highly advanced concepts without being able to deliver working strategies. The practical experience of intermediary and bank providers in recent years has shown clearly that although the exotic composite is much favoured by researchers, the ability of (a) the customers to understand them and (b) the bank to hedge them, is limited.

Inevitably, users who fail to understand the true implications of a particular structure will feel that the unknown or uncertain elements in it are to their disadvantage. This is particularly true in new markets, and for smaller companies in any market.

The solution here is for the swaps provider to remain market-oriented, not product-oriented. They must remember why the user wants the swap – not why the provider wants to provide it.

---

anxious to resolve legislative and political restrictions that remain in the path to free markets. They are acutely aware of the vast experience US companies have acquired in their domestic environment. It is clear that in a free and open market derivatives offer invaluable tools to support the marketing and structuring of contracts. With this awareness will come an entirely new and increasingly sophisticated market for these products.

In step with these developments have come the competitors to supply market-making and counterpart services. The banks are less prominent now than in the recent past and energy companies, large utilities, and trading houses (often within an investment bank) have taken their place. Insurance companies have also been drawn in to the fray due to the overlap in both clients and products. They bring with them vast resources for valuation and pricing of risk and will fuel further rapid development.

As mentioned above, another main area of expansion is likely to be in the area of exotics – that is, swaps with more complex option structures attached. As with options and other OTC instruments, the ability to structure tailored flexibility into the hedge mechanism required by the client will add value, both to the client and to the swap provider (Panel 8 provides additional comment). One important factor here is the market's growing confidence in managing curve risk. Longer-term deals are becoming more frequent, particular in the context of structured finance deals.

The increase in the range of oil indices and products traded will also have an effect, as it gives swaps providers more flexibility to manage and offset basis risk.

GROWTH SECTORS

When trying to identify growth sectors, it is useful to remember the following observation. Although it might be thought that the natural development of swaps would fit closely with the availability of exchange instruments suitable for hedging, in practice the growth has been driven very largely by end-user demand. The jet fuel and fuel oil sectors are striking proof of this.

US jet fuel swaps are one of the largest single identifiable areas of potential growth in the foreseeable future. As the fuel consumption of the larger US airlines is two or three times that of their European counterparts, the potential is vast. Airlines that currently do not hedge their jet fuel can be expected to develop hedging via swaps in a more liquid, and already technically accomplished, market.

The effect on demand of the environmental lobby is bound to increase demand for low-sulphur fuels and unleaded gasoline, and this may also lead to an increase in swaps activity in these sectors (largely to protect against basis risk).

Crude oil and integrated producers, particularly in newly risk-aware markets such as Eastern Europe, have been driven into the derivatives markets by the recent and rapid decline in oil prices from the highs of 1997. The trend on the E&P sector is toward efficient and innovative field operation at a consistent return. Although this sees the fall of the wild-cat share play it does see a maturation of a business to steady profitability. Derivatives will be a key to their sustained success.

By far the largest single area of potential growth remains the natural gas sector. As a clean fuel, its use is growing dramatically. The IPE in London has only recently established its contract for gas futures with delivery at Bacton, a key regional distribution location. This contract is beginning to stimulate a huge interest in OTC swaps for gas and for spreads against electricity called "spark spreads". The enthusiasm already evident is a clear indication of a burgeoning market. In the advance guard power generators protecting their margins on large generation projects have entered deals with maturities that reportedly extend beyond ten years. The US market for natural gas swaps is discussed in detail in Chapter 6 of this book.

The scope of the energy market, its depth of impact upon the modern economy, and the persistent ingenuity of its participants has driven a complete recovery from the troubled mid-1990s. The supervision, regulatory and financial issues that led to problems at Metallgesellschaft and elsewhere are lessons learnt. The simple elegance of the swap contract will continue to support growth and innovation in what may become the most global of markets in the 21st century.

1 *The author and publisher would like to acknowledge Chris Mason and Steve Jones, who worked on this chapter in the first edition of this book.*

2 *For a detailed discussion of the MG debacle, see* Corporate

Hedging in Theory and Practice: Lessons from Metallgesellschaft, *eds C. Culp and M. Miller, London: Risk Books, forthcoming 1999.*

2

Energy Options

Michael Hampton
HDS Shipping[1]

Energy options now comprise a huge global market, rivalling the energy swaps market as a means of managing exposures to energy prices. The size of the over-the-counter (OTC) options market is difficult to estimate, but it has grown at least as fast as the exchange-based options market. Nymex, the world's largest energy options exchange, records the volume of options traded in 1998 to be 61.7% higher than the figure four years earlier. As discussed in the Introduction and Chapter 3 of this book, oil and natural gas options have recently been supplemented by a fledgling market in electricity options.

It was not always apparent that the energy options market would grow so quickly. The introduction of exchange-traded options lagged behind the successful introduction of traded energy futures by several years. Nymex began trading crude oil WTI options in November 1986, three and a half years after it introduced its first energy futures contracts. IPE followed with gasoil options in July 1987, a full six years after its gasoil contract was launched.

However, two factors greatly spurred the growth of the young energy options market: the successful launch of an OTC market in swaps from 1986; and the extreme volatility in oil prices in 1990, the year of Iraq's invasion of Kuwait.

The emergence of an energy swaps market, described in the Introduction to this book, meant that banks and oil companies hired large numbers of commodity derivatives marketing staff. Bank marketing of OTC commodity derivatives grew steadily in Europe and Asia, and took off in the United States after the CFTC issued its safeharbour ruling in 1989 (described in Chapter 8). These new marketing people were added to the marketing staff of the exchanges, who were already scouring the market for potential business opportunities. Their marketing efforts cultivated the demand for energy derivatives, preparing the ground for the new option instruments.

Even so, explaining the concept of options to end-users in a way that related directly to the energy industry was – and still is – a challenge. The first part of this chapter therefore offers an "intuitive" approach to understanding energy option technology without algebraic equations, and acts as a foundation for the more technical discussion presented in Chapter 3. (Like the other chapters in this book, it will take the OTC market, rather than the exchange market, as its primary focus.)

The rise of crude oil prices to $40 in 1990, followed by their collapse to under $18 in 1991, was also crucial in increasing the energy option market, because it illustrated so strongly to end-users the dangers of price exposure. (The price oscillations in crude oil during 1998–99 taught a similar lesson on a smaller scale.) For buyers of call options in the early days of the price rise, options provided protection against a price rise with a limited amount of risk. For those who sold call options in late 1990 – when option volatilities exceeded 100% – they also provided a way of enhancing income by selling price insurance to a very nervous market.

Periods of extreme volatility such as 1990–91 have taught end-users (and some derivative providers) that using options in energy markets has quite specific problematics. The second half of this chapter therefore highlights the features that make using energy options different to using interest rate and currency options, before moving on to describe the simpler option-based instruments such as caps, floors, collars and swaptions. The concluding section summarises how the various instruments suit different exposure-management strategies.

An intuitive approach to energy options

SOME TRADITIONAL DEFINITIONS
The two basic types of option are traditionally defined as follows:

❑ A *call* option is the right to buy a particular

asset at a pre-determined fixed price (the strike price) at a time up to the maturity date.

❏ A *put* option is the right to sell a particular asset at the strike price up to maturity.

The problem with these conventional definitions is that they assume that the value of the option will be captured through exercise. For the call, this would mean purchasing the asset at the exercise price and then either reselling it or holding it. The traditional definitions ignore the fact that options are increasingly "settled" in cash, so that the underlying asset does not change hands.

In the oil market, OTC options are generally settled in a different way to exchange-traded options. Exchange options are exercised into futures contracts, and futures, if held to maturity, nearly always result in physical delivery of the product. (An exception is the cash-settled Brent crude oil contract offered by the IPE.) In contrast, OTC options, like OTC swaps, are generally cash-settled. Their value at settlement is normally based on the average price over a period – a calendar month is most common. The average is calculated based upon an index price derived from daily futures settlements prices or from an energy industry pricing source such as Platt's or Argus.

Cash settlement of options has advantages for many players in the market. First, it can be expensive to exercise an option and then resell the asset to capture the increase in value. This is particularly true in the case of less liquid products, but may be true even for deep-in-the-money crude oil options. For example, a refiner may hold an exchange-traded call option on crude as protection against a rise in crude prices. Selling this option at an acceptable price is usually possible. But if the options market is not liquid, the refiner would need to exercise the option by taking delivery of the underlying futures position at the strike price. However, the refiner may prefer to buy his crude from another source or for a different delivery date than the crude controlled by the futures contract. If he exercises the option and takes delivery of the future, he will need to resell it in order to capture the increase in value beyond the strike price. This may result in additional commissions to pay, or the market might move unfavourably before the futures position is disposed of.

A second reason for cash settlement of options is that many clients favour settlement against average prices. Compared to settlements based on a single point in time, they can provide a better hedge for non-specific "cashflow type"

exposures. For example, an oil trader which is buying and selling cargoes of oil can use large "lumps" of futures to hedge its large "lump" of oil. The matching of the hedge is easy. When the trader buys cargo and wants to hedge, he can sell an equal quantity of futures. And when he sells the cargo, he can buy back his short futures to unwind his hedge. For this operation, the futures are sold at a specific moment and bought back at a specific moment within the timing constraint of the ship's voyage.

But cashflow exposures are less precise, because they are made up of individual exposures too small to hedge individually. An airline may be fuelling its aircraft several times a day. Effectively, it will be paying an average price over the course of the month. Given the "flow" of small refuellings, the airline may prefer to settle its hedge against an average price. A shipping company may be running a fleet of ships, with its fleet taking on bunker fuel at unpredictable moments where and when the fuel can be obtained most cheaply. Given the unpredictability, the shipping company does not know ahead of time when the ships are going to take on fuel or from what location.

Averages are difficult or time-consuming to replicate in the futures market, particularly for options, so many end-users of derivatives prefer to buy the averaging mechanism in the OTC market and leave the mechanics of running the hedges to the OTC market-makers. (The special pricing and hedging issues created by settling against an average are discussed in Chapter 3.)

Finally, options are increasingly used to hedge cross-market risks. If the option holder does not have an interest in the underlying asset, but is merely interested in the price protection the option provides, cash settlement can be significantly cheaper. For example, a company might buy an option on gasoil as a cross-market hedge against a rise in the price of jet fuel. In this case, the option buyer is not at all interested in acquiring the underlying asset (physical gasoil or a gasoil futures contract), he merely wants a price hedge the value of which is (normally) highly correlated with his underlying price exposure. A cash-settled option is a more cost-effective solution because it does not require reselling the underlying asset, and it fits well with settlement against an average.

With the increasing tendency towards cash settlement in mind, it is possible to formulate a simple and intuitively satisfying definition of the basic options:

❏ A *call* is the "upside" in the price of a particular commodity beyond the strike price as determined by a particular settlement mechanism and limited by the maturity of the option.

❏ A *put* is the "downside" in price below the strike price with the same restrictions.

HOW DO OPTIONS RELATE TO SWAPS?

Using these definitions, the relationships between various derivatives instruments become more intuitively obvious. And the relationship between cash-settled swaps and options becomes particularly clear.

As explained in the previous chapter, a swap represents the exchange of a periodic floating payment for a fixed payment. The practice for energy swaps is that the two amounts are calculated and only the net cash difference is paid at the end of each period. Payments are required only if there is a difference, and then only one side pays. Given the settlement mechanism, the energy swap can be explained using "upside" and "downside", as illustrated in Figure 1.

The swap buyer (ie the "consumer" side of the swap which pays the fixed payment) agrees with the swap seller a fixed price for the period and a periodic quantity. Based upon this fixed price, the buyer agrees to pay the downside amount, if any, and in return receives the upside, if any. The two potential payments can be defined as follows:

❏ *upside* Amount by which the floating price exceeds the fixed price times the quantity;

❏ *downside* Amount by which the floating price is less than the fixed price times the quantity.

If the floating amount exceeds the fixed amount, then the upside difference is paid by the swap seller (floating payer) to the swap buyer (fixed payer). If the floating payment is less than the fixed amount, then the downside difference is payed by the swap buyer to the swap seller.

These payment definitions now sound very similar to the definitions of puts and calls that we provided above. In fact, a swap can be decomposed into the two options, so that being "long" a swap is the same as being "long" the upside of a strip of calls struck at the fixed swap price, and "short" the downside of a strip of puts below the swap price.

The relationship between a forward (or any individual settlement period in a swap) and its option components is illustrated in Figure 2.

There is an important relationship called put/call parity which means that a put and a call have equal (theoretical) value when they are both struck at the forward price. Similarly, a cap and a floor (option instruments described later on in Panel 5) both struck at the current market swap price have equal value.

This relationship is illustrated in Figure 2. Since a forward entered at the market price requires no upfront premium to be paid, and such forward can be decomposed into long a call and short a put with both struck at the forward price, then the two options must have equal value. The cost of the call purchased is fully covered by the value of the put sold. Otherwise a net premium would need to be paid. No logical person would pay an upfront premium for a combination of two options (long the upside through the call, short the downside through a put), when the risk characteristics of these options could be perfectly replicated through the purchase of a forward.

Another concept, called "conversion", can also be explained using Figure 2. Conversion is when one directional option is converted into an option of the opposite direction. A call can be converted into a put, or a put into a call. This can be easily explained.

If an option holder is long a call, he is long upside. If he then sells a forward at a price identical to the call strike price, he has sold the upside controlled by his call. The upward price risk inherent in the sale of the forward is therefore covered by the call, and so he has no net gain or loss if prices move higher. However, through the short created by the forward sale, he

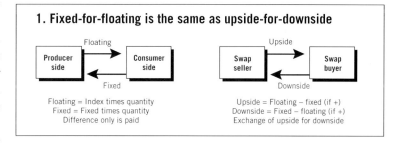

1. Fixed-for-floating is the same as upside-for-downside

Floating = Index times quantity
Fixed = Fixed times quantity
Difference only is paid

Upside = Floating – fixed (if +)
Downside = Fixed – floating (if +)
Exchange of upside for downside

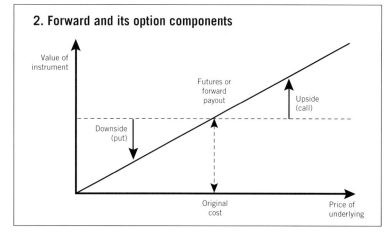

2. Forward and its option components

can benefit if the price falls below the strike price. Therefore, through the combination of being long the call and short the forward, he has acquired the downside below the strike price. So long as the maturities on the forward and the call are the same, the combined position is exactly equivalent to a long put.

In a similar fashion, a put can be converted into a call by purchasing a forward at the same price as the put strike. The downside exposures cancel each other, and the combined net position is pure upside.

OPTION VALUE AND OPTION EXERCISE

The value of an option, as compared with a forward or future, is in the flexibility it provides. The holder of an option has time to decide whether or not he wants to exercise it. The time value of delaying the decision until some future moment up to the final exercise date is that the market may give better opportunities along the way. The option provides a low risk way to wait for those better opportunities to arise.

As illustrated in Figure 3, the two basic components of an option's value are:

❑ *intrinsic value* The amount by which the option is "in-the-money" (that is, the amount the option would pay out if it were exerciseable immediately). For a call, this is the amount by which the price of the underlying commodity exceeds the strike. For a put, it is the amount by which the price of the underlying is below the strike;

❑ *time value* The value (above and beyond the intrinsic value) which the option attracts because of the possibility that, as the price for the underlying commodity fluctuates up to maturity, the option may increase in intrinsic value. All else equal, time value will be greatest when the underlying is trading at the strike price. At that point, intrinsic value is zero but can increase immediately if the price moves in the right direction. (Another way of saying this is that the flexibility provided by the option is worth most when the probability of it gaining intrinsic value is 50% – as it is when the underlying is trading at the strike price.)

Realising the value in an option is dependent upon the form of option exercise that has been stipulated. There are three basic types of option exercise:

❑ *American options* can be exercised at any time up to the maturity date;

❑ *European options* can only be exercised on the maturity date; and

❑ *Asian options* (also called average rate options) which settle in cash based upon an average price. Asian options are generally exercised automatically if they are in the money.

The exchange-traded energy options on the Nymex and the IPE are of the American type, while most OTC energy options are of the Asian variety, because of the popularity of the averaging mechanism. A few OTC options are American or European style.

Up to maturity, American and European options tend to have the same valuation except for those special cases where early exercise of an American option may enable a holder to capture more value than he could do by locking in the intrinsic value and waiting for the option to mature. (Intrinsic value can be locked in for a call by selling, and for a put by buying, the appropriate future in the same quantity.) One special case arises when options are very deeply in the money, and hence have little time value. Another occurs when the markets are very illiquid or in markets where commodities are expensive to finance or short. In this case an American option may have additional value because early exercise may enable an option holder to conclude a trade in the underlying commodity which it is impossible to achieve (cheaply) without delivery of the underlying future or commodity through early exercise.

What makes commodity options special?

Although industrial commodities may theoretically be fungible, the price for given units of an industrial commodity at a particular place and a

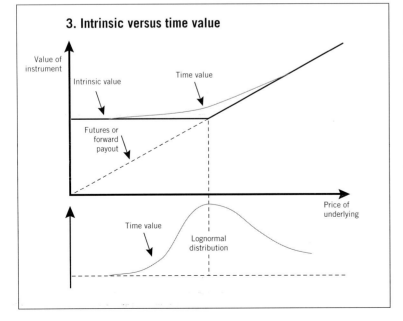

3. Intrinsic versus time value

DEFINING BASIS RISK

The term "basis risk" is used to describe the risk that the value of a hedge may not move up or down in tandem with the value of the actual price exposure that is being risk managed. Ideally, a hedge would match the underlying position in every respect, negating any chance of basis risk. But the large number of energy products, and the lack of liquid hedging markets for many of the underlying products, means that some mismatched hedges are unavoidable. The principal types of mismatch are:

❏ *Product basis* This is the most important basis risk in most risk management markets, including the energy markets. If there is a mismatch in quality, consistency, weight, or other specification then the underlying product and the hedge are not fungible. In the energy markets, there is a large number of products and only a few liquid hedging instruments (most exchange-traded futures and options and a few of the OTC indices are generally liquid). Consequently, it often happens that an illiquid underlying exposure is hedged with a liquid instrument, the price of which is linked to a different product. Even when the instrument's underlying price shows a strong historical correlation with the underlying exposure, significant basis risk can emerge if the relationship between the two products breaks down. The most famous example occurred in late 1990, after the invasion of Kuwait by Iraq: the differential between European jet fuel and gasoil quickly widened to more than five times its usual margin.

❏ *Time basis* This is a common-enough exposure in many markets. For example, in financial markets, banks will often lend money over six months, and fund this activity with one-month deposits – creating a "yield curve exposure" or "time gap". However, in energy markets, a time basis exposure can be much more dangerous, particularly when there is a sudden shift in demand or transporta-

tion bottlenecks occur. An illustration would be an electric utility needing gas in the winter time which hedges its position by purchasing January natural gas call options. If a severe cold wave were to arrive early in the winter, say in late November, then the price of December natural gas prices may surge much more than the January prices. The market knows that the price rise is likely only to last as long as the cold spell, or as long as it takes for gas pipelines to bring sufficient new supplies. In this circumstance, the January call options may not provide an efficient hedge for the December physical gas requirement.

❏ *Locational basis* As discussed in the main text, prices of exactly the same product can vary significantly from one location to another. As an illustration, Platt's reports prices for 1% sulphur fuel oil in both the US Gulf and New York Harbor, as well as a similar 1% low sulphur fuel oil in Rotterdam. An OTC swaps market has developed in trading these materials and the price differential normally shows New York Harbor at a premium which roughly reflects the cost of shipping the oil up from the Gulf. However, the trans-Atlantic differential between New York and London depends upon whether the demand for 1% fuel is greater in Europe or the United States. The premium, if great enough, will attract oil from across the ocean. But the differential is not stable and can swing with the premium on either side.

❏ Other types of basis risk can be seen in the energy markets. For example, "mixed basis" risk occurs when an underlying position is hedged with more than one type of mismatch. A January jet fuel exposure might be hedged with a February gasoil contract, leaving both time and product basis exposures. Another sort of basis risk, peculiar to the options market, arises when an option of one strike is hedged using an option with another strike.

particular time is not. This quality, which may be termed "price specificity" in the sense that the price is specific to a particular time and location, has an important impact upon the pricing and hedging of energy options.

All commodities vary in price depending upon when and where they are valued. But this is particularly true for energy commodities, which tend to be expensive to transport and dif-

ficult to store, relative to their value. A cargo of crude oil is thus worth significantly more in an importing country, such as the United States, than it is in an exporting region such as the Arabian Gulf. Likewise, natural gas prices will nearly always be much higher in the northeastern American cities, like Boston or New York, than they are at Henry Hub or Kingsport (which are near producing gas fields).

For financial commodities, like gold, there is little locational variation in value except where taxes and regulations have an effect. If this were not the case, gold could be moved quickly by air transport to the location of greatest value, and the extra supply would bring down the price. For most energy commodities, air transport is not practical. Cheaper but slower means of transport such as ships, trucks or pipelines are employed.

The more extreme and short-term variations in energy spot prices are not directly due to transportation costs. Instead they occur because bottlenecks and time delays in the normal method of transportation give rise to an extreme inflexibility in short-term supply, and this interacts with the short-term inflexiblity of demand for energy. (The price risk that this gives rise to is one form of "basis risk", as discussed in Panel 1.)

"Price specificity" is pronounced in the natural gas market because of its vulnerability to transportation bottlenecks. If, for example, cold weather in the northeastern United States causes a large drawdown of local natural gas inventories, then the local spot price may rise very quickly in the period until fresh deliveries reduce the imbalance in physical supplies. Conversely, a supply glut can cause a price to fall below replacement cost.

Through its effect on volatility, price specificity has an important impact upon option valuation. In particular, it is normal for spot energy prices to be more volatile than forward prices. This is because demand and supply disruptions which affect the physical market tend to be short-lived, while longer-term prices reflect more stable economic fundamentals.

Normally, the further forward the energy price, the lower its expected price volatility. This creates a volatility curve which is "downward sloping" as it moves forward in time. This characteristic is illustrated by Table 1.

The prices in Table 1 were sampled in a rela-

tively quiet market and so the levels shown and the degree of fall-off in the volatility curve over time is characteristic of a market without a major disruption in supply or demand. By contrast, in late 1990 and early 1991, as oil prices surged at the time of Iraq's invasion of Kuwait, short-dated oil option volatilities exceeded 100% at times. Because of the prevailing nervousness in the market, longer-dated options were also marked up. Nevertheless, there remained a pronounced downward slope in the oil volatility curve throughout the large price shifts of 1990–91.

An intuitive explanation of option pricing

This section provides an intuitive approach to option pricing, building upon concepts introduced already.[2] The approach is deliberately "non-mathematical" but, as understanding the conventional mathematical terminology is important, the principal expressions are defined in Panel 2. (Chapter 3 uses these terms to discuss, at a more advanced level, pricing and hedging methodologies for a wide range of option structures.) Panels 3 and 4 explain delta hedging – a core tactic when actively managing option positions.

There are five key inputs to an options pricing model:
❑ price of the underlying commodity;
❑ strike price;
❑ time to maturity;
❑ volatility estimate; and
❑ interest rates.

In the following, we will examine how each of the individual pricing dimensions impact on the price of an at-the-money option (if an option has intrinsic value, or is out-of-the-money, the impact of each dimension is more complex).

Price of underlying
The "character" of the underlying price affects all the other variables, and especially the volatility estimates. In particular, as explained earlier, in the case of energy options the underlying price tends to become more volatile as it moves from being a forward price to being the price of a spot commodity for physical delivery. Nearby energy prices are thus very "whippy"; that is, they move around much more than longer-dated prices.

Exchange-traded options generally settle into futures contracts maturing in, at most, a few weeks. The volatility estimates for such options can shoot up dramatically as the underlying contract approaches maturity. OTC options, on the

Table 1. Illustrative example of Nymex WTI crude oil options prices

Contract	Future	Strike	Type	Option price	Option volatility
Nearby	$16.99	$17.00	put	$0.25	28.2%
2nd	$16.99	$17.00	put	$0.58	25.5%
3rd	$17.01	$17.00	put	$0.69	24.0%
4th	$17.05	$17.00	put	$0.75	22.5%
5th	$17.08	$18.00	call	$0.50	21.7%
6th	$17.10	$18.00	call	$0.58	21.4%
8th	$17.18	$18.00	call	$0.71	20.3%

Note: This is a selection of some of the most liquid contracts for each month

PANEL 2

OPTION PRICING AND "THE GREEKS"

Throughout the risk management industry, letters of the Greek alphabet ("the Greeks") are used to describe the various assumptions underlying an option's price and its sensitivity to market moves. The four most important terms are:

Delta (δ) This term describes the change in the value of the option with respect to the change in the underlying price. (It can also be thought of as a measure of the probability of an option finishing in the money on the maturity date.) The "delta" of an option also has the very useful purpose of indicating what size of holding (or short holding) of the underlying is required to provide an effective hedge for (changes in) the option's value. Thus, a call option with a positive delta of 50% can be hedged with an equal but opposite position in the underlying; that is, a short position 50% the size of the overall quantity controlled by the option. Naturally, as the underlying price moves, the delta will change as well: a higher price increases the call delta and a lower price reduces the delta (the impact on put deltas is the reverse). Thus, delta hedges have to be modified as underlying prices move.

Gamma (γ) A second-order derivative, this term describes the change in delta with respect to the change in price. Essentially, this variable describes how much the underlying hedge for an option must be changed in order to remain "delta neutral" as prices move. A high gamma option requires more frequent adjustments to remain effectively hedged. An option is normally at its highest gamma when the underlying is trading at the strike price and when the option is approaching its moment of expiry. A low gamma option is one whose strike is far away from the underlying price, or one with a large amount of time remaining to expiry.

Theta (θ) This describes the change in the value of the option with respect to the change in time. As described in the main text, as a rule of thumb, the value of an option tends to change with the square root of time. The impact on the value of an at-the-money or out-of-the-money option is that the loss of value over time (the "time decay") starts slow and becomes increasingly rapid as an option approaches its expiry. However, if an option is deep in-the-money and nearly the whole of its value is intrinsic, there will be little time decay.

Vega This describes the change in the value of the option with respect to the change in volatility. For an at-the-money option, the option value tends to change proportionally with changes in volatility. Thus, a doubling of volatility should tend to double the value of an at-the-money option. However, volatility only affects the "time value" of an option, not its intrinsic value. Therefore, an in-the-money option which holds a large part of its value as intrinsic, will be proportionally much less affected by changes in volatility. The influence on out-of-the-money options is more complex. They may be proportionally more affected than at-the-money options, but the change in absolute value will be smaller (because they have a smaller absolute value to begin with). Below is an example showing one-year options, relative to an underlying price of $20.00.

Impact of volatility changes on value of call options with various strikes

		10% vol % change	15% vol +50.0%	20% vol +100.0%	30% vol +200.0%
Type of call option	Strike				
Out-of-the-money	$22.00	**$0.181** % change	$0.474 +161.9%	$0.814 +349.7%	$1.545 +753.6%
At-the-money	$20.00	**$0.758** % change	$1.136 +49.9%	$1.513 +99.6%	$2.265 +198.8%
In-the-money	$18.00	**$2.038** % change	$2.286 +12.2%	$2.584 +26.8%	$3.233 +58.6%

other hand, tend to settle against an average price and consequently carry a much smaller volatility estimate.

Where the underlying price is that of another instrument (as in a swaption, where the option, if exercised, settles into a swap), the volatility is likely to be relatively low. For a swaption, the longer the tenor of the swap period, the lower the appropriate volatility estimate.

Strike price Although we are describing at-the-money options, it is worth considering what happens if strike prices are shifted out of, or into, the money. Here it is important to remember that supply and demand disruptions in the physical market widen the probability distribution of price movements of energy commodities. Spot prices can move more in a few days or hours than further-out prices move over weeks. Consequently, the range of historical spot prices shows a greater deviation from the mean than would be predicted from a normal distribution. (It is sometimes said that the distribution of energy prices has a "fat tail" compared with the normal probability distribution.)

The higher probability of an extreme move, and particularly of a move upwards, creates the so-called "volatility smile" for options of varying strike prices. The traded prices of options in or out of the money, but particularly of those with higher strike prices, normally have a higher volatility estimate than options struck at-the-money. Implied volatility increases as the option strike gets further away from the at-the-money price. For the option with its strike price at the money, the resulting graph of implied volatilities (Fig. 4) looks like a slightly off-centre "smile" around the lower volatility estimate.

Time As a useful "rule of thumb", other effects being equal, an option's value varies with the square root of time. A six-month option can be expected to cost 41.4% more than a three-month option (1.414 is the square root of two), and a

one-year option double as much as a three-month option (the square root of four being two). As the intuitive expectation may be that it should increase *proportionally* with time (ie that a six-month option will be twice as expensive as a three-month option), long-dated options can appear "cheap".

In practice, there are some discounting effects which slightly reduce option values. Thus, in a 5% interest environment with flat volatilities, a one-year European call would be worth $1.36 when a 90-day call is worth $0.70 – a slightly smaller increase of 94.3% instead of the 100% increase expected in a zero interest rate environment with a fourfold increase in time.

Volatility All else equal, there is a direct correlation between volatility and the price of an option. This is easy to understand intuitively: the value of the flexibility offered by an option increases in proportion with the liklihood of price movements. As an example, if the volatility estimate embedded in an option jumps from 20% to 30%, an increase of half, the price of an at-the-money option will increase by 50%. For a three-month oil call struck at $18, when the forward price is $18, an increase in volatility from 20% to 30% would increase the value of the call 50% from $0.70 to $1.05.

Interest rates These have a much smaller impact than the other variables. An option effectively provides "free financing", since the holder of the option does not directly pay any carrying costs for the underlying physical commodity or futures contract. On the other hand, the option buyer must pay his option premium upfront. Generally, for options on futures, these effects tend to counteract each other. As an example, consider a European-style three-month oil call struck at $18, when the forward price is $18 and the implied volatility is 20%. Because this style of option may only be exercised at maturity, the discounting effect of interest rates is slightly more likely to outweigh the value of the free financing. Even so, an increase in interest rates from 5% to 10% would reduce the value of the call only slightly from $0.70 to $0.692.

Combination of effects Overall, certain effects interact in the energy market to create a very curious phenomenon: unusually slow time decay. The rise in implied volatility as an option approaches maturity, combined with the non-linear time effect (ie the square root of time, which

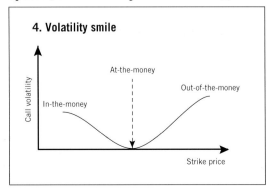

4. Volatility smile

At-the-money

In-the-money

Out-of-the-money

Call volatility

Strike price

PANEL 3

DELTA HEDGING

One way of extracting the value from an option is to hedge its value through trading in the underlying using an arbitrage strategy called "delta hedging". This strategy involves an ongoing series of trades which are designed to hedge the value of an option through frequent adjustments in the size of a commodity futures or forward position.

In the case of a call option, delta hedging involves a risk manager or trader translating the market level into a "delta equivalent" quantity of the underlying, which they then sell short. For example, an $18 call will increase in value by roughly *half a cent* if the value of the underlying rises *one cent* from $18 to $18.01. That approximate 50% "sensitivity" is the delta equivalent for an at-the-money option. As the value of the underlying increases, the percentage sensitivity, and therefore the delta equivalent, increases. (Conversely, when a trader is long a put, the delta equivalent is a negative amount such that an at-the-money put has an approximate delta equivalent of –50%.)

Having translated an options position into a delta equivalent value, an oil trader hedging an exchange-traded call can simply sell short the delta equivalent of oil futures. The amount sold short is such that any change in the underlying price will have an equal effect on both the option value and the value of the short position.

Thereafter, as the market moves up and down, the trader varies the number of contracts held short according to the delta equivalent formula. The trader thus sells at high prices and buys back (the short contracts) at lower prices. This strategy cashes a notional profit each time there is an in-and-out trade (assuming zero transaction cost and no time decay).

Normally a risk manager would use specialised option software to measure the delta exposure on a daily or a minute-to-minute basis. The program is quite complex to implement perfectly, since theoretically it requires minute adjustments in hedge positions based upon instantaneous price changes, plus adjustments for any changes in gamma, theta or vega variables. Panel 4 describes some of the problematics market-makers encounter when they are delta hedging.

The table below provides a highly simplified illustration of how to hedge the value of an $18.00 call on 1,000,000 barrels (1,000 futures contracts) of crude oil. In this example, we look at the delta equivalents on $18.00 calls at two points in time: three months prior to maturity (at 24% volatility) and with one month to maturity (at 28% volatility).

In the hedging operation, the trader needs to sell short futures contracts of the same month as those controlled by the call option.

To give some idea of how the delta hedging would work over time, let us assume the starting price level for the relevant oil contract is $18.00, which means that the option being hedged is at-the-money. Using the delta-hedging formula shown above, the trader would sell short the delta equivalent, which is 517 contracts (51.7% of 1,000 cts = 517 cts), at a price of $18.00 per barrel. For the moment, let us assume that no further delta adjustments were made, and that the relevant contract finished $1.00 lower at $17.00 with one month yet to run. The 517 contract short position would then show a profit of $517,000, ($1.00 × 517,000). This largely offsets the fall in the value of the call option, which amounts to

Simplified table illustrating hedging an $18.00 call option

Underlying price	3 months (24% vol.) option value	delta	no. cts	1 month (28% vol.) option value	delta	no. cts	Time decay option value	%	Change no. cts
$20.00	$2.203	81.8%	818	$2.055	91.2%	912	$0.148	6.7%	+94
$19.50	$1.808	75.9%	759	$1.613	85.1%	851	$0.195	10.8%	+92
$19.00	$1.446	68.8%	688	$1.209	76.3%	763	$0.237	16.4%	+75
$18.50	$1.121	60.6%	606	$0.855	64.8%	648	$0.266	23.7%	+42
$18.00	$0.840	51.7%	517	$0.564	51.4%	514	$0.276	32.9%	–3
$17.50	$0.605	42.4%	424	$0.342	37.4%	374	$0.263	43.5%	–50
$17.00	$0.416	33.2%	332	$0.188	24.6%	246	$0.228	54.8%	–86
$16.50	$0.272	24.6%	246	$0.092	14.3%	143	$0.180	66.2%	–103
$16.00	$0.167	17.3%	173	$0.040	7.3%	73	$0.127	76.0%	–100

Note: assumes 5% interest rate

$0.652 per barrel ($0.840–$0.188), or a $652,000 loss for the 1 million barrel size of the calls.

Obviously, this result can be improved upon by "trading around" the starting position or "rebalancing" the deltas on a frequent basis. (It would make little sense to consider delta hedging in this fashion unless there was an intention to regularly rebalance.) For example, if prices proved highly volatile and the oil contract first rose instantaneously by $1.50 to $19.50 (and the delta hedge was increased by 242 cts to 759 cts short at an overall average price of $18.478), and then fell $2.50 to $17.00, the entire short position could be closed out for a profit of $1,122,000.

The more volatile the underlying price over the life of the option, the more value can be extracted from delta hedging. Moreover, if a trader takes profits from delta hedging, he retains any remaining value in the call option.

Of course, it is possible that the market will move higher, and there will be a loss on the short futures contracts. For example, if the oil price were to reach $20.00 then there would be a loss of $2.00 per barrel on the starting 517 cts (1,000 × $2 × 517 = $1,034,000 loss). However, given our assumption of a large $2 jump in the underlying, and one month to maturity, the $18.00 call should be worth $2.055 per barrel or $2,055,000. The resulting gain of $1,215,000 more than covers the calculated loss of $1,034,000 on the starting short position.

Whatever level the underlying contract might settle at, any gains realised from "trading around" the deltas would be added to the gain or loss on the call. However, if there is little volatility then any gains from "rebalancing" might not fully offset the time decay of the call option.

is characteristic of all options) can mean substantially smaller time decay than for options on financial instruments which have a flatter volatility curve. As an example, in cases where prices move sideways, ie where spot prices do not change, we can see some very small time decay as shown by the following illustration:

Time left (months)	1	3	6	12
Implied volatility (%)	30	26	22	18
Theoretical price ($)	0.605	0.910	1.087	1.226

Note: Underlying price at $18, $18 strike, 5% interest rate

The decline in the value of the option over the 11 months is much less than it would be if the volatility were constant. In the example, the option value declines by $0.621, or 50.7%, as it decays from being a 12-month option to being a one-month option. If the volatility had remained at 18%, the one-month option would have been valued at $0.363, and the time decay over 11 months would have been $0.863 or 70.4%. In the example, the rise in implied volatility as the option approaches maturity reduces the time decay by $0.242 (which is 38% more slowly over the 11 months).

End-user's guide to energy option strategy

A truism discovered by those who attempt to market options is that everyone wants to buy options until they see what they cost. Corporations that use derivatives value the flexibility that energy options can provide. But because of the high volatilities, energy options

"look" expensive: corporate derivatives users do not find it easy to justify premiums which might be 4–6% of the underlying for options of less than a year's duration.

This is especially true when corporate treasurers realise that to make optimal use of any plain vanilla options that they buy, they may need to become regular participants in the energy derivatives market. Often it is only by "trading around" a core options position through effective delta hedging (see Panel 3) that an option holder can extract the full value from the flexibility that options provide.

Since most corporate users have other businesses to run, becoming an active trader in the market is not usually practical. Consequently, a key issue for most corporate users is to find ways of making the options "cheaper" than the large upfront premium on a straight option purchase.

The easiest way to reduce the upfront cost of an option is to simultaneously sell another option. This is generally done by selling off potential cash inflows which may arise from the underlying commodity being hedged or from the option purchased. The premium received from the option sold can then be used to reduce the net cost. The key challenge for the risk manager thus becomes constructing optimal combinations of sold and bought options.

"STRAIGHT" OPTIONS
These instruments, depicted graphically in Figure 5,[3] include individual puts and calls, as

PANEL 4

MANAGING OIL OPTIONS USING THE BLACK-SCHOLES MODEL

Jean-François Maurey and Patrick Perfetti, Société Générale

When using oil options, end-users have the tricky task of finding the best compromise between the perfect hedge and the cost of the envisioned strategy. However, in most cases, once the hedging tool is put into place, the position is managed passively.

Players such as market-makers or volatility traders are obliged to behave differently. By their nature, these players assume "positions" with regard to price movements, and the volatility of the underlying asset, that have to be actively managed.

To be able to conserve a spread (as a market-maker), profit from an expectation about the market (when taking a position) or a market aberration (in arbitrage), the trader needs to discover the "real" price of the option, and to have available a method of arbitrage which will capture this price with sufficient accuracy. A trader who buys an at-the-money option with an implied volatility of 20% (with, for example, an option premium of $1/bbl), and who thinks that in the future the "historical" volatility will be 25% (and therefore that the option is actually worth $1.25/bbl) should, through applying the chosen method of arbitrage, be able to gain that $0.25/bbl in whatever direction the market moves and, especially, whatever the value of the option when it expires.

The best known, and most often used, arbitrage method is that developed by Professors Black and Scholes (see Chapter 3). However, this model contains assumptions and limitations that make its application problematic – especially in the energy markets. In particular, it is based on a particular statistical hypothesis describing the behaviour of the underlying asset: it assumes that the instantaneous relative variations of the underlying asset are distributed lognormally, so that the standard deviation (volatility) is stable over time.

In theory, if this condition is met, and if a trader buys an option at the implied volatility of the market and delta hedges his position on a continuous basis as described in Panel 3, the trader will not make either a profit or a loss on maturity (the return will only be the risk-free rate on the invested premium). The trader will have "captured" the theoretical price of the option.

In practice, transaction costs (typically one cent per barrel) and the market's bid/offer spread (on long-dated contracts, the spread may be as high as 10 or 15 cents a barrel), and the fact that a trader can only hedge "discontinuously" (close to close, for example) interfere. Despite this, if all the prices chosen for hedging are derived from a lognormal price distribution, the trader will succeed in sticking pretty closely to the theoretical arbitrage price of the option (Fig. A).

Unfortunately, the distribution of prices used for hedging is not always very close to a lognormal distribution. In the case of a short-term position, for example, the number of close-to-close prices will not be sufficient to be statistically significant; if the trader increases the hedge frequency, the problem of transaction costs reappears.

More generally, any statistically representative sample of oil data is unlikely to have a lognormal distribution, especially at times of very high volatility. Graphs showing the distribution of oil prices tend to present a narrower distribution

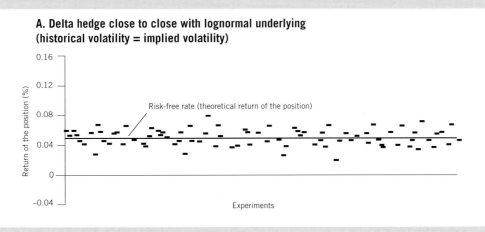

A. Delta hedge close to close with lognormal underlying (historical volatility = implied volatility)

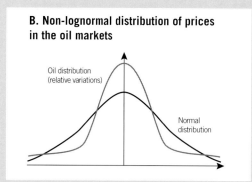

B. Non-lognormal distribution of prices in the oil markets

Oil distribution (relative variations)

Normal distribution

centre and wider borders (Fig. B). This is part of the explanation for "volatility smiles" on out-of-the-money options, and reflects the very abrupt and violent price movements manifested on the commodities markets.

There is also the problem of estimating volatility. Contrary to the hypothesis of the Black-Scholes model, this volatility is not constant over time. To get as accurate a duplication as possible of the theoretical option price, the historical volatility of the management period should be used – but for obvious reasons, this is only available in retro-

spect. The calculation of historical volatility also has to be coherent with the practicalities of risk managing the option position: for example, close-to-close delta hedging and the problem posed by weekends has to be taken into account.

On the other hand, if one wants to continuously value the portfolio by marking to market, then it is necessary to use the market's implied volatilities – which change everyday! This is a problem in the financial, as well as the commodity, risk management markets. But the problem is greatly accentuated by the fact that the underlying energy markets are relatively much more volatile.

Because of these imperfections, the effectiveness of the Black-Scholes model can only be judged statistically across multiple option positions. Globally, on a very large number of positions, it will indeed prove to be satisfactory, and the trading house will be able to duplicate the theoretical price of its portfolio. But, as Figure C indicates, in a one-off operation there may be surprises!

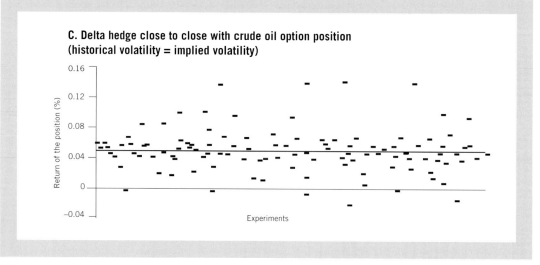

C. Delta hedge close to close with crude oil option position (historical volatility = implied volatility)

Return of the position (%)

Experiments

well as caps and floors (see Panel 5).

While the size of the upfront premium may be large, certain users find straight options acceptable as a core risk management tool. This is often because the options are being used as component pieces of a larger risk management programme. Many oil producers and refiners use a variety of derivatives and like to construct customised hedging programmes around individual futures and options.

In addition, there are some companies whose credit risk is such that it is much easier for them to buy options rather than sell options. This is because the option buyer normally pays the upfront premium one or two business days after

transacting, and thus poses a far lower credit risk than an option seller, who does not settle his obligations until maturity (or upon early exercise). Given the much smaller credit exposure, companies of lesser credit-standing can normally transact on equal terms with top credits when they are pure option buyers.

Typical examples of companies using this kind of option strategy might be a privately-owned shipping company which buys an OTC fuel oil cap as a hedge against an increase in bunker fuel prices, or a small charter airline that buys a jet fuel cap. Typically, these would settle in cash against the monthly average price of an appropriate index (typically Rotterdam HSFO,

Singapore 180cst, 380cst, 3% NY Harbor, or 3% US Gulf in the case of fuel oil; and NWE, Rotterdam barges, or the Singapore quotation in the case of jet fuel).

Caps such as these provide a cash inflow to the option buyer if the monthly average price of the relevant index exceeds the strike price. For example, the shipping company might buy a six-month cap for 5,000 tonnes per month struck at $80 per tonne of fuel oil and pay $3 per tonne for the option. For each month that the average is above $80, they would receive the "upside" times the quantity. If the average were $87 for a particular month, they would receive $7 times 5,000, (ie $35,000) for such month; if the index averages below $80 they pay nothing beyond the original premium.

There is a potential "risk control" benefit in the straight option. The option buyer limits his potential hedging cost to the upfront premium. Unlike some of the instruments described below, even if the price falls far below the option strike, the buyer only loses the premium – not the opportunity of benefiting from lower prices. This can be important in fiercely competitive industries: for example, a charter airline may be forced to pass on to its customers at least a portion of any potential fuel savings if prices fall sharply.

COLLARS

This instrument (Fig. 6) involves the simultaneous purchase of a call and the sale of a put. If a series of settlements are required, a multi-settlement collar would involve a simultaneous purchase of a cap and sale of a floor. The instrument can also be constructed the other way round so that a company trying to protect against a downside move might sell the upside (call or cap) and purchase the downside (put or floor).

Collars are often constructed as "zero cost" collars, which really means zero *upfront* cost in the sense that the value of the option sold is equal to the one purchased. (It is not necessarily "zero cost" because if prices fall the buyer of a collar may have to pay out a considerable downside below the put strike price.)

This instrument can also be thought of as a forward (or a swap) with a band in the middle (the range between the put strike and the call strike) where "nothing happens". Above the call strike, the collar seller pays out the upside; below the put strike, he receives the downside. (Payments are reversed when a company buys a collar.)

With the notion of put/call parity in mind, it might be thought that the put strike and the call

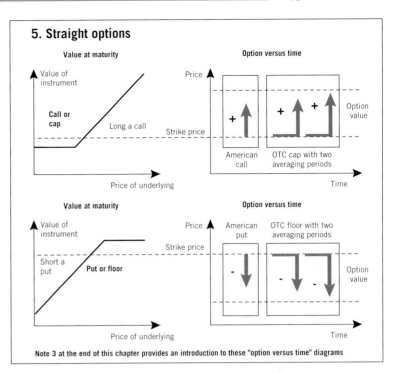

5. Straight options

Note 3 at the end of this chapter provides an introduction to these "option versus time" diagrams

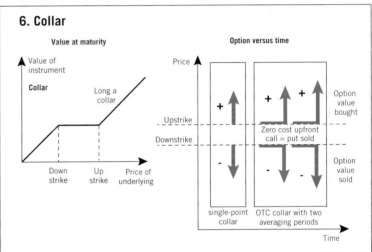

6. Collar

strike should be symmetrical around the price of a forward (or swap). This is not usually true for two reasons:

❏ As the symmetrical distance from the forward (swap) price increases, the call (cap) value increases faster than the put (floor) value due to the expected "log normal" distribution of prices. The reason is that there is a "compression effect" on potential downside prices. Because a commodity price cannot go below zero, a put has a limited potential payout. Whereas on the upside, in the case of a call, there is no theoretical limit to how high the commodity price may go. The result is that the probability of prices are distributed in an upwardly skewed distribution (a "log-normal" distribution) around the forward price. As an illustration, with forward prices at $18 and volatility at 20%, a one-year $20 call might be worth $0.68 and a one-year $16 put (also $2.00

PANEL 5

CAPS, FLOORS AND COLLARS

Jean-François Maurey and Patrick Perfetti, Société Générale

Caps, which are simply "strips", or consecutive series, of call options with the same strike price, are some of the commonest option-based instruments in energy price risk management.

To understand how they are applied, imagine that a major European refiner has decided to protect itself against price rises in crude oil over the next financial year. The company arranges to buy a cap with a strike price of $20 per barrel, a maturity of 12 months, and monthly settlement; the volume hedged is 200,000 barrels per month, and the premium charged is 60 cents a barrel.

At the end of each month, the average price over the month (representing the cost of physical supply) is compared with the strike price of $20.00 per barrel. If the average price rises above $20.00 per barrel ($24.00 for example), the seller of the cap pays the refiner ($4.00 multiplied 200,000 times = $800,000). The cap thus assures the refiner of a supply of 200,000 barrels, at a maximum price of $20.60 per barrel, for a year (Fig. A).

A floor, composed of a strip of put options, is simply a cap in reverse. By selling a floor, a consumer fixes the *minimum* price that it will pay for energy, and thus gives up any chance of profiting from a fall in prices below a certain level. But the sum raised from the sale may be used to subsidise the price the consumer pays for energy or for risk management.

For example, imagine that the management of the refinery decide they cannot afford to pay the full price of the cap (the $0.60 per barrel premium). They therefore agree to purchase a $20.00 cap and finance it through the sale of a $17.50 floor. This provides them with a "collar" at zero cost.

If the price of the crude rises above $20, to $24.00 for example, the refinery exercises its cap at $20.00 and receives $4.00 per barrel from the

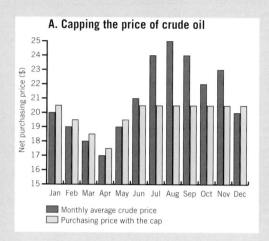

A. Capping the price of crude oil

Monthly average crude price
Purchasing price with the cap

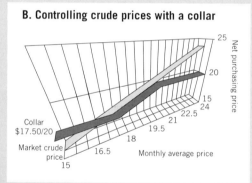

B. Controlling crude prices with a collar

collar provider. If the price of crude falls below $17.50, to $15.00 for example, the collar provider exercises its floor at $17.50 and the refinery pays out $2.50 per barrel. If the crude price stays between $17.50 and $20.00, the refinery obtains its supplies at the market price.

At first sight, using a zero-cost collar may appear to be the safest course of action for the refinery: it involves no upfront cost and offers no "speculative" return. However, if oil prices fall considerably, the refinery may end up paying much more for its feedstock than its competitors – who may lower their prices aggressively as a result. The "zero-cost" collar is thus really a "zero *upfront cost*" collar – true price insurance can be secured only by purchasing a cap.

away from the money) would be worth $0.55 (using the same volatility assumption in pricing the options). On the same assumptions, and with an $18 forward price, a zero-cost collar might be constructed using a $16.00 put which would have equal value to a $20.56 call. (Note that this level of call strike does not take account of the market maker's profit margin, or "volatility

spread".)

❏ The second reason for a lack of symmetricallity on collar structures is that an options market-maker will not take on the responsibility for managing the options inherent in a collar without building in a margin. Consequently, a market-maker might retain a "volatility edge" of some amount (a 1–2% spread on volatility is not abnormal on energy options) for transacting a collar. For example, if the one-year forward is $18.00, and a client buys a one-year collar with $16.00 as the "downstrike", the buyer might have to accept an "upstrike" of $21.14 (which gives a 2% volatility spread to the market-maker). If the client is selling the collar, he might set $16.00 as the downstrike and $20.03 as the upstrike for a zero-cost collar. Obviously, the mid-point between upstrike and downstrike is higher for the collar buyer ($18.57) than it is for the collar seller ($18.02). A market-maker can rarely find a buyer and seller for the same collar structure, so this difference in bid/offer may have to cover his cost of managing the embedded option position as well as offering a profit margin.

Many companies use collars because they like the idea of "cheap insurance". An energy consumer buying a collar gets protection from an adverse upward move through the cap, pays nothing upfront, and only has a cash outflow if prices settle below the downstrike on the floor. In a rising market, the collar buyer gets a cash inflow from the upside (beyond the cap strike) without paying anything upfront.

In a falling market, the consumer will be able to buy energy more cheaply. But the energy consumer does not give away all of the benefit of lower prices. Because the collar has a "range where nothing happens", the fall in prices below the original forward price should be greater than the cash outflow he pays on the floor. The consumer therefore pays out only a portion of his savings. However, the consumer does "give away" a volatility spread to the market-maker.

Any type of energy consumer might use a collar structure (an airline, an industrial user of oil, or an oil or gas burning electric utility). The structure can be reversed for an oil producer, with the oil producer selling the cap and buying the floor.

PARTICIPATING COLLARS AND PARTICIPATING SWAPS

These structures (Fig. 7) are essentially exchanges of options, offering a zero upfront cost. In the case of the participating collar, a company normally sells an option struck at-the-money and buys one that is out-of-the-money. Because an at-the-money option has greater value, if the options were transacted for the same quantity, then the at-the-money option sold would be worth more than the option purchased – and so the company would be due an upfront

premium. With a participating collar, the option bought is for a larger quantity than the one sold and so the options have equal premium value but different sizes.

A participating swap is like a participating collar except that the gap between the call strike and the put strike is eliminated by moving the strikes to the same point. In order to give a larger quantity to the purchased option, the strike price on the option sold is moved into the money.

To make these two participating structures clearer, we will provide examples of both. Imagine that an oil producer wants to sell a participating collar. This would involve simultaneously selling a cap struck, for example, at the swap price and buying a lower strike floor out-of-the-money for a larger quantity. To keep the example simple, we can use a single settlement. The producer might sell a one-year call on 66,700 barrels struck at $18.00 which is at-the-forward, and this call might have a value of $1.36 per barrel or a total premium received of $90,712. A one-year put struck at $16.70 might cost $0.907 per barrel, and this could be acquired in a zero-cost exchange if it were for 100,000 barrels. With this "participating" instrument, if prices were to rise and settle at $19.12, which is above the $18 upstrike, the producer would pay a cash outflow of $1.12 per barrel, or $74,704 on the 66,700 call. On the other hand, if prices fell and settled at $14.65, below the $16.70 downstrike of the put, there would be a cash inflow of $205,000 – the downside multiplied by the larger downside quantity ($2.05 × 100,000).

Alternatively, the oil producer might sell a participating swap. To keep the quantities in the same ratio of 66.7/100, a call is sold for 66,700 barrels, and the put is bought for 100,000 barrels. If we move both strikes to $17.34, both options would have equal premia (assuming the

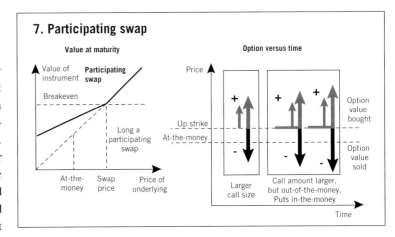

7. Participating swap

Value at maturity

Value of instrument — **Participating swap** — Breakeven — Long a participating swap — At-the-money — Swap price — Price of underlying

Option versus time

Price — Up strike — At-the-money — Larger call size — Call amount larger, but out-of-the-money, Puts in-the-money — Option value bought — Option value sold — Time

market maker that buys the participating swap from the producer retains a 1% volatility spread). If oil prices settle at $19.12, the participating swap would cost $118,726; the cash outflow is more than the participating collar described above because of the lower call strike. If prices settle at $14.65, the cash inflow is $269,000 ($17.34–14.65 = $2.69 × 100,000), which is a greater hedge benefit because of the higher strike on the put.

These instruments are described as "participating" because the company that enters into them participates in any favourable price move in the underlying commodity. For example, the oil producer can protect 100% of its downside risk (below the floor price) while selling a call on a smaller quantity and therefore retaining some portion of the upside in the underlying above the cap price. In the participating collar example, the producer pays out 66.7% of its upside on the underlying price of 100,000 barrels of production, but protects 100% below $16.70. The cost of the "participation" is the less favourable placement of the option strike prices.

BULL & BEAR SPREADS

A bull spread is a call that is partly financed by simultaneously selling back a higher strike call. A bear spread is a put that is acquired more cheaply by selling a lower strike put. These instruments (Fig. 8) are cheaper than straight options because the size of the payout is limited. The call (or cap) payment is limited to a fixed amount of the "upside" and the put (or floor) payment is limited to a fixed amount of the "downside". For example, a bull spread might be the potential upside between a $19.00 cap and a $21.00 "supercap" so that the potential cash inflow to the purchaser is limited to a maximum of $2.00 per barrel. A bear spread might be, for example, the downside between $17.00 and $15.00, also

limited to $2.00. The reason for using such instruments is that they are cheaper to buy than straight options with the same strike as the cap or floor; but the hedge protection begins to be seen at the same strike level.

An illustration of the possible cost savings for one year, single point settlement is given below. The illustration assumes a forward price of $18; other assumptions as above. The payout amounts below each instrument indicate the amount received by the holder of the instrument if the price settles at the figure indicated. For example, a $19 cap has a payout of $3 if the settlement price of the underlying is $22.

Instrument	$19 Cap	$19/21 Bull	$17 Floor	$17/15 Bear
Option premium	$0.98	$0.57	$0.90	$0.66
Payout at $22.00	$3.00	$2.00	0	0
at $20.50	$1.50	$1.50	0	0
at $15.50	0	0	$1.50	$1.50
at $14.50	0	0	$2.50	$2.00

These structures usually attract companies that would like to buy straight options, but which also want to pay a smaller upfront premium. To gain a saving they are willing to give up some of the less likely, or distant, beneficial price movements. An example might be an industrial company that wants a hedge against a rise in the price of the low sulphur fuel oil that it consumes, and which is willing to use a Brent crude oil cap as a hedge. (The company has consciously accepted the product basis risk between the price of crude and low sulphur fuel oil, because the crude option appears cheaper and is more liquid.) To make the upfront cost lower, they might agree to limit their cash inflow to $2.00 per barrel. Thus, they might buy a $19–21 bull spread at $0.57, rather than the $0.98 that a straight call option would cost. This is over 40% cheaper and yields the same payout for the first $2.00 of price move over the cap strike.

The range of payouts shown in the example above illustrates the value of using such an option where the energy price is expected to stay within a range limited by the supercap or superfloor. Often, companies use these "spread instruments" as part of a shorter maturity hedging strategy, and a standard collar as part of a longer-range hedge.

SWAPTION

A swaption (Fig. 9) is an option to buy (or to sell) a swap. As with any option, the swaption buyer pays an upfront premium for the right, but not the obligation, to buy an oil (or gas) swap at a

8. Bull spread

Value at maturity — Value of instrument — Bull spread — Long a bull spread — Cap strike — Super cap strike — Price of underlying

Option versus time — Price — Super cap strike — Cap strike — Option sold — Option bought — Higher strike calls sold to finance purchase of in-the-money calls — Time

fixed price. Compared to a cap covering the same period as the swap, the call swaption is cheaper because after the swaption is exercised, there is two-way risk on the swap, while the cap contains no downside risk for the buyer.

Swaptions are typically purchased by clients who need the assurance of a maximum fixed price, but feel that there is a reasonable prospect of a price fall before the expiry of the swaption. If prices do fall, then they will let the swaption expire unused and buy a swap at a lower cost. Typically, a swaption is held until maturity because there is normally no advantage in exercising it prior to maturity. Logically, a holder of a swaption will only exercise it if the pre-determined fixed exercise price is lower than an alternative swap purchased at the then-prevailing market price.

As an illustrative example, let us take the case of a swaption, maturing in five weeks, that is purchased in late December and expires in the middle of February; the swaption controls a six-month swap at $19.00 for February through July. Such a swaption might have cost 30 cents per barrel of the swap, or $180,000 for a swap covering 100,000 barrels per month or 600,000 barrels overall. Assuming that the swaption is exercised at maturity, then the monthly payouts over the six months, February to July, for a $19.00 fixed-price swap would be as follows:

	Average price	Fixed price	Difference	Payment on 100,000 bbl
January	18.82	Not covered	0	
February	19.05	19.00	0.05	5,000
March	18.96	19.00	(0.04)	(4,000)
April	20.22	19.00	1.22	122,000
May	20.99	19.00	1.99	199,000
June	22.36	19.00	3.36	336,000
July	21.75	19.00	2.75	275,000
Feb–Jul	20.56	19.00	1.56	933,000

From this cash inflow, the swaption cost of $180,000 could be subtracted, giving a net cash inflow of $753,000 for the swaption exercised prior to maturity. In this particular instance, where the swaption was cheap because of its short maturity, and where the market rose during the life of the swap, the net inflow is likely to have been more than for a straight call or for a collar.

However, the short maturity in the example does not fully reflect the flexibility inherent in the swaption. The advantage of the swaption is that the client need not exercise the swaption and can take advantage of any lower-cost opportunities which may be seen in the market during the period prior to maturity of the swaption.

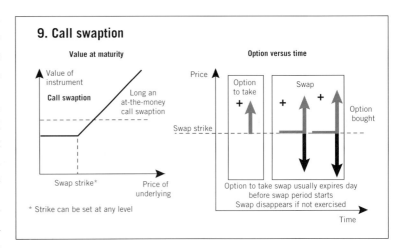

9. Call swaption

Value at maturity — Option versus time

* Strike can be set at any level

Option to take swap usually expires day before swap period starts
Swap disappears if not exercised

Conclusion: strategy summary for end-users

From the discussion above, it should be clear that different types of energy derivative are suited to quite different exposure management strategies.

❏ If an energy consumer feels certain that energy prices are at an important low (or a producer sees a high), then a swap is likely to be the most cost-effective way of locking into a low fixed price (or high price for a producer). There are no upfront premiums to pay, and the swap increases in value as soon as the price begins to move. The disadvantage is that the swap (or forward or future) leaves the client exposed to the risk of very substantial losses if he is wrong and prices move in an unfavourable direction.

❏ The more uncertain the end-user is about the future direction of prices, and the more he desires flexibility in executing his hedging requirements, the more attractive are option-related instruments, because options bring flexibility. The issue with the option is whether the cost of the flexibility provided by the option is affordable. Many combinations of buying and selling options have been developed to reduce their upfront cost.

❏ The most "swap-like" options-related instruments are collars and participating swaps. For a collar, if the "upstrike" and "downstrike" are set at the same price and there is a single fixed price, then the collar is exactly equivalent to a swap. The greater the distance between the "upstrike" and the "downstrike", the larger the range of variation where no payments will be required and the more the collar will exhibit option-like features. For a client who wants a degree of protection similar to a cap, but who does not want to pay an upfront premium, the "zero-cost" collar can be attractive. However, the client must be prepared to accept the possibility

HEDGING VERSUS SPECULATION WITH OPTIONS: SOME GUIDELINES

What is hedging and what is speculation? This question took on increasing importance during the 1990s as reports emerged of large losses suffered by corporations as a result of derivatives trading. If losses from hedging do emerge, a risk management strategy should be defensible as appropriate "hedging" if the following guidelines have been followed:

❑ The *direction* of a hedging transaction should normally be the opposite of both the specific underlying position being hedged, and the overall exposure of the company.

❑ The *size* of a hedging trade will normally relate to the underlying position, but it must also be realistic – particularly where a basis exposure is involved. For example, hedging long-term oil exposure with short-term oil futures leaves a time basis exposure. If the shape of the futures curve moves "against" a hedger, so that every month when they roll over their futures contracts on the exchange (that is, when they buy the front contract and sell the next contract) there is a big loss, the hedging company may face a significant negative cashflow. A hedge that is theoretically satisfactory in the long term is of little use if the hedging company cannot withstand the monthly losses while it waits for the basis to move back into its favour.

❑ The *risk/reward* should make sense. If combinations of options are used, there should probably be a ratio of exposures which, if prices go the "wrong" way, remains somewhere near symmetrical exposure on both the put and call sides of the trade. In the past, some companies have got into trouble using "leveraged swaps" wherein protection bought through a call was financed by selling a vastly larger exposure on the put side. When the market moved against the hedge, the losses were magnified, and the ultimate loss was far larger than any likely gain from the hedge had prices moved the other way.

❑ There should be a clear *understanding* of the hedging transaction so that the corporation can measure, monitor and anticipate the extent of its exposure on the trade (and explain the transaction to its board, if necessary).

❑ There should be a clear *hedging policy*. For example, "trading around a hedge" (ie taking profits and modifying hedge positions) can be a good tactic so long as the amount of trading is not excessive and it fits the policies and strategies agreed by the corporation's senior management.

❑ There should be close *supervision* from the senior levels of the corporation to make sure that corporate policies are being followed, and that those responsible for risk management have the ability to understand and manage the overall risk management programme.

---

of substantial losses if prices fall below the "downstrike". The more precisely an energy consumer can identify a suitable level for the "downstrike" (with little risk of cash outflows), which still provides a substantial reduction in the cost of a cap at the desired level, the more beneficial the collar structure. Producers should seek low-risk levels for placing the upstrike.

For a participating swap, if there is zero participation (ie the quantities on both sides are the same) then the instrument is exactly equivalent to a swap. As the quantity of the option purchased increases, then the strike on the option sold must be moved into-the-money to compensate for the smaller size. The participating swap is really two separate instruments sold as a combination: an offmarket swap entered with an immediate negative value which pays for an option in the desired direction. For a consumer,

this means buying a swap with a fixed swap price "above market" to pay for an out-of-the-money cap. It follows that a participating swap should be used if a corporate feels there is a high probability that prices will move so that the embedded swap will be in-the-money.

❑ The cap provides certainty of a limited maximum loss (the same is true of the floor for an energy producer). For a standard cap, with the premium payable upfront, the potential loss is limited to the upfront premium. There is normally no limitation on the cash in-flows on the cap and so the cap provides ideal risk control in a volatile market: limited risk, and unlimited return. The disadvantage is the cost: the more volatile the market, the higher the upfront cost.

❑ The swaption is a hybrid which can provide the best of both worlds (in the right circumstances), or merely a more expensive way of entering a swap (in the wrong circumstances). For the energy consumer, the call swaption gives the assurance of protecting a maximum fixed hedge price, while allowing time for prices to drop – and it normally does this at a lower cost than a cap. However, it should only be used when there is a reasonable prospect that prices may go lower, and that there may be a fall in swap prices which is large enough to at least cover the upfront premium on the swaption.

1 *The author would like to thank Vince Kaminski and Stinson Gibner of Enron Capital & Trade Resources, and Graham Wright, consultant on futures and options and visiting lecturer at the City University Business School, for reading and commenting on this chapter.* Risk *would also like to thank Kosrow Debnad of Citicorp Securities, Inc for his advice and help.*

Different option pricing models can produce different prices and delta equivalents. The figures published here are for demonstration purposes only.

2 *For the sake of clarity, the relationships described in this section are simplified and should really be regarded as approximations, or "rules of thumb".*

3 *This chapter introduces a new type of option diagram. Conventional diagrams show the option "value at maturity" with the price of the underlying on the x-axis and the option payout on the y-axis. The problem with the usual type of diagram is that it makes it impossible to compare options combinations where there are different maturities and to show how the option values are affected by time. The new type of diagram puts "time to maturity" on the x-axis and depicts an option as an arrow with the base of the arrow starting at the strike price and the length of the arrow representing the option's value. This makes it possible to compare visually the value of options of different maturities while instantly visualising how option values will change over time.*

3

Energy Exotic Options

Vincent Kaminski, Stinson Gibner and Krishnarao Pinnamaneni[1]
Enron Corp

Exotic options continue to increase in use as a means of controlling exposure to energy prices. One factor contributing to this increased popularity stems from the persistent high price volatility of many energy commodities, which results in corresponding uncertainties in future costs or revenues. Inherent exposure to various price averages and price differentials has also speeded the industry's embrace of some exotics such as Asian options and spread options.

Another factor is related to the deregulation of the US markets which, in different energy sectors, has affected both producers (natural gas) and consumers of energy (for example, airlines and utilities). Deregulation has resulted in intense competition and a concomitant sensitivity to price fluctuations. As companies have realised how vulnerable they are to fluctuations in commodity (especially energy) prices, they have tended to create or expand risk management units. Such specialised units have proven more likely to accept novel risk management instruments, such as exotic options.

One of the main reasons that exotic options have been accepted by the energy industry is that options were, in fact, embedded in many energy contracts long before they became fashionable tools of financial engineering (and even before they were analysed in academic papers). An example is provided by the "take-or-pay" contracts in the natural gas industry. Under such a contract, the buyer agreed to purchase fixed-price gas up to an annual maximum, but became subject to deficiency payments if the volume bought dropped below a minimum amount. For example, a buyer of 3,600,000 MMBtu[2] of gas per year with a minimum take of 50% could elect to purchase 1,800,000 MMBtu. But any shortfall below the 1,800,000 MMBtu level would trigger a penalty payment equal to the product of the deficiency times an agreed unit fine. In addition, many contracts allowed the buyer to vary their take amount widely from month to month – pro-

viding they bought the agreed volume over the year. The buyer effectively had an option on the timing of purchases over the year and thus could take into consideration, among other factors, the prices of alternative fuels. Until the late 1980s, these options were not explicitly recognised (or priced) by the sellers, who lacked the financial sophistication to isolate them from the other provisions of the contract.

Moreover, certain contracts in the energy industry contained, directly or indirectly, averaging provisions. For example, many contracts in the oil industry are based on the monthly or weekly averages of reference spot prices compiled by different institutions. Similarly, many natural gas contracts settle against reference prices which are, in effect, averages over some time period. This arose because the price indices compiled by newsletters in the natural gas industry – widely used as a pricing benchmark in supply contracts – represent average prices during the bid-week[3] for deliveries of gas at specified locations. It follows that the risk exposure of most producers and end-users of oil and gas is to an average price level over a period of time, and this facilitated the acceptance of Asian options.

One of the distinctive features of commodity risk management is the importance of basis risk, where basis is defined as the difference between two prices. This type of risk leads directly to another type of exotic option that is commonly traded in the energy business. Refiners are exposed to risks associated with changing crack spreads (the price differential between crude and the refined products); and producers are exposed to changing spreads between the prices of various grades of crude, or between the prices for natural gas at different geographic locations. In addition, both producers and consumers may be exposed to a "seasonal" risk (summer to winter price changes) or "annual" (year-to-year) price risk. All these types of risks have led to the prevalence of spread options in the industry.

Another major reason for the increasing pop-

PANEL 1

FIVE YEARS LATER – WHAT HAS CHANGED?

In the first edition of this book we defined exotic options in terms of the departures from the payoff definition of a standard call or put. We devoted a lot of attention to different complicated options, such as barrier options or lookbacks. Over the last few years we realised that the energy industry has rejected many option structures that were actively promoted in the past by many marketers. The authors spent much time trying to develop pricing models at the request of the sales force, trying to match in each case the most recent Wall Street structure du jour, in most cases representing a direct transplant from the fixed-income or currency markets. Most of these products never received a seal of approval from the customers. This can be explained by the fact that these options (1) did not address adequately the needs of producers and end-users of energy and/or (2) did not offer an attractive trade-off between cost and risk abatement.

As we have said before, options were traditionally used in the energy contracts long before the academic theory of derivative pricing saw the light of day. Most options represented the practical needs of doing business and were in most cases neither explicitly identified nor priced. In many cases they corresponded to the need not only to manage price exposures but also to control fluctuations in volume of production and/or demand. This is why many options in the energy industry have provisions allowing the adjustment of volumes (takes, or load factors in the industry jargon). This is especially true of the swing options that receive much more attention in this edition. Also, many contracts have been customarily structured in certain ways, and energy-related derivatives have to respect industry-wide conventions. Attempts mechanically to transfer the structures from other markets fail for these reasons.

Another reason the industry has not embraced some structures is that the nature of energy markets may increase the cost of hedging and managing the options, resulting ultimately in higher

---

ularity of exotic options is that the recent period of high price volatility in energy inputs has coincided with increased price volatility in other commodities – in particular, commodities that are associated with large energy inputs such as copper and aluminium. This volatility has seemed particularly threatening to producers because the globalisation of many industries, and worldwide excess capacity, mean that it is difficult to transfer higher input costs to customers. Certain kinds of exotic options are particularly suited to the management of multiple price exposures simultaneously.

By the same token, an energy producer with debt on the balance sheet will suffer if energy prices fall or if interest rates increase. But the real danger arises if these two conditions happen to coincide. A producer may seek protection against low prices and higher interest rates independently, but it may be more cost-efficient to seek remedies against the joint occurrence of these two related risky situations. This creates the need for an option with a payoff that is dependent on two prices: the energy index price and interest rates. Such options tend to be referred to as either exotic or hybrid contracts. We will look at some of the technical aspects of this type of option; a more detailed discussion of

their application and the concept of "integrated risk management" can be found in the next chapter.

This chapter is intended to provide a comprehensive review of the range of exotic options used in the energy industry. Our objective is to cover a rapidly expanding and highly technical area of applied finance in a way that is useful to a wide audience of professionals in the energy industry who might have had a limited previous exposure to derivatives; the chapter should also provide a useful and up-to-date summary of energy specific applications for derivative professionals. We provide the essential mathematical details and give detailed references to the most important papers; Appendix A at the end of this volume lists many of the standard formulas for pricing exotic options.

We begin by defining what exactly is an "exotic" option and then move on to discuss modelling and pricing. This overview is followed by sections describing each of the different types of contracts that have gained popularity in the energy industry: path-dependent options; dual-commodity options; compound options; digital options; and natural gas and electricity daily options. In our concluding section, we offer a résumé of some of the most pressing practical

prices. High volatility, frequent price jumps and low trading volume can make options excessively expensive. The relatively low depth of many markets can make barrier options, popular in the currency markets, prohibitively expensive in the case of energy. The same features of energy markets favour some other options, such as average price options (Asian options), in which price volatility is attenuated through the averaging process. Historically, the industry has developed other ways of handling price risks, including some provisions for risk sharing between producers and end-users.

In recognition of these trends in the energy option markets, we concentrate in this chapter on the options that have earned a permanent presence in our industry. We shall devote most attention to, and expand the treatment of, average price (Asian) options and spread options. The section devoted to digital options has been somewhat abridged, and we shall offer only very brief descriptions of options such as lookbacks and barriers. The interested reader is invited to revisit the first edition of this book.

This does not exhaust the list of changes to our chapter. Over time, we have recognised that most options in the energy markets are in some sense exotic. This reflects the fact that the behaviour of energy prices in most markets does not conform well to the theoretical assumptions underlying pricing of the financial derivatives. One obvious difference is that extremely high volatility and a tendency to jump often characterise the energy markets. Also, in spite of frequent jumps resulting from random shocks to supply and demand, prices will gravitate to the cost of production. Production costs may change over time depending on multiple factors such as available technology, inventory level, institutional framework and competition from other markets. Another obvious feature of energy prices is seasonality, derived mostly from the dependence of supply and demand on weather and climate patterns. Many of the most interesting contributions in this area made over the last few years represent the attempts to handle these features of the energy markets and to adapt the original theoretical framework for option pricing to take these features into account. We are unable to offer a full review of these contributions, but we shall signal some of them.

issues facing the providers and major end-users of exotic options.

The version of this chapter included in the second edition of this book has been updated not only to cover some most important technical developments in this field but also to address the reaction of the industry to the changing derivatives landscape. Our exposure to trading operations at Enron leads us to believe that the energy industry, saturated with people with strong quantitative skills, rejected the transplants from the financial markets that did not address adequately the needs of doing business. We have decided to reduce the amount of space devoted to less popular options and to give more attention to options that gained permanent citizenship rights in the energy markets. Additional space has been also devoted to modelling the dynamics of the underlying prices. We offer more reflections on the market trends in Panel 1.

What are exotic options?

The term exotic option is generally applied to those derivative contracts that diverge from the assumptions inherent in the early models developed by Black and Scholes (1973), Merton (1973) and Cox, Ross and Rubinstein (1979). These early models apply to call and put options with payoffs that are defined as the difference between the price of the underlying instrument, $F(T)$, at the time that the option is exercised, T, and the strike price, K, or zero if it makes no sense to exercise.

To be more precise, the payoff of these options is defined as $max(F(T) - K, 0)$, in the case of a call, or $max(K - F(T), 0)$ in the case of a put. In the case of a European option, exercise is allowed only at expiration; in the case of an American option, early exercise is possible. To price an option, one has to make assumptions regarding the dynamics of the price of the underlying instrument, with geometric Brownian motion (GBM) being by far the most popular assumption.

We may now define as exotic all option pricing models which depart from the standard assumptions either in terms of payoff definition or in terms of the stochastic process used to describe the dynamics of the underlying asset's price. Panel 2 contains the discussion of departures from standard formulations of option payoffs that convert a derivative contract from a plain vanilla variety to an exotic one. The next section reviews the properties of energy prices that require modifications of assumptions regarding the stochastic process used to construct pric-

DEFINING EXOTIC OPTIONS: MODIFIED PAYOFFS

What are the modifications to the classical payoff definition that convert a standard option into an exotic option? We can identify a few major changes, which can be classified as follows.

(1) Path-dependency. The option payoff depends not only on the price of the underlying at exercise (which is simultaneous with expiration for a European option) but also on the price trajectory during the entire life of the option (or some part of it). Examples of path-dependent options include:

❑ Asian options, which have a payoff defined as max(avg(F) – K, 0) for a call and max(K – avg(F), 0) for a put. Thus the payoff is a function of the average price, avg(F), of the underlying instrument calculated over a specified time period.

❑ Average strike options, which have a pay-off defined as max(F(T) – avg(F), 0) for a call and max(avg(F) – F(T), 0) for a put. The call payoff is equal to the price at the horizon less the average price over a certain time period.

❑ Lookback options, which offer the opportunity to obtain the best price that occurs during the life of the option. The payoff is defined as F(T) – min(F) for a call and max(F) – F(T) for a put, where max(F) and min(F) denote, respectively, the highest and the lowest price during the life of the option.

❑ Barrier options, which are extinguished or activated contingent on the occurrence of a certain event defined in terms of the price of the underlying or defined in terms of the price of an entirely different asset. For example, an option on natural gas may have a barrier defined in terms of the price of residual fuel oil.

(2) Multiple-commodity options with payoffs that depend on the prices of two or more commodities Most common are the dual-commodity options. Examples include:

❑ Spread options, which have a payoff defined as max(F$_1$ – F$_2$ – K, 0) for a call and max(K – (F$_1$ – F$_2$), 0) for a put, where F$_1$ and F$_2$ denote prices of commodities 1 and 2 at option expiration. The payoff of the option depends on the difference (spread) between the two prices.

❑ Basket options, where one or more of the underlying assets that determine the payoff of the option comprise(s) a basket of commodities.

❑ Options to exchange one asset for another or, in other words, to get the better of two assets.

(3) Compound options in which the underlying instrument is itself an option.

(4) Digital or binary options with predetermined payoffs that depend on the occurrence of events usually defined in terms of one or more prices.

This list of exotic options is by no means complete, but most of the options offered over-the-counter represent hybrids of those enumerated here.

---

ing models.

The standard assumption of the Black–Scholes framework is that the price of the underlying instrument, F, follows a geometric Brownian motion process defined by

$$dF = \mu F dt + \sigma F dz \qquad (1)$$

where μ is the drift (instantaneous expected return), σ is the volatility, dz is Wiener's variable (dz is ε√dt, ε being the standard normal random variable) and dt is an infinitesimally small step in time.

Black and Scholes (1973) proposed a formula for pricing European options on a stock that does not pay dividends. Their formula, one of the most important contributions to applied eco-

nomics, reads as follows (for a call):

$$c = S(t)N(d_1) - e^{-r(T-t)}KN(d_2) \qquad (2)$$

where

$$d_1 = \frac{\ln(S(t)/K) + (r + 0.5\sigma^2)(T-t)}{\sigma\sqrt{T-t}}$$

$$d_2 = d_1 - \sigma\sqrt{T-t}$$

where t is the valuation time, T – t is the life of the option in years, r is the risk-free interest rate, K is the strike price, S(t) is the stock price at time t, N(.) is the cumulative normal distribution function and c is the call option value.

The use of the risk-free interest rate in formula (2) is based on the principle of risk-neutral valuation. Risk-neutral valuation uses the notion of a risk-free portfolio, which is formed by combining an option with a position in the underlying and a bond. Since this portfolio has a predictable value under any circumstance, it is risk-free and should earn the same rate of return as other risk-free securities. Information about the cost of creating a risk-free portfolio allows us to price the option.

Note that the risk-free hedge can be created even if the expected rate of return on the underlying instrument is unknown. This means that the price of an option can be determined without reference to investors' preferences regarding the rate of return that they would require to hold the underlying. If investors' risk preferences do not affect option prices, one can value the options under any type of risk preference – and it makes sense to assume the simple case of risk-neutrality.

The Black–Scholes formula given by equation (2) must be modified if the standard assumption of geometric Brownian motion for the evolution of the underlying asset price is changed. Incorporation of a time-dependent or stochastic volatility is one example of a modified price evolution process. Another possibility is the selection of a different type of stochastic process altogether – for example, the jump-diffusion process. Modifications to the Black–Scholes formula are also required if the option payoff definition diverges from the original specification in Black and Scholes. Asian options and lookback options are examples of options with other payoff definitions.

In this chapter, we focus on options that have a payoff definition that is different from the standard Black–Scholes paradigm and focus on variations that are popular in the energy industry. Unless otherwise stated, none of the options discussed here aiiows for early exercise (that is, all are European-style options). We assume that the underlying instrument is a forward contract on a physical commodity, such as crude oil or natural gas, and that the price follows the geometric Brownian motion process described by equation (1), unless we explicitly change this assumption. We also address the modelling challenges related to the violations of the GBM assumption.

One of the consequences of using a forward contract as the underlying is that the drift coefficient μ in equation (1) is equal to 0. The drift of a forward price (or, technically speaking, the certainty equivalent) must be equal to zero, since the zero initial cost of entering into a forward contract is incompatible with an assumption of

positive expected return (Black, 1976). The use of futures prices is followed consistently in all the pricing formulas used in this chapter. It is important to stress that the formulas apply to options on financial contracts; they are not applicable to options on physical commodities. The call option on a forward contract has a premium given by

$$c = \exp[-r(T - t)]\{F(t)N(d_1) - KN(d_2)\} \quad (2a)$$

where

$$d_1 = \frac{\ln(F(t)/K) + 0.5\sigma^2(T - t)}{\sigma\sqrt{T - t}}$$
$$d_2 = d_1 - \sigma\sqrt{T - t}$$

and $F(t)$ is the forward price at time t.

Pricing and hedging exotic options

A natural question asked by a potential buyer or writer of exotic options is how to price such contracts and also, in the case of a seller, how to hedge them. In response, we shall offer a few general comments and give some specific examples for different types of exotics.

To price an exotic option, one should first attempt to replicate it with a package of standard options or simpler exotics. If this is possible, each component option should be priced individually, and the sum of all the long and short positions will give the desired price. As a bid–offer spread for volatility is usually included in the option valuation, one should be careful not to artificially inflate the premium by including the volatility spread for each component option.

If the replication approach does not work, in some cases one may find a closed-form expression for the option price that is comparable to the Black–Scholes formula. Such solutions are available for many exotic options. We shall discuss some of them here and give references for others. Even if an exact closed-form solution cannot be found, one may be able to find an approximation method that gives acceptable accuracy in pricing.

If neither a closed-form solution nor a good approximation method can be found, it is necessary to use one of the numerical methods. The numerical methods used for option valuation fall into three categories: Monte Carlo (simulation) methods; tree (binomial or multinomial) methods; and finite-difference or numerical integration methods. Hull (1993) discusses in detail the implementation of Monte Carlo, tree and finite-difference methods for option valuation.

PRICE PROCESS MODELLING

Traditional option pricing theory is based on the assumption that the prices of the underlying instruments follow the geometric Brownian motion process, defined in equation (1), as follows:

$$dF_x = \mu_x F_x dt + \sigma_x F_x dz \qquad (3)$$

This assumption implies that the natural logarithm of the price at the horizon, $T - t$ years from now, follows a normal distribution with the mean equal to

$$\ln\left(F_x(t)\right) + \left(\mu_x - \frac{\sigma_x^2}{2}\right)(T - t) \qquad (4)$$

and the standard deviation equal to

$$\sigma_x \sqrt{T - t} \qquad (5)$$

Note that t is the starting time measured in years (typically, t is assumed to be 0) and T is the ending date.

This approach can be extended to model the dynamics of two or more commodity prices jointly. In the case of two commodities X and Y, the assumption is that the price of Y follows the process given by

$$dF_Y = \mu_Y F_Y dt + \sigma_Y F_Y dw \qquad (6)$$

and the two Brownian motions dz and dw in equations (3) and (6) are correlated ($E\{dzdw\} = \rho dt$, where E denotes the mathematical expectation operator).

The prices described by the equations (3) or (6) are random variables. Their evolution is driven, among other factors, by the stochastic variables dz and dw. One implication of the assumption of the GBM process is the continuity of the line representing the sample trajectory of the price over time. The line could be drawn, in principle, without removing the pencil from the sheet of paper.

The assumption of geometric Brownian motion as the process that describes the dynamics of the prices of financial instruments is an approximation of the behaviour observed in real markets and has to be treated as a stylised fact. As a matter of fact, there is growing evidence that the behaviour of market prices in many past time periods did not conform to this standard assumption of financial economics. One especially troubling observation is that the empirical frequency of the occurrence of extreme outcomes is larger than the probability implied by theoretical models. This issue will be revisited below.

The assumption of GBM strikes anyone with practical experience in commodity trading as an unrealistic description of the observed behaviour of commodity prices. This has been recognised by a growing number of academics and practitioners, who have devoted a lot of attention to developing more realistic models of energy commodity price behaviour. What follows is a brief review of the most important issues that were overlooked in early modelling efforts and have been fully addressed only in recent research. One should note that energy commodities are not created equal and many observations made below apply only to some subsets of their entire universe.

❑ *Investment assets versus consumption goods* The most obvious observation is that energy commodities cannot be treated as purely financial assets, treated by owners as an investment. Energy commodities are inputs to production processes and/or consumption goods, and this explains why many models based on a mechanical extension of the approach developed for financial markets may break down in the case of energy-related contingent claims. For example, geometric Brownian motion does not allow negative prices. This assumption may be violated in practice often enough to require attention, especially in the case of electricity. In some cases, prices of electricity bid into a power pool may drop to zero if some generators want to guarantee that their plants are dispatched for contiguous blocks of time longer than a single time slot for which separate bids are accepted. In some cases, the price may become negative, as power plants have to get rid of excess output and have no option to store electricity. In other words, an assumption of free disposal, customarily made in theoretical models, does not hold. This problem has been addressed by some recently published papers (see Routledge, Seppi and Spatt, 1999).

❑ *Prices of energy commodities display seasonality* By this we mean recurring regularities in price levels and/or price volatility observed over time. Seasonality may correspond to the time of the year (winter versus summer versus shoulder months) or may be observed in intra-month, intra-week and, in some markets (like power), intra-day prices. Seasonality results primarily from regular demand fluctuations, driven in most cases by recurring weather-related factors. Fluctuations in demand interact with the supply-side factors: increased demand can be satisfied only from more expensive sources or by using more expensive production units. In many cases, increased demand resulting from weather-related factors might reach the levels at which supply becomes constrained by the capacity of the existing transportation or the transmission grid. In many markets, seasonality may change over time due to the changes in economic conditions and technology. For example, many natural gas marketers expect a change in seasonal price patterns in the US natural gas markets starting in 2000 due to increases in the gas-fired generation capacity. It is expected that, in addition to the winter peak, one will observe a more pronounced July/August peak related to the air-conditioning load.

Recognition of the existing and possibly changing patterns of seasonality creates a need for forward looking modelling. The information about future seasonality is often derived in formal models from the futures/forward prices that summarise all the information available to the market about future demand and supply patterns. Some recent papers offer ingenious methods of calibrating prices to forward price curves.

❏ *Commodity prices often display what is known as gapping or jump behaviour* This is driven in many cases by fluctuations in demand and low elasticity of supply, reflecting rigidities in the transportation and transmission system and limited inventories. One stochastic process used in financial economics to describe such a price evolution is known as the jump–diffusion process. The equation for the jump–diffusion process consists of two parts. The first part is the diffusion component, described by the equation (1). The other is an additional component which represents the Poisson process:

$$dF_X = \mu_X F_X dt + \sigma_X F_X dz + (J-1)F_X dq \qquad (7)$$

The random variable dq is the Poisson process; it tells us whether the jump took place or not. The probability of the jump will be denoted by λdt, where λ is called the intensity or rate of the process. In more technical language, the probability that the jump occurs once in the time period of length dt (that is, the probability that $dq = 1$ for this time increment) is given by

$$\lambda dt + o\left(dt\right) \qquad (8)$$

where o(dt) is such that

$$\lim_{dt \to 0} \frac{o\left(dt\right)}{dt} = 0$$

The probability of no jump ($dq = 0$) is given by

$$1 - \lambda dt + o\left(dt\right) \qquad (9)$$

and the probability of more than one jump in the time period dt is o(dt). The size and the direction of the jump are described by the variable J, which is typically assumed to have a lognormal distribution. This means that the natural logarithm of the jumps follows a normal distribution with parameters which we shall denote by α and δ ($\ln(J) \sim N(\alpha, \delta^2)$). When a jump occurs with probability λdt ($dq = 1$), the price moves from the level S to the level SJ. J, as a lognormal variable, is always positive. If it is greater than one, the jump is to the upside, and when it is smaller than one, the jump is to the downside.

❏ *Prices gravitate to the cost of production* The assumption of GBM used in simulation allows prices to wander into unrealistic levels. The same approach used in modelling two related commodities, like natural gas and power, or peak and off-peak electricity prices, may produce unrealistic spreads between them. The departures from the cost of production, or "normal" price spreads, is possible in the short run under abnormal market conditions, but in the long-term the supply will be adjusted and the prices will move to the level dictated by the cost of production.

One approach used to capture the mean-reverting behaviour of energy prices is the Ornstein–Uhlenbeck process (OU). The typical formulation assumes that there is a level, c, to which prices will revert whenever they diverge from it as a result of random shocks:

$$dF = \kappa\left(c - F\right)dt + \sigma dz \qquad (10)$$

where κ denotes the speed of mean-reversion and σ is the volatility. We can assume without loss of generality that $\kappa > 0$. The first term in the equation (10) represents mean-reversion. If the price F exceeds the long-term level, c, then $c - F < 0$ and the first term in equation (10) will make a negative contribution to the price change, dF (given that $\kappa > 0$). The second term in equation (10) is random, and its realisation may be negative or positive. If it is negative, it will reinforce the effect of the first term; if it is positive it may offset partially or completely the effect of the mean-reversion. If the starting price level is F(0), the expectation of price at time t will be given by $c + (F(0) - c)\exp(-\kappa t)$. As the term $\exp(-\kappa t)$ goes to zero, as t becomes large, the long-term expectation of price is equal to c.

One should observe that the second term in the equation (10) is similar to the diffusion part of GBM, but the interpretation of volatility changes. The change in price, dF, is measured in dollars per physical unit, dz is unitless, and therefore σ in (10) must be measured in dollars as well, unlike the volatility used in Black–Scholes option models. The important lesson is that we define and estimate volatility in the context of the stochastic process assumption, and when this changes the interpretation of volatility changes as well.

One could argue that the use of a mean-reversion process represents another case of looking for the car keys under the street light even if they were lost somewhere else. Vasicek first used the mean-reversion model for modelling interest rate dynamics, and subsequently the model was widely adopted. In the case of energy commodities, a pure mean-reversion model may not perform well. First of all, the speed of mean-reversion may be different below and above the long-term level. Second, in many markets, especially in the case of electricity, one can expect more departures to the upside than to the downside.[4] Third, a price spike in one direction is frequently neutralised by a spike of similar magnitude and opposite sign that occurs shortly after the initial spike. The mean-reversion process produces a re-adjustment that is less abrupt.

❑ *Finally, the prices of energy commodities behave differently during different periods of their lives* This is especially true of forward prices. According to the so-called Samuelson hypothesis,[5] the volatility of forward prices increases as they get closer to their maturity. This can be explained by the fact that more information becomes available as the forward contract gets closer to the delivery period – and this results in more trading, which in turn produces more volatility. The authors believe that GBM may represent a reasonable approximation to the reality of forward markets. Once a forward contract reaches maturity and we enter the delivery period, the behaviour of prices becomes more erratic and subject to frequent jumps.[6] This suggests that one can model price behaviour using more traditional apparatus like GBM or OU during the forward stages of their life, switching to more complex processes to describe the dynamics of the spot prices during the delivery month.

Many academic and applied researchers combine the features listed above in an integrated framework. A selective list of some contributions in the area of modelling energy prices is included in the bibliography at the end of this chapter.

PRICING METHODOLOGY
Monte Carlo methods The Monte Carlo approach for valuing options was first described by Boyle (1977). This approach simulates the prices of the instruments underlying the option

and allows us to compute the option payoff for each scenario of price movements. The simulations are repeated several times (typically, at least a few thousand times) and the option pay-offs for the different paths are discounted to the present time and then averaged. This average payoff represents an estimate of the option value.

A single price is often simulated over time using the assumption of geometric Brownian motion – the assumption that underlies the Black–Scholes equation. The following formula for the price at time $t + \Delta t$ follows from equation (1) and can be used to produce a path for a single price:

$$F_{t+1} = F_t \exp\left[\left(\mu - \frac{\sigma^2}{2}\right)\Delta t + \sigma\varepsilon\sqrt{\Delta t}\right] \quad (11)$$

where ε represents a drawing from the standard normal distribution. The time increment may be taken as one calendar or trading day (or week or month), with an appropriate scaling of the other parameters (which are conventionally quoted on an annual basis). The drift coefficient μ, which is usually set to the risk-free interest rate for a stock that does not pay dividends, is made zero when modelling forwards and futures prices. Volatility, σ, is usually quoted as an annualised number and should be adjusted according to the simulation frequency.

Although geometric Brownian motion is a common assumption for price behaviour, almost any type of price evolution can be simulated using the Monte Carlo approach. Monte Carlo may be the method of choice for price processes that are difficult to implement using binomial or finite-difference methods. Because of the simplicity of implementation, the Monte Carlo approach is also useful as a way of validating pricing models that are based on other approaches.

In recent years, several investigators have published methods to extend Monte Carlo to the valuation of options with American-style exercise. Tilley (1993) was the first to present an American Monte Carlo (AMC) approach, which relied on the grouping of nearby paths at each time step in the simulation to allow for a backward recursion to estimate the exercise boundary. Although somewhat computationally intensive, AMC methods and path-dependent lattice methods, discussed below, provide tools for analysing a wide range of American path-dependent options that occur in the energy industry.

Barraquand and Martineau (1995) introduce a somewhat different method of implementing AMC by using a technique that they call "stratified state aggregation" (SSA). SSA allows them to reduce the dimensionality of the problem of pricing an American option on the maximum of a basket of several assets. Using simulation, they calculate the payoffs of each state and transition probabilities between states at subsequent time steps to allow for a recursive calculation of optimal exercise. Raymar and Zwecker (1997) extend the stratified state aggregation approach by using a two-dimensional state space to attack the same problem and perform numerical experiments to verify that their models do not exhibit significant foresight biases.

Broadie and Glasserman (1997) implement AMC by using simulation to construct branching paths. The branches growing forward from each possible early exercise time are used to evaluate the exercise decision. Because the simulation paths become, in essence, bushy trees, the number of possible exercise dates must be very limited to keep computation time and memory at reasonable levels. Broadie, Glasserman and Jain (1997) suggest methods to improve the speed and convergence of this technique.

The advantage of the AMC approach is the ability to capture two critical aspects of typical energy markets options: American flavour and the need to use more complex stochastic processes in modelling price dynamics. We believe that, in spite of the relatively low speed of this valuation technique, it is one of the most promising developments of the last few years.

The main drawback of the Monte Carlo method is its relatively slow speed. Since the standard error of the result from a Monte Carlo simulation is inversely proportional to the square root of the number of price path simulations, a large number of price simulations may be required – resulting in a long "run time" for the model. Of course, in a trading environment it is critical to produce precise option premium estimates within a short period of time. As a result, variance-reduction techniques are often used to improve the convergence of simulation results and to keep the number of price scenarios within acceptable limits. One such technique, known as the "method of control variates", is discussed later in the section on Asian options. Curran (1994) discusses stratified sampling, another variance-reduction technique.

Monte Carlo methods may also be used to value options that have payoffs which are dependent on two or more underlying instruments. In this case, the simulation should take into account the correlation between the underlying prices.

An even more difficult problem is represented by options with payoffs that are dependent on the shape of the forward price curve and the yield curve (options on swaps). To price such claims it is necessary to model the entire curve. One approach to solving this problem is based on the Heath–Jarrow–Morton (1992) factor model, which, though developed originally for interest rate instruments, seems very promising for commodity options.

All Monte Carlo algorithms depend on operating system-supplied or other software to generate random drawings from a known distribution. Most software packages for numerical calculations contain programs that generate random numbers. These programs can also be implemented by any programmer who understands basic probability theory. Assuring the quality of pseudo-random number generators is critical to the implementation of simulation methods, as a poor random number generation can lead to incorrect results or poor convergence. Chaplin (1993) suggests several tests that can be used for the verification of pseudo-random number generators. Press *et al* (1992) give methods for improving system-supplied random number generators and present stand-alone random generators; they also discuss methods for sampling from various distributions.

The use of quasi-random "low-discrepancy" sequences has also received much attention in recent years. Galanti and Jung (1997) examine the use of several types of low-discrepancy sequences. Hammersley and Handscomb (1964) provide a good general reference for Monte Carlo methods, including discussions of random number generation and variance-reduction techniques. More recently, Boyle, Broadie and Glasserman (1997) have discussed recent applications of the Monte Carlo method to security pricing problems, focusing on variance-reduction methods including low-discrepancy sequences. Schmeiser (1990) gives a more concise review of simulation methods, including pseudo-random number generation, random variate generation and variance reduction.

Binomial trees Binomial (trinomial, n-nomial) trees, sometimes referred to as lattice methods, have become one of the most popular and widely used methods for pricing options. In a sense, the binomial tree approach occupies the middle ground between Monte Carlo simulation and finite-difference methods; that is, although it can be described as "organised simulation", it

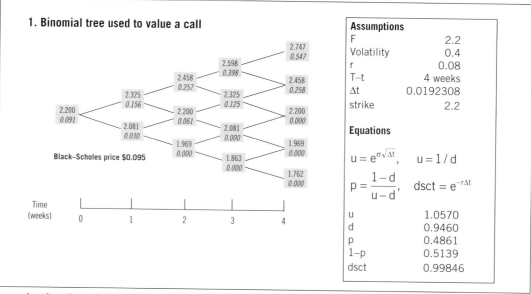

1. Binomial tree used to value a call

Assumptions	
F	2.2
Volatility	0.4
r	0.08
T–t	4 weeks
Δt	0.0192308
strike	2.2

Equations

$$u = e^{\sigma\sqrt{\Delta t}}, \quad u = 1/d$$

$$p = \frac{1-d}{u-d}, \quad dsct = e^{-r\Delta t}$$

u	1.0570
d	0.9460
p	0.4861
1–p	0.5139
dsct	0.99846

Black–Scholes price $0.095

Time (weeks): 0 1 2 3 4

can also be thought of as a special case of the finite-difference method. In a tree method the life of the option is subdivided into a number of time intervals. In each interval the price of the underlying can move into a small number of states. For example, in the binomial tree method the price in one time step can go up with a probability of, say, p and go down with a probability (1 – p). The magnitudes and probabilities of the price shifts are determined from the stochastic process assumed for the price of the underlying by requiring that the distribution of the tree prices has the correct mean and variance at each time step (see, eg, Cox, Ross and Rubinstein, 1979; Cox and Rubinstein, 1985; Hull, 1993; and Trigeorgis, 1991).

Figure 1 illustrates a binomial tree along with the numerical assumptions used to construct it. The upward price movement is determined by multiplying the price at a given node by factor u. The downward movement is given by d, the inverse of u (d = 1/u). The top value at each node of the tree in Figure 1 gives the price of the underlying at that node. The lower, italicised number is the option value at the node. At the horizon the option payoff is computed for each of the terminal nodes. The option value is then calculated by means of a backward recursion, which takes the terminal payoffs back through the tree. The payoffs are discounted and weighted by the probabilities of the upward and downward price movements. The resulting discounted, probability-weighted average of the payoffs is an estimate of the option's value.

For example, a four-week European call option can be priced using the numerical assumptions shown in Figure 1. The option payoff at the horizon is equal to the difference between the price and the strike if this difference is positive, and zero otherwise. In Figure 1 the payoffs are equal to (from top to bottom): $0.547, $0.258, $0.00, $0.00, $0.00. The value of the option one week prior to expiration, at the top node, is equal to $0.398. The value at this node is calculated as follows:

Discount factor × {Probability(up) × Payoff(up) + Probability(down) × Payoff(down)}

or

$$0.99846 \times (0.4861 \times \$0.547 + 0.5139 \times \$0.258) = \$0.398$$

Continuing backwards through the tree to calculate values for all the nodes leads us to an estimate of $0.091 for the premium. For comparison, an application of the Black–Scholes formula produces a premium of $0.095. The discrepancy between the two values is due to the imperfect approximation of a continuous distribution of prices through a discrete distribution. The accuracy of binomial tree pricing generally improves when the number of time steps used is increased. Of course, using a very large number of time steps to produce very accurate prices has the drawback of requiring more calculation time. Hull and White (1988) demonstrate how control-variate techniques can be used to accelerate the convergence of binomial option pricing methods.

Binomial methods afford great flexibility. They can be easily adapted to value American options and have also been extended to evaluate options based on two underlying instruments (for example Boyle 1988; Amin 1991). Methods have been developed to extend tree methods to the valuation of path-dependent options. Hull and White (1993) present a method for evaluating European and American path-dependent options. Cho and Lee (1997) and Chalasani, Jha and Varikooty (1998) apply binomial tree methods to the pricing of Asian options.

One of the problems that is frequently encountered in pricing energy derivatives is seasonality. Binomial trees designed for equities do not address this issue. Recently, an ingenious technique has been developed to calibrate trinomial trees to forward price curves displaying a seasonal pattern (see Clewlow and Strickland, 1999).

Finite differences and numerical integration
Two approaches that price exotic options by numerically solving the partial differential equations governing the option prices are finite-difference methods and numerical integration. Finite-difference methods were originally applied to option valuation problems by Schwartz (1977) and Brennan and Schwartz (1978), and were extended by Courtadon (1982) and Hull and White (1990). These methods start with the partial differential equation satisfied by the option price. A grid is constructed by discretising the time–price domain. In less technical terms, this means that a grid is constructed by dividing the life of the option into small time intervals and breaking the range of possible prices down into a number of intermediate discrete prices. (One may note the similarity to the binomial tree method.) The resulting grid of allowed time and price steps allows the differential equation to be approximated by a number of difference equations for which a numerical solution can be found. Dewynne and Wilmott (1993) and Wilmott, Dewynne and Howison (1993) discuss the application of finite-difference methods to valuing exotic options. These methods are generally applicable when valuing options under Black–Scholes-type price evolution and may be computationally more efficient than other methods when valuing a large number of options (Geske and Shastri, 1985).

When the option valuation problem is reduced to an integral equation, the option value can be calculated by finding the expected payoff through numerical integration. We will give an example of the application of this technique in our discussion of spread options.

DETERMINATION OF INPUTS
Deriving a pricing formula for an exotic option is a necessary but not sufficient condition for the correct valuation and determination of risk parameters. Equally important are the inputs – notably volatility and, for options which depend on two or more underlying prices, correlation.

Volatility can be inferred from the observed prices of options in the market. One can simply use the option pricing formula and vary volatility until the quoted option premium is matched. Another approach is to use one of the techniques for solving a non-linear equation, such as Newton–Raphson. One complication is that implied volatility is different for options at-the-money and options in- and out-of-the-money. This phenomenon, known as the "volatility smile", is noted in Chapter 2 and has received a good deal of attention in the literature. Derman and Kani (1994), Dupire (1994) and Rubinstein (1994) have independently developed option pricing models that attempt to incorporate the implied volatility smile. The illiquidity of traded options in many energy markets may make the practical use of such models difficult, at best, if one relies on the market to provide the implied volatilities needed in the calibration of these models.

If quoted premiums are not available, or are not reliable, one can estimate volatility from historical data. This task is not trivial and requires a combination of careful econometric analysis and common sense. The standard procedure for estimating volatility as the standard deviation of the natural logarithms of ratios of historical prices is well known; further discussion on the subject can be found in Cox and Rubinstein (1985) and Leong (1992). The price of a dual-commodity option depends on the correlation between the two underlying asset prices. Although correlation is one of the most widely used concepts in applied statistics, the use of this concept in the context of option pricing is quite difficult. First of all, correlation, like volatility, should be estimated within the framework of the assumptions made regarding the dynamics of the underlying assets' prices. Historical volatilities are estimated as the standard deviation of the natural logarithms of the price ratios, and the same approach can be taken in the case of correlations. Practitioners tend to overlook this fact and sometimes use correlations based on levels of the prices. A consistent estimator of correlation is given by

$$\rho = \frac{1}{n \times dt} \times \frac{1}{\sigma_1 \sigma_2}$$

$$\sum_{i=1}^{n} \left[\ln\left(F_1(i+1)/F_1(i)\right) - \overline{\ln\left(F_1(i+1)/F_1(i)\right)} \right]$$

$$\left[\ln\left(F_2(i+1)/F_2(i)\right) - \overline{\ln\left(F_2(i+1)/F_2(i)\right)} \right] \qquad (12)$$

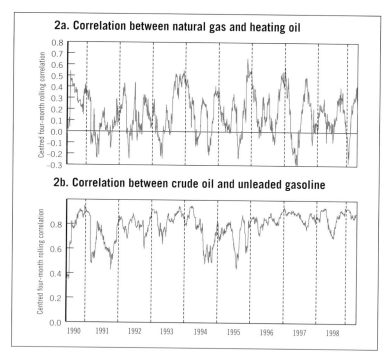

2a. Correlation between natural gas and heating oil

2b. Correlation between crude oil and unleaded gasoline

where n is the number of time periods sampled, dt is the time step between samples, σ_1 is the volatility of asset 1, σ_2 is the volatility of asset 2, F1(i) is the price of asset 1 at time period i and F2(i) is the price of asset 2 at time period i. Taking natural logarithms of price ratios in formula (12) is a conventional way of calculating price returns. The bar denotes an average.

Using accurate volatility and correlation inputs is critical when pricing dual-commodity options. Option pricing is often executed using volatilities implied in the prices of traded options. Correlations may sometimes be inferred from market option premiums as well. Implied volatility can be determined from the price of a single option through iteration. Implied correlation can be found by using the prices of three options (of which at least one must be a dual-commodity option) with similar terms by solving a system of three non-linear equations. The implied correlations and volatilities represent the market expectations of the price dynamics over the life of the option, interpreted in a risk-neutral setting. If no implied values are available, one may resort to using estimates from historical prices.

Historical correlations tend to be unstable over time. This may be a manifestation of permanent changes in the market structure or of random shocks, or it may be a reflection of seasonality. The effect of seasonality is illustrated in Figure 2, which shows centred four-month correlation between natural gas and heating oil (Nymex prompt contracts) and the correlation between crude oil and unleaded gasoline (Nymex prompt contracts). In the case of gaso-

line and crude, the correlation was affected by the Gulf War. In the case of natural gas and heating oil, correlation increases during the winter months when both prices are affected by the same underlying factor – the weather.

One of the recent developments in the estimation of correlation and volatility is the application of Garch technology, which was originally introduced by Engle (1982). The term Garch denotes a generalised autoregressive conditionally heteroscedastic econometric model. This term identifies the departures from the classical regression model given by

$$y_t = \alpha + \beta x_t + \varepsilon_t \qquad (13)$$

where α and β are regression coefficients, y_t is the dependent variable at time t, x_t is the independent variable at time t and ε_t is the random noise (error) term at time t.

In this classical regression model, the random terms are normally distributed and uncorrelated (that is, $\varepsilon_t \sim N(0, \sigma)$ for each t and $E(\varepsilon_i, \varepsilon_j) = 0$ for each i, j). The constant variance assumption for the normal distribution of random terms is known as homoscedasticity. This assumption is often violated in the case of financial time series, and special estimation techniques must be employed. The Arch model postulates that the variance of the error term is time-dependent and given, for the Arch(q) model, by

$$\sigma_t^2 = \alpha_0 + \alpha_1 \varepsilon_{t-1}^2 + \alpha_2 \varepsilon_{t-2}^2 + \ldots + \alpha_q \varepsilon_{t-q}^2 \quad (14)$$

where α is a vector of unknown parameters. The Garch(p, q) model, introduced by Bollerslev (1986), assumes that the distribution of the error term, ε_t, conditional on information ψ_t available at period t, is given by

$$\varepsilon_t | \psi_t \sim N(0, \sigma_t^2)$$

with

$$\sigma_t^2 = \alpha_0 + \alpha_1 \varepsilon_{t-1}^2 + \alpha_2 \varepsilon_{t-2}^2 + \ldots$$
$$+ \alpha_q \varepsilon_{t-q}^2 + \delta_0 + \delta_1 \sigma_{t-1}^2 + \delta_2 \sigma_{t-2}^2 + \ldots + \delta_p \sigma_{t-p}^2 \quad (15)$$

where α and δ are vectors of unknown parameters. Use of this model requires non-linear regression techniques and involves a relatively high degree of econometric sophistication. It seems, however, that the Garch technology is rapidly gaining acceptance in the dealer community.[7]

Path-dependent options

Path-dependent options have a payoff that is dependent on the price history of the underlying over part or all of the life of the option. Our review will be limited to Asian options, lookbacks and related contracts and barrier options.

ASIAN OPTIONS

Asian options have payoffs that depend on an average of prices over a period of time. For a call, the payoff of an Asian option is given by max(avg(F) − K, 0); for an Asian put the payoff is max(K − avg(F), 0), where K is the strike price and avg(F) is the average price over the specified period.

The averaging period may correspond to the entire life of the option, or it can be shorter. Many contracts in the natural gas industry, for example, are based on the average closing prices on the last two or three days of trading of the first available Nymex contract. If an Asian option is traded when it is within its averaging period, pricing the option requires supplying the average-to-date price of the underlying. For such options, averaging effectively starts – from the buyer's point of view – prior to the purchase of the contract. Averaging is typically calculated using an arithmetic average. A weighted average may be used to better fit the risk exposure of the option buyer. For example, a weighted average Asian may be used to hedge a series of planned fuel purchases that vary in volume. The weights may be chosen to vary inversely with the time until the option expires to give more importance to market conditions near expiration. An alternative to arithmetic averaging is to use a geometric average, defined as the nth root of the product of n prices. The latter is not usually used in the definition of option contracts but may be very useful in numerical algorithms used for pricing.

The average-strike option presents another type of averaging option. An average-strike option has a payoff which is defined as max(F − avg(F), 0) for the call and max(avg(F) − F, 0) for the put. For this option, the average becomes a strike price which is compared against the underlying's price on the expiration date to determine the payoff. The comments made above regarding calculation of the average apply in this case also. The volatility of an average price is lower than that of the underlying prices used in the calculation of the average. Because of this relationship, an Asian option at inception is much like a European option with a lower volatility. As a result, an Asian option will be less expensive than the corresponding European option, since premiums increase with increasing volatility. In addition to the lower cost, another advantage of Asian options is that their payoff is less sensitive to any extreme market conditions that may prevail on the expiration day (due to random shocks or outright manipulation).

Asian options are extremely important in the energy markets since, as was mentioned in our introduction, they were used long before the name or the pricing algorithms were invented. Asian options offer several advantages to both the producer and the consumer of energy products. Many buyers, such as utilities, are interested in hedging average fuel costs as the tariffs they charge to customers are based on average purchase prices. The producers are often interested in meeting budget targets that are based on average prices of energy products over the planning period. Asian options fit their risk profiles and allow them to achieve their goals at reduced costs as these contracts are typically less expensive than the corresponding European options. From the point of view of the option writer, Asian options are preferred products because they are easier to hedge. Asian options with long averaging periods do not have the high gamma risk that may befall at-the-money European options near expiry. After the Asian option enters its averaging period and the average begins to "set", the gamma risk of the option decreases and approaches zero near the end of averaging for options with reasonably long averaging periods. (If the averaging period is only two or three days, the gamma may still be sizeable at expiration.)

Pricing algorithms for Asian options have received a great deal of attention in recent years. Asian options cannot be priced using the Black–Scholes formula since an average of prices will not be lognormally distributed even though the individual component prices are. Since there is no known closed-form solution for the distribution of the average, Asian options are priced using numerical solutions or approximations. A number of different pricing algorithms have been suggested over the last few years and we shall mention a few without going into details. Levy and Turnbull (1992) give a more comprehensive review of Asian pricing methods.

The valuation methods for Asian options are based either on the application of numerical techniques or on closed-form approximations to the true value. The Monte Carlo approach can be used to price almost any option, and it is natural to apply it to Asian options in the absence of better ideas. Numerical procedures can be made more efficient by using variance-reduction techniques, which allow a reduction in the number of the simulations necessary for the desired precision. A popular approach is the use of control variates, first suggested by Boyle (1977), as a general option pricing tool. This approach exploits, in this case, the fact that a closed-form expression, similar to the Black–Scholes solution, exists for pricing an option defined in terms of geometric Asian payoffs. Enhanced simulation technology uses the history of prices for each path to calculate both the arithmetic and geometric Asian payoffs. The difference of these two payoffs is calculated and saved. At the end of the simulation process, the mean value of this difference is found and added to the known premium of the Asian option, defined in terms of the geometric average. The reader can find more details of application of this technique in the paper by Kemna and Vorst (1990), who were the first to investigate the application of Monte Carlo techniques in this area.

One can intuitively justify this approach by noting that the average difference between the arithmetic and geometric option payoffs is equal, in the expected value sense, to the difference between the corresponding premiums. By adding this difference to the known geometric option premium, we produce an estimate of the arithmetic option premium. However, the variance of the estimated arithmetic premium is lower because the Monte Carlo estimates of the arithmetic and geometric averages are highly correlated. Numerical errors in the arithmetic and geometric payoff estimates tend to cancel one another.

Among other numerical techniques, one should mention the approach proposed by Carverhill and Clewlow (1990), based on the application of fast Fourier transforms, to derive the representation of the density of the sum of random variables.

An alternative approach, proposed by Levy (1991) and Turnbull and Wakeman (1991) among others, derives an approximation for the price of an Asian option. Levy's approach is based on the assumption that the underlying distribution of the arithmetic average is closely approximated by the lognormal distribution. There is empirical evidence to support this hypothesis. The authors used Monte Carlo simulation of geometric Brownian motion and tested the empirical distribution of the average for lognormality using a Smirnov–Kolmogorov test. This test shows that the assumption of lognormality of the average price is satisfactory when the averaging period is short (up to a year) and the volatility is below 40%. These results suggest that

approximation methods should work well for short-dated options but that they become less accurate for Asians with longer tenors.

If we assume that the distribution of the average price is approximately lognormal, we have to obtain more information about the shape of the postulated distribution. This information can be extracted from the dynamics of the price used in computation of the average. The first step is to derive the formulas for the first two moments of the distribution of the average, namely the expected value of the average, $E[\text{avg}(F)]$, and the expected value of the square of the average, $E[(\text{avg}(F))^2]$. Derivation of the formulas for the moments is a straightforward application of stochastic calculus, given the assumption that the price underlying the average follows a geometric Brownian motion process. Once the moments of the distribution have been estimated, one can easily determine the drift and the volatility of the process underlying the average.

An assumption of lognormality of the average implies that its natural logarithm follows the normal distribution. This allows us to apply Wilkinson's approximation, which uses the moment-generating function for a normal variable to the natural logarithm of the average price at time T. The moments of the average price are expressed, under this transformation, in terms of the drift and volatility of the process followed by the average price. One can solve for these two parameters and use them directly in the standard Black–Scholes formula.

Turnbull and Wakeman (1991) adopt a similar approach. Their approximation is more complicated and uses the Edgeworth-series expansion to approximate the distribution of the average price.

Curran (1992) uses the technique of "conditioning", which is based on integration of the function representing the option payoff across all possible geometric mean prices (whose density is easy to obtain). A recent paper by Milevsky and Posner (1998a) derives the probability density function of the infinite sum of correlated lognormal variables. The result is then used to approximate the distribution of a finite sum of such variables, with obvious applications to pricing Asian options.

The approach proposed by Geman and Yor (1993) is a real tour de force of applied financial mathematics. This approach uses the fact that a geometric Brownian motion is a time-changed Bessel process to obtain the Laplace transform of an Asian option. The numerical challenge remains, however. One must use numerical methods for inverting Laplace transforms to solve the valuation problem. In this sense, the Geman–Yor formula is not a closed-form solution.

Figure 3 compares the price of Asian options to that of Europeans. The figure shows the Asian premium as a fraction of the premium for a European option with the same strike, volatility and tenor. The forward price and the number of days until the start of the averaging period are represented by the two horizontal axes. The time to expiration is held constant at 365 days, and the end of the averaging period corresponds to the expiration date. The figure clearly shows that the Asian price converges to that of the European as the averaging period shrinks. For a given time until expiration, the discount of the Asian premium relative to the European widens as the options move out-of-the-money. Deep in-the-money Asian options have values that again approach those of European option values, since the price of both is dominated by intrinsic rather than time value.

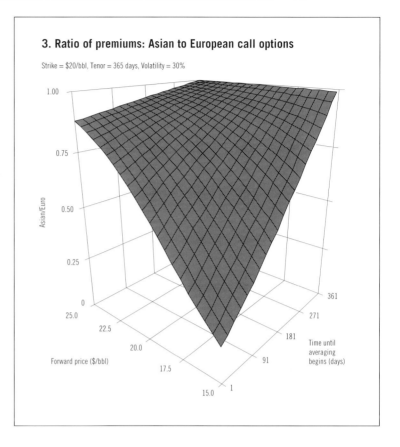

3. Ratio of premiums: Asian to European call options

Strike = $20/bbl, Tenor = 365 days, Volatility = 30%

LOOKBACK OPTIONS

A standard lookback call (put) option grants the right to purchase (sell) the underlying at the lowest (highest) price reached during the life of the option. Effectively, the best price from the point of view of the holder of the option becomes the strike price. The standard lookback call pays $(F(T) - \min(F))$ and the standard lookback put pays $(\max(F) - F(T))$. This means that the option always expires in- or at-the-money. The idea of the lookback option was introduced by Goldman, Sosin and Gatto (1979) and was explored further by Conze and Viswanathan (1991).

Conze and Viswanathan also discuss partial lookback options and options on extrema, which are similar to standard lookback options. Options on extrema are defined such that the put on minimum has a payoff equal to $\max(K - \min(F), 0)$ and the call on maximum pays $\max(\max(F) - K, 0)$. The call pays the difference between the maximum price reached over the life of the option and the strike. The put pays the difference between the strike and the minimum price. The pricing and hedging of lookback options is explored by Garman (1989) and is summarised in Appendix A at the end of this volume.

The lookback option is much more expensive than the corresponding European option, as illustrated in Figure 4. The expense dampens the

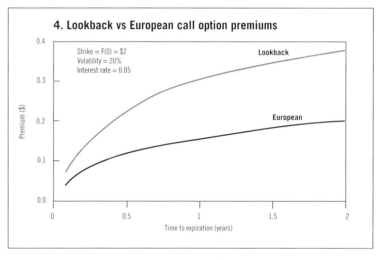

4. Lookback vs European call option premiums

Strike = F(0) = $2
Volatility = 20%
Interest rate = 0.05

lookback's popularity in the marketplace, and this type of option has never been embraced in the energy markets.

BARRIER OPTIONS

Barrier options were invented to reduce the initial cost of hedging and to allow the buyer to readjust the hedge when circumstances change. The barrier option either comes to life (is knocked in) or is extinguished (knocked out) when the underlying price passes a specified level. Most commonly, the price level (barrier, knock-out or knock-in price) may be reached at any time during the life of the option. For a call or put, the following combinations are possible:

	Event	
	Out	*In*
Up	Up-and-Out	Up-and-In
Price		
Down	Down-and-Out	Down-and-In

The barrier option may be combined with a rebate. For a knock-out option, the rebate is paid when the option is extinguished as a compensation to the holder. For knock-in options, a rebate may be paid at the expiration date for options which have failed to reach the knock-in barrier.

A typical example of a barrier option is the "up-and-out put" purchased by an energy producer to hedge its natural long position. An up-and-out put may be an attractive alternative to the vanilla put option as it is less expensive and provides the same price protection if prices move down from current levels. However, if prices move up, the increase in the underlying commodity's price reduces the need for downside price protection at the original strike. If the price moves up sufficiently to cross the barrier and extinguish the option, the owner may consider re-entering a hedge by buying another put at a higher strike price. Figure 5 illustrates prices for an up-and-out put option as compared to a standard European option and illustrates the potential savings to be derived from replacing a European option with a barrier option.

Although quite popular in foreign exchange markets, barriers options have never attained much popularity in energy markets, where end-users are typically more interested in finding structures that more closely mirror their actual energy price risk exposure. One reason why barrier options have not found many followers is that the many energy markets are relatively illiquid and it may often be relatively easy to push a price through a barrier to trigger or extinguish the option. The possibility of market manipulation is always an important consideration in the valuation of energy options. One possible practical application of a barrier option is the valuation of contracts with early termination provisions if some conditions are met. Such embedded options can be stripped from the underlying contract and valued as *barrier options*.

The barrier option value has a closed-form solution when the underlying price is continuously monitored. In practice, the option's barrier would be based on monitoring in discrete time (for example, using the closing Nymex prices) to reduce administration costs. Such an option could be priced using Monte Carlo simulation or by making an adjustment to the continuous-time formula for discrete monitoring of prices. Broadie, Glasserman and Kou (1995) present an approximate continuity correction for discretely monitored barriers, and AitSahlia and Lai (1997) provide an efficient numerical procedure for the valuation of discrete barrier and lookback options.

Merton (1973) and Black and Cox (1976) analysed the valuation of barrier options and derived closed-form solutions for some types of barriers. We provide some pricing formulas in Appendix A and also refer the reader to Rubinstein and Reiner (1991a).

From the point of view of the writers, barrier options may present formidable hedging difficulties. Benson and Daniel (1991) discuss characteristics and hedging problems associated with options that have a knock-out level which is in-the-money. Figure 6 illustrates the delta and gamma of an up-and-out put as a function of the underlying price and time to expiration. The put in Figure 6 has a knock-out level which is out-of-the-money. The delta and the gamma may change rapidly when the underlying price is near the barrier price. The gamma actually becomes infinite at the barrier price because the option's delta will suddenly change from a negative value to zero if the option is knocked out.

Multi-commodity options

Multi-commodity options have payoffs that depend on the prices of two or more underlying instruments. Modelling such options may be quite complicated, as the premiums depend on the multidimensional joint probability distribution of prices. Some types of multi-commodity options do have closed-form solutions. For example, Rubinstein (1991b) reviews concisely the valuation of two commodity "rainbow" options. For the options without closed-form formulas, Boyle (1988) and Amin (1991) suggest lattice val-

5. Up-and-out put vs European put option premiums

Strike = Forward price = $2
Tenor = 6 months
Volatility = 20%

European premium

Barrier option premium

Option premium ($) / Knock-out price ($)

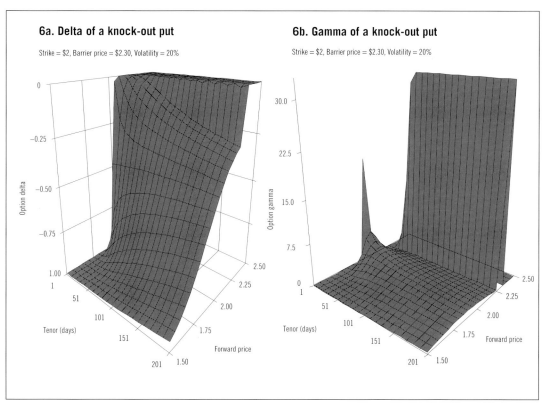

6a. Delta of a knock-out put

Strike = $2, Barrier price = $2.30, Volatility = 20%

6b. Gamma of a knock-out put

Strike = $2, Barrier price = $2.30, Volatility = 20%

uation approaches, and Barrett, Moore and Wilmott (1992) outline a numerical integration method that can be generalised to more than two underlying assets.

SPREAD OPTIONS

A spread option is written on the difference between the prices, F_1 and F_2, of two commodities, 1 and 2, with payoff defined as $\max(F_1 - F_2 - K, 0)$ for the call and $\max(K - (F_1 - F_2), 0)$ for the put. Spread options may be based on the price differences between:

❏ the prices of the same commodity at two different locations (location spreads);

❏ the prices of the same commodity at two different points in time (calendar spreads);

❏ the prices of inputs to, and outputs from, a production process (processing spreads); and

❏ the prices of different grades of the same commodity (quality spreads).

Of course, there are no clear-cut distinctions between different types of spread options, and contracts may combine location, time and quality price differences.

An example of a location spread is an option on the difference between the prices of 1% heating oil at New York Harbor and on the Gulf Coast. The price difference may induce some traders to ship heating oil from one location to the other, but they run the risk of price change when the cargo is in transit. One way to mitigate this risk is to purchase a put option on the spread between the two prices.

Examples of time spreads are provided by options on the difference between average annual ("calendar" in industry jargon) prices of natural gas (for example, the difference between the averages for calendar year 2001 and calendar 2002 gas prices) traded actively in the over-the-counter (OTC) market. Such options provide protection against reshaping of the natural gas forward price curve.

An example of a processing spread is an option on the difference between the prices of natural gas and of a basket of natural gas liquids (ethane, propane, iso-butane, normal butane and natural gasoline) that can be extracted from the natural gas stream at processing plants. Panel 3 provides a more detailed discussion.

Examples of quality spreads are the spreads between the prices of sweet and sour crude or between the prices of different grades of heating oil (defined by their sulphur content).

There are several approaches to pricing spread options. One method treats the spread between the two prices as a specific good – that is, as if it were traded separately from the two underlying commodities. This assumption may be justified in some cases. For example, in the natural gas industry an active market for the basis (ie difference) between two price indices has developed in the last few years. The next logical step is to offer options on this special commodity.

The pricing of these options is complicated

SPREADING THE CRACKS

Many companies in the energy industry are exposed to the difference in the prices of two related commodities, rather than to the price of an individual commodity. This type of exposure is generated when a company uses one commodity as an input to a process, which in turn produces another commodity. The difference between the input/output prices in such a case is known as a "crack spread".

The term "crack" refers to the technological process used in petroleum refineries – the application of vacuum, heat and catalysts to break down larger, heavier molecules of hydrocarbons into lighter ones, with higher economic value. In the natural gas industry, a corresponding process consists of the removal of liquids from the gas stream through fractionation. More recently, traders in power have coined the term "spark spread" to denote the spread between power prices and the price of fuel burned to generate power.

Common spreads are:
❏ heat spreads: the difference between the prices of No 2 heating oil and crude;
❏ gasoline spreads: the difference between the prices of unleaded gasoline and crude;
❏ resid spreads: the difference between the prices of No 6 fuel oil and crude;
❏ frac spreads: the difference between the prices of gas liquids (propane, ethane, butane, iso-butane, natural gasoline) and natural gas;
❏ spark spreads: the difference between the price of electricity and natural gas.

Market risks result from the volatile nature of both inputs and outputs, and from the imperfect correlation between the input and output commodity prices (due to the various independent factors affecting the feedstocks and products). In addition to crack spreads, refiners are sensitive to the interplay of the spreads between different grades of crude, each of which may result in a slightly different mix of refined products. Refiners are also sensitive to the spreads between the market prices of the products themselves. The high volatility of some of these spreads can be

explained if we consider that it is influenced by the volatilities of both underlying prices, moderated by their correlation (see equation (19) in the main text).

Refiners can hedge their exposure using a number of different approaches. One possibility is to use forward transactions to lock in prices of inputs and outputs. A second commonly used method is to purchase the input commodity under a netback agreement so that the price paid for the input is tied to the current level of prices commanded by the refined products. Another possibility is to enter into a basis swap under which a refiner pays a floating product price to a financial institution (a bank or a broker) and receives floating input price plus crack spread. In the normal course of business, the refiner pays a floating price for the input and receives a floating price for the processed product. When these flows are combined with a basis swap, the floating price flows cancel out and a producer is left with a fixed crack spread. The figure provides a detailed example of this type of transaction, as applied to a gasoline spread. This arrangement can be applied to a basket of outputs designed to match the mix of products marketed by the refiner.

Although the approaches described above eliminate price uncertainty, they also eliminate any opportunity for additional gain should the crack spread widen. An alternative solution is to use a spread option. As the (unhedged) producers lose if the crack spread decreases – that is, if the price of crude (input) increases relative to the price of

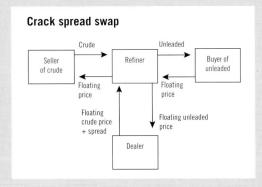

Crack spread swap

by the fact that, unlike a price, the spread can have negative values. The Black–Scholes formula cannot be used since it is based on the assumption of a lognormal distribution of prices at the horizon defined only for positive values. One can, however, assume that the spread has a nor-

mal distribution and use the pricing formula developed by Brennan (1979). This approach is used by Wilcox (1991). A shortcoming of this approach is that the distribution of the spread is not necessarily normal or even symmetric. The obvious advantage of this method is the ease of

unleaded (finished product) – they can hedge by buying a put on the spread. The payoff of the spread put option is defined as max(K – (Price of unleaded – Price of crude), 0), where K denotes the strike price. The table below provides some possible parameters for an option of this kind:

Tenor:	90 days
Forward price of unleaded:	$21.08/barrel
Forward price of crude:	$17.42/barrel
Strike (at-the-money):	$3.66
Volatility (unleaded):	25%
Volatility (crude):	24%
Correlation:	0.92
Interest rate:	5%
Put option premium:	$0.42

If the prices at expiration maintain their absolute spread, or if the spread widens, the producer lets the option expire worthless. For example, if the price of unleaded at expiration is $20.66 and crude falls to $14, then the option payoff is equal to max(3.66 – (20.66 – 14),0) = max(–3,0) = 0. The refiner allows the option to expire worthless, but benefits from the firmness of unleaded relative to crude. If the December spread narrows, let us say to $2.66, the producer can recover one dollar (less the option premium).

Refiners often use an alternative option strategy. They sell long-dated crack spread straddles to financial dealers. A straddle is a combination of a put and a call with the same expiration dates and strikes. A buyer of a straddle hopes that the volatility of the underlying prices will increase, creating profit opportunities, or that the two prices will decouple. In other words, the buyer makes a bet on decreasing correlation or increasing volatility. However, the buyers of these options may have difficulty in retrading the options to lock in a profit should the spread move their way. In fact the very poor liquidity in trading these options may oblige the purchaser to hold the options until expiration. In selling these straddles, a refiner can use the proceeds from the two options to offset changes in the crack spreads, as long as these changes are limited in size.

In the case of the electricity industry in the US, the obvious candidate for the development of an OTC spread option contract is the difference between power prices and natural gas prices. The main reason why natural gas was an obvious candidate is that among the alternative fuels used in the power industry, the market for natural gas is the most developed, both in terms of trading volume and completeness (ie existence of forward markets). Also, in some regions of the US gas-fired power plants are the marginal units to be dispatched into the power grid for most time periods. As a result, power prices are well correlated (at least, in some periods) with natural gas prices. The spread between power prices and natural gas prices is referred to as the "spark spread".

Spark spreads are often quoted using a convention based on the assumption of a heat rate of 10,000. The heat rate, in industry jargon, corresponds to the number of Btu required to produce one kilowatt of electricity. Suppose that the price of natural gas is $2.00 per million Btu (MMBtu) and the price of power is $25 per MWh. What is the spark spread? The calculation below answers this question.

Output price
$25/MWh = $25/1,000 kWh = $0.025/kWh
Input price
10,000 Btu/kWh × $2.00/MMBtu
= 10,000 Btu/kWh × $2.00/1,000,000 Btu
= $2.00/100 kWh
= $0.02/kWh

The spark spread is therefore $0.005/kWh

The obvious problem in valuation of the spark spread options is the unstable nature, discussed in the main text, of the correlation coefficient between power and natural gas prices. Valuation of the spread option requires making an assumption about the coefficient of correlation between two prices, and this correlation tends to be very unstable. The main risk that the writer and the holder of the option is running is that this correlation will change due to market factors or other circumstances. For example, power plant outages or changing hydrological conditions may alter the composition of the supply stack. In particular, an abundant water supply in the northwestern US can reduce reliance on the gas-fired power plants and lower the correlation between natural gas prices and power prices in this region.

computer implementation, as it produces a closed-form formula for option valuation.

Below, we give the formulas for call and put prices for a spread option. Note that the standard deviation of the spread, σ_A, is expressed in absolute, not relative, terms in this formula.

$$c = \exp\{-r(T-t)\}\{(S-K)N(d) + \sigma_A\sqrt{T-t}N'(d)\} \quad (16)$$

and

$$p = c - (S-K)\exp\{-r(T-t)\} \quad (17)$$

where

$$d = \frac{S - K}{\sigma_A \sqrt{T - t}}$$

S is the forward price of the spread and σ_A is the annualised standard deviation of the spread price, S.

An alternative, and possibly better, solution is to assume that the two prices defining the spread follow a joint lognormal distribution and to price the option as the discounted, expected value of the payoff in a risk-neutral world. The expected value is then simply a double integral over a relevant integration region, dependent on the forward price levels and the strike price. The specification of a joint lognormal distribution requires the calculation of the two volatilities and the correlation coefficient between the underlying prices. The integral can be evaluated using standard numerical procedures. Ravindran (1993) shows how to reduce the double integral to a one-dimensional numerical problem. The risk parameters can be found by differentiating the integral equation or can be approximated by repricing the option and using finite-difference methods. The risk parameters include two deltas, two gammas, a cross-gamma corresponding to the second mixed partial derivative, and a sensitivity with respect to the correlation coefficient. We propose that this sensitivity be called eta, η, as to the best of our knowledge no Greek letter for this risk parameter has been suggested.

OPTION TO EXCHANGE ONE ASSET FOR ANOTHER

This option, discussed by Margrabe (1978), gives the holder the ability to select the better of two assets. These options have, historically, been embedded in many futures contracts under which the short can choose the quality or type of commodity to be delivered.

For example, one can currently deliver any of 25 different types of Treasury bonds into the long Treasury bond futures contract that is traded by the Chicago Board of Trade. Given this option, the short will deliver the instrument that is the cheapest on the delivery date. In the energy markets, one possible application of this kind of option is a contract which allows the customer to buy natural gas at prices related to heating oil.

For example, if a utility is granted an option to buy 1 million Btu of natural gas at 70% of the price of 1 million Btu of 1% residual heating oil, it effectively has an option to exchange 0.7 MMBtu of "resid" for one MMBtu of natural gas. This option gives the buyer the ability to lock in the economics of cheaper fuel without necessarily investing in dual burner capacity or employing the specialised personnel necessary for handling two types of fuels. (Panel 4 provides an example of another use for this type of option.)

Energy users who elect to burn natural gas exclusively can also gain tax and "environmental" benefits. The reduction in emissions of pollutants can be monetised through a sale of emission credits, while in some states natural gas has a more favourable tax treatment than residual heating oil. Tax savings and the sale of emission credits can thus be used to defray the cost of purchasing exchange options.

The option to exchange one asset for another is actually a special case of the spread option where the strike is set to zero. The payoff for the option to exchange commodity 2 for commodity 1 can be written as $\max(F_1(T) - F_2(T), \ 0)$. Although there is no general closed-form solution for pricing spread options, an analytical solution exists for this special case. The call option to receive commodity 1 by paying with commodity 2 is given by

$$c = e^{-r(T-t)}\left[F_1 N\left(d_1\right) - F_2 N\left(d_2\right)\right] \qquad (18)$$

where

$$d_1 = \frac{\ln\left(\dfrac{F_1}{F_2}\right) + 0.5\sigma^2 \left(T - t\right)}{\sigma \sqrt{T - t}}$$

$$d_2 = d_1 - \sigma \sqrt{T - t}$$

$F_1(t)$ is the forward price of commodity 1 at time t and $F_2(t)$ is the forward price of commodity 2 at time t.

The volatility, σ, used for the inputs to expression (18) is derived from the volatilities of the underlying commodities and is given by

$$\sigma^2 = \sigma_1^2 + \sigma_2^2 - 2\rho\sigma_1\sigma_2 \qquad (19)$$

where ρ denotes the forward correlation coefficient between the two prices.

The call option described above allows the purchase of commodity 1 by paying with commodity 2 if this is advantageous to the holder of the option. Equivalently, this option allows the holder to exchange commodity 2 for commodity 1. Using our earlier example, the buyer of natural gas can pay the price of 0.7 MMBtu of "resid" when this price falls below that of natural gas. The call, priced by equation (18), which allows the purchase of commodity 1 by paying with commodity 2, is equivalent to a put that allows

BTU SWAPS

Many natural gas producers have shown interest in Btu swap contracts, under which the payments they receive for their gas are tied to the price of crude oil. One reason for the popularity of these contracts is that they allow consumers to diversify across the energy markets without having to handle different physical commodities. Another reason for entering into these contracts is the belief that the prices of energy commodities will tend to revert to certain historical relationships. When the long-term prices of crude and natural gas diverge significantly from their historical norms, Btu swaps can provide a way to profit from the expected reversion of the price ratios.

Figure A shows historical natural gas prices expressed as a fraction of the cost of an MMBtu equivalent amount of WTI. The standard conversion factor for WTI of 5.826 MMBtu/bbl was used. The figure illustrates closing prices for the nearby 12-month strip for natural gas and WTI Nymex contracts.

Near the beginning of 1994, spot gas prices were at historical highs relative to WTI, largely due to a weakness in the crude markets. This was an opportunity for producers long on gas to swap part of their gas to crude. Again when the crude markets sold off in 1998 and early 1999, the gas/crude ratio hit historical highs and presented another swap opportunity. Of course before closing on such a transaction, one must evaluate possible structural changes in the markets, such as depleting gas reserves and additions of gas-fired power generation, which could change the historical relationships between gas and crude prices.

Under a variation of the traditional Btu swap, a producer receives an initial cashflow that is equivalent to a loan. For example, for a time period prior to the beginning of the Btu swap, the pro-

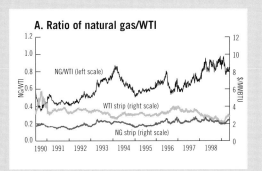

A. Ratio of natural gas/WTI

ducer receives payments that are based on a quoted index price plus an additional margin. Payment of the additional margin can be thought of as a series of loans made to the producer. During the Btu swap portion of the deal, the payments are set at a lower percentage of the crude price than for a stand-alone swap, so that the cashflows under this part of the contract repay the earlier loan amount.

Options can also be combined with Btu swaps to make them more attractive. As an example, consider a producer who wants to sell natural gas at prices that are tied to the price of crude oil. A market maker offers to purchase the natural gas at 65% of the price of crude on a MMBtu-equivalent basis. The producer requires that the gas be sold at 70% of crude or better, so a new structure is proposed whereby options are granted to the market maker in exchange for a more favourable swap price. The options grant the buyer the right to buy an additional quantity of gas at the better of either 70% of crude price or a standard gas index price. This structure, a twist on the common "double-up" deal, can be implemented using options to exchange one asset for another. This method of adding value to the deal may help to satisfy the needs of the producer, and allow the transaction to be consummated.

---

the holder to sell commodity 2 and to obtain payments in terms of commodity 1.

Rubinstein (1992) presents a binomial tree approach to valuing European- and American-type options to exchange one asset for another; a hybrid version of this type of option is discussed in Panel 5 (overleaf).

Options on the minimum or maximum of two commodities

Options on the minimum or maximum prices of two commodities are closely related to the

option to exchange one asset for another. For the special case where the strike price is zero, an equivalence relation is obtained:

$$\max(F_1(t), F_2(t)) = F_1(t) + \max(F_2(t) - F_1(t), 0) \quad (20)$$

$$\min(F_1(t), F_2(t)) = F_2(t) - \max(F_2(t) - F_1(t), 0) \quad (21)$$

An option on the maximum of two assets, $\max(F_1, F_2)$, is equivalent to a long forward position plus the option to exchange F_2 for F_1 with payin $\max(F_1 - F_1, 0)$. Similarly, a call on the min-

PANEL 5

USING HYBRID OPTIONS

The price of natural gas at the Permian Basin is one of the most volatile of the 60-plus locations in which Enron makes a market. The gas from this location traditionally flowed to California, where fluctuations in demand caused huge swings in the Permian index price. This instability resulted in a huge basis risk, basis being traditionally defined as the difference between an index and the average of the last three closing prices for the expiring Nymex contract.

Pricing of the Permian gas has been further complicated by changes in the pipeline system: in 1994 a new interconnect opened the northeastern and mid-continent markets to the production flow from this basin. In addition, the competitive situation in California was altered by the completion of the PGT (Pacific Gas Transmission) expansion, which opened this market to more Canadian gas from the Alberta region. More recently, the Northern Border pipeline added 700 million cubic feet/day of transport capacity from Alberta to the mid-western US, bringing Canadian gas into more direct competition with Permian and Gulf Coast gas in these markets. These developments may affect the gas-purchasing strategies for end-users operating in Californian markets.

Imagine the situation of a hypothetical California utility, GenCo, which is a large con-

sumer of gas. GenCo is interested in a contract that would allow it to financially lock in the price of the cheaper of the two gas supplies on a monthly basis. This type of option would allow the company to contract for long-term transportation to California in order to eliminate its exposure to fluctuations in transportation rates, and would also allow it to negotiate for preferred rates under the long-term deal. However, under a long-term transportation contract the company would have to commit to buying gas from one source and would thus incur "opportunity loss" if the gas from the other source proved to be cheaper.

GenCo therefore approaches Enron, which evaluates the factors that affect the prices of gas from both competing sources. The utility would like to maximise the benefit of having exposure to the relationship between the Permian and Alberta indexes, which, historically, has been characterised by highly seasonal volatility and correlation, as shown in the figure. The two indexes began to track each other quite closely in late 1993 and early 1994, when the PGT expansion became operational. Then for several years Canadian gas flowing south through Kingsgate traded at a significant discount to Permian Basin gas. Since the recent Northern Border expansion, Alberta gas prices have come more into line with

---

imum of two assets, $\min(F_1, F_2)$, is equivalent to taking a long forward position in F_2 and going short the option to exchange F_2 for F_1. Of course, we may be interested in valuing options on the maximum or minimum of two commodities when the strike price is non-zero. The solutions for these options, along with several interesting equivalence relations, were first published by Stultz (1982) and are reproduced, for the special case of commodity options, in Appendix A of this volume. Johnson (1987) extends these results and derives solutions for pricing options on the maximum or the minimum of several assets.

BASKET OPTIONS
Many energy price risk management situations may require options that have as the underlying asset not a single energy commodity but a basket of commodities. The weighted average price of this basket then drives the payoff of the option.

Situations in which these options can be used include hedges for gas fractionation plants that take natural gas as input and produce a basket of natural gas liquids, usually including ethane, propane, butane and natural gasoline. There are also many situations where the price of a commodity such as electricity adjusts according to an index. The index often consists of a basket of fuel prices including fuel oil and natural gas. Similarly, in Europe it is not uncommon to find natural gas priced from an index defined as a weighted average of several benchmark crude and fuel oil prices.

The simplest method of extending most option models to a basket option version is to calculate the forward price and volatility of the basket and treat the basket as the underlying commodity. In doing this, one makes the implicit assumption that the price density function of the future basket price is lognormal, which is not consistent with the assumption that the price dis-

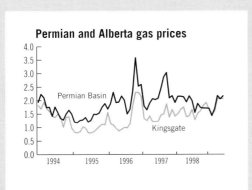

Permian and Alberta gas prices

prices in the Permian Basin.

One solution is for the company to purchase index gas at Permian Basin, where gas production is somewhat more reliable than from the Alberta supply pool, and enter into the corresponding firm transport agreement. Then the company could purchase an option from Enron that would pay the difference between the effective US dollar price of Alberta gas and the Permian price:

$$max(0, \text{Permian (\$)} - \text{Canadian (C\$)} \times \text{FX (\$/C\$)})$$

where FX is the currency exchange rate. This option, a hybrid equivalent of an option to exchange one asset for another, allows GenCo to benefit should Alberta prices again fall significantly below the Permian index. Pricing of this option is complicated by the fact that the price of one asset is a product of two related random variables. The following complicating factors must also be accounted for:

❏ the volatilities and correlations are likely to change in the future and will display a seasonal pattern that may be different from that observed in the past;

❏ all the relevant prices (the two natural gas indexes and the exchange rate) are likely to undergo discontinuous jumps – the phenomenon known as "gapping" in derivatives industry jargon; and

❏ hedging the option requires taking positions in three markets, two of which (the Permian and Alberta indexes) have historically had very high volatilities and an unstable correlation.

The provider has to be compensated for these risks, and this adds to the expense of this option. However, the attractiveness of purchasing the option ultimately depends on the expectations of the buyer. If one expects that the prices of these two indexes will continue to track one another closely, the payoff from an option to financially exchange one index for the other will be negligible. If GenCo believed in this scenario, the company could go ahead with the simple purchase of index gas and live with the risk (perceived as small) of opportunity loss. On the other hand, if GenCo came to the decision that the two indexes might again decouple in the future, the option may be quite attractive.

tribution for each individual component of the basket is also lognormal. Nonetheless, this assumption is often convenient and may produce reasonably accurate option pricing.

Milevsky and Posner (1998b) investigate use of the reciprocal gamma distribution as an approximation for the price distribution of the basket. They find that the bias in the resulting option values seems to be complementary to the bias generated under the lognormal approximation so that a combination of the two methods may generate more accurate results than either when used individually.

Compound options

An option that allows its holder to purchase or sell another option for a fixed price is called a compound option. We will use the term "overlying option" to refer to the compound option and the term "underlying option" to refer to the option which can be called or put by the holder of the compound option. In the simplest case the underlying options are simple calls or puts on an underlying commodity future or forward. Typical cases of compound options include European–European options, which may be classified as call on a call, call on a put, put on a call and put on a put. We shall use a call on a put as an illustration.

The purchase of a European call on a put means that the compound option buyer obtains the right to buy on a specified day (the expiration of the overlying option, T_o) a put option (the underlying option) at the overlying option's strike price, K_o. The underlying put has a strike of K_u and expires at an agreed time, T_u. At the overlying option's expiration the holder can either:

❏ exercise the overlying option – ie purchase the underlying put, paying a premium equal to the strike of the overlying option, K_o; or

❏ allow the overlying option to expire worthless.

Compound options offer a method of locking in commodity price protection at an initial cost

COMPOUNDING THE OPTIONS

Consider the following case study of the use of compound options. An independent exploration and production company, which we shall call Aggressive E&P, seeks to purchase additional gas-producing properties. The banks providing credit for the purchase are convinced by the geological estimates of the available gas reserves used to back the loan and are comfortable with the long-term cashflow projections. But they have a concern that loan repayment could be jeopardised if gas prices fall, and they require that some kind of price protection be arranged.

Aggressive rules out a fixed-for-floating swap as they have a bullish view of the future and want to profit from any rise in gas prices. They consider a zero-cost collar, constructed by receiving a floor (a strip of put options) in exchange for the selling of a cap (a strip of call options) of equal value. By using this "collar", Aggressive would preserve its exposure to price changes within the collar range (the range between the floor and cap levels) and thus preserve some of the "upside potential", but the company decides that the collar is still too restrictive.

The company then considers the purchase of either vanilla European puts or Asian puts, but, facing a short-term cash constraint, Aggressive decides that it really needs a structure with a smaller initial cash outlay. The purchase of a long strip of puts was unattractive for an additional reason. Aggressive expects its financial position to improve considerably over the next year, and it hopes that the banks will eventually relax the requirements for downside price insurance. In this case the puts would not be required – but selling the puts after holding them for some time would mean the loss of the time value component of the option price and of the bid–offer spread.

Marketers at Enron look for additional ways in which banks' need for price insurance and the producer's desire for participation in a rising market can be satisfied. They suggest that a compound option structure of calls on puts could provide downside protection at a low initial cost.

Price protection is required over several years, so each compound option is structured as a call on a strip of 12 monthly puts, providing price protection for one calendar year. Each call purchased by the producer expires in December of the year preceding the series of puts on which it is written. This structure allows the producer and its creditors to re-evaluate its financial position at each of these expirations and to decide at that point whether or not to purchase the puts. To minimise the premium, the strike prices of the underlying puts are set at the lowest levels satisfactory to the bank creditors. In addition to setting the underlying puts substantially out-of-the-money, the strikes of the overlying call options are set out-of-the-money as well. The resulting structure allows Aggressive to acquire the necessary price insurance for one-third of the cost of the outright purchase of a floor (floor level equal to the strike prices of the underlying put options).

The banks are satisfied that these options provide a sufficient payoff to ensure the repayment of the loan, and the producer is comfortable with the level of the up-front premiums, allowing it to complete its financing and secure the desired properties.

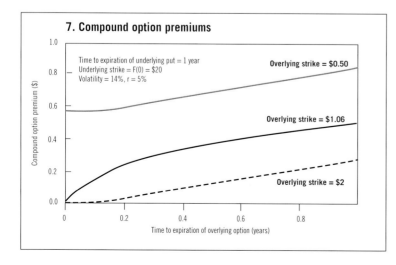

7. Compound option premiums

Time to expiration of underlying put = 1 year
Underlying strike = F(0) = $20
Volatility = 14%, r = 5%

Overlying strike = $0.50
Overlying strike = $1.06
Overlying strike = $2

Compound option premium ($)
Time to expiration of overlying option (years)

which is lower than that of the purchase of a cap or floor. These options are also useful for locking in the cost of price protection when the need for that protection is contingent on some future event (see Panel 6).

Figure 7 shows the price of compound options (calls on puts) for three different overlying strikes. At the inception of the compound option the premium of the underlying option is $1.06, so that for $K_0 = \$1.06$ the compound option has an at-the-money overlying strike price. When $K_0 = \$2.00$ the compound option is an out-of-the-money option, and when $K_0 = \$0.50$ the compound option is in-the-money with an intrinsic value of about \$0.56. Figure 7 illustrates the typical behaviour of such an option. The options lose value as they come closer to expiration, with the at-the-money and the out-of-the-money option values approaching zero for very short tenors.

The simple European on European compound options can be priced using the results of Geske (1979). These pricing formulas are reproduced in Appendix A of the present volume.

The pricing of a compound option becomes more challenging when the underlying option is more complex than a simple call or put. In some energy markets these more complicated compound option structures are seen reasonably often in the OTC markets. In the power markets, for example, purchasers of generation are accustomed to making a "capacity" payment to reserve the right to purchase fixed-price power over a specified period. Viewed financially, the capacity payment is simply the premium paid to purchase a call option on electricity, so an option on capacity becomes a compound option. This type of compound option can become complicated because of the specific terms attached to the underlying call option on power. For example, after exercising the overlying capacity option, the option buyer may be allowed to call on up to 100 MW of on-peak power for one week but is limited to a 60% capacity factor. That is, he may take a total quantity of power only up to 100 MW times 60% times the total number of hours covered by the option. In practice, the underlying option may have a number of complicated provisions specifying maximum rates and total quantities of power that may be called, minimum sizes of hourly blocks for which calls can be exercised and multiple possible delivery points (and whether the delivery option is held by the power seller or buyer).

Another type of compound option sometimes seen in the crude and natural gas markets is an option on a structure that contains options. This type of compound might be an overlying option that gives the holder the right to purchase a one-year price "collar" constructed of monthly settled caps and floors. A collar is an option transaction that involves the simultaneous sale of a call (put) and purchase of a put (call). The strikes are often calibrated to make the sale price of one option equal to the other's purchase price to create a so-called "zero-cost collar". A compound option may be defined as a right to enter into a zero-cost collar (at today's prices) at some point in the future. If, and when, this right is exercised, the market might have moved so that the collar would no longer be costless under cur-

rent market prices. Similarly, one could have a compound option where the underlying option might simply be a strip of monthly caps or floors.

Such complicated structures are offered in the OTC markets by a few of the more sophisticated marketers. Another example, an oil warrant, is an American option on an Asian option issued by Paribas Capital Markets Ltd in March 1991 (see Panel 7 overleaf). Such options can be priced using numerical procedures, and the recommended approach is a binomial or trinomial tree procedure.

Digital options

Digital options have discontinuous payoffs and, although not widely used in the energy markets, do sometimes find themselves embedded in swap and option structures. They are typically used when the customer has a strong view about the relation of future energy prices to certain specific price levels.

Digital (or binary) options typically pay either a constant value or zero depending on whether the payoff condition is satisfied or not. Examples of such options are provided by cash-or-nothing options and asset-or-nothing options (see Rubinstein and Reiner, 1991b). A cash-or-nothing call on cash amount X pays X if $F(T)$ is greater than its strike, K, or otherwise pays nothing. Similarly, a cash-or-nothing put pays X if $F(T)$ is less than K, or pays nothing. The valuation of such an option is straightforward: its expected payoff at expiration is given by the payoff amount, X, times the (risk-neutral) probability that the option will finish in-the-money. This price is equal to $XN(d_2)$, using the symbols used in formula (2a), discounted to the valuation date. The asset-or-nothing call will pay the value of the underlying instrument if the option ends in-the-money, but nothing otherwise. Its price is equal to the expected value of the asset, conditional on the price of the asset exceeding the strike at expiration. This conditional expected value is equal to $F(t)N(d_1)$ for the call $(F(t)N(-d_1)$ for the put), again using the symbols defined for formula (2a).

Some digitals are offered with the additional provision that no premium is paid for the option at inception. Cash settlement of these options occurs only if the option finishes in-the-money. Options expiring out-of-the-money require no payment by either buyer or writer. Such options are known variously as cash-on-delivery (COD), pay-later or contingent options. In the case of these options, the buyer does not receive the full

ASIAN MEETS AMERICAN

In March 1991 Paribas Capital Markets Ltd issued compound options on crude oil (January 1992 contract), with the unit size of the underlying commodity equal to 50 barrels. The offering consisted of three separate parts with the following specifications.

(1) Call on call. The overlying option was an American call with a strike of $2.00/barrel, expiring on September 27, 1991. The underlying call was Asian, with the price defined as an average of the 20 closing Nymex prices prior to December 10, 1991. The strike price of the option was equal to $21.00/barrel.

(2) Call on put. The overlying option was American with a strike of $1.50/barrel and an expiry date of September 27, 1991. The underlying Asian put was based on the average price defined as in (1), with a strike of $17.00/barrel.

The two calls described above were combined with a note floated by the issuer that had a par value equal to the strike of the overlying option. The note would be used to finance the purchase of the underlying option should the compound option be exercised. If the call remained unexercised, the holders of the options would be refunded the amount of the note proceeds.

(3) The third structure was an option with a payoff defined in the prospectus as 50 barrels × max(0, 4 − IF − 19I). This translates into a European butterfly, with a long position of two European calls on futures (strikes of $15.00 and $23.00) and a short position in two calls on futures with a strike of $19.00/barrel. The expiration date was December 13, 1991.

The figure shows that the third structure is effectively equivalent to a portfolio of options. Some of these options (in- and out-of-the-money options) are sold to the investors; at-the-money options are sold to the issuer by the buyers of the package. Valuing this "butterfly" structure is quite straightforward and is equivalent to pricing a portfolio of long and short European options on futures.

By using this butterfly structure, the issuer

effectively bought options with a strike price of $19.00, which was close to the at-the-money level, and sold calls with strikes of $15.00 and $23.00. (The price of the January 1992 crude contract on Nymex fluctuated around $19.00 at the time of the warrant issuance; it was $19.17 on March 13, $18.64 on March 25, and $19.33 on March 28.) Investors purchasing the butterfly must have believed that the future volatility would be low, since holding this structure was a bet on price stability around the $19.00 level. At-the-money call options are much more sensitive to volatility than the in-the-money and out-of-the-money options that were sold by the issuer to the investors. This allowed the issuer to effectively "buy" volatility. As we will see in a moment, the compound option structures (1) and (2) allowed the issuer to "sell" volatility. Thus the combined issuance of the butterfly structure and the compound option structures was really a volatility arbitrage. Paribas was marketing two different structures in an attempt to "buy" volatility at a low price and "sell" high.

Evaluation of the first and second investment structures offered by Paribas requires an algorithm to price a compound option involving two non-vanilla structures: American and Asian options. The technique we used employs a binomial tree with our proprietary Asian option valuation programme attached to each node. The model developed for this panel has an additional feature which allows the use of different volatilities for the

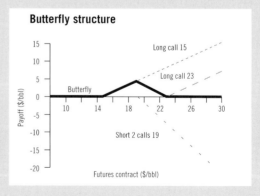

Butterfly structure

payoff given by the difference F(T) − K (K − F(T)) for a call (put). The amount deducted from the full payoff may be viewed as paying for the option. This payoff is necessarily negative for some values of F(T), making these options quite painful to the buyer on some occasions.

COD options, like other binary options, are quite difficult to hedge. This is illustrated by the behaviour of the put option's delta and gamma, which are shown in Figure 8 (overleaf). Turnbull (1992) discusses a method for hedging COD options using European options.

Pricing the calls

Call on call

	Tree volatility					
	0.15	0.20	0.25	0.30	0.35	0.40
Asian **volatility**			Option value ($/bbl)			
0.15	0.020	0.087	0.208	0.367	0.549	0.762
0.20	0.020	0.090	0.211	0.370	0.554	0.765
0.25	0.022	0.094	0.216	0.376	0.562	0.770
0.30	0.026	0.101	0.222	0.384	0.573	0.777
0.35	0.029	0.108	0.235	0.395	0.587	0.787
0.40	0.036	0.121	0.252	0.415	0.604	0.809

Call on put

	Tree volatility					
	0.15	0.20	0.25	0.30	0.35	0.40
Asian volatility			Option value ($/bbl)			
0.15	0.030	0.106	0.225	0.372	0.545	0.721
0.20	0.031	0.108	0.229	0.375	0.548	0.723
0.25	0.034	0.114	0.236	0.383	0.552	0.732
0.30	0.038	0.122	0.245	0.394	0.560	0.744
0.35	0.045	0.132	0.256	0.408	0.574	0.758
0.40	0.054	0.148	0.275	0.425	0.595	0.775

Note:
Valuation date: March 25, 1991
Closing price, January 1992 Nymex contract on crude: $18.64
Interest rate: 5%

construction of the tree and for the valuation of the underlying Asian option. (We shall explain shortly why this is a useful feature.)

Once this was accomplished, the pricing of the options was a straightforward exercise. The table shows the pricing of the call on call and call on put at different volatility levels as of March 25, 1991, using the closing Nymex price of the relevant contract on that date. We have ignored the note component of the warrant price as, on any given date, this would be a constant. Note that the option prices in the tables above are in $/barrel and must be multiplied by 50 to give the warrant values. The volatility at the top of each table refers to the tree volatility, the volatility over the life of the compound option. The volatility at the side refers to volatility over the life of the underlying Asian option.

The warrants were registered on the Luxembourg stock exchange. It seems that there was no active secondary market for these structures, which we suspect was partly due to their pioneering nature. The techniques of financial analysis required to price compound options of a complex nature were not sufficiently disseminated in 1991 to allow a wide range of potential buyers to do their "homework".

But why was this structure offered at all? The answer probably lies in the special historical circumstances prevailing in 1991. In the aftermath of the Gulf War price volatility was high by historical standards, and its future course was uncertain. Different groups of investors held diverse expectations regarding future price direction and volatility. The exotic options offered by Paribas allowed both camps to make directional bets. The compound option is really a leveraged volatility play: not only does a compound option have, all things being equal, high vega, but the use of American options as the overlying increases premium sensitivity to s. The issuer may have viewed this time period as an opportunity to "sell" volatility, expecting that the actual volatility over the life of the option would be lower than the current implied volatility level of the market. In March 1991 it seemed reasonable to expect that, by the time the underlying option was purchased (that is, by the time the overlying option was exercised), volatility would be much lower. This is why in our model we allowed the use of different volatilities for the construction of the tree (average volatility over the period terminating on September 27, 1991) and for the life of the Asian option.

Hybrid and complex structures

A number of types of options are commonly seen in the energy markets that combine aspects of the exotics mentioned above. One of the most common practices in the energy markets is to settle against an average of prices over some time period. Thus Asian options are pervasive in these markets. Perhaps the most prevalent type of average is the calendar month averaging of a daily closing price (for futures) or a daily index price (for spot or physical commodities).

Asian-style averaging is often combined with

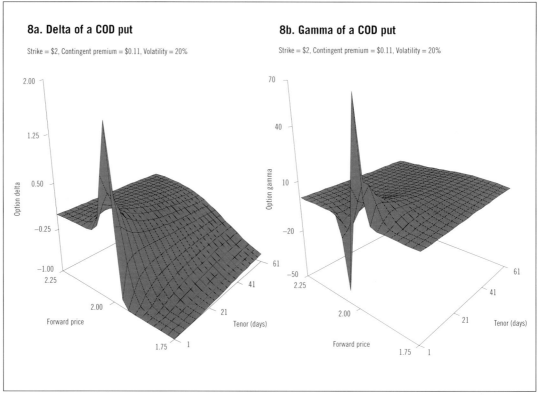

8a. Delta of a COD put

Strike = $2, Contingent premium = $0.11, Volatility = 20%

8b. Gamma of a COD put

Strike = $2, Contingent premium = $0.11, Volatility = 20%

spread options to give rise to Asian spread options. These may take the form of commodity spreads, such as an option that settles against the difference of the monthly average price of WTI futures and heating oil futures closing prices. Other Asian spread options can be written against averages that are not settled contemporaneously. Consider a customer who wants to purchase an Asian calendar spread option that settles against the actual closing prices for March versus April. One leg of the spread is determined by the average of natural gas daily prices for March, and the other leg is determined by the average prices in April. Because the two averages are determined over different, lagged time periods, we christen this option the Asian lagged spread option. Note that when the price for the early leg of the spread has been determined, this option becomes equivalent to an ordinary Asian option with a strike price defined by the determined leg of the spread.

Another twist that is sometimes added on top of the Asian option is to make the underlying asset a basket of commodities, thus giving rise to the Asian basket option. Of course, this leads to the obvious possibility of having Asian basket spreads and Asian basket lagged spreads. The possibilities open to energy marketers are endless.

Natural gas daily options

One of the interesting features of the US natural gas industry is that monthly contracts on the

physical delivery of gas in the following month are negotiated during a relatively short period at the end of each month (typically between the 20th and the 25th of each calendar month). The period when the sales/purchase contracts are negotiated is known as a bid week. Contracts negotiated during the bid week traditionally had options embedded in them long before the theory for pricing these options had been developed.

Take-or-pay contracts, discussed earlier, are an example of contracts with embedded options. Another type of option with a long history in the natural gas markets is the daily call option, which allows the buyer to take additional volumes of gas at very short notice (typically, one day). Such options have several interesting features, such as "forward start" and volume restrictions, which complicate pricing.

A forward start option written at time t_0, say, is an option with a strike price that will be set at-the-money at a later time, t_1 ($t_1 > t_0$), and which will expire at time t_2 ($t_2 > t_1$). The price of such an option at t_0 is equal to the price of a corresponding at-the-money option whose time to expiration is $t_2 - t_1$, valued at t_1 and then discounted back to t_0 (eg Rubinstein, 1991a). The forward start feature means that the strike price is made equal to the gas index for a given location at the beginning of the delivery month for which the option is written. The price indexes used for this purpose are compiled by industry newsletters, such as *Inside FERC, Natural Gas Week* and *Natural Gas Intelligence*, and are based on surveys of transaction prices during the bid week. These indexes are published in the first issues of the newsletters in each month and they closely reflect the market conditions prevailing at that time. With some qualifications, we can assume that the options are at-the-money at their inception on the first day of the month. The buyer may exercise them whenever the daily price exceeds the strike.

The ability to change on a daily basis the volume of gas purchases is usually referred to by the term swing. In addition to this daily option feature, swing options can have restrictions on the monthly volumes that the buyer can purchase. Consider a contract where one party agrees to purchase gas during a 30-day month at the first-of-the-month index price. The volume of gas purchased on any given day has a maximum of 15,000 MMBtu and a minimum of 5,000 MMBtu. Also, the contract can require the buyer to take no less than 200,000 MMBtu but no more than 300,000 MMBtu of gas for the whole month. If the volume taken during the month falls below the minimum required, the buyer may have to pay a penalty on the amount by which the volume purchased falls below the minimum. This type of provision is typical of the take-or-pay contracts so common in the natural gas industry.

In addition to the limits on daily and monthly volumes, there can be other provisions in the contract. The buyer can have the ability to change the volume from one day to the next, but only in discrete steps. This is referred to as ratcheting. For example, the contract mentioned above can require that the buyer change the daily volume by no more than 2,000 MMBtu on any given day. Also, the number of times the buyer can make such volume changes during the month can be restricted.

The market for daily gas options is quite active and evolves constantly. The options that require delivery of physical gas or electricity will be referred to as "swing options" (internally, Enron uses the term "Omicron options"). Options with similar structures but cash settled use the price indexes published by *Gas Daily*, an industry newsletter, as a reference price. *Gas Daily* prices are compiled on a regular basis from market participants through a phone and fax survey.

The volume restrictions give these options the flavour of American options combined with path-dependence. The decision to exercise an option depends on past decisions, which determine the remaining available volume, and on the number of days to expiration. If the number of remaining days is large, it usually makes economic sense to defer exercise of the option as the price could move even higher. On the last day, it makes sense to use the full daily volume available if the option is in-the-money and the monthly maximum has not been reached.

Exercise of these options presents a problem that is similar to deciding whether to call a bond. Interest rates could drop lower, increasing the benefits of retiring debt, but postponing the decision means the advantages of lower rates will accrue for a shorter period of time. Optimal timing will depend on the trade-off between the potential benefits of postponing the decision and the shrinking time period over which they will be enjoyed. One possible approach to pricing such an option is an extension of the binomial tree with additional state variables (except in the case where the monthly constraint does not effectively limit the number of days of swing).

TAKE-OR-PAY AND RATCHET OPTIONS: NOTATION
In a take-or-pay call option, the buyer agrees to purchase between a minimum v and a maximum V units of natural gas every day for the length of the contract – say, N days. The purchase (strike) price for the commodity is fixed at \$$K$/unit. Typically, the contract length is one month. The total volume for the contract period has a minimum V_{min} and a maximum V_{max}. Also, if the total volume falls below the required minimum, the buyer has to pay a fine of c\$ per unit on the volume shortfall.

A swing ratchet option is typically a monthly, seasonal or annual option with the daily volume being above v and below V units and the commodity (strike) price fixed at, say, \$$K$/unit. The daily volume can be increased (*swing up*) or decreased (*swing down*) by a constant amount, w, only. Thus, the volume purchased on any day falls into one of the volume "ratchets", namely, $v, v + w, \ldots, V$. The number of swings (ie daily volume changes) is limited to a maximum of M. A swing ratchet put option is defined similarly.

VALUATION
In this section we develop a procedure for valuing swing options by extending the lattice binomial tree approach. The binomial tree is extended to a connected set of binomial trees, for which we have coined at Enron the term "binomial forest". Thompson (1995) and Jaillet *et*

AN EXAMPLE OF PRICING SWING

Consider a simple example to illustrate the mechanics of swing option pricing. Swing options are typically exercisable daily but, to keep the example manageable, consider an option where the customer has the right to take up to 10,000 MMBtu of natural gas each week in a month (with four weeks) at a price of $2.00/MMBtu. The total volume purchased during the month must be between 10,000 and 30,000 MMBtu, with a penalty of $1.00/MMBtu for any shortfall below the 10,000 MMBtu monthly minimum.

We construct the binomial forest by first constructing the binomial tree of possible gas prices using the method shown in Figure A. The input parameters and tree parameters are given below. Recall that α is the one-period discount factor. Other parameter definitions can be found in the section titled "Valuation: take-or-pay options" and in the section on binomial trees.

To construct the binomial tree we use four time steps (with time step = 1/4 month). Once the binomial tree for the price movement is constructed, we create the forest by constructing binomial trees on four different planes corresponding to different gas quantities (k = 0, 1, 2, 3) purchased so far. The values in each of the trees in the forest are calculated by first finding the values at the terminal time step using equation (22) and then recursively finding the values of the earlier nodes using equations (23) and (24).

In Figure B, we show some of the flows of values during the recursive computation. We can start at the bottom-most tree (k = 3). Since the maximum value for k is 3, there is no optionality left here, so the option values are all zero. We can now proceed to construct the tree corresponding to k = 2. At each node we have to evaluate the two alternatives available to us: to take the minimum (0) or the maximum (10,000 MMBtu) volume. For example, for the node highlighted in italics (i = 3, j = 2, k = 2), we have

$$\text{Option value } F_{3,2}^2 = \max \begin{cases} 0*(2.089-2)+0.999*[0.501*1809+0.499*0] \\ 10,000*(2.089-2)+0.999*[0.501*0+0.499*0] \end{cases}$$

$$= \max\{906, 890\}$$

$$= 906$$

The value of taking the minimum is $906 (0 from immediate payoff plus $1,809 next week with a probability of 0.501 and 0 with a probability of 0.499). This is greater than value of taking the maximum, which is $890 (all coming from the immediate payoff since option values are all zero for k = 3).

For the node highlighted in bold (topmost node for the second week) in the tree for volume level k = 1, we have

$$\text{Option value } F_{2,2}^1 = \max \begin{cases} 0*(2.181-2)+0.999*[0.501*557+0.499*1791] \\ 10,000*(2.181-2)+0.999*[0.501*2795+0.499*906] \end{cases}$$

$$= \max\{3681, 3660\}$$

$$= 3681$$

For the initial time step and k = 0, we see that the option value comes out to be $1,422, or 4.74 cents/MMBtu on the maximum take quantity of 30,000 MMBtu.

A. Commodity price tree

Input parameters			Tree settings		Commodity price tree
S	$2	v	0	Δt	0.0208
X	$2	V	10,000	u	1.0443
r	5%	M_{min}	1	d	0.9576
σ	30%	M_{max}	3	α	0.9990
T	1/12	V_{min}	10,000	p	0.5012
N	4	V_{max}	30,000	q = 1–p	0.4988
		c	$1		

Commodity price tree:

```
                                              2.378
                                      2.277
                              2.181           2.181
                      2.089           2.089
      2.000                   2.000           2.000
              1.915           1.915
                      1.834           1.834
                              1.756
                                              1.682
```

B. Pricing a swing option using binomial forest

Volume level k = 0

Volume level k = 1

Volume level k = 2

Volume level k = 3

al (1997) consider similar approaches to pricing swing options. The method is reviewed by Pilipovic and Wengler (1998), and Barbieri and Garman (1996 and 1997) discuss pricing and hedging issues for swing options.

We assume here that the commodity price follows a geometric Brownian motion process and approximate the price evolution by a binomial tree. Under a swing ratchet option, the buyer agrees to purchase this commodity for a period of N days. Since we assume that the option on volume is exercised to maximise return using the market prices of gas over the month, it follows that the buyer will take either the minimum or the maximum volume of gas allowed on any given day (unless the minimum or maximum restriction on the total volume requires purchase of gas above the daily minimum and below the daily maximum). Using this fact, we derive recursion equations for valuing swing options. Following the notation developed in the earlier section on binomial trees, assume that the option period of N days is divided into N time steps so that each time step corresponds to one day. This choice of time interval greatly simplifies notation and provides sufficient accuracy for the option values we compute. Accuracy can be improved, if necessary, by considering time intervals of shorter length and modifying the recursion formulas appropriately.

We use below the standard notation used in the discussion of algorithms based on binomial trees. In a simple tree the forward price during each time period is assumed to make a single move, either up or down. The price is assumed to move up by a multiplicative factor of u with a probability p and to move down by a multiplicative factor of d with a probability $q = 1 - p$. It is typically assumed that $d = 1/u$. We identify a node in the tree by an ordered pair (i,j), where i stands for the number of time steps elapsed and j stands for the level of the price. The forward price at the node (i,j) is $Fu^{j}d^{i-j}$, where F is the initial price corresponding to the node $(0,0)$. The discount factor corresponding to the chosen time step is denoted by α. The pricing of swing options requires construction of more complicated trees, and additional notation will be introduced below.

VALUATION: TAKE-OR-PAY OPTIONS
For these options the daily purchase volumes are limited by a minimum quantity v and a maximum quantity V. Also, the total volume for the contract period has a minimum of V_{min} and a maximum of

V_{max}. The minimum total volume can be achieved by purchasing the maximum daily quantity for M_{min} days and the minimum daily quantity for the rest of the days – ie we compute M_{min} from $V_{min} = M_{min} V + (N - M_{min})v = Nv + M_{min}(V - v)$, where N is the option life in days. Similarly, the maximum total volume V_{max} can be achieved by taking the maximum daily quantity for M_{max} days and the minimum daily quantity for the rest of the days – ie $V_{max} = M_{max} V + (N - M_{max})v = Nv + M_{max}(V - v)$. For simplicity, we assume that both M_{min} and M_{max} are integers. Since, for the most economic use of the option, the buyer takes only the minimum or the maximum volume allowed on any given day, it follows that, to avoid paying a fine, the buyer takes the maximum daily volume for a number of days between M_{min} and M_{max} and the minimum daily volume for the remaining days. If the number of days on which the buyer takes the maximum volume V falls below M_{max}, a per unit charge of \$c will have to be paid on the volume shortfall.

For pricing ordinary American options using binomial trees (see the section devoted to numerical methods), we represent a node in the tree by the pair (i,j), where i refers to the time step and j refers to the price level. For pricing swing options, we need a triplet (i,j,k) with the additional index variable k representing the number of days the maximum daily volume V has been taken up to the current time. As illustrated in Panel 8, k determines the plane identifying the appropriate binomial tree from the forest, and i,j, determine the specific node on that tree. Let C_{ij}^k be the value of the option on day i at price level $Fu^j d^{i-j}$, given that the volume purchased during the previous i − 1 days is $(i - 1)v + k(V - v)$ (we refer to this volume as volume level k). Thus, C_{ij}^k is the option value at node (i,j) if the maximum daily volume V has been taken on k of the previous i − 1 days (with only the minimum volume v being taken on the remaining days). Also, let $x^+ = max(x,0)$.

VALUATION PROCEDURE FOR TAKE-OR-PAY OPTIONS

The recursion equations for computing C_{ij}^k using dynamic programming are given in this section. These equations may be more easily understood by going through the calculations in the example in Panel 8.

Initialisation. The value of the option at time N + 1 equals the unit penalty multiplied by the volume shortfall, if any.[8]

Thus,

For $j = 0,...,N + 1; k = 0,...,M_{max} + 1$,

$$C_{N+1,j}^k = -c(V - v)(M_{min} - k)^+ / \alpha \qquad (22)$$

where α is the 1-day discount factor.

Iteration. At node (i,j), for economic exercise of the option there are, in general, two choices for the holder of the option: to purchase the minimum volume or the maximum volume on day i. Thus C_{ij}^k can be written as the maximum of two terms corresponding to the option values using these two choices respectively. If the minimum volume, v, is purchased, the volume level remains unchanged at k. If the maximum volume, V, is taken on day i, the total number of days with maximum volume increases by one, so the new volume level is k + 1. Using these we can write,

For $i = N,...,1; j = 0,...,i; k = M_{max},...,0$:

$$C_{ij}^k = max \begin{cases} (Fu^j d^{i-j} - K)v + \alpha[pC_{i+1,j+1}^k + qC_{i+1,j}^k] \\ (Fu^j d^{i-j} - K)V + \alpha[pC_{i+1,j+1}^k + qC_{i+1,j}^{k+1}] \end{cases} \quad (23)$$

Termination. The value of the option is given by

$$C_{00}^0 = \alpha[pC_{11}^0 + qC_{10}^0] \qquad (24)$$

RATCHET OPTIONS

For a swing ratchet option the daily volume should be between v and V and cannot change by more than w units from one day to the next. Let $V = v + Lw$ so that one can change the daily volume from v to V in L days by increasing it in steps of w. Also, the number of swings (ie changes in daily volume) is limited to a maximum of M. Denote by C_{ij}^{kl} the value of the option at the node (i,j), ie on day i at price level $Fu^j d^{i-j}$, given that the volume purchased on day i − 1 is $v(l) = v + lw$ and k of the M swings have been used ($0 \le j \le i \le N$, $0 \le k \le M$, $0 \le l \le L$). The complete set of equations for computing C_{ij}^{kl} is given below. Let ϕ be 1 if the swing option is a call option and −1 if it is a put option.

VALUATION PROCEDURE FOR SWING RATCHET OPTIONS

Initialisation. We set the value of C_{ij}^{kl} to negative infinity for k = M + 1 (since the number of swings is limited to M) for all values of i, j and l, and we set C_{ij}^{kl} to zero for other values of k, j and l at the terminal time step of the tree i = N + 1.

For $j = 0,...,N + 1$; $k = 0,...,M$; $l = 0,...,L$:

$$C_{N+1,j}^{kl} = 0$$

For $i = 0,...,N + 1$; $j = 0,...,i$; $l = 0,...,L$:

$$C_{i,j}^{k+1,l} = -\infty$$

Iteration. At node (i,j) there are, in general, three choices for the holder of the option: to increase the daily volume by w, to keep the daily volume unchanged, or to reduce the daily volume by w. Thus, C_{ij}^{kl} can be written as the maximum of three terms corresponding to option values using these three choices.

For $i = N,...,1$; $j = 0,...,i$; $k = M,...,0$:

For $l = L$:

$$C_{ij}^{kl} = \max \begin{cases} (Fu^j d^{i-j} - K)\phi v(l) + \alpha\left[pC_{i+1,j+1}^{kl} + qC_{i+1,j}^{kl}\right] \\ (Fu^j d^{i-j} - K)\phi v(l-1) + \alpha\left[pC_{i+1,j+1}^{k+1,l-1} + qC_{i+1,j}^{k+1,l-1}\right] \end{cases}$$

For $l = L - 1,...,$:

$$F_{ij}^{kl} = \max \begin{cases} (Fu^j d^{i-j} - K)\phi v(l) + \alpha\left[pC_{i+1,j+1}^{kl} + qC_{i+1,j}^{kl}\right] \\ (Fu^j d^{i-j} - K)\phi v(l+1) + \alpha\left[pC_{i+1,j+1}^{k+1,l+1} + qC_{i+1,j}^{k+1,l+1}\right] \\ (Fu^j d^{i-j} - K)\phi v(l-1) + \alpha\left[pC_{i+1,j+1}^{k+1,l-1} + qC_{i+1,j}^{k+1,l-1}\right] \end{cases}$$

For $l = 0$:

$$F_{ij}^{kl} = \max \begin{cases} (Fu^j d^{i-j} - K)\phi v(l) + \alpha\left[pC_{i+1,j+1}^{kl} + qC_{i+1,j}^{kl}\right] \\ (Fu^j d^{i-j} - K)\phi v(l+1) + \alpha\left[pC_{i+1,j+1}^{k+1,l+1} + qC_{i+1,j}^{k+1,l+1}\right] \end{cases}$$

Termination. The desired option value is given by

$$C_{00}^{00} = \alpha\left[pC_{11}^{00} + qC_{10}^{00}\right]$$

IMPLEMENTATION ISSUES

In this section we discuss some issues related to the implementation and time complexity of the pricing methods given in the previous sections. The recursion method given in the above section for computing the value of a swing ratchet option requires $O(N^2LM)$ computations (ie, a simple multiple of N^2ML). Computational time can be reduced by more than half by recognising the fact that, to compute C_{00}^{00}, we need to evaluate C_{ij}^{kl} only when $k + l$ is even and $k \geq l$. Further savings are achieved by using the fact that the number of swings, k, has to be smaller than the number of periods, i. It is also important to

realise that we do not need to save all the C_{ij}^{kl} values computed since calculation of C_{ij}^{kl} for any given period i requires the values $C_{i+1,j}^{kl}$ corresponding to the next period only. This greatly reduces the memory required for computing the option price. Similar observations can be made for the recursion method for take-or-pay options, which has a time complexity of $O(N^2 M_{max})$.

Concluding remarks: practical considerations

This chapter is a product of our experience in structuring option-based risk management products at Enron. It seems that the progress in the area of exotic energy options in the last few years has happened on two fronts. One direction of research is the development of new algorithms for pricing options with complicated payoff structures, coming up with better approximations or closed-form solutions. The motivation behind it, apart from intellectual satisfaction, is to come up with solutions that are faster and more accurate. Especially impressive is the progress in the area of pricing Asian options, although many techniques have not yet been fully transferred to practical implementations. The second direction is to capture in the theoretical pricing models the salient features of the energy markets. Hopefully these two streams of research will become better integrated in the future.

The degree of market penetration for the more exotic options is very uneven and ranges from full acceptance in the case of the largest and most sophisticated companies, to very reserved, polite interest (with avoidance of any firm commitment) from many smaller energy companies. Why are many producers and end-users so wary of using some risk management products? One reason is that some of the products are relatively new and are insufficiently understood and the pricing models are not readily available to many potential buyers. They are unwilling to use these products when they cannot replicate the pricing with a high degree of certainty. And, in the case of customised products, it can be difficult to obtain comparable, simultaneous quotes from multiple market makers.

Exotic options also present some formidable problems to the institutions that offer them. One obvious problem is that many exotic options are highly customised and require, in each case, a set of indicative data that does not lend itself easily to integration with existing pricing and portfolio software. The "quants" attached to the risk management desks often struggle against time constraints to build a new and reliable option pricing model, only to learn from the risk systems manager that the new product cannot be captured and carried in the company's portfolio management system and has to be hedged and marked-to-market in a spreadsheet.

The spreadsheet method is not a sound risk management procedure and it violates the explicit policies of many companies. If option positions are dispersed in many different spreadsheets, it is difficult to monitor the risks and to rebalance the hedges in a timely manner. The "spreadsheet risk" is one of the more serious and unrecognised of the many dangers posed by exotic options. This risk may, of course, be amplified by "model risk" (flaws or approximations in the mathematical equations underlying the option pricing algorithms) and by the risk that there is a "bug" in the computer code used to implement an otherwise solid theoretical construction. One obvious question for any institution contemplating buying or selling exotic options is whether it should acquire commercially available software or develop the necessary computer programs internally. As exotic options become more and more customised they demand a flexibility that is rarely available in commercially packaged software. Another potential problem is that commercial software packages may be offered as black boxes; or, if the source code is offered, it may be prohibitively expensive. Such packages can be very useful for validating models developed internally, but we feel that most market makers need proprietary software. It is required not only for pricing but also for hedging options and marking them to market. Using a black box is risky given the high cost of even a minor mistake or interpretative error.

Another reason for purchasing source code, or generating the models internally, is accounting requirements. In most companies options have to be marked-to-market daily, and the auditors are reluctant to rely on models which cannot be easily verified and explained. Of course, some of the smaller participants in the exotic options markets simply cannot devote the resources needed to build in-house valuation software. The "trade-off" is that the packages they use will not be flexible enough to value some of the highly customised exotic products offered in the market.

Let us review some other complications. Typically, exotic options are conceived through an interaction between research groups and marketing personnel who work closely with cus-

tomers. The extensive customisation of exotics results in products with prices that are difficult to verify by comparison with similar contracts available in the OTC market or with exchange-traded benchmark options. The lack of market information can also mean that it is difficult or impossible to obtain reliable estimates of implied volatilities and correlations from the available quoted option premiums. In this situation, the trader must work closely with the research group to determine relevant inputs.

Econometric research – relatively unimportant in the option industry of the past – is vital in the case of exotic options. Many traders who understand implied volatility have had to familiarise themselves quickly with the arcane art of Arch, Garch and Egarch estimators.

An additional complication in the case of energy commodities is that many of them have a strong seasonal pattern which may evolve under the influence of various market forces. Traders typically use correlations and volatilities based on historical data for the time period corresponding to the time interval for which the option is written. For example, if an option is written in June for December expiration of the same year, one would use the historical data for the same months in the past. This heuristic approach has a major shortcoming: it necessarily fails to use the most recent market developments, which may include information that affects the seasonality of volatility and the nature of the correlations.

Once an option is written and put into the portfolio, hedging the option becomes, with many exotics, a real challenge. The difficulties arise for two different reasons. One source of problems is the definition of the option, which may result in dramatic changes of delta in some regions of the values of the underlying prices. High gamma risk is another way of describing the difficulty of maintaining a replicating portfolio which instantaneously hedges the option.

This risk may be amplified by a special property of the underlying prices. In energy markets, prices often undergo a sudden and significant change – for example, the price changes brought about in the crude markets by political or military events in the Middle East. This property, known as "gapping", violates the underlying assumptions of the option pricing models discussed in this chapter. Let us recall that the underlying assumption was that the prices follow geometric Brownian motion, which postulates continuous changes. In practical terms a sudden, drastic change in price level causes a major shift in the delta of an option and requires a rebalancing of the hedge. The speed with which prices change can make it practically impossible to readjust the hedges in a timely manner. This problem is aggravated by the need to simultaneously rebalance the hedges for a number of underlyings when hedging multi-commodity options.

Additional challenges often arise when hedging in the energy markets owing to a lack of market liquidity. Although several energy commodities enjoy respectable market liquidity, most of the trade volume is concentrated in a few nearby months. Of commodities trading on Nymex, crude oil has the largest open interest, at around 500,000 contracts. Although there are 30 consecutive monthly contracts, plus five additional long-dated contracts, the six nearby contracts account for about half of the total open interest for crude. So, even for the most active of Nymex energy commodities, there is little liquidity beyond a time horizon of three to six months.

Nymex natural gas, unleaded and heating oil markets also enjoy reasonable liquidity in the front months. But for some other commodities, such as propane, there is only a small contract volume even in the prompt month on most trading days. The total lack of liquidity in many markets, and the lack of liquidity beyond the nearby months in the more developed markets, give rise to risks that are essentially similar to the gapping risk discussed above.

Even when prices move in an orderly fashion within the energy markets, adjusting hedges for a large portfolio of options may be difficult owing to the lack of market depth. This problem is, of course, exacerbated for longer-dated contracts. The limited liquidity makes hedging any type of option risky, but this risk is amplified for exotic options that have large gammas (such as barrier and digital options) as these lead to rapid changes in hedge ratios. Given this, it could be argued that only experienced market makers, who have a substantial book of business and thus a greater ability to diversify across the OTC markets, are in a position to construct and hedge exotics.

Another complication is that not only price levels but also levels of volatility and correlation may undergo rapid change. Figure 9 illustrates the relationship between the correlation of price levels of crude oil and heating oil (Nymex prices, prompt month, six-month trailing) and the volatilities of both prices. One can see that not only does volatility change quite suddenly but also that the changes in volatility are associated with changes in correlation – typically in the

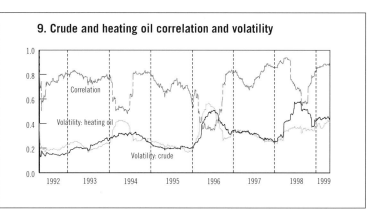

9. Crude and heating oil correlation and volatility

same direction. This phenomenon was particularly visible during the Gulf War and can be explained by the sensitivity of both prices to a common factor. When this common underlying factor disappears the relationship between the two prices grows weaker.

Derivatives specialists moving into the commodities arena should especially note this finding, as in many other derivative sectors any increased volatility in the markets typically coincides with reduced correlation. There are no easy answers to the problems involved in hedging these risks. Some dealers try to address these problems by trying to run a portfolio as a matched book of business, to the extent that this is possible. This policy, however, greatly limits the volume of business that may be taken into the book.

Another solution is to use sophisticated hedging strategies which employ a combination of options to replicate the behaviour of the underwritten option. Finding an adequate portfolio of replicating options may require the use of optimisation techniques. The main shortcoming of the option replication strategy is the expense incurred when purchasing the replicating options. Other solutions proposed by practitioners, such as stochastic replication, are still in the early stages of development.

Many of the problems outlined above tend to be mitigated by the portfolio effect, which can be exploited to the advantage of large players in the market. This effect results from the natural self-hedging which occurs between partially or totally offsetting contracts that are contained in the portfolio of a market maker who takes positions on both sides of a market. Managing a large portfolio of contracts – while avoiding excessive concentrations in any single series – provides the critical mass necessary to absorb the short-term price risks that arise out of new business; a large volume of business also helps to minimise hedging costs.

1 *We are grateful to the publishers of* Risk *for inviting us to contribute to this publication, and especially to Robert Jameson and Avril Eglinton for their comments and patience demonstrated waiting for the final version of the manuscript. We would also like to thank Darrell Duffie of Stanford University for his helpful suggestions.*

2 *MMBtu stands for million British thermal units (Btu).*

3 *Bid-week is a period of a few days few days during which gas for the next calendar month delivery is transacted in the US markets. This happens around the 25th of each month.*

4 *One should rather speak of "floor-reverting process". See Kaminski, V., 1994, "The Challenge of Pricing and Risk Managing Electricity Derivatives" in* The US Power Market, Risk Publications.

5 *See Samuelson (1965).*

6 *Dragana Pilipovic proposed a very insightful characterisation of the behaviour of energy prices: they behave as if they had split personality. The dynamics of long-term prices, as opposed to the behaviour of short-term prices, is much different.*

7 *Chapter 14 of this book compares several Garch methods with historical and implied volatilities and finds that some types of Garch estimates may be superior to simple historical volatilities.*

8 *Though the penalty is actually paid at the end of N days, it is applied here after the (N + 1)th day, one day after the option expiration. This makes it easier to write down and implement the equations for the iterative step. The penalty expression has a discount factor in the denominator to cancel the discounting that will be done in the iterative step.*

BIBLIOGRAPHY

AitSahlia, F., and T. Lai, 1997, "Valuation of Discrete Barrier and Hindsight Options", *Journal of Financial Engineering*, 6 (June), pp. 169-77.

Akgiray, V., and G. G. Booth, 1987, "Compound Distribution Models of Stock Returns", *Journal of Financial Research*, 3, (Autumn), pp. 269-80.

Amin, K., 1991, "On the Computation of Continuous Time Option Prices Using Discrete Approximations", *Journal of Financial and Quantitative Analysis*, 26, (December), pp. 477-95.

Amin, K., 1993, "Jump Diffusion Option Valuation in Discrete Time", *Journal of Finance*, 5, (December), pp. 1833-63.

Ball, C. A., and W. N. Torous, 1983, "A Simplified Jump Process for Common Stock Returns", *Journal of Financial and Quantitative Analysis*, 18 (March), pp. 53-65.

Ball, C. A., and W. N. Torous, 1985, "On Jumps in Common Stock prices and Their Impact on Call Option Pricing", *Journal of Finance*, 1, (March), pp. 155-73.

Barbieri, A., and M. Garman, 1996, "Putting a Price On Swings", *Energy & Power Risk Management*, 1, (October), pp. 17-19.

Barbieri, A., and M. Garman, 1997, "Ups and Downs of Swing", *Energy & Power Risk Management*, 1, (April), pp. 16-18.

Barraquand, J., and D. Martineau, 1995, "Numerical Valuation of High Dimensional Multivariate American Securities", *Journal of Financial and Quantitative Analysis*, 30, (September), pp. 383-405.

Barrett, J., G. Moore and P. Wilmott, 1992, "Inelegant Efficiency", *Risk*, 5, (October), pp. 82-4.

Benson, R., and N. Daniel, 1991, "Up, Over and Out", *Risk*,

4, (June), pp. 17-19 (also reprinted in: *From Black–Scholes to Black Holes*, Risk Books, London, 1992).

Black, F., 1976, "The Pricing of Commodity Contracts", *Journal of Financial Economics*, 3, (January-March), pp. 167-79.

Black, F., and J. Cox, 1976, "Valuing Corporate Securities: Some Effects of Bond Indenture Provisions", *Journal of Finance*, 31, (May), pp. 351-67.

Black, F., and M. Scholes, 1973, "The Pricing of Options and Other Corporate Liabilities", *Journal of Political Economy*, 81, (May-June), pp. 637-59.

Bollerslev, T., 1986, "Generalized Autoregressive Conditional Heteroscedasticity", *Journal of Econometrics*, 31, pp. 307-27.

Boyle, P. P., 1977, "Options: a Monte Carlo Approach", *Journal of Financial Economics*, 4, (May), pp. 323-38.

Boyle, P. P., 1988, "A Lattice Framework for Option Pricing with Two State Variables", *Journal of Financial and Quantitative Analysis*, 23, (March), pp. 1-12.

Boyle, P., M. Broadie and P. Glasserman, 1997, "Monte Carlo Methods for Security Pricing", *Journal of Economic Dynamics and Control*, 21, pp. 1267-321.

Brennan, M. J., 1979, "The Pricing of Contingent Claims in Discrete Time Models", *Journal of Finance*, 34, (March), pp. 53-68.

Brennan, M. J., and E. S. Schwartz, 1978, "Finite Difference Methods and Jump Processes Arising in the Pricing of Contingent Claims: A Synthesis", *Journal of Financial and Quantitative Analysis*, 13, (September), pp. 461-74.

Broadie, M., and P. Glasserman, 1997, "Pricing American-Style Securities Using Simulation", *Journal of Economic*

Dynamics and Control, 21(8-9), pp. 1323-52.

Broadie, M., P. Glasserman and G. Jain, 1997, "Enhanced Monte Carlo Estimates for American Option Prices", *Journal of Derivatives*, 5 (Autumn), pp. 25-44.

Broadie, M., P. Glasserman and S. Kou, 1995, "A Continuity Correction for Discrete Barrier Options", Working paper, Columbia University.

Carverhill, A. P, and L. J. Clewlow, 1990, "Flexible Convolutions", *Risk*, (April), pp. 25-9.

Chalasani, P., S. Jha and A. Varikooty, 1998, "Accurate approximations for European-style Asian options", *Journal of Computational Finance*, 1, (Summer), pp. 11-30.

Chaplin, G., 1993, "Not So Random", *Risk*, 6, (February), pp. 56-7.

Cho, H., and H. Lee, 1997, "A Lattice Model for Pricing Geometric and Arithmetic Average Options", *Journal of Financial Engineering*, 6, (September), pp. 179-92.

Clewlow, L., and C. Strickland, 1999, "Valuing Energy Options in a One Factor Model Fitted to Forward Prices", Working Paper, April.

Conze, A., and Viswanathan, 1991, "Path Dependent Options: The Case of Lookback Options", *Journal of Finance*, 46, (December), pp. 1893-907.

Courtadon, G., 1982, "A More Accurate Finite Difference Approximation for the Value of Options", *Journal of Financial and Quantitative Analysis*, 17, (December), pp. 697-703.

Cox, J., S. Ross and M. Rubinstein, 1979, "Option pricing: A Simplified Approach", *Journal of Financial Economics*, 7, (October), pp. 229-63.

Cox, J., and M. Rubinstein, 1985, *Option Markets*, Englewood Cliffs, NJ, Prentice Hall.

Curran, M., 1992, "Beyond Average Intelligence", *Risk*, 5, (November), p. 60.

Curran, M., 1994, "Strata Gems", *Risk*, 7, (March), pp. 70-1.

Derman, E., and I. Kani, 1994, "Riding on a Smile", *Risk*, 7, (February), pp. 32-9.

Dewynne, J., and P. Wilmott, 1993, "Partial to the Exotic", *Risk*, 6 (March), pp. 38-46.

Dixit A. K., and R. S. Pindyck, *Investment Under Uncertainty*, Princeton University Press, 1994.

Dupire, B., 1994, "Pricing with a Smile", *Risk*, 7 (January), pp. 18-20.

Engle, R. F., 1982, "Autoregressive Conditional Heteroscedasticity with Estimates of the Variance of United Kingdom Inflation", *Econometrica*, 50, (July), pp. 987-1007.

Galanti, S., and A. Jung, 1997, "Low-Discrepancy Sequences: Monte Carlo Simulation of Option Prices", *Journal of Derivatives*, 5, (Autumn), pp. 63-84.

Garman, M., 1989, "Recollection in Tranquillity", *Risk*, 2, (March) (also reprinted in: *From Black-Scholes to Black Holes*, Risk Books, 1992, London).

Geman, H., and M. Yor, 1993, "Bessel Processes, Asian Options, and Perpetuities", *Mathematical Finance*, 3, (October), pp. 349-75.

Geske, R., 1979, "The Valuation of Compound Options", *Journal of Financial Economics*, 7, (March), pp. 63-81.

Geske, R., and K. Shastri, 1985, "Valuation by Approximation: A Comparison of Alternative Option Valuation Techniques", *Journal of Financial and Quantitative Analysis*, 20, (March), pp. 45-71.

Goldman, M. B., H. B. Sosin and M. A. Gatto, 1979, "Path Dependent Options: Buy at the Low, Sell at the High", *Journal of Finance*, 34 (December), pp. 1111-27.

Hammersley, J. M., and D. C. Handscomb, 1964, *Monte Carlo Methods*, New York, John Wiley & Sons.

Heath, D., R. Jarrow and A. Morton, 1992, "Bond Pricing and the Term Structure of Interest Rates: A New Methodology for Contingent Claims Valuation", *Econometrica*, 60, (January), pp. 77-105.

Hull, J., 1993, *Options Futures and other Derivative Securities*, 2nd edition, Englewood Cliffs, NJ, Prentice Hall.

Hull, J., and A. White, 1988, "The Use of the Control Variate Technique in Option Pricing", *Journal of Financial and Quantitative Analysis*, 23, (September), pp. 237-51.

Hull, J., and A. White, 1990, "Valuing Derivative Securities Using the Explicit Finite Difference Method", *Journal of Financial and Quantitative Analysis*, 25, (March), pp. 87-100.

Hull, J., and A. White, 1993, "Efficient Procedure For Valuing European and American Path-Dependent Options", *Journal of Derivatives* 1, pp. 21-31.

Jaillet, P., E. Ronn, and S. Tompaidis, 1997, "Valuation of Commodity-Based "Swing" Options," working paper.

Johnson, H., 1987, "Options on the Maximum or the Minimum of Several Assets", *Journal of Financial and Quantitative Research*, 22, (September), pp. 277-83.

Jorion, P., 1988, "On Jump Processes in the Foreign Exchange Markets", *Review of Financial Studies*, 4, pp.427-45.

Kemna, A. G. Z., and A. C. F. Vorst, 1990, "A Pricing Method for Options Based on Average Asset Values", *Journal of Banking And Finance*, 14, pp. 113-29.

Kremer, J. W., and R. L. Roenfeldt, 1992, "Warrant Pricing: Jump Diffusion vs. Black Scholes", *Journal of Financial and Quantitative Analysis*, 28, pp. 255-72.

Levy, E., 1991, "Pricing European Average Rate Currency Options", *Journal of International Money and Finance*, (October), pp. 474-91.

Levy, E., and S. Turnbull, 1992, "Average Intelligence", Risk, 5, (February), (also reprinted in: *From Black-Scholes to Black Holes*, Risk Books, London, 1992).

Leong, K., 1992, "Estimates Guesstimates and Rules of Thumb", *From Black-Scholes to Black Holes*, Risk Books, London, 1992.

Mandelbrot, B., 1963, "The Variation of Certain Speculative Prices", *Journal of Business*, October, pp. 394-419.

Margrabe, W., 1978, "The Value of an Option to Exchange One Asset for Another", *Journal of Finance*, 33, pp. 177-86.

Merton, R., 1973, "The Theory of Rational Option Pricing", *Bell Journal of Economics and Management Science*, 4, (Spring), pp. 141-83.

Merton, R., 1976, "Option Pricing When Underlying Stock Returns are Discontinuous", *Journal of Financial Economics*, 3 (January/March), pp. 125-44.

Milevsky, M. A., and S. E. Posner, 1998a, "Asian Options, The Sum of Lognormals and the Reciprocal Gamma Distribution", *Journal of Financial and Quantitative Analysis*, 33 (September), pp. 409-22.

Milevsky, M., and S. Posner, 1998b, "A Closed-Form Approximation for Valuing Basket Options", *Journal of Derivatives*, 6, (Summer), pp. 54-61.

Pilipovic, D., 1998, *Energy Risk Valuing and Managing Energy Derivatives*, McGraw Hill, New York.

Pilipovic, D., and J. Wengler, 1998, "Getting Into The Swing," *Energy & Power Risk Management*, 2, (June 1998) pp. 22-24.

Press, W., B. P. Flannery, S. A. Teukolsky and W. T. Vetterling, 1992, *Numerical Recipes in C*, 2nd edition, New York, Cambridge University Press.

Ravindran, K., 1993, "Low-fat Spreads", Risk, 6, (October), pp. 66-7.

Raymar, S, and M. Zwecker, 1997, "Monte Carlo Estimation of American Call Options on the Maximum of Several Stock", *Journal of Derivatives*, 5, (Autumn), pp. 7-24.

Routledge, B. R., D. J. Seppi and C. S. Spatt, 1999, "Equilibrium Forward Curves for Commodities", manuscript, Carnegie Mellon University.

Rubinstein, M., 1991a, "Pay Now, Choose Later", Risk, 4, (February), p. 13.

Rubinstein, M., 1991b, "Somewhere Over the Rainbow", Risk, 4, (November), pp. 63-6.

Rubinstein, M., 1992, "One for Another", *From Black-Scholes to Black Holes*, Risk Books, London.

Rubinstein, M., 1994, "Implied Binomial Trees", working paper No. 232, Institute of Business and Economic Research, University of California at Berkeley, (January).

Rubinstein, M., and E. Reiner, 1991a, "Breaking Down the Barriers", Risk, 4, (September), pp. 28-35.

Rubinstein, M., and E. Reiner, 1991b, "Unscrambling the Binary Code", Risk, 4 (October), pp. 75-83.

Samuelson, P., "Proof That Properly Anticipated Prices Fluctuate Randomly", *Industrial Management Review*, 6, pp. 41-50.

Schmeiser, B., 1990, "Simulation Experiments": *Handbooks in Operations Research and Management Science Vol. 2: Stochastic Models*, D. P. Heyman and M. J. Sobel eds, North-Holland.

Schwartz, E. S., 1977, "The Valuation of Warrants: Implementing a New Approach", *Journal of Financial Economics*, 4, (August), pp. 79-93.

Stultz, R., 1982, "Options on the Minimum or the Maximum of Two Risky Assets", *Journal of Financial Economics*, 10, pp. 161-85.

Thompson, Andrew C., 1995, "Valuation of Pathe-Dependent Contingent Claims with Multiple Exercise Decisions Over Time: The Case of Take-or-Pay", *Journal of Financial and Quantitative Analysis*, 30, 2 (June), pp. 271-93.

Tilley, J., 1993, "Valuing American Options in a Path Simulation Model", *Transactions of the Society of Actuaries*, 45, pp. 83-104.

Trigeorgis, L., 1991, "A Log-Transformed Binomial Numerical Analysis Method for Valuing Complex Multi-Option Investments", *Journal of Financial and Quantitative Analysis*, 26, (September), pp. 309-26.

Turnbull, S., 1992, "The Price is Right", Risk, 5, (April), pp. 56-7.

Turnbull, S. M., and L. M. Wakeman, 1991, "A Quick Algorithm for Pricing European Average Options", *Journal of Financial and Quantitative Analysis*, 26, (September), pp. 377-89.

Wilcox, D., 1991, "Spread Options Enhance Risk Management Choices", *Nymex Energy in the News* (Autumn), pp. 9-13.

Wilmott, P., J., Dewynne and S. Howison, 1993, *Option Pricing: Mathematical Models and Computation*, Oxford, UK, Oxford Financial Press.

4

Derivatives in Energy Project Finance

Lloyd Spencer
Deutsche Bank

Project finance might be described as the art of balancing risk and reward over time. As the world's energy markets have deregulated it has become clear that major energy projects – involving extraordinary amounts of finance paid off over decades – demand particularly sophisticated risk management. Indeed, risk management techniques have underpinned many of the last decade's most innovative schemes in the financing of projects as various as deep-sea oil wells and natural gas exploration.

In this chapter we focus on risk-managing merchant power-generation projects. This is a particularly challenging area as it requires the price risk management of both the output energy and the input energy feedstocks. After looking at the rationale for project finance hedging in deregulating power markets, we consider some of the problems of implementation – which is often where disaster has struck in the past – and develop a detailed example. The example covers the impact of different levels of hedging and leverage on a power plant project.

In an extended panel we examine a key issue in oilfield project risk management: the modelling of physical oil flows in relation to project cashflows. Although the physical parameters are very different from those in power generation, the defining feature of project risk management remains the same: the need to understand the relationship between equity/debt leverage and the character of revenue flows.

Historical background

Historically, the ability of utilities to raise rates to cover capital investment or power purchase agreements (PPA) was what provided the "risk capital" to build power plants in the United States. Why is this? In most state regulatory regimes, utilities have been allowed to charge a rate per kilowatt hour that essentially provided a regulated rate of return on generation assets. As profitability fluctuated in response to changing input prices and changing operating characteristics, the price that utilities charged customers fluctuated from year to year to cover these risks. Thus, in a sense, utility customers – by bearing the risks of generation assets – were providing an essential component of the risk capital required to build generation capacity. As a result, banks were comfortable with very high leverage and high debt ratings, knowing that any problems could be resolved by charging high rates. Regardless of whether this was or was not an efficient way of allocating capital in the power generation market, it is changing in a fundamental way. These changes are occurring on a state by state level and therefore are all at different stages. Regardless of whether this was or was not an efficient way of allocating capital in the power generation market, it is changing in a fundamental way. While wholesale power markets have deregulated at a federal level, retail power markets, regulated by state legislatures, are all deregulating in different ways. In general, states with high cost retail power have the strongest incentives to deregulate.

At the heart of deregulation initiatives is a change in the way capital is allocated to capital investment projects. As a result of consumer sentiment and industry pressure, the regulatory appetite at state level for retail rate increases has changed over the past 10 years to the point where most new generation will not have risk capital provided by utilities. The market and operational risks will now rest fully with the generation owner. Although utilities may continue to be significant buyers of the output from any new or existing generation, the medium- to long-term price risk from these plants will be borne by independent generation owners. This has consequences for the funding structure of power plants as well as for the demand for price hedging services and operational expertise. It is estimated that 68.8 GW of new capacity has been proposed by various developers for the North American market, all of which will be merchant plant (ie the revenues will not depend upon guaranteed sales agreements).[1] This represents approximately 10% of existing generation capacity. A further 5.2 GW is already under construction.

On the funding side, the successful providers of capital will be those who understand the risks and opportunities inherent in leverage as well as commodity price exposure. On the marketing side, the successful providers of hedging services will provide a valuable service that enhances the risk–return profile of the equity and debt holders. In the gas market the providers of volumetric production payments were able to develop and make a market in the forward market for the underlying commodity, leading to significant market share. The same should be true for the power market.

The focus on operational expertise is shifting as merchant owners rather than regulated utilities own more generation. For example, scheduled maintenance will be adjusted to suit low-price times rather than low customer load times. The financial incentives provided by market prices will determine everything from production schedules to plant repowering.[2]

The case for derivatives in energy project finance

WHY HEDGE FORWARD OUTPUT?

A fundamental concept in project finance is the issue of selling future output from the project. One of the most active traditional forward markets is oil and gas (Panel 1). Exploration and production companies have become more familiar with selling forward production volumes in order to satisfy lenders or attract additional debt funding. The volumetric production payment (VPP) structure is in fact a forward sales contract

tied to a loan, with legal assurances satisfactory to the lenders. US law is unusual compared with other countries in allowing title to change hands for reserves still in the ground. This means that lenders can be comfortable with security to the reserves in the ground.

Owners of merchant power generation plants are faced with a similar issue. Although generation owners tend to be bullish about power prices, by the nature of their investment, the debt holders in any project will require some volume of forward sales to stabilise cashflows from the project to ensure timely debt repayment.

FORWARDS VERSUS POWER PURCHASE AGREEMENTS

Domestic power generation projects used to rely on power purchase agreements (PPAs) and long-term gas supply contracts to guarantee the cashflow from a project. Under a PPA, a buyer agrees to buy power from the facility at a predetermined price over a long time frame with very few exit clauses. For a variety of reasons – such as regulatory changes – utilities, the traditional writers of PPAs, are no longer as inclined to sign long-term contracts to buy. In many cases the construction of plants under qualifying facility (QF) rules (Public Utility Regulatory Policy Act 1978) was simply a way for utilities move the funding of new generation "off balance sheet" while still retaining many of the risk and return characteristics of ownership. The PPAs were typically structured in such a watertight fashion that banks were happy to lend a large proportion of the funds required on the basis of the creditworthiness of the utility.

How does a derivative or forward sale differ from a traditional PPA? Table 1 lists some key differences.

A SIMPLE EXAMPLE

We consider the simplified example illustrated in Figure 1. There are two decisions to be made: the funding level and the hedging level. An initial equity investment (shown in boldface) yields a return over the first year. Within each box defined by a hedging/funding combination there

Table 1. Characteristics of forwards versus power purchase agreements (PPAs)

Forward contract	Power purchase agreement
❑ Sale regardless of plant operations	❑ Generally contingent on unit operations
❑ Standardised contract specifications, eg size, timing of blocks	❑ Customised to plant specifics, operational characteristics
❑ Generally many different counterparties	❑ Generally one or two buyers
❑ Shorter terms	❑ Long-term
❑ Increasingly liquid	❑ Becoming very rare

are two possible outcomes for price and, consequently, returns. For example, with no leverage and no hedging, there is a $100 investment and the return on the investment will be either $25 or $5 depending on prices. With hedging, the cashflow is no longer dependent on prices, so in the box to the right returns are $15 regardless of the price scenario.

Note that one of the four scenarios displayed is actually not possible in the real world. With leverage but no hedging there is a chance of negative equity, which puts debt holders at risk. Debt covenants are unlikely to allow such a risk. Thus, although hedging lowers the upside for equity holders, it provides funding alternatives that otherwise would not be feasible. The leveraged, hedged alternative has a higher equity return than the other alternatives that are feasible.

In the detailed example given later in this chapter we look at a more realistic situation that shows the continuum of hedging/leverage alternatives for an energy investment.

WHICH DERIVATIVES?

For a particular commodity exposure, the most suitable hedging instrument depends on the economics of the production model. Descriptively, if the production decision is independent of price, then the value of production moves linearly with price (revenue = price × volume, where volume is independent of price). Thus it makes sense to have a hedging instrument that is linear with respect to price. So a forward sale contract is generally the most efficient way to hedge the cashflow risk of a low-cost production facility. If there is little chance that the production will be shut down by low prices, forward sales of this output usually incur lower transaction costs than other alternatives such as options.

Compare this with a high-cost production situation where the economics of the sale of output depends on short-term prices. The production function can be described as an option where: the underlying price is the market price of output; the strike price is the marginal cost of generation; and the option premium is the fixed cost of plant ownership. Thus, higher-cost production has profitability characteristics similar to options and therefore is most efficiently hedged in the options markets (or with a hedging strategy that replicates options).

Current and prospective usage

Practical implementations of derivatives in energy project finance have been limited so far

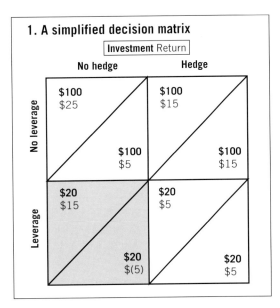

1. A simplified decision matrix

Investment Return

to the oil and gas markets. An often quoted example of a long-term project finance hedging structure is the deep-water project initiated by Shell in the Gulf of Mexico in the early 1990s, which was struggling with the operational costs caused by oil prices fluctuating above and below the marginal production cost of the project. By locking in a long-term price with Bankers Trust (BT), Shell was able to concentrate on oil production and not be concerned with monitoring day-to-day fluctuations in prices. As Paul Cambridge, of Deutsche Bank energy group, said: "By removing price risk from the equation, Shell was able to optimise the project leverage and reduce the equity capital required."[3]

New "merchant" power plants are generally more speculative today than in the past because the cashflow stream is substantially more risky than before. The few highly leveraged projects that have gone forward in recent years have generally contained some degree of risk hedging. Pat Daly, Managing Director in the Energy Investment Banking group at DB Alex Brown, summarised the situation: "It's a simple matter of probability of default: a highly leveraged power project without appropriate hedging has a higher probability of default on debt obligations"[4] (Table 2).

Deutsche Bank's Paul Naumann adds: "It's the first rule of lending: show me the security of cash flows. They certainly are not present in today's power markets without hedging, whether in the forward/derivatives market or via an off-take [PPA] agreement."[5]

In another example of the new merchant plant business paradigm, AES, a power developer with 36,000 MW of installed capacity, recently acquired six generation plants from New York

OILFIELD OPERATING CASHFLOWS

Many of the concepts described in the accompanying article were first applied in the modelling of oilfield reserves. Petroleum engineers have developed models of the flow of oil and gas out of a well or reserve that are based on the physics of the situation. Conceptually, the flow of oil from a well without production controls is similar to the escape of air from a punctured tyre. A high initial rate of flow is followed by a steeply declining production rate until, eventually, only small oil volumes are produced. Of course, various production techniques are used both to contain the initial flow and to augment the later flow. (In fact several companies make a business of taking over low-production wells and attempting to increase production through techniques such as water flooding.)

Reserve flow models

Reserve and production models are an entire field of study,[1] and a full characterisation of all the possible models is beyond the scope of this article. The range of models, which started out as very simple, has expanded to encompass the consequences of various production-enhancement techniques, such as pressure maintenance, cycling and water drive. However, for the purposes of this article we will consider a simple example.

Simple example model[2]

Reserve flow engineering models are generally based on some sort of exponential decline. Mathematically,

$$D = Kq^n$$

where D is decline as a fraction of the production rate, K is a constant and q is production rate, n is a constant $\in [0,1]$, where when $n = 0$ the decline is a constant percentage, when $n = 1$ the decline is proportional to the production rate (harmonic), and when $0 < n < 1$ the decline is proportional to a fraction of the production rate (hyperbolic).

Taking the simple example of constant percentage decline, to find total production we must first integrate the above formula to find the rate–time relationship:

$$q_t = q_i e^{-Dr}$$

where q_i is initial production rate and q_t is the production rate at time t.

Next we integrate q_t over time to find cumulative production to time t:

$$Q_t = \frac{q_i - q_t}{D} = \frac{q_i}{D}\left(1 - e^{-Dt}\right)$$

This is the most useful formula for evaluating the cashflow from an oil well project. The amount of forecast reserves available for sale at the end of the month is Q_t at the end of the month minus Q_t at the beginning of the month.

In reality, the parameters of these models are only estimates. Thus, petroleum engineers can produce a distribution or standard deviation around the estimates of D and q_i in the above example. This produces a distribution of forecast oil flows in a particular month. This distribution, when combined with a stochastic price model, produces a distribution of operating revenues for each time period modelled. So, for a particular oilfield the model of volumes and prices might suggest that the distribution of oilfield operating revenues for a particular month looks like Figure A. Thus there is a 5% probability that revenues are above $2.3 million and a 5% probability that revenues are below $0.9 million for the month of January 2000. These data can be plotted for each month and presented as in Figure B. This shows the range of monthly operating revenues that can be expected on the basis of varying prices and volumes. The lower bound is the level of revenues that can be expected to be exceeded with 95% probability. This leads to a discussion of leverage.

Leverage effects

The key use of Figure B is in comparing the 5% probable level of revenues in each month with budgeted operating and financing costs. If the

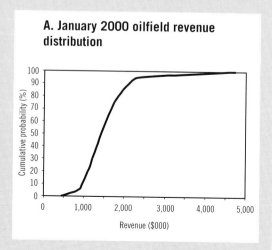

A. January 2000 oilfield revenue distribution

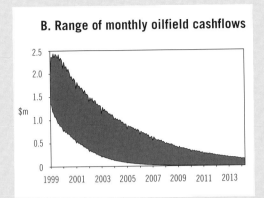

B. Range of monthly oilfield cashflows

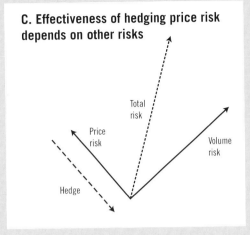

C. Effectiveness of hedging price risk depends on other risks

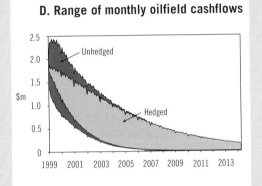

D. Range of monthly oilfield cashflows

level with 5% probability falls below this number, it is an indication that the project will be earning insufficient revenues for debt servicing. Although this will be inevitable in later years when the reserve reaches its economic limit, it is important in determining the appropriate degree of financing during the first few years of the project. (The economic limit of a petroleum reserve is the point at which the marginal revenues no longer exceed the operating costs.)

Note that, given a reserve model, a stochastic price model and a particular financing structure, a probability of default can be determined from the analysis above. For example, if operating and financing costs total $500,000 per month in 2001, there will be a 5% probability of default.

Price hedging

Clearly, hedging can act to reduce the impact of price risk on the project. The extent of this impact depends on the certainty of the volume of oil produced. If oil volumes are very uncertain, the effect of hedging is small. This can be represented as in Figure C. Since there are only two uncertainties that influence profitability, a two-dimensional representation is possible. In the example above, hedging the expected oil volumes leads to a much narrower range of cashflows in the early years, as shown in Figure D. This is because, for this particular reserve model, the uncertainty of oil volumes increases with time. Thus, from the arrow diagram, the impact of price hedging on total risk in any month becomes less significant.

The key consequence of hedging from a project finance standpoint is the effect on default probabilities. In this example, the point at which monthly cashflows have a 5% chance of falling below $500,000 is nearly six months later. Alternatively, the project will support much more debt funding in the first few years. This is more significant than many project developers realise

because of the gains from leverage. Specifically, a higher leverage may lead to higher equity returns because less equity is needed.

Most developers seek to minimise hedging given a fixed leverage ratio. This makes sense because it leaves the most room for upside in equity returns. However, it only looks at half the picture. A greater equity return may be possible by varying both leverage and hedging. This issue is developed further in the main article.

Conclusion

❑ Project leverage and forward hedging of production are intimately related.

❑ Oil and gas production projects can be modelled to determine the best combination of hedges and leverage relative to the range of possible oil reserve flows.

❑ Engineering models describe the volumetric portion or reserves.

❑ For a given time frame, price hedging is only as effective in reducing risk as the certainty of volumes.

1 Garb, F.A., 1985, "Oil & Gas Reserves Classification, Estimation, and Evaluation", *Journal of Petroleum Technology*, March, pp. 373–90.
2 Garb, F.A., and G.L. Smith, 1990, "Estimation of Oil and Gas Reserves", *Petroleum Engineering Handbook*, Chapter 40, pp. 1–38.

Table 2. Terms of recent project financing

	Calpine Pasadena	Sutton Bridge	Kincaid	Dighton
Market/region	US/ERCOT	UK	US/MAIN	US/NPCC
Rating	Ba2	Baa3/BBB	Baa3/BBB–	na
Execution market	Bank	Bond	Bond	Bank
Debt term (years)	17	25	22	20
Off-take/purchase (%)	38	100	100	100
Contract term (years)	20	15	15	20
Counterparty rating	A3, A–	Not rated	Baa2, BBB	Baa3
Initial leverage (%)	65	87	73	85
Technology	Westinghouse 501F gas turbine	GE PG 9351 FA gas turbine	Cyclone coal burner	ABB GT11N2 combustion turbine

State Electric & Gas (NYSEG). As the Vice President of Power Marketing, Jim Farrar, summarised: "Hedging of output forms an integral part of the risk management of our generation portfolio. The key differences from the old world of off-take agreements/PPAs are: shorter tenor available, variable counter-party credit quality, and greater price transparency. All of these require us to be more sophisticated than before."[7]

Implementation issues

MARKET LIQUIDITY

Energy projects tend to be highly capital-intensive. It is estimated that the installed capacity of domestic US power plants represents capital investment in excess of $400 billion. The "up-front" costs of oil and gas production as well as transportation and refining are equally capital-intensive. Consequently, the duration of any capital investment is by nature several years. The problem for many developers seeking to hedge in the derivatives market is that there do not at first appear to be instruments of adequate tenor to match the investment time horizon. Furthermore, in many power markets liquidity is limited.

There are several ways to "work around" the problem of depth of markets. The simplest is to hedge in whatever tenor of market is available in volumes that match the total commodity exposure. Thus, a 100 MW plant would hedge all 10 years' production in the 12 to 18 months of forward market that is liquid and actively "roll" these contracts out further as time progresses. The key assumption for such a strategy is that most shifts in the forward curve are parallel.

This is commonly referred to as a "stack-and-roll" approach, and is a strategy that earned a bad reputation following the Metallgesellschaft (MG) debacle in 1994. Many explanations have been offered for MG's failure with this strategy,[7] and a complete analysis is beyond the scope of this article. However, one significant problem was the mismatch between instruments requiring daily margin and those which did not require margin. When the wrong set of market conditions arose, the mark-to-market increase in value of the "non-marginable" asset did not produce a realisable cashflow to meet the margin requirements of the futures contracts. In fact this risk is present in any hedging strategy that mixes marginable assets with non-marginable assets.

This suggests that it was not so much the choice of strategy as the implementation that was to blame. Even if the futures contracts had exactly matched the tenor of the underlying gasoline contracts being hedged, with no "stack-and-roll" necessary, this cash mismatch would still have occurred.

A rigorous analysis of "stacking-and-rolling" a long-term power hedge would need to evaluate the range of collateral margin calls that may be implicit in such a strategy. One way to lower the requirements would be to transact in the over-the-counter (OTC) market with a marketer who will take forward delivery contracts from beyond the stack-and-roll time frame as collateral for shorter-term forward contracts.

Another way of dealing with a liquidity problem in one market is to hedge some volumes in a different, but correlated, market. This is sometimes referred to as a "cross-commodity" hedge. In oil markets a few hubs (areas of physical exchange that have evolved into markets) are used to price a much larger number of oil products of various qualities and locations. Oil prices are also used to hedge exposures in other fuel markets such as natural gas liquids, where there is limited market liquidity.

In a similar way, as power markets develop it is likely that many contracts will be priced and valued in relation to a regional index price. Transmission and other physical constraints are likely to prevent the development of a hub as dominant as West Texas Intermediate (WTI) in the oil markets, however. So power price exposures may be hedged in a related market, either at a regional hub price or even in a fuel market, and this provides another way of working around a liquidity problem.

As with all the other implementation issues relating to derivatives in project finance, lenders will need to be comfortable with the risk and return of a particular hedging strategy.

MARGIN CALLS, LETTERS OF CREDIT

Compared with most markets, energy is unusual in that there is inconsistent and sporadic collateral flow between trading counterparties in the OTC, or non-exchange traded, market. Several market observers, including Deutsche Bank, believe that the development of an appropriate daily collateral flow is inevitable in, and indeed a prerequisite for, a mature market. Daily collateral flows between market participants reflect changes in the mark-to-market value of the outstanding contracts. These collateral flows provide a level of comfort that, in the event of a default by one or more participants, adequate funds will be available to fund mark-to-market unrealised gains. Two scenarios will be considered here: full collateral requirements and no significant collateral requirements.

If full collateral requirements become the standard in energy commodity markets, the cashflow requirements could become a significant contingency to plan for. Consider the situation of a forward sale entered into for hedging purposes when prices rise. Although the forward sale has lost value, it is offset by a gain in value from the ownership of production from the project. However, the derivative counterparty will require a collateral flow (or, in the case of an exchange, a margin call) to fund the mark-to-market loss on the position. This short-term cash requirement could put considerable stress on the financial position of a highly leveraged project.

If no collateral requirements develop, this issue will manifest itself largely as credit risk for an energy project. Any time that a project has sold forward and prices have dropped, the mark-to-market value of the forward contracts will depend on the credit quality of the counterparty.

DERIVATIVE COUNTERPARTY CREDIT RISK

As explained above, the extent of credit risk will depend on the amount of collateral flowing between derivative counterparties in the energy markets. If there are insufficient or delayed collateral flows, significant credit risk will exist for the project whenever prices fall below the contract price. This arises because the mark-to-market value of the purchase contract by the counterparty has negative value. Of course this could be hedged by other transactions as part of the overall portfolio, but the fact remains that in a bankruptcy or financial distress scenario collateral held may be the only security against a loss to the project. Evaluation of the credit risk should include the credit ratings of counterparties, if available, as well as evaluation of balance sheet data and, to the extent possible, an understanding of the counterparties' trading strategies. For example, is a counterparty known for speculative trading or customer flow business? Some credit analysts have traditionally found more comfort in trading with an owner of physical assets, although few generation owners restrict trading activity to their physical position.

ACCOUNTING POLICY

For projects that form part of a publicly traded company, hedge accounting policy can be critical to establishing a stable earnings flow over time. If hedge accounting treatment is not achieved, the hedge instrument can be subject to periodic revaluation, with consequent swings in earnings. This is because the change in the market value of future production flows is not necessarily reflected in earnings statements. Thus, the hedge is marked-to-market but the underlying position is not. Ideally, if the hedge is defined as a "cashflow hedge"[8] as described in FASB 133 (*Accounting for Derivative Instruments and Hedging Activities*), it can be linked to a specific production position and, except for the "ineffective portion", does not require revaluation. The "ineffective portion" can be translated as basis risk. As a result, a dynamic hedging policy may have unfavourable accounting implications when compared with a hedge instrument that exactly matches the exposure but is more expensive (see also the discussion in Chapter 11).

Detailed example: a gas-fired plant in PJM

To demonstrate the joint impact of hedging and leverage on equity returns, we will now examine two hypothetical 100 MW gas-fired generation facilities in the PJM (Pennsylvania–New Jersey–Maryland) West region. The first is a new, state-of-the-art combined-cycle generation facility with a heat rate of 6,600 Btu/kWh. The second is an older steam-cycle plant with a 10,000 Btu/kWh heat rate. It will be demonstrated that the hedging, leverage and operational characteristics of the facilities are all related.

Gas prices and power prices are modelled randomly so that there are 500 different realisations of prices, each of which produces a cashflow forecast for the project. This allows a comparison of different hedging and leverage strategies to determine what is feasible and what leads to a cash shortfall.

DISTRIBUTION OF PROJECT EARNINGS
BEFORE TAX

To help understand the dynamics of the project, we chart the August 1999 and February 2000 earnings before tax against average prices in each period for each plant for many iterations of the model (Figure 2). As might be expected, the more efficient plant is profitable in both months, while the less efficient plant is only profitable sometimes. For hedging purposes it is interesting to determine the sensitivity of earnings to price. This is the slope of a best-fit line through the data. It is also defined as the hedge ratio:[9]

$$h = \rho \frac{\sigma_V}{\sigma_H}$$

where V is the value of the position being hedged (in this case pre-tax earnings for the month) and H is the hedging instrument (in this case the peak-price forward contract for the month). For hedging purposes, h is often referred to as the delta of a position. It is so named because it can be derived algebraically as

the first derivative (or rate of change) of value with respect to price. In this example, the delta of the position is 35,000 MWh for August. This means that monthly pre-tax earnings increase by $35,000 per $1 increase in the August peak price. The optimal hedging strategy here is a forward sale of 35,000 MWh.

In the same way that financing activities should not influence the operational activities of a company, neither should the hedging activities. It is important to continue to operate the plant on a marginal cost basis, dispatching power only when the value of production exceeds the cost of production. If prices are below the cost of production, it is cheaper to supply any hedging obligation from power purchased in the market.

Note that, as expected, the delta of the August positions for both plants is equivalent to 100 MW in each peak hour of the month. That is, delta = 35,000 MWh = 100 MW × 16 hours × 22 days.

In the graphs for February the slope of the line, delta, is less than 35,000 MWh. The 6,600 Btu/kWh plant has a delta of 32,000 MWh, and the 10,000 Btu/kWh plant has a delta of 22,000 MWh. The graph shows why a single delta number does not capture the risk very well. In the February graph for the steam-cycle 10,000 Btu/kWh plant, although a $1 change in average prices leads to a $22,000 change in pre-tax earnings on average, it depends on what the level of prices is. For low prices the change is less than

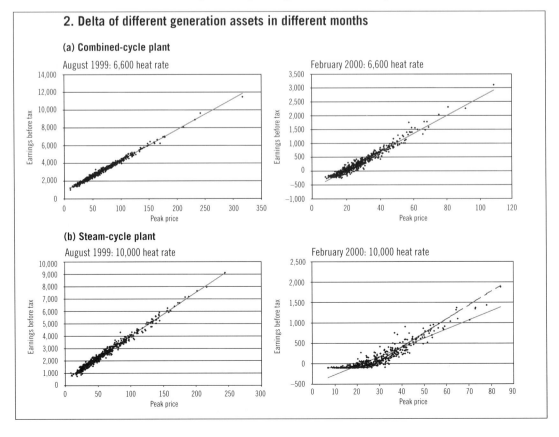

2. Delta of different generation assets in different months

(a) Combined-cycle plant

August 1999: 6,600 heat rate

February 2000: 6,600 heat rate

(b) Steam-cycle plant

August 1999: 10,000 heat rate

February 2000: 10,000 heat rate

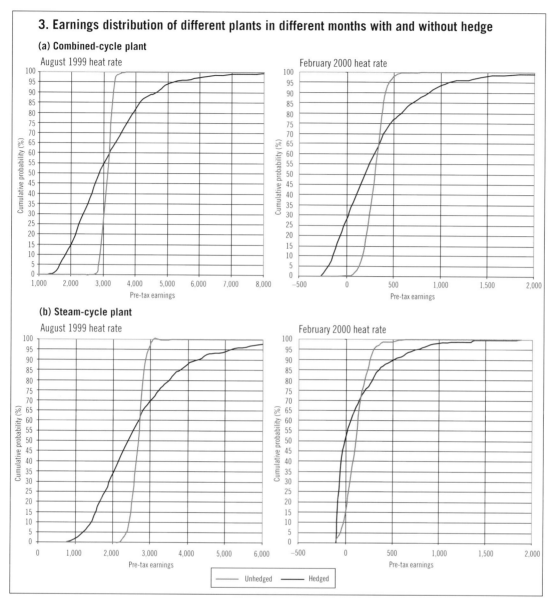

3. Earnings distribution of different plants in different months with and without hedge

(a) Combined-cycle plant

(b) Steam-cycle plant

— Unhedged — Hedged

$22,000, whereas for high prices the change is greater than $22,000. This is why the choice of derivative instrument is so important. Clearly the best choice of hedging instrument is not one that gives rise to a straight line on the graph. Options provide a profile that matches this type of generation well for the reasons outlined in an earlier section.

Another way of explaining this is that the less efficient 10,000 Btu/kWh plant has a delta of 35,000 MWh for prices over $27/MWh but a delta of almost zero for prices below $27/MWh.

The choice of options contract is more complicated than for the forward hedge described above. Balanced against the incentive to minimise the variance of cashflows is the fact that there is more limited liquidity in the options markets and a substantial bid–offer spread. However, the primary objective must be to achieve a delta position that matches the delta of the plant. So the best choice of hedge for a mid-merit or peak-

ing power plant facility is clearly an option with a strike similar to the plant's marginal (or dispatch) cost.

By selling options, the owner of a plant exchanges an uncertain cashflow that is dependent on market prices for a known up-front or periodic cashflow from the sale of options. For this example, however, we concentrate on the simpler example with forward contracts only.

Figure 3 shows the cumulative distributions of cashflows before and after hedging with forward contracts as indicated above. With hedges there is a much smaller range of outcomes, creating "room" for more debt funding of the project. This can be evaluated in terms of the fifth percentile of the distribution. For example, in August the 6,600 Btu/kWh plant will support only $1.6 million in fixed financing payments without hedging but $2.8 million with hedges.

A forward purchase of the fuel cost is another obvious way to stabilise cashflows from a pro-

104

4. Net present value of different plants for various hedging and leverage combinations

6,600 Btu/kWh combined-cycle plant

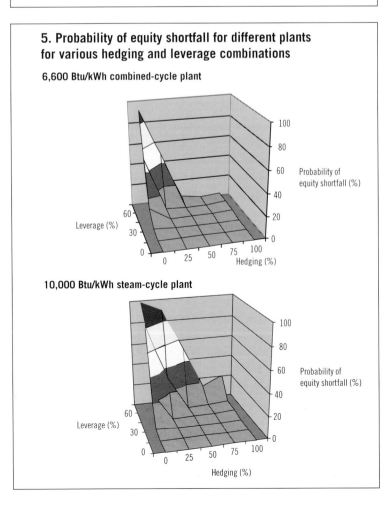

10,000 Btu/kWh steam-cycle plant

5. Probability of equity shortfall for different plants for various hedging and leverage combinations

6,600 Btu/kWh combined-cycle plant

10,000 Btu/kWh steam-cycle plant

Table 3. 15-year default probabilities for various initial ratings

S&P rating	Year 15 (%)
AAA	0.81
AA	0.87
A	1.98
BBB	4.06
BB	16.01
B	27.23
CCC	45.08
Investment grade	2.11
Speculative grade	23.03

ject. Derivative forward contracts are relatively straightforward in gas; however, nuclear and coal purchases are currently limited to long-term purchase contracts. There has been some development of a "spot" coal market in some locations.

Although the hedges shown are optimal in the sense that they create the lowest volatility of cashflow, an equity holder may wish to maintain less hedging in order to take a chance on earning higher returns. Figure 4 shows the project NPV for a range of hedging and funding alternatives for both plants. Figure 5 shows that the probability of an equity shortfall over the project life is significant for several of these alternatives, which would be unlikely to attract debt funding.

On the basis of the probability of default implicit in the free cashflow, an anticipated rating of the debt from these projects can be determined from historical default rates published by Standard & Poor's (Table 3).[9] This provides guidance on the final cost of debt funding, although investors are likely to look at a number of other measures, including coverage ratios. It is important to note that these merchant facilities have highly seasonal cashflows, which requires some degree of flexibility in the funding structure.

Investor communication

These techniques provide a very useful means of communication with investors. To get project debt rated, agencies must have confidence in the cashflow forecasts. Static forecasts can be improved with the concept of a distribution of cashflows, which allows investors to gain a better understanding of the project's dynamics. Both debt and equity holders can gain insight into the likelihood of an equity shortfall. As described above, the likelihood of default provides a means of rating the debt issue and coordinating with rating agencies, which is a key component of investor communication.

Conclusions

Energy derivative markets have developed for a number of different commodities, driven largely by increasing end-user demand for fuel supply contracts that have derivative structures embedded within them. Project finance of merchant power generation facilities is an emerging area for the application of derivative structures. This new development is being driven by the decline in the use of traditional long-term power purchase agreements.

We have seen that the hedging and leverage alternatives for a commodity-based production project are intimately related. The degree of certainty of cashflows depends critically on the hedging strategy employed, which may include derivatives. Cashflow certainty influences the amount of leverage that it is realistic to employ.

1 *Resource Data International website, Einsight.com. April 22, 1999.*

2 *"Repowering" is the term used to describe the process of increasing the production capacity or flexibility of a power generation facility.*

3 *Private communication, May 17, 1999.*

4 *Private communication, April 15, 1999.*

5 *Private communication, May 20, 1999.*

6 *Private communication, May 27, 1999.*

7 *See for example* Corporate Hedging in Theory and Practice: Lessons from Metallgesellschaft, *eds C. Culp and M. Miller, Risk Books, London, 1999.*

8 *Hull, John C., Options,* Futures, and Other Derivative Securities, *Second edition, 1997, Prentice-Hall International, New Jersey.*

9 S&P CreditWeek, *March 10, 1999. Thanks to Stuart D. Braman of Standard & Poor's.*

DEVELOPMENTS IN ENERGY MARKETS

Section Introduction

Vincent Kaminski
Enron Corp

One of the main challenges facing a professional in the energy business is that the complexity of the individual segments of the industry is growing while, at the same time, those segments are beginning to converge.

In the past, energy professionals could sail through their professional career gradually accumulating the necessary expertise and skills – using a learning-on-the-job approach – without the need for continuous formal training or exposure to other energy markets.

This world has been shattered over the last ten years. Today, it is difficult to imagine a senior or a middle-level manager in the energy industry who does not have to follow market developments, events and regulatory decisions in segments of the energy business outside his main market – and also work out their impact on the home turf. The objective of this section of the book is to facilitate this task by providing a bird's eye view of major segments of the energy industry and the key regulatory developments.

The pivotal development has been the deregulation of many sectors of the industry, a process that started in the natural gas business in the US in the late 1980s and extended to other markets and countries in the 1990s. The deregulation process typically begins "upstream", with the deregulation of production and wholesale markets. Transportation/transmission and distribution often continue to be treated as natural monopolies and remain regulated, though regulators increasingly rely on the use of free-market mechanisms to accomplish their objectives (eg the creation of the secondary market for pipeline capacity in the US). In the later stages of deregulation, competitive forces and the market mechanism are brought down to the level of retail transactions.

Even within a single country, the pace of deregulation varies across different jurisdictions, creating a complicated quilt of conflicting, overlapping and often contradictory rulings – all of which fosters regulatory uncertainty. This trend requires energy companies to dedicate significant resources to monitoring and influencing regulatory developments, and to the development of tools that allow them to ascertain the impact of future regulatory developments on their businesses.

Chapters in this section highlight the most important regulatory and structural developments in specific markets undergoing rapid deregulation. Read together, they will help the reader to understand the dynamics of this increasingly integrated industry.

The chapter on the oil markets by Etienne Amic and Philippe Lautard provides a review of the structure of the oil industry and the oil markets and explains how these markets interact in time and space. The chapter is focused on three issues:

❏ locational risks and the fundamentals driving locational price differentials;

❏ price term structure and the main factors behind it (particularly availability of storage);

❏ different spreads traded actively in the market (crack, inter-market, inter-temporal and quality spreads).

Especially important, in view of the experiences in commodity markets in the 1990s, is the question of the shape of the forward price curve (contango versus backwardation). Frequent forward price curve reshapings wreaked havoc in more than one trading portfolio in the energy and other commodity markets in the 1990s. No energy market participant of the period can forget the controversy surrounding Metallgesellschaft.[1]

The chapter on the US natural gas markets by Fred Lagrasta, Vincent Kaminski and Ross Prevatt, with a contribution on the UK gas market by Louise Kitchen, provides a history of this very dynamic market and discusses recent developments in the regulatory arena. The authors devote special attention to hedging basis risk in the natural gas markets and to the convergence of natural gas and electricity markets.

Grant Masson undertook the unenviable task of writing a chapter on a market changing so fast that analysts find it hard to keep up. He provides a taxonomy of the different power market structures implemented in different countries, including England and Wales, Australia, Scandinavia and the US (California PX). The comparative analysis of the (perpetually evolving) mandatory and voluntary pools is important because it is the only way to gain insight into the weaknesses and strengths of different solutions. We can trace an intensive exchange of information between professionals in the power industry, which is traditionally based on cooperation rather than on competition. So far, power professionals have learnt from each other's experience and the modifications of a power pool in one jurisdiction often reverberate through the power industries on many continents.

From the legal perspective, the chapter by Kenneth Raisler and Alison Gregory offers an overview of the regulatory issues related to enforceability of derivative contracts in the energy industry and the changing regulatory landscape in this area from the US perspective.

1 *Interested readers can review the controversy in the pages of* Corporate Hedging in Theory and Practice: Lessons from Metallgesellschaft, *eds C. Culp and Merton H. Miller, Risk Books (1999).*

5

The Oil Market

Etienne Amic and Philippe Lautard
Elf Trading

The trading environment of the oil markets is inherently unstable. Geology, geopolitics, economics, law, taxation, finance, technology and environmental concerns are liable at any time to make a formidable impact on the evolution of the market structure. The fundamental factors that generate risk in the oil industry, such as geological risk – on which the risk-reward relationship of the pioneering epoch of oil exploration was mainly based – may be reduced by the use of modern techniques and technology, but they cannot truly be *managed*.

Instead, the management of risk in the oil industry has tended to focus on managing the relationship between *time* and *price*. To produce crude from an oil field requires several years and a huge investment; to bring oil from the well to the customer requires at least a few weeks and sound logistics (pipelines, cargoes, storage facilities, refineries, distribution networks). These logistical facts form the backdrop to the growth in risk management in the oil industry.

The main aim of this chapter is to provide a global and up-to-date analysis of how the structure of the oil industry and the oil markets impact upon the hedging strategies of the end-user (energy consumer), the oil company and the energy derivatives' provider. We will focus on three specific issues: locational risks and the role of fundamentals; price term structure and the role of storage; and crack, product and quality spreads and the role of refining. In our conclusion we will attempt to map out how the markets in oil derivatives are likely to evolve in the future.

Introduction: market perspectives

HISTORICAL PERSPECTIVE OF THE OIL MARKET
The fundamental pricing environment for oil transactions has undergone major changes since the large price jumps of the 1970s. The shift in the ownership of producing assets from major oil companies to producing countries and national companies, through different forms of nationalisation, marked the beginning of open markets. For most companies, this meant that they could no longer simply transfer risk and added value vertically along different steps of the logistic chain. Consequently, crude oil supply contracts have evolved from being relatively fixed to being relatively flexible (Figure 1).

Another important element in the development of the oil markets has been the ambition of taxation authorities to transform the more or less arbitrary transfer prices for transactions among sister companies – for example from exploration and production to refining – into a more visible system. From an operational viewpoint, the need to balance the composition of the demand barrel, the mix of refining capacity, and the type of crude oil being run in each of the major geographical regions has fuelled the growth of a global refined products market.

The physical oil markets now play a major role in creating the supply and demand equilibrium in local markets, and in global arbitrage. Oil

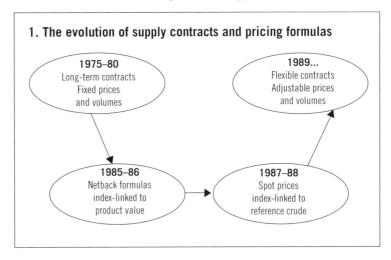

1. The evolution of supply contracts and pricing formulas

- **1975–80** Long-term contracts Fixed prices and volumes
- **1989...** Flexible contracts Adjustable prices and volumes
- **1985–86** Netback formulas index-linked to product value
- **1987–88** Spot prices index-linked to reference crude

companies and oil importing countries often consider the oil markets as a kind of dynamic counterweight to the dominance of producing countries or, more precisely, of OPEC.

Along the way, oil trading has turned from a primarily physical activity into a sophisticated financial market. It has attracted the interest of a wide range of participants who now include banks and funds managers as well as the traditional oil majors, independents and physical oil traders. In particular, retail and institutional investors hoping to enhance yield through commodity price movements, or to reduce credit exposure through the use of oil as collateral, have dramatically increased their presence in the futures markets.

Since oil is an inherently non-standard commodity, the industry has chosen a small number of "reference" or "marker" grades of crude oil and refined products to provide the physical basis for a much larger "paper" market which trades derivative instruments such as forward and futures contracts. A large volume of activity is thus concentrated through a small number of standardised trading instruments to deal with the absolute price risk; in parallel, a whole battery of price differentials has developed to fine tune the pricing of different grades, locations and delivery periods. As a result, although their physical base is rather small as compared to the overall production, free oil markets have become a major factor in the pricing mechanism for short- to medium-term crude oil and refined products – a role which was dramatically revealed to the world by the Gulf crisis of August 1990 to March 1991 and also emphasised during the price drop of 1998.

RISK MANAGEMENT AND THE END-USER
Traditionally, end-users have implemented hedging strategies using forwards, futures, options or swaps to fulfil very specific aims, such as protecting budgets, protecting inventories or as a tool in project financing. This approach has been mainly focused on eliminating financial risk, not on increasing returns.

Risk management today is also associated with strategic decisions, taken at board level, with regard to a whole range of business concerns. For an oil company, the goal may be to transfer near-term cashflow risk, generated by short-term fluctuations in oil prices or foreign exchange, to the deeper longer-term business that arises as the firm makes major investments. These investments require the longer-term provision of capital, but are far more likely to offer above-normal returns on shareholder equity. In this context, hedging does not imply any negative price view of the commodity because the total exposure of the firm on oil prices is increased by the investments. Instead, the role of risk management has shifted from that of a defensive tool to that of a proactive means of reducing the weighted cost of capital and/or changing the allocation of cashflows during business cycles. In view of this, corporate end-users should define the real objectives of their risk management strategy before taking any position on exchanges or in the over-the-counter (OTC) market.

The move to risk management may well be prompted by threats from competitors. In deregulated gas markets, for instance, distributors are often confronted with new entrants that simply buy part of their gas on the spot market, rather than obtaining supplies by means of bilateral, long-term, take-or-pay contracts that are indexed to oil prices. This indexation arose from pipeline economics. Once a pipeline is constructed, the upfront capital is sunk and it would be nonsensical to price the gas according to a fixed capital charge plus an operating cost. Such a policy might, given low competing energy prices, lead to customers switching away from gas and to a consequent loss of trade.

Pricing in relation to competing commodities is thus explicit in all the international bilateral contracts. When these contracts were first signed, a base price was agreed upon and a price escalation clause was formulated which determined the future variations in the base price. The price escalation formula is typically composed of other types of energy such as crude oil, gasoil and heavy fuel oil.[1] In more recent contracts, where gas is earmarked for the power generation market, there may be price links with coal and electricity itself.[2] The primary risk for companies with such bilateral contracts (ie most of the major European gas distributors) is the risk of being undercut by competitors when gas prices decline or are stable, while oil prices soar. The second risk is that they may be forced to take delivery of excess gas when demand is low due to warm weather conditions or when they lose market share due to high oil prices. The containment of the implicit oil, gas and temperature exposures embedded in their supply contracts has become a major challenge for companies involved in the gas business, requiring them to make use of oil as well as weather derivatives.

Corporate end-users must also set limits regarding their company's tolerance to oil market risks in terms of the amount or volume, duration, diffusion and absorption. As we describe in Chapter 7, in the recent past, privatised power producers and Regional Electricity Companies (RECs) in the UK with a large exposure to electricity, natural gas and oil prices have been obliged to start taking conscious decisions about their risk aversion. The first step of this continuing process was to gain a full understanding of the electricity market and its specific risks (nonstorability of power, sensitivity to extreme weather conditions, merit order for production, arbitrage between electricity and fuel markets) – in effect, an extended period of education, discussion and information gathering. The second stage for most of these companies was to create an internal group able to deal with risk management: contract and counterparty analysis, operational constraints, control and follow-up of positions, liquidity and valuation principles (mark-to-market). Only then were the companies able to start properly managing their global energy risk, and over the past five years some of these companies have evolved from relatively basic, risk-averse market players into sophisticated large-scale risk takers. Major utilities throughout Europe are engaged on the same learning curve and are faced with decisions regarding the role they should assign their trading divisions and the amount of market risk they are ready to bear.

As well as understanding the dynamics of the market, end-users must quantify the risks associated with their industrial or commercial activities. Risk usually arises from asymmetries between fixed versus floating or short-term versus long-term exposures. As part of corporate strategy, risk management requires that clear objectives are set for the different aspects of the business:

❏ *physical*: storage and supply optimisation;

❏ *financial*: securing budgets and cashflows, enhancing return on investment and debt-to-equity ratio;

❏ *marketing*: designing innovative marketing and tariff policies that offer a competitive advantage;

❏ *general*: gaining access to market information and arbitrage opportunities.

Several European and US oil traders have suffered from having their derivatives operations physically separate from their spot market activities. Although it may be necessary for different individuals to take responsibility, it is not practicable to run any type of derivatives book separately from a physical book (as effective use of the paper markets necessitates a close interaction between the two).

At the inception of a hedge, management must be made aware of the possibility of opportunity losses. Let us consider, as an example, an oil consumer fixing part of its yearly oil price exposure by purchasing swaps. If oil prices fall, the company may not be able to take the full advantage of the price reduction; in such a case, however, physical supplies will be less expensive than they would have been at a higher market level and the overall effect will be positive. If prices rise, and the swaps settle at a net profit, this is not necessarily good news: the end-user may well find out that its annual budget has been exceeded because the volume of its hedge was not sufficient. Rather than the marked-to-market forward cost of supplies, it is the shape of the probability distribution of this cost that should be monitored by the end-user. This can only be achieved by integrating physical and derivative transactions into a VAR-type framework,[3] the opportunity of incremental hedges being measured by their projected influence on the distribution.

Choosing the right instrument is obviously a crucial part of the hedging process. In Panel 1, we focus on one particularly active end-user market sector and tabulate the benefits and disadvantages of commonly used instruments.

Today, mastering plain vanilla energy derivatives may no longer be enough. Much activity in recent years has been directed toward designing deals to meet specific client needs. These deals tend to be highly structured, with an increasing use of options and options combined with swaps. They can be designed for a variety of purposes: monetisation of a flexibility embedded in a physical contract (eg swing options, or options on the minimum of two supply price formulas); enhancement of the yield of a cash investment with a participation in oil price movements; financing at competitive rates without credit concerns (eg syndicated loans to producers whose collateral is based on the proceeds of the sale of the commodity itself); hedging of specific processing contracts in refineries and power plants, etc. There are only a few major players willing to analyse, price and execute completely customised transactions. Whatever the expertise required, it should be remembered that most end-users are not market specialists, and it is in the interest of long-term participants in the market to adopt an "educational" approach; in partic-

INSTRUMENT SELECTION IN THE AIRLINE SECTOR

Jet fuel represents, on average, about 15% of the direct operating costs of airlines, but because the price volatility is so high it can suddenly become a much more significant cost. Price rises cannot be easily transferred to customers because of tariffs and competitive pressures. For this reason, many derivatives providers initially targeted airlines as the "ideal" user of hedging techniques.

European and, to a lesser extent, Asian airlines have been the most active in the market; their hedging operations are now very professional, and are often run just like a trading desk. For example, most airlines are fully aware not only of the behaviour of related markets, such as IPE gasoil futures and jet kerosene derivatives, but also of the price term structure and of ways to interpret or to take advantage of it.

Even so, risk management is mostly designed to stabilise short- and medium-term cashflows and to secure minimum profitability. Moreover, hedging proposals are sometimes combined with physical tenders for airport supplies. Although one might have hoped that longer-term derivatives would start to be used as part of aviation financing, the peculiarities of the air finance sector are such that this is only happening to a limited degree.

The instruments used by airlines have evolved from simple swaps to more complex or exotic types. The choice between them depends on market level and structure, on trading habits, on budget settings and cash availability (in the case of an option-like premium). It is obviously important for airlines to understand the exact characteristics and potential effects (profits/losses, volume and maturity risks) of hedging instruments. Below, we attempt to tabulate the nature of the risks and benefits associated with particular instruments.

❑ *swaps* are tailor-made to minimise the basis risks on a fixed-floating transaction. When entering the transaction, the commitment between hedgers and providers in terms of future cashflow is symmetric. However, airlines buying forward supplies at a fixed price risk an opportunity cost whenever spot prices decline during the contract period;

❑ *caps* (call options) may be purchased to hedge against the risk of a price rise, without risking the potential benefits of a drop in price. That is, caps cannot incur any opportunity cost. This payout is, of course, asymmetric, and is balanced by the upfront premium paid to the option writer;

❑ *collars* offer a hedge on the upside risk, just like caps, but the cost of this option is exchanged by assigning part of the downside to the writer. That is, collars usually have no initial cost, but entail a potential loss of opportunity (just like swaps, but at a lower level). In the past, some airlines have not fully recognised the potential impact of this opportunity cost, and found themselves in a difficult position, compared to unhedged or capped competitors, when the price of jet fuel dropped heavily;

❑ *double-ups* offer a swap-like instrument, but at a lower market price than the equivalent swap. This price benefit is offset by the fact that the provider may double the hedging quantity at the initial or a lower fixed price. In effect, the airline buys a swap and sells a put option on a similar swap (a swaption), which may later be exercised. This reduces the initial hedging cost, but the potential opportunity cost is doubled. Moreover, the implicit sale of a put does not provide enough protection with regard to the additional volume, should prices rocket upwards. Double-up strategies are therefore liable to have quite an impact if there is a large price move. Smaller or inexperienced airlines should be wary of entering into them, while airlines with large volumes to handle and a good trading organisation may find them more attractive;

❑ *combinations* between IPE gas oil futures and kerosene to gas oil spread hedging tend to be used by airlines that are very active in the market. For example, gas oil screen-hedging may be completed by the purchase of options on the kerosene-gas oil spread value over some future period. In that way, the correlation between both products is kept under control at the expense of a limited premium, while hedging the absolute price risk is achieved by means of day-to-day operations on the IPE. Users should remember that this is a sophisticated strategy that needs careful monitoring. Some airlines take positions even further ahead on their absolute price risk by buying futures on IPE crude oil, converting them into gas oil later on and finally shifting to their real kerosene exposure when their physical risk becomes more prompt. The jet fuel sector is discussed in Chapter 1, where a further panel describes the implementation of a differential swap.

ular, companies should not be led into ill-adapted deals which yield a large residual exposure.

Besides the choice of suitable instruments, potential hedgers have to take into account in-house administration risks:

❏ legal, accounting and tax considerations;

❏ operational handling and costs;

❏ information and processing systems;

❏ procedures for decision-making, authority and limits (volume or amount, maturity);

❏ procedures for reporting of positions (mark-to-market);

❏ procedures for following up positions (evolution of residual risks); and

❏ the impact of liquidity and of indexation mismatch.

Market liquidity is a crucial factor to consider in the energy markets, not only at the initiation of a transaction, but through its entire life. It has a direct impact on hedging effectiveness. Generally speaking, liquidity has both a price and a quantity dimension.[4] The price dimension, known as the spread, refers to the cost of entering and liquidating a relatively small position and is measured by the difference in the price at which traders are willing to sell (the asking price), and the price at which they are willing to buy (the bid). The quantity dimension of liquidity, on the other hand, refers to the ability of markets to handle large orders, or a large number of orders in a short period of time, without greatly distorting prices; it is usually measured by the relationship between the size of the buy order and its effect on the asking price, or the size of the sell order and its effect on the bid. A market can have low bid-ask spreads for small orders and yet still be shallow if there are not many potential orders in the neighbourhood of the market price.

The price dimension of liquidity is particularly sensitive for derivatives written on local industry indexes. The Department of Trade and Industry (DTI) indexes in the UK or the Statistisches Bundesamt indexes in Germany fall into this category; they are often used for escalation formulas in long-term supply contracts. Managing the risk associated with such local indexes is possible because of a good correlation (excluding domestic tax elements) with international oil prices (mainly Platt's assessments). However, when it exists at all, the risk management market for the local risks is much thinner than that for the direct Platt's-indexed quanto derivatives and this may justify a limited premium. On the one hand, locally indexed derivatives better represent the company exposure but, on the other, the con-

tracts are not very liquid or easily transferable and they cannot be perfectly marked-to-market. The choice of index for hedging is thus an important decision, and should be made at an appropriate level.

Finally, as on the financial markets, an end-user's strategy will be crucially affected by the shape of the term structure (backwardation or contango) and volatility of oil. Many investment opportunities involve fast-moving markets that can render potential transactions uneconomical in a very short time. Investor interest in potential derivative transactions can evaporate following almost any movement of the forward curve, price volatility or exchange rates. A unique feature of the oil market, however, is that the signals carried by oil prices are used not only as a trading tool but also as a basis for the management of stocks and processing units. In deregulated markets, it is all the more likely that refineries, power plants and other industrial facilities will be operated in even closer connection with trading decisions than they have been until now.

Trading and risk management within an oil company

Oil price risk has traditionally been at the heart of the oil business, and most oil companies have now adapted their vertical structure to the new challenges created by oil price risk trading and management. Trading in oil companies can be divided into the three main areas of business outlined below:

❏ *System trading*. This is aimed mainly at optimising the supply, import and export requirements of the oil group.

It involves the systematic researching of the most profitable markets for the crudes produced by the group. The transfer of risks from the production sector of the company to the trading sector requires that the latter should be able to handle logistics and security matters, to offer contractual and financial guarantees, and to provide adequate hedging programmes against large price fluctuations.

The supply trading entity will also arrange physical supplies at competitive prices for the oil group's refining, distribution and chemical divisions, if any. Furthermore, it will try to take advantage of any opportunities to profit from physical arbitrage: for example, the opening of export windows between the United States and North West Europe (NWE).

❏ *Third party trading*. This business sector handles trading crudes and products with large oil companies and traders. Such transactions are usually independent of direct supply concerns, but form part of global arbitrage strategies. They may also be associated with prefinancing and barter operations.

❑ *Risk management.* Risk management consists of monitoring and managing price volatility, maturity and basis risks. Third party trading clearly requires risk management, and more so if it is done through an independent entity which supplies and trades with other companies of the group under pre-agreed pricing formulas, because the amount of risks accumulated can become substantial. The risk management team acts principally for the group itself, mainly for production, transportation, refining, distribution, chemicals and international trading. Risk management may also provide the distribution subsidiaries of the oil company with additional marketing tools, such as attaching price guarantees to physical deliveries. Recently, the trend has been to fully integrate physical and derivatives operations: this integration usually aims at unleashing arbitrage opportunities and valuing flexibilities in physical supply contracts on the one hand, while better assessing physical settlements of derivatives transactions on the other hand.

At the same time, some oil companies have developed an independent portfolio of clients to whom they offer structured products: for example, airlines, shipping and transportation companies, utilities and large industries, other oil producers, refiners or traders, banks and hedge funds.

Thus, within an oil company, many elements take part in the risk management process. And a great variety of commercial opportunities may be considered. For example:

❑ the portfolio of equity crudes may be better adapted to the needs of the company's refining structure. An instance of this is the adjustment of the "sulphur balance" by buying low-sulphur crudes or by investing in hydro-desulphurisation;

❑ distribution networks may be reorganised around refineries and storage areas to enhance logistics;

❑ assets and acreage may be modified or swapped for those with better taxation or cost profiles.

In the next section we will look closely at the risk management strategy of refiners; in this introductory section we will investigate the risk management strategies of the other "fundamental" sector of the industry: exploration and production (E&P).

Oil exploration is a business with one of the highest R&D costs of any industry: the average cost of drilling oil is expressed in millions of dollars. Production also requires heavy investment, and has both a political and a strategic aspect. However, few producing companies or countries presently consider hedging their complete programmes. The taxation framework, and the risk-taking nature of the industry itself, are fundamental when assessing the potential market for E&P-oriented derivatives.

In the past, small US oil companies appear to have been more willing to use medium- to long-term hedging programmes than large North Sea producers, or national oil companies in South America, the Middle East or the Far East. However, some of these larger producers have hedged selectively, for instance, during the Gulf crisis or during periods of large contangos. From this viewpoint, the price collapse of 1998 was an alarm signal to producers and triggered a renewed activity on this segment of the market, having a direct effect on the flattening of the forward curve at the end of 1998 (Figure 6).

Ideally, an oil company's hedging programme should be designed to ensure the company's financial stability (repayment of liabilities); minimum profitability (distribution to shareholders), and the successful development of new projects (putting existing reserves on stream or discovering new reserves). The time duration and the payout structure would depend on the exact needs of the company:

❑ profitability over one or more accounting year(s);

❑ duration of liabilities if debtors require guarantee of repayments;

❑ return on investment for long-term projects.

Short-term hedging is usually made on a cargo-by-cargo basis, and must be designed to take account of tax factors because there is usually an asymmetry between taxation on oil revenues and taxation on hedging (financial) revenues or losses. The structure of market oil prices can move violently between backwardation and contango (we explore this in detail in the next section) and these different structural contexts strongly influence the hedging strategies available to producers.

One of the specific strategies suited to medium- to long-term hedging is the use of oil-linked debt to facilitate global financing. According to market circumstances, and the objectives of the strategy, the oil company can also construct an optimal combination of put options and swaps (Figure 2). The swap (or forward sale at a fixed price) is used to reward third parties, shareholders and debtors, and ensures a minimum profit and liability repayment; the put option is set up on the remainder of the production volume to hedge the down-side. The proportions of swaps and options relative to the field's production plan are adjusted according to initial market conditions, cost structure and the taxation framework. It is worth noting here that if the fixed payment for the swap is sufficient, then this will itself finance the initial premium on the option. More complex structures have been proposed recently, such as range swaps, or indexed-amortising swaps, that allow to get a better price for the forward sale of oil, provided the producer gives up some gain in case of an oil price slump.

Our brief analysis of E&P hedging suggests that risk management for the oil industry is a particularly complex process. This is particularly true in the case of an integrated company, which has the potential to take advantage of the size and variety of its own flows of risks. Yet, however sophisticated the trading, no company can afford to ignore the market fundamentals discussed later on in this chapter.

RISK MANAGEMENT AND THE DERIVATIVES PROVIDER

We would define the derivatives provider as the counterparty that bears the ultimate market risks embedded in any derivative. This may well be an oil company, as described above, an oil trader, a bank or an investment house (the so-called "Wall Street refiners"). On the one hand, the provider must develop its clientele. On the other, it needs to identify and quantify the exact residual risks in its portfolio. The derivatives' provider must pursue long-term objectives, and report and control its exposure in real time, while remaining dynamic enough to gain trading efficiency and technical advantages over competitors.

At the beginning of the 1990s, the energy derivatives market had seen a massive arrival of new entrants. However, not many have been able to sustain a long-term engagement and the exit from the sector was sometimes even quicker than the original commitment. Among the companies that have survived, even fewer are willing to keep and manage market risks (rather than only taking on those they can "back-to-back"), and are able to provide a full range of derivatives across the different markets.

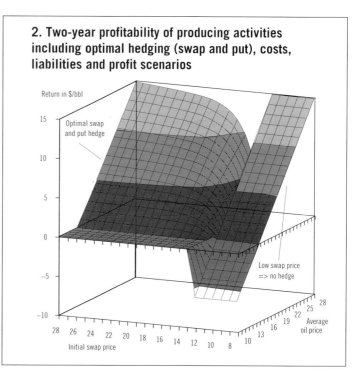

2. Two-year profitability of producing activities including optimal hedging (swap and put), costs, liabilities and profit scenarios

The involvement of commercial banks, financial houses and hedge funds has been an important factor in the development and liquidity of the market. It has been motivated by their clients' increasing demand for structured transactions, and by the prospect of higher margins – as well as contributing to a strategic diversification from their traditional business and risks (interest rates, foreign exchange and credit). However, techniques and strategies cannot be simply translated from the financial to the oil markets, largely because of the much higher volatility and lower liquidity in the commodity sector. It is all the more likely that the renewed activity in deregulated energy markets will attract a large number of new players. However, due to the intricacies of underlying markets (natural gas, power and weather) most commercial banks will be left out of the move, at least at the first stage.

The success of derivatives providers is based on two major elements: marketing and dynamic hedging. Marketing is a long process of gaining a specific relationship with potential clients, captive or not. Dynamic hedging is the constant monitoring and adjustment of the different risk portfolios. Both are intimately linked when initially pricing a transaction, but the subsequent hedging is quite independent of the origin of the risk.

Derivatives traders usually determine the price of an instrument by using empirical and mathematical models, and then by adding the bid-offer spread. In the case of "proxy hedges", there are additional risks in the relationship between the physical and the hedging indexes. The obvious risk is the correlation risk, discussed in detail in Chapter 15. Despite the recent advent of covariance swaps, this risk can rarely be hedged away as such. This is not only a technical problem, as coping with it demands an understanding of the behaviour of markets and oil fundamentals.

Because illiquidity and price gaps characterise most energy markets (Panel 2 provides an actuarial approach of the latter), the hedges actually implemented may be very different from those that were initially conceived. Compared to the "target" hedge, the actual hedge may not be well secured: it usually leaves a residual open position, and necessitates rolling contracts forward. The resulting side effects and costs, in terms of both the underlying risks and the additional hedging instruments that may be required to deal with the residual, must be anticipated when pricing and hedging derivatives. In particular, liquidity in the futures markets is often restricted to the first quoted months, and to specific hours (that is to say, when Nymex is open).

Liquidity problems inevitably affect the choice of maturities and volumes when hedging. However, it should not be assumed that a hedge will remain illiquid in the long term. The structure of liquidity in a market evolves over time, and is affected by the changing habits of traders and hedgers. For example, the growth of energy derivatives is usually acknowledged to have created similar interest in long-term West Texas Intermediate (WTI) positions. Fears of changes in tax regimes, or of further regulatory interference in paper markets, may also badly affect liquidity. In short, dynamic hedging depends on evaluating liquidity over time, managing price gaps, accessing all the available information on the market, and mastering any arbitrage opportunities.

In order to achieve profitable dynamic hedg-

ing that is based on an understanding of the global markets, and which can take advantage of portfolio effects, an increasingly sophisticated set of techniques and systems are necessary. Computing the equivalence functions of different products and maturities is an essential art when devising a hedging strategy. For example, should a specific basket of refinery margins be created or should its different elements, oil products and crudes as well, be separated out? (In fact, both strategies are justifiable.) Rational decision making can be based on a VAR-type method which takes account of the intricate correlations and volatilities of the individual components of the refinery margins (Panel 3 gives more details). Another question might be: how can one extrapolate from Nymex WTI three-year forward prices in order to price and structure a 10-year deal? If the risks of this kind of transaction are not precisely identified and measured, they will certainly accumulate and lead to heavy losses. In Figure 3 we have attempted to represent graphically the dynamic equilibrium of different expertises needed by derivatives providers.

Recently, VAR has gained popularity as a performance evaluation tool to gauge trader profits and the efficiency of market models. Traders involved in different markets – eg high sulphur fuel oil as compared to liquefied petroleum gases and to natural gas, for instance – might produce very different profit numbers simply because of the underlying volatility of the market in which they operate, rather than a difference in trading skills. Profits must therefore be composed of revenues minus expenses and expected losses to cover possible credit and market risks. Since VAR precisely represents the amount of capital economically required to support market and credit risk, it is sensible to divide trading profits by the VAR of the portfolios that generated them. From this viewpoint, the VAR approach offers a standardised base for comparing markets with different risk characteristics.

TRADING DERIVATIVES IN A MULTI-DIMENSIONAL WORLD

This chapter naturally focuses on risks that are specific and integral to the oil industry. However, most companies have to devise strategies that take account of other kinds of risk as well.

Of these, one of the most important is foreign exchange rate risk. When hedging oil price risk, an exchange rate risk may be incurred, because most contracts are traded in or indexed to the $. Many European end-users actually pay their

---

3. An equilibrium between expertise and risk

Trading
- experience in paper, physical and financial markets
- information and arbitrage
- chart and technical analysis

Dynamic hedging

Techniques
- market theory
- financial mathematics
- economics/statistics
- data processing

Portfolio
- internal flows of risk (affiliates)
- external flows of risks (marketing)
- globalisation and diversification
- strategic orientation
- speed of portfolio rotation

VAR, EVT AND THE OIL MARKET

By definition, the VAR of a trading position summarises the expected maximum loss (or worst loss) over a target horizon, with a given confidence level. Practically, VAR may for instance be defined as the left 5% quantile of the portfolio profit-loss distribution over one day.

The first step toward measurement of VAR is thus the choice of two quantitative factors:

❑ the length of the holding period, which is a trade-off between the costs of frequent monitoring of positions and the benefits of early detection of potential problems,

❑ and the confidence level, which reflects the degree of risk aversion of the company and the cost of a loss exceeding VAR.

Perhaps the greatest advantage of VAR is that it encloses in a single number, easy to understand, the total exposure of an institution to market risk. No doubt this explains why VAR has so quickly become an essential tool for conveying trading risks to senior management, directors and shareholders.

If VAR were to be measured for a single asset, the issue would be relatively simple. The problem is that it must be computed for large and complex portfolios, involving non-linear derivatives as well as physical positions, that evolve rapidly over time. There are basically three ways to compute the VAR of a portfolio:

❑ The delta-normal method assumes that all asset returns are normally distributed. Since the return of a portfolio is a linear combination of its constituents' returns, it is also normally distributed. Thus, risk is generated by a combination of factors, whose distributions are easily computed, and by the forecast of their variance-covariance matrix. Within this class of models, two methods can be used to infer the variance-covariance matrix. The latter can either be based on historical data using, for example, a model that allows for time variation in risk. Or it can be implied from options when this information is available. One of the main drawbacks of the delta-normal method is that it poorly accounts for event risk, which is crucial for energy markets.

❑ The historical-simulation method consists of going back in time, such as over the last 300 days, and applying current weights of the portfolio to a time series of historical asset returns. This method is relatively simple to implement if histori-cal data – forward curves and forward volatilities, not just returns – have been collected in-house for daily marking-to-market. By relying on actual prices, it allows non-linearities and non-Gaussian distributions and captures gamma, vega as well as correlations risks. It does not rely on specific assumptions about valuation models, or the underlying stochastic structure of the market and accounts for "fat tails" of actual distributions. One of its flaws is that random samples for market behaviour are all extracted from the same realised path (introducing correlations between trials). Moreover, it is implicitly assumed that the recent past fairly represents the immediate future.

❑ Finally, the structured Monte-Carlo method approximates the behaviour of energy prices by using computer simulations to generate random price paths. Because of its flexibility, it is by far the most powerful method to compute VAR. It can potentially account for a wide range of risks, including price risk, volatility risk and credit risk. By using different models, it can even account for that most insidious form of risk: model risk. The first, and most crucial step, in the simulation process consists of choosing a particular stochastic model for the behaviour of prices. Once thousands of fictitious price and volatility paths have been simulated, it is possible to compile a distribution of the portfolio P&L at the end of the selected horizon, and to empirically infer its VAR from the corresponding histogram.

Sound risk management procedures however, cannot rely solely on VAR, which only provides a measure of the worst loss of a portfolio under normal market conditions. Stressed (or extreme) scenarios must also be set up to evaluate quantities such as;

❑ the mean excess of VAR once VAR has been exceeded (the so-called shortfall, or "beyond VAR"),

❑ the average frequency of some rare events in the market,

❑ the distribution of the largest losses of a portfolio, or

❑ the average duration of a depression.

We thus end up with the problem of finding relevant classes of profit-loss distributions, as well as statistical fitting and tail estimation. It is a well-known fact that the latter are typically skewed, with heavy tails both at the left (losses)

and right (gains) and that volatility tends to, but does not always, cluster when a market panic occurs. A multitude of models for such phenomena has been introduced including α-stable processes (as heavy-tailed alternatives to Brownian motion), and heavy-tailed time series models, such as Arch and Garch. Most of them have already been applied to the energy markets, as Chapter 14 describes.

Before adopting any model, one should nevertheless ask the question: "what does the data tell us?" Here Extreme Value Theory (EVT) may be employed. EVT was originally developed as a modelling tool to describe distributions of river levels in hydrology and catastrophic claims in insurance, such as industrial fires and damages caused by storms, hails and floods. It is only recently that its relevance for market phenomena has been fully recognised. More than a trading tool, it should be considered as one of the best ways to analyse the tail end risks of the available price and volatility time series.

To illustrate how this method can help assess the risks of a trading portfolio, let us consider an operator holding a long position of $1 million in a WTI screen-indexed swap on the prompt month contract of the exchange (excluding the expiration dates of futures). Our aim is to fit the excesses over a given "catastrophic threshold", defined for example as a daily negative return $u_0 = -0.7\%$. The first question one might ask concerns the mean excess loss of the position once this threshold u has been exceeded:

$$e_n\left(u\right) = E\left\{R - u/R > u\right\} = \frac{\beta + \xi u}{1 - \xi} \quad (1)$$

The right-hand side of equation (1), which is linear in the variable u, is the theoretical form of this function for a distribution of returns whose left tail decreases as a power law $R^{-1/\xi}$. For a heavy-tailed (Pareto-like) time series, the mean excess function should thus resemble a straight line. For the sake of comparison, the mean excess function of the WTI first nearby time series is plotted in Figure A, with daily returns from 1986 to 1998, where it is found that $\xi \approx 0.31$. One of the consequences of this plot is that the "beyond VAR" of the position is itself a multiple of VAR:

$$\text{BeyondVAR} = E\left\{\text{Loss} - \text{VAR} / \text{Loss} > \text{VAR}\right\} \approx \frac{\xi}{1 - \xi}\text{VAR} \,(2)$$

It is then possible to fit the power-law tail of the return distribution of the swap with the help of a Hill estimator. This number is inferred from real data, with no adjustable parameter. Figure B shows the agreement of the Pareto and empirical cumulative distributions beyond the threshold $u_0 = -0.7\%$. The main difference between both marginal laws is outlined on Figure C: while the best-fit log-normal distribution gives more weight to small WTI daily returns, it dramatically understates the frequency of extreme events, and hence the probability of an extreme loss for the long position in the swap.

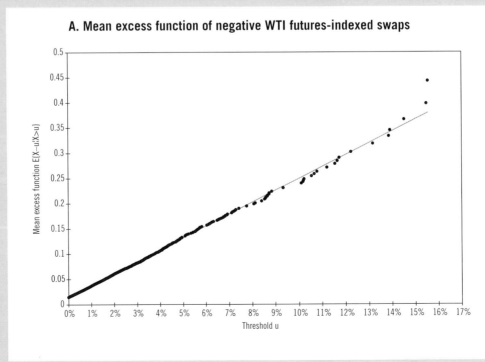

A. Mean excess function of negative WTI futures-indexed swaps

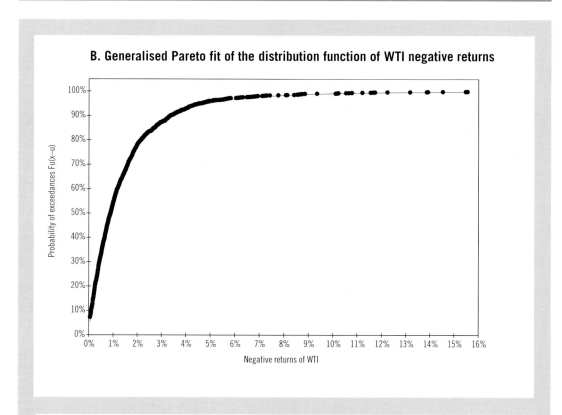

B. Generalised Pareto fit of the distribution function of WTI negative returns

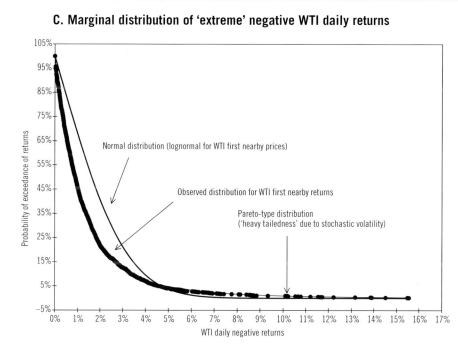

C. Marginal distribution of 'extreme' negative WTI daily returns

Another question one might ask is: "how frequently do extreme returns occur on the WTI futures market?" The answer will obviously depend on the threshold u used to define risk aversion. An extreme return of −5.0% will be much less likely than a return of −0.7%. Intuitively, the average of the time between two consecutive "catastrophes" should be roughly inversely proportional to the probability of occurrence of the threshold u, which can be read directly on Figure B. According to EVT, the overall distribution of inter-arrival times of extreme returns should be a Poisson process. Figure D compares the empirical distribution of recurrence times of returns less than −0.7% and the theoretical distribution inferred from the above argument.[1] These conclusions would be qualitatively unaffected if the length of the time series was reduced.

In short, empirical data show that:

❑ the number of exceedances of a high threshold for negative daily returns of the WTI follows a Poisson process;

❑ excesses over high thresholds can be modelled by means of a Pareto distribution;

❑ an appropriate value of the high threshold can be found by plotting the empirical mean excess function.

Other results can be obtained as well. For instance, the maximum daily loss over a longer time horizon (eg 30 business days) can be inferred from the mathematical fact that the maximum of a Poisson number of excesses over a high threshold is a Generalised Extreme Value Distribution, whose parametric form is known.[2]

It should also be noted that EVT has far reaching implications in the energy markets. First, power-law behaviour is not restricted to swaps written on futures, whose traded underlying changes as the prompt contract expires and which are thus naturally liable to display price jumps. Many OTC markets, such as gas oil, fuel oil or natural gas, follow similar patterns. Second, there are two main arguments explaining why energy time series have "fat tails": they can either be seen as a reflection of the stochastic nature of volatility, or as an inherent feature of distributions of returns caused by external shocks which are themselves Poisson distributed. For example, extreme power or gas demands usually happen to coincide with outages in transmission and power generation/gas production, thus causing price spikes when the

market is tight. EVT is a particularly useful tool to describe the "floor-reverting" process of electricity prices which arises from the non-storability of power and the exponential increase of the marginal cost of generation (in $/MWh).

Finally, it is generally possible to characterise a market by means of its power-law exponent. New or inherently unstable markets have a greater exponent ξ than mature markets. When ξ is less than 1/3, which is the case for most of futures, volatility is stochastic but can still be safely defined (and traded). For example, "catastrophes" happen more frequently on prompt futures contracts than on back months but can still be mastered by traders for hedging purposes (the market does not "gap" so often and losses incurred in dynamic hedging of positions are limited). At the other end of the spectrum, markets where replication is impossible (or at least difficult for physical reasons) have an exponent ξ greater than 1. In such a case, volatility is ill-defined and writing an option on the underlying asset is equivalent to selling a reinsurance contract[3] and turns out to be very risky indeed. The flexibility mechanism operated by Transco for short-term natural gas sales in the UK is a good example of this last category.

1 The relevance of this distribution has been checked with a χ^2 test with 10 degrees of freedom, showing a probability of 43% to make a mistake if the Poisson assumption is rejected.
2 Embrechts, Paul, Claudia Klüppelberg and Thomas Mikosch, 1997, *Modelling Extremal Events*, , Applications of Mathematics, Springer, Berlin
3 Geman, H., 1994, "Pricing Cat Calls", *Risk*, 7 (September), pp. 86–9.

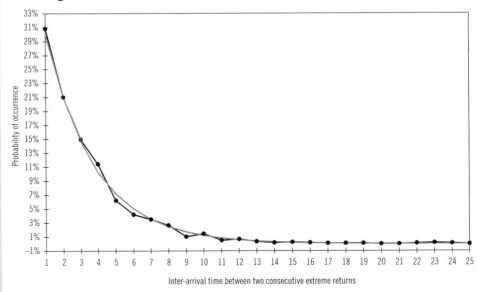

D. Poisson distribution of waiting times between two consecutive extreme negative returns

energy supplies in € and may therefore be highly sensitive to any lack of correlation between currencies, and between the currency markets and the oil markets. It should also be remembered that market behaviour is often driven by local considerations. For example, the demand in Germany for winter storage is largely related to the € price per tonne of heating oil.

The main market risks affecting oil price risk management, including exchange rate risk, are presented together in Figure 4. However, even in the case of a pure back-to-back or a perfect hedge, the different actors in the physical oil and derivatives markets are subject to credit, counterparty and contract (cc&c) risks:

❑ credit risk: credit risk expresses the exposure of forward cash-flows and deferred payments to market risks. It must be considered with regard to: the risk components of the underlying index (for example, volatility, correlation, liquidity); the maturity and type of the instrument (for example, short-term versus long-term, buying versus selling, swap versus option); and the relative level of the market;

❑ counterparty risk: credit risk must be further specified in the light of a counterparty's ability to fulfil its obligations and contractual commitments. A measure of counterparty risk is obtained from internal and credit rating analyses of the client's creditworthiness; most traders then allot to each counterparty a set "credit line" (which may, or may not, take into account the counterparty's ability to deliver physically in the event of financial difficulties);

❑ contract risk: residual exposure of a balanced portfolio to changes in, for example, the regulation of the market, taxation rules, or changes in the indexes.

These risks are very much inter-related, and assessing them will require the opinions of credit, legal and trading managers; they will need to take into account the trading habits and the nature of any potential client or counterparty. For example, some oil companies with existing relationships in the physical markets may value each other for regularity and performance in physical trading, rather than solely relying on assets-related credit rating; this tends to accelerate authorisations in the case of short-term deals.

The estimates of the value of derivative transactions at risk to "cc&c" are usually made using proprietary models. These are based on historical and market parameters, on the structure and maturity of instruments (swaps and options do not yield similar credit exposures) and on the possibility for risk reduction, diversification and

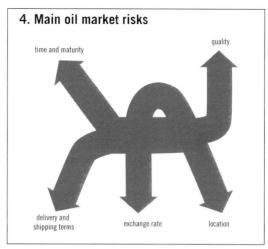

4. Main oil market risks

time and maturity
quality
delivery and shipping terms
exchange rate
location

netting of positions. There have been advances in the evaluation and trading of credit risk during the past few years. VAR methods have been successfully applied to better assess the distribution of credit events and the relationship they bear with market risk. An obvious example is that of a large oil consumer having swapped a significant part of its physical exposure during a prolonged bear market: while the mark-to-market of its paper position may show a heavy opportunity loss, its balance sheet may at the same time be improved by hefty profits on its overall procurement budget.

Finally, we should stress the importance, and difficulty, of gaining accurate information when trading in the over-the-counter energy markets. The importance of information to the efficiency of markets is well known, but the fact is that the over-the-counter oil markets, either physical, forward or derivatives, are characterised by a very poor visibility. Transactions are often private and confidential, and may be negotiated instantaneously or over the course of a few months at board or state level. Only large participants are able to get reliable and, more or less, complete information. For example, little is known about the deals made between some banks and their captive clientele, and this has sometimes led to an underestimate of this sector of the derivative market. Conversely, some traders tend to exaggerate the number and quantity of their deals. Even public exchanges, despite their legal obligations, sometimes fail to provide their regulatory bodies with enough visibility and information on the behaviour of some large traders.

This lack of transparency impairs market efficiency, and creates apparent arbitrage opportunities. But converting these apparent opportunities into cash profits requires a careful appraisal of fundamental market factors, and we will focus on these in the following sections.

STRATEGIES FOR OPTIMISING REFINING ACTIVITIES

For trading and risk management purposes, a refinery is often compared to a set of black boxes (or units) with a series of flows, and production flexibilities[1] and constraints (Figure A). Cracks spreads represent the refiner's risk/reward coefficient for each product; in aggregate they comprise the refinery margin.

One way for a refiner to protect the profitability of its activity is to fix the global refinery margin for some future period. The refiner is naturally short on crude and long on products (the net position is a short one, due to losses, and there thus remains an absolute price risk on crude oil). The index used in the margin swap is therefore the difference between the weighted sum of products and the value of a crude reference (usually dated Brent, WTI, Dubai or Tapis). The product slates of different crude oils can be varied within a refinery by adjusting the severity of the processing and by upgrading various proportions of intermediate products.[2] Selling a global margin swap consists of selling an index (basket of products: crude) at a fixed price, based on refinery yields, and buying back at a floating price the average value of the index over a contractual period. Margin swaps are sometimes complemented with double up options, giving the right to double the volume involved at buyer's or seller's convenience.

When the fixed margin is greater than the cost of refining crude, including some financing elements, the refiner may enter an arbitrage with minimum risk and almost certain return: the "cash-and-refine" arbitrage is similar to the "cash-and-carry" arbitrage described in Panel 4, though it is more complex to initiate. If a yearly refinery hedge is considered, yields are adjusted to both winter and summer seasons. Such strategies may also be used to hedge processing agreements, and they do not preclude traders or refiners from profiting from physical and operational opportunities. For example, when hedging using an average value the hedger can optimise product delivery by

A. A trader's view of a refinery

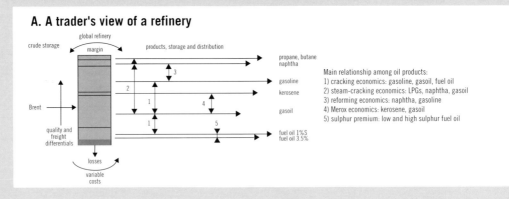

Main relationship among oil products:
1) cracking economics: gasoline, gasoil, fuel oil
2) steam-cracking economics: LPGs, naphtha, gasoil
3) reforming economics: naphtha, gasoline
4) Merox economics: kerosene, gasoil
5) sulphur premium: low and high sulphur fuel oil

Derivatives, market phenomena and correlations investigated

LOCATIONAL RISKS AND FUNDAMENTALS
When trading worldwide and on all possible indexes – Platt's assessments, for instance – it is dangerous to ignore the fundamentals of the oil industry and world economy, or the effect of the transfer mechanisms between the different consuming centres.

For example, until the economic crisis of 1997–98, Asia had been expected to generate three-quarters of the growth in the global demand for oil up to the year 2000. Since then, overall demand assessments have been continually reduced. Indeed, after the currency turmoil, many local oil companies, especially in China, have decided to husband their foreign exchange by drawing down stocks and, in turn, reducing oil imports. Futhermore, the Russian crisis of the summer 1998 and the prospect of Russia being unable to service fully its external debt have forced the Russian government to maximise oil exports to raise desperately needed hard currency and tax revenues. Russia's output will depend in the near future on the interplay between a lack of investment in its E&P sector, especially for higher cost oil fields, and the incentive to maximise exports given by the recent currency devaluation.

Any trader must also integrate fundamental elements, especially when measuring basis risk between similar grades. Geographical spreads usually reflect shipping terms and the different state of equilibrium obtaining in each market. A

selecting the most appropriate delivery dates.

Refinery risk management must also integrate a time dimension, first because of storage, and also because of the time required to transform crude into the refined product. Each product has its own price term structure, which means that refiner hedging is characteristically a multi-dimensional problem. The hedging strategy needs to be customised to the individual refiner's accounting and valuation procedures, and to the various market conditions: refinery margins, crack spreads, product and quality spreads, crude and product time-spreads.

In fact, refiners may consider locking-in individual crack-spreads as well as their overall margin. This strategy tends to be adopted by refiners who are accustomed to the paper markets, and it may offer advantages if one product has a large contribution to the refinery margin. (Over the medium term, in particular, this strategy may outperform a hedge on the overall margin.) When choosing which products to hedge, refiners have to analyse the relative contribution of each product to the refinery margin. Sophisticated refiners tend to manage the distribution of their forward overall margin with a VAR-like methodology and to hedge the outright price risk on crude losses separately.

Options on industrial or crack spreads can also prove useful to refiners. Depending on market conditions, a refiner could gain a satisfactory cash premium by selling an option on the gas oil crack spread, and thus facilitating cashflow. From the derivatives provider's viewpoint, the difficulty with spread options is that their price is critically depen-

dent on the implied correlation between product and crude, which is rarely quoted as such. For a trader with a processing contract, this premium could finance part of the processing fee. Moreover, any flexibility or constraint on the refining system may be valued and interpreted as an option or as a combination of options. For example, it is possible to increase or decrease the utilisation rate of some refinery production units. A truly sophisticated hedging programme would attempt to integrate such elements into a global risk management programme.

One final area of refinery risk management is the use of paper instruments to ensure physical delivery or distribution. On the supply side, refiners are sometimes willing to enter medium- to long-term crude oil swaps, or to use options, in order to gain a guaranteed paper access to crude. Such hedges provide financial security while enabling the refiner to optimise its supply channels.

On the distribution side, refiners and integrated oil companies may design marketing strategies which combine physical deliveries to the factory gate with derivatives that offer fixed prices (or price collars, etc).

1 This flexibility manifests itself in the ability to change crude types at short notice, to take intermediate feedstocks when they are available, for example vacuum gas oil, to meet changing proportions of products (often called "cut of the barrel") and to make new and modified products when the price is right and ship them quickly by the means the customer wants. In a refinery, flexibility comes from a combination of three elements :
❑ flexibility of the processing units
❑ flexibility of the off-plot facilities, such as tankage, blending facilities, road and rail loading, barge and shipping facilities
❑ the flexibility of organisation to use the facilities to their best advantage.

2 Average yields of different crudes are nevertheless published by oil journals and information services and provide a fair assessment of refinery margins.

colder-than-normal period in the United States may have a stronger-than-normal impact on prices, depending on the level of readily available stocks. Such local disruptions usually disconnect the US market from the European markets and, subsequently, create opportunities for moving heating oil or fuel oil cargoes to the East Coast.

Besides the fundamentals, one must remember that oil markets are not homogeneous worldwide and are subject to different pricing principles and environments. In the Asia Pacific region, price or import controls on oil products have been renewed in the most severely damaged countries, while others have slowed down the rate of liberalisation of their economies.

Even in the United States, which is considered to have a highly open market, environmental reg-

ulations, import taxes and other constraints (such as logistics) vary greatly within the country. While most American refiners already supplying reformulated gasoline have upgraded their plants to comply with the phase II specifications of year 2000, this move has only been gradually implemented from state to state.

Moreover, the different types of participants in the market behave quite differently from region to region. Typically, producer hedging is more present in the United States and, to a lesser extent, in the North Sea, than it is in other countries. Meanwhile, hedging for financial purposes is growing strongly in the Asia Pacific region. Some end-user groups may rely heavily on specific markets and introduce demand-led distortions: for example, European utilities strongly influence both high and low sulphur fuel oil, while the chemical industry focuses on naphtha.

In crude oil markets, as will be seen below, the WTI-Brent spread is the leading indicator. The price relationship is either implicit, both products being international markers that sometimes compete in the same refining area (mainly the Gulf Coast), or explicit, for example through EFPs and the delivery procedures of the Nymex Light Sweet Crude Oil (WTI) contract. In the latter case, some Brent-related crudes may be substituted for WTI, which creates arbitrage opportunities, though these are not easily or frequently achievable.

Econometrics is a useful tool for investigating cross-correlations, basis and locational risks. Various mathematical techniques exist to distinguish market trends, market cycles and other fundamental characteristics from purely random walks. Once non-random behaviour is identified, residual risks contained in serial noise may then be evaluated using a more or less modified mean-variance approach. But traders cannot take decisions and market positions on the basis of statistics alone; they must interpret such patterns in light of their own analysis and information, their portfolio orientation and their market expectations. There are so many potentially influential factors, and these are so unstable in their relationship, that any formal model of a given trading situation would be too complex, and too quickly disconnected from trading reality, to be of any use.

MODELLING TERM STRUCTURE AND THE ROLE OF STORAGE

Term structure risks arise from the deformations of forward curves of crude oil or refined products. For example, being long two futures contracts of maturity n, while simultaneously being

short one contract of maturity (n−1) and one contract of maturity (n + 1), is a direct bet on the *curvature* of the price curve rather than its absolute level. Similarly, a five-year swap on Brent could be hedged on the IPE futures market; however, contracts are traded up to 36 months, and around 80% of both volume and open interest (in other words, liquidity) are concentrated in the first three maturities, so the resulting time spread risks must be taken into account and managed. The trader will have to "roll over" its position as forward maturities start to be quoted.

Let us now investigate term structure models and related issues in the context of both physical and paper (futures and derivatives) oil markets. The notions of price term structure and convenience yield express the time component in the evaluation of crudes and products that we identified in our introduction as such a crucial factor in the energy markets. The traditional hypothesis is that the price for future delivery should reflect, on the one hand, the cost of financing and carrying physicals until the maturity date (see Panel 4) and, on the other hand, the aggregated expectations of economic agents about future oil prices. Seasonal or trend factors are usually considered as market expectations.

The theories of storage and of convenience yield provide additional insight on backwardation phenomena and on the instability of the term structure over time (Figure 5). Keynes first introduced the theory of normal backwardation, which implies that hedgers are net sellers in the medium-term market and need to pay a premium to speculators oriented toward the shorter term. Consequently, spot prices may be higher than forward prices. However, the theory is not completely descriptive of market facts for the following reasons.

❏ There is no real evidence of a downward bias in the pricing of futures.

❏ Hedgers may be either net forward buyers or sellers, or indeterminate. For example, at the end of 1998, prices had reached a 20-year historical low. Despite low absolute levels, to gain benefit from the prevailing contango, many producers, pressed by their banks, decided to sell their production forward in case of a prolonged depression. The effect was a tightening of the term structure. Figure 6 plots the deformations of the WTI forward curve (the 1st and 27th contracts are kept "attached" to their absolute price levels): as the oil price was on the downside, the stiffness of the curve appears to have increased in 1998, before regaining some curvature, and

5. Forward curves of Nymex WTI light sweet crude

finally entering a new backwardation phase at the beginning of 1999. At the same time, forward prices for back months, which had evolved in parallel for many months, started to lose that degree of correlation and fluctuate independently.

Well before that, at the end of 1993, prices had reached a five-year low and, despite the prevailing contango, many end-users had entered the market to hedge forward requirements at attractive absolute prices. In order to absorb such volumes, the forward curve adjusted itself into a significantly higher contango. Hedgers, being mostly net buyers in the swap markets, amplified the contango resulting from a depressed spot market and developed a normal contango situation. This, of course, is the reverse of the situation described by Keynes, and shows that perceived similar situations can lead to opposite forward curve deformations.

❏ Traders who cover the hedging needs of exposed clients may not be speculating on their behalf, but looking for portfolio diversification or partial covering of financial exposure to inflation. For example, portfolio managers took some preventive positions in oil markets during the Gulf crisis in order to anticipate any medium-term rise in the Consumer Price Index. In other words, trading in oil markets may have other objectives than strict hedging of physical risks or wild speculation.

In fact, short- to medium-term effects related to physical supply and demand imbalances must be taken into account. The modern theory of term structure introduces the "convenience yield", the yield which "accrues to the owner of the physical commodity but not to the owner of a contract for future delivery" (Brennan, 1989). On the industrial user side, the explicit purpose of derivative contracts is indeed to keep plants running. Factories seek to minimise their cost of production by avoiding the cost of shutting down and restarting the plant due to high prices or lack of available supplies. In other words, it is sometimes better to have the commodity at hand rather than a paper claim. Backwardation is the premium paid for earlier rather than later availability, for instance, to ensure that the planned refining operating schedule is not disrupted. In essence, normal backwardation represents the cost of holding minimum operating stocks in a just-in-time delivery environment.

Backwardation further expresses the risk of rupture or bottle-necking in the logistical chain from production to consumption. It may be linked to specific market issues like the 1989–90

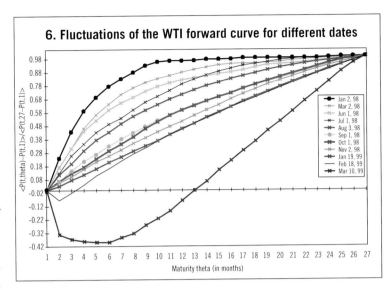

6. Fluctuations of the WTI forward curve for different dates

winter squeeze in US heating oil markets, or to general uncertainties such as the recurrent crises in the Gulf region or in Russia.

Derivatives providers are interested in developing a truly representative theory of term structure so that they can use this to guide their tactics in pricing and hedging – especially for long-term OTC transactions. The difficulty in modelling commodity prices is in specifically assessing the value that the commodity generates for the user by having it on hand as it needs it, since this value is user-specific. The aggregated concept, the convenience yield, may prove useful, for it may be modelled as a source of randomness. Intuitively, since it is a measure of the balance between the available supply and the existing demand, whose long-term equilibrium is expressed in back months prices, the convenience yield will depend on the difference between spot and forward prices. Tied to this intuition is the fact that the convenience yield appears to diminish with increasing forward price expirations.

Arbitrage relationships along the forward curve provide the mathematical background to compute a flexible and maturity-dependent form of marginal convenience yield. Since the convenience yield is extremely sensitive to short-term factors, and less so to longer-term factors, the way in which the convenience yield is absorbed over time must, ideally, be incorporated into hedging strategies. (In the very long term, other economic elements, such as the marginal cost of renewable resources or of competing energies, must also be considered, see Panel 5 for a very simplified description of those "fundamentals".)

In fact, the cost or benefit of rolling positions forward is directly dependent on movements in

PANEL 4

CONTANGO AND THE CASH-AND-CARRY ARBITRAGE

When analysing the term structure of futures and swap prices, it is important to consider the cost of carrying the commodity, especially in contango situations. If the degree of contango exceeds the carrying and financing costs of storage, then low-risk but profitable transactions (known as "cash-and-carry" arbitrages) may be entered into (Figure A). The trader buys the crude or oil product, and stores it, while at the same time selling futures or swaps of a given maturity and an equivalent quantity. The difference between the spot and the forward prices must cover the cost of financing and holding oil during the period of storage.

Generally speaking, the arbitrage is initiated whenever F(T) – Spot > r + c. Its horizon should be chosen in order to take full advantage of the market contango. At maturity, the paper settlement usually offsets the proceeds from the release of stocks: apart from the convergence process between the paper and physical prices, all the financial implications of the deal are transparent when the deal is executed. It should be noted that

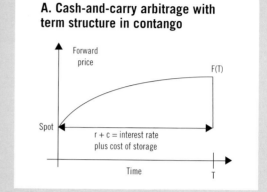

A. Cash-and-carry arbitrage with term structure in contango

cash-and-carry arbitrage cannot be implemented when the commodity is not storable, as is the case for electricity. New arbitrage mechanisms then have to be found out which involve processing of the marginal fuel in the power stack together with weather derivatives.

Let us develop a practical example, based on market gasoil prices for August 6, 1998 (Figure B).

In the example, the spot price of kerosene is $118.25/ton, while the material trades at a pre-

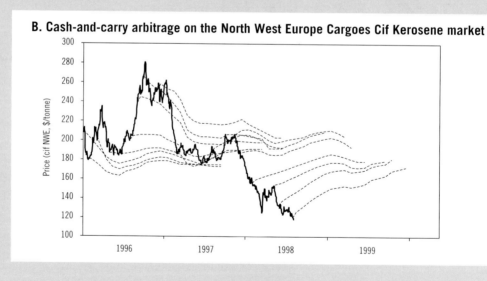

B. Cash-and-carry arbitrage on the North West Europe Cargoes Cif Kerosene market

the term structure of prices. In other words, a volumetric hedge of a long-dated position in the shorter term may cover large absolute price moves (parallel shifts), but it will not provide cover for changes in time-spreads. Maturity exposures require a kind of dynamic hedging that is based on two related concepts:
❑ the curvature of the forward price function; and
❑ volatility transfers and kinetics.

Using a term structure model of the kind described above, and making use of computed

evaluations, traders should be able to trade on bid and offer prices, using a cost function. This function is sometimes intuitive, and sometimes partly modelled; it is designed to take account of liquidity risk and the way in which certain hypotheses basic to the model may be violated over time.

In oil markets, the ability to price and hedge term structure risks, in relation to volatility surfaces, represents an important part of the value added by derivatives providers. It clearly remains the most technical element of trading, at the

C. The relationship between the shape of the forward curve and the level of stocks

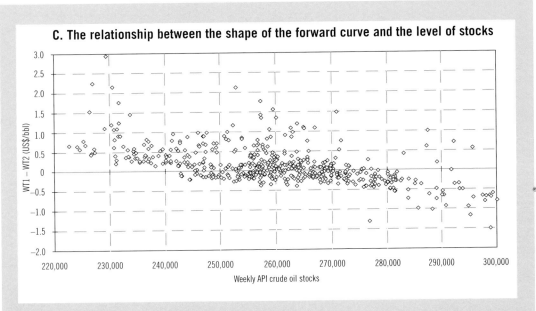

mium of $17.25/tonne for October 1998. Since storage costs amount to $2.5/tonne per month and the financing costs to roughly $1.75/tonne over the whole period, a profitable arbitrage can be set up for a profit of (17.25 − 7.50 − 1.75) = $8.00/tonne. Such operations resulted in a flattening of the forward curve between August and October in the following days, as traders exhausted the arbitrage window, buying jet on the spot and selling it forward.

Indeed, because of the opportunity for profit arising from excessive contango situations, one would expect that the size of contango should be limited to cash-and-carry costs (including financing costs). It is therefore not surprising to find a correlation of around 70% between time-spreads and stock levels during contango periods (Figure C).

But this theoretical limit is not always precisely representative of market realities. In particular:
❑ in reality, the marginal cost of storage is far from uniform for all actors;
❑ storage capacities may simply be full, with none left to initiate further cash-and-carry arbi-

trages;
❑ the premium between physical and paper prices may also impact on the economics;
❑ oil companies have an increasingly dynamic and market-oriented approach to stock valorisation and hedging – a phenomenon which must be taken into account.

The reverse of the cash-and-carry arbitrage is not workable, as there is no loan market for oil. Moreover, producing countries or integrated companies are often reluctant to release stocks when an exceptional backwardation occurs because of the high risk this strategy entails. (A large backwardation can rarely be characterised at the time as "exceptional" because it reflects unpredictable factors.)

As a result, unlike contango situations, there is no theoretical limit to the backwardation phenomenon – and the higher it is, the more unstable it becomes. Even so, some financial techniques, such as the monetisation of working or compulsory stocks, may take limited advantage of specific backwardation situations.

frontier of general market and storage theories – and, indeed, of financial mathematics.

INDUSTRIAL SPREADS AND THE ROLE OF REFINING

For convenience, we will refer here to crack, product and quality spreads as industrial spreads. These are another piece in the oil puzzle and, as summarised below, have a substantial impact on the profit and loss accounts of many participants in the market:
❑ Refiners are subject to variation in the sum

price of their products relative to that of crude oil; this variation is commonly referred to as a crack spread. Aside from fundamental factors, such as overall capacity and demand for oil products, crack spreads are the most important determinant of refiner revenues. Hedging refinery margins through the exchange and over-the-counter markets has thus become an established part of the corporate strategy of refiners.
❑ End-users and petrochemical companies may have large risks related to industrial spreads. For example, utilities that are capable of burning

THE ECONOMIC FUNDAMENTALS OF THE CRUDE OIL MARKETS

The short-term equilibrium of the oil market (production and consumption capacities are considered to be fixed) can be inferred from Figure A below. The supply curve is the histogram of total production costs for the existing oil fields and displays economic rents due to the relative ease of extraction of crude oil and the proximity to refining centers (the basic marginal cost of Middle East oil production is approximately $2/bbl, compared to $11/bbl in Canada and the North Sea, and $14/bbl in Siberia). Neither supply or demand are particularly responsive to changes in price in the short run. In some of its uses, such as transportation, oil still has no effective substitute. Moreover, since oil demand usually magnifies economic growth, the vertical curve on Figure A is liable to move violently to the left or to the right over the course of a few months time.

In a purely competitive market, when production or transportation capacities are close to saturation and demand soars, oil prices would need to reach a fairly high level before return forces became effective. At the onset, a price hike is self-realising as it triggers a cautionary demand for stocks, which in turn enhances the original imbalance. Return forces include substitution to coal or natural gas in power stations, a marginal increase in production for wells with flexibility in supply volumes or public measures for energy conservation. Price hikes are a strong incentive to invest in new production facilities and so cannot be sustained indefinitely. Because of the time required to put new fields on stream, they usually result in an over-capacity in the E&P sector one to two years later.

Inversely, when production exceeds consumption, stocks usually build up and the situation may degenerate into a price war if, in the absence of agreement between producing countries, any one of them tries to expand its market share at the expense of the others. Since the oil industry is capital-intensive, if the market were completely free, reductions in output should happen only when prices fall below the operating costs of marginal units. When this level is reached, exploration programmes are scaled down, wells are ultimately shut in and the demand side benefits from substitution in favour of oil.

In a competitive market, prices should fluctuate wildly between an upper and a lower zone whose limits are determined by purely economic constraints (they have been variously estimated at $8/bbl and $30/bbl respectively).

However, this is not quite the case. The Middle East contains two-thirds of the world's proven reserves and it produces approximately a third of total consumption. Most importantly, production is significantly cheaper and more flexible in this

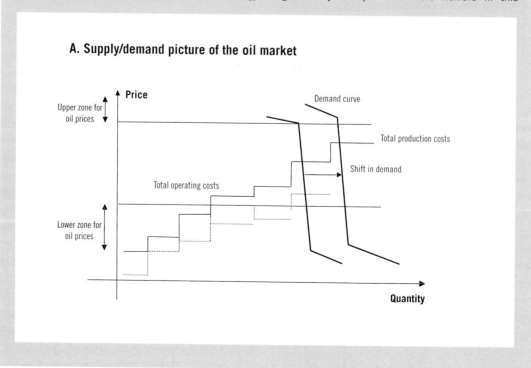

A. Supply/demand picture of the oil market

B. A dynamic view of the supply/demand equilibrium in OPEC and non-OPEC countries

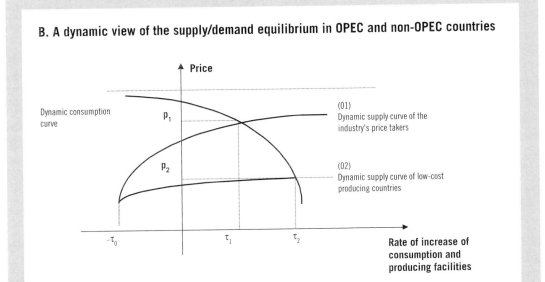

region than almost anywhere else in the world. This allows the main producers (Saudi Arabia, Iran, UAE, Iraq, Kuwait, etc) to operate "swing capacities" that can be closed well before prices drop below the variable costs of marginal units, and reactivated when demand suddenly peaks. Since such a strategy has an obvious cost (stopping facilities when they could still be operated at a profit), there must be a collective reward for its implementation. This reward is the extra profits gained by low-cost producing countries when they maintain the oil price at above "a purely competitive level" (at which level owners of the *best* oil fields would enjoy only small rents as compared to owners of *good* oil fields).

However, as the recent past has shown, OPEC is no longer able to prop up oil prices indefinitely. Due to advances in geology and drilling techniques, the cost of finding and developing new reserves outside the Middle East has been significantly reduced over the past 20 years. As a result, price takers in the industry (international oil companies and minor to medium-size producing countries) have lowered the minimum level at which it is economically sensible for them to develop new reserves. The resulting situation is summarised in Figure B above.

The "dynamic consumption curve" relates the rate of increase of worldwide consumption to the long-term oil price: it shifts to the right when economic growth increases; it is bounded upward by the price of substitutes and thus becomes flatter when alternative technologies find their way to the market. The "dynamic supply curve" (02) gives the rate of increase of oil output at a given market

price if low-cost producing countries decide to satisfy consumption increments entirely on their own, without any agreement between them. The "dynamic supply curve" (01) is identical to (02), except that it assumes that new developments are carried out only by means of price takers' reserves.

This defines an economic range of prices where low-cost producing countries can attempt to stabilise the market price of oil by varying the development rate of their own reserves. The floor of this range would be reached only if low-cost participants were acting on a purely competitive basis; below this level, an oil shock would be inevitable. On the contrary, if they tried to impose a market price above the ceiling of the range, new developments in the oil industry would only take place in the price takers' reserves and OPEC's market share would steadily decrease. Various studies have estimated these boundaries at $5/bbl and $25/bbl respectively.

From an economic standpoint, there is thus an "equilibrium range" wherein political factors can durably exert their influence on oil prices (by political factors, we mean factors that have no immediate monetary translation, ie stability in the Middle East, security of supply of importing countries, pace of development of the Gulf States). These "secondary factors" can themselves contribute to narrow the variation range of oil prices. Before 1998, it had long been widely accepted that a "political floor" at $15/bbl was a good compromise between the oil producing countries' willingness to increase their revenues and the importing countries' reluctance to aggravate their exposure to a political disruption of their source of supply.

natural gas or fuel oil can quickly alter their policies according to relative or spread values. For chemical industries, the economics of steam-cracking are mostly based on the relative prices of naphtha, gasoil and LPGs, and then on the price differential from naphtha to ethylene and propylene. Even companies that are not very flexible with regard to feedstocks must consider product spreads, as competitors may take advantage of them.

❑ In the case of hedgers, industrial spreads arise out of the way in which they assume residual risk. For example, European shipping companies willing to hedge their heavy fuel oil budget using IPE Brent futures would bear a large basis risk (as the correlation between fuel oil and crude oil is typically loose, due to substitution effects), that is, the risk of variation in the price difference between the physical index and the hedging index. If, instead, they purchase cover by means of fuel oil swaps and options, then they effectively transfer this basis risk to the derivatives provider.

The underlying indexes of industrial spreads are characterised by high volatilities and unstable correlations. Just like locational risks, industrial spreads are strongly dependent on fundamentals, for example liquidity, supply and demand, and refining economics.

Fuel oil, for example, is manufactured in two distinct forms: "straight run" and "cracked". Straight run fuel oil is the product of atmospheric distillation and is typically sold as a feedstock to refiners who have unused vacuum distillation and cracking capacity and can therefore upgrade it into more valuable gasoline and gas oil. Cracked fuel oil is what is left after upgrading and is usually less variable than straight run fuel oil; it is burnt in power stations or used for bunkers and its price depends primarily on its sulphur and

metals content, viscosity and specific gravity. In northwest Europe, the premium between both fuels is reported under the Russian grade E4[5], which acts as a market for transactions involving different viscosities. As can be seen from Figure 7, the industrial processing of straight run fuel oil has direct implications for its price: the time series of straight run fuel oil is indeed best replicated by a basket of 80% high sulphur fuel oil and 20% of gas oil 0.2% S[2] – less a premium that is seven times less volatile than the basket itself in absolute terms. In much the same way, vacuum gasoil, which is used as a feedstock for catalytic cracking and is partially converted into gasoline, can be replicated using a basket of fuel oil, gas oil and gasoline. Straight run and cracked markets for fuel oil can occasionally converge when high refinery runs mean that the straight run market is over supplied; in such a case, poorer quality grades are forced onto the oil burning market, while blenders add straight run to their cracked pool in order to reduce its viscosity.

Moreover, term structures are usually not homogeneous on both indexes of a given industrial spread. Gasoil cracks integrate seasonal factors specific to gasoil, and not those specific to Brent, as can be checked by referring to Figure 7. It can happen that the fuel oil markets are in contango, while the crude oil market is in backwardation.

It is interesting to see how correlations between quite different indexes tend to vary according to the time-horizon. For back maturities, the correlation between illiquid products, such as naphtha, and crude oil converges to 1 and the price of naphtha fluctuates around the price set by the conversion factor from tonnes to barrels. Conversely, correlations between similar indexes for different months tend to be both higher and more stable.

The observation above demonstrates that simple, or even robust, statistics are neither sufficient nor adequate to reveal and model the behaviour of term structures. They may shed light on physical and very short-term risks, but they are insufficient for the dynamic management of derivatives.

For refiners, the term structure of crack spreads is also an important indicator of forward profitability and a factor when taking strategic decisions. In particular, an investment for an upgrade or a new unit may be combined with the medium-term hedging of crack spreads or refinery margins. Panel 3 examines hedging strategies for refiners in more detail.

7. Crack gas oil versus Brent on IPE futures

The future: market developments and marketing strategies

The oil derivative markets have developed around two complementary axes: hedging the oil price exposures of large companies, and the financing operations of the oil industry. Both of these have generated rapid growth for the OTC energy derivatives industry. For the last ten years, the OTC market has also fuelled much of the growth in liquidity in the exchanges, especially for back-month trading. Below, we discuss some developments in the markets for crude oil, and oil products.

CRUDE OIL

The physical crude market is the foundation of the oil market. Prices of crude are generally quoted free on board (fob) at their loading port. Most physical crude oil is priced as a differential to an actively traded futures or forward market. Instead of buyer and seller agreeing an absolute price for the cargo of crude oil, they agree a floating price, which is generally an average of several days around the bill of lading date (when the ship loads the oil). Most oil traded in Europe and many West African crudes, for example, are priced against Brent while almost all crude exported to the US, or traded within it, is priced against Nymex futures. In the short term, the crude oil market is the trendsetter for the other energy markets; it is highly sensitive to OPEC rhetoric, to the general economic environment and to political events or uncertainties.

It is the composition and structure of the underlying physical Brent market that accounts for much of its importance. The upstream tax regulations in the UK give integrated companies producing oil an incentive to trade at arm's length in order to establish an independent and market-related price. As a result, there is always a large amount of oil available to the market, thus guaranteeing the market's liquidity. Since the blend can be traded to within a few days of physical delivery, the Brent market fills an essential gap in the term structure of the world oil market by providing a price reference over a period of one to two months ahead. Finally, because North Sea crudes are generally light and sweet, they are attractive to any refiner if the price is right.

The importance of the physical oil market in the North Sea has encouraged the development of active and liquid paper markets. WTI, on the other hand, is the leading benchmark for the US domestic crude market and the physical underlying of the deepest commodity futures market in the world. Unlike the North Sea, virtually every barrel of US domestic crude, with the exception of Alaskan North Slope (ANS), is traded, priced and transported by pipeline rather than on waterborne tankers and barges.

The main instruments of the crude oil market are futures, forwards or swaps based on WTI and Brent indexes. Cargoes of Brent blend crude oil are traded on an active forward market, so that one cargo may change hands many times before it is finally collected from Sullom Voe, its loading terminal. A forward contract requires the seller to give the buyer 15 days' notice of physical lifting dates. Once a cargo has been nominated, it is known as a "dated cargo", and specific loading dates are attached to it. Many types of physical crude oil are priced against dated Brent. Flat price risks are hedged using IPE Brent contracts and the differentials between dated Brent and the first future contract are traded through "contracts for differences" (CFDs). CFDs normally refer to calendar weeks; this means that the unwinding of these swaps takes place using Platt's quotations for the relevant Monday to Friday period.[6]

Crude oil is also the index of choice for most arbitrageurs and investment funds, since it is by far the most liquid of all energy markets. The demand generated by investment strategists for derivative funds has been growing at an impressive pace in terms of variety and volume. It is now widely acknowledged that short-term oil and natural gas futures prices are heavily affected by the trading decisions of large financial entities, including Wall Street investment banks and hedge funds. Investment transactions, which can be either private placements or public offerings such as warrants, allow financiers to assume trading positions that are indexed to oil without the bother and risk of directly managing a commodities desk. Because of their liquidity, and hence the relatively low-cost dynamic hedging they allow, futures markets for crude oil have seen the creation of many financial structured products of increasing complexity: range swaps, index-amortising swaps, corridors, etc. This activity, however, requires the development of specific distribution channels that offer access to institutional, retail and private clients (ie purchasers who are interested in oil more as an investment vehicle than as an underlying physical risk). The driving force behind any offering of structured product is investor demand, which is itself triggered by specific market configurations and proprietary views.

The market in long-term price management for financing purposes is dominated by natural gas (as described in the next chapter) and crude oil. The OTC market contracts with maturities of as long as 10 years, but specific risks are attached to such transactions. Positions may have to be "rolled over" on the longest available terms. Physical considerations have to be taken into account as well. For example, the production of both Brent and WTI is expected to decline over the years, and therefore they may become less effective as representative markers; in particular, lower production rates might make prices easier to manipulate. The Brent and Ninian fields have already been mixed, with a limited loss of quality, to form Brent Blend. However, some traders (and even Saudi Arabia) are pushing for the replacement of Brent by Forties which has a large ownership structure involving 40 companies and whose production has been rising sharply as new fields such as Scott and Nelson have been brought into the blend. In the case of WTI, there is still no real alternative crude. Companies with very long-term derivatives indexed on WTI and Brent may have to negotiate on fallback indexes, and quality differentials, or make use of early termination clauses.

OIL PRODUCTS

No refiner or marketer is really able to operate a completely balanced system and the primary function of the physical products market is to redistribute the individual surpluses and deficits that inevitably arise at each location. As a result, the broad structure of the refined products market depends on the interaction between the demand barrel, the mix of refinery capacity, and the type of crude oil being run in each of the major geographical regions. The proportion of the different products made in a refinery are indeed heavily dependent on the type of crude oil processed: the heavier crude oils of the Middle East and South America give rise to high volumes of fuel oil but little gasoline, whereas the lighter crude oils from the North Sea, North Africa and the US produce relatively small amounts of fuel oil, with a low sulphur content, which is therefore able to be cracked more easily.

Although these patterns change over time, there are regular flows of products from one region to another and the market sets relative price levels accordingly. Europe, for instance, exports gasoline to the US and gas oil to the Far East, but imports naphtha and fuel oil for use as refinery feedstocks. The US exports distillates to

South America and the Far East. And the mid-East Gulf is a structurally net exporter of naphtha and fuel oil to both the Far East and Europe. Asia Pacific was the world's fastest growing market for oil products until the economic crisis brought demand growth to an unexpected standstill in 1998. This sudden downturn has created a temporary surplus, reversing the normal pattern of trade flows between east and west. As a result, after being a net importer of refined products across the barrel, the region has now an excess which is being exported to Europe, Latin America and the US west coast when the arbitrage is open.

The growth in the derivative markets for oil products has arisen partly out of the increasing desire of end-users to ensure the profitability of their operations by hedging their energy risk, and partly out of the growth recorded in refinery margins trading (as described earlier in this chapter).

There is a great range of companies for whom oil supplies represent a substantial part of their variable costs. For example, kerosene in the case of airlines; bunker for shipping companies; motor diesel for transportation fleets; heating oil and fuel oil for utilities; fuel oil for industries. For these end-users, derivatives provide tailor-made hedges with flexibility on maturity, pricing periods and indexes. The index may, for instance, take the form of a formula that weights indexes for different geographical zones (for example, 2/3 NWE + 1/3 MED), or different products (for example, escalation formulas for natural gas prices in Europe).

The great potential of the OTC energy products market is that it allows fuel supply managers and financial officers to design a hedging programme that is exactly suited to their commercial constraints. For example, overall procurement of jet fuel for airlines is usually based on a basket of price references which depends upon the geographical split of the airline's activities. The swap market has the ability to provide instruments that exactly match those basket exposures.

Initially limited to the medium term (one, two or three accounting years), derivatives on oil products are now being proposed for long-term hedging. For example, an electricity or industrial company investing in cogeneration usually has to ensure a long-term natural gas supply contract partly or totally indexed on gas oil or fuel oil. Rather than hedging supply costs with WTI-related instruments, companies are increasingly negotiating long-term swaps or options on gas oil and fuel oil – and these may be written in local currency, such as the euro or the British pound.

The strengthening of environmental control on air pollution has also had a dramatic effect on prices. In Europe for instance, product quality standards for heating oil and automotive diesel have become much more stringent in recent years and the market is increasingly fragmented as blending opportunities are constrained. The sulphur quality for heating oil switched from 0.3% to 0.2% at the end of 1994 and was subsequently tightened to 0.05% in October 1996 for motor diesel. Sulphur is being removed from diesel and gasoline all over the world and this should widen the sweet/sour spread of both diesel and crude over the next few years. This trend should also be strengthened by the replacement of oil with natural gas for electric power generation in both the US and Europe.

Obviously these changes are liable to have an impact on the swaps or options based on the relevant underlying indexes. The problem is not only one of uncertainty: writing derivatives on the new quotations will also pose technical difficulties, because of the lack of historical data to evaluate the implied hedging risks. It is worth stressing that the lack of historical data means that traders in the "new" contracts will first have to make a precise analysis of the relevant economic and industrial fundamentals. Depending on the extent of new regulation, this is potentially true for all oil products, but is especially true for gas oil, gasoline and fuel oil.

In the US, derivatives are being marketed for hedging the sulphur differential from on-highway diesel oil to Nymex heating oil (although sales are limited at present). In Europe, the market for fuel oil has quickly grown around two main indexes, low and high sulphur fuel oil.

Since 1993, physical traders have started to make substantial use of short-term derivatives based on indexes such as gasoline and naphtha. Naphtha is used as a feedstock to produce both motor gasoline and ethylene for the petrochemical industry, but the most visible naphtha paper trade is for light petrochemical grades. Since December 1994, the Nymex futures contract has been based on regular reformulated gasoline (RFG); there is still not futures market for premium gasoline in the US. European exports are still mainly conventional grades. When a gasoline swap is discussed in the European market, it is usually based on a differential to the New York futures price. However, the liquidity of these markets for long-term deals is still sporadic

because traders often appear to have the same orientation – long or short – at the same time.

Risk management in the chemical industries is still very limited, and is restricted largely to naphtha supplies for steam-cracking. But this area of business has growth potential, especially when the chemicals business cycle moves to the "upside".

Derivatives on LPGs and, more precisely, on propane have also gained more liquidity. The underlying physical market is growing because propane can sometimes be used as a clean alternative to fuel oil; the successful introduction of a daily price report by Argus has made traders less reluctant to enter LPG swaps in their books.

MARKETING PACKAGES AND MARKET RISKS
In conclusion, it is worth observing that the vast majority of hedging strategies in the oil market are relatively basic, which is a sign of a mature and relatively liquid market. In the crude oil markets, the Nymex WTI and IPE Brent blend gather most of worldwide trading in futures and swaps as well as options and exotics. Compared to these markers, Tapis and Dubai qualities collect only marginal activity. In the past, forward Dubai trading volumes rivalled those of Brent but, since the Gulf crisis, liquidity has greatly diminished and the majority of paper Dubai deals are now either spread trades against the 15-day Brent market or inter-month spreads in the Dubai market itself. On the products side, there are now enough liquid indexes on exchanges and in OTC forward markets to hedge almost any physical exposure with a minimal basis risk. Most trading is still concentrated in swaps rather than options, but the latter have been continuously increasing in volume and complexity over the past few years.

Generally speaking, the evolution of hedging strategies has been guided by two considerations: the competitive need to propose increasingly customised packages to clients; and the need to be able to dynamically manage the market risks that arise out of these packages.

Marketing packages are often built to give more attractiveness to a strategy, for example by lowering a swap price or by limiting an option premium, or to switch from a type of risk to another (eg from an oil indexation to a gas indexation), as such they are desirable. However, endusers should remember that any flexibility or constraint given or received on either maturity or volume is generally worth an option (swaption or compound). An embedded option may add substantial risks, and these must be fully understood by clients who seek to hedge physical risks with paper strategies. Sophisticated marketing is useful as long as it is transparent and forms part of a well-defined hedging objective.

Marketing packages are increasingly being developed with reference to non-oil price risk variables: some put the emphasis on optimising taxation liability, on enhancing finance packages, on physical delivery or on weather variables. For example, oil companies and distributors in the US and in Europe have developed specific supply programmes which offer guaranteed prices for forward supplies at the client's gate (or wing, in the case of airlines). These contracts, constructed using futures, swaps and options, involve new types of risks, such as the possibility of non-performance on the physical side: the contractual agreement must closely tie together the physical arrangements and the paper arrangements.

The energy business is evolving into an integrated, multi-fuel, deregulated marketplace. The market for gas as a fuel for power generation has provided the largest area of growth in gas demand over the past few years and Combined Cycle Gas Turbines (CCGTs) are still being built at an impressive pace all over the world. In Europe, weather derivatives, which are at the crossroads of insurance and finance, seem to be following the successful path they have beaten in the US. Cross-commodity derivatives, such as spark spread options and oil versus gas swaps, are flourishing on the OTC markets. It is likely that oil and gas trading companies, which have developed a specific know-how in managing commodity price risk exposures, will have an edge over financial competitors in the near future.

1 *Gas prices to large industrial consumers are usually low and it is these customers who can most easily switch to low price fuel oil. The unit price of gas in the residential market is much higher because it is more expensive to feed small volumes of gas into individual houses at low pressure than deliver huge loads from a higher transmission line to a factory; but customers are also more captive and the competing fuel is higher priced gas oil.*

2 *In addition, there may be a non-energy component, usually an inflation index.*

3 *Value-at-risk (VAR) is traditionally defined as the maximum amount (in $) that can be lost by a trading position over a given horizon with a given confidence level (VAR is* typically *set between 1% and 5% over one day). In the case of an end-user, this merely refers to a high quantile of the distribution of the forward supply cost of a commodity over a given period of time. This limit is typically defined according to the client's break-even point and is a measure of what the firm has defined as the "critical cost" of its supplies.*

4 Crude Oil Hedging, Energy Security Analysis, Inc, *Risk Books, Energy and Power Special Reports, 1998.*

5 *Named after the Engler measure of its viscosity.*

6 *CFDs are traded up to six weeks forward.*

BIBLIOGRAPHY

Barnaud, F., 1990, "In Search of Liquidity: Hedging and Speculation in Oil Futures Markets", WPM 13, Oxford Institute for Energy Studies.

Barnaud, F., and J. Dabouineau, 1992, "Past Correction: the Volatility of Oil Prices", *Risk*, September 1992, 5(8).

Brennan, M. J., 1989, "The Price of the Convenience Yield and the Valuation of Commodity Contingent Claims", working paper, University of British Columbia.

d'Almeida, J., and F. Barnaud, 1993, "Mix and Match: Dynamic Hedging in Oil Derivative Markets", *Futures* and d'Almeida, J. and P. Lautard, 1992, "Elf Trading and Oil Derivatives", *Pipeline* Winter 1992, International Petroleum Exchange (IPE), 3, London.

Dragana and Pillipovic, 1998, *Energy Risk*, McGraw Hill.

Embrechts, P., C. Klüppelberg, and T. Mikosch, 1997, *Modelling extremal events*, Springer, New York.

Gabillon, J., 1991, "The Term Structure of Oil Future Prices", WPM 17, Oxford Institute for Energy Studies.

Gibson, R. and E. S. Schwartz, 1990, "Stochastic Convenience Yield and the Pricing of Oil Contingent Claims", *The Journal of Finance*, xlv (3).

Keynes, J.M., 1930, *A Treatise on Money, II*, Harcourt Brace, New York.

Mabro, R., et al, 1986, *The Market for North Sea Crude Oil*, Oxford Institute for Energy Studies.

Mabro, R. and P. Horsnell, 1993, *Oil Markets and Prices*, Oxford Institute for Energy Studies.

6

The Natural Gas Market

Fred Lagrasta, Vincent Kaminski and Ross Prevatt
Enron Corp[1]

T he North American natural gas industry has undergone a rapid process of evolution over the past 20 years. With annual revenues now totalling $81 billion, the market has emerged from the shadow of the crude oil market to become the leading growth sector of the US energy market.[2]

The market has not simply grown – it has also experienced radical change. Deregulation has forced market participants to compete in the wholesale, industrial and commercial sectors and, in the majority of the states, competitive forces are reaching the residential level. In this deregulated environment, market participants have found themselves increasingly exposed to price movements and to counterparty performance risk – and this has led to an exponential increase in risk management.

The most direct evidence for the growth in risk management is the success of the New York Mercantile Exchange (Nymex) natural gas futures contract: it has enjoyed the largest annual percentage volume gains of any contract launched in the history of that exchange. In 1998, the daily average volume of the Nymex Henry Hub contract exceeded 63,000 contracts, or over 10 times the average daily consumption of gas in the United States (58 billion cubic feet). Meanwhile the off-exchange, or over-the-counter (OTC), market generates a volume in structured products that is comparable to the volume traded on Nymex. Industry experts estimate that well over 10,000 OTC transactions were completed in 1998 alone.

The rapid growth in risk management is partly explained by the nature of the North American gas industry – which is structurally quite different to that of the global oil industry as described in the previous chapter. Because of the handling and transport costs, very little demand for natural gas on the North American continent is met by importing liquefied natural gas (LNG) from overseas. As a smaller, more domestically oriented industry than the global oil industry, the North American natural gas sector offers participants fewer alternatives for placing or sourcing natural gas. Additionally, for technical reasons, the transport and storage capacities of the natural gas industry are relatively inflexible compared to those of the oil industry. It follows that the natural gas price volatility is generally much higher than for other commodities, including crude oil.

Furthermore, compared to the oil industry, capitalisation is less concentrated and operations are less vertically integrated (Panel 1). Producers, gatherers, processors, transporters, storage operators and marketers are often separate economic entities – a fact that is increasingly true in the deregulated environment. These disparate companies often lack the capital and the retail distribution networks that help to buffer the oil majors against adverse price movements.

Four factors drive price volatility by affecting gas supply and demand: extreme weather increases the consumption of gas (heating in winter, air conditioning in summer); economic (industrial use); timely, reliable information is not readily available to market participants; and sentiment, or the short-term view held by different buyers and sellers. Three additional factors influence supply: stock levels, pipeline capacity and operational difficulties.

The most fundamental reason for believing that natural gas risk management will continue to grow in the future is the strength of the underlying market: natural gas usage is expected to post healthy volume gains in absolute and relative terms in the coming years. Annual US consump-

MARKET STRUCTURE

In contrast to the vertically integrated nature of much of the worldwide oil industry, the North American natural gas industry consists of a chain of distinct market segments. The chain begins with a large number of natural gas producers, who are linked by discrete gathering, processing, transportation and intermediation functions to a diverse array of gas consumers.

Most natural gas production in the US is developed from reserve basins in the Texas and Louisiana Gulf Coast (both onshore and in the Gulf of Mexico), in the Permian Basin of West Texas, the San Juan basin of New Mexico, the Hugoton/Anadarko basins of Kansas and Oklahoma, and in the Rocky Mountains region.

Significant amounts of gas are also produced in Alberta, Canada; with the recent expansion of pipeline capacity from Canada, approximately 14% of daily US demand is now met by Canadian gas.[1] That number is expected to continue to grow: interregional pipeline capacity has increased by 75% from 1990 to 1997 to reach 11,406 million cubic feet per day.[2] The US continues to be a modest net exporter to Mexico; in 1998, the US's net volume exported export to Mexico was 36 billion cubic feet.[3] The market is thus truly a North American market.

Natural gas is transported from the production regions to the market areas through pipeline systems which traverse each of the lower 48 states. In 1998, an estimated average 58 billion cubic feet (bcf) was consumed daily in the United States.

There are over 5,000 active oil and gas producers in the US, the vast majority of which are small independents. The top 10 domestic reserve-hold-ing companies accounted for approximately 28% of total annual production in 1998. The relatively small size of most natural gas producers means that they cannot justify the cost of in-house marketing and support of risk management activities. This has created a need and opportunity for natural gas gatherers and gas marketers, and has resulted in an active market for trading physical gas.

Gas processing plants are the next link in the chain. The raw natural gas stream, primarily composed of methane gas, also is rich in heavier molecules, including ethane, propane, butane and natural gasoline. These hydrocarbons are removed from the gas stream, and sold at a premium as natural gas liquids (NGLs). NGLs are used mainly for process and feedstock purposes in the chemicals industry or, in the case of propane, as an easily transportable source of energy for heating applications.

The gas processing plants are usually situated at the end of the pipeline systems that aggregate small volumes of gas into larger, more easily marketable gas pools. Generally, these processing facilities run full-time, extracting NGLs. However, at times, the price spread between natural gas and NGL prices narrows to a point which makes NGL production uneconomic; in this situation, to the extent operationally possible, the NGLs are left in the gas stream. With the emergence of longer-dated hedging markets in propane and, to a lesser extent, ethane, the forward price spreads between natural gas and the liquids stream are beginning to be actively traded and managed in much the same way as oil refinery crack spreads.

Interspersed throughout the business chain are

---

tion is predicted to grow to 35.6 trillion cubic feet by 2020 from 22.0 trillion cubic feet in 1997.[3] Driving that demand will be an increase in the use of gas for electric power generation. The amount of gas consumed by power plants is expected to almost triple, from 4.5 trillion cubic feet in 1997 to 13.0 trillion cubic feet in 2020.[4] Industrial use also will grow, but not as rapidly, from 7.3 trillion cubic feet in 1997 to perhaps 9.5 trillion cubic feet in 2020.[5] This sharp increase in demand lends credence to the oft-spoken prediction that natural gas will become the "fuel of the future".

The advantages of natural gas are numerous. Its delivered price is typically below that of most fuels on an energy-equivalent basis. Capital costs for new electricity generating units that burn natural gas are lower than those for oil-fired, coal-fired, hydroelectric and nuclear plants.[6] Increased concerns over the environmental impact of sulphur dioxide emissions from burning fossil fuels, an interest in reducing the reliance on imported energy supplies and the desire to rebuild domestic energy industries have provided the impetus to reduce regulatory and capital constraints on the natural gas industry.

The purpose of this chapter is to highlight the principal issues in risk management and

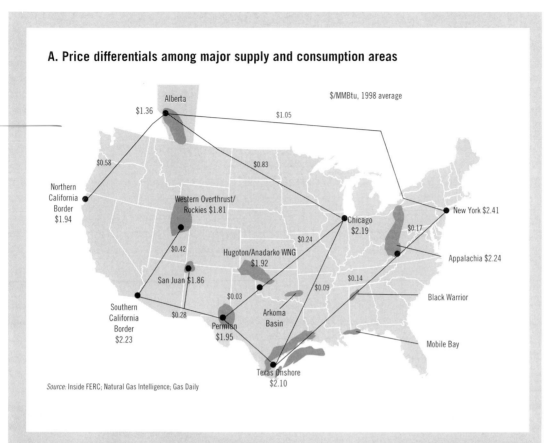

A. Price differentials among major supply and consumption areas

Source: Inside FERC; Natural Gas Intelligence; Gas Daily

natural gas marketing companies, which buy, sell and trade the commodity. Marketers add efficiency to the market by providing pooling, storage, balancing, financing and risk management services.

These marketers range from larger integrated players such as Enron, which markets over 12 bcf per day, to very small "shops" that serve niche markets. As gas marketing has gained acceptance, volume has grown. In 1998, the five largest gas marketers jointly handled an average daily volume of 9.7 billion cubic feet, while the top 20 marketers handled an average daily volume of 5.8 billion cubic feet. That compares with 3.4 billion

cubic feet and 2.2 billion cubic feet, respectively, in 1993.[4] Some of the larger players are combing operations to gain market share. Duke Energy and Mobil, NGC and Chevron, and the Coastal Corporation and Westcoast Energy are prime examples. Electric companies such as Duke and Southern Company are also entering the field, signalling the alignment of gas and power marketing, as well as pricing. Also competing with gas marketing companies are the marketing arms of production companies, pipeline marketing affiliates, and local distribution companies (LDCs).

Next in the chain are pipeline companies. Pipeline capacity is sold on the basis of firm or

changes in the gas market as the gas industry gears up to meet the energy needs of the 21st century. We begin by describing how the market structure, regulatory history and changes in the market have influenced the development of risk management in the natural gas industry. We then focus on risk management in theory and in practice, types of risk and risk instruments, and cross-commodity risk management. The relationship between company finance and risk management as well as the role of the intermediary in this market are explored. Finally, we conclude with a market outlook that describes the field's most significant emerging trends.

Market structure

A BRIEF MARKET HISTORY

Regulation has played a commanding, and often problematic, role in the evolution of the natural gas market. Government intervention in the natural gas industry dates back to the mid-1800s, but it is sufficient here to begin with the Phillips Decision of the United States Supreme Court in 1954. In deciding the case, the Court held that the primary aim of the Natural Gas Act of 1938 was the "protection of consumers against exploitation at the hands of natural gas companies". The Federal Power Commission (FPC)

interruptible service, and, in the last few years, a secondary market has developed to trade pipeline capacity. As discussed in the main text, interstate pipeline companies now act primarily as transporters, though many have non-affiliated gas marketing subsidiaries. In contrast, intrastate pipelines, not being subject to Federal Energy Regulatory Commission (FERC) oversight, can act as both transporters and gas merchants. That is not to say that the intrastate pipeline companies have a monopoly or oligopoly power – the Texas and Louisiana Gulf Coast intrastate pipelines serve the most sophisticated, competitive markets in the US, and therefore must compete strongly on price and, to a lesser extent, service. In total, more than 60 interstate pipeline companies control over 185,000 miles of natural gas pipeline throughout North America. As discussed in the main text, pipeline capacity is rapidly being increased to meet the growing market to use gas for power generation.

The largest part of the residential and commercial transportation function is handled by Local Distribution Companies (LDCs). LDCs typically serve industrial, commercial and residential needs for heat and energy. Much of the gas that is consumed in non-gas-producing states is provided by LDCs, but in gas-producing states most of the supply to large industrial and electric utility concerns is served via direct pipeline connections. In the past, natural gas commodity, transportation and service charges were fully passed through to the end-consumer, with little or no price risk accruing to the LDC. That is changing. Some 37 states are investigating and/or implementing legislation to restructure LDCs to add greater efficiency to the market. In exchange for relinquishing their

right to a set profit, LDCs have the right to market surplus gas to increase profits. LDCs, along with electric utilities, are generally overseen by state regulatory bodies such as Public Utility Commissions (PUCs), which serve to protect the public interest.

The chain ends at the natural gas burnertip. The largest end-use sector is the industrial market, which in 1998 consumed over 8.5 trillion cubic feet of gas, or approximately 40% of total annual consumption.[5] Refiners, chemical manufacturers, ammonia and methanol producers, steel and aluminium manufacturers, and paper mills account for the bulk of industrial activity. On-site industrial electricity generation makes up a large part of the industrial consumption.

Combined residential and commercial consumption comprises approximately 36% of demand; residential gas usage is about one-and-a-half times the requirement of the commercial sector. Of the remainder, electric utility consumption comprises the largest part and makes up 15% of demand but is anticipated to grow to 37% of demand by 2020, to become the largest end-user sector.[6] The vast majority of gas is used as a fuel source, although a considerable amount is used as feedstock for ammonia, methanol and other chemicals. The primary industrial markets for gas are in Texas and the Louisiana Gulf Coast region, while the primary non-industrial markets are California, the Great Lakes region of the Midwest, and the Northeast region.

1 US Department of Energy, *Natural Gas Monthly*, March 1999.
2 Energy Information Administration Natural Gas 1998: Issues and Trends.
3 US Department of Energy, *Natural Gas Monthly*, March 1999.
4 *Natural Gas Trends*, Arthur Andersen and Cambridge Energy Research Associates, 1998.
5 US Department of Energy, *Natural Gas Monthly*, March 1999.
6 1999 *Enron Energy Outlook*.

acted to carry out the Court's interpretation by mandating a cost-oriented approach to wellhead price regulation on a case-by-case basis, just as it had imposed cost-of-service regulation on pipeline companies. (Cost-of-service regulation allowed pipeline companies, which in many instances acted as monopoly utilities, to earn only what was deemed a "fair return" on the asset, based on the cost of implementing and operating that asset.) When such focused regulatory oversight of each producer proved unmanageable, the FPC adopted a system of national wellhead rates based on the concept of "vintaging". The concept of vintaging was developed as a way of assigning different values to specific gas

production based upon the date of well completion (and, in some cases, the depth of the well). Gas wells that had been developed in certain regulatory eras sold gas at a maximum lawful price that was quite different to the maximum price of gas from wells developed at a different time; "deep gas" wells produced gas that could be sold at higher prices than gas produced from shallow formations.

Many observers believe that these price schedules eventually led to the severe shortages of the 1970s, since they encouraged consumers to use the relatively cheap fuel but did not provide any incentive to producers to replace reserves. To guard against shortages in the future, pipelines entered into take-or-pay (TOP) contracts with producers. The pipelines then resold the gas to local distribution companies (LDCs) at equivalent prices with "minimum bill" provisions that mirrored their take-or-pay contracts.

Congress intervened with the Natural Gas Policy Act (NGPA) of 1978, which was designed to address the supply shortage. The NGPA provided for the gradual deregulation of wellhead gas prices and for inducements to limit gas usage, particularly for industrial consumers. The process of deregulating wellhead prices for natural gas was eventually completed with the implementation of the Natural Gas Wellhead Decontrol Act of 1989.

Limitations on industrial gas consumption imposed by the NGPA, coupled with the lifting of price controls which in some cases resulted in gas being sold for over $10/MMBtu (million British thermal units) – about 50 times greater than some vintages – quickly reversed the supply shortage. By the early 1980s a gas surplus, the so-called gas "bubble", had been created that would linger until the 1990s. To make matters worse for the pipelines, in 1984 the Federal Energy Regulatory Commission (FERC), the successor to the FPC, issued Order No 380, which declared "minimum bill" contracts between pipelines and LDCs to be invalid. Thus pipelines were faced with obligations to buy more gas than they could sell, at prices that were above market value.

In an effort to reduce their liabilities under their supply TOP contracts, pipelines began offering "special marketing programmes" through which they sold gas to non-traditional customers – typically, industrial end-users – at reduced costs. This increased sales, thus reducing the pipelines' liabilities under their supply TOP contracts. In 1985, however, the courts stopped this activity. They declared that the pipelines' practice of denying LDCs access to these lower-cost gas supplies was discriminatory. Nevertheless, this opened the door for the next step in deregulating the gas market – the unbundling of pipeline gas sales and transportation services. The first step in this unbundling process was FERC's Order No 436, issued in 1985. In effect, this order required pipelines to provide open access to capacity on their systems, making it much easier for LDCs and other end-users to purchase their gas supplies directly at the wellhead and then contract separately with the pipelines for transportation service only.

In 1987 and 1988, the FERC issued two more orders that further liberalised pipeline operations. Order No 500 provided for the sharing of TOP contract costs, including contract renegotiations, buy-outs or buy-downs, among producers, pipelines and pipeline customers.

Order No 490 removed the requirement that pipelines obtain FERC approval before terminating purchase agreements from producers. Under this regulation, either the pipeline or the producer could terminate their arrangement upon expiration of the contract and 30 days' notice. The FERC took a further significant step towards deregulating the natural gas market. Order No 636, issued in 1992, required pipelines to complete the unbundling of their sales and transportation services and to provide a system for resale of any firm capacity held by their customers. Figure 1 illustrates the history of these regulatory orders and the demand/supply balance for natural gas in the US.

Order No 636 has now been fully implemented, completing the evolution of the pipeline companies from "merchants" to "transporters". TOP is a thing of the past. This transition has paved the way for greater competition among third-party service providers and has also resulted in an active transportation-capacity trading market. A lively secondary market, bidding on this new excess of pipeline capacity, has emerged. With more counterparties involved in the bidding, short-term capacity has become increasingly competitive. Pipeline companies want to fill their systems with gas and keep them full, and many are willing to reduce rates to do so.

Further deregulation is prompting a profound evolution in how LDCs operate, and that, in turn, is creating new market dynamics for the natural gas pipelines. Specifically, deregulation on the state level is opening residential gas sales to com-

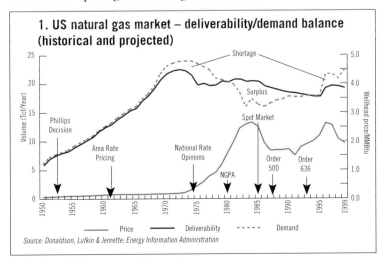

1. US natural gas market – deliverability/demand balance (historical and projected)

Source: Donaldson, Lufkin & Jenrette; Energy Information Administration

Table 1. Summary profile of completed and proposed natural gas pipeline projects, 1996–2000

Year	All type projects						New pipelines[a]		Expansions	
	Number of projects	System mileage[b]	New capacity (MMcf/d)	Project costs ($m)	Average cost /mile ($ 000)[c]	Costs/cf capacity (¢)	Average cost /mile ($ 000)[c]	Costs/cf capacity (¢)	Average cost /mile (¢)[c]	Costs/cf capacity (¢)
1996	26	1,029	2,574	552	448	21	983	17	288	27
1997	42	3,124	6,542	1,397	415	21	554	22	360	21
1998	54	3,388	11,060	2,861	1,257	30	1,301	31	622	22
1999	36	3,753	8,205	3,135	727	37	805	46	527	31
2000	19	4,364	7,795	6,339	1,450	81	1,455	91	940	57
Total	177	15,660	36,178	14,285	862	39	1,157	48	542	29

a New pipelines include completely new systems and smaller system additions to existing pipeliens, ie a lateral longer than 5 miles or an addition that extends an existing system substantially beyond its traditional terminus.

b Includes looped segments, replacement pipe, laterals and overall mileage of new pipeline systems.

c Average cost per mile is based upon only those projects for which mileage was reported. For instance, a new compressor station addition would not involve added pipe mileage. In other cases final mileage for a project in its initial phases may not yet be final and not available. In the latter case, cost estimates may not be available or be very tentative.

MMcf/d = million cubic feet per day.

Source: Energy Information Administration (EIA), EIAGIS-NG Geographic Information System, Natural Gas Pipeline Construction Database through August 1998.

petition. As of mid-1999, 37 states were investigating or implementing some form of LDC restructuring. Natural gas deregulation on the smaller user or residential level is not progressing as quickly as electricity deregulation, but ultimately it will redefine the role of the LDC. Whereas the LDC now performs all merchant functions – buying gas, buying capacity and selling gas – in the future it will serve as a distribution company only, operating its assets as a common carrier.

Changes in the natural gas market

The convergence of natural gas with electricity is irrevocably changing the marketplace. Let us look again at one dramatic figure: the amount of gas consumed by domestic power plants is expected to almost triple, from 4.5 trillion cubic feet in 1997 to 13.0 trillion cubic feet in 2020.[7] Of the 180 merchant plants in development in the US, over 94% are gas fired. In an open electricity market where the price of power is set hourly, the price of power will increasingly be set at the margin – the last plant to sell power into the pool. The lowest-kilowatt/hr cost plants

– coal and nuclear – will meet (but will not satisfy) baseload demand. The higher-kilowatt/hr cost plants – natural gas – will become the last plants to sell into the pool to meet the incremental demand. Therefore, in the future natural gas prices are likely to move in tandem with electricity prices on an energy equivalent basis and lose their association with crude oil prices.

Electricity demand is at its peak during the hot summer months, so natural gas demand will become multiseasonal. Gas no longer will be considered a winter-only fuel. As the seasonality of the business changes, gas storage is changing too (Panel 2). With virtually all new power generation fired by natural gas, demand will be year-round. The traditional pattern of injecting gas in the summer and withdrawing it in the winter will be disrupted. Storage will have to become increasingly flexible and swift to meet the needs of customers to adjust nominations on a daily basis.

This surge in demand is encouraging an unprecedented amount of pipeline construction. (Figure 2 and Table 1). From 1996 to 2000, more than 36,000 million cubic feet a day (MMcf/d) of capacity has been either completed or proposed.[8] The new supply coming out of Canada and entering the US near Chicago and in Maine is encouraging pipeline companies to expand capacity within the US (Figure 3). Two major projects, the Alliance Pipeline from Alberta, Canada to Chicago and the Vector Pipeline from Chicago to Dawn, Ontario, will alter the direction flow of gas in the US. Gulf Coast gas no longer will flow to Chicago, but rather from Chicago to points east via two additional new projects, Independence Pipeline and the Millennium Pipeline, both of which will transport gas from Chicago to New York.

More pipelines will increase supply flexibility. They also will enable producers to ship their

2. Major additions to US interstate natural gas pipeline capacity, 1991–2000

Source: Energy Information Administration

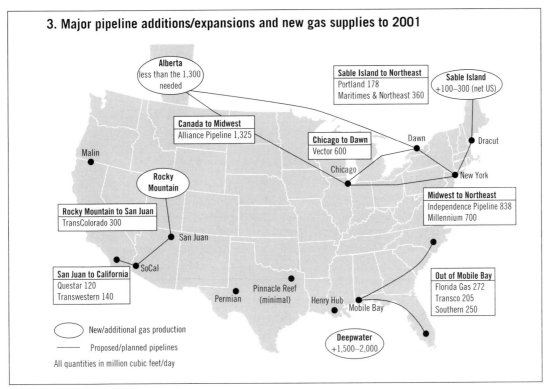

3. Major pipeline additions/expansions and new gas supplies to 2001

Alberta (less than the 1,300 needed)

Sable Island to Northeast
Portland 178
Maritimes & Northeast 360

Sable Island +100–300 (net US)

Canada to Midwest
Alliance Pipeline 1,325

Chicago to Dawn
Vector 600

Dawn

Dracut

Malin

Rocky Mountain

Chicago

New York

Midwest to Northeast
Independence Pipeline 838
Millennium 700

Rocky Mountain to San Juan
TransColorado 300

San Juan

SoCal

San Juan to California
Questar 120
Transwestern 140

Permian

Pinnacle Reef (minimal)

Henry Hub

Mobile Bay

Out of Mobile Bay
Florida Gas 272
Transco 205
Southern 250

⬭ New/additional gas production
— Proposed/planned pipelines
All quantities in million cubic feet/day

Deepwater +1,500–2,000

gas almost anywhere to obtain the best price. As regions lose their isolation and become more integrated, supply and demand surges will reverberate throughout the grid. This should ease price spikes somewhat, as nearly the entire system will be able to respond to a jump in demand. In addition, grid integration will reduce the basis differential between two points, such as Chicago and Henry Hub.

Even while pipeline capacity increases, the industry is experiencing an unprecedented reduction in long-term capacity contracts. The bulk of these agreements are set to expire by 2008. Approximately 44% of capacity contracts will expire between 1999 and 2003 (Figure 4) and are unlikely to be renewed. LDCs, faced with loss of monopoly status, are wary of renewing long-term pipeline capacity agreements. Another traditional long-term capacity customer – the independent power producer – also has lost its own long-term market. The scene for this change began to be set in 1978, five years after the oil embargo drove up energy prices, when a national concern that power would be in short supply prompted the US Congress to pass the Public Utility Regulatory Policies Act of 1978 (PURPA). PURPA was designed to encourage the development of independent power producers by requiring utilities to purchase this power under long-term power purchase agreements (PPAs), usually at terms quite favourable to the power producers. The power producers, in turn, entered into long-term capacity contracts with

pipeline firms.

However, the energy market has changed considerably in 20 years. Energy prices have not skyrocketed as predicted, and many utilities have attempted to renegotiate PPAs for shorter terms at lower prices. New independent power plants can no longer hope to sign a long-term PPA and instead must sell their output to cogeneration hosts, which purchase both electricity and steam from the power plant, or into the open electricity markets. New independent power plants are now called "merchant" plants to reflect this new status.

By necessity, without the protection of a long-term PPA, merchant plants will not commit to long-term capacity agreements with pipelines, hastening the disappearance of the long-term capacity market.

As a result, pipelines will find new ways to sell their capacity, and gas marketers are the most likely buyers. In one interesting example, a pipeline company faced a reduction of 1.2 tBtu/d of firm capacity when a gas utility allowed a contract to expire at year end 1997. A national gas marketing company bought that capacity and more – 1.3 tBtu/d in total – but its agreement with the pipeline was markedly different from the predecessor agreement. First, whereas the utility had just one contract, the marketer used three contracts to provide greater flexibility. Secondly, the marketer's contracts had shorter terms, just two years compared with the utility's six-year term. Finally, although the utility had

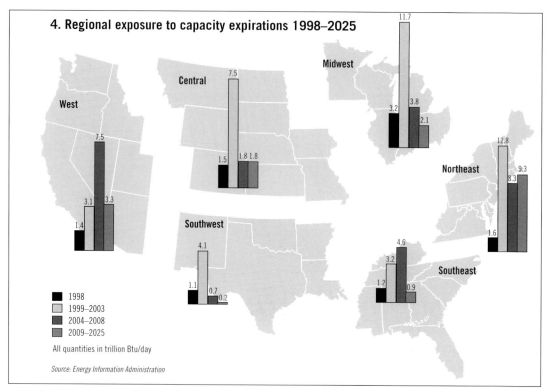

4. Regional exposure to capacity expirations 1998–2025

1998
1999–2003
2004–2008
2009–2025

All quantities in trillion Btu/day

Source: Energy Information Administration

paid the maximum tariff rate, the marketer was given a significant discount, which the pipeline company thought was necessary to ensure a buyer.

In all likelihood, gas marketers will optimise available capacity, heightening the efficiency of the market. Pipeline companies will strive to become more efficient, too. They will become more active marketers and will use their assets to flow more gas to more customers than ever before.

Another major market force is the consolidation trend rippling through the entire natural gas sector. Since 1996, producers have merged as a way to combine operations and control costs. Among the most significant mergers have been Burlington Resources' acquisition of Louisiana Land & Exploration and Union Pacific Resources' acquisition of Norcen Energy Resources of Canada, establishing these combined companies as two of the top 10 natural gas producers in the first half of 1998. The downturn in gas prices from late 1998 through to early 1999 forced many producers to seek partners.[9] The effect of this producer consolidation is unknown. Fewer producers may result in higher prices; alternatively, greater efficiencies, however, may lower the cost of gas.

There also has been a flurry of natural gas/power company mergers, although for a different reason. The eventual convergence of the industries is prompting major power companies to gain knowledge of and competency in the natural gas business, and vice versa.[10] Pipeline companies have consolidated, too, seeking the greater efficiencies and greater market presence of a larger asset base.[11]

The risk market structure

Natural gas is physically sold and traded under three different terms: intra-month (for contracts within the same month); short term (one month to one year), and long term (12 months to 20 years). This section will explain various contract terms and conditions and the role they play in the market as it evolves.

The unravelling of long-term supply contracts and the initiation of open access for interruptible transport under FERC Order No 436 has encouraged the development of a market for short-term gas supply commitments. This market has come to be called the spot or cash market. Knowledge of this market is essential when initiating a gas price hedge, as any risk management structure needs to be properly integrated with the spot market.

Three types of spot market transactions are common: "firm", "interruptible" and "baseload".[12] Firm transactions require counterparties to a transaction to perform according to the price and terms of the contract, short of a true event of *force majeure* (which is defined quite narrowly in most firm contracts). Firm transactions are usually executed under a Master Firm Purchase/Sale Agreement, which includes make-whole provisions in the form of liquidated damages and includes financial penalty provisions in

STORAGE AND NATURAL GAS RISK MANAGEMENT

The nature of natural gas storage has changed significantly during the last decade. Previously, most storage capacity was owned and utilised by the pipeline companies, which used it to secure the reliability of their supply. They needed to be certain that they could meet their regulatory obligations to end-users. Specifically, the pipeline companies used storage to help meet expected winter demand, to protect against unexpected production and transportation disruptions, and to supply peak demand during severe weather. A high premium was attached to storage because it insured the pipelines against the consequences of market disruption.

As deregulation of the natural gas industry has evolved, so has the need for storage. While storage facilities are still primarily operated by the pipelines, many of them are leased by third parties. Deregulation has also increased the number of independent storage operators, whose motivation is different from that of the pipeline companies before Order No 636 (see main text).

Following Order No 636, the pipeline companies began to function as contract carriers, offering various types of transport services to third parties. The obligation for surety of supply has thus shifted away from the pipeline companies to producer and pipeline marketing affiliates, marketing intermediaries and to the end-users themselves. To meet these obligations, marketers and major end-users enter into various supply, transport and storage agreements.

There are three major types of underground storage facilities; reservoirs (depleted oil and gas fields), aquifers (water-bearing rock formations conditioned to hold natural gas) and salt caverns (mined hollow spaces in salt beds or salt domes). Reservoirs are by far the most prevalent type of facility used, accounting for over 80% of total US working gas capacity and over 70% of total deliverability as of 1997. Aquifers rank second in working gas capacity, while salt caverns are the runners-up in deliverability.

Table A describes some of the characteristics of these facilities that affect the two most widely used measures of storage facilities, working gas capacity and daily deliverability. As the table makes clear, salt caverns offer a great deal more flexibility than the other storage facilities due to lower requirements of "cushion gas" and shorter withdrawal/injection periods. All gas storage facilities need to have cushion gas, which is the minimum volume of gas that needs to reside in the facility permanently. For reservoirs and aquifers, this requirement is typically 50% or greater of the total volume of gas in the facility, compared to the salt cavern requirement of about 33%. Further, the withdrawal period for salt caverns is only about 10 to 20 days, compared to two to three months for reservoirs and aquifers. According to the Energy Information Administration, 12 new storage facilities and 31 site expansions are planned from 1999 to 2003. By far the majority of these sites are reservoirs, as Table B illustrates.

Table A. Characteristics of natural gas storage facilities

Type	Cushion to working gas ratio	Injection period	Withdrawal period	Injection/withdrawal flexibility
aquifer	2:1	7–8 months	2–3 months	Low
reservoir	2:1	7–8 months	2–3 months	Low
salt dome	1:2	20–40 days	10–20 days	High

the event of non-performance.

Interruptible contracts provide for little in the way of obligation. Price and term are subject to renegotiation at any time. This contract market can best be characterised as a daily market. End-users tend to use it only for their daily pipeline volume "balancing" requirements.[13] Marketers and traders are the most active participants in the market for this gas, as they use interruptible transactions to balance purchases and

sales or for position trading.

Finally, baseload sales are deals that are somewhere between firm and interruptible. Although price and term are also subject to renegotiation at any time, this typically occurs only when prices move significantly one way or the other. Such interpretation is left up to the transacting parties.

The spot market mechanism has evolved into a highly institutionalised process for the active buying and selling of gas. Outside of the baseload

Table B. Expansion in natural gas storage

Type	No of expansions	No of new sites
Aquifer	1	3
Reservoir	19	9
Salt dome	11	0

Because the dominant form of gas storage will continue to be the reservoir storage facility, which cycles gas only once a year, many intermediaries and end-users find it more efficient to use the forward markets to create synthetic storage than to develop production area reservoirs or to acquire such storage facilities.

The forward markets can be used to manage seasonal price differences. However, until recently it was not possible to manage the exposure of intra-month price movements using financial swap contracts. Intra-month spot market price volatility is typically higher than that of the prompt month Nymex contract prior to its settlement. This intra-month price risk is likely to increase in the future, as production and pipeline industries operate at higher and higher utilisation rates, making the marketplace more susceptible to pricing disruptions.

Enron began offering financially settled swap and option contracts to protect customers against intra-month price swings in 1994. Two of these products are the *Gas Daily* Swap and Omicron. In the case of the *Gas Daily* Swap, discussed in more detail in the main text, the fixed price can be set well in advance of the beginning of the month, or it can take the form of a first-of-the-month index such as that published by *IFGMR*. The difference between the fixed price and the average of the reported daily prices for gas over the month is settled at the end of the month.

Omicron is the term Enron uses to define a strip of daily-settled options. Like the *Gas Daily* Swap, the strike price can be fixed and known well in advance of the beginning of the month, or the strike can be the first-of-the-month index. The customer can settle the contract financially, receiving the difference between the strike price and the daily price of gas, or they can settle physically by delivering or receiving gas priced at the strike price for the option. Omicron can also be structured as a series of contingent daily-settled options; the customer can exercise these on any day that they choose, but is limited to a known fixed number of option exercises during the month.

Storage operators are trying to build more flexibility into storage to meet the demands of power generators. While industrial users do not experience unexpected surges in demand, power generators do. If a nuclear plant is forced to shut down during a hot summer spell, a generator suddenly is faced with the need for more gas. In 1998 the Gas Industry Standards Board introduced rules allowing multiple intra-day nomination changes to give users more options to adjust supply. Users can nominate two times during the day ahead, and two times on the day of delivery. Faster injection/withdrawal rates are imperative to satisfy this need, and this is pushing companies to upgrade their storage facilities.

The shift in the type and location of storage facilities makes it more difficult for risk managers to interpret the impact of changes in storage capacity, and calculations concerning storage utilisation, on the forward market. The development of salt-dome storage within market areas and the abandonment of production-area reservoir storage facilities means that total working gas storage capability will appear to be declining in volume. But, to the contrary, the ability of the natural gas delivery system to meet peak load demand will be growing.

or firm market, most gas is traded on a 30-day basis, with pricing generally negotiated near the end of each calendar month during what is known as "bid week". Bid week coincides with the nomination deadlines for monthly pipeline capacity. While the name may imply a leisurely period of time for pricing and trading, in practice, bid week periods for the majority of pipelines have been compressed into a very short time window. Some pundits now refer to bid week as "bid day" or even "bid hour". In fact, the majority of spot market trading occurs in the hours immediately following Nymex futures contract settlement. The settlement date procedures governing the Nymex futures contract were developed to coincide as much as possible with bid week and the various pipeline nomination deadlines, to allow for the best possible convergence between cash and futures prices.

While many producers and end-users remain active sellers and buyers in the spot market for gas, in recent years many have opted to sell and buy

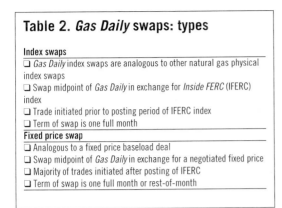

Table 2. *Gas Daily* swaps: types

Index swaps
- ❏ *Gas Daily* index swaps are analogous to other natural gas physical index swaps
- ❏ Swap midpoint of *Gas Daily* in exchange for *Inside FERC* (IFERC) index
- ❏ Trade initiated prior to posting period of IFERC index
- ❏ Term of swap is one full month

Fixed price swap
- ❏ Analogous to a fixed price baseload deal
- ❏ Swap midpoint of *Gas Daily* in exchange for a negotiated fixed price
- ❏ Majority of trades initiated after posting of IFERC
- ❏ Term of swap is one full month or rest-of-month

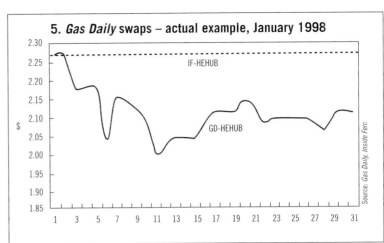

5. *Gas Daily* swaps – actual example, January 1998

Source: Gas Daily, Inside Ferc

under long-term firm contracts or "index transactions" which are referenced to published monthly prices. Index prices, which are published for a wide variety of producing area gas pooling points and major consumption areas, are generated by polling participants in the spot market. The most referenced index is McGraw Hill's *Inside FERC Gas Market Report* (IFGMR), although *Gas Daily*, *Natural Gas Week*, *Natural Gas Intelligence* and others are also frequently cited.

In 1994 Enron introduced a *Gas Daily* swap that allows market participants to financially replicate daily cash market pricing and have the opportunity to make intra-month adjustments in their positions. *Gas Daily* swap prices represent forward expectations of physical baseload gas for the current month. The swap allows buyers and sellers to change their positions immediately if their pricing outlook for the month changes, rather than waiting for the entire month before acting. Two types of *Gas Daily* swaps are available: an index swap and a fixed price swap (Table 2 and Figure 5)

The indexes used are another way in which the gas sector differs from the oil business. The natural gas industry's process of polling and publishing the responses of market participants at various pipeline points differs greatly from the practice of aggregators posting prices for wet barrels of crude oil. Crude market postings are prices at which aggregators and refiners will actually transact for crude barrels at a specified location. The natural gas indices represent a much more informal survey of how people *say* that they transacted. These surveys do not distinguish between the various contract types, described below, under which gas purchases/sales are transacted. In addition, since a response to a survey is not an offer to transact, there is little control over survey responses, which sometimes leads to the published indexes being unrepresentative of true market prices. This is one of the reasons why basis differentials

are unstable and difficult to predict. (One reason for this difference in setting spot prices is that the concentration of buyers in the crude market is greater than in the natural gas market.)

The prices in the spot market reflect the ability of the natural gas delivery system to satisfy immediate demand and to consume available supply. Unexpected weather patterns, production problems, pipeline "outages" or shutdowns, or storage injections or withdrawals, can move prices up or down significantly. Severe price movements can be very localised, and may not be dampened by the price of gas in other regions or by the price of alternative fuels; this market inefficiency is caused by the limitations of the physical delivery system, and the time and costs involved in switching fuels, although, as noted above, near-term pipeline capacity expansion should ease this market inefficiency.

Spot deals currently account for about 40% of the market, down from a high of about 70–80% in 1989. While the majority of the remaining gas bought and sold in the market is transacted under longer-term index contracts, with monthly price resets, an increasing number of long-term contracts are arranged using different price-setting mechanisms. The most common of these are fixed-price contracts for specified terms, and "trigger" contracts whereby the buyer or seller sets their price at a differential to a transparent price source such as Nymex.

On April 3, 1990, Nymex launched a natural gas futures contract. This contract brought risk management to the forefront of the natural gas industry by providing a standardised hedging vehicle and true price transparency. The delivery point for the Nymex Natural Gas futures contract is the Henry Hub gas processing plant of the Sabine Pipe Line Co at Erath, Louisiana. This delivery point was selected because it interconnects with 12 other pipeline systems: Acadian,

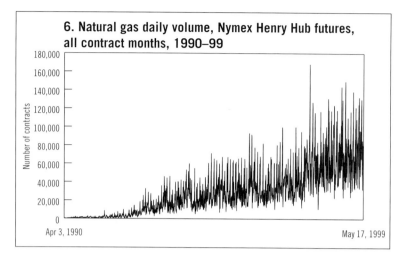

6. Natural gas daily volume, Nymex Henry Hub futures, all contract months, 1990–99

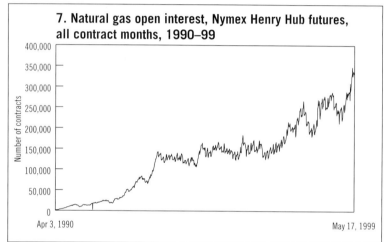

7. Natural gas open interest, Nymex Henry Hub futures, all contract months, 1990–99

8. Usage by producer type

Type of risk management product	Small independents	Medium independents	Large independents/ majors
Exchange-traded products	Limited	Moderate	High
OTC products	Moderate	High	High

As we noted above, the Henry Hub contract has been Nymex's most successful product launch to date in terms of rate of growth (Figure 6). The liquidity of the contract has allowed the over-the-counter (OTC) market to develop structured hedge transactions with their customers at narrow bid/ask spreads. Nymex, as well as OTC principals, have expended substantial time and resources to educate the market on the benefits and applications of hedging, and already there are a large number of gas industry companies active in the market, as the Nymex open interest shows (Figure 7).

The largest players are the natural gas marketing companies. Risk management capabilities have become a core component of their business, and virtually every gas marketing company has dedicated resources to providing risk management services to its customer base. It is estimated that over 80% of gas producers actively use risk management tools; and that somewhere between 60% to 80% of the larger industrial end-users of gas also manage their energy costs. Many of these companies already have experience in managing the risk of their interest rate and foreign exchange exposures, and are beginning to identify the parallels with their energy exposures. Gas and electric utilities tend to be far less active due to the regulatory restraints and uncertainty, but most have reviewed possible applications of energy risk management products in their business.

Virtually all producers participate in the gas futures market to hedge their price risk exposure. Figure 8 shows usage patterns of producers by size and type of hedge. Some producers hedge only one property, such as an acquisition, to protect their cashflow and return on investment. A financial institution may ask the producer to sell some portion of production at a fixed price to guarantee the return of monies loaned. Other producers are committed to managing risks throughout their operations. They will hedge the price risk of not only new properties but existing ones as well. For producers, hedging is seen as essential, because 100% of their revenues are derived from the energy commodity.

End-users have much less exposure in comparison; energy typically accounts for 5% to 10% of their cost of goods sold. Thus it has taken longer for all but the largest end-users to become significant players in the market.

Since 1997, another important group of institutional buyers/sellers has emerged in energy markets. This group is loosely referred to as

Coastal (ANR), Columbia Gulf, Dow Intrastate, Koch Gateway, Louisiana Resources Co (LRC), Natural Gas Pipeline of America (NGPL), Southern Natural, Texas Gas, Transco, Trunkline and Texaco's gathering system. Since 1996, Nymex has offered the Permian Basin and the Alberta contracts based on two delivery points, Keystone, Texas and Alberta, Canada–Nova Gas Pipeline, respectively, but these contracts are not actively traded. On August 1, 1995, the Kansas City Board of Trade introduced a Western futures contract based on delivery at Waha, Texas. Average daily volume for all contract months was 305 for Western, compared with 63,409 for Henry Hub.

hedge funds, or non-commercial players. These funds are largely unregulated and service the investment needs of high net-worth individuals. Typically, they do not account for much of the open interest in the energy markets, but as active traders they can and do significantly influence short-term prices. (In 1998, hedge funds accounted for 12.3% of all open interest, according to Commitments of Traders reports.)[14] They look for short-term gains rather than seeking protection over the long term (Table 3). They can enter the market quickly and exit just as rapidly, driving prices higher than the fundamentals justify, or pushing them lower than they should be.

Alongside the exchanges, a vibrant over-the-counter (OTC) market has developed. OTC contracts offer more flexibility (Table 4) Their terms can be set as long as 15 years, the load factor can vary, and physical delivery may or may not be involved. There is, however, increased counterparty risk, because these contracts do not include the guaranteed performance that exchange-based contracts have. Because contract terms can extend for more than three years, they are particularly useful for both producers and consumers, such as power plants, that no longer sign long-term supply contracts but want to lock in a price to maintain cashflow to support debt payments.

Risk management in practice

Risk management may take the form of a tactical hedge used by a company to manage its exposure to specific risks, or it can be part of a broader strategy to meet specific policy objectives or improve the company's competitive position.

In terms of the number of daily transactions, tactical hedging represents the vast majority of retail business. Typically 12 months or less in term, tactical trades are executed with the intention of protecting budgets, achieving minimum short-term cashflow levels, controlling short-term revenues or costs or protecting value differentials from location to location or between commodity prices.

Strategic hedging is much less frequent, but forms a significant fraction of the total volume of business completed. Typically longer than 12 months in term, these hedges are tied to strategic, financial or tax opportunities. Often, strategic hedging is required to obtain financing.

Purely speculative transactions make up the smallest portion of the deal spectrum. Most of these transactions are very short-term in nature, and reflect a producer or end-user's view of the

Table 3. Hedging minimises price risk – speculating means unknown outcomes

Hedging	Speculating
❏ Specific objective-driven	❏ Profit-driven
❏ Offset by cash position	❏ No offsetting cash position
❏ Reduces volatility exposure	❏ Volatility-driven
❏ Reduced likelihood of large losses or gains	❏ Increased likelihood of large losses or gains
❏ Stable production costs	❏ Full spectrum from home run to bankruptcy

Table 4. Futures vs OTC

Futures	OTC
❏ 18 consecutive months to 3 years	❏ Up to 15 years, and more
❏ Double execution risk	❏ Known price
❏ Daily mark-to-market and commissions	❏ Standard payment schedule
❏ Basis risk (location, product, timing)	❏ Customised to location
❏ Physical delivery, assigned partner	❏ No mandatory physical delivery, choose partner
❏ 100% load factor (standardised quantity)	❏ Variable load factor
❏ Regulated	❏ Non-regulated
❏ Guaranteed performance	❏ Counterparty performance risk
	❏ Less restrictive margin requirement

direction of prices for the near month. This said, many hedges contain some speculative element, regardless of the primary motivation. It is human nature to try to pick a market bottom or top at the same time as implementing a genuine hedge – tactical hedgers are the most likely to be tempted by this. However, as a result, many hedgers miss their target opportunities. At the end of 1998, the 12-month strip traded at a seasonal low of $1.981. In just over three months, the price increased 11.8% to $2.215, leaving many would-be end-user hedgers forlornly waiting for another "opportunity".

All US companies employing hedging techniques have a new mandate to account for the current market position of these hedges in their financial statements. The Financial Accounting Standards Board Statement No 133 requires all entities that use derivatives, either on their own or embedded into a contract, to recognise those instruments as either assets or liabilities in the statement of financial position and measure those instruments at fair value (Panel 3). FAS No 133 is effective for all fiscal years ending after June 15, 2000. It will force entities to recognise either the income or the loss incurred in the value of these instruments unless the derivatives are closely associated with hedging a specific financial position. If they do, the instruments

THE ART OF RISK MANAGEMENT IN THE SFAS NO 133 ERA

Ravi Thuraisingham, CFA

Enron Corp

The accounting profession has been debating for some time the standards for accounting for derivative instruments and hedging activities. The discussion over such accounting hinges on objectively addressing the following fundamental questions: What is a derivative? If your entity is using derivatives, how should you account for them so it is clear to shareholders? If a derivative is actually a position hedging a risk exposure resulting from normal business activity, then how do you formally define hedging activity? Finally, how do you demonstrate that such hedging activity is actually working?

The Financial Accounting Standards Board (FASB) addressed these issues by developing a series of pronouncements starting with Statement of Financial Accounting Standards (SFAS) No 80 and No 52 and converging on the new SFAS No 133, which answered many of these questions. To further this cause, the FASB initiated a task force that came to be known as the Derivative Implementation Group (DIG) with the explicit goal of helping entities and accounting firms successfully implement this standard. DIG has been extremely instrumental in helping all affected companies interpret and implement the standard.

In this panel, the relevant issues are discussed from the point of view of risk management, financial engineering and quantitative analysis fields and not from the perspective of an accountant or an auditor assessing the impact of the standard on the existing and new derivative activities.

Who is impacted?

This standard explicitly addresses all issues pertaining to accounting for derivative instruments and hedging activities for all entities reporting under the United States' Generally Accepted Accounting Principles (US GAAP). All affected entities must adopt the standard in its entirety for all fiscal quarters of all fiscal years beginning after June 15, 2000. For calendar year reporting entities, the effective date is January 1, 2001. Some entities may choose to adopt early.

SFAS No 133 requirements do not materially affect those portions of a trading firm's activities that are currently under Mark-to-Market (MTM)

accounting. Some energy-trading firms who in the past were not on MTM accounting are now required by the Emerging Issues Task Force (EITF) statement number 98-10 to utilise MTM accounting for fiscal years beginning after December 15, 1998. SFAS No 133 predominantly affects end-users of derivatives rather than the market makers themselves. Moreover, any other activities within the entity that would fall under the definition of derivatives under SFAS No 133 either as free standing or embedded derivatives would be affected if such activities were under accrual accounting. The definition of a derivative under SFAS No 133 is more encompassing than previous pronouncements.

Among other requirements, SFAS No 133 requires all firms seeking hedge accounting treatment[1] to document their risk management objective for using derivatives along with hedge effectiveness measurement methods that will be used to demonstrate effectiveness and subsequently to monitor such effectiveness, as part of the corporate risk management policy. A set of equations like the ones described below will have to become part of the corporate risk management policy before hedge accounting is applied.

What is in SFAS No 133?

As mentioned above, the FASB initially addressed the derivative and hedge accounting issues by initiating a long term project to stimulate industry debate on the subject. Consequently, there is a wealth of literature that has been generated by the accounting profession. Those readers wishing to study the details of the standard should start by obtaining a copy of the standard and reviewing various examples and explanations contained in it. Additionally, to address implementation issues in detail, one of the accounting firms should be consulted in addition to reviewing the available literature such as the DIG's "Statement 133 Implementation Issues" document published after each DIG meeting.

This panel will address the basic premises of the standard. The four underlying principles to the standard, as described below, apply specifically to contracts categorised as "derivatives" under SFAS

Table A. SFAS No 133 versus existing practice

SFAS No 133: Principle	SFAS No 133: Impact	Existing practice
1) Derivatives should be reported as assets or liabilities on the balance sheet	If a contract meets the definition of derivative, it must be reported as an asset or liability	Most non-trading derivatives are not explicitly recognised on the balance sheet. They are normally kept off-balance sheet with fair value and risk disclosure in the footnotes
2) Fair value is the only relevant measure for derivative value	Once a contract is determined to be a derivative under SFAS No 133, it must be carried on the books as an asset or liability at current fair value	Derivatives are often carried at historical cost. For a swap this is often zero since the deals are normally struck at the market. For options, the historical cost has less meaning as the time increases
3) Only items that are assets or liabilities should be reported as such	Gains/losses are booked through earnings or temporarily through other comprehensive income (part of equity) and not deferred as assets or liabilities on the balance sheet	Current practice of treating derivatives' unrealised gains/losses as assets or liabilities
4) Hedge accounting for qualified items	Hedge accounting applies to derivatives *only* in certain qualified circumstances. When it applies, the gains and losses from derivative contracts can be matched to the hedged item when it is recognised in earnings. All ineffective and excluded portions of qualified hedges,and derivatives not used for or not qualified as hedges, are marked-to-fair value through earnings.	Same high-effectiveness test (see definition below) is used to determine applicability of hedge accounting. However, while qualified, the entire derivative's change in value can be deferred, not just the effective portion.

No 133. The table contrasts these principles with existing practice and their impact on derivative accounting as we migrate into the new era.

SFAS No 133 groups the hedges into two major categories, each with different equity, and to some extent earnings volatility implications and effectiveness measurement challenges. These are termed Fair Value Hedges and Cash Flow Hedges. Foreign currency hedges are described as a different category in SFAS No 133, but from the risk management and modelling perspective, the majority of foreign currency hedges fall into these two categories.

Fair value hedges are designated for hedging the fair value of a recognised asset or liability, or unrecognised firm commitment, that is attributable to a particular risk. These are typically assets or liabilities that are already on the balance sheet or firm commitments that will be on the balance sheet in the future. Cashflow hedges are designated for hedging the variability of the cashflows generated by recognised assets or liabilities, or forecasted transactions that are attributable to a particular risk. Many issues arise depending on the type of hedge designation with markedly varying impact on the financial statements, particularly the equity and the earnings lines considered as part of the recurring operating income.

Risk management impact

In order to emphasise the risk management implication of changes in derivative accounting standards let us examine the issue from the perspective of typical risk management activity. Consider a risk manager who is looking to hedge their firm's exposure to certain risk factor(s). They are likely to perform a minimum-variance-hedge type of calculation to determine the number of units of the derivative to hold and its effectiveness in offsetting the underlying risk exposure. They then measure and demonstrate the effectiveness of the hedge by assessing the basis risk based on the coefficient of determination (square of the correlation coefficient, ρ, commonly referred to as the R^2) as follows:

$$\text{Basis risk} = (1 - \rho^2) \times (\text{Hedged item price risk})$$

This equation states that the basis risk is equal to the portion of the variance of the hedged item price change not "cancelled-out" by the derivative price change. Here the hedged item price risk refers to the variance of daily changes in hedged item price. In this context, the coefficient of determination is a measure (based on linear relationship) of the portion of the hedged item price change that is moving in tandem with the derivative price change. This measure is the *Hedge Effectiveness* measure referred to throughout this panel.

Under the current hedge accounting practice, if the hedge passes the effectiveness measure, the entire change in derivative value gets hedge accounting treatment. However, under SFAS No 133, the risk manager must measure the effectiveness of the hedge at least each reporting period for the entire duration of the hedge and must report any ineffective portion or excluded portion of the change in derivative value directly in earnings. In this regard, hedge effectiveness measures must serve two purposes. The first application is to determine whether hedge accounting applies for a given hedging strategy before the hedge is placed and during the period the hedge is in effect. The second application is to measure the actual ineffective portion for the reporting period that goes directly to earnings.

At the time of this writing, prevailing practice among most entities when reviewing a proposed derivative deal for hedge effectiveness is to perform the following type of calculation commonly referred to as dollar-value-offset method:

$$\text{Effectiveness measure} = \frac{\sum_{i=2}^{n}(\Delta P_H)_i}{\sum_{i=2}^{n}(\Delta P_D)_i}$$

$$\text{or another (different measure)} = \sum_{i=2}^{n}\frac{(\Delta P_H)_i}{(\Delta P_D)_i}$$

where

$$(\Delta P_H)_i = (P_H)_i - (P_H)_{i-1}$$

and

$$(\Delta P_D)_i = (P_D)_i - (P_D)_{i-1}$$

P_H and P_D are the daily price of hedged item and the derivative, respectively
i = trading day i where price of the instruments is available
n = total number of trading days in the period.

If this hedge effectiveness measure is within the range of 80% to 120% (or 125% used by some entities), then based on industry practice (stemming from a SEC speech), the hedge meets the "highly effective" test and hedge accounting applies. Otherwise, the derivative is carried on the books at mark-to-market or fair value.

This type of metric, based on the data covering the reporting period only, might not work for hedges that do not cover all hedge-item risks. Consequently, hedges may lose hedge accounting status and the future changes in derivatives' value will be marked-to-fair value without offsetting changes in the hedged item's price. In this case, the hedged item will be separately accounted for using the same GAAP that applied to it before the hedge was placed. That is, the hedges may not qualify for hedge accounting because of the hedge effectiveness test due to statistically insufficient data used in the test although the hedge may be economically effective in offsetting the underlying risk.

To address this problem, one should include more historical data in a statistically based test (perhaps including the same data and the same time period used to assess the effectiveness of the hedge before it was placed) and rolling through more data as the reporting periods progress. The limitation of using dollar-value-offset type of methods for purposes of assessing hedge effectiveness is acknowledged by the audit firms, the DIG and the FASB through the DIG process. In fact, the statistical approach to assessing hedge effectiveness was discussed at the June 1999 DIG meeting and appears to be accepted by the DIG subject to FASB approval. It should be stressed that the DIG recommends the use of the dollar-value-offset method to determine the ineffective portion that must be reported in earnings. However, a second more representative statistical test will determine if the hedge is effective (80% – 120% range test) and if hedge accounting applies. This test will be used to determine the qualification for hedge accounting before and during the hedging period.

As discussed throughout this panel, SFAS No 133 contains many quantitative issues which impact accounting methods for the first time. Additionally, many standalone and embedded derivatives involving financial and physical contracts that were not recognised on the balance sheet in the past will now have to be explicitly recognised on the balance sheet at fair value. The fair value requirement may result in demand for additional valuation models to assess the value of instruments that are not widely traded or that do not have adequate price discovery. This has profound implications since the traditional quantitative techniques and hedging strategies used for economic hedging activities customised for each market and industry, now have to be directly reflected in the financial statements through accounting standards designed to cover all reporting entities across various markets and industries.

In summary, this accounting standard will have an impact on the derivative industry with different sectors being affected differently. The energy sector is going to be affected due to the unique characteristics of energy derivatives (for example, convenience yields and basis risks) that can produce less-than-perfect hedges. Both the derivative sellers and users will be impacted by the standard. Overall, the standard is a positive step towards effective risk management by all users of derivatives.

1 A special accounting treatment whereby gains and losses from derivative contracts can be matched to a hedged item when it is recognised in earnings

qualify for hedge accounting.

In general, there must be an 80% correlation between the underlying business exposure and the instrument the company purchases in order to hedge that position. For instance, a producer that hedges its natural gas position with a crude oil derivative would not qualify for hedge accounting, since the 80% correlation standard would not apply. FAS No 133 requires that an entity establish at the inception of the hedge the method it will use for assessing the effectiveness of the derivative and the measurement approach for determining the ineffective aspect of the hedge. Those methods must be consistent with the entity's approach to managing risk. FAS No 133 will serve as a reminder that operations should have a sound risk management programme in place. (Accounting for energy derivatives is discussed in more detail in Chapter 11 of this volume.)

TYPES OF RISK

While many customised hedge transactions are sophisticated in design, and may utilise complicated contract structure, they can be disaggregated into their various risk components. Setting aside certain generic risks (credit, contract, interest rate and currency risk), the risks facing natural gas market participants can be categorised as follows:

❑ *price risk* The risk of a movement in the absolute price of gas, as defined by the price of gas traded at the Henry Hub. As we mentioned above, this is the gas processing plant and pipeline interconnect point owned and operated by the Sabine Pipeline Company in Erath, Louisiana, which serves as an interconnect for pipelines delivering gas from supply basins in the Gulf Coast to pipelines serving the Northeast and Mid-continent market areas. It is also the delivery point for the New York Mercantile Exchange (Nymex) natural gas futures contract.

❑ *basis risk* The risk of movement in price differentials between two pricing indexes. The most common price differentials quoted are those between the closing price of a Nymex futures contract on its last of trading and a specified *IFGMR, Gas Daily, Natural Gas Week* or *Natural Gas Intelligence* index. (Although a price based on the last three days of trading is also common, more and more traders use the closing price rather than the three-day average.)

❑ *physical risk* The risk that natural gas will not be delivered to, or transported from, the agreed location as required. Natural gas is transacted for

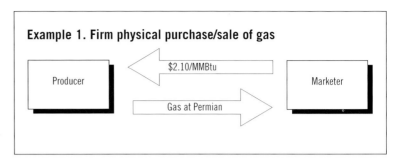

Example 1. Firm physical purchase/sale of gas

Producer — $2.10/MMBtu ← Marketer

Producer → Gas at Permian → Marketer

under firm, interruptible and baseload contracts subject to various price, production, transport and demand conditions.

❑ *cross commodity price risk* The risk that the price of natural gas will change relative to the prices of other fuels, electricity rates, gas liquids prices and other commodities or products where natural gas is a primary cost component.

HEDGING USING FORWARDS AND SWAPS

The following examples demonstrate some methods for managing price, basis and physical risk. Below, we describe alternative methods by which a producer selling its production into the El Paso pipeline system in the Permian Basin of West Texas could manage price risk.

The monetary and physical flows that occur under a firm physical transaction (executed under a Master Firm Purchase/Sale Agreement) are shown in Example 1. In this example, the producer is paid a flat $2.10 per million British thermal units (MMBtus) to deliver natural gas for a fixed term into the El Paso pipeline system. Both parties commit to gas delivery at this price regardless of factors that would cause a disruption in the flow of gas under an interruptible or baseload contract. This transaction hedges both the seller and buyer from price, basis and physical risk.

If the producer wishes to decouple the physical sale from the price risk management component, it can enter into a financial swap. A financially settled, fixed-to-floating natural gas swap that can be executed under a Master Swap Agreement is shown in Example 2 overleaf. In this example, the producer receives a fixed price and pays a floating price. Here the fixed price is $2.25 and the floating price is the closing price on the last day of trading of the Nymex contract for the delivery month. Each month, the producer will financially settle the difference between $2.25 and the final settlement price of the Nymex contract. In addition, it will sell its gas under a baseload contract into the spot market in the Permian Basin. Comparing the $2.25 Nymex price swap to the $2.10 Permian price in

Example 2. Nymex swap with index swing sale of gas

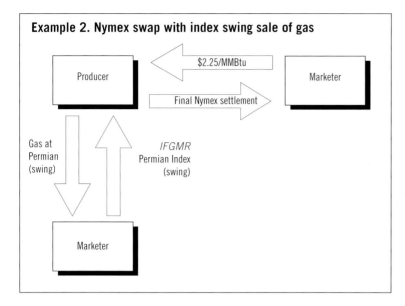

Example 1 shows that the basis between the Nymex and the IFGMR El Paso Permian index in the forward market is –15 cents.

The hedge outlined in Example 2 is the most "accessible" hedge, since it can be executed on behalf of the producer by financial intermediaries who trade on Nymex, or by the producer itself if it wants to manage a futures trading account. However, this hedge manages only price risk and does not address basis and physical risk. (Panel 4 illustrates how disastrous unmanaged basis risks can be.)

A more robust, but complicated, hedge can be initiated by the producer to manage price, basis and physical risk simultaneously. This is shown in Example 3. At the same time as executing a fixed-to-floating Nymex swap, the producer enters into a financially-settled basis swap whereby the producer receives the floating Nymex index minus 15 cents and pays the *IFGMR* El Paso Permian index for the delivery month. In addition, the producer enters into a Firm Physical Purchase/Sale Agreement whereby the producer is paid the *IFGMR* El Paso Permian index by the counterparty that is purchasing the gas.

Example 3 achieves the same results as the physical gas contract in Example 1, but because Example 3 strips the risk into its various components and manages each separately it entails higher transaction costs. However, Example 3 may appeal to those who are less risk averse, and who wish to try to time the initiation of the price, basis and physical hedges in order to gain a greater, but more speculative, return.

Options

Market participants also use options to manage risk. Like fixed-price transactions, options may be entered into using a Firm Physical Purchase/Sale Agreement or a Master Swap Agreement. As with the above examples, an option may be settled either by actually delivering the commodity or by settling financially against a Nymex, *IFGMR*, *Gas Daily* or other index.

Many market participants use options when they are taking a view on the market; the options act as insurance against adverse price moves while allowing the company to profit from the "upside" if the market moves in the expected direction.

However, many other uses exist. For example, firm fixed-price physical contracts often have monthly volumetric baseload provisions embedded in them. These provisions give the purchaser a monthly option to "turn back" a portion of the contracted volumes if the contract price is above the market prices current at the

Example 3. Nymex swap with basis swap and index firm sale of gas

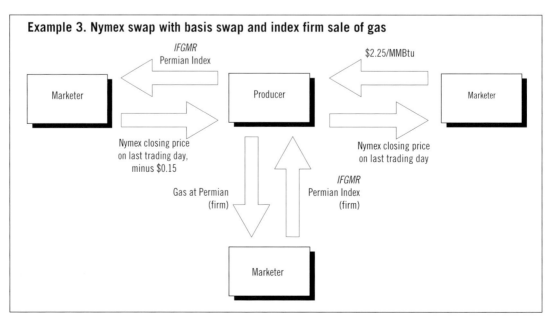

WINTER 1995–96'S BASIS BLOWOUT

Ignoring basis risk can be disastrous, as was demonstrated in the winter of 1995–96, when an unprecedented widening of basis occurred. As the figure illustrates, the index price of gas arriving at the Columbia-Appalachia interconnect reached $4.50 per million Btu in March 1996, compared with $1.30 per million Btu at the NW Canadian Border. Many producers, who participated in what is commonly called a "dirty" hedge – a Nymex hedge for price risk only – were caught unaware and suffered significant financial losses as a result.

Several circumstances combined to create this imbalance. Winter temperatures in the Midwest and the East were anywhere up to 7½ degrees colder than average. West of the Mississippi, temperatures were two to four degrees warmer. While the West had gas to spare, it was stranded: there was not sufficient pipeline capacity to deliver the extra gas to Henry Hub.

To understand the financial implications, consider this. Producers who had hoped to hedge their price had sold monthly Nymex futures. At month's end, Nymex futures prices rose, creating a loss for the producers. At the same time, at the Rocky Mountains interconnect where the producers physically delivered their gas, the price had dropped. The producers' total loss was the difference between the fixed price specified in the Nymex contract and the final settlement price – plus the drop in cash prices at the delivery point. Rather than shield themselves from risk by using a Nymex hedge, the producer exacerbated its loss because it lost both in the physical delivery and in the Nymex contract.

A basis hedge is structured in the following manner:
At the termination of the hedge the producer receives:

$$\text{Total payout to producer} =$$
$$I(T) + NX(t) - NX(T),$$

where
I is the index price of gas in the physical market,
NX is the Nymex price,
t is the time that the hedge is initiated, and
T is the time that the hedge is terminated.

Adding I(t) to both sides of the equation, we obtain the following formula which shows the gain or loss from both the physical and hedge components of the transaction:

$$\text{Total payout to producer} =$$
$$I(t) + I(T) - I(t) + NX(t) - NX(T)$$

where
$I(T) - I(t)$ = physical market gain or loss, and
$NX(t) - NX(T)$ = hedge gain or loss.

Given the recent development and expansion of pipelines, the chance that such a widespread basis blow-out will occur has been reduced. Yet the potential is still there. A rich new find of natural gas in a specific location might surpass the relevant pipeline's ability to handle the new capacity. Consumers, too, can be directly affected. Areas such as the East Coast, with relatively little pipeline development, might well experience capacity constraints during a bitterly cold winter. As discussed earlier, deregulation would now allow price signals to flow directly to the consumer. The end-user, once sheltered from basis risk, is now vulnerable.

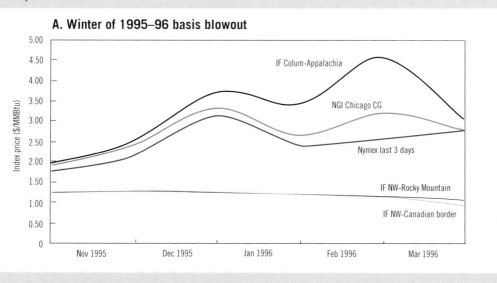

A. Winter of 1995–96 basis blowout

IF Colum-Appalachia
NGI Chicago CG
Nymex last 3 days
IF NW-Rocky Mountain
IF NW-Canadian border

Index price ($/MMBtu)

Nov 1995   Dec 1995   Jan 1996   Feb 1996   Mar 1996

time of delivery. These baseload provisions may be managed by using options that settle monthly. Some fixed-price firm physical contracts have daily baseload provisions in them; while it is relatively illiquid, there is a market in option strips that settle daily.

Many options in the energy markets are Asian options. Asian options have a payoff that depends on the average of the reference index during a specified time period. For example, the payoff might depend on the average of the last three settlement prices for a Nymex natural gas futures contract. Another example is an option that settles against the daily average of a specified *Gas Daily* Index published for a delivery month.

Spread options are also prevalent in the industry. These options have a payout that depends on the difference of two specified indexes. One common use is to hedge the basis between two published *Inside FERC* market indexes. This is known as an index spread option. Another is to hedge summer-winter price differentials by means of a time spread option.

An end-user may wish to have the option of purchasing its natural gas supply at the spot market price for either natural gas or residual fuel oil (resid) – whichever is the better. These options are often called "better of" options. Another alternative is to have the option payoff dependent upon a combination of referenced commodity prices. These "basket" options may appeal to oil and gas producers who want to hedge the total revenue received for their production. A basket option with a payoff that is determined by the value of a combined oil and gas index would be cheaper than buying separate options to hedge the oil production and to hedge the gas production.

Caps, floors, collars, swaptions, participating swaps, extendible swaps and other hedge management structures can be created using the types of options discussed above. Technical discussions of the kind of option structures used in the natural gas market and other energy markets, and how they are valued, are provided in Chapters 2 and 3 respectively of this book.

Managing cross commodity risk

Cross-commodity price risk is also a concern. Investors in oil and gas production may want to synthetically shift production from one energy commodity to another. Utilities may find it attractive to invest in plants that burn natural gas – but if they do so they run the risk that the delivered price of natural gas may change relative to that of alternative fuels. Now that the electricity markets are being deregulated, power producers are concerned with the relationship between the price of natural gas and the price of electricity. One measure, known as the "spark spread", represents the cost differential between generating electricity from natural gas or buying the electricity in the open market. It has become an effective tool for managing a power producer's spread exposure (Panel 5.)

Cross-commodity risks may be managed using a firm transaction (executed under a Master Firm Physical Purchase/Sale Agreement), whereby the price of one commodity is determined by that of another, or by means of a swap contract with financial settlements that are based on the difference between the published price indexes of two different commodities.

In Example 4, a utility located in the Northeast region of the US has retooled its plant to burn natural gas in order to comply with emissions standards set by the Clean Air Act. Instead of unwinding its current firm index-based contractual commitment to purchase residual fuel oil, the utility redelivers the "resid" and takes delivery of natural gas at the plant. It manages the price risk inherent in doing this by arranging to purchase natural gas at a price that is tied to the spot price of delivered resid in its market area.

Alternatively, the utility could enter into a financial swap to pay a formula index, based upon a published price for resid in New York Harbor, and receive the settlement price of the last day of trading of the Nymex natural gas contract. This is called a Btu swap, and is shown in Example 5. Here the utility would sell its current resid purchase commitment to the spot market, take the proceeds from this sale and combine them with the proceeds from the financial settlement of the Btu swap, and purchase gas for the

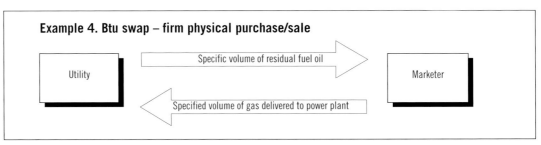

Example 4. Btu swap – firm physical purchase/sale

Utility — Specific volume of residual fuel oil → Marketer

Marketer ← Specified volume of gas delivered to power plant — Utility

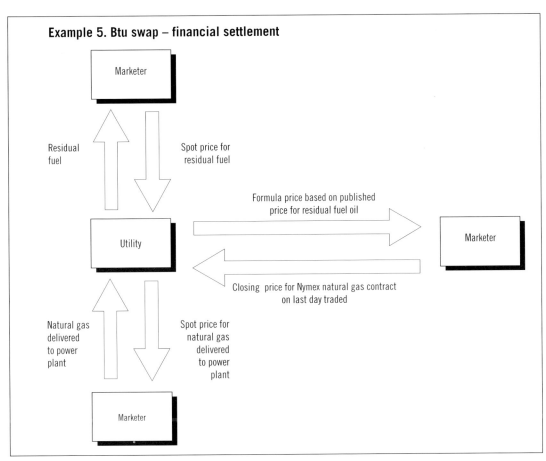

Example 5. Btu swap – financial settlement

plant. The problem with this tactic is that it leaves the utility exposed to both basis and physical risk on the resid and natural gas legs of the transaction.

To reduce the basis risk in the financial Btu swap, the utility can enter into financial basis swaps to lock in the difference between their market area indexes and those referenced in the Btu swap. To manage the physical risk of its gas supply, it can enter into a Firm Physical Purchase/Sale Agreement whereby it pays the market area index it receives in its gas basis swap in exchange for a firm commitment to deliver gas. It will also have to enter into a firm contract to sell its resid stocks against the same market area index that is referenced in its resid basis swap. As demonstrated in Example 3, it is possible to hedge any combination of risks, though this flexibility may be achieved at the expense of higher transaction costs.

The ability to manage cross-commodity risk is taken one step further in cross-commodity transactions that take one commodity and synthetically turn it into another commodity. In a "forward tolling" arrangement, for example, an energy marketer that wishes to turn gas into electricity can enter into a tolling arrangement with a power manufacturer, who will return electricity to the gas marketer (Figure 9). At no point does the gen-

erator own the gas or the electricity, but instead is paid a tolling fee. In a "reverse tolling" arrangement, the marketer sells natural gas to a power plant but has the right to "call" it back and replace it with a similar volume of power (Figure 10 overleaf). (For simplicity, operations and maintenance costs are ignored.)

The role of risk management in financing

The demand for natural gas continues to grow. By 2020, natural gas consumption is expected to grow to 43.3 trillion cubic feet in North America; 35.6 trillion cubic feet in the US alone. That com-

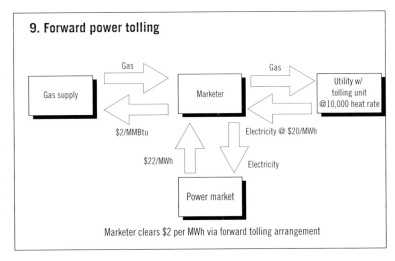

9. Forward power tolling

Marketer clears $2 per MWh via forward tolling arrangement

SPARK SPREADS

Spark spreads are commonly thought of as the fluctuating difference between the price of electricty sold by a generator and the price of the natural gas used to generate that electricity expressed in \$/MWh. However, gas turbines operate at various efficiencies. Consider the following situation. A generator has the opportunity to buy natural gas at \$2.25/MMBtu. Their turbine has a heat rate of 7 MMBtu/MWh. Here's how the generator decides whether it pays to generate power or buy power.

❑ The cost of the natural gas required to generate one megawatt-hour of electricity is \$15.75 (7 × \$2.25 = \$15.75).

❑ This amount is compared with the cost of buying power off the grid at \$25.75/MWh, thus the spark spread is \$10 (25.75 − 15.75 = 10).

❑ If the generator's variable operating and maintenance costs are less than \$10, it is cheaper to generate power than it is to buy it.

The story would change if the turbine has a heat rate of 12 MMBtu. This yields a hypothetical spark spread of \$−1.25MMBtu/MWh. This negative value indicates that generation from natural gas is more expensive than purchasing power off the grid.

If a company wishes to buy its power at a price that is based on a natural gas price index, then the power price must be converted to a natural gas index using the spark spread. The formula is as follows:

Spark spread = Price/MWh$_{power}$ − Price/MWh$_{gas}$

Example:

    Power swap: \$24.00/MWh

    Gas swap: \$2.50/MMBtu

    Heat rate: 10,000 Btu/KWh

Price per MWh

    = Power price/MWh − (Gas price/MMBtu × Heat rate (Btu/KWh) × 1,000 KWh/MWh)

    = \$24.00 − (\$2,50 × 10,000 × 1/1,000)

    = (\$1.00)

pares with 26.1 trillion cubic feet consumed in North America in 1997, of which the US accounted for 21.9 trillion cubic feet.[15]

In the early 1990s, producers in general were not replacing reserves. But in 1994, the trend was reversed. By 1997, there were more than 2,597 trillion cubic feet of recoverable natural gas reserves in the US – enough to meet anticipated demand for the next 70 years.[16] Reserve additions have exceeded US gas production five years in a row, with 104% of production replaced in 1998.[17]

While independent and major producers are increasingly interested in recovering these reserves, doing so will require a great deal of capital. Capital is required not only for exploration and production, but also for the expansion of pipeline transmission and distribution systems, and for the development of facilities to burn the gas – specifically, gas-fired electrical generation plants. Obtaining this capital is challenging, given the risk embedded in investment projects that depend upon natural gas prices.

Since the removal of natural gas price controls in 1978, there have been wide swings in natural gas prices. These price fluctuations, the financial pressures resulting from deregulation, and large write-downs resulting from take-or-pay contract settlements, led to a severe drop in the creditworthiness of many pipeline companies in the 1980s and early 1990s. The uncertainty over future price levels that was created by a large supply overhang, and by concerns over the viability of long-term contracts, led market participants to dramatically shorten the maturity of their gas supply contracts. Almost overnight, contract terms changed in duration from years to months, and the active "spot" market described above evolved to become the primary arena in which to sell and buy gas.

While dramatically shortening the maturity of transactions alleviated concerns about contract and credit risk, it also greatly increased the exposure of industry participants to changes in com-

10. Reverse power tolling

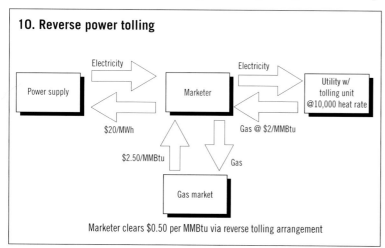

Marketer clears \$0.50 per MMBtu via reverse tolling arrangement

modity price levels. Commodity price volatility of this magnitude greatly increases the variability of the returns to investment capital, and results in high risk premiums being charged for any investment in the natural gas industry.

Other industries dependent on the price of a commodity commonly use long-term contracts that offer protection from price volatility as a way of lowering the cost of capital. Furthermore, a statistical analysis of returns from firms that have issued hybrid, commodity index-linked debt shows that their equity betas declined after the debt issuance, indicating that shareholders recognise the benefits of commodity price risk management.[18]

The objective of commodity price risk management is to reduce earnings volatility and lower the probability of financial distress. A well-designed risk management programme should allow increased financial leverage and higher, less risky returns to shareholders' equity. The benefits to the company of such a programme are enhanced creditworthiness and an increase in the supportable level of debt, higher market capitalisation and a significantly lower after-tax cost of capital. Additionally, prudent risk management helps improve the budget and planning process and allows companies to develop forward business. By means of risk management, the industry might well be able to increase its typical debt-to-equity ratios of 60/40 to 80/20 without increasing the probability of financial distress.

One established financing technique involving risk instruments is the volumetric production payment (VPP). A VPP involves the acquisition from a producer of a specified volume of gas and/or oil for future deliveries. The value of any given volume of future production is hedged and thereby transformed into a series of known cash-flows that amortise with the production profile of the financed reserves.* Producers that enter into these transactions are also able to access more debt than could be acquired via traditional non-recourse reserve-based financing.

Pre-paid financial agreements are emerging as an innovative source of producer financing (Figure 11). In this example, the producer receives a synthetic loan in the form of a lump sum payment on a present value (PV) basis. The producer maintains its price exposure by selling a swap to a marketer. Typical durations of such deals range from three to five years.

Price hedges play an integral role in the use of pre-paid agreements. The technique was developed in the latter part of 1998 and early

1999, when natural gas prices dropped dramatically. Producers experienced a severe tightening in credit as a result. To ease the crunch, many producers agreed to pre-pay financial agreements in which they consent to pre-sell a given volume of product at a pre-determined price on a present value basis. The producer receives 100% of the payment upfront. While the producer has access to the capital, the technique has a downside: it sets a fixed price for the amount of production sold. In order to regain floating price flexibility, the producer can enter into an opposite transaction to buy back their position on a non-present value basis to unwind the fixed price, thereby creating a synthetic loan. Producers who hedged their pre-pay agreements were rewarded when gas prices recovered by mid-1999.

The role of the intermediary

The primary role of the risk intermediary is to provide its customer with instantaneous liquidity for all transaction types, at all times. To do so requires an understanding of customer needs, in-depth knowledge of the products and the markets, and the ability to assume and manage the risks embedded in the customer transactions.

Many different types of intermediaries have entered the natural gas market in the last few years. Most numerous are those that intermediate in the spot market, where they match the needs of producers and end-users. Some companies focus solely on financial hedge transactions, and offer no physical services, while others bridge the physical and financial markets. During the later 1990s a number of market makers with roots in investment banking left the business. JP Morgan, United Bank of Switzerland and Merrill Lynch sold off their energy risk management business to focus on core financial products.

When entering into a transaction, intermediaries assume credit and contract exposure to the

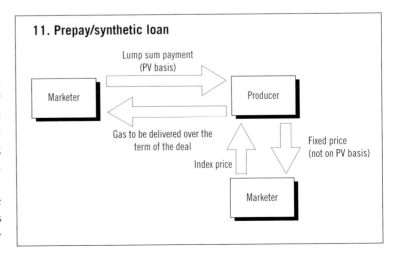

11. Prepay/synthetic loan

Lump sum payment (PV basis)

Marketer → Producer

Gas to be delivered over the term of the deal

Index price

Fixed price (not on PV basis)

Marketer

counterparty, in addition to market risks. Credit exposure is of paramount concern in the natural gas industry, and became increasingly so during the drop in energy prices in 1998–1999. The severe drop in natural gas prices, which hit a low of 1.628 on February 26, 1999 for the Henry Hub Nymex contract, forced a number of smaller producers into bankruptcy. When contracting with a counterparty, it is paramount to do a full-fledged credit analysis of that organisation. Often long-term players in the energy markets, who react calmly to sharp movements in energy prices, make the most sense as counterparties.

To mitigate credit exposure and to allow customers to engage in prudent commodity risk management practices, a number of contract provisions are used by intermediaries. These include exposure collateralisation, termination of contract upon a material adverse change in the counterparties financial condition (MAC clause) and mutual termination, if desired, at agreed forward dates.

A risk intermediary depends upon its ability to price and manage the market risk of a complex transaction portfolio. Some companies attempt to minimise risk by running a "matched book" of transactions, but this means that they often cannot respond to customer demands quickly or consistently. Dynamic portfolio management is the process of managing a "mismatched" portfolio of maturity, location, product and grade risks. It demands an understanding of the dynamics of the forward price curve of all those products for which the intermediary makes markets. The intermediary must also understand how exogenous factors may affect the curve and the relationships between the curves.

For instance, location basis (price differential) risk between various pipeline indexes is seasonally dependent, as the demand for gas varies significantly between market areas throughout the year. When pricing long-term transactions (that is, 10 years or more) where the basis risk is borne by the intermediary, market illiquidity means that the intermediary must consider the impact of pipeline expansions, reserve development, alternative fuels and the long-distance transmissions of electricty or "wheeling". The relationships between the forward curves of energy products are not obvious: for example, natural gas liquids (NGLs) prices are more closely related to the price of crude products than they are to the price of natural gas. This means that an intermediary active in the NGLs market must have a good understanding of the crude and product market, and ideally run a crude and crude product desk.

When managing an options book, the impact of these factors is magnified. As detailed in Chapter 3, the intermediary must also understand how to manage its exposure to changes in volatility (vega), changes in market prices (delta and gamma), the passage of time (theta), as well as other risks. Effectively managing these risks requires large investments in personnel, accounting, control and risk management functions, as well as computer systems. High price volatility and low liquidity in the dealer market for more exotic options, such as location basis, time spread, basket and *IFGMR*-indexed options, requires that a market maker be prepared to dynamically manage its book against an array of market factors.

The intermediary uses offsetting transactions to manage the portfolio of risks generated by its OTC business. The natural gas futures and options market on Nymex is the most visible and active of the markets used. Marketers also transfer risk to and from each other on the OTC-brokered market for swaps and options. The OTC market offers a fair degree of liquidity in long-dated swaps, physical transactions and basis swaps, as well as options and exchange for physicals (EFPs).

An EFP is defined as the conversion of a futures position into a physical position via simultaneous buy/sell transactions. EFPs often involve the exchange of a Nymex contract for the obligation to deliver or receive gas at a specified location under a firm contract at a specified differential to the price of the exchanged futures contract. In the exchange, the party delivering the contract receives the gas, and the party receiving the contract delivers the gas. This market becomes very active prior to and during bid week as market participants seek the most economical means to sell and buy their gas. In late 1998, Nymex approved the use of EFPs to settle swaps as well.

Market outlook

The combined efforts of marketers, swap counterparties and financiers in natural gas risk management have revolutionised the gas industry. Furthermore, there are strong fundamental reasons to suppose that the natural gas risk management sector will continue to grow:

❑ natural gas usage will increase because of environmental concerns and the relative economy of gas-fired combined cycle plants in electricity generation;

PANEL 6

THE UK GAS MARKET AND EUROPE

Louise Kitchen

Enron Corp – Europe

In the space of 10 years, the United Kingdom natural gas market has developed from an integrated monopoly business to a competitive market leading the way for gas markets across Europe. All users of natural gas, including 20 million household customers, can choose their supplier of gas from a range of marketers. In the same period, gas demand has increased by almost 50%, predominantly due to a surge in the use of gas for power generation and a sophisticated trading market that has developed – one which is now ready to move further into Europe.

Although competition had been enabled by legislation, in 1989 British Gas plc retained a monopoly in the transportation and sale of gas. To safeguard development capital, producers entered into "life of field" (dedicated depletion) contracts with British Gas at a fixed base price that escalated in accordance with a basket of indexes. The contracts incorporated high levels of "take-or-pay" (see main text). The UK gas regulator, Ofgas, recognised that the fact that competitors to British Gas could not access natural gas on a short-term basis was hindering competition and took two steps to address this issue. The first step prevented British Gas from purchasing more than 90% of any new gas production. Secondly, British Gas was compelled to re-sell some of the gas it had already contracted under its life-of-field contracts. At this time, Ofgas also extended the competitive market to include a further tranche of the market for small commercial consumers.

These steps led several of the upstream producers to set up marketing companies to sell directly to end-users in competition with British Gas, while others looked to develop sales to power generators. The sales to power generators, and

those to the new, non-producer marketers that emerged soon after, were conducted on a long-term, fixed-price basis, ie they were similar to traditional British Gas contracts.

The shorter term trading of gas remained limited until the spring of 1995 when aggressive competition in the consumer market forced marketers, generators and producers to trade out of long positions. The nascent trading activity was soon supported by telephone brokers and news journals, adding transparency that further promoted liquidity.

The introduction in early 1996 of the Network Code provided further stimulus to the developing market. The Network Code was introduced upon the recommendation of the Monopolies and Merger Commission report of 1993 to ensure that an equitable operating regime was applied to all parties transporting gas through British Gas' transportation division (known today as Transco). The Network Code replaced the bilateral contracts between Transco and the shippers and introduced a requirement on each shipper to match, each day, the amount of gas they put into the system with that taken off by their customers. Any imbalance between gas inputs and offtakes from the system are managed by Transco through its access to the Flexibility Mechanism, by means of which shippers post offers to buy and sell gas to Transco on a 24-hour basis. This balancing requirement increased short-term volatility significantly, leading to price deviations within the day as high as £5 per therm in extreme circumstances.

The Network Code also introduced a notional trading point, the National Balancing Point (NBP), which increased market liquidity by aggregating traditional supply points up to one trading hub

❑ open access in power transmission will increase competition and reduce margins, making commodity price risk management more important for utilities;

❑ volatility in prices will continue to be high, given the increasingly fine balance between supply and demand;

❑ access to development capital will be increasingly tied to sound price risk management prac-

tices; and

❑ market participants are becoming increasingly comfortable with risk management tools and techniques.

Other changes are already underway:

❑ the industry will increasingly manage risk exposures through contract structure rather than by investing in and managing physical assets;

❑ regulatory changes will allow utilities and

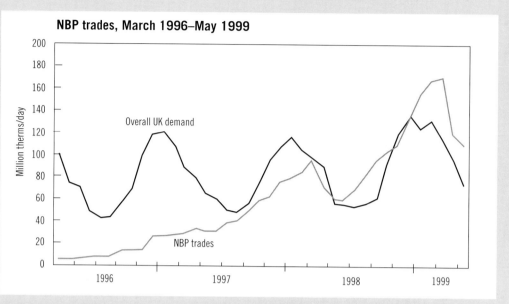

NBP trades, March 1996–May 1999

accessible to all shippers on an equal basis, thereby promoting depth and liquidity.

The rapid development of the market in 1996 enabled the International Petroleum Exchange to successfully launch its Natural Gas Futures Contract in January, 1997. The futures contract is traded via a screen-based transaction system and not by the more traditional means of open outcry. Open contracts are settled through physical delivery at the National Balancing Point. Despite a hesitant first summer, the contract is now a major part of the UK market and regularly trades over 10,000,000 MMBtus per day. The IPE continues to develop the market by extending the number of contracts.

The over-the-counter market continues to dominate forward trading, with at least 75% to 80% of the total market transactions. A significant portion of business is transacted through the numerous brokers who have been attracted to the industry due to the huge increase in transaction levels. Part of this growth has been due to an increase in the number of active participants in the spot market from only 10 or so in 1995 to over 50 in 1999. Evidence of this growth can be seen in the "churn ratio", which is the amount of gas traded

at the NBP versus total UK demand (Figure). The liquid trading period has gradually been extended out to three years, and the average trade size has doubled from 2,500 MMBtu/day to 5,000 MMBtu/day for forward contracts; trades of 50,000 to 100,000 MMBtus regularly trade within a day.

Although physical forward trading still dominates activity, a varied and liquid options market is emerging (both physical and financial). The level of sophistication within the over-the-counter market has increased significantly, so that there is presently a wide array of products for managing trading risks. Many of these products have been developed specifically to address risks specific to the UK market and require unique valuation methods.

The increasing sophistication of the UK gas market has led to new entrants with new skills. The increasing prospect of a pan-European liberalised gas and power market has attracted investment banks, commodity trading houses and European utilities, all keen to hone their skills in the UK gas market prior to the onset of full European liberalisation. The existing players have been forced to match the increased skill sets, and

LDCs to increase their use of risk management products;

❑ outsourcing is gaining acceptance among producers and end-users that wish to focus on their core businesses, such as production or manufacturing;

❑ Internet-based derivative trading will become common. Its increased efficiency and price transparency may lead to the development of a one-

day market for gas; and

❑ natural gas risk management sectors will continue to develop outside the US.

The rest of this section will discuss the first three of these changes in more detail, while Panel 6 examines the fourth.

One major effect of the development of liquid forward markets is that forward price contracts have begun to substitute for investments in

the business is well on its way to becoming a mature commodity trading market.

The development of the competitive supply market and the increasing transparency and liquidity of the traded market have created opportunities for innovative price risk management solutions, not only in gas, but across energy commodities. Late in 1996, Enron entered into the UK's first Virtual Power Station contract, which allowed the buyer access to virtual generating capacity using a combination of physical and financing commodity transactions. On a smaller scale, the gradual convergence of the gas and power markets has led to the trading of short-term (less than three months) and long-term (five year) "spark spreads" and also physical gas indexed to UK power and other commodities. Further to this, the deregulation of part of the UK's storage market in 1999 led to an expansion of risk management opportunities with various companies buying bundled storage services with the intention of unbundling the components and redesigning a more efficient and customer-focused product for resale. This development led Enron to launch another new product – Enbank – a virtual storage service that is designed to transform the storage market from a monopoly-based service physically dependent on storage assets into a market that uses risk management tools, on a contractual basis, to replace these physical assets.

The opening of the UK–Belgium Interconnector in October, 1998 has had a subtle but wide-reaching effect upon the UK market. Over the first winter, the Interconnector had a huge impact on UK winter prices, resulting in a "reverse" flow very shortly after the start of commercial operations. In essence, the newly developed UK gas market for the first time experienced the effect of external factors and was treated to a convincing display of market forces as the Interconnector carried low-priced European gas into the UK. The Interconnector was originally designed to flow out of the UK to combat an excess of supply caused

by high prices early in the 1990s. Thus, an embryonic gas market is developing at Zeebrugge (the entry/exit point for the Interconnector into the Belgian system) with daily, monthly and seasonal transactions taking place. There has been great interest in the creation of a standard contract – due to be released in late summer 1999 – for spot trading at Zeebrugge; the idea has attracted the interest of over 50 European players.

The arbitrage opportunities afforded by the Interconnector have also had the effect of exposing the UK market once again to oil prices, as continental gas prices are often related to oil. The wide arbitrage that was present for quite some time also encouraged some of the continental European gas players to take a tentative first step into the liberalised market.

We are about to see a repeat of the UK experience in continental Europe, although the development of the market and the drivers behind it will be rather different. The liberalisation of the UK gas market was largely driven by regulatory and political intervention. The EU Gas Directive may not be strong enough to force through deregulation, and the project may be further hindered by the lack of political will in some countries to drive through the Gas Directive (in most cases, there is not even a regulator in place).

The formation of a competitive European gas market will have a predominantly commercial impetus, with large end-users driving the change toward a more competitive business environment, and innovative companies with no entrenched position helping them to do so. Although the EU directive has not yet come into force, there are signs that the commercial world is impatient and unwilling to wait for legislation to catch up with commercial reality. Spot trades already have been reported at various North Western European border locations, and there are a number of anti-competition cases working their way through the courts – some of which may provide a major boost to the liquidity of the gas market.

(and management of) physical assets. For instance, a producer can now use the forward basis differential market instead of entering into a long-term transport commitment. Alternatively, end-users can lock in a summer–winter price spread by using a monthly indexed forward price contract instead of purchasing storage. In addition, gas marketers are increasingly aware that they can monetise the monthly baseload capabil-

ity in any firm physical contract that they hold by selling financial options.

In the deregulated era, the pipeline companies can no longer simply pass on capital expenditure for pipelines and storage. Decisions by pipeline companies and others to invest in these assets will be dictated by the level of real economic returns that the assets can generate. Proof of this structural change can be seen in the

WEATHER DERIVATIVES

Weather risk management is a new phenomenon – the first risk contracts were written only in 1997. It is closely associated with natural gas and power generation since the single largest influence on the volume of energy sales is temperature. While energy producers and users have been able to manage their exposure to price risk, it is only with weather derivatives that they can begin to protect themselves from "volume" risk.

As of early 1999, some 1,450 weather-related contracts with an estimated value of $2.5 billion, have been written. The majority of transactions have occurred in the US, where much of the market has been speculative.

In 1998, Enron introduced weather derivatives to Europe. European volume has been considerably less than that seen in the US, due to the absence of a speculative market. While both options and swaps are used; European buyers have tended to use swaps so as to avoid the premiums associated with options; the US market has veered toward options.

A temperature-based weather derivative is used as a proxy for energy demand because heating and cooling strongly correlate to temperature. Weather derivatives, however, can be structured to cover other conditions such as rainfall, humidity, snow, cloud cover, and river flow. A prudent weather risk management programme identifies the correlation between certain types of weather and profit margins, and then shields those margins from adverse conditions.

The first known European weather contract, a swap, was negotiated between Energie Noord West (ENW) NV and Enron. ENW's concern was that a mild winter would reduce the volume of gas sold. The three-month contract began in January. Under its terms, Enron agreed to compensate ENW if average temperatures remained above an agreed level during the winter. ENW agreed to pay Enron if temperatures remain below target levels for the period.

Weather contracts are based on totally objective measurements. In the US, all contracts are tied to the National Weather Service. In Britain, contracts are based on data from The Meteorological Office (The Met) in Bracknell, Berkshire.

Temperature-based weather derivative contracts focus on temperature as measured by "degree-days", based on either the Fahrenheit or Celsius scale. Annual heating costs are directly proportional to the total number of degree-days in the year. A degree-day (DD) is the absolute value of the difference between average daily temperature and 65° Fahrenheit or 18° Celsius. That point on the thermometer has particularly significant because when the mercury drops below 65°F or 18°C, consumers tend to turn on their heating. Above that number, they turn on their air conditioning. When the temperature falls below 65°F or 18°C, it is measured as "heating degree-days" (HDDs). Temperatures above that point are measured as "cooling degree-days".

capacity brokering (the buying and selling of various types of transport capacity) that has started to take place. This developing market can be used to manage existing transport commitments, to provide alternatives in managing physical delivery commitments, and for price discovery and hedging when making capital investment decisions.

The nature of the storage business is also changing, as investment shifts away from production area reservoir facilities and towards market area salt dome facilities. Storage fields are being developed to serve an important market need: peak load demand within market areas. The Gas Industry Standards Board has increased daily nomination from one day-ahead nomination to four nominations – twice in the day ahead and

twice during the actual day. This calls for more flexible storage that can respond to immediate market need with quicker injection/withdrawal speeds. This need will increase in the future as the industry operates at an ever-tighter supply/demand equilibrium.

Under past US regulations, LDCs and utilities have had little economic incentive to engage in risk management activities on behalf of their customers. It is widely held that if a programme was implemented that was not pre-approved by the appropriate regulatory authority, any "benefits" from hedging would accrue to ratepayers, while any "losses" would be borne by shareholders. However, most state Public Utility Commissions (PUCs) have implemented performance-based rate making, which permits LDCs to retain profits as an incentive to take on risk. In this scenario, the LDCs take on the price risk of supplying gas in exchange for keeping the profit. Utilities have become traders to support this strategy and are increasingly relying on the gas marketing firms rather than their own portfolio to manage supply. The PUCs, recognising that LDCs frequently do not manage surplus capacity effectively, are encouraging LDCs to actively trade that capacity by allowing them to retain a portion of the profit made. This has spurred increased use of risk management tools by regulated utilities.

We are likely to see an increase in outsourcing gas supply management. Customers are more comfortable securing their entire supply from one source, and they often also gain a financial advantage from doing so. In a watershed agreement, Brooklyn Union Gas (BUG) in New York outsourced its entire gas supply management to Enron in 1998. Enron provided a greater value for BUG's portfolio of capacity than the utility had achieved, and Enron guaranteed that value for the term of the contract (one year). Enron provides BUG with a full-requirements gas supply contract that approximates the manner in which the company purchased gas on its own. As the gas supply manager, Enron can trade BUG's excess capacity while using risk management tools to hedge its positions. BUG benefits because the regulators permit shareholders to keep 20% of any profits they make by trading excess capacity, and under this arrangement more capacity is available for resale.

New York State is expected to require LDCs to shed their merchant activities within the near future. Ultimately, the arrangement will help BUG make the transition from a merchant/distributor to a fully unbounded distributor.

Natural gas is becoming a more important part of the energy mix in the United States and will play a crucial role in future power generation. This is leading to greater investment in natural gas infrastructure, such as pipeline capacity storage and natural gas-fired generating plants, even as deregulation is all but eliminating the long-term contracts the industry has hitherto depended upon to finance its projects. The emergence of a vibrant risk management market is bridging the gap. Risk management has helped to temper the historical volatility of energy commodities and has enabled producers to withstand many ups and downs in the market. As price risk flows through to end-users, many large corporations are beginning to apply risk management techniques as well.

There are increasing opportunities to craft innovative risk management approaches that link commodities or protect enterprises from a variety of risks. The introduction of weather-based derivatives, which protect users from volume risk associated with weather extremes, is one such example (Panel 7). More creative products undoubtedly will follow, benefiting all.

1 *The authors would like to thank Robert Butts, Richard Causey, Jay Fitzgerald, Julie Gomez, Paige Grumulaitis, Jeannie Mandelker, Michael McCall and Richard Shapiro for their contributions.*

2 *US Department of Energy,* Natural Gas Monthly, *March 1999.*

3 *1999* Enron Energy Outlook.

4 *1999* Enron Energy Outlook.

5 *1999* Enron Energy Outlook.

6 Energy Information Administration Annual Outlook for US Electrical Power, *1991.*

7 *1999* Enron Energy Outlook.

8 Energy Information Administration Natural Gas 1998: Issues and Trends.

9 *Two prominent examples are the Exxon-Mobil merger and British Petroleum's intention to merge with not only Amoco (thereby becoming the third-largest producer of natural gas) but ARCO as well.*

10 *Mergers such as Dominion Resources and Consolidated Natural Gas; Duke Power and Pan Energy; Enova and Pacific Enterprises; and Enron and Portland General Electric, have become commonplace.*

11 *Among recent mergers are El Paso/Sonat, El Paso/Leviathan Gas Pipeline, El Paso/Tenneco, Williams/MAPCO, Williams/Transco and Koch/Delhi Gas Pipeline.*

12 *Contractually, these transactions are termed Baseload Firm, Baseload Interruptible and Swing.*

13 *Operations which purchase natural gas often vary in the amount of gas they actually need each day. However, the amount of gas entering a physical gas transportation system must be kept roughly equal to the amount being drawn out, or the integrity of the system is threatened. Thus "balancing" operations are used to adjust for the excess or shortage of gas used.*

14 *Commodities Futures Trading Commission.*

15 *1999* Enron Energy Outlook.

16 *1997* Enron Energy Outlook.

17 Energy Information Administration, US Crude Oil, Natural Gas, and Natural Gas Liquids Reserves 1997 Annual Report, *and Arthur Andersen.*

18 *"Shareholders Applaud Risk Management",* Corporate Finance, *June/July 1992.*

Competitive Electricity Markets Around the World:
Approaches to Price Risk Management

Grant S. Masson[1]
Enron Corp

The last 20 years have seen radical changes in the structure of electricity markets around the world. Prior to the 1980s it was argued convincingly that the electricity industry was a natural monopoly and that strong vertical integration was an obvious and economical model for electric utilities. Recent technological advances, however, mean that it is now possible to operate power generation and retail supply as competitive market segments.

Change came slowly at first, reflecting widespread industry concern that competition and system security were mutually exclusive. Early experiments – in particular, the UK restructuring – demonstrated clearly, however, that the lights did not go out with the institution of competition. Spurred by these successes, other countries have undertaken restructuring and deregulation, particularly during the late 1990s. By the turn of the century, more than a dozen countries will have restructured their power industries to include competition, with many more in the discussion or early implementation phases.

With restructuring come new challenges. System stability and security and reliability of supply remain the ultimate goals of the power business, and new approaches are required to ensure that competitive elements are successfully coordinated so that these goals will continue to be met. Furthermore, as competitively generated electricity becomes a commodity, there is a concomitant need to establish market structures. Although some aspects of the electricity industry are unique, many more are similar to those of other commodity businesses, and the market trends seen today are not unlike those observed in other restructured markets; the natural gas, airline, and telecommunications industries are examples.

The purpose of this chapter is to provide an overview of the state of electricity industry restructuring around the world and to show how this relates to power price risk management. First we offer an account of the industry's history, using the US and UK as models to show how technology and regulation have combined to create the markets that exist in the world today. Next we take a top-down look at the new deregulated markets, first examining global macrotrends, and then describing the risks common to all power industries and the types of risk management tools employed. Finally, we examine a few representative markets in detail, with an emphasis on the features that make them unique.

The focus in this chapter will be on wholesale markets. Although retail competition and the risks associated with it are interesting topics, space does not permit more than a few cursory observations.

History of the US and UK power industries

THE US EXPERIENCE

The US electricity business was born in 1882 when Thomas Edison built the first commercial power generation and distribution system in New York City. At first, technology did not permit the transmission of power over long distances, so most systems were local affairs, providing power only for neighbourhood street lighting and public transport. Consequently, anyone with enough daring, capital and political connections could establish a utility business in a new service territory. Soon, however, these territories began to overlap, and for the first time there was competition in electricity supply. By 1892, for example, there were more than 20 companies serving greater Chicago. In some cities customers could

168

COMPETITIVE
ELECTRICITY
MARKETS
AROUND THE
WORLD

choose any one of several providers simply by tapping different power lines strung from the same pole. At the start of the 1920s there were more than 3,000 investor-owned utilities, producing 95% of the power, and 2,500 municipal utilities scattered across the US.

Free-wheeling competition did not last long, however. As infrastructure grew in scale and cost, and as consolidation in ownership occurred, the industry began to take on the characteristics of a "natural monopoly". Determined to avoid the monopolistic abuses that had characterised the railroad business a quarter of a century before, state legislatures acted to impose effective regulatory controls. In 1907, Wisconsin and New York established the first public utility commissions (PUCs). By 1914, 43 states had followed suit. The PUCs were given authority to audit utility books and to enforce standardised accounting principles. They set rates for service that allowed utilities to cover costs and make "reasonable" returns on investment.

Although thousands of utilities existed in name, control was concentrated in a very few holding companies. By 1932 eight holding companies controlled nearly 75% of all privately owned electric utilities through elaborate pyramids of subordinated companies. Holding companies were originally designed to help diversify the risks and pool resources for several utilities. Later, the structure was corrupted to allow shareholders in the top companies to control utility assets and reap excessive profits with minimal investment. Because many of these questionable dealings were interstate in nature, the state PUCs could not regulate them. Therefore, in response to public outrage, the federal government enacted the Federal Power Act (FPA) and the Public Utility Holding Company Act (PUHCA) of 1935. The FPA established the Federal Power Authority (later the Federal Energy Regulatory Commission, or FERC) and granted it powers to regulate interstate transmission and wholesale power transactions. The PUHCA mandated the dissolution of the existing holding companies and gave the Securities and Exchange Commission (SEC) regulatory control of utility asset acquisitions and securities dealings. In passing the FPA and the PUHCA, Congress completed the process, begun by the states 20 years before, of converting the power industry into a vertically integrated, regulated monopoly – a market structure that would persist for 50 years.

The energy crises of the 1970s spurred the government to seek ways to encourage energy conservation and national energy independence. In 1978 the Public Utility Regulatory Policy Act (PURPA) was passed. Among its provisions the PURPA required utilities to purchase, at their own avoided cost, excess power that large industrial customers produced as a by-product of their operations from "qualifying facilities". Numerous stipulations concerning efficiency, size and ownership had to be met by producers if their plant was to become such a "qualifying facility". Nevertheless, the PURPA, together with rules promulgated by the state PUCs (California in particular), had the effect of guaranteeing any industrial plant with sufficient steam load the opportunity to acquire significant additional revenues through power sales to the local utility. The result was a flurry of technological and financial innovation. The PURPA had unintentionally helped to create an entirely new industry of independent power producers (IPPs), which focused exclusively on the installation of simple and combined-cycle gas turbine plants that cogenerated steam for industrial processes and electricity for sale to the local utility. Non-utility generator (NUG) capacity, including cogeneration and plants powered by renewable or waste fuel sources (which also received preferential treatment under PURPA), rose from almost non-existence in 1970 to represent nearly 10% of total US capacity by 1993.

The success of IPPs in the 1980s demonstrated clearly that small entrepreneurs could generate electricity as economically as utilities, thereby overturning the long-standing concept that only large companies in a monopolistic environment could generate electricity reliably and economically. The lesson was not lost on either the utilities or the regulators and, in 1992, despite vociferous opposition from the utility lobby, the federal government passed the Energy Policy Act (EPAct). The EPAct contains two particularly significant mandates:
❑ creation of the exempt wholesale generator (EWG) class of power production; and
❑ open and equal access to the transmission system.

The EWG provision officially opened up wholesale generation to competition by allowing the operation of merchant generation that is far less regulated than utilities and is generally allowed to charge market rates for its output. Utilities are not required to purchase EWG electricity, however. The transmission provision requires transmission owners to provide any wholesale buyer or seller with open and equal access to the transmission system. Most impor-

169

COMPETITIVE
ELECTRICITY
MARKETS
AROUND THE
WORLD

tantly, this implies that vertically integrated utilities must unbundle their services, providing separate pricing for each component. To accomplish this, the EPAct expanded the authority of FERC and directed it to develop a transmission policy that promoted a competitive wholesale electricity market. The result was FERC Orders 888 and 889, which, among other things, require all utilities to:

❏ file open access, non-discriminatory transmission tariffs and conditions of use;
❏ use transmission services, including ancillary services, for their own generation under open-access tariffs (ie no self-dealing);
❏ develop a real-time information system that provides all users with the same information and opportunity to purchase transmission services that utilities enjoy (this has led to the web-based OASIS system for transmission reservations); and
❏ separate the transmission function from generating and marketing functions.

The EPAct also specifically prohibited FERC from mandating retail access, leaving that issue to be resolved by individual states. The result is today's patchwork of rulings, which ranges from the full implementation of retail access in California to the complete absence of the issue from the legislative agenda of South Dakota.

THE UK EXPERIENCE
After a slow start, the UK electricity industry began to take off at the turn of the century. As in the US, it began as a mixture of private and municipal companies serving large urban centres with low-voltage systems of limited geographical range. Indeed, many of the earliest companies, in particular those powering the London transport system, were affiliated to growing American concerns – Edison, Westinghouse, General Electric and others – anxious to sell their product in Europe with its large and densely populated cities. The primary uses were for public transport and lighting. In commercial and residential lighting, electricity only gradually supplanted gas, and industry was the last to convert as electric motor performance and cost finally improved sufficiently to displace steam power.

The electricity business was considered a natural monopoly and was regulated as such. Service territories were franchised and tariffs set by acts of parliament or local city councils. In contrast to the US, however, the UK market did not experience a rapid consolidation of territories and ownership. Legislation that both tacitly and explicitly discouraged cooperation between

power suppliers is often cited as the principal reason for this. With some exceptions, the industry remained a patchwork of smaller companies, often with conflicting standards. Poor interconnections meant little possibility for sharing resources during emergencies. The First World War saw severe supply problems, prompting debate that resulted ultimately in legislation that created a Central Electricity Board and mandated the interconnection and standardisation of different systems via a national transmission grid. Construction began in 1928 and was largely completed by 1935.

The electrical system weathered the Second World War with surprisingly little physical damage but, because the economy was focused on the prosecution of the war, little was invested to maintain and expand the system. Consequently, the industry was ill prepared for the surge in post-war demand. The winter of 1946–47 and to a lesser extent that of 1947–48 saw chronic power rationing that seriously affected industrial output and alienated the general public. Against this backdrop of discontent, the recently elected Labour government acted to nationalise the industry on April 1, 1948, citing strategic national interests. The resulting structure remained substantially unchanged for 40 years until the 1980s, when the Thatcher government undertook a sweeping programme of industry privatisation.

While the nationalised power industry had been regarded as technically well run, it was nevertheless heavily criticised for its bureaucratic inefficiency, bloated workforce and procurement procedures that strongly favoured British over less expensive foreign products. Against this backdrop of discontent, the Conservative government acted to privatise the industry on April 1, 1990, declaring that competition was the only effective means of removing the inefficiencies latent in any publicly owned enterprise. The restructuring also furthered two very practical goals of the Thatcher government: through the sale of public assets, it created additional revenues at a time when the government was cutting taxes and reducing budgets; and it served to weaken the trade unions – the coal miners' union in particular. Privatised generation driven by competitive pressures would either buy lower-priced foreign coal or force the local coal industry to lower its prices. Either way, the miners' union would be seriously weakened. Along with privatisation, the government instituted a competitive wholesale market and timetable for

170

COMPETITIVE
ELECTRICITY
MARKETS
AROUND THE
WORLD

ANCILLARY SERVICES

The US Federal Energy Regulatory Commission (FERC) defines ancillary services generically to be those services "needed with transmission service to maintain reliability". What in practice constitutes an ancillary service is sometimes vague and varies according to market structure. In the US, FERC considers six functions to be ancillary services:

❏ *Scheduling, system control and dispatch* This provides coordination of generating assets' output. In countries with mandatory pools, this is, of course, the pool's main function and is not considered ancillary.

❏ *Regulation and frequency response* This provides for the instantaneous correction of supply/demand imbalances. A central controller monitors supply/demand balance via the system frequency (60Hz in North America, 50Hz in most other countries). As supply and demand drift out of balance, the system frequency also drifts away from its nominal value. To restore the appropriate system frequency, and thus rebalance supply and demand, the controlling operator sends signals to online generators to adjust their output up or down. Because this must be executed in real time and because the adjustment is normally very subtle, only generators with specialised Automatic Generating Control equipment (AGC) provide this service.

❏ *Reactive power supply and voltage support and control* In order to maintain transmission line voltages at their nominal values and to facilitate control of power flows around the system, generators must be able to produce or absorb reactive power. It is important to note that reactive power cannot be transmitted over large distances; it is produced (or absorbed) at specific points in order to control the local characteristics of the system. Thus, it is,

by nature, a "geographically fragmented" market and consequently prone to non-competitive pricing as described in Panel 2.

❏ *Energy imbalance* Although a generator and consumer may agree to inject and withdraw a specific volume of energy, it is rare for actual volumes to match exactly the scheduled obligations on an hour-by-hour basis. This service provides energy adjustments to correct for mismatches in energy delivery. In many markets, a specific imbalance energy pool exists where participants compete to supply this service.

❏ *Spinning reserves* This service is provided by generators that are online but not operating at their maximum output. In the event of a sudden loss of a generator, the system operator must be able to call on a subset of remaining generators to quickly ramp up to restore supply/demand balance. Typically, the combined spinning reserves capacity must at least equal the capacity of the largest single generator on the system, and the aggregate ramp rate must be sufficient to bring the system frequency back to within a "contingency tolerance" band inside a minute or so.

❏ *Supplemental reserves* Once spinning reserves have been called on to replace lost generation, the system may be incapable of responding reliably to a second contingency. Supplemental reserves are additional capacity that can be called on line over the course of several minutes to several hours to replace lost generation and allow spinning reserves to return to pre-contingency levels. Supplemental reserves are often split into several quality types that define how quickly the reserve can be brought on line. Non-spinning or 10-minute start, one-hour start, and black start are examples of such categories.

implementing retail supply competition, which would ultimately include all end-users. We shall defer discussion of the new UK electricity industry until later in the chapter.

Risk management in the new electricity market

The electricity business, competitive or otherwise, comprises five more or less mutually exclusive services:

❏ generation – the production of wholesale quantities of power;

❏ transmission – the transportation of wholesale power over large distances using high-voltage cable networks;

❏ ancillary services – products provided by generation and used by the transmission operator to balance supply and demand in real time and to maintain overall system security (Panel 1 discusses ancillary services in more detail);

❏ distribution – the transportation of power from the transmission system to the consumer; and

❏ wholesale/retail supply – services to facilitate

171

COMPETITIVE
ELECTRICITY
MARKETS
AROUND THE
WORLD

the purchase and sale of the physical commodity (for example, marketing/supply, metering and billing).

As noted earlier, the common thread running through every restructuring is the realisation that providing at least some of these services does not necessarily require a monopoly market structure. Consequently, each of these services must be unbundled and treated as a separate market. In particular, the essential features of every reformed electricity market are the separation of the generating function from the transmission (and often the distribution) functions and the provision for equal access to and fair use of the transmission service. How separation is accomplished differs from country to country. As we have seen in the history of US markets, separation can mean the establishment of distinct operating units within the existing vertically integrated utilities. In the rest of the world, where nationalised systems are the norm, separation usually means the privatisation of generating, transmission and distribution assets as three or more specialised entities. Generation and the supply of wholesale power are usually made into an explicitly competitive market, while transmission and distribution continue to be considered as natural monopolies and regulated as such. In markets where retail competition exists, distribution is further separated from the supply function, which is also opened to competition. Ancillary services are a grey area and are treated in various ways. There are no economies of scale that would argue for their remaining regulated; nevertheless, they are a submarket that is prone to abuse because the number of firms able to supply these services is often limited.

As restructuring leads to the unbundling and separation of services, the associated risks also become distinct and separate. This has led to a recent deluge of mergers, acquisitions and divestitures as incumbents attempt to redefine and partition their risks and as new entrants look to establish a presence quickly by acquiring existing expertise. The trend is clearly towards consolidation and globalisation; while not universal, the general business model is that of an integrated energy company with subsidiaries encompassing both the unregulated and the regulated sides of electricity and perhaps other energy commodities as well. (This parallels somewhat the integrated oil company model where up- and downstream activities are used to cross-hedge each other and thus reduce volatility in corporate revenues.) In the UK, for example, a visit to PowerGen's web site tells us that it is a

pan-national company with generating assets in nine countries totalling 24 GW. In 1998, it acquired East Midlands Electricity, the UK's third largest electricity distributor and supplier. In Scandinavia, the Swedish generator Vattenfall has acquired distribution and marketing companies in Sweden, Finland and several other northern European countries. In the US, more than 80 GW of capacity has been sold since 1997 or is now on the block. This represents 10% of all US generation. To date, 27 utilities have sold most or all of their generation assets. An example is San Diego Gas & Electric, which has recently sold all of its fossil-fuelled plant to recast itself as primarily a transmission and distribution company. Its holding company, Sempra Energy, however, also has subsidiaries specialising in power generation and gas pipeline assets, both domestic and international, as well as unregulated power and gas trading and marketing operations.

Other companies have chosen a different model. The UK national transmission company NGC is currently focusing exclusively on the operation of regulated transmission and distribution businesses, as evidenced by its recent purchase of NEES, a New England utility with no self-generation. In the mid-western US, the model for consolidation is the utility merger. For example, AEP and CSW, two large utilities with service territories spanning 11 states, have recently proposed a merger that, if approved, will form one of the largest utilities in the US with over four million customers, 37 GW of generation and annual sales exceeding 200 TWh. By way of comparison, the entire Australian national market has 27 GW of capacity and an annual consumption of 100 TWh.

Another interesting phenomenon is the consolidation of nuclear plant risk. Although many utilities with nuclear assets are looking for ways to reduce or eliminate their exposure to the economic and regulatory burdens of such assets, several companies are embracing nuclear power. In the US, Entergy, a utility with a franchise area covering parts of Arkansas, Louisiana, Texas and Mississippi, has established an unregulated subsidiary, Entergy Nuclear, to manage its five nuclear power plants. In addition, Entergy Nuclear recently purchased the Pilgrim One nuclear plant, an 870 MW facility located in Massachusetts, in what was the first competitively bid sale of a nuclear power plant in the US. The two British nuclear companies are active internationally as well. British Energy, in a joint venture with Philadelphia-based PECO, founded

172

COMPETITIVE
ELECTRICITY
MARKETS
AROUND THE
WORLD

ELECTRICITY PRICE VOLATILITY

Volatility in electricity prices is driven by the same supply and demand fundamentals that drive any other energy commodity. However, a number of features unique to the industry tend to exacerbate price fluctuations. One contributing factor is the high variability in demand. Fluctuations in both intraday and seasonal demand for electricity are among the largest of any energy commodity. Figure A shows typical daily load patterns for Texas in July, while Figure B shows the relative seasonal demand variability for gas, crude oil and electricity in the US.

Large differences in the cost of electricity production also contribute to price volatility. A wide variety of generating technologies with widely varying fixed and variable costs makes up a typical system's supply stack. Fixed costs range from $500/kW for simple cycle gas turbines, to $1,000/kW or more for baseload coal fired plant, to several thousands of dollars per kilowatt for nuclear units. Variable costs can range from nearly zero for run-of-river hydro to $5–20/MWh for baseload coal-fired plant to more than $100/MWh for the oldest thermal technology burning expensive fuel oils.

More important than the cost of generation, however, is the availability of generation. Because electricity cannot be stored and transported like

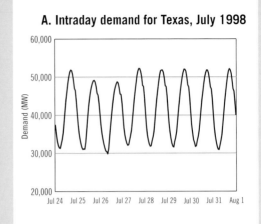

A. Intraday demand for Texas, July 1998

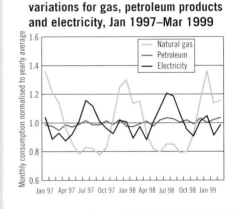

B. Comparison of US seasonal demand variations for gas, petroleum products and electricity, Jan 1997–Mar 1999

AmerGen to "purchase and operate nuclear power plants in the US". British Nuclear Fuels (BNFL), the parent of Magnox Generation, recently acquired the entire Westinghouse nuclear power business from CBS. With this acquisition BNFL is now able to offer services covering the entire spectrum of nuclear activities, including plant design, construction, instrumentation, operation and decommissioning and nuclear fuel sales. It is possible that this trend will continue into the future and that, over the next 10 to 20 years, a handful of "nuclear management" companies will emerge, perhaps specialising in a particular type or make of nuclear plant.

Derivative instruments are an integral part of the short- to medium-term risk management strategy of any wholesale power trading operation. In the new competitive wholesale market, participants face risks that are similar to those of other energy markets. Therefore, many of the techniques developed for the natural gas and oil markets find application in power as well. Below, we define the principal types of risk that exist in all restructured electricity markets and discuss how these risks are mitigated.

PRICE RISK

For reasons discussed in detail in Panel 2, electricity prices are among the most volatile of any traded commodity. Participants on both the production and consumption sides of the market are exposed to enormous revenue and costs risks, respectively, and are strongly motivated to mitigate these risks. By far the most common product is the forward agreement, be it a standardised exchange-traded futures contract or a customised over-the-counter (OTC) swap. The physical swap is a very simple contract whereby a generator agrees to sell to a consumer a given quantity of power for a fixed price. In this way, both parties are immunised against market price fluctuations. In the case of financial swaps, physi-

173

**COMPETITIVE
ELECTRICITY
MARKETS
AROUND THE
WORLD**

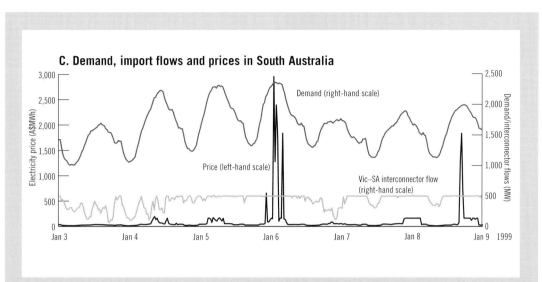

C. Demand, import flows and prices in South Australia

oil and because transmission systems have finite capacity, electricity markets are necessarily regional in nature, and consequently the number of participants in the physical market is limited. During periods of low demand, numerous agents compete at the margin ensuring that electricity is priced efficiently. In some markets, and under certain circumstances, however, it can be that, at times of high demand, only a very few participants are able to supply power. This leads to temporary "capacity constrained" markets where a few firms are able to extract substantial profits. The UK market, described later in the main text, has been cited as an example of this type of market.

Transmission congestion and other transportation-related constraints can lead to a temporary geographical fragmentation of a market. This results in a reduction in the number of suppliers physically able to compete in a given sub-market, again potentially leading to high prices. Examples of this kind of price behaviour are occasionally observed in South Australia. Normally, power flows from inexpensive generators in Victoria to "capacity short" South Australia. However, in the first week of 1999, the transmission line between the two states became constrained, while temperatures (and thus demand) in South Australia soared. Consequently, the only generating assets physically able to meet the demand were a limited number of local peaking units, which, as Figure C demonstrates, commanded prices well above production costs.

cal delivery and the risks associated with it are separated from the financial transaction. Two counterparties simply agree to exchange a fixed cashflow for one that is tied to some market price index to which both parties are exposed. In this case, generator and consumer are now assured a fixed price for the contracted volume and are free to contract with other market participants for the physical delivery component (Figure 1a).

LOCATIONAL BASIS RISK
Transmission constraints can cause a market to split into two or more submarkets, each with different prices. The constraints mean that market players cannot arbitrage the difference in prices through the physical transfer of power. A firm with a long position in one submarket and a short position in another might find it beneficial to enter into a financial float-for-float swap. Figure 1b shows an example in which a generator and

consumer may not be exposed to the same floating price. In the example, the generator retains a residual exposure to the difference in index

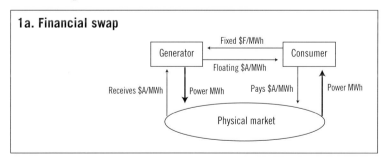

1a. Financial swap

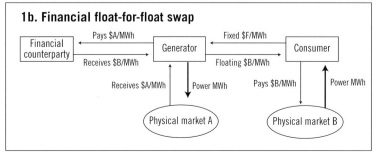

1b. Financial float-for-float swap

174

COMPETITIVE
ELECTRICITY
MARKETS
AROUND THE
WORLD

prices, which it mitigates by executing a separate float-for-float swap with a second counterparty. This might be a speculative player, or perhaps another generator with a similar but opposite exposure; it can even be the system operator. In the eastern US, the PJM pool, for example, holds auctions for the sale of fixed transmission rights (FTRs). These instruments are effectively float-for-float swaps that hedge the costs of transmission congestion.

Electricity has several quality grades that are traded as such, the most common being "baseload" and "peak". Baseload simply means a fixed volume of power delivered at a constant rate for 24 hours per day and seven days per week. Peak power is a fixed volume delivered at a constant rate over a subset of hours in the day, corresponding to the peak demand period, usually during weekdays only. In the eastern US, for example, a peak contract is denoted "5x16", meaning that power should be delivered from Monday to Friday during a single 16-hour block each day. The specific delivery hours usually follow local industry standards; in most of the US, for example, the peak period starts with the hour ending (HE) at 07.00 (ie, power starts flowing at 06.00) and runs until HE 22.00; in Australia the peak period is only 15 hours long, starting at HE 08.00 and ending at HE 22.00. In most countries all other hours of the week, including the daylight hours of the weekend, are considered off-peak and traded as a block (ie off-peak is 5x8 + 2x24). The UK is an exception in that it has standardised products for both weekday and weekend power. Occasionally, even finer quality gradations are introduced to differentiate economic value further. Argentina splits days into three unequal blocks: peak, off-peak and shoulder. In the US, super-peak periods are sometimes traded. Super-peak is defined as the eight (or even four) most expensive hours of the mid-afternoon when electricity demand and the cost of supplying it are at their highest for the day. Liquidity in super-peak power varies considerably from market to market in the US, however, and super-peak power is by no means a standard product.

Like other commodities, the tenor and maturity of electricity swaps and other forward structures vary greatly. At the long end of the spectrum are power purchase agreements (PPAs). As part of a financing package, a bank will often require independent power producers to sign long-term PPAs with the intended consumer. These are typically fixed-priced, swap-like physi-

cal contracts ranging from 5 to 30 years in length. In the shorter term, the Scandinavian electricity exchange, for example, lists forward contracts of one-year length with start dates up to three years out. More common are swaps on seasonal blocks of power with maturities typically extending only to next year's peak demand season. Because conditions in the power markets can change so rapidly, participants need to rebalance their positions continuously, sometimes right up to the point of delivery. For this reason, many markets host active trading in short-term forward contracts such as next-month, balance-of-the-month and even balance-of-the-week. At the limit are swaps on power for the next day, which are arguably more representative of a spot market. In the real-time world of electricity, however, the spot market continues almost to the moment of delivery, with sometimes frantic hour-ahead and even balance-of-the-hour trading as firms seek to realign their portfolios to account for changing loads and unexpected outages.

Options trading is common in commodity markets and electricity is no exception. It is difficult to measure, but probably the most common type of option used in the electricity industry is the option on a swap, or swaption. Here the buyer purchases the right to enter into a swap agreement of given tenor and maturity at some future date – very simple, very standard.

Probably the next most common option type is the Asian-style option. Like swaptions, Asians are sensitive to the overall market level and are relatively insensitive to short-term price fluctuations. A typical buyer of an Asian call might be an energy supplier concerned that *El Niño* will return, causing above-normal temperatures and driving up demand and market prices for the next summer. Baseload generators are the natural sellers of such options, perhaps preferring the guaranteed revenue of the option premium to the potential profits of a bull market. Of course, in a depressed market base-load generators are also potential buyers of Asian puts, as a way of protecting against decreasing margin.

The other common option structure is the European strip, which, in a sense, has a risk profile complementary to the Asian option. In particular, out-of-the-money daily or even hourly call options, bundled in monthly, seasonal or yearly blocks, are specifically designed to value the risks associated with electricity's highly volatile short-term behaviour. A variation of this type of option, called a capacity or swing option, is discussed next in the context of volume risk.

175

COMPETITIVE
ELECTRICITY
MARKETS
AROUND THE
WORLD

VOLUME RISK

Once again, because of electricity's unique characteristics (those of demand price inelasticity, non-storability and the need for real-time, near-perfect balance of demand and supply), volume risk takes on an importance not seen in other energy markets. Energy suppliers face long-, medium- and short-term volume risks. Long-term risk comes from trying to predict and hedge the uncertain trend in load growth. Historically, annual growth in electricity demand has varied from –5% to more than +10% in industrialised countries. Medium-term risk arises out of trying to predict and hedge the uncertain seasonal demand levels for the coming year. A summer in the US, for example, that is only a few degrees hotter than normal translates into millions more megawatt-hours of demand for energy. In the short term, even the best forecasts for the next day's consumption sometimes err by a few per cent or more. This error translates into hundreds of surplus or deficit megawatts, which is equivalent to the entire capacity of an average-sized power plant.

As if all this were not enough, energy suppliers must also contend with the "double-whammy" of price–volume correlation. When a supplier is short, the system as a whole is usually also short, and power therefore is likely to sell at premium prices. Conversely, when a supplier has excess volume the system is also glutted, and the supplier may have trouble unloading power at any price.

Volume risk is nothing new; utilities faced it long before deregulation. The ultimate solution was, and still is, to mitigate long-term risk by building sufficient physical capacity and to mitigate short-term risk by operating the system in such a way that forecast errors can be safely absorbed. It was not unusual, however, for neighbouring utilities to trade products to mitigate volume risks rather than build new capacity. Though couched in language peculiar to the electricity industry, many of these products have analogues in other risk management markets. In retrospect, it may be said that utilities have mitigated volume risk for many years by using derivative structures. An example of one such structure is "capacity reservation".

Originally, capacity reservation was nothing more than a power plant rental agreement. For a fee, a utility could reserve a fraction of another utility's power plant output for use over a given period. The utility would then have the right on a day-ahead basis to call on the plant to produce power to serve its own load requirements. Power from the plant would be sold either at a fixed price or indexed to fuel costs. In this way, the utility could obtain sufficient generation to satisfy its expected load at a fraction of the cost of building a power plant. As electricity has become commoditised, plant-specific language has been dropped, and capacity reservation now often simply refers to a contract that obligates the seller to deliver power at the buyer's request from one or more market sources. In the extreme all mention of the physical commodity is removed, making the contract purely financial. Capacity reservation is then exactly equivalent to the strip of daily European options mentioned above: the fee is the option premium, and the fixed price paid for power is the strike. In the case of an indexed price for electricity, this is more akin to a strip of spread options (we shall return to spread options in a moment).

Capacity reservations come in different grades, from "baseload" to "peaking". A typical baseload capacity contract might contain language obligating the buyer to take power from the plant for between 50% and 100% of the hours in the contract period. A peaking deal might stipulate that the buyer can call only up to 10% of the hours in the period (Figure 2). Those who have read Chapter 6, or who are already familiar with the natural gas industry, will recognise these as take-or-pay contracts with swing provisions.

Before leaving volume risk, it is worth mentioning weather derivatives, which have recently emerged as another way to hedge this risk. The term "weather derivative" broadly denotes a contingent claim structure where the contingency is an environmental event. For example, a hydro-generator might buy a "water put", whereby the

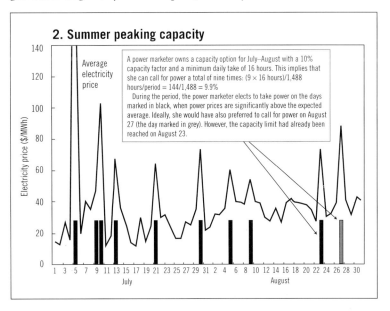

2. Summer peaking capacity

A power marketer owns a capacity option for July–August with a 10% capacity factor and a minimum daily take of 16 hours. This implies that she can call for power a total of nine times: $(9 \times 16 \text{ hours})/1{,}488$ hours/period $= 144/1{,}488 = 9.9\%$

During the period, the power marketer elects to take power on the days marked in black, when power prices are significantly above the expected average. Ideally, she would have also preferred to call for power on August 27 (the day marked in grey). However, the capacity limit had already been reached on August 23.

generator receives a payment if and only if the cumulative flow volume during the run-off season for a particular river falls below the "strike volume". In the electricity industry, weather derivatives are more often tied to the temperature measured at a specific location, averaged over a season. Electricity demand can be broadly broken down into three classes: industrial, commercial and residential. Industrial load is often insensitive to the weather, whereas commercial and residential loads respond to temperature variations, albeit in different ways and at different times of the day. An energy supplier that has a good breakdown of its customer base and can accurately measure the relationship between temperature and demand can use weather derivatives to hedge variability in demand by hedging temperature variability. Of course, the hedge is not a "pure" one; it leaves the supplier with the risk of an unexpected breakdown in the demand–temperature correlation and it does not lay off price–volume correlation risk – the "double-whammy" risk mentioned above. Nevertheless, weather derivatives represent a powerful new tool for risk managers.

MARGIN AND CROSS-COMMODITY RISK
Restructuring is forcing generators to rethink the way they create value. For many firms, power plants now assume characteristics reminiscent of refineries, where the essential function is to convert a less valuable feedstock into a more valuable commodity and the primary management goal is the optimisation of margin. For other firms that trade energy commodities, a generator becomes the converter of one form of "energy commodity" into another. Consequently, the industry has seen an increase in the use of spread options and other exotic derivatives that are sen-

sitive to cross-commodity risks. A call spread option is often referred to as a tolling agreement. For example, the owner of a power–natural gas tolling agreement has the right to toll a quantity of gas through the seller's real or virtual power plant, for which the seller receives a tolling fee to cover the plant's variable operation and maintenance (O&M) costs. The seller converts the gas with a specified efficiency, known as the heat rate, into electricity that is returned to the buyer. Thus, physical tolling agreements are simply another kind of capacity reservation used to hedge physical volume risk.

An electricity–fuel put spread can be used to hedge a power plant's profit margin. For example, a natural gas-fired base-load plant of moderate efficiency is likely to be profitable during peak hours but will probably lose money, from time to time, in the off-peak hours. Although it would be economical to shut down the plant during these intervals, operational constraints might not permit this. A put option on the spread between off-peak power and natural gas prices would allow the plant to be run optimally in the engineering sense and would guarantee revenues in the off-peak periods.

More generally, spreads and other multi-commodity derivatives allow sophisticated firms to treat electricity, natural gas, oil, coal and other fuel commodities as different "quality grades" of the same energy commodity and to use efficiency in one market to arbitrage inefficiencies in another. An example is the "coal-by-wire" contract, where an energy commodity trading house sells coal to a utility but reserves the right to substitute an equivalent amount of electricity for the physical coal. Because the utility would normally convert the coal into electricity anyway, it is indifferent to whether it receives coal or electricity. The added contract flexibility, however, allows the energy trader to look for the most economical energy product in more than one market. Figure 3 demonstrates how such flexibility might be used.

Taxonomy of the new market structures
We turn now to a discussion of specific competitive market systems that have been implemented around the world. An important characteristic of the new competitive wholesale power markets is the buying and selling of spot physical power. All restructured industries fall into one of three categories:

❑ mandatory pool;
❑ voluntary pool; and
❑ bilateral trading.

3. Coal-by-wire contract

Coal transportation: $0.50/MMBtu

Coal mine X
$1.10/MMBtu

Generator A
Efficiency:
14MMBtu/MWh

Power transportation:
$2.50/MWh

Generator B
Efficiency:
12MMBtu/MWh

Tolling fee:
$3/MWh

Coal transportation:
$0.25/MMBtu

Coal mine Y
$1.10/MMBtu

An energy marketer contracts with generator A to deliver the equivalent of 1,000MWh of coal. There are two choices. In one case, the marketer purchases coal from mine X and transports it to generator A for conversion to electricity. Given the efficiency of generator A, this strategy will cost $22.40/ MWh: ($1.10/MMBtu coal cost + $0.50/MMBtu transportation) × 14MMBtu/MWh = $22.40/MWh.

Alternatively, the marketer can deliver coal "by-wire" at a lower overall cost by exploiting the lower coal transportation costs to generator B and generator B's superior conversion efficiency. Generator B produces coal at a cost of $16.20/ MWh: ($1.10/MMBtu coal cost + $0.25/MMBtu transportation) × 12MMBtu/ MWh = $16.20/MWh. In addition, the marketer pays generator B a $3/MWh tolling fee plus a $2.50/MWh wheeling charge to the transmission provider. Thus the marketer ultimately delivers "energy" to generator A at a cost of only $21.70/MWh.

177

COMPETITIVE
ELECTRICITY
MARKETS
AROUND THE
WORLD

MANDATORY POOLS

The majority of restructured markets fall into this group, not because it is inherently superior but because mandatory pools are very similar to state-controlled systems that make up most of the world's power industries. A mandatory pool represents a compromise; it opens the market while attempting to assuage fears that too much change will jeopardise the security of the system. Under a mandatory pool system, all physical supply is controlled and coordinated by a single pool operator. All generators must sell their production to the pool, and all suppliers must purchase their requirements through the same pool. In this way, physical risk is removed from individual participants and is concentrated in the pool. To manage this risk, the pool relies on its ability to coordinate all aspects of the physical electrical system. Of course, depending on the structure of the market, firms may nevertheless remain exposed to the financial consequences of non-performance in the physical market. The archetypal mandatory pool is the UK system (more precisely, the English and Welsh system as Scotland and Ireland operate separately). It is the most studied electricity market in the world, not only because, at nine years of age, it is one of the oldest competitive markets, but also because it offers real insights into what restructuring has and has not achieved.

The United Kingdom The physical characteristics of the UK's and other countries' electricity systems are outlined in Table 1. The UK market structure is shown Figure 4. Generation totalling about 63 GW of installed capacity is divided unequally among some 22 entities. All transmission is owned by the National Grid Company

Table 1. Physical characteristics of different electricity markets

	UK	Australia	Norway	Sweden	California	US
Capacity (GW)	62	27	28	32	54	780
Peak demand (GW)	50	19.5	22	25.5	50	na
Annual production (TWh)	295	100	115	145	180	3,400
Stack mix (installed capacity)	40% coal	74% coal	99% hydro	48% hydro	41% gas	40% coal
	29% gas	17% hydro		30% nuclear	28% hydro	11% oil
	16% nuclear	6% gas		5% gas	9% nuclear	23% gas
	5% oil	2%other		9% nuclear	3% oil	13% nuclear
	10% other			17% coal/oil/biomass		12% hydro
Data source	OFFER	NEMMCO	Nordel	Nordel	EIA	EIA

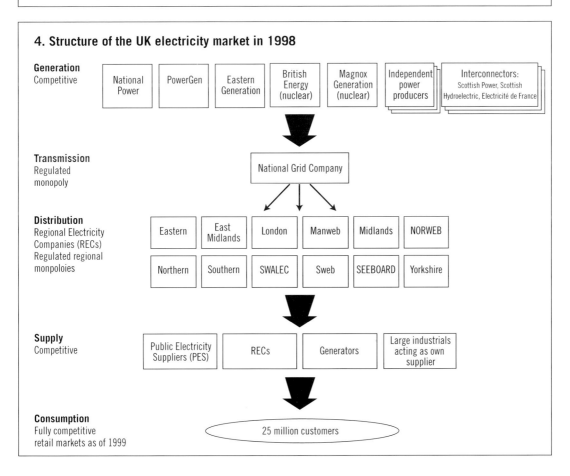

4. Structure of the UK electricity market in 1998

Generation
Competitive

National Power | PowerGen | Eastern Generation | British Energy (nuclear) | Magnox Generation (nuclear) | Independent power producers | Interconnectors: Scottish Power, Scottish Hydroelectric, Electricité de France

Transmission
Regulated monopoly

National Grid Company

Distribution
Regional Electricity Companies (RECs)
Regulated regional monpoloies

Eastern | East Midlands | London | Manweb | Midlands | NORWEB
Northern | Southern | SWALEC | Sweb | SEEBOARD | Yorkshire

Supply
Competitive

Public Electricity Suppliers (PES) | RECs | Generators | Large industrials acting as own supplier

Consumption
Fully competitive retail markets as of 1999

25 million customers

(NGC), which is responsible for its operation, maintenance and expansion. Distribution is divided geographically into 12 regional electricity companies (RECs). The electricity supplier "bubble" inserted between the RECs and consumers in Figure 4 emphasises that, although the RECs are responsible for physical delivery, retail supply is a competitive function. The NGC and the RECs operate the transmission and distribution systems as regulated monopoly services in which the prices they may charge are capped and subject to periodic review by the Office of Electricity Regulation (OFFER).

Technically, the spot market pool is a multi-lateral contract between generators and suppliers, but its operation is left to the NGC. Every day, generators – including the international interconnectors – may submit offers to supply power in each half-hour of the next day. Offers are "multi-part", containing information about start-up costs, no-load costs, ramp rates and other operational restrictions, and up to three price/capacity bands. Once submitted, generators may not alter the price points; however, they may alter the availability of capacity at any time. On the demand side, the NGC makes a prediction of load, plus necessary reserve margin, for each half-hour on the basis of forecast weather and historical demand patterns and uncertainties. Included in this projection are any expected exports submitted by the interconnectors. A limited amount of demand-side bidding occurs whereby a large consumer agrees to reduce its demand should pool prices exceed the offered price. Such bids are treated as extra generation.

Bid data are run through a computer program to obtain the most economically efficient set of generators necessary to satisfy demand – a process known as "merit order stacking". The intersection of supply and demand determines the system marginal price (SMP), with all generators who bid below SMP being dispatched for that half-hour. Figure 5 illustrates this procedure.

When the market was structured, it was felt that a mechanism was required to allow generators to recover fixed costs and to signal the need for additional capacity. The result was the creation of a capacity payment (CP), which is added to the SMP to produce the pool purchase price (PPP). The PPP is the price paid to all dispatched generators:

$$PPP = SMP + CP$$

Now, the capacity payment is a number calculated by the NGC for each half-hour based on uncertainties of demand and of generator performance and can vary in value from £0/MWh to more than £100/MWh. We shall return to the capacity payment later in Panel 3, which discusses market power and gaming. For the moment, suffice it to say that the capacity payment depends critically on the reserve margin of the system: the tighter the system, the higher the capacity payment and, hence, the larger the incentive, in principle, to add new capacity.

Electricity consumers pay the pool selling price (PSP), which is

$$PSP = PPP + Uplift = SMP + CP + Uplift$$

where "Uplift" remunerates the NGC for system operation costs, including ancillary services, transmission losses and constraint mitigation. With respect to transmission constraint relief, it is important to note that the calculation of SMP assumes an unconstrained dispatch – that is to say, it ranks each generator's bid on the basis of economics only, without regard to system reliability. If, during the course of the day, the system operator is forced to make an out-of-merit dispatch (turning off a scheduled unit or turning on an unscheduled one) to relieve a transmission constraint, a payment is made to the owners of the affected units. The cost of this compensation is lumped together as part of the uplift charge. Uplift is calculated ex post on the basis of the actual operational costs of the system and can vary significantly from hour to hour and day to day. Figure 6 shows electricity prices during a typical week and demonstrates the high variability of the CP and uplift components.

Because of the high volatility of pool prices,

5. Determination of SMP in the UK

1) Generator bids are ordered from lowest to highest price to produce the "supply stack"

2) Demand (in MW) for every half-hour is estimated by the NGC

3) The intersection of the estimated half-hourly demand with the supply stack determines the marginal generator. The marginal generator's bid price sets the SMP for that half-hour. In this example, the expected demand is 37,600MW, and the marginal generator's bid was £35/MWh

Energy bid price (£/MWh) — Cumulative capacity (MW)

there is an active OTC market for financial hedging products. By far the most common instrument is the two-way contract for differences (CFD), which is financially equivalent to a simple fixed-for-floating swap. CFDs are usually tied to PPP, but can also be linked SMP, PSP, CP or uplift. More complicated CFD structures that have option-like characteristics are also sometimes traded. The simplest of these are one-way CFDs, which are strips of simple puts and calls on half-hourly prices.

In the early stages of the UK pool, CFDs tended to be large in volume, long-dated and highly customised. In an effort to spur liquidity in the short-term market and to facilitate more finely tuned price and volume risk management, a set of standardised, brokered contracts was developed called electricity forward agreements (EFAs). In the EFA market, electricity is aggregated into four-hour blocks, six for each weekday (WD1–6) and six for weekends (WE1–6). Standardised swap contracts, usually indexed to PPP, are then constructed on the basis of this block structure. For example, a popular contract called "Load Shape 44" consists of 20 MW of 24-hour power (ie WD1–6 and WE1–6) with an additional 20 MW during WD3–5.

As the system has matured, different products, born of other commodity businesses, have also found acceptance in the electricity industry. These include Asian-style options, which settle against the average pool price, and swaptions. No organised futures market exists in the UK. Concerns about liquidity and the validity of pool prices, given the market power enjoyed by the dominant generators, have dampened interest to date. In its review of electricity trading arrangements (RETA), however, the government proposed the establishment of a forward and/or futures market as part of its overhaul of the pool system. We shall return to the RETA proposals later in this section.

The UK pool system is generally considered a success from an operational standpoint: the pool bidding system, though sometimes characterised as unduly complicated, does work. Certainly, power has continued to flow reliably, and system security has been maintained and perhaps even enhanced by the new system. Economically, however, it is widely seen as fundamentally flawed. In particular, it has fallen short of the goal of bringing competition to the British power industry. The harshest criticism has been reserved for the behaviour of some generating companies, which are perceived as exploiting

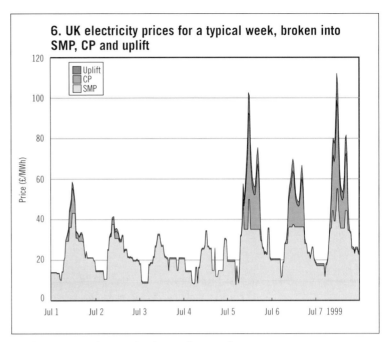

6. UK electricity prices for a typical week, broken into SMP, CP and uplift

weaknesses in the pool rules and procedures to the detriment of the system as a whole.

It was recognised from the outset that to ensure a competitive wholesale electricity market would require the separation of generation assets into at least four firms. However, there was also concern that this might create entities too small to be financially secure, so all fossil-fuel plants were ultimately spun off into just two companies, National Power and PowerGen. It is now recognised that this division created the danger of a oligopolistic market structure. Even in 1999, although more than 20 generating companies operate in the UK, just three firms control the market.[2] This is clearly suggested in Table 2 and Figure 7 overleaf, which show that, although the share of sales for National Power, PowerGen and Eastern Generation has declined steadily, they continue to set pool prices the vast majority of the time.

This paradox can be understood by examining each generator's relative operational flexibility. British Energy and Magnox Generation are the two nuclear plant operators, which, combined, generate about 24% of UK annual production. However, because their plants are designed to be run as base load, they bid their units as "must run", meaning that NGC will always dispatch them no matter what the price of power is. Another large class of generators, making up 13% of production, is the IPPs. These often have long-term take-or-pay fuel contracts and long-term power purchase agreements with the RECs. They are therefore highly motivated to (and indeed do) submit zero-price bids to ensure dispatch. Lastly, when the interconnectors export

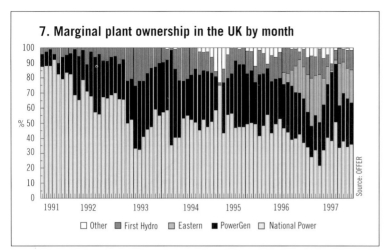

7. Marginal plant ownership in the UK by month

% 50

1991 1992 1993 1994 1995 1996 1997

☐ Other ■ First Hydro ☐ Eastern ■ PowerGen ☐ National Power

Source: OFFER

Table 2. UK generation output by company

Company	1990/91		1996/97	
	TWh	%	TWh	%
National Power	121.3	45.5	70.2	24.1
PowerGen	75.8	28.4	62.7	21.5
Eastern	0	0	19.3	6.6
Nuclear Electric	46.5	17.4	50.3	17.3
Magnox	0	0	20.2	6.9
New entrants	0	0	37.9	13.0
First Hydro	1.6	0.6	2.2	0.8
Interconnectors	20.3	7.6	27.2	9.3
Others	1.4	0.5	1.3	0.5
Total	**266.8**	**100**	**291.1**	**100**

Source: OFFER

to the UK system, they do so because they have surplus capacity on their respective systems and hence are disposed to be price-takers. The result is that only a handful of generators have the flexibility and desire to compete during the periods in which demand exceeds base-load capacity. This is a classic example of a capacity induced oligopoly, as described in Panel 2. That such arbitrage opportunities exist is not necessarily indicative of a flawed system; occasional occurrences are to be expected in any electricity market where capital costs are allocated efficiently. Its persistence in the UK market, as evidenced in Figure 7 and discussed in Panel 3, does, however, suggest a fundamental problem.

Another issue has recently come to the fore with the introduction of a competitive gas market in the UK. Briefly, there is an intra-day gas balancing market in which the price of gas can occasionally spike to 10 or 20 times its normal value. If this happens, any gas-fired plant that bid into the electricity pool the day before the spike is likely to find it profitable to declare itself unavailable for dispatch and to divert the unburned gas to the balancing market. The plant owner's decision is explicitly allowed under pool rules (though the NGC imposes a penalty if it happens when the system margin is low) and

may require the NGC to call on reserve capacity to replace the lost generation at an additional cost. This cost is passed on to consumers through the uplift charge. Although generators have the right to react economically to this cross-commodity arbitrage opportunity, critics point to such actions as an example of an inherent flaw in all mandatory pools – namely, that they tend to "socialise" costs. That is, entire classes of market participants are penalised for the actions of a single agent.

In 1997, in response to these and other criticisms, the Blair government directed regulators to undertake an in-depth review of the pool system and, where necessary, to propose measures designed to promote more competition and efficiency. One result was the *Review of Electricity Trading Arrangements: Framework Document*[3], which proposed abandonment of the mandatory pool in favour of a system that borrows elements from the Scandinavian and Californian markets. The key features of the proposal are:

❑ Establishment of physical/financial forward and futures markets.

❑ Establishment of an organised short-term bilateral physical/financial exchange operating continuously from 24 to four hours ahead of power flow. The idea of an exchange was introduced to allow participants to fine tune their positions via standardised instruments traded on a screen-based system.

❑ Binding physical positions. At the close of the short-term exchange for a given period, all participants must submit to the system operator firm schedules for physical production and consumption for that period. Pricing and other financial data would not be reported. Any differences between scheduled and actual power flows would be corrected using the imbalance energy market (see below).

❑ Imbalance energy market or pool operating continuously up to and during the physical delivery period. Generators, and perhaps certain large consumers, would submit bids and offers to the system operator that would specify the price at which they would be willing to increase or reduce generation or demand at short notice. The system operator would stack these bids and offers in order of price and use them to balance the system in real time.

Critically, the new arrangements abolish the concept of a single, mandatory electricity price. Instead, the market establishes pricing through bilateral trading. Price transparency is

181

COMPETITIVE
ELECTRICITY
MARKETS
AROUND THE
WORLD

THE PROBLEM OF CAPACITY PAYMENTS AND THE UK POOL

The capacity payment in the UK Pool, as calculated by the NGC, is the product of two terms:

$$CP = LOLP \, (VOLL - SMP).$$

The second term is the difference of VOLL and SMP, where SMP is the system marginal price described in the main text, and VOLL denotes the "value of lost load": a quantity that is intended to reflect the maximum price a consumer would be willing to pay to avoid a blackout. Because VOLL is currently set to about £2,600/MWh while SMP is typically between £20 and £60/MWh, (VOLL – SMP) is large and essentially invariant. The term, LOLP, denotes the "loss of load probability" and defines the probability that circumstances could arise that would require the system operator to black out customers.

Although the actual calculation of LOLP is complicated, the essential features are easily understood. The NGC first examines historically how actual demand in a given time period has deviated from the day-ahead forecast and determines the probability distribution of those deviations. Likewise, it sums up all generating capacity bid in for the period, reviews recent performance of that generation, and constructs the probability distribution of expected supply.

Using these two distributions, it then derives the probability distribution of the capacity margin (Available capacity – Actual demand), and calculates the probability that realised demand could exceed available capacity's ability to serve it (depicted as the grey area in Figure A). This is LOLP.

Note that LOLP is a measure of the tail of the distribution and, as such, is sensitive to the distribution's mean and shape. It should be clear from the figure that reducing the amount of available capacity has the effect of moving the distribution to the left, which can result in a dramatic increase in LOLP. Now LOLP is a very small number in the order of 0.01 or less, but its effect on the capacity payment is magnified by the large VOLL term. Thus the capacity payment can be viewed as a non-linear, highly leveraged function of capacity margin.

In the early years of the UK pool, this structure was open to abuse. There was always the danger that generation companies would declare plant unavailable for the day-ahead auction in order to tighten capacity, drive up LOLP, and increase the capacity payment. Once the NGC had completed its calculations and published the inflated capacity payment for the next day, there was nothing to prevent a generator changing the plant's status back to "available" in order to collect the capacity payment. This danger loomed large until 1993, when the regulator modified the pool rules to disallow this behaviour. However, this does not offer *certainty* that LOLP is no longer gamed in the UK or similarly structured markets. Clearly, given a large enough portfolio, it may be more profitable for a generator to selectively withhold a portion of its capacity in order drive up the capacity payment, which it then collects on the dispatch of its remaining assets.

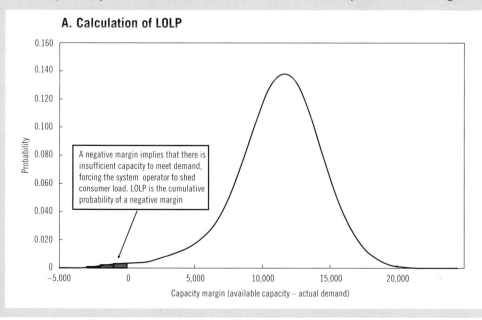

A. Calculation of LOLP

A negative margin implies that there is insufficient capacity to meet demand, forcing the system operator to shed consumer load. LOLP is the cumulative probability of a negative margin

Probability

Capacity margin (available capacity – actual demand)

182

COMPETITIVE
ELECTRICITY
MARKETS
AROUND THE
WORLD

expected to be effected through the publication of indicative pricing, as is the case in other commodity markets. The only pool-like structure in the new proposals is the balancing market, in which a significant number of generators will be able truly to compete. Generators and suppliers who deviate from their firm commitments will be expected to pay for the volume of imbalance energy that the system operator must use to correct the deviation. Although the proposed changes are considered radical in scope and a step in the right direction, some critics still question whether they do enough to reduce the market power enjoyed by some agents. In response, regulators have, in connection with recent acquisition deals, directed National Power and PowerGen to divest assets further. Whether the combination of market reorganisation and break-up of the dominant players will be sufficient to guarantee a truly competitive market, however, will only become apparent once the new system is fully implemented.

Australia The Australian National Electricity Market (NEM) spans the electricity systems of New South Wales, Victoria, South Australia, Queensland and the Australian Capital Territory (Figure 8). Queensland is at present electrically isolated from the rest of NEM but will be connected by the end of 1999. There is also a proposal to connect the hydro-dominated island state of Tasmania to the Victorian system via an undersea DC intertie, though the economics of such a connection continue to be debated. As in the UK, prior to restructuring, the Australian market was run by state-owned enterprises. It now comprises about 20 generators; some private and some state-owned corporations; three

transmission companies controlled by the respective state governments; and 13 regional distributors. Competition in retail supply is being introduced in phases according to different, state-mandated timetables. It is expected to be in place by January 2001 in all states except South Australia, where it will be introduced only by 2003.

The NEM system is modelled after the UK pool but, being younger,[3] includes important differences that seek to avoid some of the problems that have become apparent in the UK.

❑ *Simple bidding structure* The use of multi-component offers (start-up costs, no-load costs, etc) in the UK system has been criticised as unnecessarily complex. In the NEM, generators submit 10 price bands valid for an entire day up to a week ahead (although they can rebid to within 90 minutes of dispatch). Along with the price bands, generators offer the amount of capacity that they are willing to dispatch at each price level for each of the next day's 48 half-hourly blocks. Demand bids have a similar structure. Generators are expected to fold start-up costs and other quasi-variable O&M costs into their pricing information.

❑ *No capacity payment* As with variable O&M, companies are expected to determine their capital cost recovery requirements and to internalise these requirements in their pricing.

❑ *Zonal transmission pricing* Although it is dispatched as a single pool, the NEM splits the system into four regions and quotes four regional prices: New South Wales, Victoria, South Australia and Snowy (a hydro-generation facility bordering New South Wales and Victoria). Differences in regional prices reflect transmission losses and constraints. In contrast to the UK system, where average transmission costs are passed on to consumers via the uplift charge, the NEM explicitly calculates the costs of using the transmission system for each generator and supplier and adjusts bids and offers accordingly. This adjustment is taken into account both when determining dispatch order and in the settlement process.

❑ *Real-time spot pricing* Estimated prices for each half-hour, based on submitted offers and bids, are published the day before by the system operator. As part of real-time operations, the system operator runs the dispatch algorithm every five minutes, recording the marginal plant price each time. The half-hourly spot price is then calculated as the simple average of the six five-minute prices. Because transmission costs are

8. The Australian national electricity market

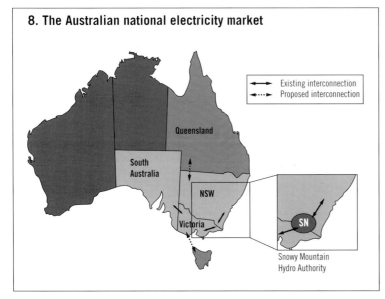

Existing interconnection
Proposed interconnection

Queensland

South Australia

NSW

Victoria

SN

Snowy Mountain Hydro Authority

183

COMPETITIVE
ELECTRICITY
MARKETS
AROUND THE
WORLD

included explicitly in the pool's dispatch mechanism, this spot price represents the true and final pool price. Additional costs, such as operations and ancillary services, are contracted for outside the spot dispatch mechanism.

Australia is one of only three countries in the world to have a commodities exchange that trades electricity futures. The Sydney Futures Exchange lists contracts for both the Victorian and New South Wales regional pricing points with the following characteristics:

❏ Contract size: 500 MWh/month based on a base-load or peaking profile.

❏ Contract months: contracts are available going out 13 months.

❏ Settlement method: the contract is cash-settled against the average of half-hourly pool prices realised over the course of a month. A unique feature is that contracts can be traded during the "delivery month".

OTC products are similar to those found in the UK; financial swaps, swaptions and Asian options are the most liquid. Borrowing from the practices of the early days in the UK market, swaps sometimes contain *force majeure* clauses. Again, because this is a mandatory pool, there is in fact no risk of physical non-delivery or non-receipt for the individual participant. However, the *force majeure* clauses tend to shift the financial burden from the non-performing firm to its counterparty.

In addition, there is some trade in "caplets" (strips of call options), settled against half-hourly pool prices. A particularly popular strike price is A\$329/MWh. Now, pool prices average around A\$20/MWh but have gone over A\$329 (sometimes exceeding A\$3,000/MWh) more than 20 times since the inception of the NEM. Often traded in blocks corresponding to the financial year, these caplet structures are more like an insurance product than a short-term speculative or hedging instrument. (The choice of A\$329/MWh as a strike has to do with the regulatory peculiarities of Victoria, which was the first jurisdiction to reform the electricity industry.)

The NEM is technically a success but, as in the UK, questions remain about the extent to which pool prices are driven by true competition. As in the UK, the system price is usually set by one of only three generators (the New South Wales generators Macquarie Generation, Pacific and Delta). In Australia, however, prices appear to be unduly depressed. One explanation is that generators are over-contracted and are using the pool as a dispatch mechanism. If a generator has hedged most of its production through vesting contracts[5] and other fixed-for-floating swap agreements, it is indifferent to pool prices – with one important caveat. To pay the floating side of the swap, the generator must ensure that it receives sufficient revenues from electricity sales to the pool. This is the situation described earlier in Figure 1a. In a mandatory pool, however, a generator's dispatch is determined entirely by its price bid. If all generators have similar positions, there is a strong incentive to bid prices down to and even below short-run marginal costs. Why would a generator elect to run when pool prices are below its operating costs? Although it would be economically rational for a generator to shut down, this can be a very risky move. It tightens the market, perhaps leading to more volatile prices, while simultaneously leaving the generator short and exposed to the volatility it has just created.

It is interesting to speculate on the future behaviour of pool prices. In the near term, pool prices must surely rise. Once the swap contracts that are now in effect expire, generators are unlikely to execute new contracts at the current depressed levels. This will lead to more price exposure for generators, which, in turn, will encourage them to drive up prices. As prices creep up, however, retailers will be increasingly motivated to negotiate fixed-priced swaps with the generators to immunise themselves against volatility in the pool. Whether this leads to yet another cycle of over-contracting and price collapse remains to be seen.

VOLUNTARY POOLS

Voluntary pools are a more recent phenomenon. The oldest is the Scandinavian system, originally established in Norway in 1992, and the youngest are the systems in California and Pennsylvania, New Jersey and Maryland (PJM), inaugurated in 1998. In voluntary pools, the bulk of physical power is traded via bilateral contracts. Participants provide details of their transactions (typically volumes, timing, point of sale, point of delivery, power ramp rates, etc) to the transmission system operator, who is expected to schedule impartially and dispatch accordingly. In addition, however, there are one or more secondary pool-like markets in which parties make offers of discretionary generation or demand flexibility and bid for supply in order to fine-tune positions. These pools are typically short-term in nature (day-ahead to hour-ahead) and are often used by the system operator to balance the system in real time.

As evidenced by the discussions and recommendations in the UK Review of Electricity Trading Arrangements, the voluntary pool may represent the next evolutionary step for mandatory pools. It removes the guaranteed counterparty that the mandatory pool represents, and moves away from the idea of a single price based on aggregate supply and demand. This forces participants to compete in a more symmetrical and traditional commodity market. At the same time, it keeps the pool intact but relegates it to a smaller, secondary role. In this way, it preserves the concept of guaranteed generator of last resort, with the perception of system security that that conveys.

Scandinavia The Nordic system is the first and only true multinational pool system, comprising Norway, Sweden and Finland. Denmark is not yet a full member of the competitive Nordic market, although it is electrically connected to the system and already exchanges substantial amounts of power with Norway and Sweden. Denmark's Jutland peninsula is expected to begin provisional participation in the market in July 1999. The system is separated, by country, into individual system operators, each run by the respective national transmission companies. Independent of the system operators is the wholesale market operator, Nord Pool, which maintains a day-ahead physical pool, called Elspot, and a financial futures and forward market, called Eltermin.

As shown in Table 3, while most of the physical power is contracted bilaterally, a significant fraction is traded through Elspot. Here participants may submit generation offers and demand bids for each hour of the next day, which Nord Pool uses to generate hourly system prices in the usual way. In contrast to the pools described above, however, once bids and offers have been accepted and posted by Elspot, they become firm physical obligations with no further adjustment allowed. All participants must then report their expected production and consumption profiles, based on both bilateral and pool-negotiated commitments, to the relevant system operator by 19.00 (7.00pm) on the day ahead.

System balancing is performed slightly differently in each country. The Norwegian system operates a single regulating market, in which generators may offer prices at which they would accept output adjustments at 15 minutes' notice or less. This market accepts bids until 19.30 (7.30pm) on the day ahead. Arguing that the Norwegian spot and regulating markets are both effectively day-ahead markets and therefore too inflexible, the Swedish grid operates its own shorter-term balancing market. The "regulation balancing" market is somewhat like the Norwegian regulation market: generators and consumers who can adjust their output at short notice can submit offers. In this case, however, the market remains open until 30 minutes before the flow hour. Sweden previously also operated a "balancing adjustment" market, which was a pool-like structure where participants could go to rectify short-term supply-demand imbalances. In March 1999 the Finnish electricity exchange EL-EX opened a day-of spot market, Elbas, which the Swedish system operator is now using in place of the balancing adjustment pool. Here, market participants may submit bids for physical purchases and sales up to two hours before delivery begins. The grid operators may also submit bids to Elbas and use the contracted power to balance the system approximately and to create counterflows on transmission lines to relieve congestion. Settlements are made one week after delivery, each participant's net commitment being compared with actual production or consumption. Any differences are assumed to have been corrected for using regulation energy and are billed to the participant at the regulation energy price.

Nord Pool's financial market, Eltermin, organises both a futures and a forward contracts exchange. Interestingly, participants can do business in any of four currencies: Norwegian kroner, Swedish kronor, Finnish markka and euros. The futures strip has a unique structure in that contract size varies according to its promptness. The "atomic" contract size is 168 MWh (1 MW base load for one week), but only the first four to seven weeks are traded as such. Further out the strip, weeks are grouped and traded as monthly blocks, which are in turn grouped and traded as three seasonal blocks at the back end (three seasonal blocks making a year). When there are less than four weekly contracts on the board, the first monthly block effectively rolls off and its four constituent weekly contracts roll on, thus increasing the number of weekly contracts to

Table 3. Nordic power trading statistics (in TWh)

	1993	1994	1995	1996	1997	1998
Elspot	10	15	20	41	44	56
Eltermin	3	7	15	43	53	89
Clearing volumes	na	na	na	na	148	352
Total generation	105	110	117	255*	258*	260*

* includes Norwegian and Swedish consumption
Source: Nord Pool

seven. Likewise, at certain times in the year, the prompt seasonal block is split into its component monthly blocks and a new seasonal block is added to the back end. Contracts are traded until the last day before the delivery week. At the end of the delivery week, the difference between the closing futures price and the average of the hourly Elspot prices is calculated, and participants who have taken the contract to "delivery" are credited or debited accordingly.

Originally, the futures market also listed annual blocks beyond the seasonal blocks, but liquidity was low because participants were unwilling to endure the cashflow swings that resulted from the daily settlement of these large futures positions. In reaction, Nord Pool replaced the annual futures blocks with a forward market for both seasonal and annual blocks going out three years. Forward contracts trade in much the same way as simple financial swaps and do not split into smaller units as time passes. Settlement occurs at the end of the delivery period.

Nord Pool continues to introduce new products in response to market demand. One example is the bilateral clearing service, introduced in 1998, in which, for a fee, Nord Pool agrees to take over financial bilateral contracts – in effect guaranteeing counterparty performance. Interest in this product has been quite respectable, as Table 3 indicates. Most recently, Nord Pool announced the introduction of an options market, which is to be launched in October 1999.

The Nordic market is often described as a success both technically and economically and the antithesis of the UK market. Certainly, the spot price and volatility time series (as seen in Figure 9), with their infrequent spikes and reasonably strong reverting tendency, are indicative of a competitive electricity market that is functioning well. What accounts for the difference? It is sometimes suggested that, although there are more than 100 generating companies in Scandinavia, two companies dominate the Norwegian–Swedish market: the state-owned Statkraft, which has 30% of the Norwegian market, and the privatised Swedish generator Vattenfall, with 50% local market share. Since both have close ties with government, it is thought that Statkraft and Vattenfall may be politically motivated to ensure price stability. This argument may have some validity, but it fails to recognise that typical winter capacity margins (ie [Total installed capacity – Peak demand]/Peak demand) in Norway and Sweden are of the order of 30%. The margin is even greater if import

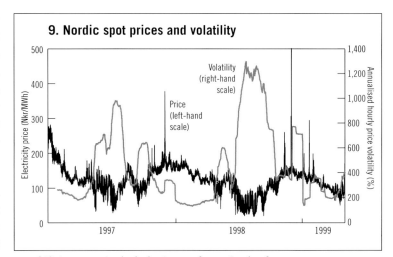

9. Nordic spot prices and volatility

capabilities are included. Apart from Statkraft and Vattenfall, there is no generator or even small of group of generators at present with a portfolio large enough to permit it to retire 30% of the country's capacity and still have enough generation in service to reap the benefits of inflated prices. This may change, however, as consolidation continues and as demand growth reduces the capacity margin.

California California was the first American state to undertake a full restructuring of its electricity market to include both wholesale and retail competition. Before restructuring, the California market was dominated by three large, vertically integrated investor-owned utilities (IOUs): Southern California Edison, Pacific Gas and Electric, and San Diego Gas and Electric. Then, in 1996, legislation was enacted to open the wholesale generating and retail marketing businesses to competition in phases over a four-year period. As in most other cases, California's restructuring consists of four elements: separation of transmission and distribution activities from generation; the establishment of open and equal transmission and distribution access; creation of an independent system operator (ISO) to operate the physical system in an unbiased fashion; and creation of a wholesale market operator, the California power exchange (PX). The first phase began in April 1998 with the debut of operations for the ISO and PX.

The function of the ISO is generally similar to that of the Nordic system operators, although there are important differences. As in the Nordic system, participants in the physical market submit requests to the ISO for transmission service on a day-ahead basis, which the ISO is required to fulfil impartially so long as system reliability is not compromised. These requests are submitted via scheduling coordinators, who act as "pre-

186

COMPETITIVE
ELECTRICITY
MARKETS
AROUND THE
WORLD

processors", performing initial consistency checks and aggregating supply and demand schedules to produce a balanced schedule (balanced in the sense of generation equalling demand plus losses), which is then submitted to the ISO. The ISO examines the schedules for possible transmission constraints, returning them unchanged if no constraints are expected or suggesting alterations to avoid constraints. The scheduling coordinators then have an opportunity to revise and resubmit their schedules to the ISO, which re-evaluates the requests one last time before issuing a final day-ahead schedule for dispatch and off-take. If transmission congestion is apparent in the revised schedules, the ISO uses participants' schedule adjustment bids (SABs) to alter schedules and assign costs for usage of constrained paths. SABs, which are voluntary bids submitted as part of the request for transmission service, are like the regulating bids in other markets: they represent a participant's willingness to alter its schedule given changes in energy price. The ISO stacks the bids in order of price, in effect using the SABs to auction rights to the transmission path. A participant submitting a low SAB is implying that it does not place much value on the transmission path. Consequently, participants with low SABs will have their scheduled flows on the path reduced more than those of a participant with a high SAB but will also pay lower congestion charges. The use of an auction, as distinct from the primary energy pool, is unique to the Californian system.

The ISO also operates four ancillary services auctions and an hour-ahead imbalance energy market. Energy procured from these markets is then used to correct over- or under-supply. The imbalance energy market is similar to Sweden's regulation market: generators submit, no later than one hour before delivery, price bids for quantities of energy that can be adjusted at short notice. The four ancillary services are regulation, spinning reserves, non-spinning reserves and replacement reserves (see Panel 1). Generators with uncommitted capacity may optionally submit bids for one or more of these auctions as part of their bid package to the scheduling coordinators. The ISO predetermines the amount of each service required for each hour of the next day and then executes the auctions sequentially. Regulation, considered the most valuable, is cleared first, followed by spinning, non-spinning and replacement reserves. Any capacity accepted in one auction is automatically withdrawn from subsequent auctions. Offers from generators consist of both a capacity and an energy price and are the financial equivalent of options on imbalance energy, the energy bid being the strike and the capacity bid being the premium. Clearing is based on the capacity price only, all winning generators receiving the marginal capacity price. During real-time operation, the ISO may then call on a generator to run if the imbalance energy price exceeds that generator's energy bid price. If dispatched, the generator receives the imbalance energy price. (Regulation service is an exception: metering limitations make it impossible to measure a generator's contribution, so participants in this market are paid according to their estimated energy production.)

The PX operates a classical pool in both the day-ahead and day-of market. The PX accepts simple offers for generation and bids for supply for each hour of the next day, stacks them in order of price and derives a market clearing price from the intersection of supply and demand. Bids and offers that make the cut are submitted to the ISO as part of the PX's balanced schedule. (As far as the ISO is concerned the PX is simply another scheduling coordinator.) In the event that the ISO assigns congestion charges to one or more transmission paths, the PX will split the market into zones, adjusting prices in each to reflect constraints and to ensure that total revenues and costs balance. Originally, the PX also conducted a more or less continuous hour-ahead market, but poor liquidity forced it to experiment with other procedures. It is now operating a day-of market with three auctions during the day. A 06.00 auction is held for power to be flowed in hours 11.00 to 16.00, a 12.00 auction for hours 17.00 to 24.00, and a 16.00 auction for 01.00 to 10.00 of the next day.

An interesting feature of the Californian system is the possibility of having more than one pool. Although the PX was created as part of the overall restructuring process, it does not hold a preferred position in the system. Scheduling coordinators are free to choose any method for arriving at a balanced schedule, including holding a pool-style auction. Indeed, there is already a privately held company, APX, which operates a web-based pool system in competition with the PX. The three IOUs are required to serve their native loads through the PX during the first four years of the phased transition to full competition, so PX volumes currently account for about 80% of all power transmitted by the ISO. At the end of the transition period, however, all retail energy suppliers will be free to choose how they go

187

COMPETITIVE
ELECTRICITY
MARKETS
AROUND THE
WORLD

about procuring power, and the PX will have to compete with other scheduling coordinators on price and quality of service.

The first electricity futures listed on Nymex were two West Coast contracts with delivery points at the California–Oregon border (COB) and the high-voltage switchyard of the Palo-Verde nuclear power station in Arizona. Nymex has since listed several more East Coast contracts, but COB and Palo Verde remain the most actively traded. The contract specifications call for 736 MWh of energy delivered at a constant 2 MW rate during peak hours of the delivery month (this will change to 864 MWh in October 1999). Futures are traded 18 months out, while options are traded on the front 12 months. Although COB and Palo-Verde contracts provide valuable information about future price expectations in western North America, neither delivery point is considered part of California by the ISO. In consequence, both the PX and APX have begun trading monthly forward contracts based on Californian delivery points in an effort to facilitate forward price discovery without basis risk.

It is still too early to tell if the restructured California market is performing as envisioned. Generally, the PX auction process appears competitive: its price–load curve exhibits a reasonably tight relationship except at the very highest load levels, where the dispersion grows and large price spikes do occur (see Figure 10). This is to be expected. Normally, there are upwards of 35 participants in the PX on any given day, but when demand peaks, only six firms, with a combined portfolio of about 17 GW of flexible gas turbine generators, participate at the margin. Also worth noting are the very low prices occasionally seen on the PX. These are the result of over-supply conditions that occur in the spring when low demand and melting snow in the Pacific Northwest can lead to a surfeit of low-priced hydro-generated power.

In contrast to the PX, the ISO's ancillary services market does not appear to have behaved competitively. In the first months of operations, capacity bids spiked to more than \$9,000/MW, far in excess of expected costs, prompting the ISO to impose first a \$500/MW cap and later a \$250/MW cap. The ISO's market surveillance committee has reviewed the market's operations and has instituted several changes and proposed several more; however, the cap remains in effect until regulators are convinced that market power issues have been satisfactorily resolved. Again, as in the case of the UK, the failure to achieve a

well-functioning market is the unintended by-product of restrictive rules and poorly designed industry procedures. Five of the most critical flaws are listed here and can be characterised as either reducing liquidity or introducing arbitrage opportunities.

❏ Because of software constraints, generators outside the ISO's control were barred from participation, reducing potential liquidity. As of August 1998, however, this constraint was removed on all ancillary services except regulation.

❏ The large IOUs are subject to a regulatory cap on rates they can earn by providing ancillary services. Consequently, there are times when an IOU may withdraw its capacity from the ancillary services market in favour of a more lucrative one.

❏ When congestion occurs, ancillary services are auctioned (and priced) on a zonal basis rather at a state level. This further segments the market.

❏ ISO procedures have not allowed it to act rationally in response to arbitrage opportunities. On numerous occasions lower-quality services have been priced higher than higher-quality services. Clearly, high-quality services can substitute for low-quality ones, but rather than simply buying more of the cheaper high-quality product, the ISO has insisted on buying fixed volumes of each designated service. Again, this tends to create fragmented markets in which a single participant can dominate.

❏ The most serious flaw is the existence of "reliability must-run" contracts (RMRs). During the design phase of the California market, concerns were voiced about some generators' excessive locational market power. In times of high

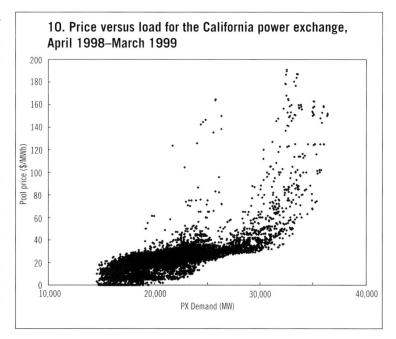

10. Price versus load for the California power exchange, April 1998–March 1999

demand, system conditions can arise that require specific generators to be turned on to prevent system failure. Under the proposed market rules, these generators could bid any price and be confident of acceptance. To mitigate this risk, most gas-fired generators were signed to RMR contracts, which stipulate that the ISO can dispatch them to help maintain system stability at a fixed rather than market-based price. Perversely, the fixed prices were typically contracted at much higher levels than market rates, some reaching $4,000/MWh. This means that when system reliability degrades, generators with RMR contracts have an incentive to withdraw from other markets in order to be available to be called. Still more perversely, generators may be using the ancillary services auctions to hedge the risk of not being dispatched under RMR. In conditions of high demand, when there is a reasonable probability that RMR contracts will be invoked, generators may elect not to participate in the energy market but to submit capacity bids to the ancillary service market at very high price levels. In this way, generators increase their expected profit by maximising the chance that their capacity is dispatched either as a high-priced ancillary service or under RMR contract.

Bilateral markets

We have seen in the previous discussions that the primary purpose of a pool is to improve or ensure liquidity in wholesale electricity or ancillary services markets. Where sufficient liquidity exists, bilateral trading between individual participants is enough to guarantee market efficiency and security of supply. This is the model used on much of the North American continent apart from the pool systems in California, New York, New England, PJM and Alberta, Canada. Bilateral trading in North America is not new; utilities have been trading power since the turn of the century. Even now, about 2,000 of the more than 3,000 North American utilities are municipalities or cooperatives that do not own generating assets and must buy power to serve their native load through long-term "full requirements" contracts. In addition to requirements transactions, a significant fraction of physical power is traded on an economic basis (ie discretionary trading, transacted to benefit the counterparties by reducing their costs). The emergence of non-traditional wholesale power players has led to an explosion in this "economy energy" market, with trading volumes exceeding 700 TWh in 1997.

The North American market has evolved into three regional networks. The Western Interconnect comprises the states and provinces in the US, Canada and parts of Mexico west of the Rocky Mountains. The Eastern Interconnect comprises most of the eastern two-thirds of the continent, from Saskatchewan to Quebec and down to Florida. Texas constitutes a separate third region. Within each Interconnect there are electric reliability councils, which are voluntary organisations with a membership encompassing the entire electricity business. Collectively they make up the North American Electric Reliability Council (NERC), whose charter is to establish standards and procedures to promote reliable electricity supply throughout North America. Each council's region is further subdivided into security areas, each with a security coordinator. The security coordinator monitors the status of its area on a real-time basis and coordinates the actions of individual control areas when threats to the system arise. A control area can be a single utility system or a group of utilities where one member is given real-time control of the entire group's assets.

Physical electricity is traded over the counter on both a spot and a forward basis. "Spot" is generally construed to mean trading for next-hour to next-day power flows. Forward contracts typically comprise larger blocks of power with delivery dates extending one year or more, although obligations beyond two years are, at best, only thinly traded. Nymex also lists futures contracts with delivery points into utility systems in the ECAR, SPP and MAAC regions. Liquidity in these contracts, which were only launched in 1998, is still low.

11. North American Reliability Councils

Source: NERC

189

COMPETITIVE
ELECTRICITY
MARKETS
AROUND THE
WORLD

Electricity trading is conducted in much the same way as gas trading. Longs and shorts transact directly over the telephone or through brokers. Although electricity flows throughout the network, it is assumed, for contractual purposes, to flow along a particular contract path. Where no independent system operator exists, firms must request transmission service from the owners of each transmission system over which the power is contracted to flow. To review available transmission capacity and to buy transmission rights, traders use the Open Access Same Time Information Service (OASIS) – the FERC-mandated, web-based transmission reservation system. With OASIS, a trader can in principle reserve transmission paths to flow power from California to Quebec. Such a transaction would not be very economical, however, since every transmission owner along the contract path is allowed to charge a regulated fee for "wheeling" power across its system.

Like other markets in the world, the North American bilateral market represents a stage in the evolution of the industry, with many issues still be resolved before it can be called fully competitive. One such issue is the treatment of transmission congestion. The present system has no mechanism for pricing transmission congestion and relies on a set of rules called transmission loading relief (TLR) procedures established by the NERC to alleviate constraints. There are six basic levels of TLRs. A Level 1 TLR is advisory, informing participants of potential problems. Level 2 imposes restrictions on flows between control areas but does not cut service. Level 3 requires curtailment of non-firm transmission service. Levels 4, 5 and 6 are progressively more severe, involving curtailment of firm services and implementation of emergency procedures to prevent system failure.

TLRs pose a significant risk to participants because they are not usually considered a *force majeure* and because there is little ability to predict them or actively manage the risk. Once cut, the short party must find an alternative way to flow power to the buyer or face non-performance penalties. More than 300 Level 2 and above TLRs were called between January 1998 and February 1999, and, although their economic effect is difficult to judge precisely, it is possible that TLRs have resulted in millions of dollars in non-performance penalties. In an effort to find a market-based alternative to TLR procedures, the NERC has proposed a "redispatch transaction" market in which transmission users would be allowed to purchase plant-specific call options. Armed with such an option, a participant could counteract the effect that its transactions might have by calling on a specific generator to alter output, creating counterflows on the affected transmission line. This is the bilateral equivalent of the schedule adjustment bids used in California.

More generally, critics charge that the present system makes it easy for transmission owners to discriminate by arbitrarily altering the declared transmission availability. In the light of these and other concerns about reliability and operations in a deregulated environment, the FERC recently issued a Notice of Proposed Rulemaking, in which it proposes the mandatory implementation of Regional Transmission Organizations (RTOs). Although the exact nature of RTOs have yet to be determined, the FERC does make it clear that, in future, transmission owners will be required to cede control of their systems to some form of independent operator.

1 *It is a pleasure to acknowledge the invaluable comments, suggestions and support of my colleagues at Enron, including Anjam Ahmad, Lynda Clemmons, Stinson Gibner, Vince Kaminski, Richard Lewis, Martin Lin, Terry Lohrenz, Mike Niman, Paul Quilkey, Bjarne Schieldrop, Michael Schilmoeller, Julian Turecek and Greg Woulfe.*

2 *In 1992 the UK government directed the regulator to review National Power's and PowerGen's trading practices. To avoid possible intervention, National Power and PowerGen agreed, among other things, to divest 4,000 MW and 2,000 MW, respectively, by 1996. The entire 6,000 MW was leased to Eastern Generation, making the competitive market a triumvirate.*

3 Review of Electricity Trading Arrangements: Framework Document, *November 1998, Office of Electricity Regulation, London.*

4 *The NEM was implemented in stages. In October 1994 the VicPool was established as competitive mandatory pool system for the Victorian system. In May 1996 New South Wales followed suit with its own statewide pool system. In May 1997 phase-one NEM was implemented whereby the Victorian and New South Wales systems were provisionally joined and dispatched jointly. The NEM formally commenced In December 1998.*

5 *To smooth the transition from regulated to market-based retail power, the state governments directed generators and retailers to sign vesting contracts designed to cover demand from customers still paying regulated tariffs. These contracts are essentially contracts for differences or fixed-for-floating swaps where the floating leg is tied to the electricity pool price.*

8

Regulatory and Legal Issues

Kenneth M. Raisler and Alison M. Gregory

Sullivan & Cromwell; Long-Term Capital Management, L.P.

W hile various forms of commodity forwards, options, swaps[1] and commodity-linked hybrid products have been in existence for years, their recent explosive growth has attracted the attention of regulators and raised questions regarding their enforceability. The central issues are whether the products are legal, and whether the market participants are permitted to enter into them, including questions about the criteria that may limit participation.

To understand the legal issues that have dominated the development of the derivatives market in the United States, we will analyse the Commodity Futures Trading Commission (CFTC) releases on swaps and hybrid instruments which provide guidance on drawing a line between permissible and impermissible products. In addition, we will examine the issuances and proposals of regulators and legislators who are examining the scope of proper participation in the derivatives markets and whether or not additional regulation is necessary and advisable. We also will review the historical division of jurisdiction between the CFTC and the Securities and Exchange Commission (SEC), as well as the role played by the states in the regulation of this market.

Law and regulation in the United States

While both federal and state regulators and laws are pertinent, the key regulator in the United States on the issue of the legality of derivative products[2] is the CFTC.

The CFTC is the regulatory agency empowered under the provisions of the Commodity Exchange Act (CEA) as amended to regulate commodity futures and options contracts as well as instruments with elements of futures or options.

The primary focus of the CFTC under the CEA is the regulation of exchange-traded futures and options contracts. Indeed, until amendments to the CEA were adopted in 1992 (see below), all futures contracts had to trade on CFTC-regulated

exchange markets, and only certain specific options could be traded outside an exchange.

The possible characterisation of commodity derivatives and hybrid products as futures or options contracts subject to CFTC regulation, including the exchange-trading requirement, was largely ignored until 1987. In 1987, the CFTC commenced and settled an enforcement action enjoining a bank from issuing gold-indexed certificates of deposit and threatened enforcement action against another bank in connection with its issuance of oil-indexed swaps.[3] That same year, the CFTC released an Advance Notice of Proposed Rulemaking with respect to hybrid instruments which questioned the legality of a full range of commodity derivatives under the CEA.[4]

Commodity derivatives, which can contain elements of commercial contracts, financial contracts, and debt or equity elements with futures-like and options-like components, are not easy to differentiate in terms of the traditional regulatory authorities of the banking regulators, the SEC and the CFTC. Not surprisingly, the 1987 Advance Notice met with considerable criticism from the other regulators. In addition, the Advance Notice, combined with the CFTC enforcement actions, chilled development of the business and drove much of it outside of the United States. The CFTC made progress with interpretations and rules issued in 1989 and 1990 (see below).

More significant progress was made with the adoption of the Futures Trading Practices Act of 1992 and the adoption by the CFTC of rules in early 1993 that broadly exempted swaps and other derivatives from CFTC regulation. These new rules go a long way to eliminate the threat of CFTC enforcement action, as well as private litigation or state enforcement action, to overturn a derivative transaction as being in violation of the CEA or state law.

However, as the growth of derivatives continues at a rapid pace, regulators and legislators continue to examine their role in this active marketplace. In addition to examining the nature of the products, which has largely been the activity of the CFTC, regulators have begun to focus on the role of the participant. Banking participants are subject to guidelines, including regulations pertaining to bank derivatives activities and guidelines that direct banks as to their extensions of credit to certain types of market participants, such as highly leveraged institutions.[5] The derivatives-related activities of pension funds, insurance companies, mutual funds and municipalities, among others, are also subject to increased scrutiny.

JURISDICTIONAL REACH OF THE SEC AND CFTC AND THE COMMODITY EXCHANGE ACT

In 1974, Congress passed the Commodity Exchange Act, granting the CFTC exclusive jurisdiction over transactions involving exchange-traded "contracts of sale of a commodity for future delivery" and commodity option contracts (exchange traded or not).[6] The term "commodity" is defined in Section 1a(3) as "wheat, cotton, rice, corn,..., and all other goods and articles, except onions..., and all services, rights, and interests in which contracts for future delivery are presently or in the future dealt in."[7]

Section 4(a)(1) requires that transactions in futures contracts be "conducted on or subject to the rules of a board of trade designated by the [CFTC] as a 'contract market' for such commodity." The CEA does not define the term "contracts for future delivery". However, case law and a CFTC Policy Statement have developed many of the elements of a "futures contract". The non-exclusive elements include that it (1) has standardised terms, (2) is usually offset, and (3) usually shifts the risk of a change in a commodity's value rather than transfers ownership.[8]

As mentioned above, the CFTC regulates commodity options. Options include "accounts, agreements (including any transaction which is of the character of, or is commonly known to the trade as, an 'option', 'privilege', 'indemnity', 'bid', 'offer', 'put', 'call', 'advance guaranty', or 'decline guaranty')."[9]

Although the CEA provides that the CFTC has regulatory powers with regard to futures contracts and options thereon, the CEA excludes or exempts certain financial instruments. First, forward contracts[10] are excluded from the CFTC's regulatory authority because the term "future delivery" does "not include any sale of any cash commodity for deferred shipment or delivery."[11]

Although the distinctions between futures and forward contracts are sometimes difficult to discern, the forward contract exclusion has provided an important basis for excluding many types of commodity agreements from the CFTC's jurisdiction and the provisions of the CEA.

Second, Section 2(a)(1)(A)(ii), often called the Treasury Amendment, excludes certain transactions, including "transactions in foreign currency".[12]

Third, CFTC Regulation 32.4(a) exempts instruments called "Trade Options". It provides that commodity option transactions (other than on agricultural commodities) "offered by a person which has a reasonable basis to believe that the option is offered to a producer, processor, or commercial user of, or a merchant handling, the commodity which is the subject of the commodity option transaction, or the products or byproducts thereof, and that such producer, processor, commercial user or merchant is offered or enters into the commodity option transaction solely for purposes related to its business as such" are generally exempt transactions.

The SEC and the CFTC have disagreed about the scope of their regulatory powers and the reach of their respective jurisdictions. One area of particular uncertainty involved the treatment of futures contracts on securities, or indices comprised of securities, and options on such futures contracts.[13] To resolve uncertainties with respect to such instruments, the CFTC and the SEC specified which instruments were under the purview of the CFTC or the SEC in the Jurisdictional Accord of 1982.[14] In other cases, courts have resolved the uncertainty regarding the jurisdictional reaches of the CFTC and the SEC.[15] Those courts that have addressed the issue have unanimously concluded that Congress' grant of exclusive jurisdiction to the CFTC provides the CFTC with the sole regulatory authority to address products within its jurisdiction. As discussed below, confusion regarding the jurisdictional reach of the SEC and CFTC has left lingering legal uncertainty with respect to securities based derivatives that was not resolved by the Futures Trading Practices Act of 1992.

THE FORWARD CONTRACT EXCLUSION AND TRANSNOR (BERMUDA) LIMITED V. BP NORTH AMERICA PETROLEUM

The breadth of the forward contract exclusion for transactions involving "any cash commodity for deferred shipment or delivery" remains uncertain because futures and forward contracts often have similar features.[16] One United States District Court for the Southern District of New York decision, *Transnor (Bermuda) Limited v. BP North America Petroleum*,[17] illustrated and exacerbated this uncertainty.

Transnor, a Bermuda corporation, argued, *inter alia*, that the defendant petroleum companies violated the CEA because Transnor contended that 15-day Brent oil contracts (on which it had defaulted) were illegal, off-exchange futures contracts, not obligations falling within the forward contract exclusion of the CEA. In denying the defendants' motion for summary judgment, the Court concluded that such contracts were illegal futures contracts and were subject to CFTC regulation because, among other things, the "relatively standardized" oil contracts were "routinely settled by means other than delivery".[18]

This ruling posed a major threat to the oil trading market. It brought into question a large number of commercial transactions that were typically cash settled and that had not been considered to be subject to the CEA. That uncertainty and the ensuing clamours for relief prompted the CFTC to issue its Statutory Interpretation Concerning Forward Transactions (the "Statutory Interpretation").[19] In the Statutory Interpretation, the CFTC clarified the forward contract exclusion. The Statutory Interpretation explained that the exclusion applied to certain commercial transactions, including 15-day Brent oil contracts, notwithstanding infrequent delivery of oil, because (1) they "create specific delivery obligations", (2) any book-out or offset required "separate, individually negotiated, new agreements" (that is, not an "exchange-style offset"), and (3) the commercial parties, who transact "in connection with their business" and are capable of making or taking delivery, bore "substantial economic risk".[20] However, it was not certain that the CFTC's Statutory Interpretation, issued after the *Transnor* decision, would be recognised as binding by the courts or would eliminate the risk of private litigation.

In addition to the Statutory Interpretation, a decision by the United States Court of Appeals for the Ninth Circuit offered some comfort to certain market participants. In the Ninth Circuit's case, *In re Bybee (Krommenhoek v. A-Mark Precious Metals, Inc.)*,[21] A-Mark transacted with a metals dealer named Bybee, who was transacting on behalf of customers. Bybee's customers did not know that Bybee purchased metals on margin and that A-Mark held a lien on the metals for purchase money owed. After the value of silver declined and Bybee paid A-Mark's margin calls, Bybee went bankrupt. A bankruptcy trustee (acting on behalf of Bybee's unpaid customers) sued A-Mark, alleging that it violated the CEA by transacting in illegal, off-exchange future contracts. Deferring to the CFTC's Statutory Interpretation, the Ninth Circuit determined that A-Mark was not liable because such contracts fell within the forward contracts exclusion. In reaching this conclusion, the Ninth Circuit determined that delivery was the "determining factor" and relied on the fact that the terms of the contracts included legal obligations to make or accept delivery (even if the parties routinely offset their obligations).[22] Because the Court concluded that certain types of commercial transactions in precious metals constituted forward contracts falling within the CEA exclusion, it implicitly rejected the reasoning of the Southern District of New York's *Transnor* decision.

Notwithstanding the comfort that the Statutory Interpretation, the *A-Mark* decision and case-by-case no-action relief provide commercial participants in the market for forward delivery of commodities, further clarification, discussed below, has been necessary.

STATE LAWS

In addition to CFTC regulatory issues, commodity transactions may also implicate the laws of the states. Section 12(e) states that nothing in the CEA "shall supersede or preempt...the application of any Federal or State statute...to any transaction in or involving any commodity...that is not conducted on or subject to the rules of a contract market, or, in the case of any State or local law that prohibits or regulates gaming or the operation of 'bucket shops'...that is not a transaction or class of transactions that has received or is covered by the terms of any exemption...." Thus, non-exempt off-exchange commodity transactions must comply with state laws, which often include various provisions that could pertain to commodity transactions.

For example, state "Blue Sky" laws may include anti-fraud provisions for transactions involving commodities. In addition, numerous states, including New York, have statutes prohibiting "bucket shops" or gambling. New York's gambling statute prohibits "all wagers, bets or stakes, made to depend upon...any lot, chance, casualty, or unknown or contingent event...".[23] Also, Section 225.00 of New York's Penal Law provides that anyone engaging in gambling when a person "stakes something of value upon the outcome of...a future contingent event not under his control or influence..." violates such Section. Arguably, numerous off-exchange commodity or energy derivative instruments could violate state statutory definitions of gambling because a party is risking "something of value" upon the outcome of a "contingent event" not under that party's control or influence (such as, say, commodity prices).

Similarly, off-exchange commodity or energy derivative transactions could arguably violate statutes that numerous states, including New York, have which prohibit "bucket shops". Around the turn of the century, operations, called "bucket shops", existed that purportedly transacted in the commodity markets or exchanges. They accepted orders to purchase or sell securities or futures contracts and then, rather than executing them on an exchange or in a market, "bucketed" them. When prices moved against their positions, the "bucket shops" failed to honour their obligations and closed.

Sections 351 and 351-e of New York's General Business Law prohibit the operation of "bucket shops". Section 351 prohibits the making or offering of a contract "without intending a bona fide purchase or sale" of the subject matter of the contract and with the intent to settle such contract by referring to general "market quotations".[24] Arguably, "bucket shop" statutes, with very broad prohibitions, could prohibit certain types of off-exchange transactions, such as over-the-counter (OTC) instruments that do not receive CEA Section 4(c) exemptive relief,[25] and their existence threatens the enforceability of such transactions.

A few courts have addressed challenges to transactions based on "bucket shop" statutes. For example, the Fourth Circuit considered a lawsuit involving a wealthy and financially sophisticated individual, named Laszlo N. Tauber, who wanted to avoid the payment of many millions of dollars that he owed on foreign currency transactions based on, among other things, a "bucket shop" statute.[26] Tauber contended, *inter alia*, that such transactions were illegal because they violated New York's "bucket shop" statute. Rejecting Tauber's argument, the Fourth Circuit determined that the transactions constituted legitimate, "bona fide contracts, resulting in legal obligations to take delivery", rather than sham transactions that would have violated the "bucket shop" statute.[27] Similarly, New York courts have upheld other legitimate commercial transactions and rejected attacks against such transactions based on gambling or "bucket shop" statutes.[28]

SWAPS POLICY STATEMENT

In 1989, the CFTC issued its Policy Statement Concerning Swap Transactions ("Swaps Policy Statement").[29] Although it lacked the force of a statutory interpretation or regulation, the Swaps Policy Statement did indicate that cash-settled swaps satisfying certain requirements would not be regulated as futures contracts or commodity options by the CFTC.

In the Swaps Policy Statement, the CFTC stated that "most swap transactions, although possessing elements of futures or options contracts, are not appropriately regulated as such under the [CEA] and regulations", and that the CFTC, accordingly, would not take action against swaps, such as interest rate, currency and commodity swaps, provided such swaps qualified for its non-exclusive safe harbour protection. To qualify for the Swaps Policy Statement protection, a swap must have (1) individually-tailored and negotiated terms, (2) an expectation that the terms would be performed and would not be terminated absent counterparty consent, (3) an absence of the indicia of an exchange market, such as a mark-to-market margin or settlement system, (4) been undertaken in conjunction with the parties' line of business, and (5) not been marketed to the public. Due to recent developments, discussed below, the safe harbour created by the Swaps Policy Statement is relevant to only a small percentage of the swap transactions that it once covered.

FUTURES TRADING PRACTICES ACT OF 1992

To provide certainty with regard to the treatment of highly successful financial instruments such as swaps, hybrids and energy contracts, and in response to the mounting pressure for clarification, Congress amended the CEA with the Futures Trading Practices Act of 1992 (FTPA).[30]

In the FTPA, Congress, among other things, granted the CFTC the authority to exempt certain agreements, contracts and transactions from various requirements of the CEA or CFTC regulations, including the CEA requirement that transactions must occur on a designated contract market.[31] One provision of the CEA that the CFTC could not exempt under the FTPA was the SEC-CFTC Jurisdictional Accord (Section 2(a)(1)). Thus, the CFTC does not have the authority to provide securities based derivatives the same scope of exemptive relief as other derivatives, and legal uncertainty continues to apply to these transactions. In assessing whether or not to grant exemptive relief, the FTPA and CEA Section 4(c) require the CFTC to consider the following: (1) whether the exemption is in the public interest and consistent with the purposes of the CEA, and (2) whether the agreement, contract or transaction (i) will only be entered into by "appropriate persons" and (ii) will not materially or adversely affect the CFTC or contract markets in discharging their CEA regulatory duties.[32] Before determining whether to issue an exemption, the CFTC was not required to find that the product to be exempted was governed by the CEA. The FTPA also amended Section 12(e) to give the CFTC authority to preempt state or local laws that prohibit gambling or "bucket shops" and to prevent the application of such laws with respect to transactions exempted by Section 4(c).

The Conference Committee Report accompanying the FTPA encouraged the CFTC to "use its new exemptive powers promptly upon enactment of this legislation in four areas where significant concerns of legal uncertainty have arisen: (1) hybrids, (2) swaps, (3) energy contracts, (4) bank deposits and accounts."[33]

Pursuant to its exemptive authority, the CFTC moved promptly in early 1993 to grant various exemptions for certain swaps agreements, hybrid instruments and energy contracts.[34]

SWAPS EXEMPTION
Although no determination had been made that swap agreements were covered by the CEA or fell under the purview of the CFTC, the CFTC approved final rules during January 1993 exempting certain swap agreements from almost all of the CEA and CFTC regulations, provided that the swap agreements meet certain criteria.[35] To qualify for an exemption, the swap agreement (1) must have been entered into by "eligible swap participants" (which resemble "appropriate persons" in Section 4(c) of the CEA and are entities of a certain size, certain individuals or entities – such as a futures commission merchant, floor broker or floor trader – or natural persons with assets exceeding at least US$10 million);[36] (2) cannot be a fungible agreement with standardised material terms; (3) must have the creditworthiness or risk of its counterparties as a material consideration; and (4) must not be traded on or through a multilateral transaction execution facility.[37]

The exemption also requires that the agreement be a "swap agreement", which includes "(i) [a]n agreement (including terms and conditions incorporated by reference therein) which is a rate swap agreement, basis swap, forward rate agreement, commodity swap, interest rate option, forward foreign exchange agreement, rate cap agreement, rate floor agreement, rate collar agreement, currency swap agreement, cross-currency rate swap agreement, currency option, any other similar agreement (including any option to enter into any of the foregoing); (ii) [a]ny combination of the foregoing; or (iii) [a] master agreement for any of the foregoing together with all supplements thereto".[38]

If the criteria are met, the "swap agreement is exempt from all provisions of the [CEA] and any person or class of persons offering, entering into, rendering advice, or rendering other services with respect to such agreement, is exempt for such activity from all provisions of the [CEA] (except in each case the provisions of Sections 2(a)(1)(B) [the Jurisdictional Accord], 4b and 4o of the [CEA (prohibiting fraud)] and § 32.9 as adopted under § 4c(b) of the [CEA], prohibiting fraud and the provisions of Section 6(c) and 9(a)(2) of the [CEA] to the extent these provisions prohibit manipulation of the market price of any commodity in interstate commerce or for future delivery on or subject to the rules of any contract market)...."[39] Also, such an agreement, to the extent it is covered by the terms of the exemption, may be exempt from state and local gambling and "bucket shop" laws, pursuant to CEA Section 12(e), as amended by the FTPA.[40]

HYBRIDS
Pursuant to its new exemptive authority, the CFTC also adopted rules exempting certain hybrid instruments from almost all of the CEA, including its exchange-trading requirement (the "Hybrid Exemption").[41] To qualify for the Hybrid Exemption's safe harbour protection, the hybrid instrument must be (1) an equity or debt security instrument according to Section 2(1) of the Securities Act[42] or (2) a time deposit, demand deposit or transaction account offered by an insured depository institution, insured credit union, or branch or agency of a bank that is federally or state regulated.[43]

Such hybrid instruments must also pass a "predominance test". It requires that, at the time of issuance, the "sum of the commodity-dependent values of the commodity-dependent components be less than the commodity-independent value of the commodity-independent component."[44] The commodity-dependent values are determined by decomposing the commodity-dependent components of the hybrid instrument into commodity options. For example, any long forward-like commodity components of the instrument are split into long call options and short put options having the same strike prices. The commodity-dependent value is "the absolute net value of the put option premia with strike prices less than or equal to the reference price[45] plus the absolute net value of the call option premia with strike prices greater than or equal to the reference price, calculated as of the time of issuance of the hybrid instrument."[46]

The Hybrid Exemption does not exempt the hybrid instruments from the Jurisdictional Accord[47] provisions of the CEA.

ENERGY CONTRACT EXEMPTION

In April 1993, the CFTC approved a Final Order exempting certain energy contracts or energy-related derivative contracts. The CFTC's Exemption for Certain Contracts Involving Energy Products ("Energy Contract Exemption") responded to an application seeking legal clarity and certainty with regard to the off-exchange market for energy products that a group of crude oil and natural gas producers, processors and merchandisers filed and provides exemptive relief for certain energy-related contracts.[48]

The CFTC's Energy Contract Exemption granted relief from almost all of the CEA and CFTC regulations to certain contracts that involve transactions in crude oil, condensates, natural gas and natural gas liquids that can be used as an energy source regardless of whether the commodities are ultimately used as an energy source.[49] Also, the Energy Contract Exemption covers derivatives of these energy products, including gasoline, diesel fuel or heating oil, that are typically used as energy sources. The Energy Contract Exemption, by its terms, does not apply to electricity contracts.

Only certain types of parties are eligible to qualify for the exemptive relief.[50] In addition, the energy contract must be an individually negotiated, bilateral contract between two eligible entities (or at least entities reasonably believed to be eligible) acting as principals. The contract cannot include a unilateral right to offset or settle by cash payment. Instead, the contract must include delivery obligations, although the CFTC recognised that the parties may later negotiate another agreement to "book out" their obligations rather

than to deliver the physical commodity.[51]

Energy contracts meeting the above criteria are exempt from all of the CEA except for the certain sections prohibiting manipulation of the market price for the energy product. Thus, unlike the Swap Exemption's relief, the Energy Contract Exemption's relief includes relief from the anti-fraud provision of the CEA.[52]

Thus, the CFTC's Energy Contract Exemption clarified that energy-related contracts that qualified for relief were exempt from CEA requirements, such as the exchange-trading requirement, and provided legal certainty in the market for energy-related contracts. In providing this relief, the CFTC avoided the futures-forwards dichotomy altogether.

Enforceability

Determining whether the underlying transaction is legal in the jurisdiction[53] in which it is entered into is but one of several legal issues that needs to be examined.[54] Legal due diligence requires scrutiny of a number of elements of the transaction and the counterparties in assessing whether the derivative contract will be enforceable.

CAPACITY

At the outset, a party entering into commodity and energy derivative transactions should ensure that its counterparty has the capacity to enter into the transactions and, if capacity is present, that the signatory has the authority to bind the entity to the transactions.

The seminal case on this point is *Hammersmith and Fulham London Borough Council v. Hazell*, 2 W.L.R. 372 (1991).[55] In *Hammersmith and Fulham*, London local authorities had engaged in hundreds of swap transactions with swap dealers during the 1987–9 fiscal years. After the Audit Commission conducted an audit of the local authorities' activities and questioned the legality of the transactions, the Council's finance director closed any swap transactions that would result in losses to the Council, and the Council received an order from the Divisional Court of the Queen's Bench Division that the transactions were contrary to law. Swap dealers appealed, and the House of Lords determined that the applicable statute did not grant the local authorities the authority to enter into swap transactions. Because the local authorities lacked legal permission to engage in them, the transactions were *ultra vires* and, thus, void.[56]

The capacity of any counterparty must, therefore, be analysed. Of particular concern are a range of constituents including governmental authorities, regulated utilities, insurance companies, pension funds and mutual funds. For example, local gas and electric utility companies in the United States are regulated by Public Utility Commissioners (PUCs). Because PUCs regulate many of the participants in the energy derivative markets, they oversee how such entities may permissibly contract to procure their fuel supplies. Some PUCs have been examining energy derivatives and determining whether or not they will permit regulated utilities companies to use such instruments to hedge their exposure to changes in the price of fuel.[57] Unless PUCs approve the use of energy derivative instruments, many regulated utilities will be severely limited in how they engage in such transactions.

Similarly, insurance companies are another group of potentially significant derivatives end-users because of their interest rate and other exposures. Like regulated utilities, however, insurance companies face state regulation. Thus, their regulatory authority to engage in derivatives activities remains uncertain without express authority from the applicable state laws and insurance regulators. The National Association of Insurance Commissioners (the NAIC), a quasi-regulatory association promoting uniformity among state regulators and comprised of the chief regulator of each US state or jurisdiction, evaluated the use of derivatives by insurance companies. The NAIC drafted and finalised a model statute authorising insurance companies to engage in derivatives activities within certain parameters, and many states are considering whether or not to adopt it or portions thereof.[58]

BANKRUPTCY

Congress amended the Bankruptcy Code with regard to "swap agreements".[59] These amendments offer considerable relief and certainty for market participants in such transactions. Parties to "swap agreements" can avoid Bankruptcy Code Section 362's automatic stay provision.[60] By avoiding the Code's automatic stay provision, parties to a master swap agreement can net their transactions, set off claims for settlement or collateral purposes and calculate one single close-out amount.[61] Based on the relief afforded by the foregoing amendments to the Bankruptcy Code, participants in derivatives markets with instruments qualifying as "swap agreements" under the Bankruptcy Code can liquidate their positions notwithstanding the filing of a bankruptcy

petition and the imposition of the automatic stay.[62]

In addition, such transactions are exempt from the Bankruptcy Code's avoidance provisions, which might, for example, have permitted a bankruptcy trustee to treat some payments made within ninety days (or, possibly, one year) of the insolvent party's petition for bankruptcy as avoidable "preferences". Any payments received or collections made during the normal course of business with respect to such transactions cannot be avoided as fraudulent transfers or preferential transfers by a bankruptcy trustee.[63]

Bankruptcy trustees cannot choose to assume or reject any executory contract, including open positions in off-exchange commodity transactions, under Section 365(a).[64]

Also, relief from the automatic stay provision, coupled with the Bankruptcy Code's interpretation of a master swap agreement and its collateral agreement as a single agreement, make it far less likely that a bankruptcy trustee could "cherry pick" among transactions between an insolvent and a solvent swap counterparty.

In addition to providing relief to participants in the US swap markets,[65] the amendments to the Bankruptcy Code also clarified that forward contracts and options were afforded similar relief. The definition of "forward contract" for purposes of the Bankruptcy Code was expanded to include physical commodities that are not currently traded on US commodity exchanges and a "repurchase transaction, reverse repurchase transaction, consignment, lease, swap, hedge transaction, deposit, loan, option, allocated transaction, unallocated transaction, or any combination thereof or option thereon."[66]

Similarly, Congress has enacted certain other laws[67] that also increased legal certainty for US derivative market participants. Nevertheless, some uncertainty remains.[68]

NETTING

Counterparties in the OTC derivatives markets recognise that they reduce their risk by broadening the use of master agreements with bilateral close-out netting provisions and by working with their counterparties to ensure that such agreements and netting provisions will be legally enforceable in all of the jurisdictions in which they transact business. Although bilateral close-out netting arrangements are increasingly common in the OTC market and their use is recommended by most regulators, many market participants remain concerned about their enforceability during bankruptcy in different jurisdictions.[69]

Some jurisdictions do recognise and enforce bilateral close-out netting arrangements. For example, as discussed below, the enforceability of such arrangements with United States counterparties in the United States is "almost certain" in insolvency proceedings involving derivatives.[70] While in other countries, such as England, that lack legislation expressly enabling a party to net derivatives obligations, such an agreement including certain provisions will likely be enforced. The lack of express authority in some jurisdictions, however, causes uncertainty when dealing with counterparties from certain jurisdictions and must be considered carefully.[71]

Derivatives and issues before the regulators

Congress, various regulatory agencies, and institutional participants in the markets for commodity and energy derivatives have focused considerable attention upon some of the issues posed by these burgeoning markets. There has been much discussion about whether these instruments increase or reduce market risk and volatility. Some have studied these issues and released reports. Others have introduced bills, guidelines or standards attempting to govern the participants in the markets for these instruments.

GROUP OF THIRTY REPORT

The Group of Thirty, a group chaired by Paul Volcker and comprised of industry representatives, central bankers, bankers, and academics spent approximately nine months assessing global derivatives markets. Upon the completion of their review, the Global Derivatives Study Group released on July 21, 1993 a lengthy study entitled Group of Thirty Study on Derivatives: Practices and Principles ("Group of Thirty Study"), consisting of a Study and three volumes of appendices.

The Study offers an overview of the derivatives markets and proffers various recommendations. Twenty of them are designed to assist end-users and dealers with the management of their derivatives activities. Among them are recommendations that senior management approve overall risk management and capital policies for derivatives; that derivative positions be marked-to-market; that market risk and credit risk be independently and regularly analysed; and that credit risk be reduced by the use of multi-product master agreements with close-out netting provisions and by attempts to insure the legal

enforceability of derivative transactions in different jurisdictions. In addition, dealers and end-users are encouraged to authorise only sophisticated professionals to execute transactions and to control and audit derivatives activities. The Study also recommends that dealers and end-users establish sophisticated management information systems to report accurately the value of derivative instruments and positions and to recognise the risks and exposures of a portfolio of positions.

The Study targeted four recommendations, intended to bolster the markets and infrastructure for derivatives, at legislators, regulators and supervisors. The Study recommends that legislators, regulators and supervisors remove legal and regulatory uncertainties with regard to derivatives instruments and markets; amend tax regulations that disadvantage derivatives; provide comprehensive and consistent accounting guidance; and recognise close-out netting arrangements and amend the Basle Accord to reflect the benefits of such arrangements with respect to bank capital regulations.

Working papers that provided the analysis and basis for the Study's recommendations are available in Appendix I of the Study. Appendix II analyses the enforceability of derivatives agreements in nine jurisdictions. Appendix III consists of the findings of a Price Waterhouse survey of industry practices.

OCC BANKING CIRCULAR 277

The Office of the Comptroller of the Currency (OCC) released Banking Circular 277 to guide national banks and federal branches and agencies of foreign banks with respect to their risk management practices for derivatives activities.[72]

For the most part, the Circular adopted recommendations of the Group of Thirty's Global Derivatives Study Group, such as recommendations that market and credit risk be regularly quantified, monitored and controlled; that auditors, operations and risk management systems be sufficiently sophisticated to manage derivatives instruments and activities; that netting arrangements and collateral agreements be considered to reduce risks; that banks ensure that counterparties have the requisite legal and regulatory authority to create enforceable agreements; and that positions and risks be marked-to-market. Similarly, the Circular, like the Group of Thirty Study, addressed legal, capital adequacy and accounting issues and emphasised the need for active supervision by senior management, and oversight by the Board of Directors to monitor the activities and authority and to control risks.

However, the Circular did not stop with the Group of Thirty recommendations. In particular, it stated that "[c]redit officers should be able to effectively analyze the impact of proposed derivatives activities on the financial condition of [the bank's] customer" and whether or not particular financial derivative instruments are applicable to managing the risk that the customer seeks to manage. According to the Circular, a national bank "approving officer" should be capable of "identify[ing] if a proposed derivatives transaction is consistent with a counterparty's policies and procedures with respect to derivatives activities, as they are known to the bank."[73] If the customer wants to proceed with the transaction, even though the credit officer (or approving officer) does not believe that the transaction would be consistent with the counterparty's policies and procedures, bank management should document its own analysis and any information provided to the customer.

This section of the Circular evoked a strong response from the banking community because many banks do not believe that such customer analysis or evaluations are appropriate when dealing with institutional counterparties. In addition, many banks remain concerned about the scope of their duty to assess the customer's risk, policies and procedures.

In part because of the strong response to this section of the Circular, the OCC released a bulletin to answer "the most frequently asked questions, and [provide] greater detail on the guidance" in the Circular.[74] After denying that the OCC adopted a suitability standard for the derivatives activities of banks,[75] it explained that the Circular's "appropriateness standard" applies to the transactions with "institutional customers", rather than transactions with dealers or, "in most cases, other market professionals".[76]

The Circular also authorised national banks to engage in physical commodity transactions in certain situations.[77] They must be undertaken to manage risks arising out of financial derivative transactions that are related to the physical commodity, and they must meet certain criteria. To fit within the Circular, the physical transactions must supplement the bank's current risk management activities, constitute a nominal percentage of such risk management activities and not be entered into for speculative purposes. National banks may engage in physical commodity transactions to manage risks arising out of per-

missible, customer-driven banking activities.[78] Also, the banks must submit a detailed plan to the OCC describing the proposed activity and receive approval before they may commence such transactions.

During the late summer and autumn of 1998 Russia defaulted on certain investments, triggering significant global market volatility. As a result losses were incurred by various banks and hedge funds, including Long-Term Capital Portfolio, L.P. These events prompted several banking regulators, including the OCC, to issue releases.

The OCC's guidance, issued on January 25, 1999 and titled "Supplemental Examination Guidance: Risk Management of Financial Derivatives and Bank Trading Activities", supplemented the guidance set forth in Banking Circular 277.[79] Upon its issuance, the OCC Deputy Comptroller for Risk Evaluation explained that the "significant volatility in global financial markets...contributed to unexpected credit losses and declines in trading reviews" and that the guidance "highlight[ed] existing shortfalls in the risk management systems within financial institutions and identif[ied] sound risk management practices that should be in place for all significant derivatives and trading activities," such as transactions between banks and hedge funds or other highly leveraged institutions.[80] The supplemental guidance includes guidance regarding price risk management, credit risk management, transaction risk management, compliance risk management and corporate risk management.[81]

FEDERAL RESERVE BOARD GUIDELINES
The Division of Banking Supervision and Regulation of the Board of Governors of the Federal Reserve System (FRB) released its guidelines, entitled "Examining Risk Management and Internal Controls for Trading Activities of Banking Organisations" (the "Guidelines") to be incorporated in the FRB's Capital Markets and Trading Activities Manual. They are designed to guide FRB examiners in their evaluations of the internal controls and risk management policies and systems established for the trading of cash and derivative instruments.[82]

In large measure, the Guidelines follow the recommendations set forth in the Group of Thirty Study and resemble the OCC's Banking Circular 277. Like Banking Circular 277, the Guidelines highlight the oversight and management responsibilities of the Board of Directors and senior management;[83] the importance of managing market, liquidity, legal and operational risks; and the necessity of sufficiently sophisticated audit procedures and internal controls. "[W]ritten policies and procedures that clearly outline the institution's risk management guidance for trading and derivatives activities" are required. The Guidelines also state that, "[i]n general, a bank should not trade a product until senior management and all relevant personnel (including those in risk management, internal control, legal, accounting and auditing) understand the product and are able to integrate the product into the bank's risk measurement and control systems".

However, the Guidelines do not adopt Banking Circular 277's customer appropriateness standard, although the Guidelines do require a bank to take some steps to ascertain a counterparty's sophistication when recommending specific transactions to some counterparties. Specifically, it states that "where a bank recommends specific transactions for an unsophisticated counterparty, the bank should ensure that it has adequate information regarding its counterparty on which to base its recommendations."

Following market events of 1998, the Board of Governors of the Federal Reserve System's Division of Banking Supervision and Regulation issued "Supervisory Guidance Regarding Counterparty Credit Risk Management" on February 1, 1999 to "[reiterate and expand] upon fundamental principles of counterparty credit risk management."[84] The "Overview" explained the "[losses] stemming from the Asian crisis and the 1998 market turbulence…indicate that basic credit risk management policies, procedures, and internal controls were insufficient at some institutions to address the risks of new, fast growing, or evolving products and activities."[85] The Guidance instructs banking institutions to focus adequate resources on these risks including the assessment of counterparty creditworthiness, adequate stress testing, exposure measurement, limit setting and use of credit enhancements.

CFTC'S OTC CONCEPT RELEASE

On May 12, 1998, the CFTC published a Concept Release on Over-the-Counter Derivatives (the "Concept Release") in the Federal Register.[86] It was issued despite objections, including the dissent of one CFTC Commissioner. Like the CFTC's Advance Notice of Proposed Rulemaking and related actions in 1987, the Concept Release triggered grave concern and uncertainty about the views and the direction of the CFTC with respect to its regulation of OTC derivatives. Without articulating the CFTC's jurisdictional basis for raising a host of regulatory questions regarding a range of swaps and hybrid instruments, the Concept Release raises questions. These questions include, but are not limited to, the possibility of modifications to the swaps exemption and hybrid instruments exemption, as well as the possible imposition of registration requirements, capital requirements, reporting requirements and sales practices requirements on OTC derivatives dealers. The Concept Release seeks comments "on whether the regulatory structure applicable to OTC derivatives under the [CFTC's] regulations should be modified in any way in light of recent developments in the marketplace…"[87]

Notwithstanding the Concept Release's statement that "[all] currently applicable exemptions, interpretations, and policy statements issued by the [CFTC] regarding OTC derivatives products remain in effect, and market participants may continue to rely on them,"further action by the CFTC threatened to disrupt existing and prospective OTC derivatives transactions. FRB Chairman Greenspan, SEC Chairman Levitt, and Treasury Secretary Rubin issued a joint statement upon the Concept Release's issuance, expressing concerns that the Concept Release increased legal uncertainty and questioning the CFTC's juridiction to act with respect to the issues raised therein. Others, including members of Congress, objected on similar grounds, and a legislative bill was passed into law that imposed a moratorium on the CFTC adopting new rules or regulations regarding OTC derivatives before March 31, 1999.[88]

LEGISLATIVE AND RELATED INITIATIVES

During 1999 and 2000, Congress will again address the reauthorization of the CFTC due to expire on September 30, 2000.[89] This process will likely involve debate regarding the CFTC's recent actions, including the issuance of the OTC Concept Release. Providing legal certainty for a variety of OTC derivatives transactions will be a primary goal of many dealers and market participants. A particular priority will be to increase legal certainty for securities derivatives left unprotected by the FTPA. In addition, the regulated futures exchanges will seek to improve their position in an increasingly competitive and technological environment. In this regard, Congress can be expected to consider the differences between regulated futures exchanges and evolving electronic trading and clearing systems for derivatives transactions. Given the rapid evolution of these trading markets, there is no likely easy solution.

In evaluating certain of those and related issues, Congress may consider the recommendations, if any, from a variety of pending studies expected by the middle of 1999. The President's Working Group on Financial Markets[90] is preparing an OTC derivatives study. The General Accounting Office is also preparing studies.

Conclusion

Given the complexity of certain commodity and energy derivative instruments and the evolving regulatory and/or legislative landscape, participants in derivatives markets must weigh the legal and regulatory implications of their transactions carefully.

First, participants must consider the legality of the derivative products in light of the CEA, CFTC regulations, pertinent CFTC or judicial interpretations of the foregoing, and any other

applicable federal, state or local laws. Second, participants must assess the enforceability of any agreements involving derivative transactions. This assessment should include an evaluation of the capacity and authority of the counterparties entering into the transactions and the laws of the applicable jurisdictions. Third, participants in the markets for derivatives must carefully monitor and manage their derivatives business. Even those entities not covered by the OCC Banking Circular 277 and its supplemental guidance or FRB Guidelines should consider comparing their activities and policies against those guidelines and those of the Group of Thirty Study.

Finally, derivatives dealers and end-users must be mindful of the changing legislative and regulatory landscape. These changes may go beyond traditional concerns about the legality of specific derivative transactions. Any entity engaging in, or planning to engage in, commodity derivatives transactions must consider the spectre of additional regulation, as well as the other legal and enforceability concerns.

---

1 *A swap is a bilateral agreement requiring each party to make periodic payments to the other party, the amounts of which are usually determined by netting the payment obligations of the parties. In such cases, neither party actually pays the notional principal amount during the term of the swap, and, on each scheduled payment date, the amount required to be paid by one party is netted against the amount required to be paid by the other party and only this net amount is paid by one party to the other. With some types of swaps, however, the parties exchange gross payments (such as gross payments in different currencies in the case of some currency swaps), not net payments.*

2 *Derivatives are instruments that derive their value from the value of underlying assets, including commodities, securities, interest or currency exchange rates, or indices of the foregoing. Derivative products include forwards, futures, options, swaps, swaptions, caps, floors, collars and other similar instruments. For the purposes of this chapter, the term "derivative" refers only to instruments traded off of an exchange, such as forwards, swaps and swap-derivatives. For a detailed discussion of exchange-traded futures and options on futures, see* Regulation of the Commodities Futures and Options Markets *by Thomas A. Russo (Colorado Springs, 1983) and the Second Edition of* Commodities Regulation *(Boston, 1989) by Philip McBride Johnson and Thomas Lee Hazen.*

3 *The CFTC acted against Wells Fargo Bank, in connection with its gold-indexed certificate of deposit programme and threatened to act against Chase Manhattan Bank, in connection with its issuance of oil-indexed swaps. See Robert B. Hiden Jr. and Donald R. Crawshaw,* Hybrids and the Commodity Exchange Act, *22* The Review of Securities &

Commodities Regulation *233, 237 (Dec. 20, 1989).*

4 *Regulation of Hybrid and Related Instruments, 52 Fed. Reg. 47,022 (1987) (Advance Notice of Proposed Rulemaking, dated Dec. 11, 1987).*

5 *In its January 1999 Report on "Sound Practices for Banks' Interactions with Highly Leveraged Institutions," the Basle Committee on Banking Supervision (a committee of central bankers from the Group of Ten countries) recommended that banks follow certain specified sound practices in dealing with highly leveraged institutions ("HLI's") including certain types of hedge funds and other forms of collective investments. These included upfront due diligence, exposure measurement methodologies, limit-setting and ongoing monitoring of counterparty exposure, especially concentrations and leverage. The Committee also suggested that more direct regulation of HLI's may be necessary if these indirect supervisory and regulatory approaches failed to alleviate potential systemic risk arising from HLI activities.*

6 *The CFTC received "exclusive jurisdiction [except for certain specified exceptions] with respect to . . . transactions involving contracts of sale of a commodity for future delivery, traded or executed on a contract market . . . or any other board of trade, exchange or market . . . ". CEA Section 2(a)(1)(A)(i); see also Section 4c(b).*

7 *See also CFTC Reg. 1.3(e). The definition of the term "commodity" includes everything except onions provided that it involves contracts for future delivery.*

8 *See, for example,* In re Stovall *[1977–1980 Transfer*

Binder] Comm. Fut. L. Rep. (CCH) ¶ 20,941 (Dec. 6, 1979);
Policy Statement Concerning Swap Transactions, 54 Fed.
Reg. 30,694 (July 21, 1989) (also printed at Comm. Fut. L.
Rep. (CCH) § 24,494).

9 CEA Sections 2(a)(1)(A)(i) and 4c(b).

10 The CFTC has listed some of a forward contract's traditional indicia, which include the following: (1) commercial
counterparties that can make or take delivery, (2) commercial transactions related to the business in that commodity,
(3) privately-negotiated transactions among principals that
cannot be assigned without consent, and (4) the absence of
a clearing house or exchange-style offset. Statutory
Interpretation Concerning Forward Transactions, 55 Fed.
Reg. 39,188 (Sept. 25, 1990), at 39,191.

11 Section 1a(11).

12 Section 2(a)(1)(A)(ii) provides that "[n]othing in [the
CEA] shall be deemed to govern or in any way be applicable
to transactions in foreign currency, security warrants, security rights, resales of instalment loan contracts, repurchase
options, government securities, or mortgages and mortgage
purchase commitments, unless such transactions involve
the sale thereof for future delivery conducted on a board of
trade."

In a recent US Supreme Court decision, the Supreme
Court was asked to determine "whether the [Treasury
Amendment's] phrase 'transactions in foreign currency'
includes transactions in options to buy or sell foreign currency." The Court held that "foreign currency options are
'transactions in foreign currency' within the meaning of the
statute." Dunn v. Commodity Futures Trading Commission,
519 U.S. 465 (1997).

13 The treatment of swap-derivative instruments with elements of options on securities was addressed in an administrative action brought by the SEC against BT Securities
Corporation ("BT Securities"), a subsidiary of Bankers Trust
New York Corporation, in connection with certain swap-
derivative instruments that Gibson Greetings Inc.
("Gibson") purchased from BT Securities. Some of the derivative transactions sold to Gibson had payment characteristics that related to, or were "linked" to, the prices or yields
of debt securities issued by the US Treasury Department.
Due to changes in interest rates, Gibson was liable to make
large payments to BT Securities on these instruments,
prompting Gibson to sue BT Securities and prompting several regulatory agencies to commence administrative proceedings against BT Securities. BT Securities settled Gibson's lawsuit and the proceedings with each of the agencies.

The SEC settlement determined that certain of the swaps
were securities. In particular, the SEC order dated December
22, 1994, deemed certain transactions involving individually negotiated, cash-settled OTC options on debt securities or
groups or indexes of securities to be securities. Simultaneously with the issuance of the settlement, the SEC issued
a temporary exemptive order exempting swap dealers
engaged in derivative transactions that were deemed by the
SEC to be securities from the broker-dealer registration
requirements of the Securities Exchange Act of 1934, provided that (1) the instruments satisfied the requirements of the
swap exemption issued by the CFTC (17 C.F.R. § 35) and (2)
the instruments were documented as swap agreements.

During 1998, the SEC issued its "Broker-Dealer Lite"
final rules, which includes certain regulations for those entities electing to engage in certain types of activities in the
United States.17 C.F.R. § 240. 36a 1-1

See also note 39, infra, discussing the simultaneous CFTC
order.

A similar issue was also considered in a US federal district court decision granting a motion to dismiss in favour
of Bankers Trust Company. The Proctor & Gamble
Company had sued Bankers Trust, alleging various violations of law, including federal and state securities laws, in
connection with certain swap transactions. The Court granted the defendants' motion, determining, inter alia, that the
relevant swap transactions did not qualify as securities
under either federal or Ohio law. Proctor & Gamble Co. v.
Bankers Trust Co., 925 F. Supp. 1270, 1283–84 (S. D. Ohio
1996).

14 See, for example, Section 2(a)(1)(B).

15 See, for example, Chicago Mercantile Exchange v.
Securities and Exchange Commission, 883 F.2d 537 (7th Cir.
1989), cert. denied, 496 U.S. 936 (1990).

16 See note 10 and text accompanying note 8, supra.

17 738 F. Supp. 1472 (S.D.N.Y. 1990).

In a subsequent CFTC enforcement proceeding, the CFTC
determined that certain energy contracts were "illegal off-
exchange futures contracts". In re MG Refining and
Marketing Inc., CFTC Docket No. 95-14 (July 27, 1995).
These contracts involved long-term contracts for the delivery
of unleaded gasoline or heating oil which allowed the purchasers to receive cash for their contracts and terminate
any remaining delivery obligations in the event of a price
spike. The CFTC's Order concluded that the contracts were
neither forward contracts nor trade options. In a related
civil case, a district court declined in a motion for summary
judgement to impose the CFTC's illegality holding to avoid
contracts (at the request of MG) with non-parties to the
CFTC proceeding. MG Refining & Marketing Inc. v. Knight
Enterprises Inc., 25 F. Supp. 2d 175 (1998).

18 738 F. Supp. at 1491. In this regard, the Court "conclude[d] that even where there is no 'right' of offset, the
'opportunity' to offset and a tacit expectation and common
practice of offsetting suffices to deem the transaction a
futures contract." Idem at 1492.

19 55 Fed. Reg. 39,188 (Sept. 25, 1990).

20 Idem at 39,191–92. One Commissioner dissented. He concluded that the oil contracts "do not sufficiently resemble
forward contracts".

21 945 F.2d 309 (9th Cir. 1991).

22 Idem at 313, 312–15. Some courts have upheld forward
contracts that are offset by adopting a different position.
Instead of emphasising the delivery obligation and the
necessity of creating a subsequent, separate transaction to
offset the forward contract, they state that "[a] set-off is in
legal effect a delivery." Board of Trade of the City of Chicago
v. Christie Grain & Stock Co., 198 U.S. 236, 250 (1905). See
also Salomon Forex, Inc. v. Laszlo N. Tauber, 8 F.3d 966, 978

(4th Cir. 1993).

23 *N.Y. Gen. Oblig. Law ∫5-401 (McKinney Supp. 1993).*

24 *N.Y. Gen. Bus. Law ∫351 (McKinney 1988).*

25 *See text accompanying note 31, infra.*

26 *See* Salomon Forex, Inc. v. Laszlo N. Tauber, *8 F.3d 966, 978 (4th Cir. 1993).*

27 *Interestingly, the court also noted that the transactions were not intended to be settled by reference to the dealings of others. Instead, they would be settled by offsetting transactions entered into by the parties.* Idem.

28 *See, for example,* Liss v. Manuel, *296 N.Y.S.2d 627 (Civ. Ct. 1968);* Holberg v. Westchester Racing Association, *53 N.Y.S.2d 490 (App. Div. 1st Dept. 1945).*

29 *54 Fed. Reg. 30,694 (July 21, 1989).*

30 *P.L. 102-546, 106 Stat. 3590.*

31 *See CEA Section 4(c); see generally* Thomas A. Russo & Marlisa Vinciguerra, Financial Regulation and Title V of the Futures Trading Practices Act of 1992, *Futures Int'l Law Letter (Nov.-Dec. 1992).*

32 *See CEA Sections 4(c)(1), 4(c)(2) and 4(c)(3).*

33 *H. Rep. No. 102-978, 102nd Cong., 2nd Sess. (1992), at 81. See also CEA Sections 4(c)(5)(A) (regarding hybrids) and 4(c)(5)(B) (regarding swaps).*

34 *See Parts 34 and 35 of the CFTC Regulations; 58 Fed. Reg. 5580 (Jan. 22, 1993); 58 Fed. Reg. 5587 (Jan. 22, 1993); and 58 Fed. Reg. 21286 (April 20, 1993).*

35 *58 Fed. Reg. 5587 (Jan. 22, 1993); see generally* A. Robert Pietrzack and Michael S. Sackheim, CFTC Exemption Procedures for Novel Derivative Transactions, *Securities & Commodities Regulation at 121-24 (July 1993).*

36 *"'Eligible swap participant' means, and shall be limited to, the following persons or classes of persons:*

(i) A bank or trust company (acting on its own behalf or on behalf of another eligible swap participant);

(ii) A savings association or credit union;

(iii) An insurance company;

(iv) An investment company subject to regulation under the Investment Company Act of 1940 (15 U.S.C. ∫ 80a-1 et seq.) or a foreign person performing a similar role or function subject as such to foreign regulations, provided that such investment company or foreign person is not formed solely for the specific purpose of constituting an eligible swap participant;

(v) A commodity pool formed and operated by a person subject to regulation under the Act or a foreign person performing a similar role or function subject as such to foreign regulation, provided that such commodity pool or foreign person is not formed solely for the specific purpose of constituting an eligible swap participant and has total assets exceeding $5,000,000;

(vi) A corporation, partnership, proprietorship, organi-

zation, trust, or other entity not formed solely for the specific purpose of constituting an eligible swap participant (A) which has total assets exceeding $10,000,000, or (B) the obligations of which under the swap agreement are guaranteed or otherwise supported by a letter of credit or keepwell, support, or other agreement by any such entity referenced in this subsection (vi)(A) or by an entity referred to in paragraph (i), (ii), (iii), (iv), (v), (vi) or (viii) of this section; or (C) which has a net worth of $1,000,000 and enters into the swap agreement in connection with the conduct of its business; or which has a net worth of $1,000,000 and enters into the swap agreement to manage the risk of an asset or liability owned or incurred in the conduct of its business or reasonably likely to be owned or incurred in the conduct of its business;

(vii) An employee benefit plan subject to the Employee Retirement Income Security Act of 1974 or a foreign person performing a similar role or function subject as such to foreign regulation with total assets exceeding $5,000,000, or whose investment decisions are made by a bank, trust company, insurance company, investment adviser subject to regulation under the Investment Advisers Act of 1940 (15 U.S.C. ∫ 80a-1 et seq.), or a commodity trading advisor subject to regulation under the Act;

(viii) Any governmental entity (including the United States, any state, or any foreign government) or political subdivision thereof, or any multinational or supranational entity or any instrumentality, agency or department of any of the foregoing;

(ix) A broker-dealer subject to regulation under the Securities Exchange Act of 1934 (15 U.S.C. ∫ 78a-1 et seq.) or a foreign person performing a similar role or function subject as such to foreign regulation, acting on its own behalf or on behalf of another eligible swap participant: Provided, however, that if such broker-dealer is a natural person or proprietorship, the broker-dealer must also meet the requirements of either subsection (vi) or (xi) of this section;

(x) A futures commission merchant, floor broker, or floor trader subject to regulation under the Act or a foreign person performing a similar role or function subject as such to foreign regulation, acting on its own behalf or on behalf of another eligible swap participant: Provided, however, that if such futures commission merchant, floor broker, or floor trader is a natural person or proprietorship, the futures commission merchant, floor broker, or floor trader must also meet the requirements of subsection (vi) or (xi) of this section; or

(xi) Any natural person with total assets exceeding at least $10,000,000." CFTC Reg. 35.1(b)(2).

37 *CFTC Reg. 35.2.*

38 *CFTC Reg. 35.1(b)(1). This definition was based on 11 U.S.C. 101 (55) (defining the term "swap agreement" for the US Bankruptcy Code).*

39 *CFTC Reg. 35.2. The exceptions to the exemption are provisions of the CEA (Section 2(a)(1)(B)) that set forth the SEC-CFTC Jurisdictional Accord delineating the jurisdictional reach of the two agencies (see text accompanying note 14,* supra*) or prohibit fraud and manipulation (Sections 4b and 4o).*

One such exception to the exemption, Section 4o of the CEA, was addressed in the CFTC order dated December 22,

1994, accepting BT Securities' offer of settlement. Among other things, the order explained that BT Securities violated Section 4o, which prohibits commodity trading advisors from engaging in fraudulent activities. The order finds that BT Securities, while acting as a commodity trading advisor (CTA) to Gibson, made material misstatements and omissions in its offer and sale of swap agreements and materially understated the value of such agreements when Gibson requested valuations for the purpose of evaluating its swaps.

In order to be a CTA, one must give advice as to the value or price of futures or commodity options. In charging BT Securities with CTA fraud, the CFTC did not identify any specific transaction as being a future or commodity option. However, the CFTC's conclusion raises questions as to whether it believes swaps generally or any specific swaps may be futures or commodity options. Also, it is interesting to note that, historically at least, swap dealers have not considered themselves to be CTAs because swap agreements are typically described as privately negotiated bilateral agreements between two counterparties. The CFTC's determination, based on the facts available regarding BT Securities' dealings with Gibson, that an advisory relationship had been established raises concerns that a dealer may have fiduciary duties to its counterparty in specific situations.

See note 13, supra, discussing the simultaneous SEC order.

40 See text accompanying notes 23–28, supra.

41 See Part 34 of the CFTC Regulations; 58 Fed. Reg. 5580 (Jan. 22, 1993).

42 For example, in 1986, The Standard Oil Company launched a public offering of Oil Indexed Units. At maturity, the Units paid Unitholders principal plus a contingent payment, if at that time oil prices surpassed a strike price. See Hiden & Crawshaw, supra note 3, at 236–237.

43 Wells Fargo Bank's gold-indexed certificate of deposit programme could be an example of such a hybrid instrument. See idem.

44 CFTC Reg. 34.3(a)(2).

45 The term reference price is defined to be the "price nearest the current spot or forward price, whichever is used to price the instrument, at which a commodity-dependent payment becomes non-zero, or, in the case where two potential reference prices exist, the price that results in the greatest commodity-dependent value." CFTC Reg. 34.2(g).

46 CFTC Reg. 34.2(e).

47 See text accompanying note 14, supra.

48 58 Fed. Reg. 21,286 (April 20, 1993).

49 The CFTC determined that the exemption did not rely on a subjective test of intent (that is, whether the energy-related product was intended to actually be used as an energy source). Idem at 21,289.

50 "[T]his order is limited to (A) commercial participants who, in connection with their business activities: (1) incur

risks, in addition to price risk, related to the underlying physical commodities; (2) have a demonstrable capacity or ability, directly or through separate bona fide contractual arrangements, to make or take delivery under the terms of the contracts; (3) are not prohibited by law or regulation from entering into such Energy Contracts; (4) are not formed solely for the specific purpose of constituting an eligible entity pursuant to this Order; and (5) qualify as one of the following entities: (i) a bank or trust company; (ii) a corporation, partnership, proprietorship, organization, trust, or other business entity with a net worth exceeding $1,000,000 or total assets exceeding $5,000,000, or the obligations of which under the agreement, contract or transaction are guaranteed or otherwise supported by a letter of credit or keepwell, support, or other agreement by any such entity or by an entity referred to in subsections (A), (B), (C), (H), (I) or (J) of section 4(c)(3); (iii) a broker-dealer subject to regulation under the Securities Exchange Act of 1934 (15 U.S.C. 78a et seq.); (iv) a futures commission merchant subject to regulation under the Act; or (B) any governmental entity (including the United States, any state, any municipality or any foreign government) or political subdivision thereof, or any multinational or supranational entity or any instrumentality, agency, or department of any of the foregoing...". 58 Fed. Reg. at 21,294.

51 Idem at 21,294.

52 One Commissioner dissented from the CFTC's determination not to apply its anti-fraud jurisdiction. Idem at 21,295.

53 Different jurisdictions have different laws affecting the legality of the derivative transaction. An examination of the laws of particular non-US jurisdictions and their application to derivatives is outside the scope of this chapter.

54 In addition to the legal issues discussed in this chapter, numerous other legal issues, including tax issues, must be examined.

55 A similar issue was raised in a lawsuit filed in connection with the Orange County bankruptcy. Orange County brought an action against Merrill Lynch and Co., Inc., among others, for restitution of the money lost on certain obligations it purchased from or through Merrill Lynch and other types of equitable relief, claiming, inter alia, that such transactions were ultra vires. See In re County of Orange, No. SA 94-22272 (Bankr. C. D. Cal. filed Jan. 12, 1995).

56 This ruling caused the swap dealers to lose an amount that represented, as of 1993, approximately one-half of the total losses incurred because of swap defaults since the beginning of the swap market. Group of Thirty Study, at 51.

57 See, for example, Catherine Good Abbott, "Rethinking Prudence: Is the Spot Gas Market too Speculative?", Cambridge Energy Forum; Adam B. Jaffe and Joseph P. Kalt, "Oversight of Regulated Utilities Fuel Supply Contracts: Achieving Maximum Benefit From Competitive Natural Gas and Emission Allowance Markets" (The Economics Resource Group: April, 1993).

58 See NAIC Investments of Insurers Model Act (Defined Limits Version); see also Michael P. Goldman and Michael J. Pinsel, "A Regulatory Overview of the Insurance Industry's

Use of Over-the-Counter Derivatives", Derivatives 202 (Vol. 1 No. 5 May/June 1996).

59 *11 U.S.C. § 101(53b). Section 101(53b) of the US Bankruptcy Code defines the term "swap agreement" as: "(A) an agreement (including terms and conditions incorporated by reference therein) which is a rate swap agreement, basis swap, forward rate agreement, commodity swap, interest rate option, forward foreign exchange agreement, spot foreign exchange agreement, rate cap agreement, rate floor agreement, rate collar agreement, currency swap agreement, cross-currency rate swap agreement, currency option, any other similar agreement (including any option to enter into any of the foregoing); (B) any combination of the foregoing; or (C) a master agreement for any of the foregoing together with all supplements." See also Section 101(53(c)) of the US Bankruptcy Code (defining the term "swap participant").*

60 *It would otherwise bar counterparties to such transactions from setting off amounts due from amounts owed to the debtor and would keep the counterparties waiting during a bankruptcy proceeding to ascertain whether any moneys remain to pay them amounts they are due.*

61 *See 11 U.S.C. § 362(b) (17).*

62 *See 11 U.S.C. § 560.*

63 *See 11 U.S.C. §§ 546(g) and 548(d)(2).*

64 *See 11 U.S.C. §§ 362 and 365.*

65 *Appendix II of the Group of Thirty Study discusses the bankruptcy laws of nine jurisdictions*

66 *See 11 U.S.C. § 101(25).*

67 *Congress enacted FIRREA in 1989. In addition to expanding the powers of the Federal Deposit Insurance Corporation (FDIC), it provided that most banks or savings institutions that are parties to "qualified financial contracts" (which include swap agreements and commodity contracts) can, among other things, offset or net obligations and exercise contractual rights to terminate or liquidate such contracts. See 12 U.S.C. § 1821(e)(8); Group of Thirty Study, Appendix II at 300–01. Then, Congress enacted the Federal Deposit Insurance Corporation Improvement Act (FDICIA) in 1991. It ensures the enforceability of a "netting contract" between two "financial institutions", "notwithstanding any other provision of law" and notwithstanding any "stay, injunction, avoidance, moratorium or similar proceeding or order, whether issued or granted by a court, administrative agency, or otherwise." The term "financial institution" includes a registered or licensed broker or dealer (and certain affiliates), a depository institution, a registered or licensed futures commission merchant or certain other institutions. 12 U.S.C. § 4402(9). FDICIA defines the term "netting contract" to mean a valid US contract between financial institutions that provides for netting present or future payment obligations or payment entitlements (including liquidation or close-out values relating to the obligations or entitlements) among the parties to the agreement...". 12 U.S.C. § 4402(14). See Group of Thirty Study, Appendix II at 302–03.*

68 *Congress has also considered more recent bills proposing various amendments to bankruptcy provisions to clarify remaining uncertainty with respect to derivative transactions, such as uncertainty regarding cross-product netting.*

69 *See Group of Thirty Study, Appendix II at 139 (July 1993); OCC Banking Circular No. 277 [Vol. 5] Fed'l Banking L. Rep. (CCH) § 58,717 (October 27, 1993) at 36,466 and OCC NR 99-3 (January 25, 1999) (supplementing the OCC Banking Circular 277 guidance). In addition, netting also significantly reduces the risk posed by derivatives because counterparties have much smaller exposures to each other. Accordingly, many have requested that the reductions in risk offered by netting agreements be recognised in the capital reserves requirements and standards. Group of Thirty Study, Appendix II at 139 (July 1993).*

70 Idem*; Appendix II at 304.*

71 *An examination of the bankruptcy laws of particular non-U.S. jurisdictions is outside the scope of this chapter.*

72 *OCC Banking Circular No. 277 [Vol. 5] Fed'l Banking L. Rep. (CCH) § 58,717 (October 27, 1993) at 36,459.*

73 Idem *at 36,462.*

74 *OCC Bulletin 94-31 [Vol. 5] Fed'l Banking L. Rep. (CCH) § 58,717 (May 10, 1994) at 36,473.*

75 Idem *at 36,478. The Bulletin explained that the Circular's section is similar to a suitability rule "in that it presumes, consistent with safe and sound banking practices, that a bank dealer will not recommend transactions it knows, or has reason to know, would be inappropriate for the customer on the basis of available information". Idem at 36,479. However, it then states that the Circular's section "requires only that the bank's credit officers determine that a proposed derivatives transaction is consistent with a counterparty's policies and procedures with respect to derivatives activities, as they are known to the bank" and that, "[if] the bank believes that a particular transaction may be inappropriate for a customer, and that customer insists on proceeding, the bank need only document its analysis and the information it provided to the customer". Idem.*

76 Idem *at 36,479. See generally* idem *at 36,478–80.*

77 *Financial derivative transactions involving precious metals such as gold, silver and platinum are already permitted and are not subject to the Circular.*

78 *Fed'l Banking L. Rep. 58,717 at 36,466.*

79 *BC 277 Supp. 1.*

80 *OCC NR 99-3 (January 25, 1999).*

81 Idem.

82 *"This guidance specifically targets trading, market making, and customer accommodation activities in cash and derivative instruments at State member banks, branches and agencies of foreign banks, and Edge corporations. The principles set forth in this guidance also apply to the risk* *management of bank holding companies, which should manage and control aggregate risk exposures on a consolidated basis, while recognising legal distinctions among subsidiaries. Many of the principles advanced can also be applied to banks' use of derivatives as end-users." Letter from Richard Spillenkothen, Director, Division of Banking Supervision and Regulation, Board of Governors of the Federal Reserve System, SR 93–69 (Dec. 20, 1993) at 1.*

83 *Boards of Directors "should regularly re-evaluate significant risk management policies and procedures with special emphasis placed on those defining the institution's risk tolerance...". Idem at 3.*

84 *FRB SR 99-3.*

85 *Idem.*

86 *63 Fed. Reg. 2614*

87 *Idem.*

88 *A majority of sitting CFTC Commissioners have represented to Congress that they have no intention to adopt rules before Congress has had an opportunity to thoroughly review all related issues.*

89 *In the past, the CFTC has continued to operate after the period of its authorization has expired. As long as budgets are appropriated by Congress, the CFTC can continue to function.*

90 *This Group is made up of the Chairmen of the SEC, CFTC and Federal Reserve Board along with the Secretary of the Treasury.*

RISK MEASUREMENT AND REPORTING

Section Introduction

Vincent Kaminski
Enron Corp

One of the consequences of the rapid growth of derivatives markets, and the emergence of energy trading companies covering a wide range of commodities (eg the Btu marketers described in the introduction to the previous section), is a great increase in the financial risks faced by companies engaging in these activities.

The history of the last ten years of energy trading is littered with the casualties – companies that have suffered significant market or credit losses and been bankrupted, or which have been forced to leave the business of energy trading. In most cases, the losses could have been avoided through the systematic and disciplined measurement and monitoring of trading risks. The chapters in this section of the volume discuss different aspects of risk measurement and management in the energy industry.

Over the past few years the measurement of market risk has become strongly associated with a particular methodology known as "value at risk" or VAR. This term is shorthand for a special way of capturing the risk generated by the market positions of a trading company. VAR can be used to assess risks resulting from fluctuations of market prices, interest rates and exchange rates.

As Brian Senior's chapter on energy VAR explains in more detail, the assessment is typically expressed in terms of the loss that may be suffered in the trading portfolio over a defined time horizon, at a specified level of probability. The estimate is typically produced using simulations, based either on a statistical model or on historically observed price returns.

An alternative approach is to derive the distribution of returns of the portfolio, which are typically assumed to be normal with a mean of zero, from the historical return volatilities and correlations of the portfolio components.

In the case of the energy industry, implementing the value-at-risk approach is fraught with challenges. The main difficulty results from the lack of historical data, and the way in which any data that is available may become irrelevant due to rapid structural change in the market.

Another serious challenge arises from the fact that returns distributions in the energy markets exhibit "fat tails". In plain English, this means that the probability of extreme outcomes is larger than the distributions conventionally used in finance might suggest. The fat tails result from the tendency of energy prices to undergo significant discontinuous changes over short periods.

In the derivative markets, the measurement of market risk is closely related to the measurement of credit risk. They are really two sides of the same coin. After all, one can lose through a counterparty default only the amount of money that one is owed, and in the case of many energy contracts this amount varies according to the level of market prices and volatilities. The relationship between credit risk and energy prices was demonstrated under very dramatic circumstances during the summer of 1998. A dramatic spike in power prices in the Northeastern United States triggered defaults by certain power marketers that had left themselves exposed to naked (uncovered or unhedged) short positions.

Their defaults caused a chain reaction that amplified the price volatility. In their chapter, Ellen Lapson and Richard Hunter discuss how credit risk can be assessed and how credit risk management can be improved under different institutional frameworks. Interestingly, they relate the lessons learned from the US to the situation that is presently evolving in certain European power markets.

Another factor affecting the energy industry is the constant evolution of accounting standards, especially with regard to hedging and trading activities. This is a very complicated area, reflecting the inherent complexity of the subject matter – witness, all the complicated structures described in detail in section 1 of this volume. It is also a very contentious discipline, as the different parties involved in the process have conflicting economic interests. One must remember that at the end of the day, the accounting rules determine the bottom line.

The chapter by Tom Lewthwaite, Hassaan Majid and Nicholas Swingler reviews recent FASB accounting guidelines that affect the accounting for hedges and their economic consequences.

9

VAR, Stress-Testing and Supplementary Methodologies:

Uses and Constraints in Energy Risk Management

Brian Senior

National Power

Competition and trading are the new features of energy supply evolving around the world. Companies engaging in these markets tend to import wholesale the culture and risk measures that have been developed and used for investment purposes in bond, equity and foreign exchange trading. However, power markets specifically, and other energy markets generally, face problems that are not present in purely financial environments.

Energy commodities are not the same as equities or bonds. Without an understanding of how energy markets function, it is not possible for a company to evaluate company-wide financial exposure, to judge the performance of traders, marketers, risk managers and their risk strategies, or to communicate effectively and accurately with senior management and shareholders.

Like many other power companies, National Power is a participant in a range of energy markets that carry with them their own special risks, including:
❑ market prices which are not available for certain periods, together with a lack of confidence in the available data;
❑ complex price distributions – both across the day and from day to day – that do not follow the rules developed for other commodity and financial markets (price jumps, curve shifts, outliers and non-normal price distributions mean that methods cannot be adopted directly from financial markets);
❑ extremely high volatility and correlations that can prove to be very unstable;
❑ prices that tend to revert to equilibrium level – a mean or a floor – over the long run;
❑ liquidity that tends to be limited and can vary significantly through time;

❑ trading of non-standard contract blocks. Frequently these include complex embedded options, which are generally not valued accurately; and
❑ counterparty default events that are significantly different from bond market events.

One of the first questions asked of risk managers concerns the purpose of trading and marketing. "Are we hedging or speculating?" For many corporations the word "speculation" has a bad connotation, whereas "hedging" is seen as a necessary activity supporting the business. (Speculation implies betting the company, whereas hedging implies sensible risk management.) Yet the distinction is in part unclear.

For most corporations a better question is: "What is our strategic objective?" In discussing risk management and risk measurement we need to describe the risk the company is taking in relevant terms, which are understood in conjunction with the defined policy and strategy of the company in relation to its trading and marketing activities.

What is risk?

Twenty years ago the average power company considered risk to be the danger of failing to deliver power to the customer. There was risk of power station failure, transmission line outage and bad weather events. There was the risk of hazard to health and the risk of fatality. Capacity planning – building enough new power stations to meet possible future demand – dominated corporate decision-making.

Now, however, power and other energy companies operating in certain countries must focus also on the risk arising from exposure to traded markets. Some observers estimate that by 2003, 85% of the world's power will be a traded com-

VAR,

STRESS-

TESTING

AND

SUPPLEMENTARY

METHODOLOGIES

modity or in deregulated markets. The world of energy and power risk management is changing rapidly.

Against this backdrop we need to be careful that what we are measuring is in fact risk; that what we are managing is exposure to that risk; and that we are not fooling ourselves and the company about what we *say* we are measuring.

The measures described here are relevant to three categories of risk:

❏ market risk – the risk the company necessarily takes in being exposed to an energy market;

❏ credit risk – the risk the company necessarily takes in being exposed to counterparties; and

❏ operational risk – the risk, other than credit and market risk, the company necessarily takes in engaging in trading and marketing activities. (For example, the risk that trading systems will crash and that as a result the company will lose money, however good its market and credit risk practices might be).

In general, we wish to measure and manage the first two while minimising the third. We wish to be paid for taking market and credit risk but at the same time to minimise the risk of losses due to operational events.

Of the three risk categories, market risk is the area for which measures are most fully developed. In the past three years, researchers have had significant success in developing quantitative measures for credit risk, and there are some early indications that operational risk can also be measured. In the remainder of this chapter, we will focus on the measures that are now becoming industry standard for market and credit risk, closing with some discussion of operational risk and the organisational challenges faced by energy companies into the next century.

Market risk

VALUE-AT-RISK

The most fashionable tool for measuring and managing market risk today is undoubtedly value-at-risk (VAR) and its extensions. The extent of the interest in VAR is shown by the number of variants that are coming into being, including daily VAR (DVAR), delta VAR (DelVAR), cash-at-risk (CAR), cashflow-at-risk (CFAR), credit-at-risk or credit-value-at-risk (CVAR), and earnings-at-risk (EAR).

VAR has been viewed as an alternative to more traditional measures, such as the Greeks (delta, gamma, vega, etc) described in Panel 4, and as a replacement for stress-testing (or scenario-testing). Numerous articles have been published that pit one type of measure against another; in reality, however, each measure has its own place. As Einstein famously commented, "The important thing is not to stop questioning."

History has it that VAR was invented to satisfy a request by the chairman of JP Morgan for a report at 4.15pm every day that would tell him how exposed the company was to movements in the markets over the next 24 hours.

This VAR measure was popularised by the G30 recommendations (Group of Thirty, 1993), the Bank for International Settlements (1996)[1] and RiskMetrics (JP Morgan, 1995). At its heart, VAR is a way of measuring possible changes in profit and loss (P&L) over a defined period with a given confidence interval. Here we have adopted a broad definition that reflects the origins of the measure.

Note particularly that the VAR figure for a given portfolio is intended to be larger than all but a certain fraction of the trading outcomes,

VALUE AT RISK CALCULATION: A SIMPLE EXAMPLE

Consider a simple forward sale of volume V at price K for delivery at time T from now. The value of this forward contract at any point in time is given by the equation $f = V(F - K)e^{-rT}$, where F is the current forward price and r is the discount rate. For this single contract, the value at risk is approximately given by $VAR = 1.645 \, \Delta \sigma \, F \sqrt{\tau}$, where σ is the volatility, Δ is the traditional (delta) measure of market risk (ie a single unit price change impact on the mark-to-market value), and τ is the unwind period. The value of Δ is Ve^{-rT}.

So, for example, if we have sold 100 MWh forward 12 months and the annualised volatility of a contract one year forward is now 10%, the value at risk is

$$1.645 \times 100 \times 0.1 \times 25 \times e^{-rT}\sqrt{\tau}$$

if the current forward price is US$25/MWh. If we allow a risk-free discount rate of 6%, the value at risk is US$387.3 with a one-year unwind period.

213

VAR,
STRESS-
TESTING
AND
SUPPLEMENTARY
METHODOLOGIES

where that fraction is determined by the confidence level specified in the measure itself.

Using VAR in the banking sector For banks, the use of VAR to measure market risk is no longer in question. Banks now need to use VAR in assessing risk capital. The recommendations of the Basle Committee (a key banking-industry body) include the calculation of risk capital based on VAR, and other influential bodies, such as the Group of Thirty, recommend that VAR forms the basis for market risk measurement in banks. The Switzerland-based Bank for International Settlements, the central bank of the central banks, sets its capital adequacy requirements for market risk in terms of a bank's own VAR estimates.

In a banking context, risk "capital" refers to the capital a bank must set aside to cover its unprotected risks. VAR is used to measure these market-related risks under very conservative assumptions. In reality, VAR has therefore moved beyond being a measure of P&L moves with a given confidence interval over a given period of time to become a "worst-case" way of estimating profit and loss change if market moves are all adverse to the position. Like factor-push analysis – in which each individual risk factor is "pushed" in the most disadvantageous direction and the combined effect of all such changes on the value of the portfolio is worked out – the Basle capital adequacy VAR represents a very conservative measure of market exposure.[2]

BACK-TESTING OF VAR
Back-testing programmes typically consist of a periodic comparison of the company's daily VAR measures with the subsequent daily profit or loss ("trading outcome").

Comparing the risk measures with the trading outcomes simply means that the company counts the number of times that the risk measured was larger than the trading outcome. The fraction actually covered can then be compared with the intended level of coverage to gauge the performance of the company's risk model. In some cases this last step is relatively informal, although there are a number of statistical tests that may also be applied.

Figure 1 shows a typical test of VAR with the best estimate of the VAR as the line and the daily movement in the P&L as the triangles. In this case, if VAR "works", the triangles will lie within the confidence intervals shown by the VAR line 95% of the time. (It is important to recognise a

95% confidence level implies that we *expect* a P&L move in excess of VAR on average one day in 20). As the figure shows, this is the case for this particular market and measure.

As an illustration of the extent of the conservatism of bank capital adequacy VAR, Figure 2 shows the best-estimate VAR given in Figure 1, together with a capital adequacy measure of VAR.

An important factor, when specifying the appropriate risk measures and trading outcomes for back-testing, is that the VAR approach to risk measurement is generally based on the sensitivity of a static portfolio to instantaneous price shocks. That is, end-of-day trading positions are input into the risk measurement model, which assesses the possible change in the value of this static portfolio due to price and rate movements over the assumed holding period.

Although this is straightforward in theory, in practice it complicates the issue of back-testing. For instance, it is often argued that VAR measures cannot be compared with actual trading outcomes because the actual outcomes will inevitably be "contaminated" by changes in portfolio composition during the holding period. Active trading therefore renders back-testing on a

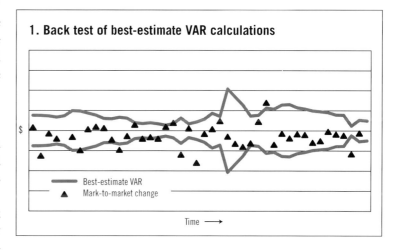

1. Back test of best-estimate VAR calculations

— Best-estimate VAR
▲ Mark-to-market change

Time ⟶

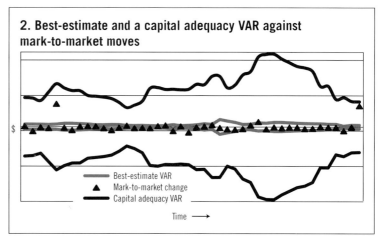

2. Best-estimate and a capital adequacy VAR against mark-to-market moves

— Best-estimate VAR
▲ Mark-to-market change
— Capital adequacy VAR

Time ⟶

static basis prone to error. In addition, the fee income should not be included in the definition of the trading outcome along with the trading gains and losses resulting from changes in the composition of the portfolio, because they do not relate to the risk inherent in the static portfolio that was assumed in constructing the VAR measure. Most recent recommendations on back-testing (Basle Committee on Banking Supervision, 1996) propose a one-day holding period (ie use of daily VAR, or DVAR) for all back-testing to minimise portfolio change effects.

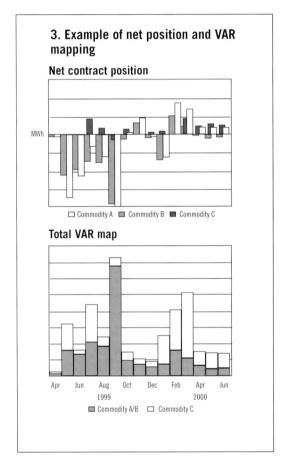

3. Example of net position and VAR mapping

Net contract position

Commodity A Commodity B Commodity C

Total VAR map

Apr Jun Aug Oct Dec Feb Apr Jun
1999   2000

Commodity A/B Commodity C

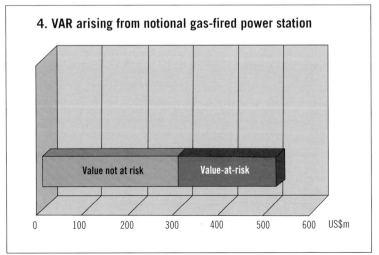

4. VAR arising from notional gas-fired power station

Value not at risk   Value-at-risk

0   100   200   300   400   500   600   US$m

Corporate sector For a corporation, VAR is not essential or required by regulatory bodies but still provides a useful tool for certain kinds of decision making.

With regard to trading decisions, VAR clearly provides a good measure of profit and loss movements for a trading position held. In addition to overall VAR for a position, we can calculate VAR for different portions of a position along the forward curve. Figure 3 presents an example of a net contract position and a map of total VAR that shows where the risk originates. The net contract position is for three underlying commodities, two of which are highly correlated and the third of which is not strongly correlated with the other two. The total VAR map shows the VAR term structure, with two values at each position along the time axis. One is for the less correlated commodity, and the second is the combined VAR for the two highly correlated commodities.

Does VAR provide all the information needed to manage the trading position? Almost certainly not. VAR is not an alternative to the Greeks, such as delta and gamma, but is a useful overall risk measure when used in conjunction with the Greeks to manage the position. In the author's experience, few traders actually use VAR to manage their positions. However, risk-aware corporations almost always use VAR as a primary risk measure in trading operations.

Making investment decisions It has become more and more practical as energy markets develop to view assets within traded markets as providing a series of physical options and forward positions. An oil refinery may be regarded as an option to swap between different products from a number of different initial feedstocks. A power station may be regarded as a series of options to convert fuel to power, with delivery at different points across the transmission system. A gas field may be considered as an option to supply, store or swing volume between periods of the year. Each asset therefore also has a risk position in the market.

Can VAR really be used to help corporations make investment decisions in traded markets? Frequently the market is such that forward prices are not available, so VAR becomes what might be termed "cashflow-at-risk". In markets such as this, the uncertainty about forecast prices or forward positions is usually more important in decision making than underlying market volatility. However, for fully liquid markets, the asset decision can be derived directly from the VAR figure.

215

VAR,

STRESS-

TESTING

AND

SUPPLEMENTARY

METHODOLOGIES

Figure 4 shows the VAR arising from a hypothetical combined-cycle gas turbine plant in a merchant situation. Here, the VAR represents a significant proportion of the total value of the merchant plant, reflecting the fact that merchant plants are indeed exposed to potentially large changes in price over time. Such an analysis informs the corporation about the extent of market risk implied by building an asset in a given energy market. But how can this be translated into a decision on whether or not to invest?

Figure 5 shows a map of the return required against the risk measured in VAR terms. The risk-free rate (RFR) on the left is associated with zero VAR. As the VAR increases, the return required to build or own the asset increases. The point shown indicates the VAR of the merchant combined-cycle gas turbine (CCGT) plant, together with an associated required return for that plant in that particular market. Returns above the line add value to the company; those below are earnings-diluting.

The risk/return line must be drawn to reflect company risk appetite; however, measures such as the risk-adjusted return on capital employed (RAROCE) also provide a framework for such investment decisions. RAROCE is widely used as an alternative to the Sharpe ratio. For any position or exposure, RAROCE is the position's returns divided by its VAR. The RAROCE measure provides a line for Figure 5, which breaks down as VAR tends towards zero.

Is VAR sufficient? Figure 6 shows US Cinergy peak spot day-ahead prices over the period May 1997 to October 1998. During this period prices peaked at over $5,000/MWh, against average prices for the season of around $30–50/MWh. The reasons for this exceptional market discontinuity were both physical (transmission lines and plant outages) and commercial (credit default events). For traders and risk managers the events in the market indicated very clearly that although VAR provides an indication of how often a P&L will move outside a particular value over a particular period, it does not say how *far* outside that value it may move. Losses in excess of $100 million were reported by some trading operations.

Such exceptional events demand other methods of risk analysis. Principal among these is stress-testing, or scenario analysis.

SCENARIO ANALYSIS AND STRESS-TESTING

The purpose of stress-testing is to identify exposure to exceptional market events by imposing scenarios or stress tests on the position. For investment banks, guidelines exist for stress-testing (Basle Committee on Banking Supervision, 1996). These specify that stress-testing should be used to cover all types of activities that generate market risks. Stress tests may also consider breakdowns of positions at the level of individual portfolios, including, in the case of banks, trading and non-trading activities. In this case, stress tests must be coupled with qualitative analysis of the actions that management might take under particular scenarios. Examples of stress scenarios include parallel shifts of the forward curve, a steepening or flattening of the curve, or a major change in correlation assumptions, such as factor-push analysis.

More generally, stress-testing should include testing the current portfolio against past periods of significant disturbance and linking scenarios to physical events in energy markets, such as major losses of transmission or OPEC decisions. Stress tests and scenario analyses provide a basis for discussions of the actions that would be taken, the amount of information which could be used to anticipate such events and the effects on market liquidity.

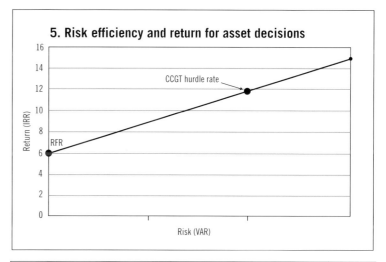

5. Risk efficiency and return for asset decisions

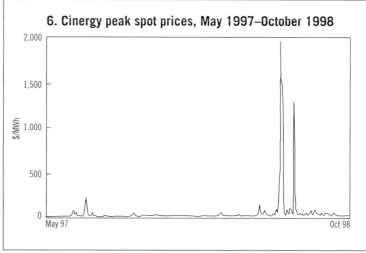

6. Cinergy peak spot prices, May 1997–October 1998

216

VAR,
STRESS-
TESTING
AND
SUPPLEMENTARY
METHODOLOGIES

PANEL 2

VAR IN CORPORATE DECISIONS: AN EXAMPLE

A natural gas supply corporation is considering the value of starting a hedging operation in the gas market. It has exposure to the market since it has agreed to supply natural gas at fixed prices to some of its customers into the future. How does it decide whether to spend the money necessary to set up the hedging operation?

For the purposes of this example we have simplified the analysis (which should actually use probabilities) and assumed:

❑ the hedging operation accesses a market that is not accessible otherwise – ie, the hedging operation hedges physical volume that is otherwise "live" in the day-ahead market;

❑ there is volumetric and price uncertainty; and

❑ the maintenance of a hedging operation has a cost which may include a discount against expected day-ahead gas market price.

The first stage of the analysis is to decompose the problem into cashflows:

	Year 1	Year 2	Year 3
Cost of operations, including any discount	C_1	C_2	C_3
Live day-ahead gas market			
Expected earnings if no hedge	$P_1^e V_1^e$	$P_2^e V_2^e$	$P_3^e V_3^e$
Worst-case revenues if no hedge	$P_1^1 V_1^1$	$P_2^1 V_2^1$	$P_3^1 V_3^1$

We begin the analysis by assuming that no hedging operation exists and by dividing the cashflows into two components:

❑ The NPV of $(P_1^1 V_1^1 \ldots P_3^1 V_3^1)$ is the cashflow not at risk. We therefore discount this at the risk-free rate (RFR).

❑ The NPV of $(P_1^e V_1^e - P_1^1 V_1^1) \ldots (P_3^e V_3^e \ldots P_3^1 V_3^1)$ is the cashflow at risk. We discount this at the relevant "risked" or "risk-adjusted" rate (RAR), and add it to the NPV of the cashflow not at risk.

The value of the hedging operation is then the value associated with moving V^e from day-ahead gas market price and volume risk exposure to fixed price (P^e), volume risk exposure.

That is, we now have a cashflow not at risk of $NPV_{RFR}(P_1^e V_1^e \ldots P_3^e V_3^e)$.

The difference in NPV for the two scenarios is then the value of the hedging operation. This is compared with the NPV of the costs, $C_1 \ldots C_3$. With this information, the gas supply corporation is able to make an informed decision.

LIQUIDITY

Value-at-risk can be calculated for positions in markets for which forward price information is known and well understood, for which options are sufficiently traded to calculate implied or average volatility, and for which correlations can be derived from market information. In practice, however, most energy markets have terms and products that are illiquid or for which the depth of trading in the market is limited. In such circumstances the corporation is forced to rely on old data or cash price forecasts, which represent company rather than market views of forward prices. In this case VAR provides only a guide. The extra risk and uncertainty is assumed as part of a business decision. The company has not chosen to hold such a position in a market in order to take advantage of price moves, but it has cho-

sen to assume an asset position in the expectation of reasonable returns from an uncertain market.

The impact of unexpected levels of market illiquidity should not be overlooked in energy markets. Some players active in the US power market during the turbulent summer of 1998 have estimated that market liquidity for power in the affected regions fell by around 90% over a two-week period. Previously liquid positions became unmanageable.

PUT THEM TOGETHER

Are VAR and stress-testing together sufficient? Provided that the stress tests are chosen carefully, representing extreme market movements, VAR and stress-testing complement one another very well. Together they provide risk managers

217

VAR,
STRESS-
TESTING
AND
SUPPLEMENTARY
METHODOLOGIES

PANEL 3

MEASURING LIQUIDITY

The characteristics of a market with poor liquidity include significant transaction costs, low market turnover, a relatively small number of traders at any time and significant bid–offer spreads. Low liquidity means that market participants who wish to liquidate positions may have to pay significant costs to do so, or do so slowly over time. Almost all energy markets exhibit some liquidity problems, and many emerging power and gas markets are highly illiquid for most of the time. Liquidity is important in assessing the holding period with measures such as VAR and is an important parameter in stress-testing or scenario analysis. Model techniques to take account of liquidity in VAR exist (Dowd, 1998).

The usual measure of liquidity is the bid–offer spread. This is sometimes expressed as the expected normalised bid–offer spread, ie the size of the bid–offer spread divided by the average of the bid and offer prices, all as expected ex ante. The bigger the spread, the less liquid the market. This is a sensible measure of liquidity because the bid–offer spread represents the risk adjustment in

the market associated with holding a position. If a trader is able to unwind a position fully in a very short space of time, the risk premium for taking on the liquidity risk in the position is close to zero and the bid–offer spread is very low.

Such measures are adequate for normal market conditions but not for crisis liquidity risk. The market can be liquid most of time but lose its liquidity in a major crisis. Typically, the trouble begins with a major change in price, which triggers a large number of sell or buy instructions and makes the market reluctant to take the other side of the transaction. The bid–offer spread therefore increases dramatically over a short space of time. The flood of orders can also overwhelm the market and slow down the time to execute. Market liquidity therefore dries up and does so at the time market participants need to use it most. Any strategy that relies on a rapid unwinding of positions then becomes unusable. There are no simple techniques for measuring or including such crisis liquidity risk in risk measures other than scenario analysis or stress-testing, including the effects of liquidity.

or other senior managers in the company with a fair view of the market risks inherent in holding an asset or trading book.

Credit risk

Credit risk is usually defined as the failure to meet contractual requirements relating to a promise to repay a loan or to pay for the delivery of goods and services within an agreed time.

Credit risk in commodity-related contracts is quite different from the credit risk of a bond. Most analytical tools developed in the literature[3] revolve around bond defaults and use the history of bond defaults or bond yield spreads to estimate the probability of default.

It is possible to argue that the probability of default on a corporate bond exceeds the probability of default on a commodity or energy transaction. This is because energy transactions with a physical component often play an important role in the production process of an end-user or a producer. It may be difficult to replicate the physical transaction financially owing to the rigidity of physical access (eg, storage or transportation) or requirements relating to reliability and the volume of delivery. It follows that, even

in bankruptcy, a counterparty that continues its economic activities will usually make an effort to perform on energy contracts. There are, of course, cases when such factors are not important and when defaulting counterparties fail to meet obligations entirely.

A second complexity in energy markets is that default on an energy transaction has many shades of grey and may not simply involve refusal to pay. Counterparties may engage in "contract frustration", including complaints about quality or timeliness of delivery, questioning the legal foundation of contracts or raising issues over physical delivery.

However, in measuring and managing credit risk we usually assume dependence on a number of factors:
❑ the current fair value of the contracts in place;
❑ the potential future credit exposure;
❑ the extent to which netting arrangements and collateral are in place and can effectively reduce exposure; and
❑ the likelihood of default by the customer.

The issue faced by many companies is how to model all of these factors so as to generate a quantitative measure of credit risk. JP Morgan

218

VAR,

STRESS-

TESTING

AND

SUPPLEMENTARY

METHODOLOGIES

ENERGY AND THE GREEKS

More traditional measures such as the Greeks provide useful additional information that is generally used in making day-to-day trading and risk management decisions. The Greeks are a set of measures used to describe the risk position and exposure of trading positions and portfolios. They are used to manage a variety of derivative instruments, including forwards, futures and options.

DELTA

Delta measures a portfolio's linear exposure to the price of an underlying commodity or product. Suppose we plot a graph of the price sensitivity of the portfolio, as in Figure A, and draw a line tangent to the curve at the current market level. The slope of the tangent line is the portfolio's delta with respect to the underlying commodity. Note

that delta approximates how a portfolio's value will respond to small changes in the price of the underlying commodity. Because it is a linear measure of risk, it does not capture the portfolio's sensitivity to curvature in the price sensitivity – which arises, for example, when options are included. To measure this sensitivity, delta is often supplemented with gamma, a second-order measure of risk.

Note that if a portfolio is exposed to multiple underlying commodities, it will have a delta for each exposure.

GAMMA

Gamma measures the second-order sensitivity of a portfolio to changes in the value of an underlying commodity. While delta measures first-order (linear) sensitivity, gamma measures the non-linearity, or curvature, of the sensitivity.

For example, consider the price sensitivity line in Figure A. The portfolio has negative gamma – ie its curvature opens downwards. Figure B shows a second portfolio with the same delta but which has curvature that opens upwards. Its gamma is positive.

VEGA

Vega measures a portfolio's linear exposure to changes in the implied volatility of an underlying commodity. In Figure C, which illustrates the sensitivity of a hypothetical portfolio to changes in implied volatility, the price sensitivity of the portfolio is described by a curve. A tangent line has

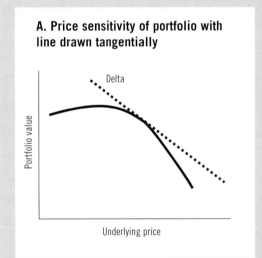

A. Price sensitivity of portfolio with line drawn tangentially

Delta

Portfolio value

Underlying price

---

recently followed up the success of the RiskMetrics package with CreditMetrics (JP Morgan, 1997). It is quite clear, that credit risk is much more complex to analyse than market risk. Nevertheless, it has become increasingly common to use VAR-type measures to estimate credit risk as well as market risk. In this case we are interested not in the amount the company can lose due to adverse market movements but in the amount the company can lose because of *favourable* market movements that are followed by credit events.

QUANTITATIVE ANALYSIS OF CREDIT RISK
The initial stage in measuring and managing credit risk is the assessment of the credit quality

of a counterparty. A number of requirements must be met for this to be performed reliably.

Credit quality is traditionally measured using a credit score or credit rating. Credit ratings developed by such companies as Standard & Poor's and Moody's Investor Services generally describe the credit quality of corporate debentures. The quality is represented by well-known symbols, such as AAA, BB, etc. Credit scores specific to a particular company are usually developed in-house using these credit ratings, but also making use of additional information that is known or specific to a particular market.

Once credit scores have been assigned to counterparties, the next step is to estimate the probability of default of each counterparty. Two

219

VAR,
STRESS-
TESTING
AND
SUPPLEMENTARY
METHODOLOGIES

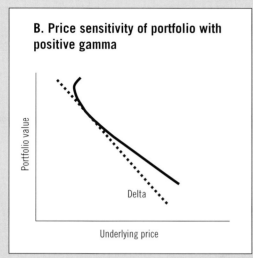

B. Price sensitivity of portfolio with positive gamma

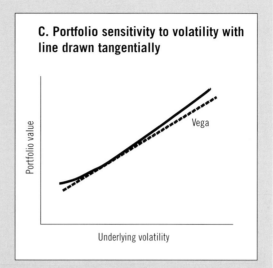

C. Portfolio sensitivity to volatility with line drawn tangentially

been fitted to the curve at the current market level. The slope of that line is the portfolio's vega. Vega can be a significant component of a portfolio's risk. This is especially true for portfolios whose delta exposures have been hedged. A portfolio that has positive vega is said to be "long" volatility. One which has negative vega is said to be "short" volatility.

RHO

Rho measures a portfolio's linear exposure to changes in an interest rate – typically the discount rate. If we replace the X axis value in Figure C with the interest rate, the slope of the line fitted to the curve at the current market level is the portfolio's rho with respect to the interest rate.

For most energy portfolios, exposure to interest rates is a less significant source of risk than is exposure to an underlying commodity or implied volatility – measured with delta and vega, respectively. Interest rate exposures arise simply because

futures and forward positions involve future cashflows, and the rate at which those cashflows is discounted affects their present value.

THETA

Theta measures a portfolio's linear exposure to the passage of time. Specifically, it tells us how rapidly a portfolio's value will change with the passage of time, assuming that all market variables (the underlying commodity, implied volatility, interest rates) do not change.

Instruments such as forwards or futures, which have no gamma or vega, have only a limited tendency to appreciate or depreciate in value with the passage of time. Their theta is often zero. Portfolios with positive gamma or vega tend to have negative theta. If other market variables remain constant, they will lose value over time. Portfolios with negative gamma or vega tend to have positive theta. If other market variables remain constant, they will gain in value over time.

methods are available for estimating such probabilities: the bond spreads method and the Markov chain method. Details of these are given in the general credit literature.[4] The result of such analyses is a table describing the probability of default as a function of the credit score.

Using credit matrices and other, simpler methodologies permits the addition of an extra level of analysis. This is the analysis of what can be termed credit risk correlation. Such correlation analysis determines how likely it is that losses will accrue in multiple exposures at the same time. It links single credit assessments to the whole portfolio of investment or trading operations.

As a final step, we need to superimpose the

likely size of an exposure to the counterparty, given likely moves in market prices, upon our estimate of the probability of default.

How is all this related to risk measures in a general sense? It is clear from the foregoing that market and credit risk calculations are intimately related. For a credit loss to accrue, the counterparty must undergo a change in credit quality, and the transactions held must be out of the money for the counterparty – that is, the counterparty must owe money on a net present value basis. VAR can bring this together. However, the calculation of the resulting VAR due to counterparty default is complex, frequently requiring the use of Monte Carlo simulation techniques. This complexity arises because credit risk is highly

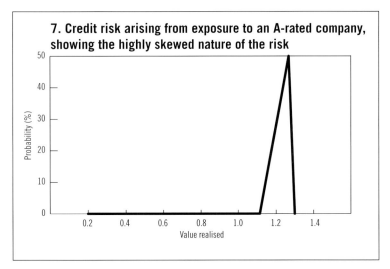

7. Credit risk arising from exposure to an A-rated company, showing the highly skewed nature of the risk

skewed and events are relatively infrequent. Credit VAR or credit-at-risk must therefore be calculated to at least a 99% confidence interval. Figure 7 shows a probability of a profit and loss for the 99% confidence interval due to credit default. The skewed nature of this distribution is extreme. It is obvious that VAR techniques using normal distributions would prove inadequate.

Operational risk

Many operational risks, such as major fraud, are clearly difficult to measure. However, some risks such as transaction processing errors can be quantified and risk measurement techniques applied to them. As with market and credit risk, risk measurement means that we attach loss estimates to particular events and also say something about the probability (or likelihood) of such events taking place.

This risk measurement begins by categorising different types of operational risk (see for example, Hoffman and Johnson, 1996). For effective measurement, each type of risk needs to fall into a clearly delineated area of responsibility. So, for example, some types of risk (such as people risks) become the responsibility of relevant line managers, whereas others (such as technology risk) become the responsibility of the risk management function.

Once the categories have been defined, information is collected and organised, covering both the size and frequency of particular types of loss. Bankers Trust (see, for example, Hoffman and Johnson, 1996) collected data from two main sources: the comparable experiences of other firms concerning fairly common risks (eg those relating to certain types of computing risk and compliance risk) and estimates based on scenario analyses supplemented by expert judgement to cover less frequent risks (the losses and risks

associated with massive computer breakdown or terrorist attack). The result of this exercise was a database that covered five main categories:

❑ people risk (covering human error, fraud, loss of staff);

❑ technology risk (covering technology failures, virus problems, losses due to unreliable systems);

❑ relationship/liability risks (covering legal and/or contractual risks);

❑ physical asset risk (covering loss of physical environment, business interruption, etc); and

❑ external risks (covering changes in regulations and external fraud).

This database was then used to quantify the relevant risk.

The expected loss is then the mean of the probability density function and the VAR of the relevant quantile of the probability distribution.

This type of analysis is undoubtedly useful in understanding and measuring operational risk, but to rely on it as a complete system of risk measurement poses several problems. For example, some operational risks which are not measurable should not be ignored. How does one quantify the risk of a major war in Europe?

Dowd (1998) comes to two important conclusions. The first is that the principal defence against operational risk is sound systems of control staffed by good people. Many operational risks cannot be handled any other way. The second is that quantitative risk measurement techniques should be used with extreme care. In theory, the methodologies are fine, but we must recognise that their use may create new and more subtle risks. Among these is perhaps the most important risk of all – that of falling into the trap of thinking that what is not measured does not exist. No operational risk measurement system captures all operational risks. If we are not careful on this point, the use of quantitative risk measures to capture operational risk could, paradoxically, leave us more exposed to operational risk than we would be without such measures.

Organisational challenges

There are perhaps two equal and opposite mistakes which are made in relation to the use of VAR measurement and associated methodologies. The first is to embrace VAR enthusiastically as a full, total and complete measurement system for all aspects of risk. The second is to ignore it and associated methodologies on the basis either that they are difficult to apply or that further work is needed. The first stance ignores the one-in-10-year event, the time when prices spike or

221

VAR,
STRESS-
TESTING
AND
SUPPLEMENTARY
METHODOLOGIES

gap, or when stance liquidity dries up as markets panic. The second stance brushes aside what is becoming an important cornerstone in market and credit risk management.

However, most commentators, users, regulators and advisers agree on one thing: for VAR and complementary measures to be effective risk measures, they must be driven through the company from top to bottom. Senior managers must be aware of the benefits and limitations of risk measures inherent in either a trading book or an asset position.

Organisations introducing new measures of risk face challenges in at least three areas.

CULTURE

For most energy companies, measures such as VAR are relatively new concepts. Traders, asset managers, project developers, senior managers and others within a company will need to be at the heart of a culture shift away from looking simply at profit and loss within a limits structure to looking at a risk–reward structure represented by measures such as RAROCE. Traders need to evaluate their own performance, including the amount of risk taken, and asset developers need to become familiar with forward risk positions

acquired when investing in an asset.

TECHNOLOGY

Energy markets are notoriously complex compared with traditional financial markets. Major issues surround the use of simple but often misleading techniques for both measuring and monitoring risk. Technology therefore needs to be developed that adequately represents the company's best view of its risk using appropriate techniques and methods. Risk measures should be continuously checked using back-testing methods.

MANAGEMENT

VAR provides information that can be used in decision-making, to limit or stop position taking, or as an ongoing tool to manage positions and support decisions. The management of risk is to some extent the duty of traders, but using risk measures such as VAR places a greater stress on the quantification of risk. For this to be effective, senior managers need to be "risk aware" – questioning and evaluating decisions on the basis of risk as well as on the basis of profit and loss.

1 *Basle Committee on Banking Supervision and Technical Committee of the International Organization of Securities Commissions (IOSCO) (1998). See also Bank for International Settlements, 1996, and relevant documentation published by committees of the Bank for International Settlements.*

2 *Ibid.*

3 *See, for example, recent articles in* Credit Derivatives: Applications for Risk Management, Investment and Portfolio Optimisation, *Risk Books, London, 1998.*

4 *Ibid.*

BIBLIOGRAPHY

Basle Committee on Banking Supervision, 1996, *Supervisory Framework for the Use of "Backtesting" in Conjunction with the Internal Models Approach to Market Risk Capital Requirements*, January.

Basle Committee on Banking Supervision and Technical Committee of the International Organization of Securities Commissions (IOSCO), 1998, *Framework for Supervisory Information About Derivatives and Trading Activities*, Joint report, September.

Bank for International Settlements, 1996, *Amendment of the Capital Accord to Incorporate Market Risk*, January.

Dowd, K., 1998, *Beyond VAR: The New Science of Risk Management*, Wiley, UK.

Group of Thirty, Global Derivatives Study Group, 1993, *Derivatives Practices and Principles*, July.

Hoffman, D., and M. Johnson, 1996, "Operating Procedures", *Risk* 9, p. 60.

JP Morgan, 1996, *Introduction to RiskMetrics*, 4th edition, December.

JP Morgan, 1997, *CreditMetrics – Technical Document, The Benchmark for Understanding Credit Risk*.

1998, *Credit Derivatives – Applications for Risk Management, Investment and Portfolio Optimisation*, Risk Books, London.

10

Credit Risk in Liberalised Power and Natural Gas Markets

Ellen Lapson and Richard Hunter

Fitch IBCA

A global trend is under way toward free markets for natural gas and electricity as a key component in liberalising public-sector utility businesses in North and South America, Europe and Australia. In the past, the electricity and natural gas sectors in most nations have been controlled by monopoly providers. To the extent that wholesale power and gas trading occurred, it took the form of agreements between substantial utilities or government agencies. However, as markets have liberalised and energy has begun to be traded more freely, the number of direct market participants has expanded in local markets and also across provincial or national borders. Electricity and natural gas are becoming ordinary wholesale commodities traded by a larger number of parties in a market similar to oil, refined products, metals and so forth. Credit risk is a concern in energy commodity markets as in other markets.

This chapter addresses the relationship of market structure and price volatility to credit risk. The first section provides an overview of counterparty credit risk within wholesale electricity and natural gas markets. The second section focuses on the outlook for counterparty credit risk in the liberalising European electricity market, discusses important implications of the European Union Directive 96/92/EC and offers profiles of the markets of the UK, Germany and Scandinavia. This is followed by a discussion of the main lessons that the US price spike of June 1998 may have for other markets, including Europe, as they liberalise the trading of power. The chapter also reviews the "best practices" in use by energy companies in liberalised bilateral markets to mitigate counterparty credit risk.[1]

Credit risk and energy market structures

Credit risk is the likelihood of economic loss due to default by a party to a contract. Credit risk arises in normal commercial contracts as well as in hedging activities. It affects contracts calling for physical settlement as well as those specifying monetary settlement. Some market participants fail to recognise that a contract to receive or deliver physical power or gas in the future in the normal course of business is a derivative; that is, the market cost of replacing the contract if the counterparty fails to perform due to insolvency will fluctuate along with changes in the market value of the underlying commodity.

Credit risk in bilateral contracts

For example, Jumbo Gas Producer has a contract to sell a fixed quantity of natural gas for delivery next month to Slick Marketing and Trading at a price of $2.50 per MMBtu. Market prices have declined since the deal was signed, and the market price today for delivery next month is $2.10. Jumbo's mark-to-market credit exposure to Slick is $0.40 per MMBtu, the difference between the contract price and the current market price, not the entire $2.50 per MMBtu contractual price. If Jumbo's contract was to sell natural gas to Slick at the market index price, there would be no credit risk associated with the contract, assuming that there is a liquid market in which Jumbo can sell natural gas at the index price at any time

Credit risk takes on different forms depending upon the nature of the market. Physical and financial (derivative) commodity markets have developed two principal market models. The first model is *bilateral contracts* between individual buyers and sellers. Bilateral contracts are prevalent

224

CREDIT RISK
IN
LIBERALISED
POWER AND
NATURAL
GAS
MARKETS

in the North American natural gas and electric power markets as well as in the emerging liberalised wholesale energy markets in most of continental Europe. In a bilateral market, each market participant must manage the risk of financial default by a contractual counterparty.

As we discuss below, counterparties manage their bilateral credit risk exposure by means such as:

❑ limiting their exposure to any individual counterparty;

❑ varying the size of transactions with counterparties based on their credit condition; and

❑ requiring each counterparty to post and maintain collateral reflecting the mark-to-market valuation of credit exposure.

Within the model of a bilateral contractual market, credit risk can be reduced for all participants by the operation of a membership organisation governed by a common set of rules. Without acting as the sole counterparty for all transactions or mutualising credit risk, an organisation of this type can reduce risk within a bilateral market by performing net settlements and carrying out systematic clearing and settlement procedures. The result is the rapid identification, containment and mitigation of a default by any counterparty and the prevention of market panics. Also, the amount of collateral that must be maintained as credit support for any counterparty's net position within this arrangement is less than the amount of collateral that would be required to collateralise positions with each individual counterparty. Efforts are underway to form an entity of this type in the North American electricity market under the name CoVar.

This development approaches the other major model, where a central administrative body of a *national pool*, a *clearing house*, or a *commodity exchange* serves as the counterparty to all buyers and sellers. In this model the exchange or the central administrator assumes the financial risk of credit default by market participants. To underwrite this risk, the exchange or administrator may require market participants to post collateral (in the form of cash margin or letters of credit, for example). Alternatively, the exchange or administrator may charge a transaction fee to fund a reserve to cover losses, adjusting the fee assessments as necessary to replenish the reserve. Some exchange mechanisms are said to mutualise credit risk; all members share proportionally in credit defaults within the pool or exchange, but if the scheme is well designed, this risk is small in comparison with the credit risk of individual bilat-

eral counterparties. In an exchange or pool, market participants are exposed to the credit risk of the exchange's insolvency and must analyse the capital adequacy and liquidity arrangements of the exchange or pool, just as they would those of a large bilateral counterparty. Variants upon this type of settlement mechanism are currently used in the Scandinavian Nord Pool, the England and Wales electricity pool, the Argentine wholesale electricity market, as well as in exchanges in which natural gas and power derivatives are traded such as New York Mercantile Exchange (Nymex), Chicago Board of Trade (CBOT) and in London the International Petroleum Exchange (IPE). Nord Pool is particularly interesting in this regard, because typically even bilateral over-the-counter (OTC) and direct contracts are cleared and settled through Nord Pool, including the assumption by Nord Pool of counterparty credit risk.

MARKET EVOLUTION
If all power and gas markets incorporated a central administrator or exchange that fully underwrote or mutualised settlement risk, credit risk would be of very little concern. However, in some of the newly liberalised schemes in Europe and the US, the market relies solely or largely on direct bilateral contracts and OTC derivatives. In some markets, such as California and Spain, physical transactions can be conducted via a pool or via bilateral arrangements outside the pool; in California, financial hedging alternatives include Nymex exchange-traded futures and options as well as OTC derivatives. When Britain revises its power pool, it is widely believed that bilateral contracting will be a feature of the new market. Indeed, it appears that markets are evolving toward increased use of the bilateral market model, albeit in most cases a very different bilateral market from the long-term, physical, delivery-oriented system of the recent past. Consequently, managing credit risk will be an important topic for energy buyers and sellers in many liberalised markets.

A major challenge of managing credit in a *transitional marketplace* is the fact that many counterparties are themselves in transition. Monopoly utilities are in the midst of a multi-year phase-in of new competitive rules that will alter their business and credit profiles over time. Also, mergers and acquisitions and the debt incurred while making the acquisition can quickly alter the financial profile of a counterparty. New and unrated market entrants will appear on the scene

CREDIT RISK
IN
LIBERALISED
POWER AND
NATURAL
GAS
MARKETS

and will change their identity, business mix, strategy and ownership many times in their early years. Finally, participants are inclined to underestimate or even to deny the importance of credit evaluation in the early stages of the new market until some dislocation in the market results in a spate of credit defaults, bringing about the rediscovery of credit risk.

The effect of liberalising power markets on credit quality

POWER LIBERALISATION IN EUROPE

The liberalisation of the European power market is a natural, if delayed, extension of the principle of the European common market to the energy sector. It is also part of a global move toward liberalisation of public-sector infrastructure. While the majority of the European market has opened for meaningful competition only relatively recently, the transformation of the European power market has been influenced by a number of international reform programmes, not least the privatisation and restructuring of the UK electricity sector in the early 1990s. Many aspects of the UK restructuring, characterised by the separation of generation, transmission and supply and the creation of a single pool through which all power clears, were also models for the reform of the electricity systems of Chile, Argentina, Victoria (Australia), and influenced the debate on restructuring in the US. Another European model for liberalisation is Nord Pool, implemented in Norway, Sweden, Finland and more recently Denmark between 1994 and 1996, as we discuss below.

The major features of electric power liberalisation are *competition in generation* (the introduction of a competitive market including both incumbents and new entrants) and *competition in supply* (consumers' ability to buy electricity from competitive sources, delivered over the generally monopolistic transmission and distribution network). Competition in the *wires-based businesses* (the transmitters of power) is currently impractical but, although changes to the risk profile of these entities is less intuitively obvious, the introduction of fundamentally different revenue and regulatory environments will also affect these industry segments. An essential ingredient for market transformation is the implementation of open access to these transmission and distribution networks for all qualified generators and consumers. The liberalisation of European electricity systems will also, in a number of cases, involve the recovery of transition costs to compensate existing utility companies for their loss of monopolistic profits from both their generation- and their wires-based activities.

The choice of pricing and dispatching system for generation capacity – pool-based, providing a reference system price, or "freedom of contract" based, where supply and demand are regulated by bilateral contracts – also has some effect on credit profiles. The former gives greater transparency as it creates a single body of reference prices, although this very concentration of price-setting can be used to distort reference bench levels and eventual settlement prices (as has been the experience in the UK).

Subsidiary issues include *private ownership, consolidation,* and *cross-border acquisitions.* Private ownership is not a prerequisite of liberalisation, but a concurrent trend. Private utilities already dominate in Belgium, Germany, Spain and the UK, although even within some of these systems, large public elements (principally distribution entities owned by municipalities) remain. Privatisation is gathering speed both for these entities, and for those markets, such as Italy, Austria and Portugal, where public ownership still dominates. It will introduce different financial imperatives and structures into the industry. Numerous small utilities owned by municipalities and regional governments will consolidate to create stronger entities. Cross-border acquisitions have already begun to make headlines and many utility companies feel under pressure to promote change ahead of the deadlines imposed by the EU timetable.

THE PACE OF CHANGE

Signs of change in the market are appearing more quickly in Europe than many considered likely at the outset, and ahead of the timetables set out in the EU Directive 96/92/EC (Panel 2) and in the statutes enacted by the national legislatures. To some extent this is the product of weak, rather than strong, liberalisation legislation. The uncertainty has led utility companies to take matters into their own hands, and to accelerate market changes faster than legislators can respond.

Change will occur at different paces in different markets. It will be almost impossible for any system to construct a Maginot line around itself, and thus faster-paced reformers will tend to pull more reluctant systems in their wake. While the actions of the French government have shown that resistance to market liberalisation is far from futile, there is no longer any chance that the

CREDIT RISK
IN
LIBERALISED
POWER AND
NATURAL
GAS
MARKETS

whole of Europe will move at the pace of the slowest member – as some had hoped.

EFFECTS ON CREDIT QUALITY

All players in the electricity supply chain will be affected by the market transformation, as will many players in support industries, most notably the power feedstock fuel sector (coal mining, natural gas extraction and supply, oil refiners). Business risks will generally be greater for generation companies and electricity traders than for network providers (transmission grids and distribution companies), but no area will escape major change.

As with all things, there will be winners and losers. *Existing utility companies* in developed and unliberalised markets currently enjoy very solid credit profiles and healthy financial conditions, based on their near-monopoly market power and the fact that the tariffs they charge are based largely on how much money they need to recover their costs. Few, if any, are experiencing as yet the pain of "stranded assets" – investments that no longer generate enough revenue to cover their costs. Companies already in the market will benefit, at least initially, from customer and regulatory inertia and "war chests" built up over the years that will increase their ability to dictate the terms of liberalisation. In most cases, the credit profiles of larger utility companies will nonetheless slip gradually, although the degree of slippage will be determined by the manner in which they respond to the new marketplace. For some smaller companies, particularly in the upstream segments, change may be quicker and more dramatic.

New entrants can be expected in power generation, retail energy supply, and wholesale power marketing and trading. Some of these will be international companies and will arrive in Europe equipped with the experience that they gained as investors and participants in competitive markets in Britain, North America, Australia and South America. New entrants will have a wide range of credit profiles, and these will generally be weaker than the credit profiles of the existing utility companies. The ability of new power generators, wholesale traders, and retail marketers to establish viable market positions will be determined by the details of each market reform – what type of transmission charging system is adopted, how licences are applied, how exchanges are run – and existing utility companies will use their political connections to influence these decisions. A number of small and

often thinly capitalised entities may also establish themselves on the fringe of the market, as has occurred in Scandinavia. However, these entities are not likely to prevail if the market is dominated by entrenched existing companies on the one hand and on the other hand by the subsidiaries of major North American and European energy companies, including such well-known names as AES, Eastern Energy, Electricité de France, Edison International, Enron Corp, National Power and PowerGen, Preussenelektra, Reliant Energy, Southern Co, and Vattenfall. Generally, even in radically reformed markets such as Nord Pool, there is not much evidence of a new breed of trading entities devoted to exploiting the potential of the power trading market.

NEW RISKS

Generation companies will experience new risks in the form of competition for "space on the grid", pressure to lower prices for generated power, and increased new entrant competition. Above all, political and regulatory risks will become increasingly dominant in the appraisal of the sector's credit profile. Wires-based businesses will generally retain their monopoly status, but will continue to rely on external agencies to set their revenue limits through tariff regulation. *Transmission* grids will face new load management risks, and wider issues involving system integrity which will include pool or dispatch management, freedom of access for competing generators, better transparency and disclosure as well as the pressures which market forces will place on them to increase their own efficiency.

Distribution companies will share some of these physical and business risks, although they will remain at the lower end of the risk spectrum. For most distributors, the risk of changing or arbitrary regulatory rules, stringent tariff regulation, and potential exposure to severe penalties for power outages will be the dominant residual risk.

The risks of electricity marketing and trading are somewhat similar to those faced by participants in commodity and financial derivative markets. They are quite new to regulated utilities and monopoly generators. The principal risks are market price volatility, counterparty credit default, and the control and human-factor risks of trading, eg mistakes, erroneous models, fraud and embezzlement (often collectively known as operational risks). In a new and evolving market,

CREDIT RISK
IN
LIBERALISED
POWER AND
NATURAL
GAS
MARKETS

price and credit management can be complex due to the lack of sufficient market liquidity and the possibility that changes in market rules and conventions will disrupt the economics of trans-actions. For example, a change in the rules of transmission access or in transmission charges can suddenly make a forward contract to unprof-itable.

Inevitably tenor of contracts will reduce dra-matically as markets develop and become liquid. Existing long-term contracts will not provide "credit substitutes" and will, in many cases, require restructuring, renegotiation or poten-tially more confrontational resolution. As a result, these contracts, a number of which have been entered into on the eve of liberalisation, as incumbents sought to "sew up" major cus-tomers, may create negative pressure on the credit profiles of both contracted parties, rather than support their position. Initially, such con-tracts can initiate a price war and help to depress margins across the market, a particular danger in markets where pricing is opaque. The EU Commission's intervention to reduce exclu-sive supply contracts in Belgium from 30 years to just 10 years is another example. In extreme cases, such long-term contracts might encourage entities to invest in generating capacity – either in the form of physical plants or contracts for power – that would subsequently not be used. To what extent power companies are compen-sated for such long-term contracts – in effect they form "stranded assets" – under the transi-tion regimes will be a matter decided jointly by national and Brussels-based EU authorities.

This process has fundamental implications for Europe's new power markets.

NEW OPPORTUNITIES
Investment opportunities will take the form of domestic and cross-border *acquisitions* of existing participants, as well as the chance to construct *new generation* plant and to enter the new *power trading markets*. Power traders will require little in the way of fixed asset investment but will require capital to develop information and trading systems, develop adequate staffing, establish credit in the market, and cover short-term liquidity. *Refinancing* of state debt and restructuring of post-privatisation balance sheets will also pro-vide fixed-income investors with opportunities within the marketplace. The securitisation of *transition costs* has also proved attractive in more advanced markets, and may provide an

irregular flow of large-ticket transactions.

Here again, one of the primary risks is politi-cal. The widely discussed transition package for the Spanish power market has already been passed by the Spanish parliament, and went so far as to identify the "ballpark" amounts of com-pensation due to individual market participants. However, it has begun to suffer delay as Brussels deliberates over the implementation of transi-tion costs in the EU as a whole. Another political dimension is added by the different national approaches to nuclear power, which have often been endorsed by referendums. The Austrian operator Verbund has claimed compensation for substantial transition costs and a "rethink" of the reciprocity clause, maintaining that the demo-cratic decision of Austria to reject nuclear power will be rendered meaningless if the importing of nuclear generated power begins to undercut Verbund's own hydro-powered pro-duction.

Finally, development of appropriate *hedging instruments* and a liquid market for *risk man-agement products* has been rightly recognised as a precondition of a successful and stable market.

Such a market will create substantial invest-ment opportunities for both traditional commod-ity investors and traditional power sector entities. The preconditions for investing in this kind of business are a willingness to challenge major preconceptions about power as a com-modity market and a fundamental understanding of the risks involved.

Market structure in Europe

EU DIRECTIVE 96/92/EC
While the EU Directive provides goals for Europe as a whole, the overriding principle of "subsidiar-ity" – effectively the right of national govern-ments to amend legislation – has left a number of soft "options" within each area of reform. In addition, under Article 27, derogations are granted to Belgium and Ireland of one year and Greece of two years to allow for the "specific technical characteristics" of their systems. The timeframe for the opening of competitive supply, regarded as a primary catalyst for change, has also been left open to national variation. Article 19 of the Directive recommended opening about 25% of the market in 1999, rising to 28% in 2000 and 33% in 2003. However, the majority of coun-tries have opted for faster implementation, and as of June 1999 four have already implemented 100% access nominally at least.

CREDIT RISK
IN
LIBERALISED
POWER AND
NATURAL
GAS
MARKETS

STRUCTURAL REQUIREMENTS

For countries where such separation has not already occurred, the Directive requires separation of management and of accounting for *generation*, *transmission* and *distribution*. The Directive stopped short of mandating full separation, ie separate legal entities and/or separate ownership, but requires "Chinese walls" to be erected to ensure fair access of competitors to monopoly elements of incumbents' systems. Beyond the purely competition-related issues, assessment of credit profiles will include the degree to which largely national *ring-fencing* proposals effectively prohibit or support the cross-subsidy of the debt burden of one part of a company with the cashflow of another.

GENERATION

Access for new generation capacity is a critical element of the new directive. Under Article 4, the Directive foresaw two methods of licensing entry – *authorisation*, where proposals are judged on the basis of individual "speculative" applications and *tendering*, where the individual state would establish the country's new generation requirements and hold an auction. At the moment, virtually all of the EU's countries have opted for authorisation rather than tendering, although there is ample scope within the authorisation procedure for obstacles to be placed in the way of competition, slowing the pressure on incumbents. One much reported example of this is the requirement in France that workers in independent generation facilities be paid on the same, generous scale enjoyed by Electricité de France (EdF) employees. Other potentially restrictive requirements include general planning permission, energy efficiency, nature of primary fuel source and the ominously vague heading of "public service obligation".

TRANSMISSION

Transmission costs are central to cross-border and intra-border trading. The determination of transmission costs revolves around three issues: the *nature* of *access* (mandatory or negotiated); the *pricing formula* (distance-based, or flat-fee/"postage stamp") and *multiple charges* cumulative ("pancaked") or consolidated (ie netted-out) between producers and transmitters. Most countries, including France, have rejected the ultra-monopolistic, single-buyer system, and the majority have gone for mandatory, or regulated, third-party access, which requires publication of "across-the-board" fees for all network users.

The most notable exception to this is Germany, where access is negotiated (although tariff publication is recommended under the EnWG) and it is also one of the few countries to pursue a distance-based rather than flat-fee structure. This choice has been highly controversial, as it limits the ability of new entrants to compete in Germany, and simultaneously impairs Germany's ability to act as a major exchange point. The notoriously complicated agreement in May 1998 which regulates access to the German market terminates in September 1999 and discussions between Germany's major utilities are underway which may reverse this policy. In general, if transmission costs are too high, this will protect local utility companies at the expense of competitors, but will also support the credit profiles of "better located" energy generators, ie those that are closer to major consumption areas rather than major fuel sources.

TRANSITION COSTS

The issue of *transition* is addressed towards the end of the Directive, under Article 24, which provides for transitional regimes. Countries were given a deadline of one year after the Directive came into force to apply for such transitional regimes, and all but Finland, Italy and Sweden appear to have done so in one form or another. As of mid-1999, the progress of individual transition plans is varied. Spain is quite advanced, though the concrete numbers are being disputed by the Spanish regulator before authorities in Brussels; Austria is similarly far down the path. Decisions on the 12 plans submitted, which would set important precedents, were expected early in 1999 but had not been published by mid-1999. Delay is a feature of EU regulation, as it is of regulation the world over, and represents another source of "event risk" to market participants and investors.

Liberalisation in three European markets: UK, Nord Pool and Germany

Three very different approaches to market liberalisation are revealed by examining the UK, Nordic and German experiences.

UK ELECTRICITY MARKET

The 1990/91 privatisation of the UK industry succeeded on a number of significant counts. Prices for the consumer fell, as costs (primarily relating to manpower and fixed-asset bases) were stripped out of the distribution and generation elements of the chain. Consumers were able to

CREDIT RISK
IN
LIBERALISED
POWER AND
NATURAL
GAS
MARKETS

choose their supplier, starting with major industrial customers from as early as 1990. The nuclear generator, British Energy, presently Britain's largest single power producer, was successfully privatised – a notable first. The UK demonstrated a commendable lack of economic nationalism in its approach to acquisitions by foreign firms in key sectors of the industry.

Other elements were less successful. The smaller *Scottish* and *Ulster* markets remained vertically integrated, and with no real pool or trading systems aided by their inherent geographical isolation, were able to inhibit competition. In the much more significant England and Wales market, a number of structural problems became apparent. Abortive attempts to include nuclear capacity in the first wave of privatisation left the country with two dominant fossil-fuel generators. The ability of these two companies to dictate prices in the generation sector is only just diminishing nine years later, after the disposal or closure of more than half of their inherited capacity. Long-term contracts skewed the market. The two largest generators entered into coal-backed contracts, in a politically-motivated move that was intended to prepare the UK coal industry for privatisation. Additionally, overpriced contracts entered into by distributors on their "new entrant" capacity were tolerated by the regulator as the price for encouraging greenfield development. More recently, political interference – a ban on gas-fired plant, that had already gained partial consent, and "horse-trading" over merger preconditions – has also clouded the pool for investors and companies alike.

This said, the generation market is about to undergo a profound change when proposals under consideration will bring about the full overhaul of the pool, including *demand-side bidding*. The changes will incorporate a new three-tier market as well as a "spot balancing market". All of this implies both a shift of emphasis in favour of flexible generating plant, as well as potentially complicated renegotiations of current bilateral agreements, "contracts for differences", which are based on prices taken from the existing power pool.

The regulator's assumptions on the cost-saving potential within *distributors* also erred (necessarily) on the cautious side, allowing politically unpopular levels of profitability to be achieved in this monopoly segment. In turn this led to a widely-flagged, but largely arbitrary, windfall tax levy. *Regulatory transparency* in pricing reviews has also been poor compared to the natural gas and water sectors in the UK, as have provisions for financial supervision and ring-fencing. Partly as a result of all the above, but largely as a result of hefty "leveraging up" undertaken by new owners of the distributors, ratings of the monopolists have fallen from the AA range to the lowA/BBB range in less than three years. The pressure to leverage up utility companies is a consequence of privatisation rather than liberalisation – the latter is only of relevance insofar as it creates a more conducive environment for privatisation. Once privatised, often with little debt, many power sector companies have faced private sector shareholder pressure to rebalance this capital structure to improve shareholder returns, or face the prospect of being acquired by a firm that will do the job for them. The low business-risk profile of wires-based assets, in particular, can support higher levels of leverage than industrials pegged within the same credit-rating category, although the increasing instances of regulatory risk can negatively affect these companies and is beginning to chip away at this effective "premium".

GERMANY

The German market is the linchpin of the European electricty system, and the site of some of the continent's largest private utility companies. The German market will be crucial in determining how fast and deep reform enters other continental markets and, once again, the signs are that developments on the ground are outpacing regulatory reforms.

German utility companies have faced a demanding 12 months, after the election of an initially hostile government which threatened their substantial investment in nuclear power; the implementation of the EU Directive in national law; the creation of a controversial agreement governing transmission charges; and the first salvo in a price war designed to protect German industrial customers, largely, one suspects, from siren voices and deep pockets across the border in France.

The traditionally strong credit profiles of the utilities have come under strain, although the major private utility companies have been quick to respond. First, they appear to have successfully stymied, at least temporarily, attempts by ecologists in the new government to shut down their nuclear capacity or tear up reprocessing agreements signed with British and French agencies. Second, the May 1998 *Verbändevereinbarung* (Agreement of the Associations –

CREDIT RISK
IN
LIBERALISED
POWER AND
NATURAL
GAS
MARKETS

Power and Industrial Users) governing transmission access charges has succeeded in rendering export into and transit through Germany extremely unattractive to non-German competitors. This agreement, however, is understood to be under renegotiation, as it seriously hampers Germany's chances of operating as an export hub. The argument revolves around the hefty distance-related element in the access charge, in contrast to the "postage stamp" (flat-rate) system used in almost all the other EU countries. Such discussions are entirely in the hands of the utility companies themselves as Germany does not have an energy regulator, *oversight* being carried out by the competition authority (Kartellamt). Half a dozen high-profile cases were considered by the Kartellamt in early 1999 – notably all involving domestic plaintiffs – and decisions by the Kartellamt have not gone entirely in favour of the companies. They will be wary of the experience of Deutsche Telekom, which now has a regulator, and whose access charges are based on a benchmark of international operators' rates.

Perhaps the most dramatic step was the move by utilities to conclude long-term contracts with large customers at significant discounts prior to the opening of the single market in late 1998. This resulted in industrial tariffs for some customers being cut by up to 20%. The response is typical of European utility companies driven by the fear of increased French exports, and will induce a sense of déjà vu in those who observed the US market during the 1994–95 period.

All of these events will help accelerate the process of consolidation already underway in the Federal Republic – much of the last tier of the system, the distribution/supply companies, is owned by municipalities. Partial privatisation of some of these entities has already begun and is likely to become a trend. Understanding the credit profiles of these entities requires both a thorough understanding of the German legal framework relating to municipal entities and an independent assessment of the utility companies' operations. *Stadtwerke* do not enjoy the kind of explicit legal guarantee granted, for example, to Germany's municipally-owned banks. In addition, they are forbidden to trade outside the local region and, consequently, the issue of possible "ultra vires" exposure has to be assessed (Panel 1).

NORD POOL

The integrated power market operating in Scandinavia, Nord Pool, is often cited as Europe's most liquid and competitive power market, with over 200 participants trading in futures and forward contracts up to three years ahead. Participants now include overseas players who have come simply to trade on financial basis. Although the longer-term contracts are still having trouble attracting substantial liquidity, overall traded volumes have grown at a sharp rate, up 50% in 1998 to 145TWh or roughly 40% of total power consumed within the three-core partner countries. In addition, Nord Pool increasingly fulfils a clearing role for bilateral over-the-counter transactions, many of which are benchmarked to Nord Pool power prices.

Traders in Nord Pool face the same risks as those faced by commodity traders in most markets, but there are some important differences. Not least are the high margin requirements for futures and forwards contracts (which comprise about 60% of traded volumes), where all transactions are marked to market on a daily basis. For futures contracts, daily changes in value are settled between seller and buyer up to the date of the contract's settlement. For forward contracts, the difference between the market and the face value is only settled daily during the delivery period itself. These payments are in addition to the security margin requirements (typically 3%–10% of a portfolio's value) posted to cover potential losses by the exchange in its function as clearer. This all means that traders have to make a substantial liquidity investment in the market, against a background of what is a reasonably volatile spot price – in part due to the considerable weather dependency of the Norwegian market, where almost 100% of the generation stock is hydro-powered.

Nord Pool also operates a clearing service, which covers the bulk of the remainder of the electricity traded in Scandinavia (ie the bilateral trades). Nord Pool thus becomes the counterparty credit risk for the cleared trade, for which service a fee of between Nkr0.04 and Nkr0.08 per MWh is levied, in addition to clearing and entry fees of $13,000 and $6,500 respectively. This fee, which has been the subject of some controversy, is based on the volume of power traded by each entity in the previous quarter, and does not currently contain any credit-related element.

One issue that could prove of key interest as more European networks apply commercial rules to their interconnector capacity is the mechanism by which the constraints imposed by interconnector capacity between areas of low-cost power and areas of high-cost power are balanced

231

CREDIT RISK

IN

LIBERALISED

POWER AND

NATURAL

GAS

MARKETS

KNOW YOUR COUNTERPARTY

In evaluating and negotiating bilateral contracts, whether for physical delivery or financial settlement, the identity of the counterparty is a key factor. What kind of entity will sign the contract – a highly rated utility or a non-recourse subsidiary without credit rating or capital? And is the counterparty legally authorised under its corporate charter and bye-laws (or by statute, if it is a municipal or state agency) to enter into contractual obligations of this type and in this amount?

The "halo effect"

Some active participants in the North American energy market are subsidiaries of financially strong energy companies or utilities. These affiliates often cite the parent's credit ratings in their marketing materials and emphasise the strategic importance of trading and marketing to the parent's core business. It is rare for a US or Canadian parent to provide a general guarantee applicable to all creditors, but many parents pro- vide limited guarantees to individual counterparties. Practice is mixed in the energy market upon the acceptance of such subsidiaries as counterparties without explicit parent guarantee or other forms of credit enhancement. Some counterparties accept exposure to a subsidiary based on the "halo effect" of the illustrious parent's implied financial support.

The North American energy and power markets are in the midst of a gradual shake-out, and it is not uncommon for a corporate parent to reinterpret its strategic direction and close down its marketing and trading affiliate. Every energy credit manager can recall cases in which a parent has advanced funds and taken losses to wind down the affairs of its unsuccessful subsidiary; Consolidated Natural Gas, LG&E Corp, and Cilcorp are three examples from 1998. But on occasion, a corporate parent may decide it is not in its economic interest to support the obligations of a wholly-owned non-recourse subsidiary.

by a "capacity fee", which is added to the transmission charge. This mechanism further underlines the significance of transmission charges in the competitive marketplace. It also demonstrates how neighbouring markets may have effects on one another over and above the extent to which their physical systems are inter-connected. A key development will be the creation of a similar mechanism to operate in "freedom of contract" systems (as opposed to the pool model used in Scandinavia). "Freedom of contract" systems in Europe generally do not have a uniform benchmark price, although such benchmarks have been artificially created in the US. This has led to complications in assessing the impact of transmission constraints on individual deals as opposed to their impact on pool-system price.

Best credit practices in bilateral markets

Senior managers of many utility companies in Europe, North America and Australia now face the challenge of transforming their business practices and control systems for a new marketplace and industry structure. Although liquidity and transparency are not as great in the natural gas and power commodity markets as in established financial derivatives markets, managers in the energy industry can nonetheless apply many of the techniques developed in liquid financial and commodity markets to manage bilateral counterparty credit risk.

In 1993 the Group of Thirty (G30), published a compendium of recommendations reflecting the experience of leading worldwide financial institutions on "best practices" for derivatives risk management. Five of the 15 recommendations in the G30 report specifically addressed credit risk management. The G30 recommendations have been updated and supplemented over time. Drawing upon these recommendations and Fitch IBCA's reviews of the best practices currently in use by major energy market participants, the following summarises some key credit risk management policies and practices in bilateral markets.

❑ *Contracts with counterparties should incorporate strong credit terms.* Terms which should be included in master contracts governing all deals with a particular counterparty are:

TERMINATION PROVISIONS. If the contract counterparty defaults on payment terms in this agreement or other similar agreements, fails to post required collateral, or is insolvent or bankrupt, the other party to the contract should have the right to terminate future commitments and liqui-

232

CREDIT RISK
IN
LIBERALISED
POWER AND
NATURAL
GAS
MARKETS

A good example was the bankruptcy of Dutch aircraft-maker Fokker, majority-held subsidiary of German conglomerate Daimler Benz (now DaimlerChrysler). Although German commercial law generally requires a parent to offer financial support where a subsidiary is majority-owned and controlled by the parent, Fokker was allowed to enter protective bankruptcy. After the June, 1998 Midwestern US electric power price spike and the consequent credit defaults, it came to light that some counterparties had accepted exposures to Power Company of America, based in part on the impressive names of its shareholders. However, when PCA became insolvent, these minority investors did not support the marketer's non-recourse obligations. In the wake of the US credit defaults of the summer of 1998, market practice has become more conservative, and most counterparties now require explicit parent company guarantees, evidence of parental support, or other forms of credit enhancement.

Legal competence and authority
Another concern is the contract counterparty's legal ability to enter the transaction, and the authority of the individual signer to bind the counterparty. A famous case involved the Hammersmith and Fulham London Borough Council which, as Chapter 8 discusses, managed to avoid liability for an "ultra vires" (unauthorised) transaction. In the same vein, German local utility companies ("*Stadtwerke*", etc.) are prohibited from transacting power exchanges outside their locality; thus any such contract signed by an officer of the *Stadtwerke* could easily be deemed ultra vires. In June, 1998 the Water Light & Power Dept of Springfield, Illinois abrogated its contracts to deliver power under options, defending its breach on the grounds that city council authorisation was necessary for the municipal utility to contract a financial exposure; the utility also asserted that the defaulted options contracts were the work of a junior officer without the authority to bind the city. The municipal utility has made payments to settle suits brought by two counterparties, settlement discussions are underway with several others, and other suits are still pending in court against the municipal utility.

date any outstanding positions.

CREDIT ENHANCEMENT. When one counterparty has strong credit and the other counterparty is of inadequate credit quality, the agreement will call for the weaker counterparty to post collateral such as cash or liquid and low-risk government securities, a guarantee from a creditworthy parent, or letters of credit from financial institutions with acceptable credit ratings (in an amount equal to the mark-to-market credit exposure). When the counterparties are of equivalent credit quality, the agreement may call for bilateral security, ie collateral will be posted and adjusted on the daily mark-to-market value by whichever party has a net exposure. The cost of providing collateral is high, and the daily supervision of collateral also entails high internal administrative and safekeeping costs.

Even when a counterparty's credit is acceptable without enhancement at the time the contract is opened, the agreement should call for the party to provide credit enhancement against net exposure in the event of an adverse credit event. Typically, when counterparties have published ratings, the adverse credit event trigger is the lowering of the credit rating of the counterparty (or its parent) below a specified level. However, when a counterparty is unrated, the agreement may specify other credit event triggers, such as "net worth in any quarterly financial statement less than $10 million" or "at any time XYZ corporation owns less than 90% of the common stock of the counterparty", as well as the termination events listed above.

GUARANTEES AS CREDIT ENHANCEMENT. If the credit enhancement offered is a guarantee or letter of credit, it should be reviewed initially and on a daily or frequent basis to make sure that the exposure to the counterparty is adequately covered (including any reasonably likely change in forward market prices) and that the credit party or guarantor remains creditworthy.

❑ *Measure and monitor credit exposures.* The firm should establish and implement systems to track and value individual counterparty and portfolio exposures. It is impossible to manage credit effectively without reliable systems to monitor overall positions and mark positions to market on a frequent basis. Implementing consistent

CREDIT RISK
IN
LIBERALISED
POWER AND
NATURAL
GAS
MARKETS

position reporting and valuation within the firm is a particular challenge for corporations currently expanding via frequent mergers in the rapidly consolidating electric power and natural gas industry. Techniques to measure credit exposures and expected credit loss are explored at the end of this chapter.

❏ *Implement portfolio modelling and stress tests.* In addition to mark-to-market valuation and reporting systems, the firm should develop more modelling capabilities to measure the sensitivity of individual counterparty exposures and the overall portfolio to changes in economic conditions, unusual market events and various levels of market volatility. "Value-at-risk" (VAR) methodologies and stress-modelling techniques should be used to analyse portfolios of liquid financial instruments and to measure risk exposures at predicted confidence levels; these concepts can be adapted to help managers understand risk in emergent commodity markets with limited trading history and imperfect liquidity, albeit with lower confidence levels than in more established and liquid markets.

❏ *Establish internal risk rating systems and/or obtain external ratings from a credit rating agency to categorise counterparties and exposures by credit quality.* When there is insufficient information to perform a credit analysis in-house and no published credit ratings are available, the counterparty should be assigned to an unrated category, ie at the bottom of the credit scale. The credit risk management unit must also monitor credits on an ongoing basis. Credit surveillance techniques may include monitoring news media, confirming credit experience with other market participants or banks, reviewing the counterparty's availability of bank credit, and monitoring counterparties' stock or bond prices for signs of change in circumstance.

❏ *Establish credit limits.* Typically, credit limits are applied on the basis of both dollar exposures and product volume. Limits are applied to:

■ individual counterparty exposures;

■ aggregate product exposures, eg electricity, natural gas and gas liquids;

■ aggregate portfolio exposure to credits of various ratings categories, eg "A", "BBB", "BB" and "unrated"); and

■ permissible exposure duration at various ratings.

Firms must monitor and enforce daily the policies regarding credit exposure limits and collateral arrangements. Credit policies which are kept in a manual on the shelf and not routinely and systematically implemented are not effective. The credit policies should clearly identify the actions to be taken in the event of a non-conforming credit exposure.

❏ *Establish reserves to cover estimated credit losses and apply risk adjustments in internal systems.* Firms should institute credit reserves at the counterparty and portfolio level that incorporate the estimated cost of the credit risk. Reserves should reflect counterparty credit quality as well as the term of the exposure.

■ Such credit risk adjustments should be applied whenever the performance or profitability of business units, products, customer categories and counterparty relationships is measured.

■ Credit risk adjustments should also be incorporated in evaluating the performance of traders, marketers and risk managers. Incentive compensation systems should be based on risk-adjusted performance measures to avoid providing financial incentives to personnel to fill the book with exposure to weak counterparties.

Quantifying expected credit loss

As discussed in the previous section, the most effective practices for dealing with bilateral credit risk require identification and measurement of credit exposures. Some rough quantification tools are available to help managers perform these tasks.

Risk managers need to quantify the expected or maximum likely level of credit loss associated with an individual transaction or the net credit exposure to a single counterparty in order to establish the appropriate credit reserves against counterparty credit exposures. Another use of this data is to factor expected credit loss into pricing decisions, risk-adjusted profitability measures, and risk-adjusted personal compensation.

The first step in this process is determining the value of the credit risk exposure. For an account receivable or a note, the amount of the exposure is either static over time or changes predictably by accretion. For market contracts and derivatives, however, credit risk exposure varies with the market price of the commodity as that changes.[2] The methodology for calculating a contract's credit risk exposure is based upon the mark-to-market value of the contract currently and the distribution of future potential values over the contract's remaining life. The higher the volatility of the commodity's market price, the greater the potential credit risk exposure.

234

**CREDIT RISK
IN
LIBERALISED
POWER AND
NATURAL
GAS
MARKETS**

LESSONS LEARNED FROM THE JUNE 1998 US POWER PRICE SPIKE

In late June 1998, the US wholesale power market experienced an extreme dislocation. Abnormally high power prices resulted in losses and profits for many market participants far in excess of the statistically expected amounts, and many participants' risk management systems proved to be woefully deficient.

To recap those events, during the period between June 22 and June 26, next-day electricity prices in the Midwestern market rose from $25 per megawatt hour (MWh) to $2,600 per MWh, and a legendary hourly trade took place at $7,500. The causes of the abnormal market events included: hot weather; generating-unit outages; transmission constraints; inexperienced traders and trading organisations; absence of market transparency and clear price signals for large users and interruptible users of electricity. Physical defaults on contract deliveries lowered confidence about supplies and contributed to a market panic, accelerating the price spiral. Most market participants who failed to deliver paid

compensation to counterparties for the replacement cost, but some poorly capitalised market participants became insolvent because of the unexpected magnitude of the amounts owed for failure to deliver

Two power marketers, Federal Energy Sales (FES) and Power Company of America (PCA) filed in bankruptcy, and there were several notable defaults that did not result in bankruptcy. A number of large energy companies brought lawsuits against Springfield Illinois' municipal utility after the utility defaulted on contractual deliveries and attempted to reject its ongoing contractual obligations. Further effects of the price spike and contractual defaults include large losses reported by half a dozen large utilities or their parent holding companies and announcements that several energy marketing and trading organisations would withdraw from the market or substantially curtail activities.

Some companies that were long power were able to achieve sizeable trading gains, but some of the gains were absorbed by the establishment of

Electricity prices are often more volatile than the price for natural gas, which in turn is somewhat more volatile than other commodities.

In the case of a large portfolio of individually small consumer receivables, credit managers may be able to apply historical data about their own collections to calculate the experience of default by different types of accounts types (households, small retail businesses, etc.) and estimate future default probabilities. However, for a wholesale

energy portfolio consisting of large exposures to a limited number of major accounts, that methodology will not work. No individual energy company has a large enough sample of data on wholesale market transactions over a long enough period to estimate credit default probabilities. Therefore, as a reasonable proxy, historical bond market data regarding actual defaults on US corporate bonds over a 10-year or longer period ("mortality rates") is often used.

The historical bond default data illustrate two major trends:
❑ The probability of credit default increases with the duration of the credit exposure
❑ The lower the credit rating of the counterparties at the beginning of a 10-year period, the higher the experience of actual credit default (Figure 1).

However, the weakest credits (below investment grade ratings) tend to concentrate their default experience in the first several years, whereas the credits originally rated in the high investment grade category tend to have fewer defaults in the early years and an increasing probability of downgrades and defaults as the time hori-

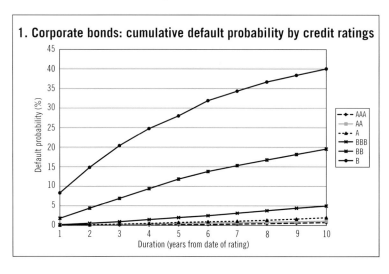

1. Corporate bonds: cumulative default probability by credit ratings

235

CREDIT RISK
IN
LIBERALISED
POWER AND
NATURAL
GAS
MARKETS

larger risk reserves occasioned by the revelation that the magnitude of actual losses can deviate substantially from those predicted by normal statistical models.

Among the most important lessons learned by risk managers and senior corporate management were the following:

❑ Market disruptions are accompanied by reduced liquidity, which in turn produces extreme price volatility.

❑ Price volatility for short periods can exceed reasonable statistical expectations.

❑ Statistical modelling techniques that assume a normal distribution of prices may not be suited to electricity, which cannot be stored and is subject to transmission constraints. "Value-at-risk" (VAR) models which produce an estimated probable loss at a certain confidence level can be misleading or deceptive, unless combined with other forms of modelling (sensitivity and scenario or "what-if" analyses) that estimate portfolio losses under unlikely or abnormal circumstances.

❑ Contract terms are extremely important. Contracts should specify netting of positions with a single counterparty and provide for termination in the event of adverse credit circumstances unless the counterparty posts adequate collateral.

❑ Counterparties should be aware that guarantees or security taken as collateral may not prove to be large enough to protect against loss when the market price changes so rapidly.

❑ Companies need to formulate and enforce credit limits on positions with individual counterparties both in volume terms and in monetary amounts.

❑ Owning or controlling physical assets is not a perfect hedge against market price risk. Some of the largest losses were experienced by generators that had contracted to deliver power at fixed prices from capacity which was not in service at the time of the price spike, or that could not deliver power at the contractual delivery point due to transmission constraints; their losses resulted from their purchases of replacement power at market prices.

It is worthwhile to recall that the North American natural gas market experienced two or three major shake-outs over the period 1994–97, each time occasioned by abnormal price movements and unexpected change in normal price relationships among related commodities or markets. While this episode is the first shake-out in the young US power market, it will not be the last.

zon is extended beyond five or six years. Of course, it would be preferable to use an historical database of credit defaults on energy contracts rather than corporate bonds, but no database of sufficient size or history exists, so bond data is used as a substitute. Also, to date the available information on bond defaults describes only US corporate bonds. There has not been sufficient data on European or emerging market bonds to do a meaningful study of default experience in those markets. Until such data is available, credit managers generally apply the US corporate bond experience

The discussion above supposes that the credit manager has access to credit ratings for all of his counterparties corresponding in some way to the credit ratings of the historical database of corporate bond default data. This will be true for many

large utility companies, major oil and natural gas producers, and transmission companies, but in a market sector that is so new and so rapidly evolving, there are many unrated counterparties, including marketing and trading companies, new-entrant generation companies, or subsidiaries of large corporations transacting business without a parent's guarantee (as described in Panel 1). In the case of unrated counterparties, market participants typically perform their own analysis or check list and assign proxy credit ratings, or hire advisors to perform this type of evaluation; when no information is available, the counterparty is assigned the lowest rating and business is only conducted within very small limits and on a fully collateralised basis.[3]

CREDIT RISK
IN
LIBERALISED
POWER AND
NATURAL
GAS
MARKETS

1 *The authors wish to thank the following individuals who advised on aspects of this article, reviewed drafts, and offered their valuable comments: Richard Apostolik of Bankers Trust, James Whelan of Eastern Energy plc and Mark Schroeder of Enron Europe Ltd.*

2 *For a detailed explanation of techniques to estimate expected credit loss of individual transactions and for a single counterparty in energy portfolios, see Ellen Lapson,"Managing Credit Risk in the Electricity Market",* The US Power Market: Restructuring and Risk Management, *London: Risk Publications, 1997, pp. 281-91.*

3 *One approach to proxy ratings is discussed in detail by Richard Buy, Vincent Kaminski et al. in "Actively Managing Corporate Credit Risk: New Methodologies and Instruments for Non-financial Firms" in* Credit Derivatives: Applications for Risk Management, Investment and Portfolio Optimisation, *Risk Books: London, 1998, pp. 65-82.*

11

Accounting for Derivative Contracts in an Energy Environment

Tom Lewthwaite, Hassaan Majid and Nicholas Swingler
Arthur Andersen

U ntil recently, limited formal guidance has existed in respect of accounting practices for energy derivatives. The accounting applied to date has been based on general principles developed by various regulatory bodies, interpretations of accounting standards applicable to other, related areas and industries and an evaluation of individual circumstances. With the growth in the range of available energy products and the size of derivatives markets generally, along with the liberalisation of energy markets in many parts of the world, the ability for energy companies to enter into complex energy derivatives has increased substantially. However, over this same period of change, accounting standards have often failed to keep up with the new developments. This is not because the standards-setting bodies have failed to recognise the importance of derivative markets and thereby ignored the critical issues associated with their use, but rather that the discussions have frequently been contentious. The major points of contention are:

❑ how the value of derivatives should be reflected in the financial statements of the user; and

❑ how to account for the various ways in which derivatives are used – ie as hedges or for speculative/trading purposes.

Current practice for accounting for energy derivatives is mainly based on US, International or UK generally accepted accounting principles (GAAP). US GAAP is currently the most advanced in the provision of detail and prescriptive guidance, while International and UK GAAP lag behind in terms of issuing formal guidance. However, recent discussion papers and projects indicate that this gap will close in the near future as International and UK standards move closer to US GAAP.

The objective of this chapter is to draw the attention of management to the latest developments in accounting for derivative contracts in an energy environment from a US, UK and international point of view.

US accounting and disclosure requirements

As mentioned above, US standards are more advanced in terms of providing formal guidance in accounting practices for energy derivatives. Primary guidance in the US is set out in two publications issued by the Financial Accounting Standards Board (FASB):

❑ *Accounting for Derivative Instruments and Hedging Activities* (Statement of Financial Accounting Standards (SFAS) 133); and

❑ *Accounting for Energy Trading and Risk Management Activities* (Emerging Issues Task Force Consensus (EITF) 98-10).

SFAS 133: ACCOUNTING FOR DERIVATIVE INSTRUMENTS AND HEDGING ACTIVITIES
SFAS 133, issued in June 1998, replaces the existing accounting pronouncements and practices with a single, integrated accounting framework for derivatives and hedging activities (among others, SFAS 133 supersedes SFAS 80, 105 and 119 and amends SFAS 52, 107 and 115). It was originally applicable for all quarters of all fiscal years beginning after June 15, 1999. However, in May 1999, the FASB proposed an amendment which effectively defers the implementation of the standard by one year. Therefore, calendar year companies will need to adopt the new statement with effect from January 1, 2001. The standard should be adopted prospectively, ie prior years should not be restated.

ACCOUNTING

FOR

DERIVATIVE

CONTRACTS

IN AN

ENERGY

ENVIRONMENT

SFAS 133 expands the previous accounting definition of a "derivative" – which focused on freestanding contracts such as options, forwards, futures and swaps – to include embedded derivatives as well as various commodity contracts (including energy contracts). Every derivative instrument has to be recorded on the balance sheet at fair value as an asset or a liability. The statement further requires that changes in the fair value of derivative instruments be included in current earnings unless specific hedge accounting criteria are met. The key principles underlying SFAS 133 are set out in Figure 1.

It is evident from the above that this statement will dramatically affect market participants in the energy business from oil and gas producers to energy marketers. Below is a summary of some consequences and provisions of SFAS 133:

❑ it advances the FASB's objective of measuring all financial assets and liabilities at fair value;

❑ it casts a wide net, sweeping in a broad range of transactions;

❑ new volatility in earnings and equity has to be reflected as changes in fair value in current earnings;

❑ hedging eligibility criteria are more difficult to meet than under SFAS 80;

❑ there is to be no grandfathering of existing hedges; and

❑ a restricted exception allows written options as hedges.

A "derivative" is defined by SFAS 133 as a financial instrument or other contract with all three of the following characteristics:

❑ it has (1) one or more underlyings (a reference rate or price such as a commodity price, interest rate, security price, foreign exchange rate or any index of prices or rates) and (2) one or more notional amounts or payment provisions that require settlement if an underlying changes in a specified way;

❑ the initial net investment is not significant (for example, the initial net investment on most option contracts is insignificant compared to the notional amount of the derivatives); and

❑ net settlement is permitted or required, a market mechanism exists for net settlement, or the asset to be delivered is readily convertible to cash.

This definition of a derivative instrument includes contracts that may not previously have been recognised and recorded as derivative instruments for accounting purposes, such as natural gas and power sales and purchase contracts. However, the statement provides an exemption in respect of "normal purchases and normal sales". This exemption excludes contracts with "no net settlement provision and no market mechanism to facilitate net settlement" from the definition of a derivative.

It should be noted that natural gas and power contracts will constitute derivative instruments if the contracts allow net cash settlement even though the contracts permit net cash settlement only on default and the parties intend to settle the contracts via physical delivery. For example, the following contracts could be classified as derivative instruments under SFAS 133:

❑ exchange-traded futures and options contracts;

❑ over-the-counter ("OTC") forward, swap and option contracts;

❑ physical delivery contracts negotiated by an exploration and production entity for the sale of future production/reserves; and

❑ physical delivery/purchase contracts negotiated by an electric generation facility for the sale of future production or purchase of natural gas.

A further consequence of SFAS 133 is that it also covers derivatives embedded in broader non-derivative contracts. Specifically, if the economic characteristics of an embedded derivative and its host contract are not clearly and closely related, SFAS 133 requires that the embedded derivative be separated and accounted for as a stand-alone derivative. The FASB has granted a one-off exemption in respect of embedded derivatives included in contracts acquired or issued prior to January 1, 1998. However, the exemption has to be applied consistently for all embedded derivative instruments.

SFAS 133 prescribes specific treatment for changes in the fair value of derivatives that meet defined hedge criteria. It is important to note that not all contracts deemed to be hedges by management will meet the hedge criteria as specified

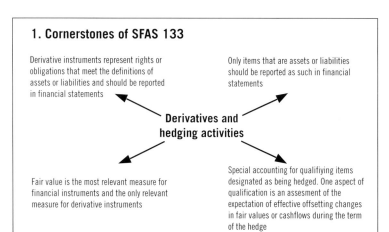

1. Cornerstones of SFAS 133

Derivative instruments represent rights or obligations that meet the definitions of assets or liabilities and should be reported in financial statements

Only items that are assets or liabilities should be reported as such in financial statements

Derivatives and hedging activities

Fair value is the most relevant measure for financial instruments and the only relevant measure for derivative instruments

Special accounting for qualifiying items designated as being hedged. One aspect of qualification is an assesment of the expectation of effective offsetting changes in fair values or cashflows during the term of the hedge

239

ACCOUNTING
FOR
DERIVATIVE
CONTRACTS
IN AN
ENERGY
ENVIRONMENT

by the statement. Furthermore, management has to elect specifically whether or not to designate a transaction as a hedge. Before being able to opt for hedge accounting, management must:

❏ at inception of the transaction, formally document the hedging relationship, the entity's risk management objective and the hedging strategy (it should be noted that a calendar year-end company will have to formally redesignate all existing derivative instruments as at January 1, 2000, if it wishes to adopt hedge accounting for those instruments – transitional provisions do not allow post-inception recognition); and

❏ be satisfied that the hedging relationship is highly correlated at inception and on an ongoing basis. Note that SFAS 133 requires, unlike earlier GAAP, that all hedge inefficiencies, irrespective of size, be recorded in current earnings. Furthermore, requirements for assessing hedge effectiveness are complex and perhaps onerous.

SFAS 133 considers three types of hedges where the accounting treatment differs from the default position. These hedges are considered in more detail in Figure 2.

Written options may be designated as hedges even if they have previously been accounted for as speculative contracts. However, the combination of the written option and the hedged item must provide at least as much potential for gains as exposure to losses due to changes in the combined fair value. This effectively limits the use of written options to hedge purchased options.

EITF 98-10 ACCOUNTING FOR ENERGY TRADING AND RISK MANAGEMENT ACTIVITIES
EITF 98-10 is applicable to all financial statement with fiscal years beginning after December 15, 1998. This means that adoption is required two years prior to SFAS 133 for calendar year companies. Adoption is on a prospective basis.

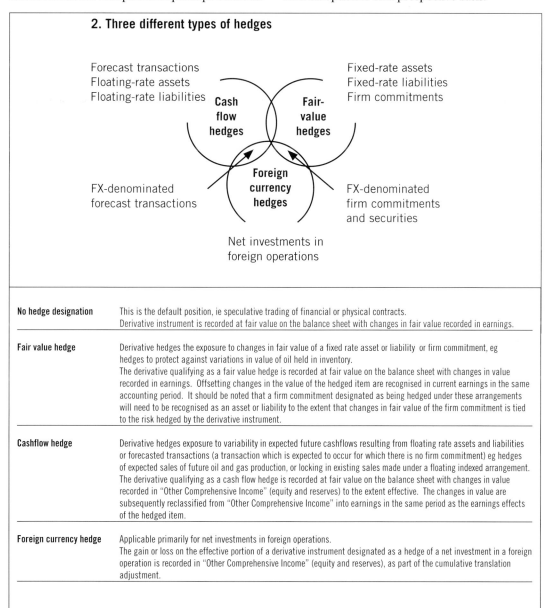

2. Three different types of hedges

Forecast transactions
Floating-rate assets
Floating-rate liabilities — **Cash flow hedges**

Fair-value hedges — Fixed-rate assets
Fixed-rate liabilities
Firm commitments

Foreign currency hedges

FX-denominated forecast transactions

FX-denominated firm commitments and securities

Net investments in foreign operations

No hedge designation	This is the default position, ie speculative trading of financial or physical contracts. Derivative instrument is recorded at fair value on the balance sheet with changes in fair value recorded in earnings.
Fair value hedge	Derivative hedges the exposure to changes in fair value of a fixed rate asset or liability or firm commitment, eg hedges to protect against variations in value of oil held in inventory. The derivative qualifying as a fair value hedge is recorded at fair value on the balance sheet with changes in value recorded in earnings. Offsetting changes in the value of the hedged item are recognised in current earnings in the same accounting period. It should be noted that a firm commitment designated as being hedged under these arrangements will need to be recognised as an asset or liability to the extent that changes in fair value of the firm commitment is tied to the risk hedged by the derivative instrument.
Cashflow hedge	Derivative hedges exposure to variability in expected future cashflows resulting from floating rate assets and liabilities or forecasted transactions (a transaction which is expected to occur for which there is no firm commitment) eg hedges of expected sales of future oil and gas production, or locking in existing sales made under a floating indexed arrangement. The derivative qualifying as a cash flow hedge is recorded at fair value on the balance sheet with changes in value recorded in "Other Comprehensive Income" (equity and reserves) to the extent effective. The changes in value are subsequently reclassified from "Other Comprehensive Income" into earnings in the same period as the earnings effects of the hedged item.
Foreign currency hedge	Applicable primarily for net investments in foreign operations. The gain or loss on the effective portion of a derivative instrument designated as a hedge of a net investment in a foreign operation is recorded in "Other Comprehensive Income" (equity and reserves), as part of the cumulative translation adjustment.

ACCOUNTING
FOR
DERIVATIVE
CONTRACTS
IN AN
ENERGY
ENVIRONMENT

The EITF refers to the term "energy contracts", which are defined as contracts entered into for (or indexed to) the purchase or sale of electricity, natural gas, natural gas liquids, crude oil, refined products and other hydrocarbons. It specifically includes energy-related contracts, such as capacity contracts, requirements contracts and transportation contracts. Note that the range of contracts affected by EITF 98-10 is broader than those that fall under the definition of derivatives in SFAS 133 and includes certain physical delivery contracts. However, non-energy derivatives are clearly not within the scope of EITF 98-10 but remain subject to SFAS 133 and other hedge-accounting guidance.

The EITF reached a consensus that energy contracts used in trading activities should be marked-to-market (that is, measured at fair value determined as at the balance sheet date), with resulting gains and losses recognised in current earnings. Contracts that have been designated as hedges for non-trading activities are not considered to be energy-trading contracts and should be accounted for in accordance with the appropriate hedge-accounting guidance.

Determining whether an entity is involved in energy-trading activities depends on the relevant facts and circumstances relating to that entity, and an element of judgement will be involved in reaching a conclusion. Energy-trading activities refer to entering into energy contracts with the objective of generating profits on or from exposure to changes in market prices. Ultimately, a company has to consider whether its business focus is physical receipt and delivery of commodities and other related services or whether it is generating profits by taking on and managing financial risk. Examples of factors to consider include:
❑ the operation has little or no generation/production/distribution/transmission capabilities;
❑ its major competitors are traders;
❑ the portfolio has a high turnover rate;
❑ the entity communicates internally in terms of a "trading strategy"; and
❑ there is infrastructure similar to that of a trading operation in a financial institution or investment bank.

The guidance is not limited to legal entity status but includes divisions or business units/groupings within a legal entity. Companies that have trading operations within their business should scrutinise closely whether those operations meet the requirements of EITF 98-10 and, if they do, its energy-trading contracts should be marked-to-market.

DISCLOSURES

Derivative disclosures apply to all derivatives and are not specific to the energy industry. Basic disclosures include setting out the objectives of holding/issuing derivative instruments, the context required to understand those objectives and the strategies for achieving those objectives. Furthermore, the disclosures should distinguish between those instruments designated as fair-value hedges, cashflow hedges and foreign currency hedges (as defined in SFAS 133), with additional detailed disclosure requirements depending on the type of hedge. The detailed additional disclosures include quantifying the impact of the hedge on the different elements (earnings, other comprehensive income/equity, assets and liabilities) of a company's financial statements. In addition to the above, cashflow hedges require disclosure of the underlying transactions that are being hedged and the existing gains and losses that will be reclassified from other comprehensive income to earnings within the next 12 months.

Companies with publicly traded stock or debt quoted on US exchanges fall under the rules of the Securities and Exchange Commission (SEC). The SEC rules require such companies to provide additional disclosures, both quantitative and qualitative, about market risk. The qualitative disclosures are similar to those specifed under SFAS 133, while the quantitative disclosures require disclosure of the inherent risk in a company's portfolio using value-at-risk, sensitivity analysis or tabular presentation.

UK accounting and disclosure requirements

In the UK there is currently no formal guidance on accounting practice for derivatives. The Accounting Standards Board (ASB) issued a discussion paper in 1996 that covered issues relating to measurement, hedge accounting and disclosures. Since the release of the paper the only formal guidance from the ASB has been Financial Reporting Standard (FRS) 13, *Derivatives and Other Financial Instruments: Disclosures*.

The 1996 discussion paper recognises that historical measurement practices are no longer adequate owing to the development of markets and risk management techniques that point towards greater use of current value as opposed to historical costs (currently, certain financial instrumental are valued at historic cost while others are valued at current value).

ACCOUNTING

FOR

DERIVATIVE

CONTRACTS

IN AN

ENERGY

ENVIRONMENT

The ASB considers a number of different approaches to measurement but has concluded that all financial instruments should be measured at current value, with all gains and losses recognised as and when they occur. However, it also recognises that it would be wholly inappropriate to put all gains and losses through the income statement and that use should be made of the "Statement of total recognised gains and losses" (similar to "Other Comprehensive Income" used in the US). Clearly, these proposals represent a significant change from current practices, and significant discussion is ongoing in this area.

The 1996 discussion paper also identifies issues relating to hedge accounting. It is of the opinion that, should its proposals on measurement be accepted, many of the hedge-accounting issues would become irrelevant. A number of different hedge-accounting options are identified and two approaches (or a combination of these approaches) are suggested. One possibility is to measure hedges at fair value and defer the resulting gains and losses within liabilities and assets, respectively. Deferring the hedging gain (loss) as a liability (asset) is seen as an alternative to recognising the change in value of the underlying hedged position where the hedged item is an existing asset, liability or firm commitments – ie the equivalent of fair-value hedges under SFAS 133. Alternatively, the discussion paper suggests that hedges should be measured at fair value, with the resulting gains or losses recognised in the "Statement of total recognised gains and losses". Gains and losses should be transferred to earnings when the hedged transaction occurs – ie as for cashflow hedges under SFAS 133.

It is evident that there is a high degree of similarity between the approach suggested in the UK discussion paper and that adopted in SFAS 133. Generally in the UK, companies involved in energy trading have used guidance from other countries or industries – for example, the US or the banking industry. This approach has resulted in the adoption of a US GAAP-like approach whereby items are marked-to-market to reflect the actual impact of market changes. Furthermore, the move towards US GAAP is also driven by the fact that a large number of energy companies are US-based or quoted on US exchanges and are therefore required to comply with US GAAP.

DISCLOSURES

As mentioned above, the only formal guidance from the ASB has been Financial Reporting Standard (FRS) 13. FRS 13 is effective for accounting periods ending on or after March 23, 1999, and is applicable to companies that have one or more of their capital instruments publicly traded on a stock exchange or market. Cash-settled commodity contracts should be treated as financial instruments and are subject to FRS 13 disclosure requirements.

FRS 13 relies on both narrative and numerical disclosures to enable users of the financial statements to assess the entity's objectives, policies and strategies for holding or issuing financial instruments. Furthermore, the users should be able to assess the risk profile of the entity for each of the major financial risks arising from financial instruments as well as the significance of the instruments to the entity's reported financial performance.

Companies should consider the following in relation to FRS 13:

❏ a company has to have defined objectives, policies and strategies for the financial instruments it holds;

❏ comprehensive, lengthy and detailed disclosures are required;

❏ whether the quantitative disclosures reflect the objectives; and

❏ that fair values may not always be available or reliable.

IASC accounting and disclosure requirements

The IASC has issued IAS 39 – *Financial Instruments: Recognition and Measurement*, and is currently working on "Financial Instruments – Comprehensive Project", which has a target date for completion by the end of 2001.

IAS 39 – FINANCIAL INSTRUMENTS:
RECOGNITION AND MEASUREMENT
IAS 39 will be effective for annual accounting periods beginning on or after January 1, 2001, and requires that all financial trading assets and liabilities should be recognised on the balance sheet at fair value.

All financial assets should be revalued to fair value except for the following, which should be carried at amortised cost subject to an impairment test:

❏ loans and receivables originated by the company but not held for trading;

❏ other fixed-maturity investments that the company intends and is able to hold to maturity; and

❏ financial assets whose fair value cannot be reli-

ACCOUNTING

FOR

DERIVATIVE

CONTRACTS

IN AN

ENERGY

ENVIRONMENT

ably measured (limited to some equity instruments with no quoted market price and some derivatives that are linked to, and must be settled by, delivery of such unquoted equity instruments)

Financial liabilities should be reflected at original recorded amount less principal repayments and amortisation. All derivatives and liabilities held for trading should be revalued to fair value.

Subsequent changes in the fair value of financial assets and liabilities can be accounted for in one of two ways (the approach adopted has to be applied consistently in respect of all fair-value assets and liabilities):

❑ recognise the entire adjustment in the net profit and loss (P&L) account for the period; or

❑ recognise only the changes in fair value related to trading in the net P&L and recognise fair-value changes relating to non-trading as a change in equity (until disposal, when the full change will be reflected in the P&L).

Hedge accounting (for changes in fair value or cashflows) is permitted under IAS 39 provided that the hedging relationship is clearly defined, measurable and effective. Specific hedging instruments have to identified and linked to corresponding hedged items. The criteria for applying hedge accounting are similar to those under US GAAP and equally complex to apply in practice.

DISCLOSURES

The IASC addresses disclosure requirements in IAS 32 – *Financial Instruments: Disclosure and Presentation*, which is applicable to all derivative financial instruments. However, a contract that requires the receipt or delivery of physical assets is deemed not to give rise to a financial asset or liability unless the corresponding payment is deferred past the date on which the physical assets are transferred.

A company's policies for managing risks associated with financial instruments (such as hedging policies, avoidance of undue concentration of risk, etc) have to be disclosed, together with additional disclosure to ensure that the users of the financial statements are able to assess the extent of the risks associated with financial instruments. Additional disclosures include price risk (currency, interest rate and market), credit risk, liquidity risk and cashflow risk (fluctuations of future cashflows of a monetary instrument).

The standard requires disclosure of the fair value of financial assets and liabilities and the difference, if any, between the fair value and the carrying value in the balance sheet. Financial assets and liabilities should be disclosed on a net basis when it is a reflection of a company's expected future cashflows from settling two or more separate financial instruments.

In instances where a financial instrument has been accounted for as a hedge of an anticipated transaction, the disclosures should include a description of the hedged item and hedging instrument and whether or not related gains or losses have been deferred.

Conclusions

❑ Current accounting practices for derivative contracts in an energy environment are mainly based on or aligned to the US GAAP. There is an increasing move to recognising the value of derivatives as assets or liabilities in the balance sheet regardless of whether they are used for trading or hedging purposes.

❑ The recently issued and proposed accounting standards under US, UK and international GAAP represent a major change from historical practices and will require companies to assess carefully their approach to the use of derivatives. Companies may find that the revised standards have a significant effect on their balance sheets and may result in volatile earnings.

❑ The rules for applying hedge accounting are growing ever more complex and will place a significant burden on management in terms of documentation, initial and ongoing evaluation and measurement of the values of derivatives and hedged items. Companies need to consider whether their current and future approaches to the use of derivatives will result in the desired accounting treatment.

❑ Disclosures are also becoming more and more detailed and comprehensive. Qualitative disclosures require companies to disclose their approach to the use of derivatives – shareholders may be surprised to discover the information they were previously unaware of or, worse, may not understand it at all. Companies also need to assess whether they currently collect, maintain and report the information required at the relevant time periods and with the necessary level of detail and accuracy.

❑ Controls and information systems may need to be developed to support the company's requirements under the new accounting rules. The company will also need to be able to demonstrate such compliance to auditors and other regulatory bodies.

TOOLS FOR RISK ANALYSIS

Section Introduction

Vincent Kaminski
Enron Corp

The growing complexity of the energy markets demands the introduction of increasingly sophisticated tools for the analysis of market structures and for the modelling of the dynamics of spot market and forward prices.

One of the most fundamental problems facing any energy trading operation is how to generate a forward price curve. In principle, the problem is very simple. In any market, a forward curve comprises a collection of prices, transacted today, for the delivery of the asset in question at some future point. When these prices are sorted by maturity and plotted on a graph, they map out the term structure of the forward price of the asset: the forward price curve.

In the energy markets, price discovery is often imperfect and constructing a price curve can depend upon an assembly of eclectic techniques – a combination of art and science. The typical procedure followed in the industry is to make use of any available futures prices (ie the prices of standardised forward contracts traded on a public exchange), with or without any adjustments necessary to distinguish between futures and forward prices.

The futures prices are the most reliable way of tracing out the "closest" part of the forward curve, however most of the time market participants want their forward curve to extend beyond the reach of the maturity of the furthest out (or longest dated) futures contract. At this point it is necessary to switch to the over-the-counter (OTC) markets.

The OTC forward prices, often extracted from the price of calendar spreads and/or calendar swaps, are available from brokers and/or traders for tenors that vary from market to market. As one goes out in time, the reliability of the price information, and the frequency at which this information is updated, deteriorates. At this point, the science of building forward curves becomes an art. An additional challenge arises from the fact that, in many markets, forward prices display a seasonality that has to be reflected in the curve.

Shankar Nagarajan has written a chapter in this section, focused on the electricity markets. Power prices offer special challenges to builders of forward curves. Investment projects in the electricity industry typically have a long gestation period and a long economic life – often over 20 years. This creates the need for very long-term "forward price curves" that can be used in project valuation.

Typically, such curves are in fact derived from forecasts of future spot prices. The forecasts are generated from fundamental models which bring together in a unified framework a whole variety of assumptions about future loads, generation capacity (often using exogenous or model determined capacity expansion forecasts), fuel prices, transmission grid topology, and the availability of generating plant. Such models attempt to construct supply and demand curves for power, hour by hour, for future periods. Most sophisticated models generate the most likely internal "commitment decisions" regarding the dispatch of individual generating units and attempt to model transmission flows, all based on sophisticated optimisation algorithms.

However, all this depends on whether we are correct to equate the forecast of future spot prices with forward prices – and this assumes that the latter are unbiased predictors of realised spot prices. This assumption is not satisfied in practice: in most cases, forward markets are asymmetric, ie in most cases the natural "long" positions dominate the natural "shorts", or vice versa. So in practice, the prices at which the traders will be willing to enter into forward contracts will deviate from the prices generated from a fundamental model, even in the unlikely event that everyone in the market agreed on the inputs to the fundamental model in the first place.

Shankar Nagarajan's chapter focuses on an alternative technique of generating forward price curves, using econometric techniques. As any econometric model has to be calibrated to the historical data, such models are "backward looking", and thus contrast to fundamental models based on guesses and forecasts of future values of the critical variables (eg future fuel prices).

In the second chapter in this section, Kaushik Amin, Victor Ng and Craig Pirrong offer a unified framework for the valuation of energy derivative products. Their approach recognises that the term structure of futures prices depends upon convenience yields ie the flow of benefits that accrues to the holder of a physical commodity. They proceed to incorporate the convenience yield in a pricing algorithm, first assuming that the convenience yield is non-stochastic and then eliminating this restriction.

The third chapter in this section is by Darrell Duffie, Stephen Gray and Philip Hoang and provides a review of various volatility models. The paper concentrates on stochastic volatility models known in finance as Garch and Egarch, developed to capture in a parsimonious way the phenomena of volatility persistence and clustering that is observed in many financial and commodity markets. By a "persistence of volatility", we mean that if volatility rises above "normal" levels, volatility will tend to stay above that normal level for some time. Similarly, if volatility drops below the "normal" level, it will stay below this level for some time.

The chapter reveals the results of parameter estimation for different markets and models and discusses the implications of these results for energy option hedging and valuation. One important conclusion is that option-implied volatility is a better predictor of future volatility than either unconditional historical volatility or Arch-based model forecasts.

The chapter written by Carol Alexander will hopefully become a standard reference for energy industry practitioners responsible for portfolio management, derivation of the hedge ratios, correlation analysis and the statistical analysis of market trends. Correlation is one of the most widely used tools in risk analysis, but its limitations, especially in relation to the energy markets, are not widely appreciated. One especially important concept, cointegration, offers an alternative way to measure the co-movement of two prices and is a very powerful tool in the determination of hedge positions.

12

Power Forward Curves:

A Managerial Perspective

Shankar Nagarajan
Deloitte & Touche L.L.P.

The deregulation of energy and power markets in the US, the UK, Argentina, Australia and other countries has given rise to a number of risks which the utilities and power companies previously either did not face or handled through fixed-price, long-term contracts. The history of deregulation in various industries – financial services, oil and natural gas and, more recently, power and telecommunications – suggests the following evolution of events.

First, one observes a trend towards de-contracting, whereby long-term contracts are allowed to expire and are quickly replaced by spot trades. Soon, market players realise that they require transactions with maturity longer than one year, and the tenor of contracts is slowly extended as liquidity develops in various segments of the market. Part of the difficulty in this tenor-extension process is that, because of the fast-changing market structure, forward prices and associated volatilities are not easily obtained. Hence, managing the term structure risk becomes difficult for market players attempting to enter into longer-term contracts and for those who own long-lived generation assets. The power market may be characterised as being in this stage of evolution at the present time.

This chapter starts out by describing the special features that make electricity a challenging commodity to analyse and how these features influence the risk of its prices. The forward curve is defined and its various determinants are discussed. The chapter then discusses existing econometric models that are presently available for constructing a forward curve before proposing a new model that can be used to model the forward prices either directly or indirectly through spot prices. Next, a number of applications of forward curves are presented from a senior managerial perspective. The chapter con-

cludes with some thoughts on future directions.

While gas and oil markets are important and are linked to the power markets, excellent treatments of forward curves in these markets can be found elsewhere (eg, Gabillon, 1995). This chapter will instead focus on forward curves in power markets. To the extent that there is a long-term trend toward convergence in energy markets, however, gas curves may contain information that is relevant for power curves as well. Unfortunately, correlations between gas and power curves can be seasonal and weak. In any case, as will be argued, much of this type of information is likely to be subsumed in the information that is directly contained in the spot and forward curves.

The focus here will be on managerial applications of power forward curves rather than on the technical issues, which, because of their complexity, require separate treatment. Given the relative infancy of power markets and the profusion of sophisticated statistical models, it is easy to get carried away with the statistical nuances. However, the current lack of quality and quantity of data can make this exercise frustrating. This chapter, therefore, adopts a more practical approach to modelling forward curves. The hope is that, as more quality data become available in the course of time, further refinement of forward curves can – and should – be attempted.

The determinants of electricity prices

Electricity is a commodity like no other. Hence, before discussing forward curves, it is useful to understand the properties of electricity as a commodity and the various determinants of electricity prices. Compared to oil and natural gas, which are also energy-related, electricity presents a host of difficulties in pricing and trading. These are outlined below.

Non-storability First of all, electricity cannot be stored in a conventional manner.[1] Any electricity that is generated must be either consumed instantaneously within the grid or transmitted to another location. This fact underlies all the other difficulties that arise in analysing this commodity. The non-storability of electricity means that the usual arbitrage arguments, which are commonly invoked to determine forward prices, do not apply to electricity markets.

Transmission constraints To compound the storability problem, electricity grids tend to be highly

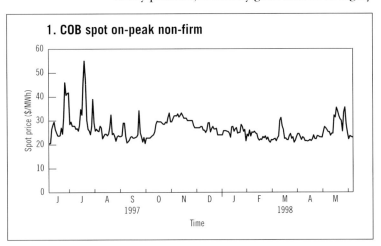

1. COB spot on-peak non-firm

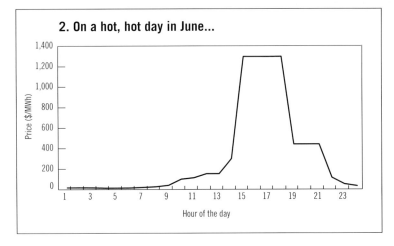

2. On a hot, hot day in June...

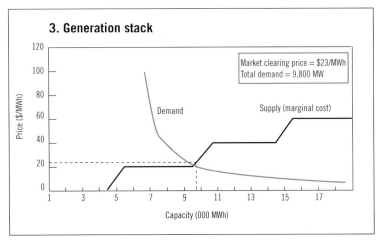

3. Generation stack

segmented. There are several reasons for this, some of them historical. Historically, the high cost of transporting fuel meant that plants were located and designed around the availability of fuel. Demand patterns tend to be related to weather and economic activity, and so are localised. Furthermore, the interconnection of grids raises the risk that outages in one part of the system may affect others. Transmitting power over longer distances may also increase line losses. Finally, regulatory jurisdiction in the US tends to be at state or local Public Service Commissions, further localising the efforts of management. For example, the US system is divided into several grids (NERC regions), some of which (eg Texas) are virtually power islands. Some grids are interconnected with DC lines, while others are interconnected with small-capacity lines. Moreover, given the lack of clear incentives in the present regulatory structure to invest in transmission lines, this constraint is likely to remain for some time. The presence of transmission constraints implies that imbalances in supply and demand in any given region cannot always be smoothed out by exporting or importing the commodity.

Seasonality and weather-dependence There are also seasonal and weather-related variations in the demand and supply of electricity, giving rise to strong seasonal and intra-day price patterns. Figure 1 illustrates a spot price peak in the summer months arising from an increased use of air-conditioning, while a smaller, heating-driven peak is evident in the winter months.

In addition, because of the patterns of electricity consumption by industrial and residential users, electricity demand peaks during the day but drops off at night and over weekends. Figure 2 shows the intra-day price pattern on June 7, 1999, a particularly hot and humid day. This feature gives rise to at least two sets of prices – the on-peak (6 am to 10 pm weekdays) and off-peak prices – and they are not highly correlated. For example, the 5 × 16 contract supplies power for the 16 peak hours Monday to Friday. The off-peak contracts cover nights and weekends (5 × 8 + 2 × 24) and are cheaper. In addition, the so-called "super-peak" contracts cover four to eight hours during the peak hours and exhibit even higher prices. Around the clock (ATC) contracts offer power 24 hours a day, seven days a week.

Swing risk and delivery Unlike other commodity markets, the supplier of power (utility) faces a "swing" demand risk. At short notice (one day)

249

POWER
FORWARD
CURVES:
A
MANAGERIAL
PERSPECTIVE

the buyer can demand more or less power within certain limits. From a delivery point of view, electricity poses an additional set of problems. Since electrons can not be tagged, electricity is produced and dumped into pools much like water entering a water reservoir. A buyer merely taps into the pool supplied by many generators and marketers. The issue of who pays whom is decided on a notional basis rather than on an actual delivery basis.

Electricity must be generated from calorific fuels such as oil, coal and natural gas. A major determinant of power prices is therefore fuel prices and generation costs, which can affect the supply curve for electricity.

Generation stack From the supply side, a utility or, more likely, a pool operator (ie independent service operator, or ISO) will "stack" the various available plants that have been "bid in" in increasing order of their marginal costs. That is, the first plants to be turned on in any day are those with the cheapest marginal costs (hydro, nuclear) – the so-called base-load units. Then the more expensive coal- and oil-fired plants are run, and, finally, the most expensive gas-fired plants are turned on. The supply curve is the locus of all these marginal costs arranged in increasing order (Figure 3). The market clearing price is given by the point at which the supply curve intersects the demand curve. Because of their high marginal costs, the oil- and gas-fired units are likely, though not always, to be the marginal units at this intersection, and they therefore play a key role in determining the market price.

The notion of the gas- or oil-fired unit as a "price setter" is the basis for the popularity of spark spreads. The spark spread between power and gas prices, say, is computed using a notional conversion rate called the heat rate (eg 10,000 MMBtu/MWh) for gas-generated electricity. More importantly, since the market clearing price cannot be below the marginal cost of production, the marginal cost of a gas unit is sometimes viewed as the lower bound. However, it is important to keep in mind that the gas unit's marginal cost may not represent a lower bound to power prices when demand is low because the marginal unit may turn out to be a lower-cost base-load unit. If so, the lower bound would reflect the marginal cost of that particular unit. Hence, although the marginal costs of gas-fired units may be a key determinant of electricity prices in peak periods and in summer, the marginal cost of base-load units may help to drive power prices at off-peak times and in

"shoulder" months (spring and autumn).

It has also been argued, on the other hand, that the gas marginal cost may represent the upper bound for power prices (Leong, 1997). The reason is that if the power price is too high relative to the marginal cost of peakers, more such units will be fired up, bringing more supply and helping to lower prices. The problem here is that such instant competition may not happen on very hot days when peak demand exceeds all available capacity – and certainly not until there is sufficient competition on the supply side.

An implication of these unique features is that electricity prices are much more likely to be driven by spot demand and supply considerations than some of the other energy commodities. We now turn to the forward curve.

Electricity forward curve

Although most risk professionals can recognise a forward curve when they see one in the financial markets, the notion of a forward curve is not so obvious in the context of the energy – especially power – markets. Often, the term is confused with the *price forecast* curves many utilities generate using forward-looking economic information, such as demand and supply variables. Strictly speaking, a *forward curve* is defined as one that allows market participants to lock in the indicated prices in advance at reasonable levels of liquidity. The forward curves for the NEPOOL (North-East Pool) and NYPP (New York Power Pool) hubs as of May 9, 1999, are shown in Tables 1 and 2 overleaf. Options are traded only on the NYPP. Note that the curve is available only for the next 12–18 months; longer maturities, if they exist, are simply not publicly observable. How are these forward prices set?

CLASSICAL ARBITRAGE
As we have argued, electricity is a very distinct type of commodity, and it is instructive to first review the classical arbitrage argument that is used to derive the forward price of oil. Suppose that the forward price of oil is too expensive relative to its spot price; it then pays to buy the oil now on the spot, store it and deliver it in the future. As long as the cost of "carry" (interest plus storage costs minus any convenience value from physically owning the oil) is less than the difference between the forward and the spot, an arbitrage profit can be made. Such a situation tends to draw more arbitrageurs into the market, who proceed to bid up the cheaper instrument and bid down the expensive one, eventually wip-

Table 1. NEPOOL

Month(s	Demand period	Bid (MWh)	Ask ($/MWh)
June			
E+0	5 × 16	$36.25	$37.00
E+0	5 × 8, 2 × 24	$24.00	$25.00
ICAP		$0.40	$0.50
July–August			
E+I	7 × 24	n/a	n/a
E+0	5 × 16	$53.00	$58.00
E+0	5 × 8, 2 × 24	$24.00	$26.00
ICAP		$0.50	$0.70
September			
E+0	5 × 16	$31.25	$31.75
ICAP	7 × 24	$0.40	$0.65
Q4			
E+0	5 × 16	$28.50	$29.75
E+0	5 × 8, 2 × 24	n/a	n/a
ICAP	7 × 24	$0.40	$0.60
2000			
E+I	7 × 24	n/a	n/a
E+0	5 × 16	$34.00	$35.50
E+0	5 × 8, 2 × 24	n/a	n/a
ICAP	7 × 24	$0.80	$1.25

Table 2: NYPP

Month(s)	Demand period	Bid (MWh)	Ask ($/MWh)
Frontier			
Bal May	5 × 16	$32.00	$36.00
Jun	5 × 16	$34.50	$37.00
Jul–Aug	5 × 16	$59.00	$64.00
Sep	5 × 16	$28.00	$30.25
Q4	5 × 16	$24.25	$26.25
Jan–Feb 2000	5 × 16	$29.00	$31.75
Mar 00	5 × 16	$25.00	$26.50
Apr 00	5 × 16	$23.00	$25.50
May 00	5 × 16	$26.00	$29.00
Cal 2000	5 × 16	$31.50	$35.00
Central			
Jul–Aug	5 × 16	$60.00	$65.00
ICAP			
Jun–Oct West NY		$0.50	$1.00
Nov–Mar East NY		$2.20	$2.50
Options			
$40DPC Jul–Aug	West NY	$21.00	$26.00
$50DPC Jul–Aug	West NY	$17.50	$22.00
$55DPC Jul–Aug	West NY	$15.00	$19.00
$65DPC Jul–Aug	West NY	$12.00	$15.00

Notation guide:

A × B denotes demand period as A days by B hours; eg 7 × 24 is 7 days by 24 hours

ATB = At the border

All prices are 100% firm system power except noted otherwise; eg 90% means that there is a 90% availability on the power

ICAP = Installed capacity

E = Energy

0 = Operable capacity

Installed capacity is priced as a function of kilowatt month when no power is associated with it

DPC = daily physical call

ing out the imbalance. If, on the other hand, the spot is too expensive relative to the forward – again by the amount of the carry costs – traders can and will short the spot and buy the forward, and the same conclusion holds. In the case of electricity, the absence of storage means that the first type of arbitrage cannot be performed. The second type of arbitrage is also not feasible, since selling the spot short is out of the question because borrowed spot electricity can not be replaced later.

Although storing and arbitraging electricity is clearly ruled out, there may be opportunities for some market participants to use one of the fuels that generate electricity to store and indulge in indirect arbitrage. For instance, if the forward price of electricity is too high relative to spot, a generation company may buy the fuel, store it and sell the expensive electricity forward. So long as the marginal cost of fuel, storage and generation is less than the spread between forward and spot, the company can lock in a sure profit. On the other hand, if the forward price of electricity is low relative to the cost of generating it by hoarding fuel, the company may just decide to buy power in the forward market and forgo generation altogether.

However, in contrast to other commodity or financial markets, the ability to undertake this type of carry arbitrage is not widespread in the electricity market. As is evident from the above argument, first and foremost the arbitrageur must have access to generation and storage facilities. Also, storage and generation costs may vary from company to company, giving rise to differing arbitrage opportunities for different players. The upshot of all this is that significant arbitrage opportunities may exist at various points in time and may persist for sufficiently long periods, so much so that arbitrage arguments alone are not sufficient to determine forward prices in the electricity market. At best, they can be viewed as setting fairly loose bounds for forward prices.

CONSTRUCTING A FORWARD CURVE

Given that liquidity in energy, and especially power, markets is limited to short maturities (12–18 months), a forward curve needs to be synthetically constructed from market data. Constructing a forward curve that is useful for trading and risk management purposes often involves an elaborate extrapolation exercise, perhaps using an econometric model. The resulting curve is typically partly market-based and partly model-based, and hence may not be entirely transactable. If a majority of price setters end up using similar econometric models – for example, mean-reverting – it is possible (but by no means guaranteed) that model-based forward prices will converge to market prices at the longer end of the curve. In any case, as the markets become deeper and more liquid, longer-dated instruments will begin to appear and the forward curve will become more market-based and less model-based in the course of time. While longer-dated contracts are currently transacted in over-the-counter (OTC) markets, the forward curves underlying these transactions are not publicly available.[2]

A current forward curve allows traders, marketers and asset owners to lock in today's prices into the future, but it is also important to understand the dynamics of these forward price changes. Figures 4–7 plot the forward contracts for on-peak firm power in PJM (Pennsylvania–New Jersey–Maryland) for the months of July, August, September and October. Note that the contract starts trading a few months before the month in question and ends before the contract month.

VOLATILITIES

In addition to the forward curve mentioned above, forward-looking volatilities at selected maturities are also necessary for pricing and risk management. There are essentially two approaches to obtaining these volatilities. The first involves obtaining historical forward prices at the maturity in question and computing the historical volatility, possibly by employing a volatility model such as Garch. Assuming that the historical volatility patterns are stable over time, these estimates could be used as proxies for future volatilities. In the second approach implied volatilities are obtained from available option contracts traded at these maturities (Table 2) using an option pricing model (eg modified Black–Scholes).

It is well known that in many markets, including commodity markets, implied volatilities incorporate all the information that is available from historical volatility estimates, and possibly more. This is a version of the "semi-strong" form of market efficiency touted in finance textbooks. Although the richness of the information content may appear to vindicate the implied volatility approach, there are a few caveats to consider. First, option price quotes for maturities longer than a year are even more difficult to obtain than forward prices. Second, the implied volatilities

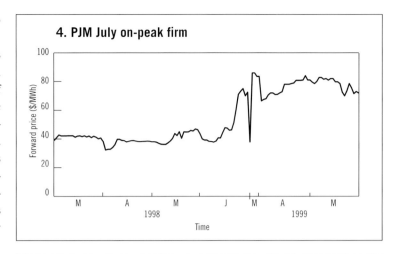

4. PJM July on-peak firm

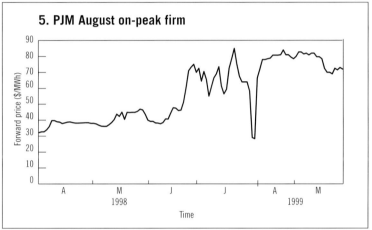

5. PJM August on-peak firm

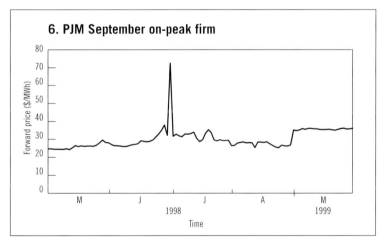

6. PJM September on-peak firm

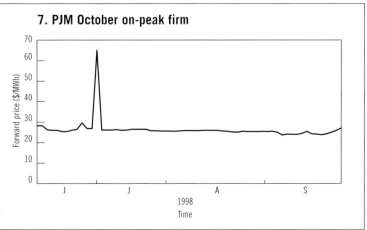

7. PJM October on-peak firm

are a function not only of the data but also of the option pricing model used, and hence are subject to so-called "model risk". For example, using a simple Black–Scholes model instead of the Black (1976) model – as some commercial software do – can yield quite different volatility estimates. This implies that first one must have an appropriate option pricing model, taking into account the proper price behaviour of the underlying forward, and available hedging opportunities. The third, and rarely mentioned, point is that the implied volatilities represent an average of the expected (spot) volatilities up to maturity. Finally, the implied volatilities can vary with whether the option is in-, at- or out-of-the money (the volatility smile/smirk). Liquidity, and consequently data reliability, is a problem in the case of out-of-the-money options.

Electricity forward curve models

The role of an econometric model, as mentioned above, is to extend the forward and volatility curves over longer maturities – at the cost of making certain assumptions. A number of models have been discussed in the literature.[3] Without pretending to be exhaustive, we discuss one such model below, before proposing a new one.

THE JUMP–DIFFUSION MODEL

The jump–diffusion model belongs to a category of models called three-factor models, so named because the spot price risk comes from three sources: a Brownian motion (diffusion); a Poisson jump process; and the size of the jump itself, which follows a lognormal process. All three processes are assumed to be independent.[4] The equation of motion for the spot price can be written as

$$dP_t = \mu P_t \, dt + \sigma P_t \, dz_t + (J - 1) \, P_t \, dq_t$$

where dP_t is the instantaneous change in the spot price, P_t; μ is the drift rate; σ is a volatility parameter; dz_t is a random variable that follows a standard Wiener process; J is a lognormal random variable that describes the size and the direction of the jumps, where $\ln(J)$ is distributed as $N(\alpha, \delta^2)$; and dq_t is a Poisson random variable that takes the value 1 if a jump takes place with probability $\lambda \, dt$, and zero otherwise.

The appeal of the jump–diffusion process is that it is able to take into account sudden and discrete events that may affect spot prices. For example, unscheduled outages in nuclear or coal base-load plants or transmission failures in the grid may cause supply-side shocks that are dis-

---

Table 3. Jump-diffusion model estimates for COB daily on-peak non-firm spot prices

Diffusion mean	−0.01
Diffusion volatility	0*
Jump rate	4.07
Jump mean	0*
Jump volatility	0.05

* Not statistically significant

---

crete and can be rather large. On the demand side, an unexpected warm or cold front moving into a major metropolitan area may cause sudden shift in the demand curve for electricity.

To apply the above specified jump–diffusion model, we examine the COB on-peak, non-firm spot prices from June 5, 1997, to June 5, 1998, as illustrated in Figure 1. The prices show a definite seasonal pattern, peaking in summer (possibly due to air-conditioning demand) but not much in the winter. The parameters of the jump–diffusion model specified above were estimated for these data using the maximum likelihood method. Intuitively, this method asks what set of parameters would give rise to the maximum likelihood of observing the given data. The method performs well and yields estimators that are consistent for "large" samples such as the one used here.

The results are given in Table 3. There is hardly any drift or volatility of significance in the pure diffusion component. The biggest explanatory variables seem to be the Poisson jump rate and the volatility of the magnitude of the jumps. This translates to a particularly high probability of a jump (90%) in any given period. Overall, the tests suggests that, at least during the period for which the data were obtained, the key determinants of the spot on-peak prices on the COB hub were either supply shocks or demand shocks or both.

MEAN-REVERTING HETEROSCEDASTIC
VOLATILITY MODEL

One of the striking aspects of electricity prices (at least, the spot prices) is that they are fairly stable at low price levels (eg $25/MWh) but become increasingly volatile at higher prices. In the language of statisticians, such a property of variable volatility is called heteroscedasticity. By combining a heteroscedastic volatility and the familiar mean-reversion, one can propose the following specification of the spot price dynamics:[5]

$$dP_t = \kappa(\mu - P_t) + \sigma(P_t - \underline{P})^\alpha \, dz_t$$

where dP_t is the instantaneous change in the

spot price, P_t; $\underline{P}$ is the absolute floor for the spot price; μ is the long-run mean; κ is the speed of mean-reversion; σ is a volatility scaling parameter; α is a parameter that describes the strength of the floor-reversion; and dz_t is a random variable that follows a standard Wiener process.

The first term captures the mean-reversion, while the second term captures heteroscedasticity. This specification is such that for $\alpha > 1$, spot prices will exhibit high volatility at higher levels of the spot price but low volatility near the floor levels, allowing them to stay above ("reflect off") the floor. Because the prices have a lower bound (theoretically, the marginal cost of generation) but no real upper bound, the model should be able to capture the extreme volatility exhibited by electricity spot prices. This lower bound is reflected by the spread option inherent in the operation of peaking generation units, which often (but not always) represent the marginal units in a stack. This model incorporates stochastic volatility, and in this respect is related to Garch-type models. The main difference from the Garch models is the floor-reflection property of the prices, which allows a more intuitive specification. Another advantage is that there is no need to specify seasonality separately, as the the price-dependence of the volatility will take care of this market characteristic. Finally, since for $\alpha = 0$ MRHV becomes a simple mean-reverting model, there is no need to specify separate models for oil, gas or other commodities in a firm's overall portfolio.

Note that it is a one-factor model in the sense that there is only one source of randomness. It is well known that in other markets (eg US Treasury), single-factor models fail to capture the richness of the entire forward curve dynamics. The forward curve for the mean-reverting heteroscedastic volatility (MRHV) model can be derived by performing some tedious stochastic calculus.[6] As is the case with these types of models, the derived forward curve will not fit all possible current market forward curve shapes exactly, but should provide good approximation.[7]

Figures 8–10 plot the daily historical on-peak, spot (mid-) prices at the PJM (firm), NEPOOL (non-firm) and MAIN (firm) hubs from January 1, 1996, to June 3, 1999. The data were obtained from Bloomberg LP. Note that the spot prices never fall below \$14/MWh and have risen as high as \$201 at PJM, "only" \$45 at NEPOOL and a whopping \$1,650 at MAIN during this time period. More interestingly, the spot prices seem

to be less volatile at low levels but appear to become more volatile at higher levels.

The discrete version of the MRHV model for spot prices was estimated for the PJM, NEPOOL and MAIN hubs using daily mid-price data from January 1, 1996, to June 3, 1999. The estimation procedure used here is generalised least squares, a version of the familiar ordinary least squares technique that involves volatility weighting.[8] The results are given in Table 4. In general, the model performs much better than a pure mean-reversion model. The floor price was preset at \$14/MWh, reflecting the lowest prices histori-

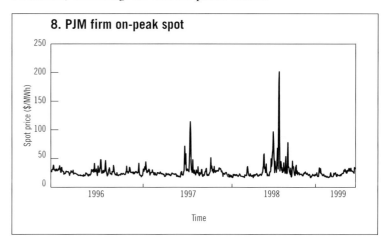

8. PJM firm on-peak spot

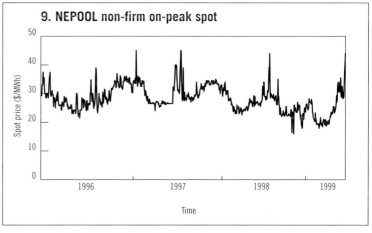

9. NEPOOL non-firm on-peak spot

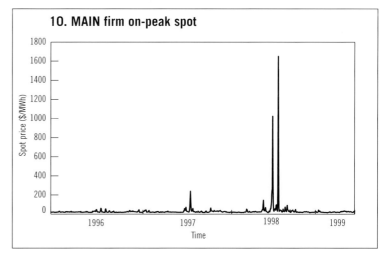

10. MAIN firm on-peak spot

254

POWER

FORWARD

CURVES:

A

MANAGERIAL

PERSPECTIVE

Table 4. MRHV model estimates for PJM, NEPOOL and MAIN daily firm (except NEPOOL) on-peak spot prices

	PJM	NEPOOL	MAIN
Long-run mean	$25.06	$23.88	$38.06
Speed of mean reversion	0.16	0.90	0.04*
Volatility	$0.04	$0.04	$0.10
Exponent	2	2	4
Floor price	$14.00	$14.00	$14.00

* Not statistically significant

cally observed in these hubs.[9] For simplicity, only (even) integer values of the exponent α were admitted. Note that the estimate of the exponent α for MAIN is 4, reflecting the recent higher levels of volatility there, while $\alpha = 2$ for PJM and NEPOOL. The test also confirms what is evident from Figures 1–3: mean-reversion appears to be strongest in the NEPOOL spot prices, whereas MAIN spot prices exhibit statistically insignificant mean-reversion. Although the MRHV model appears to capture the dynamics of electricity spot prices reasonably well, further tests directly comparing it with the standard Garch and the jump–diffusion models are required to verify its performance.

AN ECONOMETRIC MODEL OF FORWARD PRICES

Rather than model the spot prices first and then derive forward prices from them, one could model forward prices directly using historical data. This method has two advantages. First, it avoids the intermediate steps and goes directly to the heart of the matter. Second, and more subtle, some of the assumptions (eg arbitrage) required to move from a spot price model to the forward price model described above may not hold.[10]

We shall use the MRHV approach to model forward prices directly, using the July–August on-peak forward (OTC) contracts on PJM for 1998 and 1999. Referring to Figure 4, note that the July 1998 contract was trading peacefully until it hit the (now notorious) price spike in the third week of June. Interestingly, the forward market does exhibit a long memory, for the next July contract (1999) opened for trading in March with a large spike before settling down at a much higher average price ($77/MWh, versus $43/MWh in 1998). It appears that the price spike of June 1998 had a significant persistence effect.

Using the generalised least squares technique outlined above, the parameters were estimated

for the MRHV model, and the results are shown in Table 4. The exponent for the forward contract turns out to be 0.4, the long-run mean is estimated to be $51, and the daily volatility scaling parameter is $2. These are consistent with the high prices and high volatilities to be expected in peak summer months. Note that these estimates were obtained by combining 1998 and 1999 data. But a casual examination of Figure 4 reveals that a structural shift had occurred since the June 1998 peak, so strictly speaking the model should be estimated by omitting the pre-June 1998 data.[11]

APPLICATIONS OF THE FORWARD CURVE: A MANAGERIAL PERSPECTIVE

We now turn to the question of what all this fuss about electricity forward curves means for a senior manager. In short, the forward curve represents the basic building block for all valuation, trading, risk management and shareholder value management. Some applications of the forward curve in the new deregulated power markets are outlined below.

PLANT VALUATION

An important application of the forward curves for a power producer is in the valuation of a generating unit. A generation unit fuelled by a fossil fuel (ie a commodity) can be viewed as a series of spread options over the life of the plant. The value of the plant is given by

$$V = \sum_{t=1}^{T} \frac{Max(Powerprice_t - Fuelprice_t * Heatrate - O\&M,0)}{(1 + r_t)}$$

where T is the estimated life of the plant and r_t is its appropriate discount rate. This formula needs to be modified if the plant is not completely flexible and requires significant ramp-up time – for example, a coal-fired unit may need 16 hours of preheat time. In such cases it may be optimal for the plant to run even if the "option" is out of the money, as this loss can be offset by more efficient overall dispatching capabilities.[12] Such baseload plants are better modelled as forwards or call options.

The inputs for the spread option formula include the forward curves, especially the volatility term structure. Ideally, a Monte Carlo simulation should be used to perform a full valuation of the spread option.

CAPITAL BUDGETING

Forward curves are also useful in evaluating new

255

POWER
FORWARD
CURVES:
A
MANAGERIAL
PERSPECTIVE

projects for selection. The classical criteria for project selection include NPV (net present value) and IRR (internal rate of return) methods, which have the drawback of being static, subjective and not being tied to market prices. By directly incorporating market information from the forward curves, a much more market-based analysis can be performed.

Let us consider a hypothetical case in which the choice is between two gas turbines. Turbine A is a conventional unit with a heat rate of 10,000 MMBtu/MWh that can be fired up with very little lead time and shut down quickly. Turbine B also runs on gas but has a super-efficient heat rate of 6,500 MMBtu/MWh. However, to run it at this better rate, Turbine B needs to be in continuous operation and cannot be switched on or off at will. Both are rated at 100 MW but, while Turbine A costs $100 million, Turbine B is more expensive because of its superior technology, costing $120 million.

To choose between the two, a conventional analysis would run as follows. The average price of electricity for the next 10 years is projected to be $25/MWh, allowing for inflation at 2% a year. The price of natural gas is forecast to be $2.20/MMBtu, again inflated at 2% a year. The capacity utilisation of Turbine A, being a peaking unit, will be about 30%, whereas Turbine B will be run around the clock, approximately 85% of the time. A brief session with a calculator suggests that the present value of the revenue stream from Turbine B is higher than from Turbine A but that Turbine B is perhaps too costly to justify its recommendation.

This analysis correctly assumes that Turbine A will not be running all the time, but it misses a very important point. Turbine A will be optimally run only when prices peak (and are likely to exceed the assumed average price, $25/MWh), justifying the marginal cost of running the unit (fuel + variable O&M), and not when prices are low. This is the so-called spread option embedded in peaker units. In order to correctly take into account the prices at which Turbine A would run, one needs information on likely price levels into the future and, more importantly, on the future volatilities of prices, since the value of the spread option depends on the latter. The forward curve is precisely the source of such information.

PERFORMANCE MEASUREMENT

The application of forward curves to the capital budgeting process gives rise to interesting new issues in the area of managerial performance measurement and compensation. To appreciate this, note that the present value of the project calculated using forward curves can, and will, vary with fluctuations of the curve on a daily basis. Furthermore, as new information about various aspects of the project becomes available, it will give rise to a number of real options to increase or reduce the rate of investment or abandon the project altogether. This is to be expected, and is – at least conceptually – perfectly sound.

On a more practical level, however, many corporations may have difficulty evaluating the project-selection skills of their managers if the values of the chosen projects vary on a daily basis. It is important to recognise that the problem here has nothing to do with the methodology of using forward curves for valuation. If anything, it suggests a need for different benchmarking techniques. Rather than assessing the performance of a project in absolute terms, as is conventional, the firm needs to evaluate the success of the project on an ex ante basis, relative to the forward curves prevailing at the time the project selection was made. This is in some ways no different from evaluating hedges on an ex ante basis (did the hedge make sense at the time it was put on?) rather than on an ex post basis (did we lose money?).

There is another twist to performance measurement in this brave new world. As the project is essentially being "marked-to-market", it gives rise to a slew of real options that the management can then choose to exercise over the development cycle. The managers must also be evaluated on the basis of their skills in identifying, quantifying and exercising such options.

PRODUCT PRICING AND STRUCTURING

The electricity market is somewhat unique in the bewildering complexity of products, especially as regards the structure of power derivatives, that are currently being traded. Many of them involve "swing risk" (volumetric risk) and several layers of compound and path-dependent options. Many features, including the swing load features, are vestiges from a regulated past when pricing risk was virtually non-existent (except for rate payers) but which have nevertheless remained intact. In the new world of electricity deregulation these contracts are highly sensitive to pricing risk. While pricing models are still being developed to price the more complicated options, an important input for all of these mod-

256

**POWER
FORWARD
CURVES:
A
MANAGERIAL
PERSPECTIVE**

els will be the term structure of volatilities gleaned from forward curves. (The reader is referred to Chapter 3 of this volume for a more detailed discussion of the pricing and risk management of exotic energy and power derivatives.)

An example of a product that requires proper pricing is the full reserve requirements contract, which subjects the supplier to considerable swing risk. One version of the contract has a three-block structure for each billing cycle. This is designed to give adequate incentives to consumers to smooth out their peak load, which can be taxing on the power supplier. An indicated pricing for the three blocks is as follows:

❏ $55/MWh for the first 150 hours;
❏ $45/MWh for the next 150 hours; and
❏ $38/MWh thereafter.

The first block is priced at a flat $55/MWh assuming a peak load of 20 MW. Depending on the actual usage, a credit is given against this flat charge during the second block of time. If total usage exceeds 20 × 150 MWh during the second block, the additional consumption is charged at $45/MWh. If it does not, this credit is carried over and eventually wiped out in the third block, when the $38/MWh tariff applies. With this type of a contract there is a strong incentive for the end-user to stay within the peak load of 20 MW. But how do we know that the three prices and the block lengths are optimal? By combining the load forecast information and forward curve information, the contract can be valued using a Monte Carlo simulation. By varying the pricing and block parameters, the optimal contract can be designed.

ASSET OPTIMISATION

As pointed out earlier, the physical generation assets can be monetised by treating them as either spread options or forward contracts. The optimisation of all generation and storage assets

can be achieved by optimally synchronising the real-time dispatching of the units and fuel storage decisions with the trading of electricity and fuels. Many utilities have begun to recognise the importance of asset optimisation by setting up separate asset optimisation groups with responsibility for trading, storage and dispatching units. An important ingredient in the entire asset optimisation activity is the availability of forward curves, including the term structure of volatilities and forward pricing models.

VALUATION OF TRANSMISSION OPTIONS

As mentioned earlier, transmission is a scarce commodity and, hence, the proper valuation of transmission capacity is important. As in the case of the generation assets, the transmission capacity can be valued as a spread option between the spot prices at the two nodes of a transmission line. However, this is more complicated than the generation option, since the ability to exercise the transmission option is also linked to exercising the option of using different generation units owned by the same utility. For example, as the spread between the two nodes widens, a utility will be able to bring on line other (back-up) units with higher marginal costs. This gives rise to a series of compound options, as shown in Figure 11. Clearly, pricing of the transmission option requires forward curve information, especially about the volatilities.

RISK MANAGEMENT

As is well known, a major prerequisite for risk management is the availability of not only the current forward curve but also a model of forward curve dynamics. First, the positions have to be marked-to-market using the current forward curve. Then, as discussed in Chapter 8, the portfolio value-at-risk (VAR) must be calculated, using Monte Carlo simulation or other methods, taking into account the dynamics of the forward curve. In addition, stress-testing and scenario analyses also require the forward curve model. These help to set the trading limits for individual positions as well as for the whole trading portfolio. Once the VAR has been calculated and the position limits set, the risk capital can be allocated to portfolios and sub-portfolios. This allows the measurement of performance of the asset optimisation group and its various portfolios by properly benchmarking them. In short, a host of very important risk management activities are predicated on the availability of good forward curve information.

11. Transmission options

257

POWER
FORWARD
CURVES:
A
MANAGERIAL
PERSPECTIVE

Future directions

As more data become available the statistical models proposed here and elsewhere can be fine-tuned to produce better forward curves. Ultimately, the true forward curve is a tradable curve; it will not become available until longer-dated and more liquid transactions become commonplace. Because of the difficulty of arbitraging in the power markets, statistical models borrowed from other commodity applications that implicitly use arbitrage arguments will continue to remain suspect. Nevertheless, they can serve as useful benchmarks on which market participants can base their longer-dated transactions.

Price seasonality is likely to remain in the intermediate term as generation assets are restructured and new merchant plants come on line. For summer price spikes to disappear completely, a number of conditions must be satisfied. End-user consumption must be truly interruptible and properly market-priced. The costs of peaking and stand-by capacity must decline substantially to allow units to follow the spiking load closely. The promise of more investment in transmission capacity, and better incentives for such investment, may alleviate price squeezes in congested regions. Finally, proper credit risk management throughout the industry can go a long way towards alleviating the credit risk that often exacerbates price spikes.

1 *Currently, the only feasible method of "storing" high-voltage electricity in bulk is by means of a pumped storage mechanism. Electricity is used to pump water into a reservoir on higher ground, which can later be run off to generate electricity. Two factors limit such schemes. First, pumped storages typically have limited capacity. Second, the laws of thermodynamics mean that a substantial amount of energy is lost in the hysteresis process.*

2 *Understandably, the traders participating in these transactions are reluctant to reveal their forward curves.*

3 *For a recent collection of technical essays on modelling power prices, see* Energy Modelling and the Management of Uncertainty, *London: Risk Publications, 1999.*

4 *Instead of a constant volatility in the Brownian motion, the volatility can be assumed to be stochastic as well, which gives rise to a Garch specification. See Kaminski (1997).*

5 *Although I am not aware of any previous work using this specification for modelling electricity spot prices, the elements of mean-reversion or heteroscedasticity are hardly novel in the econometric literature (see Greene, 1997).*

6 *As usual, further assumptions are needed. See endnote 10.*

7 *The fit can be made more precise by modifying the model to allow for the drift term to be a function of time, ie $\mu(t)$, at the risk of additional complexity.*

8 *Alternatively, one could use the method of maximum likelihood estimation. Each method has strengths and weak-nesses, a discussion of which is beyond the scope of this chapter.*

9 *The floor price could also be directly estimated from the model. Note that it is easier to specify exogenously the floor price than, say, the long-run average price, as is required in some commercial software that incorporates both short-term and long-term means.*

10 *It is often suggested that moving from a specification such as a mean-reversion model for spot prices to the forward curve is strictly a matter of solving some messy stochastic partial differential equations which the busy reader would be grateful to avoid (Pilipovic, 1997). This is misleading, as the solutions presume the existence of a unique equivalent martingale measure, which cannot be guaranteed if the market is not complete – which, as we have already argued, the electricity market patently is not. In plain English, what this means is that such solutions, while mathematically elegant, cannot be representations of the true market prices when, as discussed, arbitrage arguments do not apply. The same criticism holds for most of the real-option pricing models.*

11 *Of course, this is not statistically sound and falls under the sins of "data mining".*

12 *Alternatively, the decision to shut down a coal plant can be viewed as an American option, which can be exercised early, but the restart can be costly as reflected by the time delay. Some independent service operators allow utilities to fudge the marginal costs of the plants they bid into the pool to prevent some base-load plants from cycling.*

258

POWER
FORWARD
CURVES:
A
MANAGERIAL
PERSPECTIVE

BIBLIOGRAPHY

Gabillon, J., 1995, "Analysing the Forward Curve", in *Managing Energy Price Risk,* First Edition, Risk Publications, London, pp. 29-38.

Greene, W., 1997, *Econometric Analysis,* Third Edition, Prentice Hall, New York.

Kaminski, V., 1997, "The Challenge of Pricing and Managing Energy Derivatives", in *The US Power Market: Restructuring and Risk Management,* Risk Publications, London, pp. 149-71.

Leong, K., 1997, "The Forward Curve in the Electricity Market", in *The US Power Market: Restructuring and Risk Management,* Risk Publications, London, pp. 133-47.

Pilipovic, D., 1997, *Energy Risk: Valuing and Managing Energy Derivatives,* McGraw-Hill, New York.

Arbitrage-Free Valuation of Energy Derivatives

Kaushik Amin, Victor Ng and Craig Pirrong[1]
Lehman Brothers; Goldman Sachs; Washington University in St Louis

The great expansion in the variety and the volume of trading in energy derivatives in recent years has created a need for new analytical tools to price energy-contingent claims. In this chapter, we review some of the relevant techniques available in the literature to value energy claims, and we develop an arbitrage-free framework to value energy derivatives.

In particular, we focus on models that take the current term structure of futures or forward prices as given, and then value options and other types of derivatives based on this term structure. The use of the entire term structure makes the models more general than the standard Black (1976) model that is often used to price commodity-contingent claims. Moreover, the simultaneous modelling of the evolution of the entire term structure unifies the pricing and risk management of a portfolio of energy derivative positions. This is of great practical importance to the market participants who trade these claims.

Since we are interested in valuing claims that are based on the entire term structure of futures prices, we first need to understand the relationship between futures contracts of different maturities. This will provide some guidelines on how we can model the evolution of futures prices. Therefore, in the first section of this chapter, we discuss the implications of the theory of storage for the relationship between spot, forward and futures prices, and how that relationship is affected by fundamental supply and demand conditions. In particular, since supply and demand conditions for energy products have strong seasonal elements, the relationship between the spot and futures prices will be seasonal as well. These patterns need to be modelled and explicitly considered in the pricing of energy derivatives.

Furthermore, such relationships can be stochastic in nature, as supply and demand conditions change unpredictably – and this must also be incorporated into the valuation exercise. Therefore, in the second section of this chapter, we present an extension of the framework in Black (1976) which allows for seasonality in a deterministic way. A closed-form solution for the price of a European futures option is given for a one-factor model that only permits parallel shifts in the term structure of futures prices. A binomial-tree approach for the valuation of American options is also introduced. Further, the valuation of options in a multi-factor model using a Monte Carlo approach, such as that described in Cortazar and Schwartz (1992), is discussed.

In the third section of this chapter we consider the more general case, in which the relationship between the spot and futures prices is stochastic. A two-factor model which extends the Gibson and Schwartz (1990) model is presented. However, in contrast to Gibson and Schwartz, we model the evolution of the entire term structure of futures prices.[2] The model permits non-parallel shifts in the term structure; a closed-form solution for the price of a European futures option is provided, and a tree approach to valuing American options is also introduced.

Relationship between the spot, forward and futures prices

A distinguishing feature of the energy futures market is the behaviour of the term structure of futures prices. This term structure describes how futures prices depend upon time-to-contract expiration. For energy products, the term structure exhibits a variety of shapes. Moreover, the energy futures term structure varies substantially and unpredictably over time.

Given that the behaviour of the term structure is such a salient feature of energy prices, a contingent claim pricing model should be predicated upon a firm understanding of the factors that determine this behaviour. This section provides an analysis of the relationship between spot, forward and futures prices, and a brief discussion of the factors that determine the evolution of the term structure of energy futures prices. The sections below build upon this theory of the term structure to derive contingent claim pricing models that are applicable to energy derivatives.

Let $S(t)$ be the current spot price of a commodity and $F(t,T)$ be the forward price at date t to deliver one unit of the commodity at date T. For simplicity, we assume that the commodity can be delivered against the forward contract only on the expiration date T. We also assume that there exists a forward price for every maturity date T up to some finite maturity date T_m.

Since we focus on the term structure of futures prices, and its effect on the valuation of energy derivatives, we further assume that interest rates are known (deterministic). Given deterministic interest rates, forward prices will equal futures prices, as described by Jarrow and Oldfield (1981). Therefore, the futures price of the commodity at date t for delivery at date T is also equal to $F(t,T)$. This assumption of deterministic interest rates can be relaxed, as described by Amin and Bodurtha (1994), only at the expense of added complexity.

Arbitrage implies a mathematical relationship between futures prices with different maturities, and between spot and futures prices. The textbook example of such a relationship is the traditional "cost-of-carry" model, which states that the futures price must exceed the spot price by the cost of carrying inventory. Formally, let $r(u)$ be the instantaneous forward interest rate at date u, and $w(u)$ be the instantaneous storage cost at date u measured as a proportion of the spot price, which is also known at time t. Then,

$$F(t,T) = S(t)\exp\left[\int_t^T [r(u) + w(u)]du\right] \quad (1)$$

An examination of spot and futures prices reveals that this relationship seldom, if ever, holds in the energy markets. With a few exceptions (such as occurred in 1986, or late 1993 and early 1994 when the price of oil collapsed), energy futures prices are typically lower than predicted by the simple cost-of-carry model. This is because of the phenomenon known as the "convenience yield", described in other chapters.

The convenience yield affects the relationship between the energy spot and futures prices in

the same way that a dividend yield affects the relation between the value of a stock index and a futures contract on that index. Specifically, it drives the futures price below the level implied by the pure cost-of-carry model because it reduces the opportunity cost of holding inventories.

Formally, one may define $y(t,u)$ as the instantaneous convenience yield, as perceived by the marginal storers at date t, arising from having a unit of the commodity in inventory at date u. The relation between the spot and futures prices is then given by:

$$F(t,T) = S(t)\exp\left[\int_t^T [r(u) + w(u) - y(t,u)]du\right] \quad (2)$$

To avoid excessive notation, we can rewrite the above equation as:

$$F(t,T) = S(t)\exp\left[\int_t^T [r(u) - z(t,u)]du\right] \quad (3)$$

where $z(t,u) = y(t,u) - w(u)$ is now the instantaneous forward convenience yield net of physical storage cost. To avoid confusion, we will still refer to $z(t,u)$ as the instantaneous forward convenience yield. Further, $z(t) \equiv z(t,t)$ will be referred to as the spot convenience yield.

Intuitively, the above relationship suggests that, in equilibrium, the marginal holder of inventories must be indifferent as to whether she holds the spot commodity or a futures contract. If this investor holds the spot, she has to finance the initial purchase price $S(t)$ at prevailing interest rates, but she also receives the convenience yield of holding the spot asset in inventory. If expression (3) holds, the payoffs to the futures contract and a position in the spot commodity are identical over the interval from t to T. Put another way, in equilibrium the convenience yield earned on stocks in inventory exactly offsets the expected capital loss on these stocks when (3) holds.

It is evident from an examination of (3) that the behaviour of the convenience yield has an important effect on the dynamics of energy futures prices, and therefore upon the prices of energy options, swaps, and swaptions as well.

An economic model called the "theory of storage" has important implications regarding the evolution of the convenience yield. These implications can be incorporated into a model for pricing energy contingent claims. Specifically, the theory predicts that the convenience yield should increase as supplies decline and/or demand increases. This is true because the convenience yield measures the marginal value of a unit of the commodity in store. Given demand, this marginal value should increase as the available supply declines. Similarly, given the avail-

261

ARBITRAGE-
FREE
VALUATION
OF ENERGY
DERIVATIVES

able supply, this marginal value should increase as the demand for the commodity increases. This also necessarily implies a relation between the level of inventory and the convenience yield. In particular, the convenience yield should vary inversely with the level of inventory.[3]

As a concrete example, consider the heating oil and natural gas markets. During a cold snap, the demand for these products increases. This is typically associated with a decrease in the level of inventory, an increase in the overall levels of natural gas and heating oil prices and an increase in convenience yields. That is, during cold snaps the price of gas or heating oil for immediate delivery increases relative to its price for deferred delivery. In this situation, the term structure of futures prices exhibits less "carry", or a more pronounced backwardation.

Moreover, since demand for some energy products (especially natural gas and heating oil) is seasonal, this relation between demand and the convenience yield implies that the term structure of futures prices may exhibit pronounced seasonalities. For example, the ratio between the January and March heating oil futures prices is typically greater than the ratio between the March and June heating oil futures prices. This pattern reflects the fact that the demand for heating oil is high in the winter months, and low in the summer months.

Furthermore, since supply and demand vary unpredictably, the convenience yield should vary unpredictably as well. Uncertain and changing weather conditions are primary sources of convenience yield variability in some energy products. Similarly, unexpected disruption of supply, such as that caused by the Gulf War, or the current problems in oil refineries in California, have caused pronounced shifts in the shape of the term structure in the past. Business cycle fluctuations can also unexpectedly change the term structure. All else equal, an unexpected increase in aggregate economic activity tends to cause a rise in convenience yields.

No discussion of the supply conditions in the energy markets would be complete without mentioning the effects of the Organisation of Petroleum Exporting Countries (OPEC). The collapse of the cartel in 1986 caused an unexpected glut of oil which drove down the general level of oil prices and forced the crude oil futures price term structure into a nearly full "carry" situation. A similar glut in early 1994 had a similar effect on the level and shape of the crude oil term structure.

Finally, the convenience yield should be mean-reverting. That is, if the convenience yield is unusually high (low) at time t, it should tend to decline (increase) as time progresses after t. This mean reversion reflects the ability of economic agents to adjust supply and demand over time. For example, a high convenience yield for heating oil implies that inventories are very valuable. Refiners can respond to such a situation by increasing production runs, or perhaps activating idle capacity, in order to expand output and replenish stocks. These activities tend to reduce the convenience yield, but they cannot be effected instantaneously. Thus, a large increase or decrease in the convenience yield tends to induce consumption and production responses that gradually drive the yield back towards a "normal" level. The expectation of a long-run adjustment process also tends to make the short end of the term structure more volatile than the long end.[4]

In the next section of this chapter, we will discuss the valuation of energy derivatives when the term structure of convenience yields is deterministic, but can exhibit seasonality. In the following section, we will consider the more general case when the convenience yields are stochastic and mean reverting.

Option valuation with deterministic convenience yields

The simplest framework used to value general commodity options is that of Black (1976). Some additional details on the valuation of American options in this framework are given in Brenner, Courtadon and Subrahmanyam (1985). This framework can be used to value energy options. However, Black (1976) focuses only on the valuation of options based on a single futures price.

In the first subsection immediately below, we will modify Black's framework in a simple manner to incorporate the entire term structure of futures prices in the spirit of term-structure models by Ho and Lee (1986), Heath, Jarrow and Morton (1992), and Amin and Jarrow (1991). Matching the initial term structure and modelling the evolution of the entire term structure of futures prices in a consistent way are important to guarantee that the model is arbitrage free, and that it can be applied to more general types of options such as American options on the spot price or swaptions – which cannot be valued in the Black (1976) framework. The subsections after this will examine, in turn, the valuation of European-type contracts; American-type options; and the valuation of options in a multifactor model, like that in Cortazar and Schwartz (1992), using a Monte Carlo approach.

AN EXTENSION OF THE BLACK (1976) FRAMEWORK

Since futures prices of different maturities are related indirectly through the spot-futures parity relation expressed in equation (3), one approach when building a consistent model for the evolution of the entire term structure of futures prices is to specify the dynamics of the spot price and the term structure of convenience yields to preclude arbitrage.

Initially, we assume that the convenience yields are deterministic. In this case, specifying the dynamics of the spot price and the initial term structure of convenience yields completely specifies the model, since the futures prices at future dates can be determined from the spot/futures parity relation (3) and the known convenience yields. In this setup, the spot price and the futures prices of all maturities are governed by the same underlying source of uncertainty. The model is based on a single risk factor and, therefore, all the futures prices are instantaneously perfectly correlated. In practice, we would observe futures prices in the market and back out the convenience yields to ensure that they are consistent with market futures prices as described below.

Let the spot price at date t evolve over time according to the stochastic differential equation:

$$dS(t) = \mu(t)S(t)dt + \sigma S(t)dW_1(t) \qquad (4)$$

where $\mu(t)$ is the deterministic drift of the spot price, σ is the constant instantaneous volatility, and $W_1(t)$ is a Brownian motion. It is possible to permit σ to be a deterministic function of time without changing the essence of the arguments to follow. For simplicity, we will initially maintain the constant volatility assumption. Writing the spot price process in stochastic integral form, we have:

$$S(t) = S(0)\exp\left[\int_0^t \left(\mu(u) - \sigma^2/2\right)du + \sigma W_1(t)\right] \quad (5)$$

Since $W_1(t)$ is normally distributed with mean 0 and variance t, the logarithm of the relative spot price (S(t)/S(0)) at date t is normally distributed with mean $\int_0^t(\mu(u) - \sigma^2/2)du$ and variance $\sigma^2 t$.

The theory of storage developed in the previous section implies that the forward price at date 0 for delivery at date T is given by the relation:

$$F(0,T) = S(0)\exp\left[\int_0^T\left(r(u) - z(0,u)\right)du\right] \qquad (6)$$

where $z(0,u)$ is the forward convenience yield at date 0 for maturity date u and $r(u)$ is the spot interest rate at date u. Since we assume that interest rates are deterministic, $r(u)$ is equal to the current instantaneous forward interest rate for maturity u. Therefore, the current term structure of interest rates is easily incorporated. Given the current spot price and the term structure of forward or futures prices for every maturity, we can compute the initial term structure of convenience yields from equation (6).

At any future date t, given the spot price and the assumption of deterministic convenience yields and interest rates, the term structure of futures prices for all maturities can be computed using the theory of storage relation:

$$F(t,T) = S(t)\exp\left[\int_t^T\left(r(u) - z(t,u)du\right)\right]. \qquad (7)$$

With deterministic convenience yields, $z(t,u) = z(0,u)$.

Therefore, to compute option prices, it is sufficient to model the evolution of the spot price. All of the futures prices can be computed using the storage relation in (7).

To understand the dynamics of the futures prices implied by equation (7), we will now write down the stochastic integral representation for all the futures prices. Using (7),

$$d\log F(t,T) = d\log S(t) - \left[r(t) - z(t,t)\right]dt \qquad (8)$$

Substituting for $d\log S(t)$ from (4), we obtain

$$d\log F(t,T) = \\ \left[\mu(t) - \sigma^2/2 - r(t) + z(t,t)\right]dt + \sigma dW_1(t) \qquad (9)$$

or, in stochastic integral form,

$$F(t,T) = F(0,T) \\ \exp\left[\int_0^t\left(\mu(u) - \sigma^2/2 - r(u) + z(u,u)\right)du + \sigma dW_1(t)\right] \qquad (10)$$

Therefore, given the futures price for maturity T at the initial date 0, the logarithm of the relative futures price (F(t,T)/F(0,T)) for that maturity at any subsequent date t is normal with mean $\int_0^t(\mu(u) - \sigma^2/2 - r(u) + z(u,u))du$ and variance $\sigma^2 t$.

A crucial feature of this framework is that the futures prices of all maturities are governed by the same shock $W_1(t)$. Therefore, the model is based on a single risk factor and the futures prices of all maturities are instantaneously, perfectly correlated. If the volatility parameter σ is independent of the futures maturity date T, then

263

ARBITRAGE-
FREE
VALUATION
OF ENERGY
DERIVATIVES

it is apparent from (9) that the futures term structure is subject only to parallel shocks. In that sense, our model is analogous to the Ho and Lee (1986) model of the term structure of interest rates.

Another possible approach is to specify the model directly in terms of the different futures prices, and to simply define the spot price as $S(t) = F(t,t)$. That is, we can specify the entire futures term structure as:

$$d\log F(t,T) = \left[\alpha(t,T) - \sigma^2/2\right]dt + \sigma dW_1(t) \quad (11)$$

or

$$F(t,T) = \quad (12)$$
$$F(0,T)\exp\left[\int_0^t \alpha(u,T) - \sigma^2/2\right]du + \sigma dW_1(t)$$

The entire term structure of futures prices is governed by the same Brownian motion $W_1(t)$. The link between the specifications specified by (12) and (9) is readily apparent if we simply redefine $\alpha(u,T)$ in equation (12) to be $\mu(u) - r(u) + z(u,u)$. In this case, the two specifications are equivalent. Further, the term structure of convenience yields in (12) is given implicitly by the relation:

$$F(t,T) = F(t,t)\exp\left[\int_t^T (r(u) - z(t,u))du\right] \quad (13)$$

In this framework, we can also permit the futures prices of different maturities to be affected differently by the shock $W_1(t)$ by specifying σ to be a function of the futures maturity T. However, the futures prices are still instantaneously perfectly correlated. In this case, we obtain a one-factor version of the model in Cortazar and Schwartz (1992). To permit independent variation in futures prices of different maturities, we can add additional Brownian motions on the right-hand side in (11), with different volatility coefficients for different maturities. For example, consider the following specification for futures prices:

$$d\log F(t,T) =$$
$$\left[\alpha(t,T) - \sigma_1^2(t,T)/2 - \sigma_2^2(t,T)/2\right]dt \quad (14)$$
$$+ \sigma_1(t,T)dW_1(t) + \sigma_2(t,T)dW_2(t)$$

This specification permits futures prices to be affected by two independent shocks (Brownian motions) $W_1(t)$ and $W_2(t)$. Each of these shocks can impact futures contracts of different maturities in different ways. That is, the volatility corresponding to each of these shocks can be different for different maturities. Therefore, we represent each of the volatilities $\sigma_1(t,T)$ and $\sigma_2(t,T)$ as explicit functions of the futures maturity. These

volatility functions can be determined by a principal component analysis or a maximum likelihood factor analysis, as in Cortazar and Schwartz (1992). Furthermore, in a more general setup, the number of independent shocks (factors) that affects the entire term structure of forward prices can also be estimated jointly with the volatility functions.

The model specified directly in terms of the futures prices, as in (14), is very general. However, for the valuation of more complicated derivatives such as swaptions or American options, it is not easily amenable to numerical computations and requires the use of tedious procedures such as Monte Carlo simulation or path-dependent models (see Amin and Bodurtha, 1994) except under restrictive specifications of the type specified in the penultimate section of this chapter. A brief description of the Monte Carlo simulation method to value European-style options is given later in this section.

Furthermore, computing American option prices is difficult. In contrast, our simple model represented by (4) and (9) or (11) is easily amenable to computations for most kinds of derivatives, as we will show in the next subsection of this chapter.

The major innovation in our framework, as compared to Black (1976), is its simultaneous modelling of the evolution of the entire futures term structure using (10), conditional upon the initial futures term structure (or the convenience yields). This feature permits the valuation of options on futures with different maturities, options on the spot asset, commodity swaptions etc in a single unified framework. It also permits us to hedge all these claims within a single "book". This feature is in the spirit of Ho and Lee (1986) and Heath, Jarrow and Morton (1992), who take the initial term structure of interest rates as given and then model the simultaneous evolution of the entire term structure of interest rates. The specific model developed above is a special case of the model in Amin and Jarrow (1991) which contains a stochastic term structure of interest rates, a stochastic asset and a stochastic term structure of yields. Our model obtains if we assume a deterministic yield and deterministic interest rates in the Amin and Jarrow (1991) framework. The model is similar to that proposed by Jamshidian (1992).

This completes the description of our model setup. Now we will focus on the valuation of options based on the term structure of futures prices.

RISK-NEUTRAL VALUATION OF EUROPEAN OPTIONS

We will refer to the economic model described so far as the "true model" or the "true economy". However, for the purpose of option valuation, we will transform the true economy into a risk-neutral economy. This transformation is now the standard technique for option valuation. For a description of this technique, see Jarrow and Rudd (1983).

In the risk-neutral economy, investors value all future cash flows at their expected values, discounted back to the current date using the risk-free interest rate. Alternatively, the expected return on all assets (both risky and risk-free) in this risk-neutral economy equals the riskless rate of return. Therefore, once the transformation to the risk-neutral economy is accomplished, we can value an option by computing its expected payoff when it is exercised, and then discounting this payoff to the current date using the riskless interest rate. In our model, there is only one source of uncertainty, $W_1(t)$, affecting the entire term structure of futures prices. Therefore, we can replicate the cash flows from any option dependent on the term structure of futures prices by dynamically trading a riskless bond and a single futures contract. This condition implies that our economic model is dynamically complete and permits the construction of the risk-neutral economy. We now describe its construction.

Since the futures contract does not require an initial investment and continuously pays the change in the futures price, in a risk-neutral world, the expected change in the futures price must be zero. In the risk-neutral economy, the futures prices of all maturities therefore satisfy the equation:

$$dF(t,T)/F(t,T) = \sigma dW_1^*(t) \qquad (15)$$

where $W_1^*(t)$ is a Brownian motion in the risk-neutral economy.

Similarly, since the spot asset requires an initial investment equal to the spot price, unlike the futures contract, an investment in the spot asset must earn a return equal to the riskless return less the convenience yield earned from holding the riskless asset. That is, the spot price distribution is specified by:

$$dS(t)/S(t) = \left[r(t) - z(t,t)\right]dt + \sigma dW_1^*(t) \qquad (16)$$

or

$$d\log S(t) = \left[r(t) - z(t,t) - \sigma^2/2\right]dt + \sigma dW_1^*(t) \qquad (17)$$

Since investors are risk-neutral in this economy, options can be valued by their expected discounted payoffs. A European call option with maturity date τ on the futures contract with futures maturity T will have a price given by:

$$c[t,F(t,T)] = E_t^*\left[\exp\left[-\int_t^\tau r(u)du\right]Max\left[F(\tau,T) - K,0\right]\right] \qquad (18)$$

where K is the strike price of the option and E is the conditional expectation given the information set at date t under the risk-neutral distributions given by equations (15) and (16).

By substituting the futures price distribution from (15) into (18) and simplifying, we obtain:

$$c[t,F(t,T)] = \exp\left[-\int_t^\tau r(u)du\right]\left[F(t,T)N(d_1) - KN(d_2)\right] \qquad (19)$$

where $N(.)$ is the normal cumulative distribution function,

$$d_1 = \left[\log[F(t,T)/K + \sigma^2(\tau - t)/2]/\left[\sigma\sqrt{(\tau - t)}\right]\right]$$

and

$$d_2 = d_1 - \sigma\sqrt{(\tau - t)}$$

Similarly, a European futures put option has a value:

$$p[t,F(t,T)] = \exp\left[-\int_t^\tau r(u)du\right]\left[KN(-d_2) - F(t,T)N(-d_1)\right] \qquad (20)$$

Since the futures price equals the spot price at the futures maturity, a European call (put) option on the spot commodity has the same value as a European futures call (put) option with the same maturity if the underlying futures maturity is the same as the option maturity. We can also rewrite these formulae in terms of the spot price by substituting equation (7) into the above formulae.

It is interesting to note that the formulae (19) and (20) for the European call and put options on the spot and the futures are identical to those in Black (1976). Further, they still hold even if the model for the evolution of futures prices is specified as a multifactor Cortazar and Schwartz (1992) model, as in a K-factor version of equation (14). All we require is that the volatility functions $\sigma_j(.)$ be a function only of calendar time and maturity. Then, the futures price of a given maturity is lognormal and European call and put prices at date t are given by (19) and

265

ARBITRAGE-
FREE
VALUATION
OF ENERGY
DERIVATIVES

(20) with σ^2 replaced by the average proportional variance of the futures price during the remaining life of the option, that is:

$$\int_t^\tau Var\big[dF(t,T)/F(t,T)\big]/(\tau - t) \quad (21)$$

The key is that this variance is deterministic, and therefore can be computed at the current date t. For additional details, see Amin and Jarrow (1991).

VALUATION OF AMERICAN OPTIONS AND OTHER OPTIONS

Most listed and OTC options are of the American type, whereby the owner is permitted to exercise the option at any date prior to maturity. Further, closed-form solutions cannot be derived for other types of derivative securities such as swaptions. In this section, therefore, we show how our simple model can be discretised so that option values for which closed-form solutions are not available can also be computed.

To value an American option, we need to evaluate the expression:

$$C(t) = max_\theta E_t^*\left[exp\left[-\int_t^\theta r(u)du\right]g(\theta)\right] \quad (22)$$

Where $g(\theta)$ is the cashflow to the American option if exercised at date θ and the maximum is taken over all possible early exercise strategies θ. For example, one possible early exercise strategy is to exercise the option the first time that it crosses a particular boundary in the futures price versus time state space. The standard technique to compute option values is to approximate the spot price or futures price distribution by a discrete binomial-type model. The option value at the option maturity date τ is known as a function of the spot or futures price at that date. Given the terminal option prices, we can obtain the option price by working backwards in time through the tree representing the state space of the futures prices over time. The option value at any given node in the tree is equal to the maximum of the value if exercised at the current node, and the expected value in the next period, discounted back to the current period.

Consider an option with maturity τ years. Suppose we wish to value this option using a discrete approximation with N time steps. Therefore, the length of each time step is:

$$h = \tau/N \quad (23)$$

The spot commodity is the primary security in our framework. All futures (forward) prices can be computed as a function of the spot price using equation (7). Therefore, to value any claim,

it is sufficient to build a discrete-time model which approximates the risk-neutral spot price distribution given by:

$$S(t) =$$
$$S(0)exp\left[\int_0^t\big[r(u) - z(u,u) - \sigma^2/2\big]du + \sigma W_1^*(t)\right] \quad (24)$$

Over a small time interval of duration h, the commodity price change can be represented by the equation:

$$S(t+h) =$$
$$S(t)exp\Big[\int_t^{t+h}\big[r(u) - z(u,u) - \sigma^2/2\big]du$$
$$+\sigma\big[W_1^*(t+h) - W_1^*(t)\big]\Big] \quad (25)$$

This distribution can be approximated with a binomial distribution given by:[5]

$$S(t = h) =$$
$$S(t)exp\big[\mu*(t)h + \sigma\sqrt{h}\big] \text{ with prob } \frac{1}{2}$$
$$S(t)exp\big[\mu*(t)h - \sigma\sqrt{h}\big] \text{ with prob } \frac{1}{2} \quad (26)$$

where,

$$\mu*(t)h = \int_t^{t+h}\big[r(u) - z(u,u) - \sigma^2/2\big]du \quad (27)$$

is the drift of the term inside the exponent in (25). Figure 1 depicts the evolution of the commodity price using this binomial distribution (26) over three periods, each of length h.

Any option can now be valued on the state space tree depicted by Figure 1 overleaf and (26). We first compute the value of the option at each of the nodes at maturity as a function of the spot commodity price at that node. If the option value depends on the futures or forward prices, then these prices can be computed using the cost-of-carry relationship in (7). Then, we step back one time-step and value the option as the expected value in the next time period, discounted back to the current time period. That is, when C(t) is the value of the option at time t, the computation of option prices is given by the equation:

$$C(t) = E_t^*\left[C(t+h)exp\left[-\int_t^{t+h}r(u)du\right]\right] \quad (28)$$

An American-style option which can be exercised early, can be valued by using the alternative equation:

$$C(t) = Max\left[g(t),E_t^*\left[C(t+h)exp\left[-\int_t^{t+h}r(u)du\right]\right]\right] \quad (29)$$

where g(t) is the payoff if the option is exercised

266

ARBITRAGE-
FREE
VALUATION
OF ENERGY
DERIVATIVES

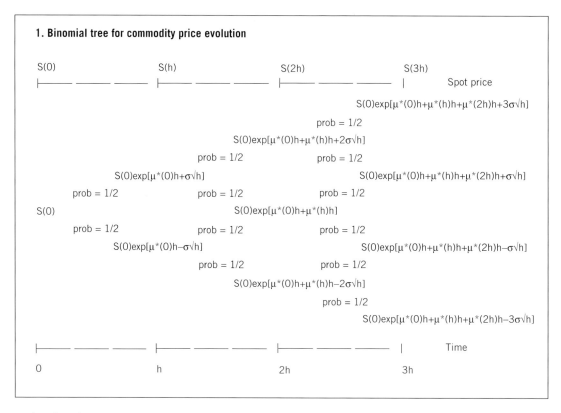

1. Binomial tree for commodity price evolution

at date t in the current state.

For an American call option on the spot asset with a strike price K, $g(t) = Max[S(t) - K, 0]$. For the corresponding American futures call option on the futures contract with maturity T, $g(t) = Max[F(t,T) - K, 0]$. This model can now be used to value very general claims dependent on the term structure of futures prices.

VALUATION OF EUROPEAN-STYLE OPTIONS USING MONTE CARLO METHODS

The discrete-time binomial style model developed in the previous section, as well as its continuous-time limit used to compute closed-form solutions for European option prices, impose strong restrictions on the volatility of the commodity price. In particular, we required the volatility to be constant. Further, the model implies that the volatilities of the futures prices of all maturities are also identical. When we wish to incorporate more general volatility functions (for example, as a function of the levels of futures prices), then closed-form solutions for European options cannot be derived and binomial-style discrete approximations are also very difficult to build. In this situation, Monte Carlo simulation can be used to compute European-style option prices, but with significant computation effort. However, it is difficult to value American options in this framework.

Consider a multifactor generalisation of the two-factor model in (14):

$$dlog\, F(t,T) = \left[\alpha(t,T) - \sum_{j=1}^{N}\sigma_j^2(t,T)/2\right]dt + \sum_{j=1}^{N}\sigma_j(t,T)dW_j(t) \tag{30}$$

In this specification, the volatility functions $\sigma_j(t,T)$'s can be some arbitrary functions of time t, maturity T or even the level of futures prices.

In the risk-neutral economy, as we argued earlier, the expected change in the futures price should be zero. Therefore, for option valuation, the risk-neutral distributions of the futures prices are represented by:

$$dlog\, F(t,T) = \left[-\sum_{j=1}^{N}\sigma_j^2(t,T)/2\right]dt + \sum_{j=1}^{N}\sigma_j(t,T)dW_j^*(t) \tag{31}$$

where W_j^*'s are independent Brownian motions in the risk-neutral economy. Equation (31) is the starting point of the approach in Cortazar and Schwartz (1992). In this case, the number of factors and the volatility functions can be determined by a principal component analysis or maximum likelihood factor analysis, as in Cortazar and Schwartz (1992).

Specifically, suppose $\sigma_i(t,T_j)$ is a constant for all i and maturity T_j, then $\sigma_i(t,T_j)$ can be estimated as $\beta_{ij}\sqrt{\alpha_i}$. Where α_i is the ith largest eigenvalue of the covariance matrix of the vector of futures returns: $(dlog\, F(t,T_1), dlog\, F(t,T_2), ..., dlog\, F(t,T_m))'$, and β_{ij} is the jth element of the eigenvector corresponding to α_i. As another example, suppose $\sigma_i(t,T_j)$ takes the functional

267

ARBITRAGE-
FREE
VALUATION
OF ENERGY
DERIVATIVES

form $\delta_{ij}\exp(-(T_j - t))$, then $\sigma_i(t, T_j)$ can be estimated as $\exp(-(T_j - t))\beta_{ij}\sqrt{\alpha_i}$, where α_i is the ith largest eigenvalue of the covariance matrix of the vector of transformed futures returns: $(w_1 d\log F(t, T_1), w_2 d\log F(t, T_2), ..., w_m d\log F(t, T_m))'$, w_j is defined as equal to $\exp(T_j - t)$ and β_{ij} is the jth element of the eigenvector corresponding to α_i. If $\sigma_i(t, T_j)$ takes a very general nonlinear functional form, then the computationally simple principal component analysis cannot be conveniently applied. In this case, a full fetch maximum likelihood factor analysis needs to be performed.

Since we are in a risk-neutral economy, the value of a European option which pays $g(\tau)$ at the expiration date τ is given by:

$$C(t) = E_t^*\left[g(\tau)\exp\left[-\int_t^\tau r(u)du\right]\right] \quad (32)$$

To compute the value of this expression, we need to compute the distribution of the futures prices at date τ and then integrate the option payoff with respect to this distribution. In general, this distribution cannot be obtained in closed form. However, we use the fact that increments to a Brownian motion are normally distributed with mean zero and variance equal to the elapsed time to build the distribution of the futures prices. Consider a discretisation of (31) to generate the distribution of futures prices at some future date. Let the time interval be discretised by: [0, h, 2h, ..., t, t + h, t + 2h, ...] for some sufficiently small time interval h. Suppose we consider the increment to the log of the futures prices of all maturities over the time interval [t, t + h], that is, $\log F(t + h, T) - \log F(t, T)$ for all maturities T. Then, equation (31) implies that $\log F(t + h, T) - \log F(t, T)$ can be approximated by:

$$\log F(t + h, T) - \log F(t, T)$$
$$= \left[-\sum_{j=1}^N \sigma_j^2(t, T)/2\right]h + \sum_{j=1}^N \sigma_j(t, T)\varepsilon_j^*(t)\sqrt{h} \quad (33)$$

where $\varepsilon_j^*(t)$'s are independent at date t and are also serially independent and normally distributed random variables with mean zero and variance 1.

The term $\varepsilon_j^*(t)\sqrt{h}$ approximates the increment to the jth Brownian motion from t to t + h. We can generate a sequence of $(\varepsilon_1^*(t), \varepsilon_2^*(t), ..., \varepsilon_N^*(t))$'s, one for each discrete date 0, h, 2h, ... and then recursively compute the value of the futures prices at future dates using (33). This yields one possible realisation (path of futures prices) in the approximation scheme represent-

ed by (33). Note that the futures prices of all maturities are simultaneously computed using the same values of $(\varepsilon_1^*(t), \varepsilon_2^*(t), ..., \varepsilon_N^*(t))$ for $t = 0, h, 2h, ...$. Therefore, the single realisation corresponds to a path of all the futures prices of all maturities. To generate the entire distribution of futures prices, we need to repeatedly sample $(\varepsilon_1^*(t), \varepsilon_2^*(t), ..., \varepsilon_N^*(t))$ for $t = 0, h, 2h, ...$ and generate futures prices from (33). Option prices can be computed by integrating (averaging over the different realisations) over this distribution.

For example, consider an option which has a payoff of $g(\tau)$ at date τ as some function of the realisation of the path of futures prices up to date τ. Then, the price of the option is given by:

$$C(t) = E_t^*\left[\exp\left(-\int_t^\tau r(u)du\right)g(\tau)\right] \quad (34)$$

The option being considered above can also be an Asian option or other type of exotic option, as long as the option does not permit early exercise. For example, the price of an Asian call option which is dependent on the average futures price from time s to τ is given by:

$$C(t) = E_t^*\left[\exp\left(-\int_t^\tau r(u)du\right)\right.$$
$$\left. Max\left(0, (1/(\tau - s))\int_s^\tau F(u, T)du\right) - K\right] \quad (35)$$

where K is the exercise price and τ is the expiration date of the option. To compute the option price, we need to compute the expectation in (34) as described below.

For each simulated price path, the term inside the expectation can be computed. This yields the realised price of the option under that realisation. To compute the current price of the option today, we take the average over a large number of realisations so that the price of the option does not change if we increase the number of realisations (in most cases, 10,000 realisations will prove sufficient).[6]

Option valuation with stochastic convenience yields

Our treatment above allows deterministic (but seasonal) convenience yields. However, since relative supply and demand conditions can also change unpredictably from time to time, the convenience yields are likely to have a stochastic component. Allowing the convenience yields to be random enriches the one-factor model we described in the previous section. In the one-factor model, futures prices of all maturities are perfectly correlated and the term-structure of futures prices is subject only to parallel shocks. By permitting the convenience yields to be stochastic, independent variation between the futures prices of different maturities can occur.

We will model the entire term structure of convenience yields, and then price options based on the evolution of this term structure. Our approach is arbitrage-free, as we do not require any additional assumptions except the absence of arbitrage once the dynamics of the futures prices are specified. It is worthwhile to mention an alternative modelling method in which only the evolution of the spot price and the instantaneous convenience yield is specified. Futures prices (in addition to the prices of options) in these models are endogenously determined within the model, as a function of the spot price and the instantaneous convenience yield only.

For an example of this approach, see Gibson and Schwartz (1990). Their approach requires additional assumptions on investors' preferences, and requires the specification of the market price of risk of the instantaneous convenience yield. Further, it has difficulty matching the initial term-structure of futures prices. Since our main objective in this chapter has been to price options rather than the underlying futures contracts, we do not discuss these issues in more detail. In order to price futures within the same framework, the approach followed by Gibson and Schwartz (1990) would be necessary.

THE EVOLUTION OF THE TERM STRUCTURE
OF CONVENIENCE YIELDS
For simplicity, we will focus on a model in which forward convenience yields of all maturities are subject to a single source of uncertainty. Furthermore, we will directly specify the evolution of convenience yields in the risk-neutral economy rather than in the true economy. Let the term structure of forward convenience yields $z(t,T)$ for all maturities T, in the risk-neutral economy, be governed by the stochastic differential equation:

$$dz(t,T) = \beta(t,T)dt + \delta(t,T)dW_2^*(t) \quad (36)$$

It is worthwhile to note that the entire term structure of convenience yields is governed by the same Brownian motion $W_2^*(t)$. Further, we permit the Brownian motion $W_2^*(t)$ to have a constant correlation ρ with $W_1^*(t)$. For simplicity, we assume that $\delta(t,T)$ is a deterministic function of time and maturity. This function and the correla-

tion parameter ρ constitute the parameter inputs. The function $\beta(t,T)$ is determined inside the model, as we will show in following paragraphs.

In the risk-neutral economy, the convenience yield drift $\beta(t,T)$ must be such that the expected change in the futures prices of all maturities is zero. A futures contract does not require any initial investment. Therefore, its expected price change in a risk-neutral economy must be zero. This condition provides the relationship between the convenience yield drifts, $\beta(t,T)$, and the volatility structure of convenience yields. The value of $\beta(t,T)$ in the true economy is irrelevant for valuation.

The relationship between the futures and spot price derived earlier is given by:

$$F(t,T) = S(t)\exp\left[\int_t^T \left(r(u) - z(t,u)\right)du\right] \quad (37)$$

By substituting the stochastic differential equation for $z(t,u)$ and $S(t)$ into the above equation and simplifying, we can write down the stochastic differential equation for $F(t,T)$ as:[7]

$$dF(t,T)/F(t,T) = \sigma dW_1^*(t) - \left[\int_t^T \delta(t,u)du\right]dW_2^*(t) \quad (38)$$

Further, our Appendix to this chapter also shows that the drift $\beta(t,T)$ must satisfy the relation:

$$\beta(t,T) = \delta(t,T)\left[\int_t^T \delta(t,u)du - \sigma\rho\right] \quad (39)$$

That is,

$$dz(t,T) =$$
$$\delta(t,T)\left[\int_t^T \delta(t,u)du - \sigma\rho\right]dt + \delta(t,T)dW_2^*(t) \quad (40)$$

From (38), the instantaneous proportional variance of the futures price of maturity T at date t is therefore given by:

$$\zeta^2(t,T) = \sigma^2 + \left[\int_t^T \delta(t,u)du\right]\left[\int_t^T \delta(t,u)du - 2\rho\sigma\right] \quad (41)$$

The volatility is given by the square root of the above expression, that is $\zeta(t,T)$. Further, the futures price is lognormal with volatility $\zeta(t,T)$. Therefore, the value of a European futures option is given by the Black (1976) formula, by substituting $\zeta(t,T)$ for the volatility.

That is, the price of a European call option with maturity date τ on the futures contract with futures maturity T is given by:

$$c[t,F(t,T)] =$$
$$\exp\left[-\int_t^\tau r(u)du\right]\left[F(t,T)N(\gamma_1) - KN(\gamma_2)\right] \quad (42)$$

where $N(.)$ is the normal cumulative distribution function,

$$\gamma_1 = \left[\log\left[F(t,T)/K\right] + \eta^2(t,\tau,T)(\tau - t)/2\right] / \left[\eta(t,\tau,T)\sqrt{(\tau - t)}\right]$$

$$\gamma_2 = \gamma_1 - \eta(t,\tau,T)\sqrt{(\tau - t)}$$

and

$$\eta^2(t,\tau,T) = \left(1/(\tau - t)\right)\int_t^\tau \zeta^2(u,T)du$$

Our framework with a stochastic convenience yield term structure is therefore similar to Black's (1976) framework, except that we explicitly specify the link between futures contracts of different maturities and the link between the spot and futures prices. This link is important for valuing American options on the spot price based on the current term structure of futures prices. It is also important for valuing options whose prices depend on the entire term structure of futures prices, for example swaptions. At any date, the swap value is a function of the entire futures curve. Therefore, the theory must *simultaneously* model the evolution of futures prices of all maturities.

In actual implementation, we need to assume a parsimonious form for $\delta(t,T)$. The exact function, $\delta(t,T)$, can then be estimated from the futures returns based on (38) with the drift term included or, more appropriately, from the return on the price spread between futures contracts of different maturities. To the extent that the $\delta(.)$ functions are reasonably stable through time, these can be estimated historically using the maximum likelihood technique. The model then contains only two unestimated parameters, σ and ρ, which can be implied out from the previous day's option prices.

To the extent that the correlation parameter is reasonably stable, it can also be determined by historical data analysis. In this case, only σ needs to be determined by the implied method. Alternatively, if the function $\delta(.)$ involves only one or two parameters, which are common across all maturities, then, provided that a relatively large number of options are available, these parameters can be implied out simultaneously from the previous day's option prices.

An alternative method of constructing a two-factor model is to model the term structure of futures prices directly with two factors, as in equation (14). It is possible to show that these methods are equivalent from a theoretical perspective. However, specifying the model in terms of convenience yields is more intuitive, since it permits a better understanding of the relation-

ship between futures contracts of different maturities. Moreover, if we choose a particular volatility structure for the convenience yields, our model permits the construction of a discrete time approximation with a lattice structure similar to Figure 1. This discretisation will be described in the following subsection.

A TREE APPROACH TO VALUING AMERICAN AND OTHER OPTIONS

Simple European-style options on the spot or futures can be valued using the Black (1976) formula with the volatility $\eta(t,T)$. To value more complicated options, such as Asian options or lookback options or European-style swaptions, we can use a Monte Carlo simulation of equations (17) and (36) or (38). It is straightforward to implement our model using this technique.[8]

American-style options can be valued with a discrete-time version of our model. With general volatility functions, the techniques developed in Amin and Bodurtha (1994) are applicable. A detailed description of the discretisation procedure is beyond the scope of the current chapter. Here, we describe a discretisation procedure when $\delta(t,T) = \delta$ is a constant (independent of t or T). Then, it is possible to build a path-independent discrete-time tree such that the discrete-time distribution of the state variables converges to the continuous-time distributions given by (5) and (38) as the discrete time interval $h \rightarrow 0$.

The tree for the state variables describes the evolution of the spot price $S(t)$ and the entire term structure of convenience yields $z(t,T)$. The futures prices at any date can be computed as functions of these state variables. Suppose the tree up to date t has already been constructed. We permit four possible states given by A, B, C, and D, to occur at the next date $t + h$. Under each of these states, the spot price $S(t)$ and all the convenience yields $z(t,T)$ can be updated for their possible values at date $t + h$, according to Table 1 overleaf.

Table 1 yields a tree for the evolution of the state variables in which, given a current state, there are four possible nodes at the next date. For example, state A corresponds to both the spot price and the convenience yields increasing, whereas state C corresponds to the spot price decreasing and the convenience yields increasing. Another notable feature is that the entire term structure of convenience yields can be updated at each date using the table. Further, from a computational perspective, the tree is path independent: the order of occurrence of

Table 1: Single period distribution of the spot price and convenience yields

Variable	Increment over (t,t+h)	Risk-neutral probability	State
$\log[S(t+h)/S(t)]$ $z(t+h,T)-z(t,T)$	$[r(t)-\sigma^2/2]h + \sigma\sqrt{h}/2$ $\beta(t,T)h + \delta\sqrt{h}$	$[1- z(t,t)\sqrt{h}/\sigma]/4$	A
$\log[S(t+h)/S(t)]$ $z(t+h,T)-z(t,T)$	$[r(t)-\sigma^2/2]h + \sigma\sqrt{h}/2$ $\beta(t,T)h - \delta\sqrt{h}$	$[1- z(t,t)\sqrt{h}/\sigma]/4$	B
$\log[S(t+h)/S(t)]$ $z(t+h,T)-z(t,T)$	$[r(t)-\sigma^2/2]h - \sigma\sqrt{h}/2$ $\beta(t,T)h + \delta\sqrt{h}$	$[1 + z(t,t)\sqrt{h}/\sigma]/4)$	C
$\log[S(t+h)/S(t)]$ $z(t+h,T)-z(t,T)$	$[r(t)-\sigma^2/2]h - \sigma\sqrt{h}/2$ $\beta(t,T)h - \delta\sqrt{h}$	$[1 + z(t,t)\sqrt{h}/\sigma]/4$	D

the different states over time is irrelevant.

For example, the occurrence of state A in the first period, followed by state D in the second period, yields the same values of all the state variables as state D in the first period followed by state A in the second period. Therefore, the number of nodes in the tree after n time steps is only $(n+1)^2$. This implies that the computational effort for computing even long maturity option values is quite manageable.

An important feature of our tree is that the probability that each state (A, B, C, or D) will occur is not the same at all nodes in the tree. The probabilities depend on the current spot convenience yield $z(t,t)$. Once the state space represented by a tree has been constructed, option values can be computed using the same procedure as described in the previous section of this chapter, using equation (27).

This completes our description of the model with stochastic convenience yields.

Applications and limitations

In this chapter, we have presented a unified approach for pricing energy derivative products. One of the salient features of energy derivative products is that the term structure of futures prices depends upon convenience yields. These convenience yields can cause the term structure of futures prices to slope upwards or slope downwards, or to vary non-monotonically with maturity. The models derived herein explicitly incorporate this convenience yield feature in order to determine how it influences the pricing of energy contingent claims. Our first, and simpler, model assumes that convenience yields are deterministic; whereas the model described in the last section considers the more complex and more realistic case in which the convenience yields vary stochastically.

In addition to the added realism arising from the incorporation of convenience yields into the pricing formulae, the valuation models presented herein offer several advantages to the practitioner. Specifically, unlike the standard Black (1976) model, these models can be used to price American options, Asian options and swaptions. Moreover, all of these various types of contingent claims can be priced within a single unified framework. Finally, and perhaps most importantly, using these models, a portfolio of energy-contingent claims can be hedged within a single "book". This last feature simplifies substantially the task of managing the risk of a portfolio of energy derivatives.

Finally, we should discuss some of the limitations of our approach in this chapter. We have assumed that the maturity of each futures contract is known and that delivery occurs only on the maturity date. However, there are delivery timing options embedded in exchange-traded futures contracts. Incorporating this feature is quite difficult since it requires an explicit framework to value the delivery option of the short. For long-term options, ignoring this delivery option is not likely to introduce significant valuation errors. However, for short-term options, this delivery option may be quite important.

A second limitation of our approach is the assumption that the volatility of the spot asset is constant. In the energy markets, the theory of storage implies that the volatility is higher when inventories are low, and that the volatility is lower when inventories are high. Since there is a negative relationship between the convenience yield and inventories, this implies a positive relationship between the spot volatility and the level of convenience yields. This feature cannot be incorporated in our simple framework without significantly complicating the model and making the computational task much more difficult.[9]

Finally, we have assumed deterministic interest rates. For long-term options (with maturities greater than three years), the stochastic nature of interest rates will also have some influence on option values. Incorporating a stochastic term structure of interest rates is straightforward, but increases the computational cost.[10, 11]

271

ARBITRAGE-
FREE
VALUATION
OF ENERGY
DERIVATIVES

1 *Kaushik Amin, Lehman Brothers; Victor Ng, Goldman Sachs International; S. Craig Pirrong, Olin School of Business, Washington University in St. Louis.*

The authors would like to thank Vince Kaminski of Enron, Frédéric Barnaud of Elf Trading SA and, particularly, the editor, Robert Jameson for very useful comments.

2 *As in Heath, Jarrow and Morton (1992) for interest rates or Amin and Jarrow (1991) for risky assets.*

3 *See Ng and Pirrong (1993) and (1994) for an analysis of the theory of storage.*

4 *See Ng and Pirrong (1993) and (1994) for evidence on the mean reversion of convenience yields in refined petroleum and industrial metal products, and the greater volatility of the spot than the futures prices associated with this*

long-run adjustment process.

5 *See Amin (1991) for a similar discretisation.*

6 *For details, see Boyle (1977).*

7 *See Appendix A for details.*

8 *See Boyle (1977) for a description of Monte Carlo methods applied to option pricing.*

9 *For details on how the above issues can be accommodated, see Amin, Ng and Pirrong (1994).*

10 *Some work along these lines is given in Amin and Jarrow (1991a).*

11 *Some work along these lines is given in Amin and Jarrow (1991b).*

BIBLIOGRAPHY

Amin, K.I., 1991, "On the Computation of Continuous Time Options Prices Using Discrete Approximations", *Journal of Financial and Quantitative Analysis*, 26, pp. 477-96.

Amin, K.I., and J.N. Bodurtha, 1994, "Discrete-time Option Valuation with Stochastic Interest Rates", forthcoming, *Review of Financial Studies*.

Amin, K.I., and R.A. Jarrow, 1991a, "Pricing Foreign Currency Options Under Stochastic Interest Rates", *Journal of International Money and Finance*, 10, pp. 310-30.

Amin, K.I., and R.A. Jarrow, 1991b, "Pricing Options on Risky Assets in a Stochastic Interest Rate Economy", *Mathematical Finance*, no. 2, pp. 217-38.

Amin, K.I., V.K. Ng, and C. Pirrong, 1994, "Arbitrage Free Valuation of Commodity Options with Stochastic Volatility and Convenience Yields", technical report, University of Michigan.

Black, F., 1976, "The Pricing of Commodity Contracts", *Journal of Financial Economics*, 3 (1/2), pp. 167-79.

Boyle, P.P., 1977, "Options: A Monte Carlo Approach", *Journal of Financial Economics*, 4, pp. 323-8.

Brenner, M., G. Courtadon, and M. Subrahmanyam, 1985, "Options on the Spot and Options on Futures", *Journal of Finance*, 40, pp. 1303-17.

Cortazar, G., and E. Schwartz, 1992, "The Valuation of Commodity Contingent Claims", technical report, Anderson Graduate School of Management, University of California, Los Angeles.

Gibson, R. and E.S. Schwartz, 1990, "Stochastic Convenience Yield and the Pricing of Oil Contingent Claims", *Journal of Finance*, vol. XLV, no. 3, 959-76.

Heath, D., R.A. Jarrow and A. Morton, 1992, "Bond Pricing and the Term Structure of Interest Rates: A New Methodology", *Econometrica*, 60, pp. 77-105.

Ho, T.S.Y., and S.B. Lee, 1986, "Term Structure Movements and Pricing Interest Rate Contingent Claims", *Journal of Finance*, 41, pp. 1011-29.

Jamshidian, F., 1992, "Commodity Option Evaluation in the Gaussian Futures Term Structure", *Review of Futures Markets*, 11, pp. 325-46.

Jarrow, R.A., and G. Oldfield, 1981, "The Relationship Between Forward and Futures Prices", *Journal of Financial Economics*, 9 (4), pp. 373-82.

Jarrow, R.A., and A. Rudd, 1983, *Option Pricing*, Irwin, New York.

Ng, V.K., and S.C. Pirrong, 1992, "The Relation Between Crude Oil, Heating Oil, and Gasoline Futures and Spot Prices", *Mid-America Institute Research Report*, Mid-America Institute, Chicago, IL.

Ng, V.K., and S.C. Pirrong, 1993, "Price Dynamics in Physical Commodity Spot and Futures Markets: Spread, Spillovers, Volatility and Convergence in Refined Petroleum Products", Mitsui Life Financial Research Center Working Paper, University of Michigan.

Ng, V.K., and S.C. Pirrong, 1994, "Fundamentals and Volatility: Storage, Spreads, and the Dynamics of Metal Prices", *Journal of Business*, vol. 67, no.2 (April), pp. 203-30.

14

Volatility in Energy Prices

Darrell Duffie, Stephen Gray and Philip Hoang

Stanford University and University of Queensland[1]

P rices in the energy markets are marked by a volatility that is both high and variable over time. These characteristics mean that energy markets are an ideal testing ground for volatility models, which is our primary concern in this chapter, and that the ability to track and forecast volatility is of paramount importance when trading and hedging energy-related portfolios of derivatives.

When making markets, for example, a trader will need to track the exposure of a book of positions to market changes of various types, including volatility. What is a 95% worst-case mark-to-market on a given position? What is the risk (standard deviation) of the current book? Which desk is above its risk limit, and how should such limits be set? Which traders have shown acceptable or superior performance in light of the volatility of the markets in which they trade? The answers to all these questions rely on estimates of past or future volatility.

A model of stochastic volatility is also useful when estimating a fair price for a given option, cap, or other volatility-dependent derivative, or when calculating the delta of a given portfolio of energy-related securities – and the option positions that would make a reasonable delta hedge against that portfolio.

We hope that this chapter will provide a useful review of the modelling and empirical behaviour of volatility in energy prices. As a point of departure, we first review the standard constant-volatility model. Then we describe stochastic volatility models of a Markov variety, in which current volatility is a function of the past level of volatility and a new "shock", which may or may not be correlated with the current return on the underlying price. We then move on to examine a range of Arch-based models. We conclude by comparing and contrasting these time series

models of volatility with market quoted implied volatilities.

Throughout the chapter, we refer to a series of tests that we performed in order to discover which of the most commonly used and discussed models of volatility is the most effective forecaster. For the purposes of this experiment, we use historical data supplied by the energy industry to compare the forecasts of the models, at a given point in time, to the level of volatility that was subsequently realised in the markets. In our conclusion, we highlight our most important findings and suggest some directions for future work.

A few preliminary comments are necessary on the different applications of volatility estimation. Some investors speculate on energy volatility, attempting to predict changes in volatility before those changes are impounded into generally available market prices. This is perhaps as much of an art as it is a science. Changes in volatility are not generated by a mathematical model, but rather by real-world events that have a significance which may at first only be apparent to engineers, geologists, economists or geopolitical analysts. Armed with a solid understanding of the Black–Scholes formula, a well-informed trader with advance knowledge of volatility-related events (or a superior ability when analysing the implications of such events) would not need the modelling approaches we offer here in order to be successful.

Instead, this chapter is aimed at the managers of systems that are designed to cope with energy portfolios. A buyer of long-term natural gas contracts for an electric power utility, a heating oil supplier, a major oil refiner and marketer, or a market maker in energy derivatives would naturally rely on the sort of models that we present here.

Constant volatility

For a given asset, "volatility" is the standard deviation of the rate of return, conditional on all available information. The starting point for almost any model of volatility is the constant volatility model exploited by Black and Scholes (1973), in which the volatility is a constant over time.

The constant-volatility model can be presented in a simple form. The return on an asset, say on a daily basis, is the percentage change in the value of the investment. We ignore dividends or storage costs, since, being comparatively small and predictable over limited time horizons, they have a relatively minor effect on volatility in energy markets over the time horizons that we study here. Instead, we will concentrate on price returns. On a continuously compounded basis, the price return over a given period can be computed as the logarithm of the ending price less the logarithm of the beginning price.

For example, if the price of a barrel of a oil at the close on Monday is \$16.00, and at the close on Tuesday is \$16.20, then the close-to-close price return is $\ln(16.20) - \ln(16.00) = 0.0124$. On an annualised basis ($252 \times 0.0124 = 3.12$), this results in an annual return of 312%.

Whether in a discrete or continuous time setting, the constant volatility model assumes that the underlying prices S_1, S_2, ..., S_t of the asset in question have returns $R = \ln(S_t) - \ln(S_{t-1})$ given by:

$$R_t = \mu + \sigma \varepsilon_t \qquad (1)$$

where μ is a constant mean return coefficient, σ is a constant volatility parameter, and ε_1, ε_2, ... is *white noise* (by which we mean independent, normally distributed random variables of zero mean and unit variance). Sticking to daily frequency (mainly for expositional reasons), the annualised volatility is the standard deviation of $R_1 + \cdots + R_{252}$, which is $\sqrt{252}\sigma$ in our constant-volatility model (1).

In the continuous-time setting of Black and Scholes, it is well known that the price of an option at time t, say a European call, is given explicitly by the famous Black–Scholes formula $C_t = C^{BS}(S_t, \tau, K, r, \sigma)$, given the strike price K, the time τ to expiration, the continuously compounding constant interest rate r, and the volatility σ.

It also well known that this formula is strictly increasing in σ, so that, from the option price C_t, one may theoretically infer, without error, the volatility parameter:

$$\sigma_t = \sigma^{BS}(C_t, S_t, \tau, K, r). \qquad (2)$$

The function σ^{BS} is known as Black–Scholes implied volatility.[2] While no explicit formula for σ^{BS} is available, one can compute implied volatilities readily with a simple numerical search routine such as Newton–Raphson. For these and many other details on the Black–Scholes model and extensions, one may refer to Cox and Rubinstein (1985), Stoll and Whaley (1993), and Hull (1997), among many other sources.

If an option price is not available, one may estimate σ from returns data. The *historical* volatility $\hat{\sigma}_{t,T}$ implied by returns R_t, R_{t+1},..., R_T is the usual maximum likelihood estimator for σ given by:

$$\hat{\sigma}_{t,T}^2 = \frac{1}{T-t} \sum_{s=t+1}^{T} \left(R_s - \hat{\mu}_{t,T}\right)^2 \qquad (3)$$

where $\hat{\mu}_{t,T} = (R_{t+1} + ... + R_T)/(T - t)$. If, as in the Black–Scholes setting, the constant-volatility returns model (1) applies at arbitrarily fine data frequency (with suitable adjustment of μ and σ for period length), then one can learn the volatility σ within an arbitrarily short time interval from the historical volatility estimator.[3]

In reality, however, price data frequency is limited. Moreover, returns at exceptionally high frequency have statistical properties that are heavily dependent on the institutional properties of the market, and these are of less importance over longer time periods. Given a fixed number of observations over a given period, the optimal sampling times for estimation of σ are not necessarily evenly spaced, as shown by Genon-Catalot and Jacod (1993).

When estimating σ in the Black–Scholes setting one can also take special advantage of additional financial price data, such as the high and low prices for the period, as shown by Garman and Klass (1980), Parkinson (1980), and Rogers and Satchell (1991).

For energy prices, and indeed for many other assets, historical volatility data strongly indicate that the constant-volatility model does not apply. For example, the returns of heating oil, crude oil, natural gas and electricity shown in Figure 1 appear to indicate that volatility is changing, in some manner, over time and this is confirmed by the volatility estimates in Figure 2.

For petroleum products and natural gas, volatility tends to cluster through time. There are some periods of high volatility and other periods of low volatility. The realised volatility for the electricity markets appears to behave very differently. This is simply a function of the large spikes in price that occur from time to time. These price spikes can be driven by weather events, generator outages and institutional features of particular markets. Our measure of realised volatility is severely affected by these price spikes. Since we take a 25-day moving average of squared log price changes, a large price spike inflates our measure of realised volatility, and continues to do so for the following 24-days, at which point it drops out of the moving average calculation and our measure of realised volatility falls. This measure is misleading in the sense that these price spikes tend to be one-off events or "jumps" that do not have a permanent effect. We offer a more detailed interpretation of this issue in the context of specific volatility models below.

Even in the constant-volatility setting, one expects the historical volatility estimate to vary over time, sometimes dramatically, merely from random variation in prices. (This is sometimes called "sampling error".) One can perform various tests to find out whether changes in historical volatility are so large as to cause one to reject the constant volatility hypothesis at a given confidence level. For example, under the constant volatility hypothesis, the ratio $F_{a,b} = \hat{\sigma}^2_{t(a),T(a)}/\hat{\sigma}^2_{t(b),T(b)}$ of squared historical volatilities over non-overlapping time intervals has the F distribution (with degrees of freedom given by the respective lengths of the two time intervals). From standard tables of the F distribution, one can then test the constant-volatility hypothesis, rejecting it at, say, the 95% confidence level, if $F_{a,b}$ is larger than the associated critical F statistic. (One should take care not to select the time intervals in question in light of one's impression, based on observing prices, that volatility apparently differs between the two periods. This would introduce a selection bias that makes such classical tests inappropriate.)

In any case, most energy price data, including those considered in this chapter, generate rejections of the constant volatility hypothesis in tests such as this, and it seems inappropriate here to go into the subtleties designed to refine such tests. Although rejections in such classical tests are, by nature, subject to random errors, the Black–Scholes implied volatility trajectories (from the next-to-mature option contract) shown in Figure 2 certainly suggest that options traders do not believe that the constant-volatility model applies to heating oil, crude oil, or natural gas. Implied volatilities are unavailable for the elec-

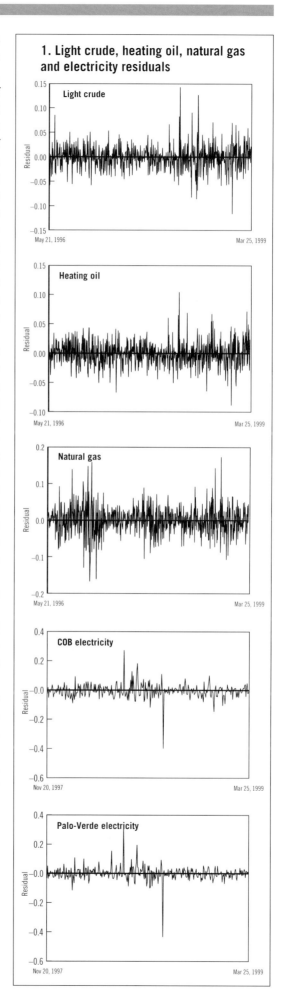

1. Light crude, heating oil, natural gas and electricity residuals

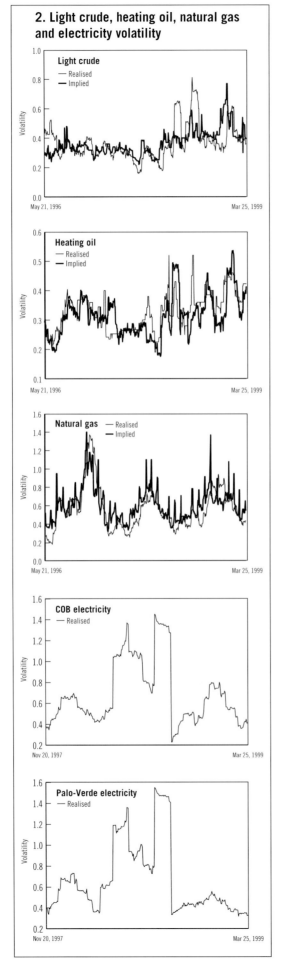

2. Light crude, heating oil, natural gas and electricity volatility

tricity markets that we examine.

In other words, when buying or selling options, each trader has in mind a fair price that reflects the likelihood of reaching each possible level of the underlying price. If the constant-volatility model were correct and believed by traders to be correct, then the prices paid for options would have constant implied volatilities. That is not what we see in Figure 2. Of course, it is theoretically possible that volatility is constant and that the evidence in Figure 2 is due to failures of one or more assumptions in the Black–Scholes model other than constant volatility, but it seems unlikely that the extent of the failure of these other assumptions could be responsible for the dramatic variation of the implied volatilities shown in Figure 2, especially given the alignment of sharp changes in implied volatility with identifiable market events such as the Gulf War.

If traders have in mind something other than constant volatility, then one can learn something about their forecasts of volatility from the prices at which they buy and sell options. For example, even if the Black–Scholes model is incorrect, the Black–Scholes implied volatilities could have forecasting power for volatility. Indeed, Figure 2 shows that this seems to be the case, as the plot of Black–Scholes implied volatility "leads" historical volatility.

That is, we can view $\sigma^{BS}(C_t, S_t, T-t, K, r)$ as a useful predictor of $\hat{\sigma}_{t,T}$ the former known at time t, the latter only at the expiration date T of the option. Even though Figure 2 plots historical volatility for 25-day periods, regardless of the expiration dates of the options underlying the implied volatility, the ability of implied volatility to forecast changes in historical volatility is apparent. Later, we will compare the forecasting quality of implied volatility with that of other volatility predicators.

The seasons of the year play an important role in the markets for energy products. For example, the demand for heating oil depends on winter weather patterns, which are obviously only determined in the winter. The demand for gasoline is greater, and shows greater variability, in the summer, and gasoline prices therefore tend to show greater variability during the summer months. The demand for electricity peaks during the summer (due to air conditioning demand) and also has a strong intra-day seasonal peaking early in the evening. There is even a day-of-the-week effect in the volatility of most futures markets that reflects institutional market features, including the desire of market makers to close out their positions over weekends.

One can "correct" for seasonality, for example by estimating volatility separately by season. Even after correcting volatility for seasonality, however, there are still persistent and random changes in volatility. That is, a model in which volatility is constant, but in which the constant level of volatility depends on the season in some regular way such as this, can also be safely ruled out. This is not to say that seasonality is not important. Indeed, one would probably want to include seasonality in a detailed model of volatility, but seasons alone do not adequately account for the patterns of volatility that we see in the energy markets.

It seems safe to conclude that, at least for energy markets, we can benefit by moving beyond the constant volatility model.

Stochastic volatility

The word "stochastic" simply means "random". It is reasonable, and has become popular, to treat "volatility" as a stochastic process. A reasonably large class of extensions of the constant-volatility model can then be built on a "stochastic-volatility" model of returns, given by:

$$R_t = \mu + \sigma_{t-1}\varepsilon_t \qquad (4)$$

where the constant[4] mean return and random return shocks $\varepsilon_1, \varepsilon_2, ..., \varepsilon_t$ are as above, and where σ_{t-1} is the standard deviation of the return R_t, conditional on information available at time $t - 1$.

Knowledge of the *stochastic volatility* process $\sigma_1, \sigma_2, ...$ would, under certain conditions, allow us to handle the applications described in the introduction. For example, if we knew the random manner in which σ varies over time, we could estimate the risk (standard deviation) of a portfolio of energy positions simply by Monte Carlo simulation of σ and of the returns process R from (4). Likewise, from such a simulation, we could estimate the position in an energy derivative, such as a futures contract, that minimises the risk of a portfolio of energy market commitments. As we shall see, with a model of σ, depending on the technical assumptions that one is willing to make, one can price an option-embedded derivative on the underlying energy price. Other applications, such as trading performance evaluation, can be improved if we can estimate a stochastic model for volatility, since that would allow one to estimate the level of volatility that existed over a historical period.

While the current return R_t is normally dis-tributed in the stochastic-volatility model (4), conditional on information available at time $t - 1$, the unconditional distribution of returns can be thought of as mixture of normal distributions – each observation being drawn from a distribution with a different standard deviation. In particular, the unconditional distribution of returns would typically be skewed and leptokurtic, consistent with the distribution of returns observed in most markets, including the energy markets.[5]

The basic objective here is to model the stochastic volatility process, and from such a model, forecast future volatility from past data, options prices, and perhaps prices from related energy markets. Before getting into the details, it may help to focus on what it is about "volatility" that one wants to estimate. Ideally, we want to specify completely the joint behaviour of returns and volatility as stochastic processes. For comparison purposes, however, and given the sorts of applications one may have in mind, it makes sense to consider forecasts of volatility.

We concentrate especially on forecasting the average future squared volatility:

$$v_{t,T}^2 = \frac{1}{T-t}\left(\sigma_t^2 + ... + \sigma_{T-1}^2\right) \qquad (5)$$

This is a reasonable objective, for, as one can show by the law of iterated expectations, an unbiased forecast of $v_{t,T}^2$ is the same as an unbiased forecast of:

$$\frac{1}{T-t}\sum_{s=t+1}^{T}(R_s - \mu)^2 \qquad (6)$$

which in turn is almost identical to the historical volatility measure $\hat{\sigma}_{t,T}^2$. (These differ only by the replacement of the estimated mean return $\hat{\mu}_{t,T}^2$ with the true value μ, and this substitution has a negligible effect in practice.)

Another advantage of concentrating on $v_{t,T}^2$ is that, under well-understood conditions that we review below, it is straightforward to convert Black–Scholes implied volatilities into unbiased forecasts of $v_{t,T}^2$, and vice versa. Finally, from forecasts of $v_{t,T}^2$, one can estimate risk exposures (such as standard deviations or 95% worst-case scenarios), and more generally feed the needs of a risk-management system.

Markovian models of stochastic volatility

One can envision a model for stochastic volatility in which the current level of volatility depends in a non-trivial way on the path that volatility has taken in the past. For example, one might say that volatility tends to decline if it is currently higher than its average level over some period in the past. It is also realistic, in energy markets, to believe that volatility depends on the quantities of the asset, say heating oil or crude oil, currently held in readily accessible inventory. See, for example, Ng and Pirrong (1994) for such a model in the context of metal markets. In this context, future volatility in electricity markets might depend more on supply shocks such as new plants or interconnections coming on line. While we advocate the consideration of volatility models that include potential path dependencies, dependencies on inventory levels, and other potential determinants of volatility, for simplicity of illustration we will focus here only on the simplest forms of volatility models that have commonly appeared in the literature. These models are mainly of the Markovian form:

$$\sigma_t = F(\sigma_{t-1}, z_t, t) \qquad (7)$$

where F is some smooth function in three variables and $z_1, z_2, \ldots, z_t$ is white noise. The term "Markovian" means that the probability distribution of the next period's level of volatility depends only on the current level of volatility, and not otherwise on the path taken by volatility. This form of volatility also rules out, for reasons of simplification, dependence of the distribution of changes in volatility on other possible state variables, such as inventory levels (as mentioned above) and macro-economic factors. Later, we do consider Markov models in which other state variables, such as price levels or volatilities in related markets, play a role. Moreover, we do not necessarily assume that the volatility shock z_t and the return shock ε_t are perfectly correlated.

In the following sections, we will consider several basic classes of the Markovian stochastic volatility model (7). Each of these classes has its own advantages, both in terms of empirical reasonability and tractability in an option-pricing framework. The latter is particularly important, since option valuation may, under certain conditions, provide volatilities implicitly – as in the Black–Scholes setting.

AUTO-REGRESSIVE VOLATILITY

A standard Markov model of stochastic volatility is given by the log-AR(1) model:

$$\ln(\sigma_t^2) = \alpha + \gamma \ln(\sigma_{t-1}^2) + \kappa z_t \qquad (8)$$

where α, γ, and κ are constants. We always assume that z_t and ε_s are independent for $t \neq s$, and that z_t and ε_t have some constant correlation ρ. Volatility

persistence is captured by the coefficient γ. A value of γ that is near zero implies low persistence, while a value that is near one implies high persistence. We always assume that $-1 < \gamma < 1$, otherwise volatility becomes "explosive".

From (4) we may write:

$$\ln(R_t - \mu)^2 = \ln(\sigma_{t-1}^2) + \ln(\varepsilon_t^2). \qquad (9)$$

Harvey, Ruiz, and Shepard (1992) and Harvey and Shepard (1993) have shown that one can estimate the coefficients of (8) and (9) by quasi-maximum likelihood,[6] which is indeed consistent under certain technical restrictions. We have not estimated this volatility model for energy prices, but for completeness we provide the calculation by Heynen and Kat (1993) of the expected average squared future volatility associated with (8):

$$\bar{v}_{t,T}^2 = \frac{\bar{\sigma}^2}{T-t} \sum_{k=1}^{T-t} \sigma_t^{2\gamma^k} \exp\left(\frac{-\alpha\gamma^k}{1-\gamma} - \frac{\kappa^2\gamma^{2k}}{2(1-\gamma^2)}\right) \qquad (10)$$

where $\bar{\sigma}^2$ is the steady-state[7] expectation of σ_t^2.

OPTION-IMPLIED AND FORECASTED VOLATILITY

A natural continuous time version of the Markov model (7) is given by the stochastic differential equation:

$$d\sigma_t = a(\sigma_t, t)dt + b(\sigma_t, t)dZ_t \qquad (11)$$

where a and b are continuous functions in two variables and Z is a Standard Brownian Motion. (Regularity conditions on a and b are required. See, for example, Karatzas and Shreve, 1988.) The associated continuous-time model for the underlying asset price, analogous to (4), is:

$$dS_t = \mu S_t dt + \sigma_t S_t)dB_t \qquad (12)$$

where B is a Standard Brownian Motion. With (11) and (12), we can extend the Black–Scholes approach to option valuation, and obtain a generalisation of the notion of implied volatility. A standard example of that is Heston (1993).

For example, we can follow Hull and White (1987), Scott (1987), and Wiggins (1987) in assuming that, after switching to risk-neutral probabilities, a stochastic differential equation of the form (11) and (12) still applies, in which the innovation process Z^*, driving stochastic volatility, is independent of the returns innovation process B^*. With this, one obtains the option pricing formula:

$$C_t = C^{SV}(S_t, \sigma_t, T, K, r)$$
$$\equiv E^*[C^{BS}(S_t, \sigma_t, T-t, K, r) \mid S_t, \sigma_t] \qquad (13)$$

where E* denotes risk-neutral expectation and

$$v_{t,T}^2 = \frac{1}{T-t}\int_t^T \sigma_s^2 ds. \qquad (14)$$

The fact that (13) and (14) is a valid option-pricing model follows from the fact that, if volatility is time-varying but deterministic, then one can substitute $v_{t,T}$ in place of the usual constant volatility coefficient to get the correct option price $C^{BS}(S_t, v_{t,T}, T - t, K, r)$ from the Black–Scholes model.

With the independence assumption above, one can simply average this modified Black–Scholes formula over all possible (probability-weighted) realisations of $v_{t,T}$ to get the result (13). One may note that we use the same notation $v_{t,T}$ in (5) and (14), as these two definitions of $v_{t,T}$ coincide in the limit as the length of a time period goes to zero.

As with any stochastic differential equation, an increase in σ_t implies an increase in σ_s for all $s \geq t$. Thus, under mild technical conditions on a and b, expected future average squared future volatility $\bar{v}_{t,T}^2$ is strictly increasing and continuous in σ_t. Since the Black–Scholes implied volatility σ^{BS} is likewise strictly monotone and continuous in volatility, each of the following is a strictly increasing continuous function of the other (in particular, knowledge of any one implies knowledge of others):

❑ the current option price $C_t = C^{SV}(S_t, \sigma_t, t, T, K, r)$;
❑ the current volatility σ_t;
❑ the expected average squared future volatility $\bar{v}_{t,T}^2$; and
❑ the Black–Scholes implied volatility $\sigma^{BS}(C_t, S_t, T - t, K, r)$.

Neither the current volatility σ_t, nor the expected average square volatility $\bar{v}_{t,T}^2$, are directly observable, but there may be traded options from whose prices they can be inferred.[8]

Knowing how to convert the option price or Black–Scholes implied volatility to the current or forecasted volatility depends on knowledge of the functions a and b determining the random behaviour of volatility in (11) – and these functions must themselves be estimated from data. This programme has been carried out in various ways by Renault and Touzi (1992), Poteshman (1998), Chernov and Ghysels (1998) and Benzoni (1998). In this setting, one can synthetically replicate (and therefore perfectly hedge) a given option with positions in the underlying asset, risk-free borrowing and lending, and positions in any other option. In other words, stochastic volatility risk is *spanned* in this setting. We

revisit this spanning property later in our discussion.

For many specifications of (11), and with empirically fitted parameters, one obtains from (13) the well-documented "smile-shaped" dependence of the Black–Scholes implied volatility on this strike price.

There are several methods for computing option prices under the continuous-time model (11) and (12), such as Monte Carlo simulation, or numerical solution of the associated partial differential equation.[9] Hull and White (1987) and Lu and Yu (1993) point out that option valuation with this stochastic volatility model can be well approximated by a Taylor-series expansion in the moments of volatility, given by:

$$C^{SV}(S_t, \sigma_t, T, K, r) = C^{BS}(S_t, \bar{v}_{t,T}, t, T, K, r)$$
$$+ \frac{1}{2}\frac{\partial^2}{\partial\sigma^2}C^{BS}(S_t, \bar{v}_{T-t}, T - t, K, r)\,\text{var}_t(v_t, T) + \frac{1}{6}\cdots (15)$$

where $\text{var}_t(\cdot)$ denotes conditional variance.

While the Black–Scholes option-implied volatility $\sigma^{BS}(C_t, S_t, T - t, K, r)$ is generally a biased forecast of $v_{t,T}$ the bias can be corrected when one knows the functions a and b in (11). In fact, as we have already seen from Figure 2, the bias is not large for our data set. (For the purposes of that figure, the well-documented "smile" aspect of the bias is mitigated by taking as the "Black–Scholes implied volatility" the average of the implied volatility for several near-to-the-money puts and calls.)

Several special cases of (11) have been analysed. The log-AR(1) model of discrete-time volatility given by (8) has the continuous-time counterpart $\sigma_t^2 = v_t$ where:

$$dv_t = (\alpha + \gamma v_t)dt + \kappa\,z_t \qquad (16)$$

for constants α, γ and κ. With $\gamma < 0$, we have "mean reversion", by which we mean that the expected rate of change of log-volatility is negative when v_t is above its steady-state mean $\bar{v} = -\alpha/\gamma$ and is positive when $v_t < \bar{v}$. The special case with $\alpha = 0$ (no mean reversion) is considered by Hull and White (1987), Scott (1987), and Wiggins (1987).

In a closely related model, Lu and Yu (1993) propose the special case of (11) given by $\sigma_t = \sqrt{V_t}$ where:

$$dV_t = (\alpha + \gamma V_t)dt + \kappa V_t\,dZ_t \qquad (17)$$

where the coefficients α, γ and κ have interpretations similar to those for (16). When $\alpha = 0$, the two volatility models (16) and (17) both have the standard lognormal volatility assumed by Hull and White (1987).

The Lu-Yu model has expected average squared future volatility :

$$\bar{v}_{t,T}^2 = \frac{1}{\gamma^2(T-t)}\left[(\gamma\sigma_t^2 - \alpha)(1 - e^{-\gamma(T-t)}) + \alpha\gamma(T-t)\right] \quad (18)$$

Other continuous-time Markovian models for stochastic volatility have been considered. For example, Heston (1993) uses a stochastic volatility of the "square root" style, and incorporates the impact of risk premia for volatility .

DATA

In the sections below, we estimate a number of volatility models using data from various energy markets. Enron Capital and Trade Resources has provided New York Mercantile Exchange (Nymex) energy commodity data for light crude, heating oil, natural gas, as well as the electricity futures contract data for the Palo-Verde and California-Oregon-Border (COB) hubs. (Contract specifications can be obtained from the Nymex web site at http://www.nymex.com/contracts.htm.) The daily data, starting from December 2, 1991 and ending on April 29, 1999, provided a considerable sample of 1,859 data points for the raw commodities, after filtering for non-trading days. The electricity futures series commenced on April 15, 1996, providing a smaller sample of 764 data points.

GARCH VOLATILITY

Many modellers have turned to Arch (autoregressive conditional heteroscedasticity) models of volatility, proposed by Engle (1982), and the related Garch (generalised Arch) and Egarch (exponential Garch) formulations, because they capture volatility persistence in a simple and flexible way.

For example, the Garch[10] model of stochastic volatility proposed by Bollerslev (1986) assumes that:

Table 1. Garch estimates

	α	β	γ
Heating oil	$4.18 (10^{-6})$	0.0647	0.9233
	(3.1710)	(7.4605)	(87.3438)
Light crude	$1.67 (10^{-6})$	0.0428	0.9529
	(1.9101)	(6.0805)	(118.1744)
Natural gas	$1.58 (10^{-4})$	0.3440	0.5831
	(6.9153)	(10.7401)	(16.9339)
Electricity (Palo-Verde)	$1.94 (10^{-4})$	−0.0048	0.9278
	(0.3258)	(−0.3005)	(4.0992)
Electricity (COB)	$7.93 (10^{-4})$	0.1490	0.5097
	(3.2187)	(3.3867)	(3.6777)

$$\sigma_t^2 = \alpha + \beta\varepsilon_t^2 + \gamma\sigma_{t-1}^2 \quad (19)$$

where α, β, and γ are positive constants[11] and $\varepsilon_t = R_t - \mu$. Here, γ is the key persistence parameter: a high γ implies a high carry-over effect of past to future volatility, while a low γ implies a heavily damped dependence on past volatility.

One can estimate α, β, and γ from returns data. For example, Table 1 illustrates the estimated Garch parameters (t-statistics in parentheses) associated with crude oil, heating oil, natural gas, and electricity obtained by maximum likelihood estimation. The data indicates a relatively high persistence of daily volatility, with γ estimated at over 90% for heating oil and light crude oil. The volatility process for natural gas appears to be much less persistent. (Another explanation is measurement error, which may be greater in natural gas due to the lower liquidity and greater volatility.) For natural gas, β is relatively high, indicating the increased importance of recent shocks in this market. The parameter estimates are noticeably inconsistent in the two electricity markets. The Palo-Verde market appears to exhibit much stronger persistence, and the estimate of β in that market is negative. This leaves open the possibility of negative volatilities being generated by the model (if ε_t is large in magnitude), which of course should be impossible. The implication of these results is that Garch models do not provide a good description of volatility in electricity markets. In Figure 1, the volatility of the petroleum products and natural gas tends to cluster through time. There are periods of high volatility followed by periods of low volatility. It is this type of volatility clustering that Garch models seek to capture. Volatility in the electricity markets behaves quite differently, being characterised by rapid and extreme changes brought about by spikes in prices. These price spikes do not tend to be followed by periods of high volatility and, therefore, Garch-type models seem inappropriate. It is likely that a model that formally incorporates jumps, such as described in Clewlow and Strickland (1998) will be more promising in this setting.

Bollerslev (1986) demonstrates that the squared residuals can be written as an ARMA process:

$$\varepsilon_t^2 = \alpha + (\beta + \gamma)\varepsilon_{t-1}^2 + \eta_t$$

Therefore, $\delta = \beta + \gamma < 1$ is a condition required for "non-explosivity". Heynen and Kat (1993) demonstrate that if this condition is satisfied, the forecasted (expected average square future)

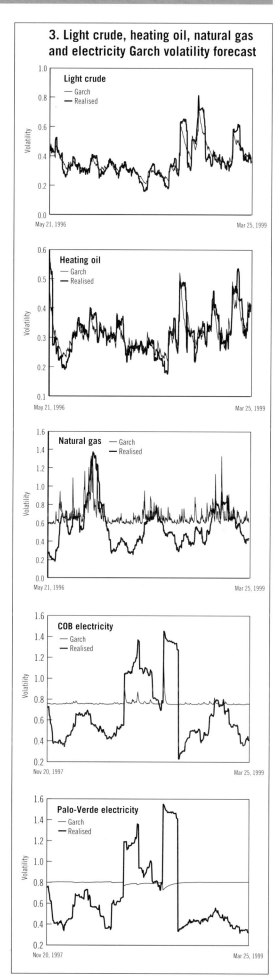

3. Light crude, heating oil, natural gas and electricity Garch volatility forecast

volatility associated with the Garch model is given by:

$$\bar{v}_{t,T}^2 = (T - t)\bar{\sigma}^2 + \left(\sigma_{t+1}^2 - \bar{\sigma}^2\right)\frac{1 - \delta^{T-t}}{1 - \delta} \quad (20)$$

where $\bar{\sigma} = \alpha/(1 - \delta)$.[12]

Figure 3 compares the 25-day Garch forecast of volatility, and the ultimately realised historical volatility for the same 25-day period, in the cases of heating oil, light crude oil, natural gas, and electricity. A casual review of the figures shows that the Garch model performs very poorly in modeling electricity volatility. There is some apparent forecasting ability for the other products, but one might also notice a potential disadvantage of the Garch model, in that the impact of the current return R_t on σ_{t+1}^2 is quadratic. This means that a day of exceptionally large absolute returns can have a dramatic impact on forecasted volatility, and cause "overshooting" in forecasted volatility. Moreover, if the persistence parameter is high, the effect on the volatility process of this single observation can take a long time to die out.

The main reason for the poor performance of the Garch model in the electricity markets is the fact that squared shocks enter the conditional variance. Volatility in the electricity markets is characterised by occasional large shocks. These large shocks have a dramatic impact on volatility and, therefore, heavily influence the parameter estimates of the Garch model. To reduce the impact of these "outliers", the Garch model can be re-estimated capping the influence of lagged shocks. For example, the modified Garch equation could be written as:

$$\sigma_t^2 = \alpha + \beta(\varepsilon^*)_t^2 + \gamma\sigma_{t-1}^2$$

where ε^*_t equals ε_t if the magnitude of $|\varepsilon_t|$ is less than two times the unconditional standard deviation of ε_t and is equal to two times the unconditional standard deviation of ε_t otherwise. We examine this model in our cross-model comparisons below.

EGARCH VOLATILITY

A potentially more flexible model of persistence is the Egarch model proposed by Nelson (1991), which takes the form[13]:

$$\log\sigma_t^2 = \left(\alpha - \beta_2\sqrt{\frac{2}{\pi}}\right) + \gamma\log\sigma_{t-1}^2$$

$$+ \beta_1\left(\frac{R_{t-\mu}}{\sigma_{t-1}}\right) + \beta_2\left(\left|\frac{R_t - \mu}{\sigma_{t-1}}\right|\right) \quad (21)$$

Maximum likelihood estimates of the Egarch

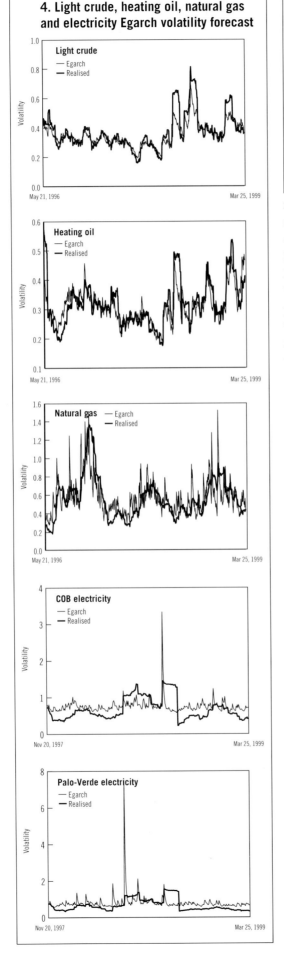

4. Light crude, heating oil, natural gas and electricity Egarch volatility forecast

Table 2. Egarch estimates

	α	γ	β_1	β_2
Heating oil	−0.2192	0.9869	0.0345	0.1465
	(5.0705)	(221.0038)	(2.3653)	(8.0978)
Light crude	−0.1446	0.9926	0.0110	0.1108
	(4.4421)	(293.1672)	(0.9285)	(6.7532)
Natural gas	−1.0358	0.8967	0.0577	0.4409
	(7.7545)	(51.9999)	(3.4895)	(13.5356)
Electricity	−1.9856	0.7150	0.2031	0.4340
(Palo-Verde)	(4.6622)	(11.1144)	(3.3809)	(4.5867)
Electricity (COB)	−2.2084	0.6727	−0.0905	0.2869
	(3.4120)	(6.6590)	(2.1132)	(4.3732)

model for crude oil, heating oil, natural gas and electricity are shown in Table 2. Again, a strong degree of volatility persistence is evident in the heating oil and light crude oil markets. Persistence in natural gas volatility is estimated to be much lower. As for the Garch model on the previous page, the Egarch model does not capture the important features of electricity volatility. Volatility in electricity markets tends to take the form of non-persistent "jumps" rather than the clustering of small and large price changes that Arch-type models seek to capture. For the Egarch model, some asymmetry[14] in the impact of return shocks to volatility is permitted, as these shocks appear in both levels, and in their absolute values.

For heating oil, crude oil and natural gas the coefficient β_1 on return shocks is positive, indicating that an increase in price is estimated to increase volatility more than does a decrease in price. Figure 4 illustrates volatility forecasts for the Egarch model.

The expected average squared future volatility implied by the Egarch model is:

$$\bar{v}_{t,T}^2 = \sum_{k=0}^{T-t-1} C_k \sigma_t^{2\gamma^\kappa} \qquad (22)$$

where C_k is relatively complicated constant given by Heynen and Kat (1993).

Nelson (1990) has shown that the Egarch model (21) and the log-AR(1) model (8) converge with decreasing period length, and appropriate normalisation of coefficients, to the same continuous-time model (16).

MULTIVARIATE GARCH VOLATILITY

When, as in many energy markets, one can infer volatility-related information for one commodity from changes in the volatility of returns in another market, one can generally do better by incorporating such cross-market information rather than using a model in which the volatility for the given commodity is affected only by its own past price behaviour.

A simple model that accounts for cross-market inference is the multivariate Garch model. For example, a simple two-commodity version of this model takes the form:

$$\begin{pmatrix} \sigma_{a,t}^2 \\ \sigma_{ab,t} \\ \sigma_{b,t}^2 \end{pmatrix} = \alpha + \beta \begin{pmatrix} R_{a,t}^2 \\ R_{a,t} R_{b,t} \\ R_{b,t}^2 \end{pmatrix} + \gamma \begin{pmatrix} \sigma_{a,t-1}^2 \\ \sigma_{ab,t-1} \\ \sigma_{b,t-1}^2 \end{pmatrix} \quad (23)$$

where:
$R_{a,t}$ is the return on commodity a at time t
$R_{b,t}$ is the return on commodity b at time t
$\sigma_{a,t-1}$ is the conditional volatility of $R_{a,t}$
$\sigma_{b,t-1}$ is the conditional volatility of $R_{b,t}$
$\sigma_{ab,t-1}$ is the conditional covariance between $R_{a,t}$ and $R_{b,t}$
σ is a vector with three elements
β is a 3×3 matrix
γ is a 3×3 matrix.

With β and γ assumed to be diagonal for simplicity and tractability, a maximum likelihood estimate for the bivariate Garch model (23) for heating oil (a) and crude oil (b) is given by:

$$\begin{pmatrix} \sigma_{a,t}^2 \\ \sigma_{ab,t} \\ \sigma_{b,t}^2 \end{pmatrix} = \begin{bmatrix} \underset{(2.717)}{2.29(10^{-6})} \\ \underset{(3.118)}{2.47(10^{-6})} \\ \underset{(4.141)}{4.83(10^{-6})} \end{bmatrix} + \begin{bmatrix} \underset{(8.349)}{0.046} & 0 & 0 \\ 0 & \underset{(7.819)}{0.040} & 0 \\ 0 & 0 & \underset{(9.689)}{0.064} \end{bmatrix}$$

$$\begin{pmatrix} R_{a,t}^2 \\ R_{a,t} R_{b,t} \\ R_{b,t}^2 \end{pmatrix} + \begin{bmatrix} \underset{(146.408)}{0.949} & 0 & 0 \\ 0 & \underset{(138.840)}{0.950} & 0 \\ 0 & 0 & \underset{(108.373)}{0.923} \end{bmatrix} \begin{pmatrix} \sigma_{a,t-1}^2 \\ \sigma_{ab,t-1} \\ \sigma_{b,t-1}^2 \end{pmatrix}$$

with *t*-statistics shown in parentheses. Note the difference between the univariate and multivariate Garch parameters for heating oil (alone) and crude oil (alone). In principle, cross-market information can only improve the quality of the model if the multivariate model is appropriate. Figure 5 illustrates the fit of the multivariate Garch model estimated above.

STOCHASTIC VOLATILITY AND DYNAMIC HEDGING POLICIES

Park and Bera (1987), Cecchetti, Cumby and Figlewski (1988), and Kroner and Sultan (1993) discuss the application of bivariarte Garch models to the choice of hedging positions. In general, there is an improvement, both within and outside of the sample period over which the model is estimated, of the quality of hedging

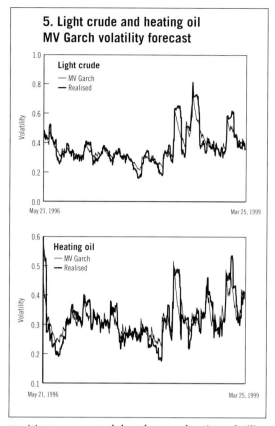

5. Light crude and heating oil MV Garch volatility forecast

positions suggested by the stochastic volatility model over those suggested by assuming constant covariances. These studies are limited to one-period hedges.

The dynamic-programming solution of multiperiod hedges in the bivariate Garch setting would, in general, imply different hedging coefficients, period by period, than those suggested by myopic (one-period-at-a-time) hedging. This is true even in deterministic volatility settings, as shown by Duffie and Richardson (1991). The extent to which prices are martingales, however, improves the robustness of myopic hedges. See, for example, Duffie and Jackson (1990). Further progress in the ability to exploit stochastic volatility models in selecting dynamic hedging policies is reported by Schweizer (1993).

Cross-model comparisons

Table 3 provides a comparison of the performance of several stochastic volatility models as applied to heating oil, light crude oil, natural gas and electricity. Except where noted, we are comparing the quality of each of the following five models with regard to forecasting realised historical volatility:
(i)   Garch
(ii) Egarch
(iii) bivariate Garch
(iv) past historical volatility
(v)   Black–Scholes implied volatility.

Table 3. Volatility forecast quality

%	Light crude	Heating oil	Natural gas	Palo-Verde electricity	COB electricity
In-sample period					
Garch	30	35	78	58 (42)	70 (44)
Egarch	28	32	53	66	65
MV Garch	31	34	–	–	–
Historical	29	33	55	65	70
Implied	30	28	40	–	–
Out-of-sample period					
Garch	30	26	55	83 (53)	62 (39)
Egarch	29	25	37	85	99
MV Garch	29	24	–	–	–
Historical	36	30	37	85	91
Implied	26	21	40	–	–

For all five models, the forecast $\bar{v}_{t,t+25}$ is as outlined on the previous page. For the "historical volatility" (volatility), we take $\bar{\sigma}_{t-25,t}$ as the forecast of its own future value, $\bar{\sigma}_{t,t+25}$. For the Black–Scholes implied volatility, we take the time series supplied to us by Enron. In each case, the root mean square forecast error is in terms of annualised percentage volatility – that is, the unit normally used to quote implied volatility.

The bracketed figures in the Garch row for the electricity markets relate to the modified Garch model where the impact of past shocks is capped at two standard deviations. This model performs much better than the standard Garch model, indicating that the presence of large price spikes in electricity markets are not well modelled by standard Garch models.

Table 3 is divided into two parts: "In-sample" and "Out-of-sample". The distinction is important for those models, (i)–(iii), for which parameters must be estimated before a forecast can be calculated.

In the case of the in-sample forecasts, the parameters were estimated from the same historical period over which the forecasts were made. These "forecasts" are therefore not possible to make contemporaneously. The out-of-sample forecasts for models (i)–(iii) are based on parameters estimated during the earlier (in-sample) period. Such forecasts are therefore possible to obtain contemporaneously, and are perhaps more realistic for practical purposes.

The "in-sample" period (ie from which model parameters were calculated) for the light crude, heating oil and natural gas contracts starts on January 10, 1992 and ends on May 20, 1996, and the "out-of-sample" period starts on May 21, 1996 and ends on March 25, 1999. The "in-sample" period for the electricity contracts starts on May 21, 1996 and ends on November 19, 1997, and the "out-of-sample" period starts on November

20, 1997 and ends on March 25, 1999.

Incidentally, one should not attempt to compare directly the out-of-sample forecast quality with the in-sample forecast quality, as these apply over different time periods, and the level of volatility appears to have been reduced during the out-of-sample period.

The Black–Scholes implied-volatility forecasts, which are always contemporaneously feasible, generally outperformed the other models during both the in-sample and the out-of-sample periods. It seems fair to conclude that, when available from options data, the Black–Scholes implied volatility is likely to be a more reliable method for forecasting volatility than the other methods that we examined. Somehow, implied volatility is capturing expectations of volatility held by traders, and those expectations appear to contain useful information that is not captured in a simply way by past returns.

Of course, our empirical study is very preliminary; our principal ambition was to use this empirical test to illustrate some of the issues. In fact, we remain quite hopeful that sophisticated and carefully estimated econometric models of stochastic volatility will turn out to be much more useful when used in conjunction with additional information (such as inventory levels, trading volume, price levels and cross-market volatility).[15]

Most promisingly, when options data are available, models of stochastic volatility can be constructed in which one uses options prices, possibly in conjunction with historical returns data, to estimate current volatility. In this case, one would estimate the parameters of a stochastic volatility model of the form (11) and (12) and apply a formula such as (13) (or extensions for more general cases) so as to infer the current level of volatility, σ_t. From σ_t and (11), one can then forecast volatility over future periods – by

Monte Carlo simulation, if by no other means. The confounding effect of imperfect parameter estimation on volatility forecasts can be treated, again by Monte Carlo simulation if no more computationally efficient method can be designed.

Other volatility models and option hedging

Rubinstein (1994), Dupire (1992, 1994), and Derman and Kani (1994) have shown that one may take:

$$\sigma_t = F(S_t, t) \qquad (24)$$

for some continuous function F so as to match the modelled prices of traded options with the prices for these options that are observable in the market. For example, appropriate choice of F allows one to match the well known "smile" curve of Black–Scholes implied volatility as a function of the exercise price. This is reminiscent of the idea of calibrating the parameters of a term-structure model of interest rates to the prices of bonds and option-embedded securities, as pursued earlier by Ho and Lee (1986), Black, Derman and Toy (1991), and Black and Karasinsky (1993).

The Rubinstein model treats a family of options with a particular expiration date and varying strike prices, while the Derman–Kani and Dupire approach addresses options with different exercise dates and strikes. Underlying the approach is the idea that one can infer, from the family of available options prices, something about the risk-neutral probability distribution of the underlying asset or, equivalently, the "state prices", in the sense of Breeden and Litzenberger (1978).

The computation of the implied probability distribution function (or state prices) has been taken up by Banz and Miller (1978), Shimko (1993), and, in the context of crude oil markets, by Melick and Thomas (1993). Given the implied risk-neutral probability distribution function, one then determines the stochastic process for the underlying asset price, using some simple rules to construct a "tree" that is consistent with the probabilities assigned to prices at the exercise dates. The Derman–Kani and Rubinstein trees are "binomial" (two branches out of each node), while the Dupire tree is "trinomial". Dupire also has in mind a continuous-time process that is consistent with a binomial or trinomial discretisation.

An implication of the price-dependent volatility model (24) is that all options can be hedged merely by taking positions in the underlying asset, along with riskless borrowing and lending – an important distinction from the Markov models of stochastic volatility considered previously.

In the latter case, hedging also call for positions in other volatility-related positions, such as options. It seems likely that, in the energy markets, volatility is broadly affected by market-wide events of an unpredictable nature, such as wars, natural disasters, cartel discussions, and in the case of electricity markets, weather and new generation. The onset of such events apparently raises volatility in many markets simultaneously in a way that has little to do with the levels of individual asset prices. If this is indeed the case, then (24) may be an inappropriate model for energy derivatives valuation and hedging.

For example, in times of dramatically changing volatility, we would guess that a hedge of a position in the energy markets with embedded options that is based on the "delta" from a model such as (24) could be improved by taking positions in the underlying commodity as well as positions in another option-related instrument.

It may be useful to model volatility that is both stochastic, as well as dependent on the price of the underlying commodity. For example, we may wish to replace the univariate Markovian stochastic volatility model (7) with:

$$\sigma_t = F(\sigma_{t-1}, S_t, z_t, t) \qquad (25)$$

so that one combines the stochastic volatility approach with that of Rubinstein, Dupire and Derman–Kani. To our knowledge, this combined approach has not yet been explored in any practical way.

In continuous time, such a combined form of stochastic volatility might supplant the simpler model (11) and (12), under risk-neutral probabilities, with a stochastic differential equation for the volatility σ and asset price S of the form:

$$d\sigma_t = a^*(\sigma_t, S_t, t)dt + b(\sigma_t, S_t, t)dZ_t^* \qquad (26)$$
$$dS_t = rS_t dt + \sigma_t S_t dB_t^*$$

where we can assume for simplicity that the risk-free rate r is constant and that the risk-neutral Brownian motions Z* and B* have constant correlation. In this setting, the prices $C(\sigma_t, S_t, t)$ and $A(\sigma_t, S_t, t)$ of any two distinct options (having, for example, distinct strike prices or distinct expiration dates) would generally have different deltas with respect to both σ_t and S_t. These deltas (partial derivatives) are denoted $C_\sigma(\sigma_t, S_t, t)$ and $C_S(\sigma_t, S_t, t)$ for the first option and $A_\sigma(\sigma_t, S_t, t)$ and $A_S(\sigma_t, S_t, t)$ for the second option. From Ito's lemma and the absence of arbitrage, the first option price $Y_t = C(\sigma_t, S_t, t)$ satisfies:

$$dY_t = rY_{dt} + C_\sigma(\sigma_t, S_t, t)b(\sigma_t, S_t, t)dZ_t^*$$

$$+ C_S(\sigma_t, S_t, t)\sigma_t S_t dB_t^*$$

This option can therefore be hedged by a dynamic trading strategy consisting of a portfolio (α_t, β_t) in the underlying asset and the second option, respectively given by:

$$\alpha_t = \frac{C_\sigma(\sigma_t, S_t, t)}{A_\sigma(\sigma_t, S_t, t)} A_S(\sigma_t, S_t, t)$$

$$\beta_t = \frac{C_\sigma(\sigma_t, S_t, t)}{A_\sigma(\sigma_t, S_t, t)}$$

(27)

The residual capital necessary to finance this hedging strategy would, in theory, be obtained by risk-free borrowing and lending. The option prices, deltas and trading strategies above can be computed for practical purposes using numerical methods, such as finite-difference schemes or Monte Carlo simulation, for solving the partial differential equations for C and A that arise in the usual way. See, for example, Hull (1997) or Duffie (1992) for a review. The major unknowns, of course, are the functions a^* and b in (26) – or, in discrete-time, the risk-neutral analogue of F in (25) – that determine the stochastic behaviour of volatility under risk-neutral probabilities. The simple models (25) and (26) could easily be expanded so as to allow path-dependence, or additional dependence on other state variables, as we have mentioned.

Of course, there are alternative models for volatility that go well beyond those that we have covered here. See, for example, Levy, Avellaneda and Paras (1994).

Concluding remarks

We have reviewed some of the basic approaches to modelling volatility that have been adopted for energy prices (and, in fact, most asset prices). This review is not entirely comprehensive, but it does support the following basic conclusions.

First, constant-volatility models, such as Black–Scholes, are a necessary starting point at a conceptual level, but are unreasonable for energy price data. They are, nevertheless, adequate for pricing near-to-expiration options, provided that the volatility coefficients used are consistent with contemporaneous option prices.

Second, stochastic volatility is persistent for energy prices. That is, when volatility is higher than "normal", it tends to stay higher for some time; when volatility is lower than "normal", it tends to say lower for some time. This fact is apparent from market data (on square returns and implied volatility), as well as from the estimated coefficients of several standard models that we examined.

Third, Black–Scholes option-implied volatility, when available, provided a more reliable forecast of future volatility than either historical volatility, or than can be obtained from the standard Arch-based models of volatility that we have examined. That is, although volatility is clearly stochastic, standard Arch-based models do not capture all of the important features of volatility in energy prices. This is especially true in the electricity markets.

Fourth, a reasonable test for the quality of a stochastic-volatility model is an out-of-sample measure of volatility forecast error. In-sample tests can be misleading. We also recommend, as a check of the quality of a stochastic volatility model, a measure of the accuracy of implied option hedges, such as the extent to which the payoff of a (possible fictitious) option can be replicated by a dynamic trading strategy, such as that in (27), involving the underlying asset price and, possibly, other options for which market prices are available.

Finally, there is good reason to explore stochastic volatility models that incorporate one or more of the following features:
❑ spreads between spot and forward prices;[16]
❑ inventory levels;
❑ price levels of the underlying asset;[17]
❑ the estimated level of volatility of related commodities;
❑ volumes of trade;[18]
❑ implied volatilities from stochastic-volatility models.

Given the explanatory power of simple, unadjusted Black–Scholes implied volatility, the use of contemporaneous estimates of volatility based on available options prices and models of stochastic volatility – the last feature – seems especially promising to us.

A reasonable place to start is a model such as (26), in which the probability distribution of volatility shocks is assumed to depend on the current levels of the underlying asset price and of volatility itself.

1 *Darrell Duffie can be contacted at the Graduate School of Business, Stanford University, Stanford, CA 94305-5015; telephone +1-415-723-1976. Stephen Gray can be contacted at the Department of Commerce, University of Queensland, Brisbane, Qld 4072, Australia; telephone +61-7-3365 6586; www.commerce.uq.edu.au/gray; Philip Hoang is at the Department of Commerce, University of Queensland, Brisbane, Qld 4072, Australia; telephone +61-7-3365 6420. We are grateful for assistance in obtaining data to Robert Jameson of Risk and Vince Kaminsky and Stinson Gibner of Enron.*

2 *This idea goes back at least to Beckers (1981).*

3 *Literally, $\lim_{T\to\infty}\hat{\sigma}_{t,T} = \sigma$ almost surely, and since an arbitrary number of observations of returns is assumed to be possible within an arbitrarily small time interval, this limit can be achieved in an arbitrarily small amount of calendar time.*

4 *There are of course good reasons to allow the mean return μ to vary with volatility, but we shall avoid this generality for expositional reasons.*

5 *For early models of this, see Clark (1973).*

6 *Except that $\log \varepsilon_t^2$ (by our assumption on ε_t) is not normally distributed, this would be a standard set-up for Kalman filtering of volatility. In such a setting, we would have access to standard methods for estimating volatility given the coefficients α, γ, and κ, and for estimating these coefficients by maximum likelihood. See for example, Brockwell and Davis (1992) for the consistency of the estimators in this setting.*

7 *That is, $\bar{\sigma} = \lim_{t\to\infty}E(\sigma_t^2)$, this limit existing if $0 < \gamma < 1$.*

8 *A qualification: if the underlying price process is continuously observable, σ_t is observable as the limit of historical volatility $\hat{\sigma}_{t-\delta,t}$, as $\delta \downarrow 0$, and the data frequency goes to infinity. This is not, however, a practical recipe.*

9 *For this equation, see for example Hull and White (1987).*

10 *This is known more precisely as the Garch(1,1) model. For specifics and generalisations, as well as a review of the Arch literature in finance, see for example Bollerslev, Chou and Kroner (1992).*

11 *The Garch model is in the class (5) of Markov models since we can write $\sigma_t = F(\sigma_{t-1},z_t) = [\alpha + \beta\sigma_{t-1}^1 z_t + \gamma\sigma_{t-1}^2]^{1/2}$ where $z_t = \varepsilon_t$ is white noise. Formally, this is known as Garch(1,1) model.*

12 *Note that $\bar{\sigma}^2$ is in fact the steady-state mean squared volatility,*

13 *The term $\sqrt{2/\pi}$ is equal to $E_t[|(R_t - \mu)/\sigma_{t-1}|]$.*

14 *This asymmetry was originally viewed by Nelson (1991), Schwert (1989), and Campbell and Kyle (1993) as important for stock returns.*

15 *See Lamoreux and Lastrapes (1993).*

16 *See Ng and Pirrong (1992, 1994).*

17 *See Dupire (1992, 1994), Derman and Kani (1994) and Rubinstein (1994).*

18 *See Lamoreux and Lastrapes (1993).*

BIBLIOGRAPHY

Baillie, R., and R. Myers, 1991, "Modelling Commodity Price Distributions and Estimating the Optimal Futures Hedge", *Journal of Applied Econometrics*, vol. 2, pp. 109-24.

Banz, R., and M. Miller, 1978, "Prices for State-contingent Claims: Some Evidence and Applications", *Journal of Business*, vol. 51, pp. 653-72.

Beckers, S., 1981, "Standard Deviations Implied in Option Process as Predictors of Future Stock Price Variability", *Journal of Banking and Finance*, vol. 5, pp. 363-82.

Benzoni, L., 1998, "Pricing Options Under Stochastic Volatility: An Econometric Analysis", working paper, J.L. Kellog Graduate School of Management, Northwestern University.

Black, F., and P. Karansinsky, 1993, "Bond and Option Pricing when Short Rates are Log-Normal", *Financial Analysts' Journal*, pp. 52-9.

Black, F., and M. Scholes, 1973, "The Pricing of Options and Corporate Liabilities", *Journal of Political Economy*, no. 81, pp.637-59.

Black, F., E. Derman and W. Toy, 1991, "A One-Factor Model of Interest rates and its Applications to Treasury Bond Options", *Financial Analysts' Journal*, January-February, pp. 33-9.

Bollerslev, T., 1986, "Generalised Autoregressive Conditional Heteroskedasticity", *Journal of Econometrics*, vol. 31, pp. 307-27.

Bollerslev, T., R. Chou and K. Kroner, 1992, "ARCH Modelling in Finance: A Review of Theory and Empirical Evidence", *Journal of Econometrics*, vol. 52, pp. 5-59.

Breeden, D., and R. Litzenberger, 1978, "Prices of State-Contingent claims Implicit in Options Prices", *Journal of Business*, vol. 51. 621-51.

Brockwell, P., and R. Davis, 1987, *Time Series: Theory and Methods*, New York.

Campbell, J., and A. S. Kyle, 1993, "Smart Money, Noise Trading and Stock Price Behaviour", *Review of Economic Studies*, vol. 60. pp. 1-34.

Cecchetti, S., R. Cumby and S. Figlewski, 1988, "Estimation of the Optimal Futures Hedge", *Review of Economics and Statistics*, vol. 70, pp. 623-30.

Chernov, M., and E. Ghysels, 1998, "What Data Should Be Used To Price Options?", working paper, Department of Finance, Pennsylvania State University.

Clark, P., 1973, "Subordinated Stochastic Process Model with Finite Variance for Speculative Prices", *Econometrica*, vol. 41, pp. 135-55.

Clewlow L., and C. Strickland, 1998, "A Multi-factor Model for Energy Derivatives Risk Management", Working Paper, School of Finance and Economics, University of Sydney.

Cox J., and M. Rubinstein, 1985, *Options Markets*, Englewood Cliffs.

Dasgupta, S., 1992, *Pricing Futures Options with Stochastic Volatility: Early Exercise, Incomplete Markets, and Maximum Likelihood Estimation of Parameters*, New York.

Derman, E., and I. Kani, 1994, "Riding on the Smile", *Risk*, February, pp. 32-9.

Duffie, D., 1992, *Dynamic Asset Pricing Theory*, Princeton University Press.

Duffie, D., and M. Jackson, 1990, "Optimal Hedging and Equilibrium in a Dynamic Futures Market", *Journal of Economic Dynamics and Control*, vol. 14, pp. 21-33.

Duffie, D., and H. Richardson, 1991, "Mean-Variance Hedging in Continuous-Time", *Annals of Applied Probability*, vol. 1, pp. 1-15.

Dupire, B., 1992, "Arbitrage Pricing with Stochastic Volatility", Société Générale, Paris.

Dupire, B., 1994, "Pricing with a Smile", *Risk*, January, pp. 18-20.

Engle, R., 1982, "Autoregressive Conditional Heteroskedasticity with Estimates of the Variance of United Kingdom Inflation", *Econometrica*, vol. 50, pp. 987-1008.

Garman, M., and M. Klass, 1980, "On the Estimation of Security Volatilities from Historical Data", *Journal of Business*, vol. 53, pp. 67-78

Genon-Catalot, V., and J. Jacod, 1993, "On the Estimation of the Diffusion Coefficient for Multi-Dimensional Diffusion Processes", *Annales Institut Henri Poincare*, vol. 29, pp. 119-51.

Harvey, A., and N. Shepard, 1993, "The Econometrics of Stochastic Volatility", LSE Financial Markets Group Discussion Paper Number 166, London School of Economics.

Harvey, A., E. Ruiz and N. Shepard, 1992, "Multivariate Stochastic Variance Models", LSE Financial Markets Group Discussion Paper, London School of Economics.

Heston, S., 1993, "A Closed-Form Solution for Options with Stochastic Volatility, with Applications to Bond and Currency", *Review of Financial Studies*, vol. 6, pp. 327-44.

Heynen, R., and H. Kat, 1993. "Volatility Prediction: A Comparison of the Stochastic Volatility, GARCH(1,1) and EGARCH(1,1) Model", Department of Operations Research, Erasmus University.

Ho, T., and S. Lee, 1986, "Term Structure Movements and Pricing Interest Rate Contingent claims", *Journal of Finance*, vol. 41, pp. 1011-29.

Hull, J., 1997, *Options, Futures, and Other Derivative Securities*, Third Edition, Englewood Cliffs.

Hull, J., and A. White, 1987, "The Pricing of Options on Assets with Stochastic Volatilities", *Journal of Finance*, vol. 42, pp. 281-300.

Johnson, H., and H. Shanno, 1987, "The Pricing of Options when the Variance is Changing", *Journal of Financial and Quantitative Analysis*, vol. 22, pp. 143-51

Karatzas, I., and S. Shreve, 1988, *Brownian Motion and Stochastic Calculus*, New York.

Kroner, K., and J. Sultan, 1993, "Time-Varying Distributions and Dynamic Hedging with foreign Currency Futures", *Journal of Financial and Quantitative Analysis*, vol. 28, pp. 535-51

Lamoreux, C., and W. Lastrapes, 1993, "Endogenous Trading Volume and Momentum in Stock Return Volatility", Olin School of Business, Washington University, St. Louis.

Levy, A., M. Avellaneda and A. Paras, 1994, "A New Approach for Pricing Derivatives Securities in Markets with Uncertain Volatilities: A 'Case Study' on the Trinomial Tree", Courant Institute of Mathematical Sciences, New York University.

Melick, W., and C. Thomas, 1993, "Recovering an Asset's Implied PDF from Option Prices: An Application to Crude Oil during the Gulf Crisis", Federal Reserve Board, Washington DC.

Melino, A., and S. Turnbull, 1990, "Pricing Foreign Currency Options with Stochastic Volatility", *Journal of Econometrics*, vol. 45, pp. 239-65.

Nelson, D., 1990, "ARCH Models as Diffusion Approximations", *Journal of Econometrics*, vol. 45, pp. 7-39.

Nelson, D., 1991, "Conditional Heteroskedasticity in Asset Returns: A New Approach", *Econometrica*, vol. 59, pp. 347-70.

Nelson, D., 1992, "Filtering and Forecasting with Mispecified ARCH Models I: Getting the Right Variance with the Wrong Model", *Journal of Econometrics*, vol. 52, pp. 61-90

Ng, V., and C. Pirrong, 1992, "The Relation between Oil and Gasoline Futures and Spot Prices", School of Business, University of Michigan, and Midamerica Institute.

Ng, V., and C. Pirrong, 1994, "Fundamentals and Volatility: Storage, Spreads, and the Dynamics of Metals Prices", *Journal of Business*, vol. 67, pp. 203-30.

Park, A., and A. Bera, 1987, "Interest Rate Volatility, Basis Risk, and Heteroskedasticity in Hedging Mortgages", *AREUEA Journal*, vol. 15, pp. 79-97.

Parkinson, M., 1980, "The Extreme Value Method for Estimating the Variance of the Rate of Return", *Journal of Business*, vol. 46, pp. 434-52.

Poteshman, A., 1998, "Estimating a General Stochastic Variance Model from Options Prices", working paper, Graduate School of Business, University of Chicago.

Renault, E., and N. Touzi, 1992, "Stochastic Volatility Models: Statistical Inference from Implied Volatilities Working Paper", GREMAQ, IDEI, and CREST, France.

Rogers, C., and L. Satchell, 1991, "Estimating Variance from High, Low and Closing Prices", *Annals of Applied Probability*, vol. 1, pp. 504-12.

Rubinstein, M., 1994, "Implied Binomial Trees", Haas School of Business, University of California, Berkeley.

Schweizer, M., 1993, "Approximating Random Variables by Stochastic Integrals", Working Paper, University of Bonn.

Schwert, W., 1989, "Why does Stock Price Volatility Change Over Time?", *Journal of Finance*, vol. 44, pp. 1115-53.

Scott, L., 1987, "Option Pricing when the Variance changes Randomly" Theory, Estimation, and an Application", *Journal of Financial and Quantitative Analysis*, vol. 22, pp. 419-38.

Shimko, D., 1993, "Bounds of Probability", *Risk*, April, pp. 33-7.

Stoll, H., and R. Whaley, 1993, *Futures and Options: Theory and Applications*, Cincinnati.

Wiggins, J., 1987, "Optional Values under Stochastic Volatility: Theory and Empirical Estimates", *Journal of Financial Economics*, vol. 19, pp. 351-72.

15

Correlation and Cointegration in Energy Markets

Carol Alexander
University of Oxford

Successful risk management requires an understanding of the nature of volatility and of the correlations between financial markets, as well as of the problems inherent in calculating statistical estimates of these quantities.[1] While volatilities are based on the variances of individual returns distributions, correlations depend on the characteristics of the joint distributions between two related markets. This extra dimension adds a great deal of uncertainty to measures of correlation risk.

It is generally assumed that individual return processes are stationary. That is, they are mean-reverting to a constant mean, at a rate that is stable over time. Volatility is a standardised form of the variance of this process, which is finite and constant when returns are stationary. So it is reasonable to assume that volatilities do indeed exist. But it is by no means always the case that two returns processes will be *jointly* stationary. That is, while they are individually stationary, the cross-correlations may not be stable over time. Indeed, unconditional correlations may not even exist.

Of course, it is always possible to calculate a number that supposedly represents correlation, but often these numbers change considerably from day to day. This is a sign that the two returns processes are not in fact jointly stationary. It is unfortunate that some standard correlation estimation methods induce an apparent stability that is purely an artefact of the method, while the true nature of underlying correlations is obscured.

The primary aim of this chapter is to review the different approaches to measuring energy correlations, pointing out their advantages and limitations, and their applications to energy markets. The crude oil and natural gas markets are used to illustrate some applications.[1] We use daily data on West Texas Intermediate (WTI)

crude oil spot and near futures prices from July 1, 1988 to February 26, 1999, and the New York Mercantile Exchange (Nymex) sweet crude prices from 1 to 12 months from February 4, 1993 to March 24, 1999. For the natural gas market we use the Nymex prompt month future with the *Gas Daily* time series for natural gas from April 10, 1992, and the Kansas City "Western" natural gas contract from December 18, 1995 to March 3, 1999.

In efficient markets the logarithm of prices follows a random walk. Not all energy markets are efficient, since prices are dominated by supply constraints (storage, transport, cartel restrictions, etc) and by demand fluctuations (weather conditions and so on). For example, the natural gas market discussed in Panel 1 is clearly not efficient. Prices are mean-reverting, so they cannot be generated by a random-walk model.

However, if the market is efficient, the stochastic trend in the data must be removed before any analysis of volatility and correlation. This is the first limitation of correlation analysis. Since data are detrended before the analysis, this precludes any chance of investigating long-term common trends in asset prices using volatility or correlation analysis. Because of this, correlation-based hedges may require frequent rebalancing. There is nothing in the computation of correlation-based hedge ratios that guarantees that the hedge will remain tied to the underlying over the longer term.

As an aside, it is worth giving some thought to how the data should be detrended before the calculation of volatility and correlation. If the random-walk model for log prices has a drift, the log prices will trend upwards or downwards, depending on whether the drift is positive or negative. But even if there is zero drift, random walks have a "stochastic" trend. That is, they are

292

CORRELATION
AND
COINTEGRATION
IN ENERGY
MARKETS

non-stationary and only stationary after first differencing. Thus the appropriate stationarity transform is to take first differences of the log prices; this means that volatilities and correlations should be calculated on *returns*. Note that detrending price data by fitting a linear trend, and taking deviations from that trend, is not appropriate. In fact this process only removes the drift in the random walk, and the stochastic trend remains.

Another limitation of correlation is that it is essentially a static measure, so it cannot reveal any dynamic causal relationships. This introduces the danger that hedges might be based on spurious correlations that appear high even though there is no underlying causal relationship, particularly when some of the rather misleading correlation measures are employed. The advanced management of correlation risks must take account of any lead-lag relationships, for example the "price discovery" between spot and futures, but correlation is not an adequate tool for such analyses.

The last part of this chapter introduces a method of measuring comovements between markets that overcomes some of the limitations of correlation. Cointegration, a methodology that has become standard practice in econometrics during the last decade, is now showing itself to be a very useful tool for hedging financial assets.

Cointegration refers not to comovements in returns, but comovements in asset prices. If spreads are mean-reverting, asset prices are tied together in the long-term by a common stochastic trend, and the prices are said to be "cointegrated". Hedges based on cointegration may deviate from the underlying in the short term, but are tied to the underlying by a long-run equilibrium relationship and hence require less frequent rebalancing.

Cointegration is a two-step process: first, any long-run equilibrium relationships between prices are established, and then a dynamic correlation model of returns is estimated. This "error correction model", so-called because short-term deviations from equilibrium are corrected, reveals the dynamic causalities that must be present in a cointegrated system. The chapter concludes with an empirical example of a cointegration model for crude oil spot and futures.

Statistical measures of correlation

Returns to financial assets, the relative price changes, are well approximated for short holding periods by the difference in log prices. For ease

of exposition we consider daily returns $R_t = \log P_t - \log P_{t-1}$ although correlation methods apply equally well to different returns frequencies, provided data are synchronous.

It is reasonable to assume that returns are generated by a stationary stochastic process. That is:

$E(R_t)$, the unconditional mean, is a finite constant;

$V(R_t)$, the unconditional variance, is a finite constant;

$COV(R_t, R_{t-s})$, the unconditional autocovariance, depends only on the lag s.

The mean-reversion property of stationary series is well known. A stationary process is mean-reverting, not in the sense of a mean-reverting term structure, but mean-reverting over time. They can never drift too far from their mean because of the finite variance.

The speed of mean-reversion is determined by the autocovariance: mean-reversion is quick when autocovariances are small, and slow when autocovariances are large. At one end of the spectrum we have "white noise", when returns are independent so $COV(R_t, R_{t-s})$ is zero, and mean-reversion is instantaneous. At the other extreme $COV(R_t, R_{t-s}) = V(R_t)$ so autocorrelations are unity, there is no mean-reversion, and returns are not stationary.

Two stationary returns processes R_1 and R_2 are jointly covariance stationary if $COV(R_{1,t}, R_{2,t-s})$ depends only on the lag s. In particular the contemporaneous covariance $COV(R_{1,t}, R_{2,t})$ is a constant, irrespective of the time at which it is measured.

For jointly stationary returns we may define a contemporaneous cross-correlation as:

$$Corr(R_{1,t}, R_{2,t}) = COV(R_{1,t}, R_{2,t}) / \sqrt{(V(R_{1,t})V(R_{2,t}))}$$

or in alternative notation $\rho = \sigma_{12}/\sigma_1\sigma_2$. So the extension of the constant volatility assumption to constant unconditional cross-correlations requires joint stationarity. This is quite an heroic assumption, except in special circumstances. So it should be clear from the outset that the computation of unconditional correlations may be a meaningless exercise. Nevertheless it is standard practice, so one focus of this chapter is to point out the dangers of using such measures when they are not, in fact, valid.

If it exists, the unconditional correlation is one number, ρ, that is the same throughout the process. Correlations always lie between +1 and –1. High positive values indicate that the returns move together in the same direction, and high negative values indicate that they tend to move in opposite directions. Orthogonal or uncorrelated returns have zero correlation.

Any differences between estimates of ρ at different times arise from differences in samples. The smaller the sample the bigger these differences, because sampling errors are inversely proportional to sample size. But when returns have a high degree of joint stationarity correlation estimates should not jump around too much even for small sample sizes. On the other hand, if correlation estimates are highly unstable this is a sure sign of non-joint stationarity. So, while it is always possible to calculate a number based on some formula or model for correlation, it does not always make sense to do so.

It may also be that correlations appear quite high for a long period, even when they are spurious. For example, contemporaneous data on live hog spot prices and crude oil prompt futures may be available from Nymex, and correlations estimates could be calculated. But it is probable that little underlying causal relation exists between live hogs and crude oil, except perhaps in transportation costs. Their returns are unlikely to be jointly stationary, but correlation calculations according to some methods might result in apparently high and stable correlations.

The next section shows how the most common correlation estimates of all, the equally weighted "historical" correlations, will have apparent stabilities that are, in fact, just an artefact of the estimation method. Using a more appropriate correlation model, such as an exponentially weighted average or a Garch model of the kind described in detail below, would reveal greater instabilities in correlation, particularly if returns are not jointly stationary.

But then, if unconditional correlations do not exist because returns are not jointly stationary, and if conditional correlations are jumping around all over the place, what can be done to hedge correlation risk? In the absence of correlation swaps or a futures contract based on equally weighted averages it may be better to look for alternative measures of comovements between assets. For example, it would be possible to base hedging strategies on the cointegration error correction models of asset prices that are introduced at the end of this chapter.

EQUALLY WEIGHTED MOVING AVERAGES
Unbiased estimates of unconditional correlation are usually calculated by a weighted moving aver-

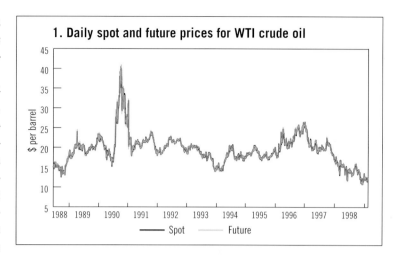

1. Daily spot and future prices for WTI crude oil

age, with either equal or exponential weighting. A standard method is to estimate variance as a weighted average of squared returns and to divide the covariance, estimated as a similarly weighted average of cross products of returns, by the square root of the product of the variances.

Consider for example the WTI crude oil spot[2] and Nymex near-futures prices shown in Figure 1. They should be very highly correlated because the major price changes arise from supply constraints, such as the Gulf crisis in 1990/1991, rather than demand fluctuations. This is in marked contrast to the natural gas market discussed in Panel 1.

However, crude oil spot-futures correlations are also quite variable, because the market has oscillated between backwardation and contango during the course of the decade (Panel 2). Fluctuations in the convenience yield arise as perceptions of inventory and financing costs change, and these perceptions are governed by micro- and macroeconomic factors that can vary considerably between the different players in the oil market.

Figure 2 shows correlations between spot and futures crude oil prices calculated using equal weighting over three months, six months,

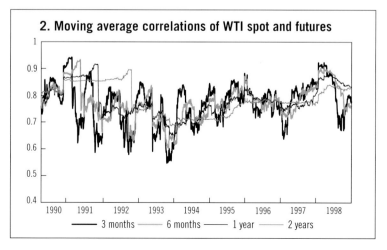

2. Moving average correlations of WTI spot and futures

294

CORRELATION
AND
COINTEGRATION
IN ENERGY
MARKETS

one year and two years. The longer the averaging period, the more stable the correlations appear to be. This is because the pronounced effect on correlations that always follows an extreme event in the markets will last for exactly n days, where n is the length of the averaging period.

For example on January 17, 1991 when spot and future prices dropped from about $32 to about $22 overnight following the outbreak of war in the Gulf, equally weighted correlations increased substantially by an amount that was in inverse proportion to the length of the average. On January 18, 1991 the three-month correlation rose from 0.8 to 0.91, staying above 0.9 until April 17, 1991 when it jumped down from 0.94 to 0.83. The two-year correlation jumped from 0.81 to 0.86, staying at around this level for exactly two years, long after the other averages had returned to more realistic levels. But nothing special happened on April 17, 1991, or on July 18, 1991 or one year or two years after the outbreak of the Gulf war. The sharp reduction in the correlation figures on these dates is simply an artefact of the estimation method.

These "ghost" effects of extreme events on correlation become less intense, but longer lasting, as the averaging period increases. So if equal weighting is to be applied for measuring correlations and hedge ratios there is a case for ignoring extreme events. Otherwise they can bias estimates for a long time after an extreme event has occurred.

EXPONENTIALLY WEIGHTED MOVING AVERAGES

One of the advantages of using exponential rather than equal weighting is that shocks to correlation die out exponentially, at a rate determined by the smoothing constant.

Exponential smoothing takes the form

$$(1-\lambda)\sum_{i=1}^{\infty}\lambda^{i-1}x_{t-i-1}$$

where $0 < \lambda < 1$. Another time series is created, the exponentially weighted moving average (EWMA) that is "smoother" than the original. The degree of smoothing is determined by the size of the smoothing constant λ.

To calculate an exponentially weighted correlation, take three EWMAs with the same value of λ. First calculate each of the two returns variances by smoothing the squared returns in each market. Then calculate the EWMA covariance, so that x is the cross product of returns, and finally divide this by the square root of the product of the two variances.

Exponential weighting is a simple method of measuring correlations that has advantages over both the "historical" equally weighted averages and the more technical Garch models that are introduced in the next section. But the big question with exponential weighting is which value of λ should be used?

The larger λ is, the smoother the correlation becomes because observations far in the past still effect the current average. The smaller λ is, the more responsive the correlation to daily moves in the markets. There is no one best method for optimising the value of λ. And even if an optimal value is found for any particular market, there are considerable advantages in using the same value of λ for all markets in a large risk system.

The RiskMetrics data provided by JP Morgan that is downloadable every day free of charge from the Internet, estimates volatilities and correlations of hundreds of markets for many different types of financial assets (see Alexander, 1996). The RiskMetrics exponentially weighted moving average daily data use the value $\lambda = 0.94$ for all volatilities and correlations, and the EWMA examples in this chapter all take this value for λ.

In fact the exponentially weighted moving average with $\lambda = 0.94$ has a half-life of about 30 days, so its variability is similar to that of the 30-day equally weighted moving average (see Figure 3). The main difference between the two methods is that the equally weighted measure has 30 day "ghost" effects, whereas shocks die out exponentially in the EWMA. It would therefore be more realistic to base spot-futures or forward curve arbitrage on exponentially rather than equally weighted correlation estimates.

Figure 3 shows the exponentially weighted correlation between spot and prompt future prices of crude oil. It is quite evident from Figure 3

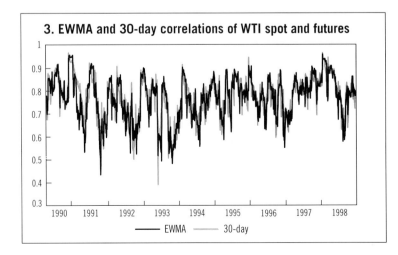

3. EWMA and 30-day correlations of WTI spot and futures

— EWMA   — 30-day

295

CORRELATION
AND
COINTEGRATION
IN ENERGY
MARKETS

THE CORRELATION BETWEEN NATURAL GAS SPOT AND PROMPT FUTURE

Low or unstable correlation between spot and futures prices can lead to considerable basis risk. Consider hedging natural gas spot prices, as indicated by the *Gas Daily* index, by purchasing the Nymex future contract for delivery over the next month shown in Figure A. The *Gas Daily* price is the price transacted for delivery of gas on the following day. The futures contract represents the price for delivery of equal volumes over the entire calendar month represented by the futures contract.

Natural gas storage facilities play a crucial role in balancing supply and demand in North America, and there are substantial seasonal effects. In the summer months excess production is injected into storage and in the winter months the stored gas is withdrawn to supply any excess load. In cold winters, when demand typically exceeds production, one would expect to see *Gas Daily* prices rise sharply during periods of extreme cold. Futures prices might also rise because depletions in the amount of stored gas may raise expectations for future prices. However, because storage costs are high, there can be a substantial decoupling of these two prices under certain conditions, as was seen when the spot prices spiked in February 1996. The net effect is that correlations between spot and future prices are quite variable, and may be rather low when storage is filled to capacity.

The winters of 1997/98 and 1998/99 were very mild. During the autumn of 1998 one could hardly give away spot natural gas during some weeks, since storage was completely full. This was apparent in the downward price spikes in *Gas Daily* prices for both October and November. Because of these two warm winters the exponentially weighted moving average (EWMA) correlation between spot and futures prices decreased, as shown in Figure B. More recently the correlation actually became negative. Storage was filled to capacity during the autumn months of 1997 and 1998, so futures prices responded hardly at all to daily demand fluctuations.

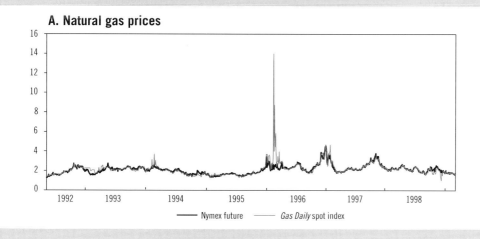

A. Natural gas prices

—— Nymex future   —— *Gas Daily* spot index

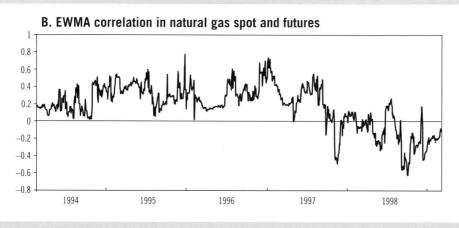

B. EWMA correlation in natural gas spot and futures

296

CORRELATION
AND
COINTEGRATION
IN ENERGY
MARKETS

CORRELATION IN THE CRUDE OIL TERM STRUCTURE

The Nymex sweet crude oil contracts from 1 to 24 months are illustrated in Figure A. An immediate feature to note is that the volatility of futures prices decreases with maturity, the 1-month future being the most volatile and the 24-month future the least. This is true for all term structures, because short-term expectations are more volatile than long-term expectations and open interest and trading volume are concentrated at the low end. Slicing through the data gives the futures term structure on any given day, and both downwards and upwards sloping term structures are evident as the market oscillates between backwardation and contango.

Correlations of the 1-month future with futures of other maturities are illustrated in Figure B, calculated using an EWMA with $\lambda = 0.94$. They reduce as the spread increases, as would be expected. But what is interesting about these correlations is their variability over time, a feature that is most pronounced in the less liquid longer maturities.

For example, on March 13, 1996 the 1-month to 6-month correlation stood at 0.9, the 1-month to 2-month correlation at 0.92. One week later the

1-month to 2-month correlation had fallen to 0.8 but the 1-month to 6-month had dropped substantially, to 0.57. Even greater changes in correlations can occur with longer maturities, because most of the trading is in the shorter futures.

Interestingly, the relatively stable periods in correlation did not necessarily occur when the term structure itself was flat and/or stable. For example, correlations were relatively high and stable during the entire year from October 1996 to October 1997. But during this time both strong and weak backwardation, and weak contango situations occurred. On the other hand, correlations were quite unstable in 1998 and the early part of 1999, although the market experienced a strong contango throughout.

The expected price rises occurred at the end of the data period, in March 1999 when OPEC producers restricted supply. At the time of writing the contango has been replaced by a wobbly but flat term structure. Uncertain expectations about the direction of the next price move have had the effect of increasing volatility and reducing correlation at the end of the sample.

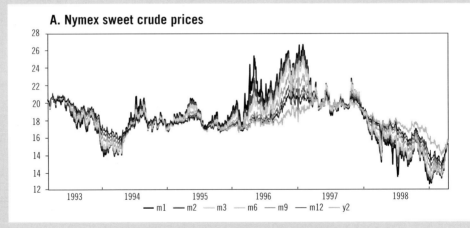

A. Nymex sweet crude prices

— m1 — m2 — m3 — m6 — m9 — m12 — y2

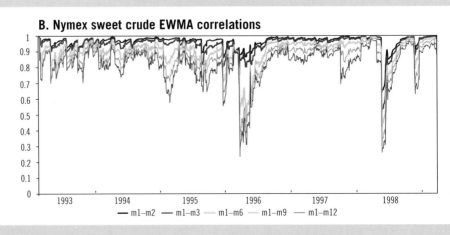

B. Nymex sweet crude EWMA correlations

— m1–m2 — m1–m3 — m1–m6 — m1–m9 — m1–m12

297

CORRELATION
AND
COINTEGRATION
IN ENERGY
MARKETS

that these estimates are less stable then those in Figure 2. But in both figures it is the same correlation that is being estimated.

Exponentially and equally weighted moving average correlation measures are all estimating the same thing: the constant unconditional correlation that is assumed by the weighted average model. So how can it be that so many different results are obtained from estimating correlation on the same data? A generic problem with correlation estimation is that wildly different results may be obtained, depending on the time period of the data and the estimation method used. For any given model, be it an equally weighted average over a fixed number of days, or an exponentially weighted average with some value for λ, the variation in results at different time periods can only be attributed to "noise" arising from differences in samples. There is nothing else in these models to explain time variation in correlation.

When correlation estimates are found to be unstable the constant correlation assumption that underlies weighted average correlation measures should be questioned. Conditions in many energy markets may not be conducive to joint stationarity. For example, the correlations between Nymex sweet crude futures of various maturities can be very unstable, particularly when there are big differences in trading volume and open interest (Panel 2).

Readers interested in statistical tests for joint stationarity are referred to standard econometrics texts such as Hamilton (1994). They are based on the eigenvalues of coefficient matrices from a vector autoregressive model: if they lie within the unit circle the series are jointly covariance stationary.[3] But it should not really be necessary to go into such details: if correlations are found to be unstable, returns are unlikely to be jointly stationary. In this case it is not correct, strictly speaking, to use a model based on constant correlation, such as the weighted average models that have been discussed above.

GARCH

Weighted average methods only provide an estimate of the unconditional variance or covariance, which are constants. The variance and covariance estimates do change over time, but this can only be ascribed to "noise" or sampling errors in a moving average model. There is nothing else in the model that allows for variation in return distributions.

In a Generalised Autoregressive Conditional Heteroscedasticity (Garch) model, the same returns data are now assumed to be generated by a stochastic process with time varying volatility. Instead of collapsing the data into a single unconditional distribution, a Garch model introduces more detailed assumptions about the conditional distribution of returns. It is allowed to change over time in an autocorrelated way. In particular the conditional variance is assumed to be an autoregressive process.

Why are these models given such an unpronounceable name? "Heteroscedasticity" means changing variance, so conditional heteroscedasticity means changing conditional variance. "Autoregressive" means regression on itself, so a time series displays autoregressive conditional heteroscedasticity if it has highly volatile periods interspersed with tranquil periods. In other words volatility comes in bursts or clusters. And "generalised" simply refers to the fact that the first Arch model introduced by Robert Engle (1992) was later generalised by Tim Bollerslev (1986). Most financial markets are better modelled by Garch than Arch processes, and there are many different Garch models from which to choose.

However, it is rarely necessary to use more than a Garch(1,1) to model volatility, which has one lag of the squared unexpected return ε^2 and one autoregressive term:

$$\sigma_t^2 = \omega + \alpha \varepsilon_{t-1}^2 + \beta \sigma_{t-1}^2$$
$$\omega > 0, \alpha, \beta \geq 0$$

The size of the parameters α and β determine the short-run dynamics of the resulting volatility time series. Large "persistence" coefficients β indicate that shocks to conditional variance take a long time to die out. Large "reaction" coefficients α mean that volatility is quick to react to market movements, and volatilities tend to be more "spiky". In financial markets it is common to find lag coefficients in excess of 0.7 but returns coefficients tend to be smaller, often less than 0.2. If these coefficients sum to one, the Garch model is integrated, and volatility term structure forecasts do not mean-revert.

Although Garch estimates are based on a time-varying model for returns distributions, and EWMA estimates are not, they are quite similar. In fact the EWMA is a simple integrated Garch model without a constant term. But when it comes to modelling volatility, Garch models have many advantages over EWMA. In particular:

❑ Garch parameters are estimated independently and optimally using maximum likelihood.

Whereas in the EWMA model the persistence and reaction coefficients (λ and $1-\lambda$ respectively) are constrained to sum to one. Also there is no single optimal technique for estimating the parameter of an EWMA.

❑ The Garch stochastic volatility model gives convergent term structure forecasts, whereas the EWMA model assumes constant volatility. The EWMA is an estimate, not a forecast. It is commonly assumed that current levels of volatility will persist forever (the "square root of time" rule), which is rather unrealistic.

Garch may also be used to estimate and forecast correlation, but with much less success. The multivariate Garch model may be used to obtain conditional correlation estimates that are supposed to be time-varying, because they are based on the assumption of stochastic rather than constant correlation.

But whereas Garch volatility models are easy enough to implement, multivariate models often experience convergence problems. This is because the likelihood function becomes very flat and difficult to optimise as the number of parameters increases. The bivariate BEKK model has 11 parameters compared to the three parameters of a symmetric univariate Garch, so often parameters are imposed. For example, the diagonal vech multivariate Garch has only nine parameters, but it assumes that the cross-market effects are zero which is not very realistic. The multivariate Garch volatilities and correlations that are estimated depend very much on the parameterisation chosen, and it is extremely difficult to determine which is the best Garch model.

Given the uncertainty in correlation estimates, and the difficulty of doing anything other than assuming that the current correlation estimate is the forecast, the advantages of multivariate Garch are nothing like as clear as those of univariate Garch. Readers who wish to find out

more about the subject have a huge literature to choose from. See for example the surveys in Bollerslev, Chou and Kroner (1992), Bollerslev, Engle and Nelson (1994) and Alexander (1998).

To summarise the correlation models introduced here, the simple weighted average methods are easy to implement and are recommended for use in various circumstances, for different reasons. Long-term equally weighted averages can provide a good indication of the average correlation over a large number of months, and preferably years. But for short-term correlation, exponentially weighted moving averages are recommended because they are similar to Garch estimates and do not suffer from the "ghost" features of equally weighted averages following extreme market events.

Some applications of correlation

Several of the chapters in this book describe the type of products being traded in energy markets, why they are traded and by whom, and the growth in volumes on such markets. So there is no need to reiterate those discussions here. Instead, this section focuses on the way correlation affects the pricing of hedges, spreads and multi-asset options.

What should be done if a trade is based on a correlation that does not materialise? Even when energy markets are sufficiently liquid to admit correlation hedging, these correlations may be too unstable for hedging to be effective. In some cases the short-term equally weighted averages or exponentially weighted averages jump around all over the place, and the long-term averages will be very misleading for some time after an extreme event in the markets. It is, therefore, very important to conduct a thorough empirical testing of any model in which derivative prices are affected by correlations, to assess how realistic the correlation measure is.

SPREADS

A spread is a first-order correlation product, so called because correlation has a direct influence on price through the volatility of the spread. Spread volatility, which is based on the formula $\sigma_{x-y}^2 = \sigma_x^2 + \sigma_y^2 - 2\rho\sigma_x\sigma_y$, is lowest when underlyings are highly correlated.

For example, consider the price spread between the Kansas City Board of Trade (KCBOT) "Western", and the Nymex natural gas future contract. The Nymex contract has always traded at a premium, as shown by the positive spread in Figure 4. When the KCBOT was first

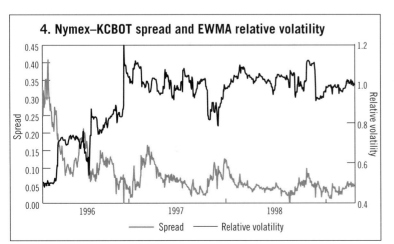

4. Nymex–KCBOT spread and EWMA relative volatility

introduced both volume and volatility were very low relative to the Nymex contract. But as the KCBOT contract trading volume increased so did its relative volatility and the spread decreased substantially. In recent years the correlation between the two contracts has been very high and stable; although the KCBOT closes later, trading on this contract after Nymex has closed is still very thin. Consequently, spread volatility is now relatively low and this affords a certain degree of predictability in the spread.

However close the contracts appear to be, caution should always be exercised when equally weighted correlation measures are used. The exponentially and equally weighted correlations shown in Figure 5 were indeed very similar during the second half of the data period. But in the earlier days of the KCBOT, the use of equally weighted correlations created some misleading measures.

A small decoupling on a single day will affect the 30-day correlation for exactly 30 days, as for example, following the sharp contraction in the spread and the increase in relative volatility on March 26, 1996. Then 30 days later, on May 9, 1996, the 30-day correlation fell from 0.94 to 0.74, although nothing particular happened in the market on that day. The fall in correlation is simply an artefact of the equal weighting of historical data. These effects are not apparent with the exponentially weighted correlation measure.

Traders who are fully hedged over a long period of time often wish to take advantage of short-term profits or losses arising from movements in the spread. Such trades are usually based on the assumption that the spread is a stationary (mean-reverting) process. Certainly many spreads are stationary – time spreads and crude spreads in particular. In that case not only will spread trading be relatively predictable, but also spread options will be reasonably cheap since the high correlation between prices serves to reduce spread volatility.

On the other hand, in some energy markets there is empirical evidence that certain spreads are non-stationary. For example, crack spreads that are heavily traded by refiners, speculators and arbitrageurs alike may evolve into efficient markets so that spreads become random walks. When spreads are not stationary the unconditional variance is infinite, the standard formula for spread volatility will not be valid, and univariate statistical models of non-stationary spreads will have little forecasting power. However, it may be possible to use cointegration between

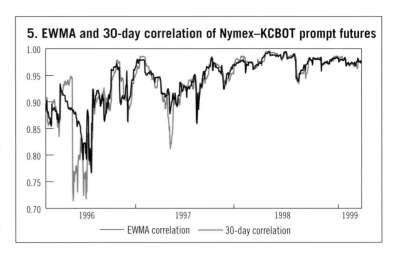

5. EWMA and 30-day correlation of Nymex–KCBOT prompt futures

related spreads to build an error correction model for trading, as the last section of this chapter explains.

HEDGING

Hedging is a very uncertain activity in energy markets, given the unique supply and demand structures that frequently decouple the spot price from prices of futures and forwards, and given the extreme volatility and unstable correlations that are inherent in these markets. Some producers may be unwilling to hedge at all, but there are still very many players, from end-users to speculators and arbitrage traders, who have created a large and growing demand for energy derivatives.

When hedging a spot exposure with a forward for the forward delivery date the hedge ratio should be 1. Energy consumers purchase exactly the number of contracts they expect to require on the delivery date, and any unexpected demand fluctuations are met from storage. The basis risk, which depends on the difference between spot and forward prices, should converge to zero on the delivery date.

The same applies when hedging with futures that correspond exactly to the underlying asset price, although the hedge ratio will be a bit less than one in general, to reflect the interest on margin calls and payments. But if the futures price is an average of daily prices, as it is in the natural gas market, spot and futures returns may have low or unstable correlation and this would induce substantial basis risk (Panel 1). Even in the very liquid crude oil market, where the Cushing prices represent an underlying asset that is exactly the same as that represented by the futures contract, the basis risk can be considerable (Figure 3), so short-term arbitrage is a possibility.

When equivalent forward or futures markets

300

CORRELATION

AND

COINTEGRATION

IN ENERGY

MARKETS

are not available, a proxy hedge must be used. In this case the basis of the cross-hedge has two components: the difference between the spot price of the two underlyings, and the difference between spot and futures prices of the hedging instrument. So when the two instruments are not perfectly correlated there is an additional source of risk arising from the first component of the cross-hedge basis.

For example, the Kansas City Western contract for delivery in "Waha" might be proxied by Nymex natural gas futures for delivery at Henry Hub, Louisiana. The KCBOT contract was particularly illiquid in the early days and it is still very thinly traded compared to the Nymex contract. Figure 6 illustrates how the hedge ratio has changed since the beginning of 1996. For example, during 1996 a natural gas trader may have hedged 1 billion cubic feet, equivalent to 100 Western contracts, with 60 Nymex contracts. The expectation would be that by the delivery date the Nymex contracts could be sold at a price that was sufficient to purchase 1 billion cubic feet on the swing market.

Suppose each unit of an exposure x is hedged by β units of a proxy y. The hedge ratio β, which depends on the correlation and relative volatility between x and y, is given by $COV(R_{x,t}, R_{y,t})/V(R_{y,t})$ or in alternative notation, σ_{xy}/σ_y^2. This is equivalent to $\rho(\sigma_x/\sigma_y)$ so when the spread is stable, ie the correlation is close to 1, the hedge ratio is the relative volatility of the underlying with respect to the hedge.

More generally, hedge ratios depend heavily on correlation and so they too display features that areartefacts of the model used to measure correlations. For example, in Figure 6 the exponentially weighted hedge ratios with a half-life of 30 days often differ substantially from the 30-day equally weighted hedge ratios, but it is not clear a priori which ratio should be used.

MULTI-ASSET OPTIONS

There are many products on related energy markets that are tailor-made for end-users and producers alike. For example, energy producers that are exposed to many commodities will hedge revenues with basket options that are cheaper than buying options on individual markets. "Best of" options allow end-users to purchase energy supply at either the natural gas price or the oil price (say), whichever is better.[4] Long-term swaptions and options on related markets diversify the risks from hedging all costs with derivatives based on a single market. Currency-protected products allow the purchaser to hedge all foreign exchange risk, and derivatives for end-users can be based upon several indexes.

The prices of all these products depend to a greater or lesser extent on cross-market correlations. Many of these derivatives are second-order correlation products, so called because correlation has a lesser effect on price, affecting it only through changes in discount rates rather than directly through volatility. For example, the price of a currency-protected derivative depends on the "quanto" correlation between the underlying and the exchange rate, but only in so far as it changes the discount rate in the Black–Scholes formula.

Although these quanto correlations are likely to be low, they can also be very unstable. But the instability of cross-market correlations is not so much of an issue with second-order products. It is the first-order correlation products that will be very difficult to price when correlation is unpredictable.

Consider, for example, a basket option on crude oil and natural gas near-month futures. The basket option should be cheaper than buying separate options on each underlying, because basket volatility is related to the volatility of individual options as $\sigma_{x+y}^2 = (\sigma_x + \sigma_y)^2 - 2(1-\rho)\sigma_x\sigma_y$. Thus the basket volatility is less than the sum of individual volatilities unless $\rho = 1$.

Figure 7 shows equally weighted correlation measures between Nymex prompt futures on crude oil and natural gas. The longer term correlations in Figure 7 are very small, in the region of 0.1 to 0.2, so long-term basket options on natural gas and crude oil should be relatively cheap. But in addition to other factors, differences in settlement dates and procedures across different markets produce highly unstable short-term correlations, as, for example, in the 30-day correlation shown in Figure 7. So even though they may be cheaper, prices of short-term basket options will be subject to great variability.

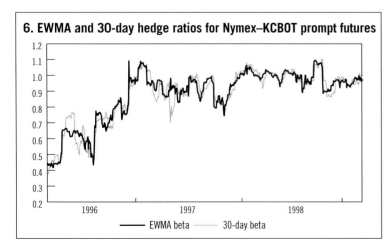

6. EWMA and 30-day hedge ratios for Nymex–KCBOT prompt futures

—— EWMA beta ⋯⋯ 30-day beta

Introducing cointegration

The classic paper on cointegration by Engle and Granger (1987) engendered a revolution in applied economic methods. Cointegration has emerged as a powerful technique for investigating common trends in multivariate time series, and provides a sound methodology for modelling both long-run and short-run dynamics in a system.

Although models of cointegrated financial time series are now relatively commonplace in the literature their importance has, until very recently, been mainly theoretical. This is because the traditional starting point for risk management is a correlation analysis of returns, whereas cointegration is based on the prices themselves.

In standard risk-return models the price data are differenced before the analysis is even begun, which removes a priori any long-term trends in the data. Certainly these trends are implicit in the returns data, but in correlation models any decision based on long-term common trends in the price data is excluded.

Cointegration extends the traditional model of correlation to include a preliminary stage in which the multivariate price data are analysed for long-term equilibria defined by "cointegrating vectors". Then in a dynamic correlation model called the "error correction model" (ECM) the causal flows between returns are investigated.

Here we can only provide a rather simplistic version of the theory, but the more general theory is more than adequately covered in standard econometric texts such as Hamilton (1994) and Hendry (1985, 1995).

Two price processes are cointegrated if there is a linear combination of these prices that is stationary, and any such linear combination is called the "cointegrating vector". The cointegrating vector is a spread, often taken to be a difference in *log* prices rather than prices themselves, so that the error correction model is based on returns. So, generally speaking, when spreads are stationary prices are cointegrated. Certainly prices may deviate in the short term, and correlations may be low at times, but they are "tied together" by a long-term common trend because of the mean-reversion in the spread.

Spot and futures prices are cointegrated when the basis is mean-reverting. Related commodity prices may be cointegrated if costs of carry are well behaved, but that is not always the case. Cointegration arises naturally in many other financial markets: equities within an index, along or between yield curves, in currency systems and

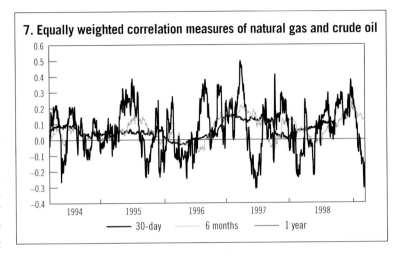

7. Equally weighted correlation measures of natural gas and crude oil

between international market indexes. The interested reader may consult Alexander (1999) and the references there for more details.

Panel 3 (overleaf) analyses cointegration and error correction models in the crude oil market. This serves both to introduce some basic concepts in cointegration and to analyse how dynamic relationships can behave in energy markets. Although spot and prompt future prices are taken in this analysis, similar methods could be applied to any points in the term structure, to related non-stationary crack spreads, and indeed to any energy markets that have common stochastic trends.

Before commencing cointegration analysis the non-stationarity of data should be established. There are many statistical tests for stationarity described in the voluminous econometric literature on unit root tests. The test described in Phillips and Perron (1988) is perhaps the most appropriate given the fat-tailed nature of energy markets. But for simplicity only a basic test is described here.

The augmented Dickey–Fuller (ADF) statistic is based on a regression of Δx on a constant, one lag of Δx and one lag of x, where Δ denotes the first difference. The t-ratio on the lag of x is the ADF statistic, which has a 5% critical value of −2.88 and 1% critical value of −3.46. If the ADF exceeds the α% critical value then x is stationary at the α% level (see Alexander and Johnson, 1994, Dickey and Fuller, 1979 and MacKinnon, 1994). Results of ADF tests on crude oil price data are shown in Panel 3.

The next step in cointegration is to establish that a "cointegrating vector" exists between related price series. This is a linear combination of non-stationary prices that is stationary.

In the simple case that only two series are considered, one would perform a regression of one log price y on the other log price x and then

302

CORRELATION
AND
COINTEGRATION
IN ENERGY
MARKETS

COINTEGRATION AND ERROR CORRECTION IN CRUDE OIL PRICES

The first step in cointegration is to check that the price data are non-stationary. In major equity, currency and fixed income markets daily prices are almost always governed by integrated processes, if not a random walk. However, unusual demand and supply constraints influence the very uncertain prices and extreme variability that is a characteristic of many energy markets, and it is by no means certain that prices will be non-stationary.

The augmented Dickey–Fuller (ADF) statistics from WTI crude oil log spot prices are shown in Figure A. Each regression was based on five years of data, a somewhat arbitrary choice but not a choice that hugely influenced the qualitative

nature of the results. The regressions were rolled over the whole data period, each time recording the ADF, giving the data in Figure A. Although it exceeds the 5% critical value marked for a brief period in 1996 (an artefact of the Gulf War five years earlier) it stays well above the 1% level in recent years. So we conclude that WTI crude oil prices are significantly non-stationary.

Spot and futures prices are cointegrated if there is a stationary linear combination. While there may be more stationary combinations than the basis $z = \log F - \log S$, there is no doubt that the basis is stationary and it is more intuitive to use this as the cointegrating vector in error correction models.

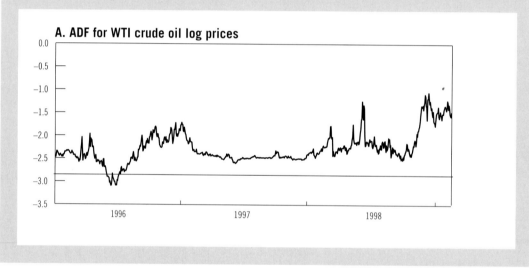

A. ADF for WTI crude oil log prices

test the residual for stationarity. If the residuals indicate that the error process is indeed stationary, then the cointegrating vector is $z = y - \beta x$ where β is the regression coefficient. This is the method proposed by Engle and Granger (1987). For more details on this and other methods see Alexander (1999).

The final step is to estimate an error correction model (ECM) on returns, which may have quite a complex lag structure. If only the first lags are used the ECM takes the simple form:

$$R_x = \alpha_0 + \alpha_1 R_x(-1) + \alpha_2 R_y(-1) + \alpha_3 z(-1) + \varepsilon_s$$
$$R_y = \beta_0 + \beta_1 R_x(-1) + \beta_2 R_y(-1) + \beta_3 z(-1) + \varepsilon_f$$

The ECM is the mechanism that ties cointegrated series together in the long run. It takes its name from the fact that α_3 is positive and β_3 is negative. Thus if the cointegrating vector z is above its equilibrium value, next period price of x will

tend to increase, the price of y will tend to decrease and both serve to reduce the size of cointegrating vector.

The ECM may be used to analyse "Granger" causality, which must be present in cointegrated series. Granger causality means that turning points in one series lead turning points in the other (Granger, 1988). If the ECM coefficients α_2 and/or α_3 are significant, there is a dynamic causality from y to x. If the coefficients β_1 and/or β_3 are significant, there is a causality from x to y. Granger causality between crude oil spot and futures is investigated in Panel 3.

In many financial markets one can argue the case for "price discovery", where futures prices lead spot prices (for example, see Bopp and Sitzer 1987, Schroeder and Goodwin 1991, Schwartz and Laatsch 1991, Schwartz and Szakmary 1994, and Wang and Yau, 1994). However, the relationship between spot and

303

CORRELATION
AND
COINTEGRATION
IN ENERGY
MARKETS

Error correction models are estimated using ordinary least squares. Then simple t tests on the significance of the coefficients in rolling regressions show how the lead-lag relationship between spot and futures prices evolves over time. Figure B shows t-statistics on α_2 (future to spot), α_3 (basis to spot), β_1 (spot to future) and β_3 (basis to future) for the crude oil data using rolling regressions on a four-year window.

Note that after the structural break on January 17, 1995, when the dramatic fall in prices on January 17, 1991 drops out of the data, part of the error correction mechanism broke down. The coefficient α_3 is no longer positive. However, the t-statistics on β_3 are very large indeed, and negative (as they should be). So the error correction mechanism is currently working through changes in futures prices.

Figure B gives a very clear message that it is futures and not spot prices that are being driven; there are very significant causalities from both spot prices and the basis into futures prices on the next day.

It is not surprising that futures prices are not good forecasts of spot prices in the crude oil market. In fact in any energy market, demand fluctuations produce an immediate response in spot prices because of the inelastic supply curve. The subsequent effect on inventory levels changes the convenience yield, but it may take time for futures prices to respond. It is the spot price, and in the crude oil market the basis even more so, that predicts futures prices. However, spot prices themselves are difficult to predict. This is to be expected, since demand fluctuations are governed by so many unpredictable quantities.

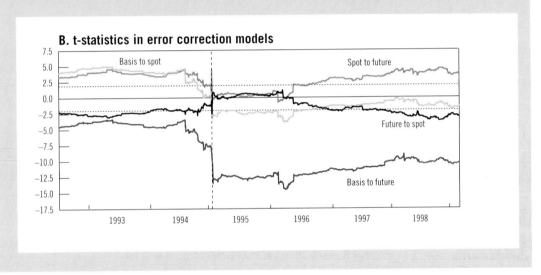

B. t-statistics in error correction models

futures prices in energy markets is quite unique, as is demonstrated by the cointegration analysis of crude oil prices in Panel 3. For example, in equity indexes it is the future that is actually traded – completely the other way round to energy markets, where spot prices alone govern the physical delivery.

The information that is revealed in a dynamic correlation model, such as an error correction model, should be very useful for short-term trades in and between many other energy markets. All the methods described here may be implemented in statistical packages such as Excel, so readers are invited to experiment.

1 *Many thanks to Vincent Kaminski, Stinson Gibner and Allan Firstenberg of Enron Corp for providing the data used in this analysis and for much help with its interpretation.*

2 *Spot is the 1st Month Cushing until the future's expiry, then the 2nd Month Cushing until the 25th, then back to the 1st Month Cushing. The "Cushing" prices are quoted by Platts and represent market prices paid for crude to be delivered over the next (or 2nd nearest) calendar month. Thus the underlying asset is exactly the same as that repre-*

sented by the futures contract. This "cash" market trades for only about 30 minutes each day during a period which is after the Nymex contract closes trading for the day.

3 *Hence the term "unit root" to indicate non-stationarity.*

4 *In "best of" options the price depends on correlation through the volatility of the price ratio (not the ratio of price volatilities).*

304

CORRELATION
AND
COINTEGRATION
IN ENERGY
MARKETS

BIBLIOGRAPHY

Alexander, C. and A. Johnson, 1994, "Dynamic Links", *Risk* 7(2) pp. 56–61.

Alexander, C.O., 1996, "Evaluating the use of RiskMetrics™ as a risk measurement tool for your operation: What are its advantages and limitations", *Derivatives Use, Trading and Regulation* 2(4).

Alexander, C., 1998, "Volatility and correlation: measurement, models and applications" in *Risk Management and Analysis (second edition) Volume 2: Measuring and Modelling Financial Risk*, edited by C. Alexander, John Wiley & Sons.

Alexander, C., 1999, "Optimal hedging using cointegration", *Philosophical Transactions of the Royal Society* (Series A, 354, August 1999).

Bollerslev, T., 1986, "Generalized autoregressive conditional heteroskedasticity", *Journal of Econometrics*, 31, pp. 307–27.

Bollerslev, T., R.Y. Chou and K.F. Kroner, 1992, "ARCH modeling in finance", *Journal of Econometrics*, 52, pp. 5–59.

Bollerslev, T., R.F. Engle and D.B. Nelson, 1994, "ARCH models" in *Handbook of Econometrics*, vol. 4 edited by R.F. Engle and D.L. McFadden, North Holland.

Bopp, A.E. and S. Sitzer, 1987, "Are petroleum prices good predictors of cash value?", *Journal of Futures Markets*, 7, pp. 705–719.

Choi, I., 1992, "Durbin-Hausmann tests for a unit root", *Oxford Bulletin of Economics and Statistics*, 54(3), pp. 289–304.

Chowdhury, A. R., 1991, "Futures market efficiency: evidence from cointegration tests" *The Journal of Futures Markets* 11(5), pp. 577–89.

Covey, T. and D.A. Bessler, 1992, "Testing for Granger's full causality", *The Review of Economics and Statistics*, pp. 146–153.

Dickey, D.A. and W.A. Fuller, 1979, "Distribution of the estimates for autoregressive time series with a unit root", *Journal of the American Statistical Association*, 74, pp. 427–9.

Engle, R.F., 1982, "Autoregressive conditional heteroscedasticity with estimates of the variance of United Kingdom inflation", *Econometrica* 50(4), pp. 987–1007.

Engle, R.F. and C.W.J. Granger, 1987, "Co-integration and error correction: representation, estimation, and testing", *Econometrica*, 55(2), pp. 251–76.

Granger, C.W.J., 1988, "Some recent developments on a concept of causality", *Journal of Econometrics*, 39, pp. 199–211.

Hamilton, J.D., 1994, *Time Series Analysis*, Princeton University Press.

Hendry, D.F., 1986, "Econometric modelling with cointegrated variables: an overview", *Oxford Bulletin of Economics and Statistics*, 48(3), pp. 201–12.

Hendry, D.F., 1995, *Dynamic Econometrics*, Oxford University Press.

Mackinnon, J.G., 1994, "Approximate asymptotic distribution functions for unit-root and cointegration tests", *Journal of Business Economics and Statistics*, 12(2), (April), pp. 167–176.

Phillips, P.C.B. and P. Perron, 1988, "Testing for a unit root in time series regressions", *Biometrika*, 75, pp. 335–46.

Schroeder, T.C. and B.K. Goodwin, 1991, "Price discovery and cointegration for live hogs", *Journal of Futures Markets*, 11(6), pp. 685–696.

Schwartz, T.V. and F.E. Laatsch, 1991, "Dynamic efficiency and price discovery leadership in stock index cash and futures market", *Journal of Futures Markets*, 11(6) pp. 669–684.

Schwartz, T.V. and A.C. Szakmary, 1994, "Price discovery in petroleum markets: arbitrage, cointegration, and the time interval of analysis", *Journal of Futures Markets*, 14(2), pp. 147–167.

Wang, G. H. K. and J. Yau, 1994, "A Time Series Approach To Testing For Market Linkage: Unit Root And Cointegration Tests", *Journal of Futures Markets*, 14(4).

APPENDIX A
Chapter 3: Energy Exotic Options
Formulas for Option Pricing

THROUGHOUT THIS APPENDIX, the following definitions apply:

t = valuation time,

$T - t$ = life of the option in years,

r = risk-free interest rate,

K = strike price,

$F(t)$ = forward price at time t, sometimes abbreviated F, and

$N(.)$ = cumulative normal distribution function.

A.1 Vanilla options

The premium for a call option on a forward contract is given by

$$C = \exp\left[-r(T-t)\right]\left[F(t)N(d_1) - KN(d_2)\right] \; , \tag{A.1}$$

and the premium for a put option on a forward contract is given by

$$P = \exp\left[-r(T-t)\right]\left[-F(t)N(-d_1) - KN(-d_2)\right], \tag{A.2}$$

where

$$d_1 = \frac{\ln(F(t)/K) + 0.5\sigma^2(T-t)}{\sigma\sqrt{T-t}}$$

and

$$d_2 = d_1 - \sigma\sqrt{T-t}$$

A.2 Barrier options

The equations (A.3) to (A.8) are for pricing barrier options which have no rebates; barrier options with rebates can be found in Rubinstein and Reiner (1991a).

These equations are for knock-out options. Knock-in options can be priced using the parity relationship that holds between knock-in, knock-out and vanilla options with the same strike price. When all three options have the same strike and the knock-out and knock-in options have the same barrier price, then the knock-in call (put) premium plus the knock-out call (put) premium is equal to the premium of a standard call (put) option.

Down-and-out call option (B<K)

$$C_{dao(B<K)} = \exp[-r(T-t)]\{[FN(d_1) - KN(d_2)] - [BN(z_1) - K(F/B)N(z_2)]\} \tag{A.3}$$

Down-and-out call option (B>K)

$$C_{dao(B>K)} = \exp[-r(T-t)]\{FN(x_1) - KN(x_2) - BN(y_1) + K(F/B)N(y_2)\} \tag{A.4}$$

Up-and-out call option (B<K)

$$C_{uao(B>K)} = \exp[-r(T-t)]\{[FN(d_1) - KN(d_2)] + [BN(-z_1) - K(F/B)N(-z_2)]$$
$$-[FN(x_1) - KN(x_2)] - [BN(-y_1) - K(F/B)N(-y_2)]\} \tag{A.5}$$

Down-and-out put option (B<K)

$$P_{dao(B<K)} = \exp[-r(T-t)]\{[-FN(-d_1) + KN(-d_2)] - [BN(z_1) - K(F/B)N(z_2)]$$
$$+[FN(-x_1) - KN(-x_2)] + [BN(y_1) - K(F/B)N(y_2)]\} \tag{A.6}$$

Up-and-out put option (B<K)

$$P_{uao(B<K)} = \exp[-(\ - \ )]\{- \quad (F \ _1) + \quad (- \ _2)\mp[\quad (- \ _1) - (\ \text{\textit{t}} \ ) \quad (- \ _2)]\}$$ (A.7)

Up-and-out put option (B>K)

$$P_{uao(B>K)} = \exp[-r(T-t)]\{[-FN(-d_1) + KN(-d_2)] + [BN(-z_1) - K(F/B)N(-z_2)]\}$$ (A.8)

Where we use the following definitions:

B = barrier price level;

$$d_1 = \frac{\ln(F/K) + 0.5\sigma^2(T-t)}{\sigma\sqrt{T-t}} \ ; d_2 = d_1 - \sigma\sqrt{T-t} \ ;$$

$$x_1 = \frac{\ln(F/B) + 0.5\sigma^2(T-t)}{\sigma\sqrt{T-t}} \ ; x_2 = x_1 - \sigma\sqrt{T-t} \ ;$$

$$y_1 = \frac{\ln(B/F) + 0.5\sigma^2(T-t)}{\sigma\sqrt{T-t}} \ ; y_2 = y_1 - \sigma\sqrt{T-t} \ ;$$

$$z_1 = \frac{\ln(B^2/FK) + 0.5\sigma^2(T-t)}{\sigma\sqrt{T-t}} \ ; \text{ and } \ z_2 = z_1 - \sigma\sqrt{T-t} \ .$$

A.3 Compound options

For the valuation of compound options, we use the following additional definitions:

F = F(t), the price of the underlying at time t.

F^* = underlying price which makes the underlying option price equal to K_0 at time T_0. F^* must be found by solving equation (A.1) or (A.2) with the premium set equal to K_0, with $T = T_u$, and with $t = T_0$.

K_0 = strike of the overlying option

K_u = strike of the underlying option

T_0 = time of expiration of the overlying option

T_u = time of expiration of the underlying option

r = risk-free rate

σ = annualised volatility

$M(x,y,\rho)$ = bivariate cumulative normal distribution function.

ρ = correlation coefficient

Call on a call:

$$C_C = \exp[-r(T_u - t)] \{FM(x_1, y_1, \rho) - K_u M(x_2, y_2, \rho)\} - \exp[-r(T_0 - t)] K_0 N(x_2)$$ (A.9)

where we have additionally defined

$$x_1 \quad = \quad \frac{\ln(F/F^*) + (\sigma^2/2)(T_0 - t)}{\sigma\sqrt{T_0 - t}}$$

$$x_2 \quad = \quad x_1 - \sigma\sqrt{T_0 - t}$$

$$y_1 \quad = \quad \frac{\ln(F/K_u) + (\sigma^2/2)(T_u - t)}{\sigma\sqrt{T_u - t}}$$

$$y_2 \quad = \quad y_1 - \sigma\sqrt{T_u - t}$$

$$\rho \quad = \quad \sqrt{\frac{T_0 - t}{T_u - t}}$$

The additional type of compound options are given in a very similar fashion. A put on a call is given by

$$P_C = \exp[-r(T_u - t)]\{K_u M(-x_2, y_2, -\rho) - F M(-x_1, y_1, -\rho)\} + \exp[-r(T_o - t)]K_o N(-x_2) \quad (A.10)$$

Similarly the value of a call on a put is

$$C_P = \exp[-r(T_u - t)]\{K_u M(-x_2, -y_2, \rho) - F M(-x_1, -y_1, \rho)\} - \exp[-r(T_o - t)]K_o N(-x_2) \quad (A.11)$$

Finally, the value of a put on a put is given by

$$P_P = \exp[-r(T_u - t)]\{F M(x_1, -y_1, -\rho) - K_u N(x_2, -y_2, -\rho)\} + \exp[-r(T_o - t)]K_o N(x_2) \quad (A.12)$$

A.4 Options on the minimum or maximum of two assets

For options involving two assets, we use the following definitions:

F_1 = Forward price of commodity 1 at time t,

F_2 = Forward price of commodity 2 at time t,

σ_1 = volatility of commodity 1

σ_2 = volatility of commodity 2

ρ = correlation between commodity 1 and commodity 2, and

$M(x, y, \rho)$ = bivariate cumulative normal distribution function.

We further define

$$\sigma^2 = \sigma_1^2 + \sigma_2^2 - 2\rho\sigma_1\sigma_2$$

$$y_1 = \frac{\ln(F_1/F_2) + (\sigma^2/2)(T-t)}{\sigma\sqrt{T-t}},$$

$$y_2 = \frac{\ln(F_2/F_1) + (\sigma^2/2)(T-t)}{\sigma\sqrt{T-t}},$$

$$a_1 = \frac{\ln(F_1/K) + (\sigma_1^2/2)(T-t)}{\sigma_1\sqrt{T-t}},$$

$$a_2 = \frac{\ln(F_2/K) + (\sigma_2^2/2)(T-t)}{\sigma_2\sqrt{T-t}}, \quad \text{and}$$

$$b_1 = a_1 - \sigma_1\sqrt{T-t},$$

$$b_2 = a_2 - \sigma_2\sqrt{T-t},$$

$$z_1 = \frac{(\rho\sigma_2 - \sigma_1)}{\sigma},$$

$$z_2 = \frac{(\rho\sigma_1 - \sigma_2)}{\sigma}.$$

Having made these definitions, we can now express the premium of a call on the maximum of two commodities or cash (in the amount K) as

$$C_{max(F,F,K)} = \exp[-r(T-t)]\{F_1(N(y_1) - M(-a_1, y_1, z_1)) + F_2(N(y_2) - M(-a_2, y_2, z_2) + KM(-b_1, -b_2, \rho)\} \quad (A.13)$$

and the value of a call on the maximum of two commodities is simply given by

$$C_{max(F,F)-K} = C_{max(F,F,K)} - K\exp[-r(T-t)] \quad (A.14)$$

If the strike price is zero, then this formula reduces to

$$C_{max(F,F)-0} = \exp[-r(T-t)]\{F_2 + F_1 N(y_1) - F_2 N(y_1 - \sigma\sqrt{T-t})\} \quad (A.14B)$$

The purchase of call on the minimum of two commodities is equivalent to buying vanilla calls on the two individual commodities and selling a call on their maximum, ie

$$C_{min(F,F)-K} = C(F_1, K) + C(F_2, K) - C_{max(F,F)-K}, \quad (A.15)$$

where $C(F_1, K)$ and $C(F_2, K)$ represent plain vanilla calls on F_1 and F_2 with strike price K.

A put on the maximum of two commodities can be valued as holding a call on the maximum of two commodities (with strike = K), being short a call on their maximum (with strike = 0), and holding a loan of the present value of the strike price.

$$P_{max(F,F)-K} = K \exp[-r(T-t)] - C_{max(F,F)-0} + C_{max(F,F)-K} \tag{A.16}$$

Finally, a put on the minimum of two commodities (strike = K) is equivalent to having a call on the minimum (strike = K) and a loan of the present value of the strike price and being short a call on the minimum of the two commodities (strike = 0).

$$P_{min(F,F)-K} = K \exp[-r(T-t)] - C_{min(F,F)-0} + C_{min(F,F)-K} \tag{A.17}$$

A.5 Lookback options

The pricing and hedging of lookback options is explored by Garman (1989). Garman presents a replication strategy that consists of hedging a lookback call (put) using an option with a strike equal to the current minimum (maximum) price. At inception this price is equal to the price of the underlying. When the underlying price establishes a new minimum (maximum), the option is sold and the proceeds are rolled into a new at-the-money contract. This roll results in a negative cashflow since the new option is more expensive than the old one. In the absence of transaction costs this strategy will produce a payoff equal to that of the lookback option and therefore has the same value. At any point in time, the lookback option has a value that is equal to the current replicating option plus the option on the uncertain cashflows related to the replication strategy (which Garman calls a "strike-bonus option"). The value of the strike bonus option for a call, C_{sb}, is given by

$$C_{sb} = F \exp\left[-r(T-t)\right]\sigma\sqrt{(T-t)}\left[N'(d_L) + d_L N(d_L)\right]$$

where

$$d_L = -\frac{\ln\left(F/\min(F)\right) + 0.5\sigma^2(T-t)}{\sigma\sqrt{(T-t)}}$$

$\min(F)$ = minimum price attained to date during the life of the option, and N' denotes normal density function. Similarly, the strike bonus component of a lookback put is given by

$$P_{sb} = F \exp\left[-r(T-t)\right]\sigma\sqrt{(T-t)}\left[N'(d_H) + d_H\left(N(d_H) - 1\right)\right]$$

where

$$d_H = -\frac{\ln\left(F/\max(F)\right) + 0.5\sigma^2(T-t)}{\sigma\sqrt{(T-t)}}$$

and $\max(F)$ = maximum price attained to date during the life of the option.

The formula above is the rule given by Garman (1989), modified for those cases in which the drift, m, is equal to 0. The other component of the lookback option price, in addition to C_{sb} (P_{sb}), is the price of an ordinary call (put) option struck at the minimum (maximum) price achieved over the life of the option.

APPENDIX B

Chapter 13: Arbitrage-Free Valuation of Energy Derivatives

IN THIS APPENDIX, we derive the stochastic differential equation for the futures prices (equation 38 in the main text) when the convenience yields are stochastic. We begin with the cost-of-carry relation:

$$F(t,T) = S(t) \exp\left[\int_t^T \left(r(u) - z(t,u)\right) du\right]$$

Substituting the stochastic differential equation for $z(t,u)$, we obtain:

$$F(t,T) = S(t) \exp\left[\int_r^T r(u) du\right] \exp\left[-\int_t^T \left\{z(0,u) + \int_0^t \beta(v,u) dv + \int_0^t (v,u) dW_2^*(v)\right\} du\right]$$

Writing in differential form,

$$d\log F(t,T) = d\log S(t) + r(t) dt + z(0,t) dt - \left[\int_t^T \beta(t,u) du\right] dt + \left[\int_0^t \beta(v,t) dv\right] dt$$

$$- \left[\int_t^T \delta(t,u) du\right] dW_2^*(t) + \left[\int_0^t \delta(v,t) dW_2^*(v)\right] dt$$

Since equation (34) implies that:

$$z(t,t) = z(0,t) + \int_0^t \beta(v,t) dv + \int_0^t \delta(v,t) dW_2^*(v)$$

$$d\log F(t,T) = -\left(\sigma^2 / 2\right) dt + \sigma dW_1^*(t) - \left[\int_t^T \beta(t,u) du\right] dt - \left[\int_t^T \delta(t,u) du\right] dW_2^*(t)$$

For the expected futures price change to be zero, the drift of the log of the futures price must be equal to minus one half the variance of the log of the futures price. To derive the condition, necessary to ensure this relationship, rewrite the previous equation as:

$$d\log F(t,T) = \left[-\left[\int_t^T \beta(t,u) du\right] dt + (1/2)\left[\int_t^T \delta(t,u) du\right]^2 dt - \rho\sigma\left[\int_t^T \delta(t,u) du\right] dt\right]$$

$$+ \left[-\left(\sigma^2 / 2\right) dt + \sigma dW_1^*(t) - \left[\int_t^T \delta(t,u) du\right] dW_2^*(t) - (1/2)\left[\int_t^T \delta(t,u) du\right]^2 + \rho\sigma\left[\int_t^T \delta(t,u) du\right] dt\right]$$

Therefore, to ensure that the futures price has zero expected increment, the following must hold:

$$-\int_t^T \beta(t,u) du + (1/2)\left[\int_t^T \delta(t,u) du\right]^2 - \sigma\rho\int_t^T \delta(t,u) du = 0$$

that is,

$$\int_t^T \beta(t,u) du = (1/2)\left[\int_t^T \delta(t,u) du\right]^2 - \sigma\rho\int_t^T \delta(t,u) du$$

By taking the derivative with respect to T on both sides, we obtain:

$$\beta(t,T) = \delta(t,T)\left[\int_t^T \delta(t,u) du - \rho\sigma\right]$$

Therefore, the futures price evolves according to:

$$d\log F(t,T) = \sigma dW_1^*(t) - \left[\int_t^T \delta(t,u) du\right] dW_2^*(t) - \left(\sigma^2 / 2\right) dt - 1/2\left[\int_t^T \delta(t,u) du\right]^2 dt + \rho\sigma\left[\int_t^T \delta(t,u) du\right] dt$$

or

$$dF(t,T) / F(t,T) = \sigma dW_1^*(t) - \left[\int_t^T \delta(t,u) du\right] dW_2^*(t)$$

QED

GLOSSARY

This glossary provides short definitions of terms and abbreviations that are used, often without further explanation, in the developing power and energy risk management industry. The glossary has been designed for general reference so not all the terms below are used elsewhere in this book. Longer definitions of derivative and risk management terms are available in a glossary called The Chase/Risk Magazine Guide to Risk Management, *while energy risk management terms are more fully covered in* The Energy & Power Risk Management Glossary, *both published by Risk Publications.*

Alternative Delivery Procedure (ADP) is the provision made in certain futures contracts, whereby buyers or settlers may make or take delivery under circumstances that differ from those stipulated in the contract

American-style option Option that may be exercised at any moment during its lifetime, up to and including the expiration date, in contrast to a European-style option (qv)

API or American Petroleum Institute

API gravity Industry-standard scale devised by the American Petroleum Institute for expressing the specific gravity of oils

Asian option Path-dependent option with a payout that depends on the *average* price or rate of the underlying instrument during all or part of the life of the option, rather than the price of the underlying at a single moment in time. Asian options are one of the most popular exotic options in the energy markets

ASTM, or American Society for Testing Materials. The quality of a petroleum product may be described using ASTM specifications

ATK, or aviation turbine kerosene, is a medium-light fuel consumed in jet and turbo-prop aircraft engines

average price/rate option *see* Asian option

back-to-back Deal in which an intermediary is able to offset the price exposure generated by a derivative contract sold to one party with the price exposure of a contract undertaken with another. Ideally, a back-to-back transaction would leave the intermediary with no market risk at all, although it may still be exposed to other risks (notably credit risk)

backwardation Term used to describe an energy market in which the anticipated value of the spot (or prompt) price is lower than the current spot price (ie the market is inverted). That is, when a market is in backwardation the market participants expect the spot price to go down. The reverse situation is described as contango (qv)

barrel (bbl) is the standard measure for oil and oil products. One barrel = 35 imperial gallons, 42 US gallons, or 159 litres. In energy units, one barrel = 5.8 million British Thermal Units (Btu)

barrier options are exotic options which either come into life (are knocked-in) or are extinguished (knocked-out) under conditions stipulated in the option contract. The conditions are usually defined in terms of a price level (barrier, knock-out, or knock-in price) that may be reached at any time during

the life of the option

base-load units Power generating plant that is used almost continuously, usually because it provides power at an economical rate and also often because it is difficult or uneconomic to shut down. The nature of base-load units varies from market to market but coal, hydropower and nuclear power units are often important constituents. Base-load units are not usually the units that set power prices, unlike the more expensive-to-run but flexible mid-merit and peaking units (qv)

basis risk The risk that the value of a futures contract or an over-the-counter hedge will not move in line with that of the underlying price exposure that is being risk managed. Alternatively, the risk that the spot–futures spread will widen or narrow between the time when the hedge position is implemented and the time when it is liquidated. Basis risk is thus a form of inefficiency, and sometimes a source of worrying or misunderstood financial exposures, in hedging programmes

basis swap Basis swaps are used to hedge exposure to basis risks, such as locational risk or time exposure risk. For example, a natural gas basis swap could be used to hedge a locational price risk: the seller receives from the buyer a Nymex settlement value (usually the average of the last three days closing prices) plus a negotiated fixed basis, and pays the buyer the published index (qv) value of gas sold at a specified location

bbl *see* barrel

b/d, B/D Abbreviation for "barrels per day". Also written as bpd/BPD

benzene Derived from petroleum, benzene is one of the most important feedstocks in the chemical industry. It is the simplest aromatic (hydrocarbons with a ring structure) compound

bilateral contracts *see* over-the-counter (OTC) contracts

binary options *see* digital options

bpd, BPD Abbreviation for "barrels per day". Also written as b/d, B/D

break Sudden downward movement in futures prices on an exchange

Brent Blend Crude oil blended from the output of the Brent and Ninian fields in the North Sea

British thermal unit (Btu) Measure of the heat content of coal and other fuels. Formally, the amount of heat required to raise the temperature of 1lb of water by 1 degree Fahrenheit (from 60° to 61°). It is equivalent to 0.252kcal and 1.055kJ

BS&W, or Bottom Sediment and Water, describes the wastage often found in crude oil and residual fuel

Btu see British thermal unit

Btu swap Commodity swap under which the floating price of one commodity is calculated as a percentage of the price of another commodity, both prices being expressed in terms of MMBTU (million BTU) equivalents

bunker fuel Term used to describe the heavy fuel oil purchased by shipping companies

buy-back price is the price that an oil company pays to a state for oil that the company has produced but which is owned by the state

"calendar" or time spreads describe the price differential, or spread, that may arise between differently dated futures contracts. For example, the price difference between contracts for first and second month Brent offered on the IPE. Time spreads can be mitigated by purchasing options on the difference between average annual

prices. In effect, such options provide protection against a reshaping of the forward price curve

capacity In the power industry, this describes the generating or transmission (ie load carrying) capabilities of generators or transmission lines, typically expressed in megawatts or megavoltamperes

CCPG, or combined cycle power generation *see* combined heat and power (CHP)

CEA *see* Commodity Exchange Act

C&F, or Cost and Freight, indicates that the quoted price/contract includes freight

CFTC or Commodity Futures Trading Commission (United States)

charm describes an option risk parameter which measures the amount that delta (qv) will change due to the passage of time

CHP *see* Combined Heat and Power

CIF, or Cost Insurance Freight, indicates that the price/contract includes freight and insurance, but excludes customs duties

combination hedging describes the use of a combination of hedges to construct a risk management strategy. For example, a hedging strategy for jet fuel price exposure might make use of IPE Gasoil futures combined with an options on the kerosene/gasoil spread value over the risk-managed period

combined-cycle gas turbines (CCGT) Energy efficient gas turbine systems where the first turbine generates electricity from the gas produced during fuel combustion. The hot gases pass through a boiler and then into the atmosphere. The steam from the boiler drives the second generating turbine

combined heat and power (CHP), is used to describe power generation where fuel is burnt to produce both electricity and heat

(or steam), both forms of energy being used to power the host industrial site. If the heat is not used on-site it can be used to generate further electricity using steam turbines, in which case the process is called Combined Cycle Power Generation (CCPG)

Commodity Exchange Act (CEA), was passed in 1974 by the United States' Congress, granting the Commodity Futures Trading Commission exclusive jurisdiction over transactions involving exchange-traded "contracts of sale of a commodity for future delivery" and commodity option contracts (exchange traded or not). However, *see also* Futures Trading Practices Act (FTPA)

compound option Option that allows its holder to purchase or sell another option for a fixed price. For example, the purchase of a European "call on a put" means that the compound option buyer obtains the right to buy on a specified day (the expiration of the overlying option) a put option (the underlying option) at the overlying option's strike price

contango Term used to describe an energy market in which the anticipated value of the spot price into the future is higher than the current spot price. That is, when a market is in contango, market participants expect the spot price to go up. The reverse situation is described as backwardation (qv)

contracts for difference, Contracts for Difference This term is sometimes used (uncapitalised) as an alternative to the term swap. In a more specialised sense, CFDs are the OTC derivatives (again, usually swaps) used extensively by generators and suppliers in the UK electricity market to manage their exposures. For example, in return for an option fee, a contract seller may agree to pay a contract buyer the difference between the UK electricity "pool" price and the contract exercise price in each settlement period (half hour) when the pool price exceeds the exercise price

convenience yield The modern theory of term structures in commodity prices introduces this concept to describe the yield that accrues to the owner of a physical inventory but not to the owner of a contract for future delivery. It represents the value of having the physical product immediately to hand, and offers a theoretical explanation (of limited predictive value) for the strength of backwardation (qv) in the energy markets

cost-plus pricing Price setting policy that is a characteristic feature of regulated power markets, whereby power companies are allowed to set prices for electricity in line with the costs they incur supplying that power plus a margin for profit. As power markets deregulate, cost-plus pricing is being gradually supplanted by prices discovered through competitive sales and purchases of power in power markets, pools and exchanges

"cracking" describes the technological process used in petroleum refineries; that is, the application of vacuum, heat and catalysts to break down larger, heavier molecules of hydrocarbons into lighter ones, with higher economic value

crack spread describes the difference in the prices of two or more commodities, where one of the (unrefined or input) commodities is used to produce the other (refined or output) commodity(ies). Crack spreads are particularly important to refiners, as their profit margin is dependent upon the price differential between unrefined crude oil and a basket of refined products

cross-market derivative Derivative instrument designed to manage simultaneously price exposures generated in different markets. For example, an interest rate swap, with payments linked to energy prices, can be used to manage jointly the firm's exposure to energy prices and to changes in interest rates

crude spreads The price difference between different varieties of crude. For example, the difference between the price of the May WTI

crude oil futures contract on Nymex and the May Brent crude oil futures contract on the IPE

cubic foot Standard unit for measuring gas. 1 cubic foot = 0.0283 cubic metres

curve-lock swap Swap that "locks" the counterparty into an existing price relationship in the forward curve, with the aim of benefiting from any shifts in the forward curve, eg between backwardation and contango

daily call option The daily call option, which has a long history in the natural gas markets, allows the buyer to take additional volumes of gas at very short notice (typically one day)

degree day *see* weather derivative

delta Option risk parameter that measures the sensitivity of an option price to changes in the price of the underlying instrument

demurrage Sum paid as damages for delay in loading or discharging cargo from a chartered ship

depletion control Any restriction placed on the speed with which oil or gas can be extracted from a given field

digital, or binary, options pay either a fixed sum or zero depending on whether the payout condition is satisfied or not, eg cash-or-nothing options, and asset-or-nothing options

distillates Products of the refinery process, condensed out of crude oil during fractional distillation. They include naphtha, petrol, kerosene and gasoil

double-up swap This instrument grants the swap provider an option to double the swap volume before the pricing period starts; by granting this option, swap users can achieve a swap price which is better than the actual market price. The mechanism by which this is achieved involves consumers (who are buying fixed) selling a put swaption, or producers (who are selling fixed) selling a call swaption; in either case, the

premium earned from the sale is used to subsidise the swap price

"downstream", as opposed to "upstream", activities include the refining and marketing of crude oil and oil products and, in fact, any activity after the crude oil has been produced and loaded

dual-commodity options have payouts that depend on the prices of two or more underlying instruments

EFA *see* Electricity Forward Agreements

Electricity Forward Agreements, or EFAs, are standardised and brokered swap-like instruments used in the UK electricity derivative market to hedge or trade pool prices. Regional Electricity Companies and generators use EFAs as a means of fine-tuning their CFD (qv) transactions

E&P Abbreviation for "Exploration and Production"

European-style option Option that may only be exercised on its expiration date, in contrast to an American-style option (qv)

extendable swap The extendable swap is constructed on the same principle as the double-up swap (qv), except that instead of doubling the swap, the provider has the right to extend the swap, at the end of the agreed period, for a further pre-determined period

Federal Energy Regulating Commission (Ferc) US government agency charged with regulating electricity and natural gas industries at an interstate level in the US

feedstock Raw material used by any processing unit. For example, crude oil is a feedstock of oil refineries and petrochemical plants

FERC 888 This Federal Energy Regulating Commission order in 1996 represented an important milestone in the restructuring of the US wholesale electricity industry, dealing with issues such as open access to transmission lines, non-discriminatory service for wholesale transactions, and approaches to the recovery of stranded costs

"fixed-for-floating" contracts Alternative name for a swap

force majeure This legal term describes the contract clauses that relieve a counterparty of responsibility to perform under the terms of the contract, after disruption of the contract by uncontrollable forces – such as riot, flood, act of God, or war. Defining and interpreting *force majeure* events in the liberalising power markets is a potentially contentious but vital part of managing contract risk

forward contract Contract by means of which one counterparty agrees to sell to another counterparty a specified amount of a commodity for a certain price at a designated date in the future

"frac" spread Difference between the price of natural gas and of natural gas liquids (eg propane, ethane, butane, iso-butane). The equivalent term in the oil industry is "crack spread" (qv)

free on board (FOB) Under an FOB contract, the seller provides a product such as heating oil at a lifting or loading installation and the buyer takes responsibility for shipping and freight insurance

FTPA *see* Futures Trading Practices Act

fuel oil Heavy distillates produced during the refining process and used as fuel for power stations, ships, etc

futures contract Similar to a forward contract, a futures contract is an agreement to buy or sell a commodity for a certain price at a designated time in the future. Unlike forward contracts, futures contracts are traded on an exchange which specifies standard terms for the contracts and guarantees their performance. Exchanges normally require that margins (qv) are posted by holders of open contract positions

Futures Trading Practices Act, or

FTPA, of 1992. By this Act, Congress granted the CFTC the authority to exempt certain agreements, contracts and transactions from various requirements of the CEA or CFTC regulations, including the CEA requirement that transactions must occur on a designated contract market

gamma Option risk parameter that measures the sensitivity of the option delta (qv) to a change in the price of the underlying instrument. It is thus a second-order risk parameter of the option price with respect to the price of the underlying

gasoil Medium distillates produced in refineries during the fractional distillation of crude oil. Gasoil is burned in central heating systems, and is used as a feedstock for the chemical industry; it is also used to produce diesel fuel

gasoline spread The difference between the price of unleaded gasoline and crude oil

gigawatt One billion watts

GOR, or gas-to-oil ratio, expresses the volume of gas/volume of oil produced from a given well

heat rate This measure is used to describe how efficiently a generator converts thermal energy into electricity. More technically, it is the ratio of British thermal units of fuel consumed to kilowatt hours of electricity produced. The *lower* the heat rate, the higher the efficiency of the generator

heat spread Jargon used to describe the difference between the price of No. 2 heating oil and the price of crude oil

heavy crude Crude oil that possesses a high proportion of heavy hydrocarbon fractions (and a low API gravity)

HSFO Abbreviation of High Sulphur Fuel Oil

independent power producer (IPP) Non-utility power generating company

independent system operator (ISO) In the US, an entity responsible for ensuring the efficient use and reliable operation of the transmission grid. ISOs are also sometimes responsible for managing generation facilities and/or managing power exchange facilities

index Published indices are often agreed upon as the price references for energy derivative contracts. For example, in the US natural gas industry, indices provide an average price of contracts for delivery during the calendar month at a given location. The average is based upon a survey of prices transacted during "bid week" (typically, the 20th to the 25th of the month). The best known indices are published by *Inside FERC*, *Gas Week* and *Gas Daily*

index swap In the natural gas market in North America, index (qv) swaps are often used to hedge against location price risk (a form of basis risk). The seller receives a fixed, or otherwise determined, price and pays the buyer the published index value for natural gas from a specified location

International Petroleum Exchange (IPE) This institution, based in London, is one of the world's leading energy futures and options exchanges

interruptible service Electricity or natural gas sales contracts that are subject to interruption for a specified number of days or hours, perhaps during times of peak demand, high prices or in the event of system emergencies. In exchange for interruptibility, purchasers pay lower prices

kappa *see* vega

kerosene Medium-light product of the fractional distillation of crude oil, used for lighting, heating and the manufacture of jet fuel

kilowatt (KW) One thousand watts

lambda *see* vega

LDC, or local distribution company. Term used to describe companies at the end of the natural gas supply chain in the US

light crude Crude oil that possesses a high proportion of light hydrocarbon fractions (and a high API gravity)

"limit up" The maximum move that is allowed in the price of an exchange contract, as specified in the United States by the CFTC (qv)

LNG, or Liquefied Natural Gas, is natural gas that has been liquefied by cooling to about −161 degrees Celsius at atmospheric pressure. Liquefied gas is hundreds of times denser than natural gas and much easier to transport

load The power industry's term for the amount of power carried by an electricity system, or the amount of power drawn down from a power system by an electric device at some specific time or point. In other words, "load" is simply another word for the realised *demand* for power

load factor Ratio between the *average* and *peak* usage of electricity (and natural gas) in a particular energy or power system. The higher the load factor, the smaller the difference between average and peak demand

location spread Differential between the prices quoted for the same commodity at two different locations, eg between the price of 1% heating oil at New York Harbor and at the Gulf Coast

lookback option A lookback call (put) option grants the right to purchase (sell) the underlying energy commodity at the lowest (highest) price reached during the life of the option. Effectively, the best price from the point of view of the holder of the option becomes the strike price

LSFO Abbreviation for Low Sulphur Fuel Oil

margin Cash or securities that must be deposited with the clearing house of a broker or exchange for security against any losses which could result if the investor should fail to honour the obligations of

any open futures position

margin swap *see* refining margin swaps

mark to market (MTM) To "mark to market" is to calculate the value of a financial instrument such as a power option (or a portfolio of such instruments) using the *current* market price of the underlying market variable – which may be very different from the price of the underlying when the contract was originally entered into. Marking instruments to market is thus an important risk management activity for corporations with major contracts that fluctuate in value, and some corporations mark their portfolios to market on a daily or more frequent basis

mean reversion The tendency of prices to revert to a long-term mean (or average) level. The long-term mean is often taken to represent an equilibrium price in the market, and the nature and level of this long-term equilibrium price is a key focus of debate in many energy markets. Prices that exhibit quite strong mean reversion may still be extremely volatile in the short or medium term

megawatt (MW) One million watts (sometimes MMW)

MTBE, or Methyl tertiary butyl ether, is a gasoline additive used to reduce pollution

naphtha Term used to describe a range of distillates from the heavier gaseous fuels to the lighter varieties of kerosene. Naphtha is used as a feedstock in the manufacture of petrol, and in the chemical industry (as a feedstock for ethylene, etc)

natural gas liquids, or NGLs, are the hydrocarbons extracted from the natural gas stream at processing plants by means of fractionation. The liquids include ethane, propane, normal butane, iso-butane and natural gasoline

Net Present Value (NPV) Technique for assessing the worth of future payments by looking at

the present value of those future cashflows discounted at today's cost of capital

New York Mercantile Exchange (Nymex) The world's largest physical commodity and energy exchange, with a range of contracts that includes futures and options in natural gas and electricity

NGL *see* natural gas liquids

Nord Pool One of the world's leading regional power exchanges, Nord Pool lists spot market, futures and forward contracts based on the Scandinavian (Norway, Sweden, Finland, Denmark) power markets

North American Electric Reliability Council (Nerc) Group formed in the US in 1968 after a series of blackouts on the East Coast, to promote the reliability of bulk power supply in the electric utility systems of North America. It has assumed responsibility for ensuring the reliability of the US power grid, and consists of 10 regional councils

NWE Common abbreviation for the oil market in North-West Europe

Nymex *see* New York Mercantile Exchange

off-market swap In this type of swap, a premium is built into the swap price to fund the purchase of options or to allow for the restructuring of a hedge portfolio. Off-market swaps are generally used to restructure or cancel old swap/hedge deals: essentially, they simulate a refinancing package

OIP, or Oil in Place, signifies an estimate of the actual amount of oil present in a reservoir; only a proportion of OIP is likely to be recoverable (for technical and economic reasons)

OPEC, or Organisation of Petroleum Exporting Countries

open interest Sum of all the long positions (or short positions) taken in a given futures contract

option Contract that gives the purchaser the right, but not the obligation, to buy or sell the underlying commodity at a certain price (the exercise, or strike, price) on or before an agreed date. With European-style options, purchasers may take delivery of the commodity only at the end of the option's life. American-style options may be exercised at any time over the life of the option. Most exchange-traded options are of American type; most OTC energy options are Asian (qv) options

OTC *see* over-the-counter contracts

outage The loss of a generating unit, transmission line or other facility due either to scheduled inspection or maintenance (planned outage) or due to failure or mishap (unplanned outage)

over-the-counter (OTC) contracts Term used to describe private contracts negotiated between two parties (bilateral contracts) as opposed to the standardised contracts traded on a formal exchange. OTC options and swaps are usually arranged with an intermediary such as a major bank, energy major or energy marketer. They can be carefully tailored to a counterparty's specific risk management or trading needs but they are relatively illiquid and usually generate credit risk – in contrast to heavily traded exchange contracts where the exchange itself often becomes the formal counterparty

participation swap Similar to a regular swap in that the fixed price payer is fully protected when prices rise above the agreed (fixed) price, with the difference that the client "participates" in any price decrease. For example, a participation swap agreed at a level of $80/mt for high sulphur fuel oil, with a 50% participation, would offer full protection against prices above $80/mt. But the buyer would retain 50% of the savings generated when prices fell below $80/mt

path-dependent options have a payout that is dependent on the price history of the underlying over all or part of the life of the option. The commonest form of option in OTC energy risk management (the

Asian option) is a path-dependent option, as are lookback and barrier options

peaking units (peak-lopping plant) Power generating plant that is operated only during the hours or days when electricity consumption reaches an unusually high level or "peaks". Peaking units are often relatively expensive to run but also relatively cheap to build and flexible to operate: for example combustion turbines that run on natural gas as opposed to base-load (qv) generating units such as hydro or nuclear plant

peak-lopping plant *see* peaking units

pool Power pools are formal systems for trading bulk or wholesale power according to pre-defined "pool rules". The pool operates to ensure that the demand for power is met – in other words pools are one way of ensuring that consumers can rely on their electricity supply. Most pool rules specify how generator owners can "bid" or sell their power into the pool to meet expected demand for power, as well as specifying how the price the generators receive is calculated. The question of whether electricity systems really need pools in order to ensure reliability, and if so how pools should be structured in order to promote competition, fairness and price transparency, has dominated much of the debate about the liberalisation of the world's power markets

PPP, or Pool Purchase Price, is a term used to describe a component of the pricing formulae used in the UK electricity Pool

pre-paid swap By means of a pre-paid swap, the fixed payments that form one side of the cash-flows generated by a standard swap, and which are normally paid over the life of the swap, are discounted back to their net present value and paid as an immediate cash sum to one of the swap counterparties. That counterparty will then make floating price payments over the life of the swap, just as in a standard swap. Pre-paid swaps are often used as a source of project

finance or pre-export financing

price-process model Formal approach to describing how the price of an asset such as a quantity of natural gas or power evolves over time, often taking the form of a mathematical equation and an associated set of assumptions

"processing spread" is a general term for an option on the difference between the price of feedstock and products. For example, the difference between the price of natural gas and of a basket of the natural gas liquids (ethane, propane, iso-butane, normal butane and natural gasoline) which can be extracted from the natural gas stream at processing plants. See also crack spread, "frac" spread and spark spread

PSP, or Pool Selling Price, is the price paid by suppliers to the UK electricity industry "pool", consisting of the PPP (qv) plus an "uplift" payment

"quality spreads" describe the price differential between different qualities of the same energy product. Examples are the spreads between the prices of sweet and sour crude (also known as "crude spreads"), or between the prices of different grades of heating oil (defined by their sulphur content)

reactive power supply In order to maintain transmission line voltages at their nominal values and to facilitate control of power flows around the system, system operators and the generators they despatch must be able to produce or absorb reactive power. It is important to note that reactive power cannot be transmitted over large distances; it is produced (or absorbed) at specific points in order to alter the local characteristics of the system

RECs, or Regional Electricity Companies, are the electricity supply companies in the UK electricity industry

refining margin swaps simultaneously hedge the price of the products (or output) of a refinery, and the price of the crude oil feedstock (or input). That is, the products are sold, and the crude is bought, for equivalent forward periods. Refinery margin swaps effectively "lock-in" the profitability of a refinery

reserve margin The amount of reserve capacity set by the North American Electric Reliability Council regions that needs to be held by an electric utility, over and above the utility's peak requirements. The reserve margin, which is calculated using probabilistic methods, helps ensure that the electricity system in each region will be able to respond to unusual but possible levels of demand for electricity

spark spread The difference between the price of electricity sold by a generator and the price of the fuel (eg natural gas) used to generate that power

spikes Sudden upward or downward movements in price that can be extremely large but which are quickly reversed. Dramatic price spikes are a particular feature of power markets

spinning reserves This service is provided by generators that are online but not operating at their maximum output. In the event of a sudden loss of a generator's output, the system operator must be able to call on a subset of remaining generators to quickly ramp up to restore supply/demand balance. Typically, the combined spinning reserves capacity must at least equal the capacity of the largest single generator on the system, and the aggregate ramp rate must be sufficient to bring the system frequency back to within a "contingency tolerance" band inside a minute or so. See also supplemental reserves

spot price The price paid for a commodity in the short-term physical or cash markets. In the power markets the term refers to the shortest term markets that are available such as the day-ahead market – as opposed to the price paid for power under long-term contracts or under futures and other financial contracts

spread options are options written on the differential between the prices of two commodities. Spread options may be based on the price differences between prices of the same commodity at two different locations (location spreads); prices of the same commodity at two different points in time (calendar spreads); prices of inputs to, and outputs from, a production process (processing spreads); and prices of different grades of the same commodity (quality spreads). See also crack spread, "frac" spread and spark spread

"stacking contract" is the generic term for a type of Contract for Difference used in the UK electricity market

straddle Combination of a put and a call with the same expiration dates and strikes. A buyer of a straddle hopes that the volatility of the underlying prices will increase, creating profit opportunities

strip Industry jargon for any series of transactions with consecutive settlement or expiration dates. For example, an annual strip of futures denotes a purchase/sale of 12 consecutive futures contracts on the same commodity

supplemental reserves Once spinning reserves (qv) have been called on to replace lost generation, a power system may be incapable of responding reliably to a second contingency. Supplemental reserves are additional capacity that can be called on line over the course of several minutes to several hours, to replace lost generation and allow spinning reserves to return to pre-contingency output levels

supply stack The supply stack describes the nature of the universe of generating units available to generate power within any given power system, and the order in which a system operator is likely to despatch these units. For example, a supply stack may be composed of a certain number of cheap-to-run hydro and nuclear units that supply the baseload (qv); coal and oil-fired generating plant in the middle of the supply stack; and natural gas plant acting as

peaking units (qv) when demand and power prices are very high

swap Agreement whereby a floating price is exchanged for a fixed price over a specified period. It is an off-balance sheet financial arrangement which involves no transfer of physical energy; both parties settle their contractual obligations by means of a transfer of cash. The agreement defines the volume, duration and fixed reference price. Differences are settled in cash for specific periods – monthly, quarterly or six-monthly. Swaps are also known as "contracts for differences" and as "fixed-for-floating" contracts

swaption Option to purchase (call swaption) or sell (put swaption) a swap at some future date

sweet crude Crude oil with a low level of hydrogen sulphide or mercaptans

"swing" options Options that allow customers to "swing" or vary the volume of energy or electricity that they take from a supplier, often within predetermined limits. Such options are a common feature of traditional contracts in the power and energy markets, but with the liberalisation of markets the costs incurred under these clauses are increasingly regarded as a source of price exposure that needs to be risk managed

take or pay contracts Under these contracts, an important but now declining feature of the natural gas market, the counterparty is obliged to pay for a specified amount of natural gas whether it takes the natural gas or not, although it may be able to carry forward some part of the commitment to the next contract period (depending on the individual contract terms)

theta Option risk parameter that measures the speed of time decay of the option premium

time spreads *see* calendar spreads

transmission capacity Load-carrying capability of electrical equipment such as generators or transmission lines, usually expressed in megawatts

"trend" Term usually applied to movements in the short-term (spot) prices, where these are not thought to imply any change in the term structure itself. An upward trend may thus sustain or increase the market backwardation, and a downward trend will have the same effect on a contango

ULCC, or Ultra-Large Crude Carrier, is a tanker of over 300,000 tonnes deadweight

"upstream" All oil industry activities prior to the delivery of crude oil to the production terminal, eg exploration and production. The opposite of "downstream" (qv)

value-at-risk (VAR) Put simply, the VAR figure for any financial position is the worst loss that might arise from that position within a given period and within a specified degree of certainty. The measure was developed to allow banks and other financial houses to represent complex risks in a way that made them easy to comprehend and compare. More formally, it represents the probabilistic bound of market losses (arising from a single position or portfolio of positions) over a given period of time (known as the holding period) expressed in terms of a specified degree of certainty (known as the confidence interval). The VAR figure is not, however, the worst loss that could *conceivably* arise, and it is very dependent upon the assumptions made in the calculation. For instance, a portfolio with a VAR of $20 million over a one-day holding period, with a 95% confidence level, would have only a 5% chance of suffering an overnight loss greater than $20 million. However, a 5% chance of loss implies that the loss might arise around once every 20 trading days, and when the loss happens it might be much greater than the VAR figure of $20 million. Adapting VAR measures to allow for the complex option risks, market illiquidity, longer holding periods and high volatilities seen in the energy markets is still work in progress

vega Option risk parameter that measures the sensitivity of the option price to changes in the price volatility of the underlying instrument. Also known as kappa or lamda

"vintaging" In the past, the regulated natural gas market in the United States used the concept of "vintaging" to assign different permitted maximum prices to gas produced from specific wells, based upon the date of well completion and, in some cases, the depth of the well

VLCC, or Very Large Crude Carrier, is a tanker of over 200,000 tonnes deadweight

weather derivative Financial instruments used to hedge against or speculate on weather. Weather derivatives are one way for utilities to hedge volumetric weather risk: the risk that weather will be unexpectedly warmer or cooler than expected and thus drastically affect the demand for power (and power prices and revenues). Although precipitation or other weather factors may be used in the future, to date most weather derivatives define their underlying variable in terms of temperature using the concept of "degree days". The degree day measure is used to count the variation of one day's temperature against a standard reference temperature – typically 65° Fahrenheit (18° Centigrade). The cumulative variation can then be monetised according to the terms of the contract

INDEX